Books of Enoch, Jasher, Jubilees:
Forbidden Books:
These Books Were Omitted From The Bible

**Translated
by R.H. Charles**

CONTENTS

THE BOOK OF THE COURSES OF THE HEAVENLY LUMINARIES 58

THE DREAM-VISIONS 66

THE CONCLUDING SECTION OF THE BOOK 75

THE BOOK OF ENOCH

INTRODUCTION: THE APOCALYPTIC LITERATURE

As the Book of Enoch is, in some respects, the most notable extant apocalyptic work outside the canonical Scriptures, it will not be inappropriate to offer a few remarks here on the Apocalyptic Literature generally. In writing about the books which belong to this literature, Prof. Burkitt says very pointedly that "they are the most characteristic survival of what I will venture to call, with all its narrowness and its incoherence, the heroic age of Jewish history, the age when the nation attempted to realize in action the part of the peculiar people of God. It ended in catastrophe, but the nation left two successors, the Christian Church and the Rabbinical Schools, each of which carried on some of the old national aims. And of the two it was the Christian Church that was most faithful to the ideas enshrined in the Apocalypses, and it did consider itself, not without some reason, the fulfilment of those ideas. What is wanted, therefore, in studying the Apocalypses is, above all, sympathy with the ideas that underlie them, and especially with the belief in the New Age. And those who believe that in Christianity a new Era really did dawn for us ought, I think, to have that sympathy. . . . We study the Apocalypses to learn how our spiritual ancestors hoped again that God would make all right in the end; and that we, their children, are here to-day studying them is an indication that their hope was not wholly unfounded." [1]

Hope is, indeed, the main underlying motive-power which prompted the writers of the Apocalypses. And this hope is the more intensive and ardent in that it shines forth from a background which is dark with despair; for the Apocalyptists despaired of the world in which they lived, a world in which the godly were of no account, while the wicked seemed too often triumphant and prosperous. With evil everywhere around, the Apocalyptists saw no hope for the world as it was; for such a world there was no remedy, only destruction; if the good were ever to triumph it must be in a new world. Despairing, therefore, of the world around them, the Apocalyptists centred their hope upon a world to come, where the righteous would come to their own and evil would find no place. It is this thought which underlies the opening words of the Book of Enoch: "The words of the blessing of Enoch, wherewith he blessed the elect and righteous, who will be living in the day of tribulation, when all the wicked and godless are to be removed." Nowhere in this book is the essence of this hope more beautifully expressed than in a short metrical piece in the first chapter:

---

[1] *Jewish and Christian Apocalypses*, p, 16 (1913).

"But with the righteous He will make peace,

And will protect the elect,

And mercy shall be upon them.

"And they shall all belong to God,

And they shall all be prospered,

And they shall all be blessed.

"And He will help them all,

And light shall appear unto them,

And He will make peace with them" (1 Enoch i. 8).

In all the books belonging to this literature which have come down to us this hope is expressed more or less vividly; nor is the dark background wanting. with prophecies of coming wrath. It will, therefore, be realized that the Apocalyptic Literature is almost wholly concerned with the future; it is true that again and again the Apocalyptist glances at the contemporary history of the world around him, to which many a cryptic reference is made--a fact which necessitates some knowledge of the history of this period (*circa* 200 B.C.-A.D. 100) for a full understanding of the books in question--but these references are only made with a view to comforting the oppressed and afflicted with the thought that even the most mighty of earthly powers are shortly to be overthrown by. the advent of the new and glorious era when every injustice and all the incongruities of life will be done away with. So that every reference to the present is merely a position taken up from which to point to the future. Now, since, as we have seen, the Apocalyptists despair of any bettering of the present world, and therefore contemplate its destruction as the preliminary of the new order of things, they look *away* from this world in their visions of the future; they conceive of other-worldly forces coming into play in the reconstitution of things, and of society generally; and since these *are* other-worldly forces the supernatural plays a great part in the Apocalyptic Literature. This supernatural colouring will often strike the reader of this literature as fantastic, and at times *bizarre*; but this should not be permitted to obscure the reality which often lies behind these weird shadows. Mental visions are not always easily expressed in words; the seer who in a vision has received a message in some fantastic guise necessarily has the impress upon his mind of what he has seen when giving his message; and when he describes his vision the picture he presents is, in the nature of the case, more fantastic to the ear of the hearer than to the eye of him who saw it. Allowance should be made for this; especially by us Westerns who are so lacking in the rich imaginativeness of the Oriental. Our love of literalness hinders the play of the imagination because we are so apt to "materialize" a mental picture presented by another. The Apocalypses were written by and for Orientals, and we cannot do justice to them unless we remember this; but it would be best if we could get into the Oriental mind and look at things from that point of view.

Another thing which the reader of the Apocalyptic Literature must be prepared for is the frequent inconsistency of thought to be found there, together with variableness of teaching often involving contradiction. The reason of this is not to be sought simply in the fact that in the Apocalypses the hand of more than one author is frequently to be discerned, a fact which would easily account for divergence of views in one and the same book-no, the chief reason is that, on the one hand, the minds of the Apocalyptists were saturated with the traditional thoughts and ideas of the Old Testament, and, on the, other, they were eagerly absorbing the newer conceptions which the spirit of the age had brought into being. This occasioned a continual conflict of thought in their minds; the endeavour to harmonize the old and the new would not always succeed, and in consequence there often resulted a compromise which was illogical and which presented contradictions. Inconsistency of teaching on certain points is, therefore, not surprising under the circumstances.

Again, to realize the significance of much that is found in these Apocalypses one has to reckon with a rigid predestinarianism which was characteristic of the Apocalyptists as a whole. They started with the absolute conviction that the whole course of the world, from beginning to end, both as regards its physical changes and also in all that concerns the history of nations, their growth and decline, and of every single individual, was in every respect predetermined by God Almighty before all time. This belief of the Apocalyptists is well illustrated in one of the later Apocalypses by these words:

"For He hath weighed the age in the balance,

And by number hath He numbered the seasons;

Neither will He move nor stir things,

Till the measure appointed be fulfilled."

(ii. (iv.) Esdras iv. 36, 37.)

Thus "the times and periods of the course of the world's history have been predetermined by God. The numbers of the years have been exactly fixed. This was a fundamental postulate of the Apocalyptists, who devoted much of their energy to calculations, based upon a close study of prophecy, as to the exact period when history should reach its consummation . . . the underlying idea is predestinarian."[2] But all these things, according to the Apocalyptists, were divine secrets hidden from the beginning the world, but revealed to God-fearing men to whom was accorded the faculty of peering into the hidden things of God and of understanding them; upon these men was laid the privilege and duty of revealing the divine secrets to others, hence their name of Apocalyptists or "revealers." It was because the Apocalyptists believed so firmly in this power which they possessed of looking into the deep things of God that they claimed to be able to measure the significance of what had happened in the past and of what was happening in the present; and upon the basis of this knowledge they believed that they also had the power, given them by God, of foreseeing the march of future events; above all, of knowing when the end of the world would come, a consummation towards which the whole history of the world had been tending from the beginning.

In spite of all the mysticism, sometimes of a rather fantastic kind, and of the frequently supra-mundane vision with which the Apocalyptic Literature abounds, the Apocalyptists fully realized the need of practical religion; they were upholders, of the Law, the loyal observance of which they regard as a necessity for all God-fearing men. In this the Apocalyptists were at one, in principle, with Pharisaism; but their conception of what constituted loyal observance of the Law differed from that of the Pharisees, for, unlike these, the Apocalyptists laid all stress on the spirit of its observance rather than upon the letter. Characteristic of their attitude here are the words in 1 Enoch v. 4:

"But ye--ye have not been steadfast, nor done the commandments of the Lord,

But ye have turned away, and have spoken proud and hard words

With your impure mouths against His greatness,

O ye hard-hearted, ye shall find no peace."

And again, in xcix. 2:

"Woe to them that pervert the words of uprightness,

And transgress the eternal Law."

We do not find in this Literature that insistence on the literal carrying-out of the minutest precepts of the Law which was characteristic of Pharisaism. Veneration for the Law is whole-hearted; it is the real guide of life; punishment awaits those who ignore its guidance; but the Pharisaic interpretation of the Law and its requirements is alien to the spirit of the Apocalyptists.

As a whole, the Apocalyptic Literature presents an universalistic attitude very different from the nationalistic narrowness of the Pharisees. It is true, the Apocalyptists are not always consistent in this, but normally they embrace the Gentiles equally with the men of their own nation in the divine scheme of salvation; and, in the same way, the wicked who are excluded are not restricted to the Gentiles, but the Jews equally with them shall suffer torment hereafter according to their deserts. [3]

The Apocalyptic Literature, as distinct from the Apocalyptic Movement owing to which it took its rise, began to come into existence about the period 200-150 B.C.; at any rate, the earliest extant example of this Literature--the earliest portions of the Book of Enoch--belongs to this period. Works of an Apocalyptic character, continued to be written for about three centuries; the Second (Fourth) Book of Esdras, one of the most remarkable Apocalypses, belongs to the end of the first Christian century, approximately. There are Apocalypses of later date, some of subordinate interest are of much later date; but the real period of the Apocalyptic Literature is from about 200 B.C. to about A.D. 100; its beginnings date, therefore, from a time prior to that great landmark in Jewish history, the Maccabæan Era.

THE BOOK OF ENOCH: ITS COMPONENT PARTS AND THEIR DATES

The Book of Enoch is now usually designated 1 Enoch, to distinguish it from the later Apocalypse, *The Secrets of Enoch*, known as 2 Enoch. The former is also called the Ethiopic Enoch, the latter the Slavonic Enoch, after the languages of the earliest versions extant of each respectively. No manuscript of the original language of either is known to be in existence.

---

[2] G. H. Box, *The Ezra Apocalypse*, p, 36 (1912).
[3] The general Pharisaic point of view regarding this may be gathered from Matt. iii. 7-10.

According to Canon Charles, the various elements of which our book in its present form is made up belong to different dates. The following table will show the dates of the different parts of the book. Canon Charles believes that these are approximately correct, without committing himself to the certainty of this in each case:

CHAPTERS		
xii.-xxxvi.	"The Apocalypse of Weeks."	The oldest pre-Maccabæan portions.
xclii.		
xci. 12-17		
vi.-xi.	Fragments of "The Book of Noah."	Pre-Maccabæan at the latest.
liv. 7-lv. 2		
lx.		
lxv.-lxix. 25		
cvi., cvii.		
lxxxiii.-xc.	"The Dream-Visions,"	165-161 B.C.
lxxii.-lxxxii.	"The Book of the Heavenly Luminaries."	Before 110 B.C.
xxxvii.-lxxi.	"The Parables," or "Similitudes."	circa 105-64 B.C.
xci. 1-11, 18, 19-civ.		
i.-v.	The latest portion,	but pre-Christian.

Chapter cv, which consists of only two verses, cannot be dated; while cviii. is in the nature of an appendix, probably added subsequently, to the whole work.

While these dates may be regarded as approximately correct, it should be pointed out that differences of opinion exist among scholars on the subject. Schürer holds, for example, that, with the exception of chapters xxxvii.-lxxi. (the "Parables," or "Similitudes"), the entire book belongs to the period 130-100 B.C.; the "Parables" he assigns to a time not earlier than Herod the Great. Beer thinks that the "Dream-Visions" (chapters lxxxiii.-xc.) belong to the time of John Hyrcanus (135-105 B.C.), and he includes under the pre-Maccabæan portions only xci. 12-17, xcii. xciii. 1-14; and holds that the rest of the book was written before 64 B.C. Dalman maintains that it cannot be proved that the important section xxxvii.-lxxi. (the "Similitudes") is "the product of the pre-Christian period," though he fully recognizes its Jewish character. Burkitt regards the writer as "almost contemporary" with the philosopher Posidonius (135-51 B.C.). There is thus some diversity of opinion as to the date of the book among leading authorities. That it is, as a whole, pre-Christian, may be regarded as definitely established. More difficult is the question whether any portions of it are pre-Maccabæan; Charles gives various reasons for his belief that considerable parts are pre-Maccabæan; we are inclined to agree with him, though it may be questioned whether the last word on the subject has been spoken.

AUTHORSHIP

As the various parts of the book [4] clearly belong to different dates, diversity of authorship is what one is naturally led to expect; and of this there can, indeed, be no shadow of doubt. The author of the earliest portions was a Jew who lived, as Burkitt has shown, in northern Palestine, in the land of Dan, south-west of the Hermon range, near the headwaters of the Jordan. This is important, as it tends to show that the book, or books, is really Palestinian, and one which, therefore, circulated among Jews in Palestine. "If, moreover, the author came from the north, that helps to explain the influence the book had upon the Religion that was cradled in Galilee." [5] Of the authors of the other three books of which "Enoch" is made up (viz. "The Dream-Visions," "The Book of the Heavenly Luminaries," and "The Similitudes") we know nothing save what can be gathered from their writings as to their religious standpoint.

Charles holds that though there is not unity of authorship there is, none the less, uniformity; for, according to him, all the books were written by *Chassidim*, [6] or by their successors, the Pharisees. This contention has been strongly assailed and much weakened by Leszynsky in a recent work on the Sadducees. [7] While frankly recognizing the composite character of the book, Leszynsky holds that the original portions of it emanate from Sadducæan circles; and that the special object of the book originally was the bringing about of a reform of the

---

[4] Burkitt rightly insists that we should speak of the collection as the books, not the book, of Enoch.
[5] Burkitt, op. cit., 28-30.
[6] *i.e.* the " Pious ones." or " Saints."
[7] *Die Saddurder* (1912).

calendar. He points to the ascription of the book to Enoch as supporting his contention, for Enoch lived 365 years, [8] *i.e.* is years correspond to the number of days in the solar year; the basis of reckoning time was one of the fundamental points of difference between the Pharisees and Sadducees, for whereas the former reckoned time by the lunar year (360 days), the latter did so by the solar year. Here a significant remark of Burkitt's is worth recalling; in writing about the false titles given to all the Apocalyptic books, he says: "There is another aspect of pseudonymous authorship to which I venture to think sufficient attention has not been given. It is this, that the names were not chosen out of mere caprice; they indicated to a certain extent what subjects would be treated and the point of view of the writer." [9] Further, the fact that "Enoch walked with God; and he was not; for God took him," (Gen. v. 24) *i.e.* that he ascended into the heavens, is also significant; for he would thereby be just the one to know all about the heavenly luminaries; he was just the most appropriate author of a book which was to deal with astronomical questions. "The Sadducæan character of the original work," says Leszynsky, "is seen most clearly in the discussion regarding the calendar; chapters lxxii.-lxxxii. are rightly called the Book of Astronomy: [10] 'the book of the courses of the luminaries of the heaven, the relations of each, according to their classes, their dominion and their seasons, according to their names and places of origin, and according to their months . . . with regard to all the years of the world and unto eternity, till the new creation is accomplished which endureth till all eternity' (lxxii. 1). That sounds almost as though the author of the Book of jubilees had written it. That it is not a merely scientific interest which impels the writer to give expression to his astronomical theories may be seen from the words at the conclusion of the section: 'Blessed are all the righteous, blessed are all those who walk in the way of righteousness, and sin not as the sinners in the reckoning of all their days, in which the sun traverseth the heaven, entering into and departing from the portals for thirty days . . .' (lxxxii. 4-7). Herein one can discern quite clearly the tendency of the writer. He desires the adoption of the solar year, while his contemporaries wrongly followed a different reckoning, and therefore celebrated the feasts at the wrong time. The 'sinners who sin in the reckoning of the year' are the Pharisees; and the righteous ones who are blessed, the *Zaddikim*, [11] who walk upon the paths of righteousness (*Zedek*) as the name is made to imply, are the Sadducees." [12] The point may appear small to us, but we may compare with it the Quartodeciman controversy in the Church during the second century. It is, at any rate, a strong point in favour of the Sadducæan authorship of "The Book of the Heavenly Luminaries."

The pre-Maccabæan portions (assuming that some portions of it are pre-Maccabæan) of the book of Enoch must certainly be ascribed to the *Chassidim*; but it is not on that account necessary to ascribe *all* the later portions to the Pharisees. Three points especially militate against this: some of the teaching concerning the Messiah; the, generally speaking, universalistic spirit, which is quite un-Pharisaic, and the attitude towards the Law, which is not that of the Pharisees. It is not to be denied that some portions (*e.g.* cii. 6 ff.) are from the hands of Pharisees; nor can it be doubted that the whole collection in its present form has been worked over by a Pharisee, or Pharisees; but that all the post-Maccabæan portions in their original form emanated from Pharisaic circles does not appear to have been proved. It seems more likely that, with the exceptions already referred to, the various component parts of the book were written by Apocalyptists who belonged neither to Pharisaic nor yet to Sadducæan circles.

LANGUAGE

The Book of Enoch exists only in the Ethiopic Version; this was translated from the Greek Version, of which only a few portions are extant. [13] The Latin Version, which was also made from the Greek, is not extant, with the exception of i. 9, and cvi. 1-18; the fragment containing these two passages was discovered by the Rev. Al. R. James, of King's College, Cambridge, in the British Museum. The book was originally written either in Hebrew or Aramaic; Charles thinks that chapters vi.-xxxvi., lxxxiii.-xc. were Aramaic, the rest Hebrew. It is, however, very difficult to say for certain which of these two languages was really the original, because, as Burkitt says, "most of the most convincing proofs that the Greek text of Enoch is a translation from a Semitic language fit equally well with a Hebrew or an Aramaic original"; his opinion is that Aramaic was the original language, "but that a few passages do seem to suggest a Hebrew origin, yet not decisively." [14]

---

[8] See Gen. v. 21-23.

[9] *Op. cit.*, .

[10] *i.e.* "The Book of the Heavenly Luminaries." as Charles calls it.

[11] *i.e.* "the righteous"; a play on the word *Zaddûkîm*, the "sons of Zadok," *i.e.* the Sadducees.

[12] Leszynsky, *op cit.*, p3 ff.

[13] Chaps. i.-xxxii. 6. and xix. 3-xxi. 9 in a duplicate form were discovered at Akhmîm in 1886-1887; vi.-x. 14. xv. 8-xvi. x, and viii. 4-ix. 4 in a duplicate form, have been preserved in Syncellus; lxxxix. 42-49 occurs in a Greek Vatican MS. (No. 1809); there are also a few quotations in early Greek ecclesiastical writings; and i. 9, v.4. xxvii. 2 are quoted in the Epistle of St. Jude 14, 15

[14] *Op. cit.*, .

GENERAL CONTENTS

The reader who comes to peruse the Book of Enoch for the first time will find much that appears to him strange and unattractive; he must not, however, be repelled by this; for in due time he will come to other arts of the book which he will soon see to be of real value from many points of view. But even regarding the less attractive parts, he will find that when these are carefully studied they contain more that is of interest than appears upon the surface. Unfortunately, the opening portion (i.-xxxvi.), which is naturally read first, contains a good deal of the least important parts of the whole book; some passages are even repellent. It is well to remember the point, already referred to, that there are at least four quite independent books included in the "Book of Enoch," exclusive of certain "Noah" fragments and other pieces (see below); the student is, therefore, advised to treat these as separate works, and to read them as such. There is no reason to begin with the book which happens to come first, especially as the first thirty-six chapters do not all belong together.[15] But, in any case, it will be found most useful to have some general idea of the contents of each of the different books before beginning to read them. For this purpose a brief *résumé* of each is given here.

i. *The Book of Enoch* (chapters xii.-xxxvi.). The book begins With a Dream-Vision of Enoch. In this dream Enoch is asked to intercede for the watchers of heaven, *i.e.* the angels, who had left their heavenly home to commit iniquity with the daughters of men. He writes out the petition (cp. the title "Enoch the Scribe") the fallen angels make, and then retires to await the answer, which comes to him in a series of visions. These visions are not quite easy to follow; they are evidently incomplete and somewhat confused; in all probability the text has suffered in transmission. At any rate, the petition is refused; Enoch declares to the fallen angels the doom which, as he has been taught in the visions, is to be their lot; the final words of the message which he is bidden to give them are: "You have no peace" (xii.-xvi.). There follow then accounts of the different journeys which Enoch makes, being conducted by angels of light, through certain parts of the earth, and through Sheol. After the account of the *first journey* (xvii.-xix.) a short enumeration is made of the archangels, seven in number, and their functions (xx.). In the *second journey* is described the place of final punishment of the fallen angels: "This place is the prison of the angels and here they will imprisoned for ever." From thence Enoch is taken to Sheol; then to the west, where he sees the luminaries of heaven. After that the angels show him "seven magnificent mountains," upon one of which is the throne of God; he sees also the Tree of Life, which is to be given to the holy and. righteous after the great judgement. From thence he comes back to the centre of the earth and sees the "blessed place," Jerusalem, and the "accursed valley" (xxi.-xxvii.). The book concludes with what appear to be fragments of other journeys, to the east, to the north, and to the south. Of special interest here is the mention of the Garden of Righteousness, and the Tree of Wisdom (xxviii.-xxxvi.).

Much that is written in these chapters may appear pointless and uninspiring; but we must bear in mind the purpose that lies behind it all. The fallen angels were believed to have brought sin on to the earth; all the wickedness of the world the Apocalyptist traces back to them. This cause of sin must be wholly destroyed before righteousness can come truly to its own. Therefore the Apocalyptist has a practical aim in view when describing in much detail the final place of punishment of the fallen angels; for here, too, are to come all those who by sin are the offspring of this race. No less does he delight in telling of the abode of joy prepared for the righteous. That all these descriptions were constructed out of the imagination of the Apocalyptist, based largely, no doubt, upon popular tradition, did not detract from their practical value for the people of his day. He was a preacher of righteousness who looked forward in absolute conviction to the final overthrow of sin; and all his visions have as their motive-power the yearning for and belief in the triumph of righteousness over sin. One of a like mind wrote later on, in a kind of preface to his book, these significant words, which sum up the essence of the teaching of this book:

And destroy all the spirits of the reprobate, and the children of the Watchers. because they have wronged mankind. Destroy all wrong from the face of the earth, and let every evil work come to an end: and let the plant of righteousness and truth appear: and it shall prove a blessing: the works of righteousness and truth shall be planted in truth and joy for evermore.

ii. *The Parables* (chapters xxxvii.-lxxi.). There are three Parables. or Similitudes, and they all have as their underlying thought the destruction of evil and the triumph of righteousness, as in the preceding book. But here some new and important elements are introduced which give special value to this book.

The *first parable* (xxxviii.-xliv.) is a prophecy of coming judgement upon the wicked, and especially the kings and mighty ones on the earth. On the other hand, the Apocalyptist sees in his vision the abode and resting-places of the righteous who are continually praising the "Lord of Spirits "; this is the usual title given -

---

[15] It is a great pity that one system of chapter-enumeration runs through the whole volume; if each separate book began with chap. i. it would be much better. For obvious reasons this cannot be done here; see Editors' General Preface.

to God in this book. Here occurs the first mention of the "Elect One" (cp. Luke xxiii. 35). In the presence of the Lord of Spirits are also the four Archangels and innumerable companies of other angels. Here he learns many secrets of the heavens; a fragment on Wisdom (xlii.), which recalls some passages in Ecclus. xxiv., comes in the middle of the secrets, and is clearly out of place. The *second parable* (xlv.-lvii.) continues the same theme and further develops it. Of special importance is the sitting of the Elect One on the throne of glory as Judge (xlv. 3), and the mention of His title, "Son of Man" (xlvi. 2). The thought of the vindication of the righteous is marred by their joy at vengeance upon the wicked. A particularly striking passage is chapter xlviii. 1-7, which speaks of the inexhaustible fountain of righteousness reserved for the holy and elect in the presence of the Son of Man and of the Lord of Spirits. The Apocalyptist prophesies further of the repentance of the Gentiles (chapter l.), an universalistic note of significance, and speaks of the Resurrection of the dead in a notable passage:

And In those days shall the earth also give back that which has been entrusted to it, And Sheol also shall give back that which it has received, And Hell shall give back that which it owes.

The parable ends with an account of the judgement, followed by two short passages on the last struggle of the heathen powers against Israel (lvi. 5-8), and the return from the Dispersion (lvii.), which do not appear to be in their original place. The *third parable* (lviii.-lxxi.) has clearly suffered largely from the intrusion of alien matter, and is probably incomplete. Its main theme is the final judgement upon all flesh, and especially upon the great ones of -the earth; the judge is the Son of Man. Some of the passages which speak of the future reward of the righteous are full of beauty; the following is well worth quoting:

And the righteous and elect shall have risen from the earth,

And ceased to be of downcast countenance.

And they shall have been clothed with garments of glory.

And they shall be garments of life from the Lord of Spirits: And your garments shall not grow old.

Nor your glory pass away before the Lord of Spirits.

A large Noah fragment comes in the middle of the Parable (see p. xxvi below). The close of this Parable is contained in lxix. 26-29; the account of Enoch's final translation (lxx.), and two of Enoch's visions (lxxi.) are out of place.

iii. *The Book of the Courses of the Heavenly Luminaries* (chapters lxxii.-lxxxii.). In lxxiv. 12 it says: "And the sun and the stars bring in all the years exactly, so that they do not advance or delay their position by a single day unto eternity; but complete the years with perfect justice in 364 days." [16] This gives the key-note of this book, viz. that time is to be reckoned by the sun, not by the moon (see further on this the section on Authorship, above). Until we come to chapter lxxx. this book is uninteresting in the extreme; it purports to tell in detail of the laws by which the sun, moon, stars and the winds are governed; they are described by Uriel, "the holy angel," to the Apocalyptist. The four quarters of the world, the seven mountains and the seven rivers are also dealt with. "The author has no other interest save a scientific one coloured by Jewish conceptions and beliefs." [17] It is, however, different when we come to chapter lxxx. 2-8; the whole tone alters in these verses, in which it is said that owing to the sin of men the moon and the sun will mislead them. An ethical thought is thus brought in which is wholly lacking in the previous chapters of this book; this is also true of chapter lxxxi.; it is probable that neither of these chapters stood here originally.

Regarding the point of the 364 days to the year which the writer of this book makes, Charles says that "he did this only through sheer incapacity for appreciating anything better; for he must have been acquainted with the solar year of 365¼ days. His acquaintance with the Greek cycles shows this. . . . The author's reckoning of the year at 364 days may be partly due to his opposition to heathen systems, and partly to the fact that 364 is divisible by seven, and amounts to fifty-two weeks exactly." [18] In any case, he is opposed to the lunar year, the Pharisaic way of reckoning time; and this is an important point in favour of Sadducæan authorship. It will be noted that this book was written in post-Maccabæan times; it was after the Maccabæan struggle that the Sadducees and Pharisees appeared as parties definitely opposed to one another. [19]

iv. *The Dream-Visions* (chapters lxxxiii.-xc.). This book consists of two dream-visions; the first deals with the judgement brought upon the world by the deluge on account of sin; the origin of sin is again traced to the angels who fell. It concludes with a hymn of praise to God in which a prayer is offered that all flesh may not be destroyed (lxxxiii.-lxxxiv.). The second dream-vision is much longer; it gives in brief outline the history of the

---

[16] See also lxxxii. 4-6. it.

[17] Charles, *The Book of Enoch*, 7 (1912).

[18] *Op. cit.*

[19] For the points of difference between the Pharisees and Sadducees see the present writer's *The Books of the Apocrypha, their Origin, Teaching, and Contents*, chap. vii.

world to the founding of the Messianic Kingdom. First, the patriarchs, symbolized by bulls, etc. (lxxxv.); then the fallen angels, also described in symbolic language, and their punishment (lxxxvi.-lxxxviii.). The history then proceeds to deal more specifically with Israel from the time of Noah to the Maccabæan revolt (lxxxix.-xc. 19).

Throughout the dream-vision symbolic language is used; the faithful in Israel are spoken of as the sheep, while the Gentiles are symbolized by wild beasts and birds of prey.

The dream-vision concludes with some familiar eschatological notes: the judgement and condemnation of the wicked; the establishment of the New Jerusalem; the conversion of the Gentiles, who become subject to Israel; the gathering-in of the dispersed Israelites; the resurrection of the righteous dead and the setting-up of the Messianic Kingdom on the appearance of the Messiah (xc. 20-38).

v. *The Concluding Section* of the Book (xcii.-cv.; xci. x-10, 18, 19 also belong here) is a complete, though short, work; but there are some obvious interpolations, and it is quite possible that some parts of the text are dislocated. This makes the understanding of the book difficult; but if we follow Charles's guidance here the difficulties will disappear. He says that this concluding piece has in some degree suffered at the hands the final editor of the book, both in the way of direct interpolation and of severe dislocations of the text. The interpolations are: xci. 11, xciii. 11-14, xciv. 7^d, xcvi.

2. The dislocations of the text are a more important feature of the book. They are confined (with the exception of xciii. 13-14, and of cvi. 17^a which should be read immediately after cvi. 14) to xci.-xciii. All critics are agreed as to the chief of these. xci. 12-17 should undoubtedly be read directly after xciii. . . . Taken together xciii. 1-10, xci. 12-17 form an independent whole--the Apocalypse of Weeks--which has been incorporated in xci.-civ. . . . The remaining dislocations need only to be pointed out in order to be acknowledged. On other grounds we find that xci.-civ. is a book of different authorship from that of the rest of the sections. Now, this being so, this section obviously begins with xcii.: 'Written by Enoch the Scribe.' etc. On xcii. follows xci. 1-10, 18, 19 as a natural sequel, where Enoch summons his children to receive his parting words. Then comes the Apocalypse of weeks, xciii. 1-10, xci. 12-17. The original order of the text, therefore, was: xcii. xci. 1-10, 18, 19, xciii. 1-10, xci. 12-17. xciv. These dislocations were the work of the editor, who put the different books of Enoch together, and added lxxx. and lxxxi." (*Op. cit.*, 8).

This book is concerned with the question of the final reward of the righteous and the final punishment of the wicked. . But a new teaching of great importance is put forth here. Hitherto it had been taught that although much incongruity and apparent injustice were to be found on this earth owing to the suffering of the righteous and the prosperity of the wicked,. nevertheless all things would be righted in the world to come, where the wicked would receive their deserts, and the righteous would come to their own. In this book it is taught that retribution will overtake the wicked, and the righteous will have peace and prosperity, even on this earth, with the setting-up of the Messianic Kingdom; and that at the last there will come, with the final judgement, the destruction of the former heaven and earth, and the creation of a new heaven. Then will follow the resurrection of the spirits of the righteous dead who will live for ever in peace and joy, while the wicked will perish everlastingly. The important point, which is a development, is the idea of the punishment of the wicked taking place on this earth, the very scene of their unrighteous triumphs.

vi. *The Noah Fragments* (vi.-xi, lvii. 7-lv. 2, ix. lxv.-lxix. 25, cvi., cvii.). These fragments are not of much importance; the main topics touched upon are the fall of the angels and sin among men in consequence; judgement on mankind, *i.e.* the Deluge, and the preservation of Noah. The first five chapters are generally field to be as late as any part of the whole collection; they deal with the punishment hereafter of the wicked and the blessedness of the righteous. Chapter cviii., which reads like a final word to the whole collection, touches upon the same theme.

THE IMPORTANCE OF THE BOOK FOR THE STUDY OF CHRISTIAN ORIGINS

This is a subject which cannot be thoroughly appreciated without studying the book in detail, especially from its doctrinal standpoint, and seeing in how many aspects it represents the doctrine and the popular conceptions of the Jews during the two last pre-Christian centuries. To do this here would involve a far too extended investigation; it must suffice to indicate a few of the many points which should be studied; from these it will be seen how important the book is for the study of Christian origins. Charles says that "the influence of 1 Enoch on the New Testament has been greater than that of all the other apocryphal and pseudepigraphical books put together"; and he gives a formidable list of passages in the New Testament which "either in phraseology or idea directly depend on, or are illustrative of, passages in 1 Enoch," as well as a further list showing that various doctrines in 1 Enoch had "an undoubted share in moulding the corresponding New Testament doctrines." These passages should be studied--and they will be found to be a most interesting study-

-in Charles's work already referred to several times, pp. xcv.-ciii.; and with these should be read the section on the Theology of the Book of Enoch, pp. ciii.-cx. Another book of great value and interest--also already quoted--is Burkitt's *Jewish and Christian Apocalypses*. In dealing with the subject of 1 Enoch and the Gospels, this writer points out that the former "contains a serious attempt to account for the presence of Evil in human history, and this attempt claims our attention, because it is in essentials the view presupposed in the Gospels, especially in the Synoptic Gospels.

It is when you study Matthew, Mark, and Luke against the background of the Books of Enoch that you see them in their true perspective. In saying this I have no intention of detracting from the importance of what the, Gospels report to us. On the contrary, it puts familiar words into their proper setting. Indeed, it seems to me that some of the best-known Sayings of Jesus only appear in their true light if regarded as *Midrash* upon words and concepts that were familiar to those who heard the Prophet of Galilee, though now they have been forgotten by Jew and Christian alike" (). He then gives an illustration of this from Matt. xii. 43-45, Luke xi. 24--26. Of still greater interest are his remarks upon the relationship between 1 Enoch lxii. and Matt. xxv, 31-46; he believes that "the Similitudes of Enoch are presupposed in the scene from Matthew." The whole of the discussion which follows should be read.

The special points of interest that should be studied in seeking to realize the importance of these books of Enoch for the study of Christian origins are the problems of evil, including, of course, the subjects of dæmonology, and future judgement; the Messiah and the Messianic Kingdom--the title "Son of Man" is of special importance--and the Resurrection. There are, of course, other subjects which will suggest themselves in studying the book.

ABBREVIATIONS, BRACKETS, AND SYMBOLS SPECIALLY USED IN THE TRANSLATION OF 1 ENOCH

E denotes the Ethiopic Version.

G^s denotes the fragments of the Greek Version preserved In Syncellus: in the case of 8^b-9^b there are two forms of the text, G^{s1} G^{s2}.

G^g denotes the large fragment of the Greek Version discovered at Akhmîm, and deposited in the Gizeh Museum, Cairo.

The following brackets are used in the translation of 1 Enoch:

⌈ ⌉. The use of these brackets means that the words so enclosed are found in G^g but not In E.

⌈⌈ ⌉⌉. The use of these brackets means that the words so enclosed are found in E but not in G^g or G^s.

⟨ ⟩ . The use of these brackets means that the words so enclosed are restored.

[ ] The use of these brackets means that the words so enclosed are interpolations.

( ). The use of these brackets means that the words so enclosed are supplied by the editor.

The use of **thick type** denotes that the words so printed are emended.

† † corruption in the text.

. . . = some words which have been lost.

CHAPTER I.

1. The words of the blessing of Enoch, wherewith he blessed the elect ⌈⌈and⌉⌉ righteous, who will be living in the day of tribulation, when all the wicked ⌈⌈and godless⌉⌉ are to be removed.

2. And he took up his parable and said--Enoch a righteous man, whose eyes were opened by God, saw the vision of the Holy One in the heavens, ⌈which⌉ the angels showed me, and from them I heard everything, and from them I understood as I saw, but not for this generation, but for a remote one which is for to come.

3. Concerning the elect I said, and took up my parable concerning them:

The Holy Great One will come forth from His dwelling,

4. And the eternal God will tread upon the earth, (even) on Mount Sinai,
[And appear from His camp]
And appear in the strength of His might from the heaven of heavens.
5. And all shall be smitten with fear
And the Watchers shall quake,
And great fear and trembling shall seize them unto the ends of the earth.
6. And the high mountains shall be shaken,
And the high hills shall be made low,
And shall melt like wax before the flame
7. And the earth shall be [wholly] rent in sunder,
And all that is upon the earth shall perish,
And there shall be a judgement upon all (men).
8. But with the righteous He will make peace.
And will protect the elect,
And mercy shall be upon them.
And they shall all belong to God,
And they shall be prospered,
And they shall [all] be blessed.
[And He will help them all],
And light shall appear unto them,
[And He will make peace with them].
9. And behold! He cometh with ten thousands of [His] holy ones
To execute judgement upon all,
And to destroy [all] the ungodly: And to convict all flesh
Of all the works [of their ungodliness] which they have ungodly committed,
And of all the hard things which ungodly sinners [have spoken] against Him.

CHAPTER II.

1. Observe ye everything that takes place in the heaven, how they do not change their orbits, [and] the luminaries which are in the heaven, how they all rise and set in order each in its season, and transgress not against their appointed order.

2. Behold ye the earth, and give heed to the things which take place upon it from first to last, [how **steadfast** they are], how [none of the things upon earth] change, [but] all the works of God appear [to you].

3. Behold the summer and the winter, [[how the whole earth is filled with water, and clouds and dew and rain lie upon it]].

CHAPTER III.

Observe and see how (in the winter) all the trees [[seem as though they had withered and shed all their leaves, except fourteen trees, which do not lose their foliage but retain the old foliage from two to three years till the new comes.

CHAPTER IV.

And again, observe ye the days of summer how the sun is above the earth over against it. And you seek shade and shelter by reason of the heat of the sun, and the earth also burns with growing heat, and so you cannot tread on the earth, or on a rock by reason of its heat.

CHAPTER V.

1. Observe [[ye]] how the trees cover themselves with green leaves and bear fruit: wherefore give ye heed [and know] with regard to all [His works], and recognize how He that liveth for ever hath made them so.

2. And [all] His works go on [thus] from year to year for ever, and all the tasks [which] they accomplish for Him, and [their tasks] change not, but according as [[God]] hath ordained so is it done.

3. And behold how the sea and the rivers in like manner accomplish and [change not] their tasks [from His commandments].

4. But ye--ye have not been steadfast, nor done the commandments of the Lord,
But ye have turned away and spoken proud and hard words
With your impure mouths against His greatness.
Oh, ye hard-hearted, ye shall find no peace.
5. Therefore shall ye execrate your days,
And the years of your life shall perish,
And [the years of your destruction] shall be multiplied in eternal execration,
And ye shall find no mercy.
6a. In those days ye shall make your names an eternal execration unto all the righteous,
b. And by you shall [all] who curse, curse,
And all the sinners [and godless] shall imprecate by you,
7c. And for you the godless there shall be a curse.
6d. And all the . . . shall rejoice,
e. And there shall be forgiveness of sins,
f. And every mercy and peace and forbearance:
g. There shall be salvation unto them, a goodly light.
i. And for all of you sinners there shall be no salvation,

j But on you all shall abide a curse.

7*a*. But for the elect there shall be light and joy and peace,

b. And they shall inherit the earth.

8 And then there shall be bestowed upon the elect wisdom,

And they shall all live and never again sin,

Either through ungodliness or through pride:

But they who are wise shall be humble.

9 And they shall not again transgress,

Nor shall they sin all the days of their life,

Nor shall they die of (the divine) anger or wrath,

But they shall complete the number of the days of their life.

And their lives shall be increased in peace,

And the years of their joy shall be multiplied,

In eternal gladness and peace,

All the days of their life.

VI-XI. *The Fall of the Angels: the Demoralisation of Mankind: the Intercession of the Angels on behalf of Mankind. The Dooms pronounced by God on the Angels: the Messianic Kingdom* (a Noah fragment).

CHAPTER VI.

1. And it came to pass when the children of men had multiplied that in those days were born unto them beautiful and comely daughters.

2. And the angels, the children of the heaven, saw and lusted after them, and said to one another: 'Come, let us choose us wives from among the children of men and beget us children.'

3. And Semjâzâ, who was their leader, said unto them: 'I fear ye will not indeed agree to do this deed, and I alone shall have to pay the penalty of a great sin.'

4. And they all answered him and said: 'Let us all swear an oath, and all bind ourselves by mutual imprecations not to abandon this plan but to do this thing.'

5. Then sware they all together and bound themselves by mutual imprecations upon it.

6. And they were in all two hundred; who descended [in the days] of Jared on the summit of Mount Hermon, and they called it Mount Hermon, because they had sworn and bound themselves by mutual imprecations upon it.

7. And these are the names of their leaders: Sêmîazâz, their leader, Arâkîba, Râmêêl, Kôkabîêl, Tâmîêl, Râmîêl, Dânêl, Êzêqêêl, Barâqîjâl, Asâêl, Armârôs, Batârêl, Anânêl, Zaqîêl, Samsâpêêl, Satarêl, Tûrêl, Jômjâêl, Sariêl.

8. These are their chiefs of tens.

CHAPTER VII.

1. And all the others together with them took unto themselves wives, and each chose for himself one, and they began to go in unto them and to defile themselves with them, and they taught them charms and enchantments, and the cutting of roots, and made them acquainted with plants.

2. And they became pregnant, and they bare great giants, whose height was three thousand ells:

3. Who consumed all the acquisitions of men. And when men could no longer sustain them,

4. the giants turned against them and devoured mankind.

5. And they began to sin against birds, and beasts, and reptiles, and fish, and to devour one another's flesh, and drink the blood.

6. Then the earth laid accusation against the lawless ones.

CHAPTER VIII.

1. And Azâzêl taught men to make swords, and knives, and shields, and breastplates, and made known to them **the metals** ⟨of the earth⟩ and the art of working them, and bracelets, and ornaments, and the use of antimony, and the beautifying of the eyelids, and all kinds of costly stones, and all colouring tinctures.

2. And there arose much godlessness, and they committed fornication, and they were led astray, and became corrupt in all their ways. Semjâzâ taught enchantments, and root-cuttings, Armârôs the resolving of enchantments, Barâqîjâl, (taught) astrology, Kôkabêl the constellations, Ezêqêêl the knowledge of the clouds, ⟨Araqiêl the signs of the earth, Shamsiêl the signs of the sun⟩, and Sariêl the course of the moon. And as men perished, they cried, and their cry went up to heaven . . .

CHAPTER IX.

1. And then Michael, Uriel, Raphael, and Gabriel looked down from heaven and saw much blood being shed upon the earth, and all lawlessness being wrought upon the earth.

2. And they said one to another: 'The earth made †without inhabitant cries the voice of their crying† up to the gates of heaven.

3 ⟦And now to you, the holy ones of heaven⟧, the souls of men make their suit, saying, "Bring our cause before the Most High.".'

4. And they said to the Lord of the ages: 'Lord of lords, God of gods, King of kings, ⟨and God of the ages⟩, the throne of Thy glory (standeth) unto all the generations of the ages, and Thy name holy and glorious and blessed unto all the ages!

5. Thou hast made all things, and power over all things hast Thou: and all things are naked and open in Thy sight, and Thou seest all things, and nothing can hide itself from Thee.

6. Thou seest what Azâzêl hath done, who hath taught all unrighteousness on earth and revealed the eternal secrets which were (preserved) in heaven, which men were striving to learn:

7. And Semjâzâ, to whom Thou hast given authority to bear rule over his associates.

8. And they have gone to the daughters of men upon the earth, and have slept with the women, and have defiled themselves, and revealed to them all kinds of sins.

9. And the women have borne giants, and the whole earth has thereby been filled with blood and unrighteousness.

10. And now, behold, the souls of those who have died are crying and making their suit to the gates of heaven, and their lamentations have ascended: and cannot cease because of the lawless deeds which are wrought on the earth.

11. And Thou knowest all things before they come to pass, and Thou seest these things and Thou dost suffer them, and Thou dost not say to us what we are to do to them in regard to these.'

CHAPTER X.

1. Then said the Most High, the Holy and Great One spake, and sent **Uriel** to the son of Lamech, and said to him:

2. ' ⟨Go to Noah⟩ and tell him in my name "Hide thyself!" and reveal to him the end that is approaching: that the whole earth will be destroyed, and a deluge is about to come upon the whole earth, and will destroy all that is on it.

3. And now instruct him that he may escape and his seed may be preserved for all the generations of the world.'

4. And again the Lord said to Raphael: 'Bind Azâzêl hand and foot, and cast him into the darkness: and make an opening in the desert, which is in Dûdâêl, and cast him therein.

5. And place upon him rough and jagged rocks, and cover him with darkness, and let him abide there for ever, and cover his face that he may not see light.

6. And on the day of the great judgement he shall be cast into the fire.

7. And heal the earth which the angels have corrupted, and proclaim the healing of the earth, that they may heal the plague, and that all the children of men may not perish through all the secret things that the Watchers have disclosed and have taught their sons.

8. And the whole earth has been corrupted through the works that were taught by Azâzêl: to him ascribe all sin.'

9. And to Gabriel said the Lord: 'Proceed against the bastards and the reprobates, and against the children of fornication: and destroy[the children of fornication and] the children of the Watchers from amongst men [and cause them to go forth]: send them one against the other that they may destroy each other in battle: for length of days shall they not have.

10. And no request that they (i.e. their fathers) make of thee shall be granted unto their fathers on their behalf; for they hope to live an eternal life, and that each one of them will live five hundred years.'

11. And the Lord said unto Michael: 'Go, bind Semjâzâ and his associates who have united themselves with women so as to have defiled themselves with them in all their uncleanness.

12. And when their sons have slain one another, and they have seen the destruction of their beloved ones, bind them fast for seventy generations in the valleys of the earth, till the day of their judgement and of their consummation, till the judgement that is for ever and ever is consummated.

13. In those days they shall be led off to the abyss of fire: ⟨and⟩ to the torment and the prison in which they shall be confined for ever.

14. And whosoever shall be condemned and destroyed will from thenceforth be bound together with them to the end of all generations.

15. And destroy all the spirits of the reprobate and the children of the Watchers, because they have wronged mankind.

16. Destroy all wrong from the face of the earth and let every evil work come to an end: and let the plant of righteousness and truth appear: [and it shall prove a blessing; the works of righteousness and truth] shall be planted in truth and joy for evermore.

17 And then shall all the righteous escape,

And shall live till they beget thousands of children,

And all the days of their youth and their old age

Shall they complete in peace.

18 And then shall the whole earth be tilled in righteousness, and shall all be planted with trees and be full of blessing.

19. And all desirable trees shall be planted on it, and they shall plant vines on it: and the vine which they plant thereon shall yield wine in abundance, and as for all the seed which is sown thereon each measure (of it) shall bear a thousand, and each measure of olives shall yield ten presses of oil.

20. And cleanse thou the earth from all oppression, and from all unrighteousness, and from all sin, and from all godlessness: and all the uncleanness that is wrought upon the earth destroy from off the earth.

21. [And all the children of men shall become righteous], and all nations shall offer adoration and shall praise Me, and all shall worship Me. And the earth shall be cleansed from all defilement, and from all sin, and from all punishment, and from all torment, and I will never again send (them) upon it from generation to generation and for ever.

CHAPTER XI.

1. And in those days I will open the store chambers of blessing which are in the heaven, so as to send them down [upon the earth] over the work and labour of the children of men.

2. And truth and peace shall be associated together throughout all the days of the world and throughout all the generations **of men**.'

XII-XVI. *Dream Vision of Enoch: his intercession for Azâzêl and the fallen Angels: and his announcement to them of their first and final doom.*

CHAPTER XII.

1. Before these things Enoch was hidden, and no one of the children of men knew where he was hidden, and where he abode, and what had become of him.

2. And his activities had to do with the Watchers, and his days were with the holy ones.

3. And I, Enoch was blessing the Lord of **majesty** and the King of the ages, and lo! the Watchers called me--Enoch the scribe--and said to me:

4. 'Enoch, thou scribe of righteousness, go, †declare† to the Watchers of the heaven who have left the high heaven, the holy eternal place, and have defiled themselves with women, and have done as the children of earth do, and have taken unto themselves wives: "Ye have wrought great destruction on the earth:

5. And ye shall have no peace nor forgiveness of sin: and inasmuch as †they† delight themselves in †their† children,

6. The murder of †their† beloved ones shall †they† see, and over the destruction of †their† children shall †they† lament, and shall make supplication unto eternity, but mercy and peace shall ye not attain."'

CHAPTER XIII.

1. And Enoch went and said: 'Azâzêl, thou shalt have no peace: a severe sentence has gone forth against thee to put thee in bonds:

2. And thou shalt not have toleration nor †request† granted to thee, because of the unrighteousness which thou hast taught, and because of all the works of godlessness and unrighteousness and sin which thou hast shown to men.'

3. Then I went and spoke to them all together, and they were all afraid, and fear and trembling seized them.

4. And they besought me to draw up a petition for them that they might find forgiveness, and to read their petition in the presence of the Lord of heaven.

5. For from thenceforward they could not speak (with Him) nor lift up their eyes to heaven for shame of their sins for which they had been condemned.

6. Then I wrote out their petition, and the prayer in regard to their spirits and their deeds individually and in regard to their requests that they should have forgiveness and length ⟨of days⟩ †.

7. And I went off and sat down at the waters of Dan, in the land of Dan, to the south of the west of Hermon: I read their petition till I fell asleep.

8. And behold a dream came to me, and visions fell down upon me, and I saw visions of chastisement, ⌈and a voice came bidding (me)⌉ I to tell it to the sons of heaven, and reprimand them.

9. And when I awaked, I came unto them, and they were all sitting gathered together, weeping in 'Abelsjâîl, which is between Lebanon and Sênêsêr, with their faces covered.

10. And I recounted before them all the visions which I had seen in sleep, and I began to speak the words of righteousness, and to reprimand the heavenly Watchers.

CHAPTER XIV.

1. The book of the words of righteousness, and of the reprimand of the eternal Watchers in accordance with the command of the Holy Great One in that vision.

2. I saw in my sleep what I will now say with a tongue of flesh and with the breath of my mouth: which the Great One has given to men to converse therewith and understand with the heart.

3. As He has created and given ⟦⌈to man the power of understanding the word of wisdom, so hath He created me also and given⌉⟧ me the power of reprimanding the Watchers, the children of heaven.

4. I wrote out your petition, and in my vision it appeared thus, that your petition will not be granted unto you ⟦⌈throughout all the days of eternity, and that judgement has been finally passed upon you: yea (your petition) will not be granted unto you⌉⟧.

5. And from henceforth you shall not ascend into heaven unto all eternity, and ⌈in bonds⌉ of the earth the decree has gone forth to bind you for all the days of the world.

6. And (that) previously you shall have seen the destruction of your beloved sons and ye shall have no pleasure in them, but they shall fall before you by the sword.

7. And your petition on their behalf shall not be granted, nor yet on your own: even though you weep and pray and speak all the words contained in the writing which I have written.

8. And the vision was shown to me thus: Behold, in the vision clouds invited me and a mist summoned me, and the course of the stars and the lightnings sped and hastened me, and the winds in the vision caused me to fly and lifted me upward, and bore me into heaven.

9. And I went in till I drew nigh to a wall which is built of crystals and surrounded by tongues of fire: and it began to affright me.

10. And I went into the tongues of fire and drew nigh to a large house which was built of crystals: and the walls of the house were like a tesselated floor (made) of crystals, and its groundwork was of crystal.

11. Its ceiling was like the path of the stars and the lightnings, and between them were fiery cherubim, and their heaven was (clear as) water.

12. A flaming fire surrounded the walls, and its portals blazed with fire.

13. And I entered into that house, and it was hot as fire and cold as ice: there were no delights of life therein: fear covered me, and trembling got hold upon me.

14. And as I quaked and trembled, I fell upon my face.

15. And I beheld a vision, And lo! there was a second house, greater than the former, and the entire portal stood open before me, and it was built of flames of fire.

16. And in every respect it so excelled in splendour and magnificence and extent that I cannot describe to you its splendour and its extent.

17. And its floor was of fire, and above it were lightnings and the path of the stars, and its ceiling also was flaming fire.

18. And I looked and saw⌈⌈therein⌉⌉ a lofty throne: its appearance was as crystal, and the wheels thereof as the shining sun, and there was the vision of cherubim.

19. And from underneath the throne came streams of flaming fire so that I could not look thereon.

20. And the Great Glory sat thereon, and His raiment shone more brightly than the sun and was whiter than any snow.

21. None of the angels could enter and could behold His face by reason of the magnificence and glory and no flesh could behold Him.

22. The flaming fire was round about Him, and a great fire stood before Him, and none around could draw nigh Him: ten thousand times ten thousand (stood) before Him, yet He needed no counselor.

23. And the most holy ones who were nigh to Him did not leave by night nor depart from Him.

24. And until then I had been prostrate on my face, trembling: and the Lord called me with His own mouth, and said to me: 'Come hither, Enoch, and hear my word.' 25. ⌈And one of the holy ones came to me and waked me⌉, and He made me rise up and approach the door: and I bowed my face downwards.

CHAPTER XV.

1. And He answered and said to me, and I heard His voice: 'Fear not, Enoch, thou righteous man and scribe of righteousness: approach hither and hear my voice.

2. And go, say to ⌈⌈the Watchers of heaven⌉⌉, who have sent thee to intercede ⌈⌈for them: "You should intercede"⌉⌉ for men, and not men for you:

3. Wherefore have ye left the high, holy, and eternal heaven, and lain with women, and defiled yourselves with the daughters of men and taken to yourselves wives, and done like the children of earth, and begotten giants (as your) sons?

4. And though ye were holy, spiritual, living the eternal life, you have defiled yourselves with the blood of women, and have begotten (children) with the blood of flesh, and, as the children of men, have lusted after flesh and blood as those ⌈also⌉ do who die and perish.

5. Therefore have I given them wives also that they might impregnate them, and beget children by them, that thus nothing might be wanting to them on earth.

6. But you were [formerly] spiritual, living the eternal life, and immortal for all generations of the world.

7. And therefore I have not appointed wives for you; for as for the spiritual ones of the heaven, in heaven is their dwelling.

8. And now, the giants, who are produced from the spirits and flesh, shall be called evil spirits upon the earth, and on the earth shall be their dwelling.

9. Evil spirits have proceeded from their bodies; because they are born from men, [[and]] from the holy Watchers is their beginning and primal origin; [they shall be evil spirits on earth, and] evil spirits shall they be called.

[10. As for the spirits of heaven, in heaven shall be their dwelling, but as for the spirits of the earth which were born upon the earth, on the earth shall be their dwelling.]

11. And the spirits of the giants, the nephilim, afflict, oppress, destroy, attack, do battle, and work destruction on the earth, and cause trouble: they take no food, [but nevertheless hunger] and thirst, and cause offences. And these spirits shall rise up against the children of men and against the women, because they have proceeded [from them].

CHAPTER XVI.

1. From the days of the slaughter and destruction and death [of the giants], from the souls of whose flesh the spirits, having gone forth, shall destroy without incurring judgement--thus shall they destroy until the day of the consummation, the great[judgement] in which the age shall be consummated, over the Watchers and the godless, yea, shall be wholly consummated."

2. And now as to the Watchers who have sent thee to intercede for them, who had been [[aforetime]] in heaven, (say to them): "You have been in heaven, but [all] the mysteries had not yet been revealed to you, and you knew worthless ones, and these in the hardness of your hearts you have made known to the women, and through these mysteries women and men work much evil on earth."

4. Say to them therefore: "You have no peace."'

XVII-XXXVII. *Enoch's Journeys through the Earth and Sheol.*
XVII-XIX. *The First Journey.*

CHAPTER XVII.

1. And they took [and] brought me to a place in which those who were there were like flaming fire, and, when they wished, they appeared as men.

2. And they brought me to the place of darkness, and to a mountain the point of whose summit reached to heaven.

3. And I saw the places of the luminaries [and the treasuries of the stars] and of the thunder [and] in the **uttermost depths**, where were a fiery bow and arrows and their quiver, and [[a fiery sword]] and all the lightnings.

4. And they took me to the living waters, and to the fire of the west, which receives every setting of the sun.

5. And I came to a river of fire in which the fire flows like water and discharges itself into the great sea towards the west.

6. I saw the great rivers and came to the great [river and to the great] darkness, and went to the place where no flesh walks.

7. I saw the mountains of the darkness of winter and the place whence all the waters of the deep flow.

8. I saw the mouths of all the rivers of the earth and the mouth of the deep.

CHAPTER XVIII

1. I saw the treasuries of all the winds: I saw how He had furnished with them the whole creation and the firm foundations of the earth.

2. And I saw the corner-stone of the earth: I saw the four winds which bear [the earth and] the firmament of the heaven.

3. [[And I saw how the winds stretch out the vaults of heaven]], and have their station between heaven and earth:[[these are the pillars of the heaven]].

4. I saw the winds of heaven which turn and bring the circumference of the sun and all the stars to their setting.

5. I saw the winds on the earth carrying the clouds: I saw [[the paths of the angels. I saw]] at the end of the earth the firmament of the heaven above. And I proceeded and saw a place which burns day and night, where there are seven mountains of magnificent stones, three towards the east, and three towards the south.

7. And as for those towards the east, ⟨one⟩ was of coloured stone, and one of pearl, and one of jacinth, and those towards the south of red stone.

8. But the middle one reached to heaven like the throne of God, of alabaster, and the summit of the throne was of sapphire.

9. And I saw a flaming fire. And beyond these mountains 10. is a region the end of the great earth: there the heavens were completed.

11. And I saw a deep abyss, with columns [[of heavenly fire, and among them I saw columns]] of fire fall, which were beyond measure alike towards the height and towards the depth.

12. And beyond that abyss I saw a place which had no firmament of the heaven above, and no firmly founded earth beneath it: there was no water upon it, and no birds, but it was a waste and horrible place.

13. I saw there seven stars like great burning mountains, and to me, when I inquired regarding them, 14. The angel said: 'This place is the end of heaven and earth: this has become a prison for the stars and the host of heaven.

15. And the stars which roll over the fire are they which have transgressed the commandment of the Lord in the beginning of their rising, because they did not come forth at their appointed times.

16. And He was wroth with them, and bound them till the time when their guilt should be consummated (even) [for ten thousand years].'

CHAPTER XIX.

1. And Uriel said to me: 'Here shall stand the angels who have connected themselves with women, and their spirits assuming many different forms are defiling mankind and shall lead them astray into sacrificing to demons [[as gods]], (here shall they stand,) till [[the day of]] the great judgement in which they shall be judged till they are made an end of.

2. And the women also of the angels who went astray shall become sirens.' 3. And I, Enoch, alone saw the vision, the ends of all things: and no man shall see as I have seen.

CHAPTER XX.
Name and Functions of the Seven Archangels.

1. And these are the names of the holy angels who watch.

2. Uriel, one of the holy angels, who is over the world and over Tartarus.

3. Raphael, one of the holy angels, who is over the spirits of men.

4. Raguel, one of the holy angels who †takes vengeance on† the world of the luminaries.

5. Michael, one of the holy angels, to wit, he that is set over the best part of mankind [[and]] over chaos.

6. Saraqâel, one of the holy angels, who is set over the spirits, who sin in the spirit.

7. Gabriel, one of the holy angels, who is over Paradise and the serpents and the Cherubim.

8. Remiel, one of the holy angels, whom God set over those who rise.

CHAPTER XXI.
Preliminary and final place of punishment of the fallen angels (stars).

1. And I proceeded to where things were chaotic.

2. And I saw there something horrible: I saw neither a heaven above nor a firmly founded earth, but a place chaotic and horrible.

3. And there I saw seven stars of the heaven bound together in it, like great mountains and burning with fire.

4. Then I said: 'For what sin are they bound, and on what account have they been cast in hither?'

5. Then said Uriel, one of the holy angels, who was with me, and was chief over them, and said: 'Enoch, why dost thou ask, and why art thou eager for the truth?

6. These are of the number of the stars [of heaven], which have transgressed the commandment of the Lord, and are bound here till ten thousand years, the time entailed by their sins, are consummated.'

7. And from thence I went to another place, which was still more horrible than the former, and I saw a horrible thing: a great fire there which burnt and blazed, and the place was cleft as far as the abyss, being full of great descending columns of fire: neither its extent or magnitude could I see, nor could I conjecture.

8. Then I said: 'How fearful is the place and how terrible to look upon!'

9. Then Uriel answered me, one of the holy angels who was with me, and said unto me: 'Enoch, why hast thou such fear and affright?' And I answered: 'Because of this fearful place, and because of the spectacle of the pain.'

10. And he said [[unto me]]: 'This place is the prison of the angels, and here they will be imprisoned for ever.'

CHAPTER XXII.
Sheol, or the Underworld.

1. And thence I went to another place, and he showed me in the west [another] great and high mountain [and] of hard rock.

E	G^g

| **E** | **G^g** |

2 And there was in it †four† **hollow** places, deep and wide and very smooth. †How† smooth are **the hollow places** and deep and dark to look at.

2. And there were †four† hollow places in it, deep and very smooth: †three† of them were dark and one bright; and there was a fountain of water in its midst. And I said: '†How† smooth are these hollow places, and deep and dark to view.'

3. Then Raphael answered, one of the holy watchers who was with me, and said unto me: 'These hollow places have been created for this very purpose, that the spirits of the souls of the dead should assemble therein, yea that all the souls of the children of men should assemble here. And these places **have been made** to receive them till the day of their judgement and till their appointed period [till the period appointed], till the great judgement (comes) upon them.'

| **E** | **G^g** |

5. I saw the spirits of the children of men who were dead, and their voice went forth to heaven and made suit.

5. I saw (the spirit of) **a dead man** making suit, and his voice went forth to heaven and made suit.

6. Then I asked Raphael the watcher who was with me, and I said unto him: 'This spirit--whose is it whose voice goeth forth and maketh suit?'

6. And I asked Raphael the angel who was with me, and I said unto him: 'This spirit which maketh suit, whose is it, whose voice goeth forth and maketh suit to heaven?'

7. And he answered me saying: 'This is the spirit which went forth from Abel, whom his brother Cain slew, and he makes his suit against him till his seed is destroyed from the face of the earth, and his seed is annihilated from amongst the seed of men.'

E

8. Then I asked regarding it, and regarding all the **hollow places**: 'Why as one separated from the other?'

9. And he answered me and said unto me: 'These three have been made that the spirits of the dead might be separated. And such a division has been made ⟨for⟩ the spirits of the righteous, in which there as the **bright** spring of **water**.

10. **And** such has been made for sinners when they die and are buried in the earth and judgement has not been executed on them in their lifetime.

11. Here their spirits shall be set apart in this great pain till the great day of judgement and punishment and torment of those who †curse† for ever, and retribution for their spirits. There He shall bind them for ever.

12. And such a division has been made for the spirits of those who make their suit, who make disclosures concerning their destruction, when they were slain in the days of the sinners.

13. Such has been made for the spirits of men who were not righteous but sinners, who were

Gᵍ

8. Then I asked regarding all the **hollow places**: 'Why is one separated from the other?'

9. And he answered me saying: 'These three have been made that the spirits of the dead might be separated. And **this** division has been made for the spirits of the righteous, in which there is the bright spring of water.

10. And **this** has been made for sinners when they die and are buried in the earth and judgement has not been executed upon them in their lifetime.

11. Here their spirits shall be set apart in this great pain, till the great day of judgement, scourgings, and torments of the accursed for ever, **so that** (there maybe) retribution for their spirits. There He shall bind them for ever.

12. And **this** division has been made for the spirits of those who make their suit, who make disclosures concerning their destruction, when they were slain in the days of the sinners.

13. And **this** has been made for the spirits of men who shall not be righteous but sinners, who are godless, and of the lawless they shall be companions: but their

complete in transgression, and of the transgressors. they shall be companions: but their spirits shall not be slain in the day of judgement nor shall they be raised from thence.

14. Then I blessed the Lord of glory and said: 'Blessed be my Lord, the Lord of righteousness, who ruleth for ever.'

spirits shall not be punished in the day of judgement nor shall they be raised from thence.

14. Then I blessed the Lord of Glory and said: 'Blessed art Thou, Lord of righteousness, who rulest over the world.'

CHAPTER XXIII.

The Fire that deals with the Luminaries of Heaven

1. From thence I went to another place to the west of the ends of the earth.

2. And I saw a [[burning]] fire which ran without resting, and paused not from its course day or night but (ran) regularly.

3. And I asked saying: 'What is this which rests not?'

4. Then Raguel, one of the holy angels who was with me, answered me [[and said unto me]]: 'This course [of fire] [[which thou hast seen]] is the fire in the west which †persecutes† all the luminaries of heaven.'

XXIV. XXV. *The Seven Mountains in the North-West and the Tree of Life.*

CHAPTER XXIV.

1. [[And from thence I went to another place of the earth]], and he showed me a mountain range of fire which burnt [[day and night]].

2. And I went beyond it and saw seven magnificent mountains all differing each from the other, and the stones (thereof) were magnificent and beautiful, magnificent as a whole, of glorious appearance and fair exterior: [[three towards]]the east, [[one]] founded on the other, and three towards the south, one upon the other, and deep rough ravines, no one of which joined with any other.

3. And the seventh mountain was in the midst of these, and it excelled them in height, resembling the seat of a throne: and fragrant trees encircled the throne.

4. And amongst them was a tree such as I had never yet smelt, neither was any amongst them nor were others like it: it had a fragrance beyond all fragrance, and its leaves and blooms and wood wither not for ever: and its fruit [[is beautiful, and its fruit]] resembles the dates of a palm.

5. Then I said: '[How] beautiful is this tree, and fragrant, and its leaves are fair, and its blooms [[very]] delightful in appearance.' 6. Then answered Michael, one of the holy [[and honoured]] watchers who was with me, and was their leader.

CHAPTER XXV.

1. And he said unto me: 'Enoch, why dost thou ask me regarding the fragrance of the tree, and [why] dost thou wish to learn the truth?'

2. Then I answered him [[saying]]: 'I wish to know about everything, but especially about this tree.'

3. And he answered saying: 'This high mountain [[which thou hast seen]], whose summit is like the throne of God, is His throne, where the Holy Great One, the Lord of Glory, the Eternal King, will sit, when He shall come down to visit the earth with goodness.

4. And as for this fragrant tree no mortal is permitted to touch it till the great judgement, when He shall take vengeance on all and bring (everything) to its consummation for ever. It shall then be given to the righteous and holy.

5. Its fruit shall be for food to the elect: it shall be transplanted to the holy place, to the temple of the Lord, the Eternal King.

6 Then shall they rejoice with joy and be glad,

And into the holy place shall they enter;

And its fragrance shall be in their bones,

And they shall live a long life on earth,

Such as thy fathers lived:

And in their days shall no [[sorrow or]] plague

Or torment or calamity touch them.'

7 Then blessed I the God of Glory, the Eternal King, who hath prepared such things for the righteous, and hath created them and promised to give to them.

CHAPTER XXVI.
Jerusalem and the Mountains, Ravines and Streams.

1. And I went from thence to the middle of the earth, and I saw a blessed place [in which there were trees] with branches abiding and blooming [of a dismembered tree].

2. And there I saw a holy mountain, [[and]] underneath the mountain to the east there was a stream and it flowed towards the south.

3. And I saw towards the east another mountain higher than this, and between them a deep and narrow ravine: in it also ran a stream [underneath] the mountain.

4. And to the west thereof there was another mountain, lower than the former and of small elevation, and a ravine [deep and dry] between them: and another deep and dry ravine was at the extremities of the three [mountains].

5. And all the ravines were deep [[and narrow]], (being formed) of hard rock, and trees were not planted upon them.

6. And I marveled [[at the rocks, and I marveled]] at the ravine, yea, I marveled very much.

CHAPTER XXVII.
The Purpose of the Accursed Valley.

1. Then said I: 'For what object is this blessed land, which is entirely filled with trees, and this accursed valley [[between]]?'

2. [[Then Uriel, one of the holy watchers who was with me, answered and said: 'This]] accursed valley is for those who are accursed for ever: Here shall all [the accursed] be gathered together who utter with their lips against the Lord unseemly words and of His glory speak hard things.

E	Gg
Here shall they be gathered together, and here shall be their place of judgement.	Here shall they be gathered together, and here shall be the place of their habitation.
3. In the last days there shall be upon them the spectacle of righteous judgement in the presence of the righteous for ever: here shall the	3. In the last times, in the days of the true judgement in the presence of the righteous for ever: here shall the **godly**

merciful bless the Lord of glory, the Eternal King.

bless the Lord of Glory, the Eternal King.

4. In the days of judgement over the former, they shall bless Him for the mercy in accordance with which He has assigned them (their lot).'

5. Then I blessed the Lord of Glory and set forth His [glory] and lauded Him gloriously.

XXVIII-XXXIII. *Further Journey to the East.*

CHAPTER XXVIII

1. And thence I went [[towards the east]], into the midst [[of the mountain range of the desert]], and I saw a wilderness and it was solitary, full of trees and plants.

2. [[And]] water gushed forth from above.

3. Rushing like a copious watercourse [which flowed] towards the north-west it caused clouds and dew to ascend on every side.

CHAPTER XXIX.

1. And thence I went to another place in the desert, and approached to the east of this mountain range.

2. And [[there]] I saw aromatic trees exhaling the fragrance of frankincense and myrrh, and the trees also were similar to the almond tree.

CHAPTER XXX.

1 .And beyond these, I went afar to the east, and I saw another place, a valley (full) of water.

2. And [therein there was] a tree, the colour (?) of fragrant trees such as the mastic.

3. And on the sides of those valleys I saw fragrant cinnamon. And beyond these I proceeded to the east.

CHAPTER XXXI.

1. And I saw other mountains, and amongst them were [groves of] trees, and there flowed forth from them nectar, which is named sarara and galbanum. 2. And beyond these mountains I saw another mountain [to the east of the ends of the earth],[[whereon were aloe trees]], and all the trees were full of stacte, being like almond-trees.

3. And when one burnt it, it smelt sweeter than any fragrant odour.

CHAPTER XXXII.

E	G^g
1. And after these fragrant odours, as I looked towards the north over the mountains I saw seven mountains full of choice nard and fragrant trees and cinnamon and pepper.	1. To the north-east I beheld seven mountains full of choice nard and mastic and cinnamon and pepper.

2. And thence I went over the summits of [all] these mountains, far towards the east [of the earth], and passed above the Erythraean sea and went far from it, and passed over [[the angel]] Zotîêl.

E	G^g
3. And I came to the Garden of Righteousness, and saw beyond those trees many large trees growing there and of goodly fragrance, large, very beautiful and	3. And I came to the Garden of Righteousness, and from afar off trees more numerous than these trees and great--†two† trees there, very great, beautiful, and glorious,

| glorious, and the tree of wisdom whereof they eat and know great wisdom. | and magnificent, and the tree of knowledge, whose holy fruit they eat and know great wisdom. |

4. ⌈That tree is in height like the fir, and its leaves are⌉ like (those of) the Carob tree: and its fruit is like the clusters of the vine, very beautiful: and the fragrance of the tree penetrates afar.

5. Then I said: '⌈How⌉ beautiful is the tree, and how attractive is its look!' 6. Then Raphael the holy angel, who was with me, answered me ⟦⌈and said⌉⟧: 'This is the tree of wisdom, of which thy father old (in years) and thy aged mother, who were before thee, have eaten, and they learnt wisdom and their eyes were opened, and they knew that they were naked and they were driven out of the garden.'

CHAPTER XXXIII.

1. And from thence I went to the ends of the earth and saw there great beasts, and each differed from the other; and (I saw) birds also differing in appearance and beauty and voice, the one differing from the other.

2. And to the east of those beasts I saw the ends of the earth whereon the heaven rests, and the portals of the heaven open.

3. And I saw how the stars of heaven come forth, and I counted the portals out of which they proceed, and wrote down all their outlets, of each individual star by itself, according to their number and their names, their courses and their positions, and their times and their months, as Uriel the holy watcher who was with me showed me.

4. He showed all things to me and wrote them down for me: also their names he wrote for me, and their laws and their companies.

XXXIV. XXXV. *Enoch's Journey to the North.*

CHAPTER XXXIV.

1. And from thence I went towards the north to the ends of the earth, and there I saw a great and glorious device at the ends of the whole earth.

2. And here I saw three portals of heaven open in the heaven: through each of them proceed north winds: when they blow there is cold, hail, frost, snow, dew, and rain.

3. And out of one portal they blow for good: but when they blow through the other two portals, it is with violence and affliction on the earth, and they blow with violence.

CHAPTER XXXV.

1. And from thence I went towards the west to the ends of the earth, and saw there three portals of the heaven open such as I had seen in the †east†, the same number of portals, and the same number of outlets.

CHAPTER XXXVI.
The Journey to the South.

1. And from thence I went to the south to the ends of the earth, and saw there three open portals of the heaven: and thence there come dew, rain, †and wind†.

2. And from thence I went to the east to the ends of the heaven, and saw here the three eastern portals of heaven open and small portals above them.

3. Through each of these small portals pass the stars of heaven and run their course to the west on the path which is shown to them.

4. And as often as I saw I blessed always the Lord of Glory, and I continued to bless the Lord of Glory who has wrought great and glorious wonders, to show the greatness of His work to the angels and to **spirits** and to men, that they might praise His work and all His creation: that they might see the work of His might and praise the great work of His hands and bless Him for ever.

THE PARABLES

SECTION II . (CHAPTERS XXXVII LXXI)

THE PARABLES. INTRODUCTION

A. Critical Structure.

This Section is in a fragmentary condition, and many of the critical questions connected with it can only be tentatively solved or merely stated. It consists in the main of three Parables — 38-44, 45-57, 58-69. These are introduced by 37 and concluded by 70 which records Enoch's final translation. 71 appears to be out of place, and belongs to one of the three Parables. The two visions recorded in it were witnessed in Enoch's lifetime.

There are many interpolations. 60 65-69-23 are confessedly from the Book of Noah. 39 1-2a 54-7 -55-2 are probably from the same work. These interpolations are adapted by their editor to their adjoining contexts in Enoch. This he does by borrowing characteristic terms, such as 'Lord of Spirits', 'Head of Days', to which, however, either through ignorance or of set intention he generally gives a new connotation.

There now remain the following chapters and verses: 37-41-2; 42; 45-54; 55-3; 58; 62-63: 69-23 to 71. But these passages can hardly have been derived from the same hand originally. There are traces of a composite origin. Beer, in Kautzsch's Apok. und Pseudep. ii. 227, has drawn attention to the fact that behind the Parables there appear to lie two distinct sources — one dealing with the Elect One (40-5; 45-3; 49 2-4; 51-3, 5; 52 6-9; 53-6; 55-4; 61-5, 8, 19; 62,1) and the other with the Son of Man (46-2, 3, 4; 48-2; 62-7,9,14; 63-11; 69-26,27,28; 70-1; 71-17) and that in the former the angelus *interpres* was designated ' the angel of peace who went with me ' and in the latter ' the angel who went with me'. This observation is just, and even with the present text it is possible, I think, to distinguish these sources, though Beer has not attempted it. But these two sources do not account for the whole of the Parables. In 71 there are two distinct visions, 71 1-4 and 71 5-17', where the angelus interpres is Michael and not either of the former angels, unless we identify him with one of them, which is indeed possible : see my edition of the Test. XII Patriarchs, pp. 39-40. Whence 42 is drawn is a difficulty. But returning to the two sources above-mentioned, we might assign to the ' Son of Man ' source and the angelic interpreter — ' the angel who went with me.'

40.3-7; 46 – 48.7; 52.3-4; 61 3-4; 62.2-63; 69.26—29; 70-71.

And to the source dealing with the Elect One and the angelic interpreter — ' the angel of peace.'

38-39; 40.1-2, 8-10; 41. 1-2, 9; 45; 48.8-10; 50-52.1-2, 5-9; 53-54.6; 55.3-57; 61.1-2, 5-13; 62.1.

The above analysis of the sources can of course only be provisional until the Greek version of the original is recovered. The second source differs from the former in recognizing the judgement of the sword, 38-5; 48.8-10, and the attack of the hostile Gentiles on Jerusalem, 56, the progressive conversion of the Gentiles who had no part in oppressing Israel, 50 2.4, and the triumphant return of the Dispersion, 57.

55.3 – 57.3 looks like an independent source adapted to a new context. There is no hint of the judgement of the sword in the first source.

These two sources had much material in common. 52.1-2 apparently belonged to both in some form. The Elect One and the Son of Man alike judge the kings and the mighty, and the same attributes are to a great extent ascribed to each, save that of pre-existence, which as it happens, is attributed only to the Son of Man, 48.2 sqq,

B. Relation of 37-71 to the rest of the book.

As all critics are now agreed that the Parables are distinct in -origin from the rest of the book, there is no occasion for treating exhaustively the grounds for this conclusion. Accordingly, we shall give here only a few of the chief characteristics which differentiate this Section from all the other Sections of the book,

(a) Names of God found only in 37-71. ' Lord of Spirits ' (passim) ; ' Head of Days' (46-2); 'Lord of the mighty' (63-2); 'Lord of the rich' (63-2); •Lord of wisdom' (63-2).

(b) Angelology. The four chief angels in 37-71 are Michael, Raphael, Gabriel, and Phanuel. Phanuel is not mentioned elsewhere in the book, which gives Uriel instead. In 14-11 God is surrounded by Cherubim; but in 61.10; 71.6 by Cherubim, Seraphim, and Ophannim, angels of power, and angels of principalities. The angel of peace (40.8) is also peculiar to the Parables,

(c) Demonology. In the other Sections of the book the sins of the angels consisted in their lusting after the daughters of men (6-8), but in 54-6 in their becoming subjects of Satan. In 37.71 an evil spirit-world is presupposed from the beginning, but not in the rest of the book. Satan and the Satans, 40.7; 53.3; 54.6, are not even mentioned in the other Sections. These have access to heaven, 40-7, whereas in the other Sections only good angels have access there. The angels of punishment also are found for the first time in 37-71.

(d) The Messianic doctrine in 37-71 is unique, not only as regards the other Sections of Enoch, but also in Jewish literature as a whole. The Messiah pre-exists, 48.2 (note), from the beginning ; he sits on the throne of God, 51-3, and possesses universal dominion, 62-6; all judgement is committed unto him, 69-27, and he slays the wicked by the word of his mouth, 62-2. Turning to the other Sections we find that there is no Messiah in 1-36 and in 91-104, while in 83-90 the Messiah is evidently human and possesses none of the great attributes belonging to the Messiah of the Parables.

(e) The scene of the Messianic kingdom in 1-36 is Jerusalem and the earth purified from sin; in 83-90, a heavenly Jerusalem set up by God Himself; in 91-104, Jerusalem and the earth as they are ; but in 37-70, a new heaven and a new earth, 45- 4-5. Again, the duration of the Messianic kingdom in 1-36 is eternal, but the life of its members limited. The duration of the Messianic kingdom in 83-90 is eternal, and the life of its members eternal (?). The duration of the Messianic kingdom in 91-104 is limited, and the life of its members limited. (In 91-104 the real interest centres, not in the Messianic kingdom, but in the future spiritual life of the righteous.) But the duration of the Messianic kingdom in 37-71 is eternal, and the life of its members eternal.

C. Date.

From a full review of the evidence, -which is given and discussed in the notes on 38-5, it appears that the Kings and the mighty so often denounced in the Parables are the later Maccabean princes and their Sadducean supporters — the later Maccabean princes, on the one hand, and not the earlier ; for the blood of the righteous was not shed, as the writer complains (47 1-2-4), before 95 B.C. : the later Maccabean princes, on the other hand, and not the Herodians; for (1) the Sadducees were not supporters of the latter, and (2) Rome was not as yet known to the writer as one of the great world-powers — a fact which necessitates an earlier date than 64 b. c, when Rome interposed authoritatively in the affairs of Judaea. Thus the date of the Parables could not have been earlier than 94 B.C. or later than 64 B.C. But it is possible to define the date more precisely. As the Pharisees enjoyed un- broken power and prosperity under Alexandra 79-70 B. c, the Parables must be assigned either to the years 94-79 or 70-64. Finally, if we consider that 56-5 – 57-3a is an interpolation, and that this passage must have been written before 64 b. c, the Parables might reasonably be referred to the years 94-79. See also Gen, In trod.

D. The Problem and its Solution.

Seeing that God is a just God, how comes it that wickedness is throned in high places and that righteousness is oppressed ? Is there no end to the prosperity and power of unbelieving rulers, and no recompense of reward for the suffering righteous ? The author (in the genuine portions) finds the answer in a comprehensive view of the world's history : only by tracing evil to its source can the present wrongness of things be understood, and only by pursuing the world's history to its final issues can its present inequalities be justified. The author has no interest save for the moral and spiritual worlds, and this is manifest even in the divine names ' Lord of Spirits ', ' Head of Days ', ' Most High '. Whole hierarchies of angelic beings appear in 61 10-12. His view is strongly apocalyptic, and follows closely in the wake of Daniel. The origin of sin is traced one stage further back than in 1-36. The first authors of sin were the Satans, the adversaries of man, 40' (note). The Watchers fell through becoming subject to these, and leading mankind astray, 54-6. Punishment was at once meted out to the Watchers, and they were confined in a deep abyss, 54-5, to await the final judgement, 54-6, 55-4, 64.

In the meantime sin flourishes in the world : sinners deny the name of the Lord of Spirits, 38-2; 41-2, and of His Anointed, 48-10; the Idngs and the mighty of the earth trust in their sceptre, and glory, 63-7, and oppress the elect of the children of God, 62-11. But the prayer of the righteous ascends, and their blood goes up before the Lord of Spirits crying for vengeance, 47-1; and the angels unite in the prayer of the righteous, 47-2. But the oppression of the kings and the mighty will not continue for ever : suddenly the Head of Days will appear and with Him the Son of Man, 46 2-3-2; 48-2, to execute judgement upon all alike— on the righteous and wicked, on angel and on man. And to this end there will be a Resurrection of all Israel, 51-1; 61-5; the books of the living will be opened, 47-3; all judgement will be committed unto the Son of Man, 41-9;' 69.27; the Son of Man Avill possess universal dominion, 02", and sit on the throne of his glory, 62-3,5; 69 27-29, which is likewise God's throne, 47-3; 51-3. He will judge the holy angels, 61-8, and the fallen angels, 55.4, the righteous upon earth, 62-3, and the sinners, 62-3 ; but particularly those who oppress his saints, the kings and the mighty and those who possess the earth, 48 5-8,9; 53-3; 62 3-11'. All are judged according to their deeds, for their deeds are weighed in the balance, 41-1. The fallen angels are cast into a fiery furnace, 54-6; the kings and the mighty confess their sins, and pray for forgiveness, but in vain, 63; and are given into the hands of the righteous, 38-5 ; and their destruction will furnish a spectacle to the righteous as they burn and vanish for ever out of sight, 48 9-10; 62.12; to be tortured in Gehenna by the angels of punishment, 53 3-5; 54 1-2. The remaining sinners and godless will be driven from off the face of the earth, 38-3; 41-2; 45-6. The Son of Man will slay them with the word of his mouth, 62-2. Sin and wrongdoing will be banished from the earth, 49-2; and heaven and earth will be transformed, 45 4-5 ; and the righteous and elect will have their mansions therein, 39-5,' 41-2. And the light of the Lord of Spirits will shine upon them, 38-4 ; they will live in the light of eternal life, 58-3. The Elect One will dwell amongst them, 45-4; and they will eat and lie down and rise up with him for ever and ever, 62-14. They will be clad in garments of life, 62-15,16; and shine as fiery lights, 39-7. And they will seek after light and find righteousness and peace with the Lord of Spirits, 58-4; and grow in knowledge and righteousness, 58-5.

CHAPTER XXXVII.

1. The second vision which he saw, the vision of wisdom--which Enoch the son of Jared, the son of Mahalalel, the son of Cainan, the son of Enos, the son of Seth, the son of Adam, saw.

2. And this is the beginning of the words of wisdom which I lifted up my voice to speak and say to those which dwell on earth: Hear, ye men of old time, and see, ye that come after, the words of the Holy One which I will speak before the Lord of Spirits.

3. It were better to declare (them only) to the men of old time, but even from those that come after we will not withhold the beginning of wisdom.

4. Till the present day such wisdom has never been given **by** the Lord of Spirits as I have received according to my insight, according to the good pleasure of the Lord of Spirits by whom the lot of eternal life has been given to me.

5. Now three parables were imparted to me, and I lifted up my voice and recounted them to those that dwell on the earth.

XXXVII-XLIV. The First Parable.

CHAPTER XXXVIII.
The Coming Judgement of the Wicked.

1. The First Parable.

When the congregation of the righteous shall appear,

And sinners shall be judged for their sins,

And shall be driven from the face of the earth:

2. And when the Righteous One shall appear before the eyes of the righteous,

Whose elect works hang upon the Lord of Spirits,

And light shall appear to the righteous and the elect who dwell on the earth,

Where then will be the dwelling of the sinners,

And where the resting-place of those who have denied the Lord of Spirits?

It had been good for them if they had not been born.

3. When the secrets of the righteous shall be revealed and the sinners judged,

And the godless driven from the presence of the righteous and elect,

4. From that time those that possess the earth shall no longer be powerful and exalted:

And they shall not be able to behold the face of the holy,

For the Lord of Spirits has caused His light to appear

On the face of the holy, righteous, and elect.

5. Then shall the kings and the mighty perish

And be given into the hands of the righteous and holy.

6. And thenceforward none shall seek for themselves mercy from the Lord of Spirits,

For their life is at an end.

CHAPTER XXXIX.
The Abode of the Righteous and of the Elect One: the Praises of the Blessed.

1. [And it †shall come to pass in those days that elect and holy children †will descend from the high heaven, and their seed †will become one with the children of men.

2. And in those days Enoch received books of zeal and wrath, and books of disquiet and expulsion.]

And mercy shall not be accorded to them, saith the Lord of Spirits.

3. And in those days a whirlwind carried me off from the earth,

And set me down at the end of the heavens.

4. And there I saw another vision, the dwelling-places of the holy,

And the resting-places of the righteous.

5. Here mine eyes saw their dwellings with His righteous angels,

And their resting-places with the holy.

And they petitioned and interceded and prayed for the children of men,

And righteousness flowed before them as water,

And mercy like dew upon the earth:

Thus it is amongst them for ever and ever.

6a. And in that place mine eyes saw the Elect One of righteousness and of faith,

7a. And I saw his dwelling-place under the wings of the Lord of Spirits.

6b. And righteousness shall prevail in his days,

And the righteous and elect shall be without number before Him for ever and ever.

7b. And all the righteous and elect before Him shall be †strong† as fiery lights,

And their mouth shall be full of blessing,

And their lips extol the name of the Lord of Spirits,

And righteousness before Him shall never fail,

[And uprightness shall never fail before Him.]

8. There I wished to dwell,

And my spirit longed for that dwelling-place:

And there heretofore hath been my portion,

For so has it been established concerning me before the Lord of Spirits.

9. In those days I praised and extolled the name of the Lord of Spirits with blessings and praises, because He hath destined me for blessing and glory according to the good pleasure of the Lord of Spirits.

10. For a long time my eyes regarded that place, and I blessed Him and praised Him, saying: 'Blessed is He, and may He be blessed from the beginning and for evermore.

11. And before Him there is no ceasing. He knows before the world was created what is for ever and what will be from generation unto generation.

12. Those who sleep not bless Thee: they stand before Thy glory and bless, praise, and extol, saying: "Holy, holy, holy, is the Lord of Spirits: He filleth the earth with spirits."'

13. And here my eyes saw all those who sleep not: they stand before Him and bless and say: 'Blessed be Thou, and blessed be the name of the Lord for ever and ever.'

14. And my face was changed; for I could no longer behold.

XL. XLI. *The Four Archangels.*

CHAPTER XL.

1. And after that I saw thousands of thousands and ten thousand times ten thousand, I saw a multitude beyond number and reckoning, who stood before the Lord of Spirits.

2. And on the four sides of the Lord of Spirits I saw four presences, different from those that sleep not, and I learnt their names: for the angel that went with me made known to me their names, and showed me all the hidden things.

3. And I heard the voices of those four presences as they uttered praises before the Lord of glory.

4. The first voice blesses the Lord of Spirits for ever and ever.

5. And the second voice I heard blessing the Elect One and the elect ones who hang upon the Lord of Spirits.

6. And the third voice I heard pray and intercede for those who dwell on the earth and supplicate in the name of the Lord of Spirits.

7. And I heard the fourth voice fending off the Satans and forbidding them to come before the Lord of Spirits to accuse them who dwell on the earth.

8. After that I asked the angel of peace who went with me, who showed me everything that is hidden: 'Who are these four presences which I have seen and whose words I have heard and written down?'

9. And he said to me: 'This first is Michael, the merciful and long-suffering: and the second, who is set over all the diseases and all the wounds of the children of men, is Raphael: and the third, who is set over all the powers, is Gabriel: and the fourth, who is set over the repentance unto hope of those who inherit eternal life, is named Phanuel.' And these are the four angels of the Lord of Spirits and the four voices I heard in those days.

CHAPTER XLI.

1. And after that I saw all the secrets of the heavens, and how the kingdom is divided, and how the actions of men are weighed in the balance.

2. And there I saw the mansions of the elect and the mansions of the holy, and mine eyes saw there all the sinners being driven from thence which deny the name of the Lord of Spirits, and being dragged off: and they could not abide because of the punishment which proceeds from the Lord of Spirits.

XLI. 3-9. *Astronomical Secrets.*

3. And there mine eyes saw the secrets of the lightning and of the thunder, and the secrets of the winds, how they are divided to blow over the earth, and the secrets of the clouds and dew, and there I saw from whence they proceed in that place and from whence they saturate the dusty earth.

4. And there I saw closed chambers out of which the winds are divided, the chamber of the hail and winds, the chamber of the mist, and of the clouds, and the cloud thereof hovers over the earth from the beginning of the world.

5. And I saw the chambers of the sun and moon, whence they proceed and whither they come again, and their glorious return, and how one is superior to the other, and their stately orbit, and how they do not leave their orbit, and they add nothing to their orbit and they take nothing from it, and they keep faith with each other, in accordance with the oath by which they are bound together.

6. And first the sun goes forth and traverses his path according to the commandment of the Lord of Spirits, and mighty is His name for ever and ever.

7. And after that I saw the hidden and the visible path of the moon, and she accomplishes the course of her path in that place by day and by night--the one holding a position opposite to the other before the Lord of Spirits.

And they give thanks and praise and rest not;

For unto them is their thanksgiving rest.

8. For the sun changes oft for a blessing or a curse,

And the course of the path of the moon is light to the righteous

And darkness to the sinners in the name of the Lord,

Who made a separation between the light and the darkness,

And divided the spirits of men,

And strengthened the spirits of the righteous,

In the name of His righteousness.

9. For no angel hinders and no power is able to hinder; for He appoints a judge for them all and He judges them all before Him.

CHAPTER XLII.
The Dwelling-places of Wisdom and of Unrighteousness.

1. Wisdom found no place where she might dwell;

Then a dwelling-place was assigned her in the heavens.

2 Wisdom went forth to make her dwelling among the children of men,

And found no dwelling-place:

Wisdom returned to her place,

And took her seat among the angels.

3 And unrighteousness went forth from her chambers:

Whom she sought not she found,

And dwelt with them,

As rain in a desert

And dew on a thirsty land.

XLIII. XLIV. *Astronomical Secrets.*

CHAPTER XLIII.

1. And I saw other lightnings and the stars of heaven, and I saw how He called them all by their names and they hearkened unto Him.

2. And I saw how they are weighed in a righteous balance according to their proportions of light: (I saw) the width of their spaces and the day of their appearing, and how their revolution produces lightning: and (I saw) their revolution according to the number of the angels, and (how) they keep faith with each other.

3. And I asked the angel who went with me who showed me what was hidden: 'What are these?' 4. And he said to me: 'The Lord of Spirits hath showed thee their parabolic meaning (lit. 'their parable'): these are the names of the holy who dwell on the earth and believe in the name of the Lord of Spirits for ever and ever.'

CHAPTER XLIV.

Also another phenomenon I saw in regard to the lightnings: how some of the stars arise and become lightnings and cannot part with their new form.

XLV-LVII. The Second Parable.
The Lot of the Apostates: the New Heaven and the New Earth.

CHAPTER XLV.

1. And this is the Second Parable concerning those who deny the name of the dwelling of the holy ones and the Lord of Spirits.

2. And into the heaven they shall not ascend,

And on the earth they shall not come:

Such shall be the lot of the sinners

Who have denied the name of the Lord of Spirits,

Who are thus preserved for the day of suffering and tribulation.

3. On that day Mine Elect One shall sit on the throne of glory

And shall **try** their works,

And their places of rest shall be innumerable.

And their souls shall grow strong within them when they see Mine Elect Ones,

And those who have called upon My glorious name:

4. Then will I cause Mine Elect One to dwell among them.

And I will transform the heaven and make it an eternal blessing and light

5. And I will transform the earth and make it a blessing:

And I will cause Mine elect ones to dwell upon it:

But the sinners and evil-doers shall not set foot thereon.

6. For I have provided and satisfied with peace My righteous ones

And have caused them to dwell before Me:

But for the sinners there is judgement impending with Me,

So that I shall destroy them from the face of the earth.

CHAPTER XLVI.
The Head of Days and the Son of Man.

1. And there I saw One who had a head of days,

And His head was white like wool,

And with Him was another being whose countenance had the appearance of a man,

And his face was full of graciousness, like one of the holy angels.

2. And I asked the angel who went with me and showed me all the hidden things, concerning that Son of Man, who he was, and whence he was, (and)

why he went with the Head of Days? And he answered and said unto me:

This is the son of Man who hath righteousness,

With whom dwelleth righteousness,

And who revealeth all the treasures of that which is hidden,

Because the Lord of Spirits hath chosen him,

And whose lot hath the pre-eminence before the Lord of Spirits in uprightness for ever.

4, And this Son of Man whom thou hast seen

Shall †raise up† the kings and the mighty from their seats,

[And the strong from their thrones]

And shall loosen the reins of the strong,

And break the teeth of the sinners.

5. [And he shall put down the kings from their thrones and kingdoms]

Because they do not extol and praise Him,

Nor humbly acknowledge whence the kingdom was bestowed upon them.

6. And he shall put down the countenance of the strong,

And shall fill them with shame.

And darkness shall be their dwelling,

And worms shall be their bed,

And they shall have no hope of rising from their beds,

Because they do not extol the name of the Lord of Spirits.

7. And these are they who †judge† the stars of heaven,

[And raise their hands against the Most High],

†And tread upon the earth and dwell upon it†.

And all their deeds manifest unrighteousness,

And their power rests upon their riches,

And their faith is in the †gods† which they have made with their hands,

And they deny the name of the Lord of Spirits,

8. And they persecute the houses of His congregations,

And the faithful who hang upon the name of the Lord of Spirits.

CHAPTER XLVII.
The Prayer of the Righteous for Vengeance and their Joy at its coming.

1. And in those days shall have ascended the prayer of the righteous,

And the blood of the righteous from the earth before the Lord of Spirits.

2. In those days the holy ones who dwell above in the heavens

Shall unite with one voice

And supplicate and pray [and praise,

And give thanks and bless the name of the Lord of Spirits]

On behalf of the blood of the righteous which has been shed,

And that the prayer of the righteous may not be in vain before the Lord of Spirits,

That judgement may be done unto them,

And that they may not have to suffer for ever.

3. In those days I saw the Head of Days when He seated himself upon the throne of His glory,

And the books of the living were opened before Him:

And all His host which is in heaven above and His counselors stood before Him,

4 And the hearts of the holy were filled with joy;

Because the number of the righteous **had been offered**,

And the prayer of the righteous had been heard,

And the blood of the righteous been required before the Lord of Spirits.

CHAPTER XLVIII.
The Fount of Righteousness; the Son of Man--the Stay of the Righteous: Judgement of the Kings and the Mighty.

1. And in that place I saw the fountain of righteousness

Which was inexhaustible:

And around it were many fountains of wisdom;

And all the thirsty drank of them,

And were filled with wisdom,

And their dwellings were with the righteous and holy and elect.

2. And at that hour that Son of Man was named In the presence of the Lord of Spirits,

And his name before the Head of Days.

3. Yea, before the sun and the signs were created,

Before the stars of the heaven were made,

His name was named before the Lord of Spirits.

4. He shall be a staff to the righteous whereon to stay themselves and not fall,

And he shall be the light of the Gentiles,

And the hope of those who are troubled of heart.

5. All who dwell on earth shall fall down and worship before him,

And will praise and bless and celebrate with song the Lord of Spirits.

6. And for this reason hath he been chosen and hidden before Him,

Before the creation of the world and for evermore.

7. And the wisdom of the Lord of Spirits hath revealed him to the holy and righteous;

For he hath preserved the lot of the righteous,

Because they have hated and despised this world of unrighteousness,

And have hated all its works and ways in the name of the Lord of Spirits: For in his name they are saved,

And according to his good pleasure hath it been in regard to their life.

8. In these days downcast in countenance shall the kings of the earth have become,

And the strong who possess the land because of the works of their hands;

For on the day of their anguish and affliction they shall not (be able to) save themselves.

9. And I will give them over into the hands of Mine elect:

As straw in the fire so shall they burn before the face of the holy:

As lead in the water shall they sink before the face of the righteous,

And no trace of them shall any more be found.

10. And on the day of their affliction there shall be rest on the earth,

And before them they shall fall and not rise again:

And there shall be no one to take them with his hands and raise them: For they have denied the Lord of Spirits and His Anointed.

The name of the Lord of Spirits be blessed.

CHAPTER XLIX.
The Power and Wisdom of the Elect One.

l. For wisdom is poured out like water,

And glory faileth not before him for evermore.

2. For he is mighty in all the secrets of righteousness,

And unrighteousness shall disappear as a shadow,

And have no continuance;

Because the Elect One standeth before the Lord of Spirits,

And his glory is for ever and ever,

And his might unto all generations.

3. And in him dwells the spirit of wisdom,

And the spirit which gives insight,

And the spirit of understanding and of might,

And the spirit of those who have fallen asleep in righteousness.

4. And he shall judge the secret things,

And none shall be able to utter a lying word before him;

For he is the Elect One before the Lord of Spirits according to His good pleasure.

CHAPTER L.
The Glorification and Victory of the Righteous: the Repentance of the Gentiles.

1. And in those days a change shall take place for the holy and elect,

And the light of days shall abide upon them,

And glory and honour shall turn to the holy,

2. On the day of affliction on which evil shall have been treasured up against the sinners.

And the righteous shall be victorious in the name of the Lord of Spirits:

And He will cause the others to witness (this)

That they may repent; And forgo the works of their hands.

3. They shall have no honour through the name of the Lord of Spirits,

Yet through His name shall they be saved,

And the Lord of Spirits will have compassion on them,

For His compassion is great.

4. And He is righteous also in His judgement,

And in the presence of His glory unrighteousness also shall not maintain itself:

At His judgement the unrepentant shall perish before Him.

5. And from henceforth I will have no mercy on them, saith the Lord of Spirits.

CHAPTER LI.
The Resurrection of the Dead, and the Separation by the Judge of the Righteous and the Wicked.

1. And in those days shall the earth also give back that which has been entrusted to it,

And Sheol also shall give back that which it has received,

And hell shall give back that which it owes.

5a. For in those days the Elect One shall arise,

2. And he shall choose the righteous and holy from among them:

For the day has drawn nigh that they should be saved.

3. And the Elect One shall in those days sit on My throne,

And his mouth shall pour forth all the secrets of wisdom and counsel:

For the Lord of Spirits hath given (them) to him and hath glorified him.

4. And in those days shall the mountains leap like rams,

And the hills also shall skip like lambs satisfied with milk,

And the faces of [all] the angels in heaven shall be lighted up with joy.

5b. And the earth shall rejoice,

c. And the righteous shall dwell upon it,

d. And the elect shall walk thereon.

CHAPTER LII.
The Seven[20] Metal Mountains and the Elect One.

l. And after those days in that place where I had seen all the visions of that which is hidden--for I had been carried off in a whirlwind and they had borne me towards the west-- 2. There mine eyes saw all the secret things of heaven that shall be, a mountain of iron, and a mountain of copper, and a mountain of silver, and a mountain of gold, and a mountain of soft metal, and a mountain of lead.

3. And I asked the angel who went with me, saying, 'What things are these which I have seen in secret?' 4. And he said unto me: 'All these things which thou hast seen shall serve the dominion of His Anointed that he may be potent and mighty on the earth.'

5. And that angel of peace answered, saying unto me: 'Wait a little, and there shall be revealed unto thee all the secret things which surround the Lord of Spirits.

6. And these mountains which thine eyes have seen,

The mountain of iron, and the mountain of copper, and the mountain of silver,

And the mountain of gold, and the mountain of soft metal, and the mountain of lead,

All these shall be in the presence of the Elect One

As wax: before the fire,

And like the water which streams down from above [upon those mountains],

And they shall become powerless before his feet.

7. And it shall come to pass in those days that none shall be saved,

Either by gold or by silver,

And none be able to escape.

8 And there shall be no iron for war,

Nor shall one clothe oneself with a breastplate.

Bronze shall be of no service,

---

20 [Only six are mentioned; see Charles' note in his large edition--EDD.]

And tin [shall be of no service and] shall not be esteemed,

And lead shall not be desired.

9 And all these things shall be [denied and] destroyed from the surface of the earth,

When the Elect One shall appear before the face of the Lord of Spirits.'

LIII. LVI. *The Valley of Judgement: the Angels of Punishment: the Communities of the Elect One.*

CHAPTER LIII.

1. There mine eyes saw a deep valley with open mouths, and all who dwell on the earth and sea and islands shall bring to him gifts and presents and tokens of homage, but that deep valley shall not become full.

2. And their hands commit lawless deeds,

And the sinners devour all whom they lawlessly oppress:

Yet the sinners shall be destroyed before the face of the Lord of Spirits,

And they shall be banished from off the face of His earth,

And they shall perish for ever and ever.

3. For I saw all the angels of punishment abiding (there) and preparing all the instruments of Satan.

4. And I asked the angel of peace who went with me: 'For whom are they preparing these instruments?' 5. And he said unto me: 'They prepare these for the kings and the mighty of this earth, that they may thereby be destroyed.

6. And after this the Righteous and Elect One shall cause the house of his congregation to appear: henceforth they shall be no more hindered in the name of the Lord of Spirits.

7. And these mountains shall not stand as the earth before his righteousness, But the hills shall be as a fountain of water,

And the righteous shall have rest from the oppression of sinners.'

CHAPTER LIV.

1 And I looked and turned to another part of the earth, and saw there a deep valley with burning fire.

2. And they brought the kings and the mighty, and began to cast them into this deep valley.

3. And there mine eyes saw how they made these their instruments, iron chains of immeasurable weight.

4. And I asked the angel of peace who went with me, saying: 'For whom are these chains being prepared?'

5. And he said unto me: 'These are being prepared for the hosts of Azâzêl, so that they may take them and cast them into the abyss of complete condemnation, and they shall cover their jaws with rough stones as the Lord of Spirits commanded.

6. And Michael, and Gabriel, and Raphael, and Phanuel shall take hold of them on that great day, and cast them on that day into the burning furnace, that the Lord of Spirits may take vengeance on them for their unrighteousness in becoming subject to Satan and leading astray those who dwell on the earth.'

7. 'And in those days shall punishment come from the Lord of Spirits, and he will open all the chambers of waters which are above the heavens, and of the fountains which are beneath the earth.

8. And all the waters shall be joined with the waters: that which is above the heavens is the masculine, and the water which is beneath the earth is the feminine.

9. And they shall destroy all who dwell on the earth and those who dwell under the ends of the heaven.

10. And when they have recognized their unrighteousness which they have wrought on the earth, then by these shall they perish.

CHAPTER LV.

1. And after that the Head of Days repented and said: 'In vain have I destroyed all who dwell on the earth.'

LV 2. *Noachic Fragment on the first World Judgement.*

2. And He sware by His great name: 'Henceforth I will not do so to all who dwell on the earth, and I will set a sign in the heaven: and this shall be a pledge of good faith between Me and them for ever, so long as heaven is above the earth. And this is in accordance with My command.'

LV. 3-LVI.

4. *Final Judgement of Azâzêl, the Watchers and their children.*

3. When I have desired to take hold of them by the hand of the angels on the day of tribulation and pain **because of** this, I will cause My chastisement and My wrath to abide upon them, saith God, the Lord of Spirits.

4. Ye †mighty kings† who dwell on the earth, ye shall have to behold Mine Elect One, how he sits on the throne of glory and judges Azâzêl, and all his associates, and all his hosts in the name of the Lord of Spirits.'

CHAPTER LVI.

1. And I saw there the hosts of the angels of punishment going, and they held scourges and chains of iron and bronze.

2. And I asked the angel of peace who went with me, saying: 'To whom are these who hold the scourges going?' 3. And he said unto me: 'To their elect and beloved ones, that they may be cast into the chasm of the abyss of the valley.

4. And then that valley shall be filled with their elect and beloved,

And the days of their lives shall be at an end,

And the days of their leading astray shall not thenceforward be reckoned.

LVI. 5-8. *Last struggle of heathen Powers against Israel.*

5. And in those days the angels shall return

And hurl themselves to the east upon the Parthians and Medes:

They shall stir up the kings, so that a spirit of unrest shall come upon them, And they shall rouse them from their thrones,

That they may break forth as lions from their lairs,

And as hungry wolves among their flocks.

6. And they shall go up and tread under foot the land of His elect ones,

[And the land of His elect ones shall be before them a threshing-floor and a highway:]

7 But the city of my righteous shall be a hindrance to their horses.

And they shall begin to fight among themselves,

And their right hand shall be strong against themselves,

And a man shall not know his brother,

Nor a son his father or his mother,

Till there be no number of the corpses through their slaughter,

And their punishment be not in vain.

8 In those days Sheol shall open its jaws,

And they shall be swallowed up therein

And their destruction shall be at an end;

Sheol shall devour the sinners in the presence of the elect.'

CHAPTER LVII.
The Return from the Dispersion.

1. And it came to pass after this that I saw another host of wagons, and men riding thereon, and coming on the winds from the east, and from the west to the south.

2. And the noise of their wagons was heard, and when this turmoil took place the holy ones from heaven remarked it, and the pillars of the earth were moved from their place, and the sound thereof was heard from the one end of heaven to the other, in one day.

3. And they shall all fall down and worship the Lord of Spirits. And this is the end of the second Parable.

LVIII-LXXI. The Third Parable.

CHAPTER LVIII.
The Blessedness of the Saints.

1. And I began to speak the third Parable concerning the righteous and elect.

2. Blessed are ye, ye righteous and elect,

For glorious shall be your lot.

3. And the righteous shall be in the light of the sun.

And the elect in the light of eternal life:

The days of their life shall be unending,

And the days of the holy without number.

4. And they shall seek the light and find righteousness with the Lord of Spirits:

There shall be peace to the righteous in the name of the Eternal Lord.

5. And after this it shall be said to the holy in heaven

That they should seek out the secrets of righteousness, the heritage of faith:

For it has become bright as the sun upon earth,

And the darkness is past.

6. And there shall be a light that never endeth,

And to a limit (lit. 'number') of days they shall not come,

For the darkness shall first have been destroyed,

[And the light established before the Lord of Spirits]

And the light of uprightness established for ever before the Lord of Spirits.

CHAPTER LIX.
The Lights and the Thunder

[1. In those days mine eyes saw the secrets of the lightnings, and of the lights, and the judgements they execute (lit. 'their judgement'): and they lighten for a blessing or a curse as the Lord of Spirits willeth.

2. And there I saw the secrets of the thunder, and how when it resounds above in the heaven, the sound thereof is heard, and he caused me to see the judgements executed on the earth, whether they be for well-being and blessing, or for a curse according to the word of the Lord of Spirits.

3. And after that all the secrets of the lights and lightnings were shown to me, and they lighten for blessing and for satisfying.]

CHAPTER LX.
Book of Noah--a Fragment.

Quaking of Heaven: Behemoth and Leviathan: the Elements.

1. In the year five hundred, in the seventh month, on the fourteenth day of the month in the life of †Enoch†. In that Parable I saw how a mighty quaking made the heaven of heavens to quake, and the host of the Most High, and the angels, a thousand thousands and ten thousand times ten thousand, were disquieted with a great disquiet.

2. And the Head of Days sat on the throne of His glory, and the angels and the righteous stood around Him.

3. And a great trembling seized me,

And fear took hold of me,
And my loins gave way,
And dissolved were my reins,
And I fell upon my face.

4 And Michael sent another angel from among the holy ones and he raised me up, and when he had raised me up my spirit returned; for I had not been able to endure the look of this host, and the commotion and the quaking of the heaven. And Michael said unto me: 'Why art thou disquieted with such a vision? Until this day lasted the day of His mercy; and He hath been merciful and long-suffering towards those who dwell on the earth.

6. And when the day, and the power, and the punishment, and the judgement come, which the Lord of Spirits hath prepared for those who worship not the righteous law, and for those who deny the righteous judgement, and for those who take His name in vain--that day is prepared, for the elect a covenant, but for sinners an inquisition.

7. And on that day were two monsters parted, a female monster named Leviathan, to dwell in the abysses of the ocean over the fountains of the waters.

8. But the male is named Behemoth, who occupied with his breast a waste wilderness named †Dûidâin†, on the east of the garden where the elect and righteous dwell, where my grandfather was taken up, the seventh from Adam, the first man whom the Lord of Spirits created.

9. And I besought the other angel that he should show me the might of those monsters, how they were parted on one day and cast, the one into the abysses of the sea, and the other unto the dry land of the wilderness.

10. And he said to me: 'Thou son of man, herein thou dost seek to know what is hidden.'

11. And the other angel who went with me and showed me what was hidden told me what is first and last in the heaven in the height, and beneath the earth in the depth, and at the ends of the heaven, and on the foundation of the heaven.

12. And the chambers of the winds, and how the winds are divided, and how they are weighed, and (how) the portals of the winds are reckoned, each according to the power of the wind, and the power of the lights of the moon, and according to the power that is fitting: and the divisions of the stars according to their names, and how all the divisions are divided.

13. And the thunders according to the places where they fall, and all the divisions that are made among the lightnings that it may lighten, and their host that they may at once obey.

14. For the thunder has †places of rest† (which) are assigned (to it) while it is waiting for its peal; and the thunder and lightning are inseparable, and although not one and undivided, they both go together through the spirit and separate not.

15. For when the lightning lightens, the thunder utters its voice, and the spirit enforces a pause during the peal, and divides equally between them; for the treasury of their peals is like the sand, and each one of them as it peals is held in with a bridle, and turned back by the power of the spirit, and pushed forward according to the many quarters of the earth.

16. And the spirit of the sea is masculine and strong, and according to the might of his strength he draws it back with a rein, and in like manner it is driven forward and disperses amid all the mountains of the earth.

17. And the spirit of the hoar-frost is his own angel, and the spirit of the hail is a good angel.

18. And the spirit of the snow has forsaken his chambers on account of his strength--There is a special spirit therein, and that which ascends from it is like smoke, and its name is frost.

19. And the spirit of the mist is not united with them in their chambers, but it has a special chamber; for its course is †glorious† both in light and in darkness, and in winter and in summer, and in its chamber is an angel.

20. And the spirit of the dew has its dwelling at the ends of the heaven, and is connected with the chambers of the rain, and its course is in winter and summer: and its clouds and the clouds of the mist are connected, and the one gives to the other.

21. And when the spirit of the rain goes forth from its chamber, the angels come and open the chamber and lead it out, and when it is diffused over the whole earth it unites with the water on the earth. And whensoever it unites with the water on the earth . . .

22. For the waters are for those who dwell on the earth; for they are nourishment for the earth from the Most High who is in heaven: therefore there is a measure for the rain, and the angels take it in charge.

23. And these things I saw towards the Garden of the Righteous.

24. And the angel of peace who was with me said to me: 'These two monsters, prepared conformably to the greatness of God, shall feed . . .

25. When the punishment of the Lord of Spirits shall rest upon them, it shall rest in order that the punishment of the Lord of Spirits may not come, in vain, and it shall slay the children with their mothers and the children with their fathers. Afterwards the judgement shall take place according to His mercy and His patience.'

CHAPTER LXI.
Angels go off to measure Paradise: the Judgement of the Righteous by the Elect One: the Praise of the Elect One and of God.

1. And I saw in those days how long cords were given to those angels, and they took to themselves wings and flew, and they went towards the north.

2. And I asked the angel, saying unto him: 'Why have those (angels) taken these cords and gone off?' And he said unto me: 'They have gone to measure.'

3. And the angel who went with me said unto me:

'These shall bring the measures of the righteous,

And the ropes of the righteous to the righteous,

That they may stay themselves on the name of the Lord of Spirits for ever and ever.

4. The elect shall begin to dwell with the elect,

And those are the measures which shall be given to faith

And which shall strengthen righteousness.

5. And these measures shall reveal all the secrets of the depths of the earth,

And those who have been destroyed by the desert,

And those who have been devoured by the beasts,

And those who have been devoured by the fish of the sea,

That they may return and stay themselves

On the day of the Elect One;

For none shall be destroyed before the Lord of Spirits,

And none can be destroyed.

6. And all who dwell above in the heaven received a command and power and one voice and one light like unto fire.

7. And that One (with) their first words they blessed,

And extolled and lauded with wisdom,

And they were wise in utterance and in the spirit of life.

8. And the Lord of Spirits placed the Elect one on the throne of glory.

And he shall judge all the works of the holy above in the heaven,

And in the balance shall their deeds be weighed

9. And when he shall lift up his countenance

To judge their secret ways according to the word of the name of the Lord of Spirits,

And their path according to the way of the righteous judgement of the Lord of Spirits,

Then shall they all with one voice speak and bless,

And glorify and extol and sanctify the name of the Lord of Spirits.

10. And He will summon all the host of the heavens, and all the holy ones above, and the host of God, the Cherubic, Seraphin and Ophannin, and all the angels of power, and all the angels of principalities, and the Elect One, and the other powers on the earth (and) over the water.

11. On that day shall raise one voice, and bless and glorify and exalt in the spirit of faith, and in the spirit of wisdom, and in the spirit of patience, and in the spirit of mercy, and in the spirit of judgement and of peace,

and in the spirit of goodness, and shall all say with one voice: "Blessed is He, and may the name of the Lord of Spirits be blessed for ever and ever."

12. All who sleep not above in heaven shall bless Him:

All the holy ones who are in heaven shall bless Him,

And all the elect who dwell in the garden of life:

And every spirit of light who is able to bless, and glorify, and extol, and hallow Thy blessed name,

And all flesh shall beyond measure glorify and bless Thy name for ever and ever.

13. For great is the mercy of the Lord of Spirits, and He is long-suffering,

And all His works and all that He has created He has revealed to the righteous and elect, In the name of the Lord of Spirits.

CHAPTER LXII.
Judgement of the Kings and the Mighty: Blessedness of the Righteous.

1. And thus the Lord commanded the kings and the mighty and the exalted, and those who dwell on the earth, and said: 'Open your eyes and lift up your horns if ye are able to recognize the Elect One.'

2. And the Lord of Spirits seated him on the throne of His glory,

And the spirit of righteousness was poured out upon him,

And the word of his mouth slays all the sinners,

And all the unrighteous are destroyed from before his face.

3. And there shall stand up in that day all the kings and the mighty,

And the exalted and those who hold the earth,

And they shall see and recognize How he sits on the throne of his glory,

And righteousness is judged before him,

And no lying word is spoken before him.

4. Then shall pain come upon them as on a woman in travail,

[And she has pain in bringing forth]

When her child enters the mouth of the womb,

And she has pain in bringing forth.

5. And one portion of them shall look on the other,

And they shall be terrified,

And they shall be downcast of countenance,

And pain shall seize them,

When they see that Son of Man Sitting on the throne of his glory.

6. And the kings and the mighty and all who possess the earth shall bless and glorify and extol him who rules over all, who was hidden.

7. For from the beginning the Son of Man was hidden,

And the Most High preserved him in the presence of His might,

And revealed him to the elect.

8. And the congregation of the elect and holy shall be sown,

And all the elect shall stand before him on that day.

9. And all the kings and the mighty and the exalted and those who rule the earth

Shall fall down before him on their faces,

And worship and set their hope upon that Son of Man,

And petition him and supplicate for mercy at his hands.

10. Nevertheless that Lord of Spirits will so press them

That they shall hastily go forth from His presence,

And their faces shall be filled with shame,

And the darkness grow deeper on their faces.

11. And He will deliver them to the angels for punishment,

To execute vengeance on them because they have oppressed His children and His elect

12. And they shall be a spectacle for the righteous and for His elect:

They shall rejoice over them,

Because the wrath of the Lord of Spirits resteth upon them,

And His sword is drunk with their blood.

13. And the righteous and elect shall be saved on that day,

And they shall never thenceforward see the face of the sinners and unrighteous.

14. And the Lord of Spirits will abide over them,

And with that Son of Man shall they eat

And lie down and rise up for ever and ever.

15. And the righteous and elect shall have risen from the earth,

And ceased to be of downcast countenance.

And they shall have been clothed with garments of glory,

16. And these shall be the garments of life from the Lord of Spirits:

And your garments shall not grow old,

Nor your glory pass away before the Lord of Spirits.

CHAPTER LXIII.
The unavailing Repentance of the Kings and the Mighty.

1. In those days shall the mighty and the kings who possess the earth implore (Him) to grant them a little respite from His angels of punishment to whom they were delivered, that they might fall down and worship before the Lord of Spirits, and confess their sins before Him.

2. And they shall bless and glorify the Lord of Spirits, and say:

'Blessed is the Lord of Spirits and the Lord of kings,

And the Lord of the mighty and the Lord of the rich,

And the Lord of glory and the Lord of wisdom,

3. And splendid in every secret thing is Thy power from generation to generation,

And Thy glory for ever and ever:

Deep are all Thy secrets and innumerable,

And Thy righteousness is beyond reckoning.

4. We have now learnt that we should glorify

And bless the Lord of kings and Him who is king over all kings.'

5. And they shall say:

'Would that we had rest to glorify and give thanks

And confess our faith before His glory!

6. And now we long for a little rest but find it not:

We follow hard upon and obtain (it) not:

And light has vanished from before us,

And darkness is our dwelling-place for ever and ever:

7. For we have not believed before Him

Nor glorified the name of the Lord of Spirits, [nor glorified our Lord]

But our hope was in the sceptre of our kingdom,

And in our glory.

8. And in the day of our suffering and tribulation He saves us not,

And we find no respite for confession

That our Lord is true in all His works, and in His judgements and His justice,

And His judgements have no respect of persons.

9. And we pass away from before His face on account of our works,

And all our sins are reckoned up in righteousness.'

10. Now they shall say unto themselves: 'Our souls are full of unrighteous gain, but it does not prevent us from descending from the midst thereof into the †burden† of Sheol.'

11. And after that their faces shall be filled with darkness

And shame before that Son of Man,

And they shall be driven from his presence,

And the sword shall abide before his face in their midst.

12. Thus spake the Lord of Spirits: 'This is the ordinance and judgement with respect to the mighty and the kings and the exalted and those who possess the earth before the Lord of Spirits.'

CHAPTER LXIV.
Vision of the fallen Angels in the Place of Punishment.

1. And other forms I saw hidden in that place.

2. I heard the voice of the angel saying: 'These are the angels who descended to the earth, and revealed what was hidden to the children of men and seduced the children of men into committing sin.'

CHAPTER LXV.
Enoch foretells to Noah the Deluge and his own Preservation.

1. And in those days Noah saw the earth that it had sunk down and its destruction was nigh.

2. And he arose from thence and went to the ends of the earth, and cried aloud to his grandfather Enoch: and Noah said three times with an embittered voice: Hear me, hear me, hear me.'

3. And I said unto him: 'Tell me what it is that is falling out on the earth that the earth is in such evil plight and shaken, lest perchance I shall perish with it?'

4. And thereupon there was a great commotion, on the earth, and a voice was heard from heaven, and I fell on my face.

5. And Enoch my grandfather came and stood by me, and said unto me: 'Why hast thou cried unto me with a bitter cry and weeping?

6. And a command has gone forth from the presence of the Lord concerning those who dwell on the earth that their ruin is accomplished because they have learnt all the secrets of the angels, and all the violence of the Satans, and all their powers--the most secret ones--and all the power of those who practice sorcery, and the power of witchcraft, and the power of those who make molten images for the whole earth:

7. And how silver is produced from the dust of the earth, and how soft metal originates in the earth.

8. For lead and tin are not produced from the earth like the first: it is a fountain that produces them, and an angel stands therein, and that angel is pre-eminent.'

9. And after that my grandfather Enoch took hold of me by my hand and raised me up, and said unto me: 'Go, for I have asked the Lord of Spirits as touching this commotion on the earth.

10. And He said unto me: "Because of their unrighteousness their judgement has been determined upon and shall not be withheld by Me for ever. Because of the sorceries which they have searched out and learnt, the earth and those who dwell upon it shall be destroyed."

11. And these--they have no place of repentance for ever, because they have shown them what was hidden, and they are the damned: but as for thee, my son, the Lord of Spirits knows that thou art pure, and guiltless of this reproach concerning the secrets.

12. And He has destined thy name to be among the holy; And will preserve thee amongst those who dwell on the earth; And has destined thy righteous seed both for kingship and for great honours, And from thy seed shall proceed a fountain of the righteous and holy without number for ever.

CHAPTER LXVI.
The Angels of the Waters bidden to hold them in Check.

1. And after that he showed me the angels of punishment who are prepared to come and let loose all the powers of the waters which are beneath in the earth in order to bring judgement and destruction on all who [abide and] dwell on the earth.

2. And the Lord of Spirits gave commandment to the angels who were going forth, that they should not cause the waters to rise but should hold them in check; for those angels were over the powers of the waters.

3. And I went away from the presence of Enoch.

CHAPTER LXVII.
God's Promise to Noah: Places of Punishment of the Angels and of the Kings.

1. And in those days the word of God came unto me, and He said unto me: 'Noah, thy lot has come up before Me, a lot without blame, a lot of love and uprightness.

2. And now the angels are making a wooden (building), and when they have completed that task I will place My hand upon it and preserve it, and there shall come forth from it the seed of life, and a change shall set in so that the earth will not remain without inhabitant.

3. And I will make fast thy seed before me for ever and ever, and I will spread abroad those who dwell with thee: it shall not be unfruitful on the face of the earth, but it shall be blessed and multiply on the earth in the name of the Lord.'

4. And He will imprison those angels, who have shown unrighteousness, in that burning valley which my grandfather Enoch had formerly shown to me in the west among the mountains of gold and silver and iron and soft metal and tin.

5. And I saw that valley in which there was a great convulsion and a convulsion of the waters.

6. And when all this took place, from that fiery molten metal and from the convulsion thereof in that place, there was produced a smell of sulphur, and it was connected with those waters, and that valley of the angels who had led astray (mankind) burned beneath that land.

7. And through its valleys proceed streams of fire, where these angels are punished who had led astray those who dwell upon the earth.

8. But those waters shall in those days serve for the kings and the mighty and the exalted, and those who dwell on the earth, for the healing of the body, but for the punishment of the spirit; now their spirit is full of lust, that they may be punished in their body, for they have denied the Lord of Spirits and see their punishment daily, and yet believe not in His name.

9. And in proportion as the burning of their bodies becomes severe, a corresponding change shall take place in their spirit for ever and ever; for before the Lord of Spirits none shall utter an idle word.

10. For the judgement shall come upon them, because they believe in the lust of their body and deny the Spirit of the Lord.

11. And those same waters will undergo a change in those days; for when those angels are punished in these waters, these water-springs shall change their temperature, and when the angels ascend, this water of the springs shall change and become cold.

12. And I heard Michael answering and saying: 'This judgement wherewith the angels are judged is a testimony for the kings and the mighty who possess the earth.' 13. Because these waters of judgement minister to the healing of the body of the **kings** and the lust of their body; therefore they will not see and will not believe that those waters will change and become a fire which burns for ever.

CHAPTER LXVIII.
Michael and Raphael astonished at the Severity of the Judgement.

1. And after that my grandfather Enoch gave me the teaching of all the secrets in the book in the Parables which had been given to him, and he put them together for me in the words of the book of the Parables.

2. And on that day Michael answered Raphael and said: 'The power of the spirit transports and **makes me to tremble** because of the severity of the judgement of the secrets, the judgement of the angels: who can endure the severe judgement which has been executed, and before which they melt away?' 3. And Michael answered again, and said to Raphael: 'Who is he whose heart is not softened concerning it, and whose reins

are not troubled by this word of judgement (that) has gone forth upon them because of those who have thus led them out?' 4. And it came to pass when he stood before the Lord of Spirits, Michael said thus to Raphael: 'I will not take their part under the eye of the Lord; for the Lord of Spirits has been angry with them because they do as if they were the Lord. Therefore all that is hidden shall come upon them for ever and ever; for neither angel nor man shall have his portion (in it), but alone they have received their judgement for ever and ever.'

CHAPTER LXIX.
The Names and Functions of the (fallen Angels and) Satans: the secret Oath.

1 And after this judgement they shall terrify and make them to tremble because they have shown this to those who dwell on the earth.

2 And behold the names of those angels [and these are their names: the first of them is Samjâzâ, the second Artâqîfâ, and the third Armên, the fourth Kôkabêl, the fifth †Tûrâêl†, the sixth Rûmjâl, the seventh Dânjâl, the eighth †Nêqâêl†, the ninth Barâqêl, the tenth Azâzêl, the eleventh Armârôs, the twelfth Batarjâl, the thirteenth †Busasêjal†, the fourteenth Hanânêl, the fifteenth †Tûrêl†, and the sixteenth Sîmâpêsîêl, the seventeenth Jetrêl, the eighteenth Tûmâêl, the nineteenth Tûrêl, the twentieth †Rumâêl†, the twenty-first †Azâzêl†.

3. And these are the chiefs of their angels and their names, and their chief ones over hundreds and over fifties and over tens].

4. The name of the first Jeqôn: that is, the one who led astray ⌈all⌉ the sons of God, and brought them down to the earth, and led them astray through the daughters of men.

5. And the second was named Asbeêl: he imparted to the holy sons of God evil counsel, and led them astray so that they defiled their bodies with the daughters of men.

6. And the third was named Gâdreêl: he it is who showed the children of men all the blows of death, and he led astray Eve, and showed [the weapons of death to the sons of men] the shield and the coat of mail, and the sword for battle, and all the weapons of death to the children of men.

7. And from his hand they have proceeded against those who dwell on the earth from that day and for evermore.

8. And the fourth was named Pênêmûe: he taught the children of men the bitter and the sweet, and he taught them all the secrets of their wisdom.

9. And he instructed mankind in writing with ink and paper, and thereby many sinned from eternity to eternity and until this day.

10. For men were not created for such a purpose, to give confirmation to their good faith with pen and ink.

11. For men were created exactly like the angels, to the intent that they should continue pure and righteous, and death, which destroys everything, could not have taken hold of them, but through this their knowledge they are perishing, and through this power it is consuming me†.

12. And the fifth was named Kâsdejâ: this is he who showed the children of men all the wicked smitings of spirits and demons, and the smitings of the embryo in the womb, that it may pass away, and [the smitings of the soul] the bites of the serpent, and the smitings which befall through the noontide heat, the son of the serpent named Tabââ'ĕt.

13. And this is the task of Kâsbeêl, the chief of the oath which he showed to the holy ones when he dwelt high above in glory, and its name is Bîqâ.

14. This (angel) requested Michael to show him the hidden name, that he might enunciate it in the oath, so that those might quake before that name and oath who revealed all that was in secret to the children of men.

15. And this is the power of this oath, for it is powerful and strong, and he placed this oath Akâe in the hand of Michael. 16 And these are the secrets of this oath . . .

And they are strong through his oath:

And the heaven was suspended before the world was created,

And for ever.

17. And through it the earth was founded upon the water,

And from the secret recesses of the mountains come beautiful waters,

From the creation of the world and unto eternity.

18. And through that oath the sea was created,

And †as its foundation† He set for it the sand against the time of (its) anger,

And it dare not pass beyond it from the creation of the world unto eternity.

19. And through that oath are the depths made fast,

And abide and stir not from their place from eternity to eternity.

20. And through that oath the sun and moon complete their course,

And deviate not from their ordinance from eternity to eternity.

21. And through that oath the stars complete their course,

And He calls them by their names,

And they answer Him from eternity to eternity.

[22. And in like manner the spirits of the water, and of the winds, and of all zephyrs, and (their) paths from all the quarters of the winds.

23. And there are preserved the voices of the thunder and the light of the lightnings: and there are preserved the chambers of the hail and the chambers of the hoarfrost, and the chambers of the mist, and the chambers of the rain and the dew.

24. And all these believe and give thanks before the Lord of Spirits, and glorify (Him) with all their power, and their food is in every act of thanksgiving: they thank and glorify and extol the name of the Lord of Spirits for ever and ever.]

25. And this oath is mighty over them

And through it [they are preserved and] their paths are preserved,

And their course is not destroyed.

Close of the Third Parable.

26. And there was great joy amongst them,

And they blessed and glorified and extolled

Because the name of that Son of Man had been revealed unto them.

27. And he sat on the throne of his glory,

And the sum of judgement was given unto the Son of Man,

And he caused the sinners to pass away and be destroyed from off the face of the earth,

And those who have led the world astray.

28. With chains shall they be bound,

And in their assemblage-place of destruction shall they be imprisoned,

And all their works vanish from the face of the earth.

29. And from henceforth there shall be nothing corruptible;

For that Son of Man has appeared,

And has seated himself on the throne of his glory,

And all evil shall pass away before his face,

And the word of that Son of Man shall go forth

And be strong before the Lord of Spirits.

This is the Third Parable of Enoch.

CHAPTER LXX.
The Final Translation of Enoch.

1. And it came to pass after this that his name during his lifetime was raised aloft to that Son of Man and to the Lord of Spirits from amongst those who dwell on the earth.

2. And he was raised aloft on the chariots of the spirit and his name vanished among them.

3. And from that day I was no longer numbered amongst them: and he set me between the two winds, between the North and the West, where the angels took the cords to measure for me the place for the elect and righteous.

4. And there I saw the first fathers and the righteous who from the beginning dwell in that place.

CHAPTER LXXI.
Two earlier visions of Enoch.

1. And it came to pass after this that my spirit was translated
And it ascended into the heavens:
And I saw the holy sons of God.
They were stepping on flames of fire:
Their garments were white [and their raiment],
And their faces shone like snow.

2. And I saw two streams of fire,
And the light of that fire shone like hyacinth,
And I fell on my face before the Lord of Spirits.

3. And the angel Michael [one of the archangels] seized me by my right hand,
And lifted me up and led me forth into all the secrets,
And he showed me all the secrets of righteousness.

4. And he showed me all the secrets of the ends of the heaven,
And all the chambers of all the stars, and all the luminaries,
Whence they proceed before the face of the holy ones.

5. And he translated my spirit into the heaven of heavens,
And I saw there as it were a structure built of crystals,
And between those crystals tongues of living fire.

6. And my spirit saw the girdle which girt that house of fire,
And on its four sides were streams full of living fire,
And they girt that house.

7. And round about were Seraphin, Cherubic, and Ophannin:
And these are they who sleep not
And guard the throne of His glory.

8. And I saw angels who could not be counted,
A thousand thousands, and ten thousand times ten thousand,
Encircling that house.
And Michael, and Raphael, and Gabriel, and Phanuel,
And the holy angels who are above the heavens,
Go in and out of that house.

9. And they came forth from that house,
And Michael and Gabriel, Raphael and Phanuel,
And many holy angels without number.

10. And with them the Head of Days,
His head white and pure as wool,
And His raiment indescribable.

11. And I fell on my face,
And my whole body became relaxed,
And my spirit was transfigured;
And I cried with a loud voice,

. . .with the spirit of power,

And blessed and glorified and extolled.

12. And these blessings which went forth out of my mouth were well pleasing before that Head of Days.

13. And that Head of Days came with Michael and Gabriel, Raphael and Phanuel, thousands and ten thousands of angels without number.

[Lost passage wherein the Son of Man was described as accompanying the Head of Days, and Enoch asked one of the angels (as in 46³) concerning the Son of Man as to who he was.]

14. And he (*i.e.* the angel) came to me and greeted me with His voice, and said unto me:

'This is the Son of Man who is born unto righteousness;

And righteousness abides over him,

And the righteousness of the Head of Days forsakes him not.'

15. And he said unto me:

'He proclaims unto thee peace in the name of the world to come;

For from hence has proceeded peace since the creation of the world,

And so shall it be unto thee for ever and for ever and ever.

16. And all shall walk in his ways since righteousness never forsaketh him: With him will be their dwelling-places, and with him their heritage,

And they shall not be separated from him for ever and ever and ever.

17. And so there shall be length of days with that Son of Man,

And the righteous shall have peace and an upright way

In the name of the Lord of Spirits for ever and ever.'

THE BOOK OF THE COURSES OF THE HEAVENLY LUMINARIES

(LXXII-LXXXII.)

CHAPTER LXXII. *The Sun.*

1. The book of the courses of the luminaries of the heaven, the relations of each, according to their classes, their dominion and their seasons, according to their names and places of origin, and according to their months, which Uriel, the holy angel, who was with me, who is their guide, showed me; and he showed me all their laws exactly as they are, and how it is with regard to all the years of the world and unto eternity, till the new creation is accomplished which dureth till eternity.

2. And this is the first law of the luminaries: the luminary the Sun has its rising in the eastern portals of the heaven, and its setting in the western portals of the heaven.

3. And I saw six portals in which the sun rises, and six portals in which the sun sets and the moon rises and sets in these portals, and the leaders of the stars and those whom they lead: six in the east and six in the west, and all following each other in accurately corresponding order: also many windows to the right and left of these portals.

4. And first there goes forth the great luminary, named the Sun, and his circumference is like the circumference of the heaven, and he is quite filled with illuminating and heating fire.

5. The chariot on which he ascends, the wind drives, and the sun goes down from the heaven and returns through the north in order to reach the east, and is so guided that he comes to the appropriate (lit. 'that') portal and shines in the face of the heaven.

6. In this way he rises in the first month in the great portal, which is the fourth [those six portals in the east].

7. And in that fourth portal from which the sun rises in the first month are twelve window-openings, from which proceed a flame when they are opened in their season.

8. When the sun rises in the heaven, he comes forth through that fourth portal thirty mornings in succession, and sets accurately in the fourth portal in the west of the heaven.

9. And during this period the day becomes daily longer and the night nightly shorter to the thirtieth morning.

10. On that day the day is longer than the night by a ninth part, and the day amounts exactly to ten parts and the night to eight parts.

11. And the sun rises from that fourth portal, and sets in the fourth and returns to the fifth portal of the east thirty mornings, and rises from it and sets in the fifth portal.

12. And then the day becomes longer by †two† parts and amounts to eleven parts, and the night becomes shorter and amounts to seven parts.

13. And it returns to the east and enters into the sixth portal, and rises and sets in the sixth portal one-and-thirty mornings on account of its sign.

14. On that day the day becomes longer than the night, and the day becomes double the night, and the day becomes twelve parts, and the night is shortened and becomes six parts.

15. And the sun mounts up to make the day shorter and the night longer, and the sun returns to the east and enters into the sixth portal, and rises from it and sets thirty mornings.

16. And when thirty mornings are accomplished, the day decreases by exactly one part, and becomes eleven parts, and the night seven.

17. And the sun goes forth from that sixth portal in the west, and goes to the east and rises in the fifth portal for thirty mornings, and sets in the west again in the fifth western portal.

18. On that day the day decreases by †two† parts, and amounts to ten parts and the night to eight parts.

19. And the sun goes forth from that fifth portal and sets in the fifth portal of the west, and rises in the fourth portal for one-and-thirty mornings on account of its sign, and sets in the west.

20. On that day the day is equalized with the night, [and becomes of equal length], and the night amounts to nine parts and the day to nine parts.

21. And the sun rises from that portal and sets in the west, and returns to the east and rises thirty mornings in the third portal and sets in the west in the third portal.

22. And on that day the night becomes longer than the day, and night becomes longer than night, and day shorter than day till the thirtieth morning, and the night amounts exactly to ten parts and the day to eight parts.

23. And the sun rises from that third portal and sets in the third portal in the west and returns to the east, and for thirty mornings rises in the second portal in the east, and in like manner sets in the second portal in the west of the heaven.

24. And on that day the night amounts to eleven parts and the day to seven parts.

25. And the sun rises on that day from that second portal and sets in the west in the second portal, and returns to the east into the first portal for one-and-thirty mornings, and sets in the first portal in the west of the heaven.

26. And on that day the night becomes longer and amounts to the double of the day: and the night amounts exactly to twelve parts and the day to six.

27. And the sun has (therewith) traversed the divisions of his orbit and turns again on those divisions of his orbit, and enters that portal thirty mornings and sets also in the west opposite to it.

28. And on that night has the night decreased in length by a †ninth† part, and the night has become eleven parts and the day seven parts.

29. And the sun has returned and entered into the second portal in the east, and returns on those his divisions of his orbit for thirty mornings, rising and setting.

30. And on that day the night decreases in length, and the night amounts to ten parts and the day to eight.

31. And on that day the sun rises from that portal, and sets in the west, and returns to the east, and rises in the third portal for one-and-thirty mornings, and sets in the west of the heaven.

32. On that day the night decreases and amounts to nine parts, and the day to nine parts, and the night is equal to the day and the year is exactly as to its days three hundred and sixty-four.

33. And the length of the day and of the night, and the shortness of the day and of the night arise--through the course of the sun these distinctions are made (lit. 'they are separated').

34. So it comes that its course becomes daily longer, and its course nightly shorter.

35. And this is the law and the course of the sun, and his return as often as he returns sixty times and rises, *i.e.* the great luminary which is named the sun, for ever and ever.

36. And that which (thus) rises is the great luminary, and is so named according to its appearance, according as the Lord commanded.

37. As he rises, so he sets and decreases not, and rests not, but runs day and night, and his light is sevenfold brighter than that of the moon; but as regards size they are both equal.

CHAPTER LXXIII.

1. And after this law I saw another law dealing with the smaller luminary, which is named the Moon.

2. And her circumference is like the circumference of the heaven, and her chariot in which she rides is driven by the wind, and light is given to her in (definite) measure.

3. And her rising and setting change every month: and her days are like the days of the sun, and when her light is uniform (*i.e.* full) it amounts to the seventh part of the light of the sun.

4. And thus she rises. And her first phase in the east comes forth on the thirtieth morning: and on that day she becomes visible, and constitutes for you the first phase of the moon on the thirtieth day together with the sun in the portal where the sun rises.

5. And the one half of her goes forth by a seventh part, and her whole circumference is empty, without light, with the exception of one-seventh part of it, (and) the fourteenth part of her light.

6. And when she receives one-seventh part of the half of her light, her light amounts to one-seventh part and the half thereof.

7. And she sets with the sun, and when the sun rises the moon rises with him and receives the half of one part of light, and in that night in the beginning of her morning [in the commencement of the lunar day] the moon sets with the sun, and is invisible that night with the fourteen parts and the half of one of them.

8. And she rises on that day with exactly a seventh part, and comes forth and recedes from the rising of the sun, and in her remaining days she becomes bright in the (remaining) thirteen parts.

CHAPTER LXXIV.

1. And I saw another course, a law for her, (and) how according to that law she performs her monthly revolution.

2. And all these Uriel, the holy angel who is the leader of them all, showed to me, and their positions, and I wrote down their positions as he showed them to me, and I wrote down their months as they were, and the appearance of their lights till fifteen days were accomplished.

3. In single seventh parts she accomplishes all her light in the east, and in single seventh parts accomplishes all her darkness in the west.

4. And in certain months she alters her settings, and in certain months she pursues her own peculiar course.

5. In two months the moon sets with the sun: in those two middle portals the third and the fourth.

6. She goes forth for seven days, and turns about and returns again through the portal where the sun rises, and accomplishes all her light: and she recedes from the sun, and in eight days enters the sixth portal from which the sun goes forth.

7. And when the sun goes forth from the fourth portal she goes forth seven days, until she goes forth from the fifth and turns back again in seven days into the fourth portal and accomplishes all her light: and she recedes and enters into the first portal in eight days.

8. And she returns again in seven days into the fourth portal from which the sun goes forth.

9. Thus I saw their position--how the moons rose and the sun set in those days.

10. And if five years are added together the sun has an overplus of thirty days, and all the days which accrue to it for one of those five years, when they are full, amount to 364 days.

11. And the overplus of the sun and of the stars amounts to six days: in 5 years 6 days every year come to 30 days: and the moon falls behind the sun and stars to the number of 30 days.

12. And the sun and the stars bring in all the years exactly, so that they do not advance or delay their position by a single day unto eternity; but complete the years with perfect justice in 364 days.

13. In 3 years there are 1092 days, and in 5 years 1820 days, so that in 8 years there are 2912 days.

14. For the moon alone the days amount in 3 years to 1062 days, and in 5 years she falls 50 days behind: [*i.e.* to the sum (of 1770) there is to be added (1000 and) 62 days.] 15. And in 5 years there are 1770 days, so that for the moon the days in 8 years amount to 2832 days.

16. [For in 8 years she falls behind to the amount of 80 days], all the days she falls behind in 8 years are 80. 17. And the year is accurately completed in conformity with their world-stations and the stations of the sun, which rise from the portals through which it (the sun) rises and sets 30 days.

CHAPTER LXXV.

1. And the leaders of the heads of the thousands, who are placed over the whole creation and over all the stars, have also to do with the four intercalary days, being inseparable from their office, according to the reckoning of the year, and these render service on the four days which are not reckoned in the reckoning of the year.

2. And owing to them men go wrong therein, for those luminaries truly render service on the world-stations, one in the first portal, one in the third portal of the heaven, one in the fourth portal, and one in the sixth portal, and the exactness of the year is accomplished through its separate three hundred and sixty-four stations.

3. For the signs and the times and the years and the days the angel Uriel showed to me, whom the Lord of glory hath set for ever over all the luminaries of the heaven, in the heaven and in the world, that they should rule on the face of the heaven and be seen on the earth, and be leaders for the day and the night, *i.e.* the sun, moon, and stars, and all the ministering creatures which make their revolution in all the chariots of the heaven.

4. In like manner twelve doors Uriel showed me, open in the circumference of the sun's chariot in the heaven, through which the rays of the sun break forth: and from them is warmth diffused over the earth, when they are opened at their appointed seasons.

5. [And for the winds and the spirit of the dew† when they are opened, standing open in the heavens at the ends.] 6. As for the twelve portals in the heaven, at the ends of the earth, out of which go forth the sun, moon, and stars, and all the works of heaven in the east and in the west.

7. There are many windows open to the left and right of them, and one window at its (appointed) season produces warmth, corresponding (as these do) to those doors from which the stars come forth according as He has commanded them, and wherein they set corresponding to their number.

8. And I saw chariots in the heaven, running in the world, above those portals in which revolve the stars that never set.

9. And one is larger than all the rest, and it is that that makes its course through the entire world.

CHAPTER LXXVI.

The Twelve Windows and their Portals

1 And at the ends of the earth I saw twelve portals open to all the quarters (of the heaven), from which the winds go forth and blow over the earth.

2. Three of them are open on the face (*i.e.* the east) of the heavens, and three in the west, and three on the right (*i.e.* the south) of the heaven, and three on the left (*i.e.* the north).

3. And the three first are those of the east, and three are of †the north, and three [after those on the left] of the south†, and three of the west.

4. Through four of these come winds of blessing and prosperity, and from those eight come hurtful winds: when they are sent, they bring destruction on all the earth and on the water upon it, and on all who dwell thereon, and on everything which is in the water and on the land.

5. And the first wind from those portals, called the east wind, comes forth through the first portal which is in the east, inclining towards the south: from it come forth desolation, drought, heat, and destruction.

6. And through the second portal in the middle comes what is fitting, and from it there come rain and fruitfulness and prosperity and dew; and through the third portal which lies toward the north come cold and drought.

7. And after these come forth the south winds through three portals: through the first portal of them inclining to the east comes forth a hot wind.

8. And through the middle portal next to it there come forth fragrant smells, and dew and rain, and prosperity and health.

9. And through the third portal lying to the west come forth dew and rain, locusts and desolation.

10. And after these the north winds: from the seventh portal in the east come dew and rain, locusts and desolation.

11. And from the middle portal come in a direct direction health and rain and dew and prosperity; and through the third portal in the west come cloud and hoar-frost, and snow and rain, and dew and locusts.

12. And after these [four] are the west winds: through the first portal adjoining the north come forth dew and hoar-frost, and cold and snow and frost. And from the middle portal come forth dew and rain, and prosperity and blessing; and through the last portal which adjoins the south come forth drought and desolation, and burning and destruction.

14. And the twelve portals of the four quarters of the heaven are therewith completed, and all their laws and all their plagues and all their benefactions have I shown to thee, my son Methuselah.

CHAPTER LXXVII. *The Four Quarters of the World: the Seven Mountains, the Seven Rivers, &c.*

1. And the first **quarter** is called the east, because it is the first: and the second, the south, because the Most High will descend there, yea, there in quite a special sense will He who is blessed for ever descend.

2. And the west quarter is named the diminished, because there all the luminaries of the heaven wane and go down.

3. And the fourth quarter, named the north, is divided into three parts: the first of them is for the dwelling of men: and the second contains seas of water, and the abysses and forests and rivers, and darkness and clouds; and the third part contains the garden of righteousness.

4. I saw seven high mountains, higher than all the mountains which are on the earth: and thence comes forth hoar-frost, and days, seasons, and years pass away.

5. I saw seven rivers on the earth larger than all the rivers: one of them coming from the west pours its waters into the Great Sea.

6. And these two come from the north to the sea and pour their waters into the Erythraean Sea in the east.

7. And the remaining four come forth on the side of the north to their own sea, ⟨two of them⟩ to the Erythraean Sea, and two into the Great Sea and discharge themselves there [and some say: into the desert].

8. Seven great islands I saw in the sea and in the mainland: two in the mainland and five in the Great Sea.

CHAPTER LXXVIII. *The Sun and Moon: the Waxing and Waning of the Moon.*

1. And the names of the sun are the following: the first Orjârês, and the second Tômâs.

2. And the moon has four names: the first name is Asônjâ, the second Eblâ, the third Benâsê, and the fourth Erâe.

3. These are the two great luminaries: their circumference is like the circumference of the heaven, and the size of the circumference of both is alike.

4. In the circumference of the sun there are seven portions of light which are added to it more than to the moon, and in definite measures it is s transferred till the seventh portion of the sun is exhausted.

5. And they set and enter the portals of the west, and make their revolution by the north, and come forth through the eastern portals on the face of the heaven.

6. And when the moon rises one-fourteenth part appears in the heaven: [the light becomes full in her]: on the fourteenth day she accomplishes her light.

7. And fifteen parts of light are transferred to her till the fifteenth day (when) her light is accomplished, according to the sign of the year, and she becomes fifteen parts, and the moon grows by (the addition of) fourteenth parts.

8. And in her waning (the moon) decreases on the first day to fourteen parts of her light, on the second to thirteen parts of light, on the third to twelve, on the fourth to eleven, on the fifth to ten, on the sixth to nine, on the seventh to eight, on the eighth to seven, on the ninth to six, on the tenth to five, on the eleventh to four, on the twelfth to three, on the thirteenth to two, on the fourteenth to the half of a seventh, and all her remaining light disappears wholly on the fifteenth.

9. And in certain months the month has twenty-nine days and once twenty-eight.

10. And Uriel showed me another law: when light is transferred to the moon, and on which side it is transferred to her by the sun.

11. During all the period during which the moon is growing in her light, she is transferring it to herself when opposite to the sun during fourteen days [her light is accomplished in the heaven], and when she is illumined throughout, her light is accomplished full in the heaven.

12. And on the first day she is called the new moon, for on that day the light rises upon her.

13. She becomes full moon exactly on the day when the sun sets in the west, and from the east she rises at night, and the moon shines the whole night through till the sun rises over against her and the moon is seen over against the sun.

14. On the side whence the light of the moon comes forth, there again she wanes till all the light vanishes and all the days of the month are at an end, and her circumference is empty, void of light.

15. And three months she makes of thirty days, and at her time she makes three months of twenty-nine days each, in which she accomplishes her waning in the first period of time, and in the first portal for one hundred and seventy-seven days.

16. And in the time of her going out she appears for three months (of) thirty days each, and for three months she appears (of) twenty-nine each. 17. At night she appears like a man for twenty days each time, and by day she appears like the heaven, and there is nothing else in her save her light.

1. *Recapitulation of several of the Laws.*

CHAPTER LXXIX.

1. And now, my son, I have shown thee everything, and the law of all the stars of the heaven is completed.

2. And he showed me all the laws of these for every day, and for every season of bearing rule, and for every year, and for its going forth, and for the order prescribed to it every month and every week: 3. And the waning of the moon which takes place in the sixth portal: for in this sixth portal her light is accomplished, and after that there is the beginning of the waning: 4. ⟨And the waning⟩ which takes place in the first portal in its season, till one hundred and seventy-seven days are accomplished: reckoned according to weeks, twenty-five (weeks) and two days.

5. She falls behind the sun and the order of the stars exactly five days in the course of one period, and when this place which thou seest has been traversed.

6. Such is the picture and sketch of every luminary which Uriel the archangel, who is their leader, showed unto me.

CHAPTER LXXX.

1. And in those days the angel Uriel answered and said to me: 'Behold, I have shown thee everything, Enoch, and I have revealed everything to thee that thou shouldst see this sun and this moon, and the leaders of the stars of the heaven and all those who turn them, their tasks and times and departures.

LXXX. 2-8. *Perversion of Nature and the heavenly Bodies owning to the Sin of Men.*

2. And in the days of the sinners the years shall be shortened,

And their seed shall be tardy on their lands and fields,

And all things on the earth shall alter,

And shall not appear in their time:

And the rain shall be kept back

And the heaven shall withhold (it).

3. And in those times the fruits of the earth shall be backward,

And shall not grow in their time,

And the fruits of the trees shall be withheld in their time.

4. And the moon shall alter her order,

And not appear at her time.

5. [And in those days the sun shall be seen and he shall journey in the evening †on the extremity of the great chariot† in the west]

And shall shine more brightly than accords with the order of light.

6. And many chiefs of the stars shall transgress the order (prescribed).

And these shall alter their orbits and tasks,

And not appear at the seasons prescribed to them.

7. And the whole order of the stars shall be concealed from the sinners,

And the thoughts of those on the earth shall err concerning them,

[And they shall be altered from all their ways],

Yea, they shall err and take them to be gods.

8. And evil shall be multiplied upon them,

And punishment shall come upon them So as to destroy all.'

CHAPTER LXXXI.
The Heavenly Tablets and the Mission of Enoch

1. And he said unto me:

'Observe, Enoch, these heavenly tablets,

And read what is written thereon,

And mark every individual fact.'

2 And I observed the heavenly tablets, and read everything which was written (thereon) and understood everything, and read the book of all the deeds of mankind, and of all the children of flesh that shall be upon the earth to the remotest generations.

3. And forthwith I blessed the great Lord the King of glory for ever, in that He has made all the works of the world,

And I extolled the Lord because of His patience,

And blessed Him because of the children of men.

4. And after that I said:

'Blessed is the man who dies in righteousness and goodness,

Concerning whom there is no book of unrighteousness written,

And against whom no day of judgement shall be found.'

5. And those seven holy ones brought me and placed me on the earth before the door of my house, and said to me: 'Declare everything to thy son Methuselah, and show to all thy children that no flesh is righteous in the sight of the Lord, for He is their Creator.

6. One year we will leave thee with thy son, till thou givest thy (last) commands, that thou mayest teach thy children and record (it) for them, and testify to all thy children; and in the second year they shall take thee from their midst.

7. Let thy heart be strong,

For the good shall announce righteousness to the good;

The righteous with the righteous shall rejoice,

And shall offer congratulation to one another.

8. But the sinners shall die with the sinners,

And the apostate go down with the apostate.

9. And those who practice righteousness shall die on account of the deeds of men,

And be taken away on account of the doings of the godless.'

10. And in those days they ceased to speak to me, and I came to my people, blessing the Lord of the world.

CHAPTER LXXXII.
Charge given to Enoch: the four Intercalary Days: the Stars which lead the Seasons and the Months.

1. And now, my son Methuselah, all these things I am recounting to thee and writing down for thee, and I have revealed to thee everything, and given thee books concerning all these: so preserve, my son Methuselah, the books from thy father's hand, and (see) that thou deliver them to the generations of the world.

2. I have given Wisdom to thee and to thy children,

[And thy children that shall be to thee],

That they may give it to their children for generations,

This wisdom (namely) that passeth their thought.

3. And those who understand it shall not sleep,

But shall listen with the ear that they may learn this wisdom,

And it shall please those that eat thereof better than good food.

4. Blessed are all the righteous, blessed are all those who walk in the way of righteousness and sin not as the sinners, in the reckoning of all their days in which the sun traverses the heaven, entering into and departing from the portals for thirty days with the heads of thousands of the order of the stars, together with the four which are intercalated which divide the four portions of the year, which lead them and enter with them four days.

5. Owing to them men shall be at fault and not reckon them in the whole reckoning of the year: yea, men shall be at fault, and not recognize them accurately.

6. For they belong to the reckoning of the year and are truly recorded (thereon) for ever, one in the first portal and one in the third, and one in the fourth and one in the sixth, and the year is completed in three hundred and sixty-four days.

7. And the account thereof is accurate and the recorded reckoning thereof exact; for the luminaries, and months and festivals, and years and days, has Uriel shown and revealed to me, to whom the Lord of the whole creation of the world hath subjected the host of heaven.

8. And he has power over night and day in the heaven to cause the light to give light to men--sun, moon, and stars, and all the powers of the heaven which revolve in their circular chariots.

9. And these are the orders of the stars, which set in their places, and in their seasons and festivals and months.

10. And these are the names of those who lead them, who watch that they enter at their times, in their orders, in their seasons, in their months, in their periods of dominion, and in their positions.

11. Their four leaders who divide the four parts of the year enter first; and after them the twelve leaders of the orders who divide the months; and for the three hundred and sixty (days) there are heads over thousands who divide the days; and for the four intercalary days there are the leaders which sunder the four parts of the year.

12. And these heads over thousands are intercalated between leader and leader, each behind a station, but their leaders make the division. And these are the names of the leaders who divide the four parts of the year which are ordained: Mîlkî'êl, Hel'emmêlêk, and Mêl'êjal, and Nârêl.

13. And the names of those who lead them: Adnâr'êl, and Îjâsûsa'êl, and 'Elômê'êl--these three follow the leaders of the orders, and there is one that follows the three leaders of the orders which follow those leaders of stations that divide the four parts of the year.

15. In the beginning of the year Melkejâl rises first and rules, who is named †Tam'aini† and sun, and all the days of his dominion whilst he bears rule are ninety-one days.

16. And these are the signs of the days which are to be seen on earth in the days of his dominion: sweat, and heat, and calms; and all the trees bear fruit, and leaves are produced on all the trees, and the harvest of wheat, and the rose-flowers, and all the flowers which come forth in the field, but the trees of the winter season become withered. 17. And these are the names of the leaders which are under them: Berka'êl, Zêlebs'êl, and another who is added a head of a thousand, called Hîlûjâsĕph: and the days of the dominion of this (leader) are at an end.

18. The next leader after him is Hêl'emmêlêk, whom one names the shining sun, and all the days of his light are ninety-one days. 19. And these are the signs of (his) days on the earth: glowing heat and dryness, and the trees ripen their fruits and produce all their fruits ripe and ready, and the sheep pair and become pregnant, and all the fruits of the earth are gathered in, and everything that is in the fields, and the winepress: these things take place in the days of his dominion.

20. These are the names, and the orders, and the leaders of those heads of thousands: Gîdâ'îjal, Kê'êl, and Hê'êl, and the name of the head of a thousand which is added to them, Asfâ'êl': and the days of his dominion are at an end.

THE DREAM-VISIONS

(LXXXIII-XC.)
LXXXIII. LXXXIV. *First Dream-Vision on the Deluge.*

CHAPTER LXXXIII.

1. And now, my son Methuselah, I will show thee all my visions which I have seen, recounting them before thee.

2. Two visions I saw before I took a wife, and the one was quite unlike the other: the first when I was learning to write: the second before I took thy mother, (when) I saw a terrible vision. And regarding them I prayed to the Lord.

3. I had laid me down in the house of my grandfather Mahalalel, (when) I saw in a vision how the heaven collapsed and was borne off and fell to the earth.

4. And when it fell to the earth I saw how the earth was swallowed up in a great abyss, and mountains were suspended on mountains, and hills sank down on hills, and high trees were rent from their stems, and hurled down and sunk in the abyss.

5. And thereupon a word fell into my mouth, and I lifted up (my voice) to cry aloud, and said: 'The earth is destroyed.'

6. And my grandfather Mahalalel waked me as I lay near him, and said unto me: 'Why dost thou cry so, my son, and why dost thou make such lamentation?'

7. And I recounted to him the whole vision which I had seen, and he said unto me: 'A terrible thing hast thou seen, my son, and of grave moment is thy dream-vision as to the secrets of all the sin of the earth: it must sink into the abyss and be destroyed with a great destruction.

8. And now, my son, arise and make petition to the Lord of glory, since thou art a believer, that a remnant may remain on the earth, and that He may not destroy the whole earth.

9. My son, from heaven all this will come upon the earth, and upon the earth there will be great destruction.

10. After that I arose and prayed and implored and besought, and wrote down my prayer for the generations of the world, and I will show everything to thee, my son Methuselah.

11. And when I had gone forth below and seen the heaven, and the sun rising in the east, and the moon setting in the west, and a few stars, and the whole earth, and everything as †He had known† it in the beginning, then I blessed the Lord of judgement and extolled Him because He had made the sun to go forth from the windows of the east, †and he ascended and rose on the face of the heaven, and set out and kept traversing the path shown unto him.

CHAPTER LXXXIV.

1. And I lifted up my hands in righteousness and blessed the Holy and Great One, and spake with the breath of my mouth, and with the tongue of flesh, which God has made for the children of the flesh of men, that they should speak therewith, and He gave them breath and a tongue and a mouth that they should speak therewith:

2. 'Blessed be Thou, O Lord, King,

Great and mighty in Thy greatness,

Lord of the whole creation of the heaven,

King of kings and God of the whole world.

And Thy power and kingship and greatness abide for ever and ever,

And throughout all generations Thy dominion;

And all the heavens are Thy throne for ever,

And the whole earth Thy footstool for ever and ever.

3. For Thou hast made and Thou rulest all things,

And nothing is too hard for Thee,

Wisdom departs not from the place of Thy throne,

Nor turns away from Thy presence.

And Thou knowest and seest and hearest everything,

And there is nothing hidden from Thee [for Thou seest everything].

4. And now the angels of Thy heavens are guilty of trespass,

And upon the flesh of men abideth Thy wrath until the great day of judgement.

5. And now, O God and Lord and Great King,

I implore and beseech Thee to fulfil my prayer,

To leave me a posterity on earth,

And not destroy all the flesh of man,

And make the earth without inhabitant,

So that there should be an eternal destruction.

6. And now, my Lord, destroy from the earth the flesh which has aroused Thy wrath,

But the flesh of righteousness and uprightness establish as a plant of the eternal seed,

And hide not Thy face from the prayer of Thy servant, O Lord.'

LXXXV-XC. *The Second Dream-Vision of Enoch: the History of the World to the Founding of the Messianic Kingdom.*

CHAPTER LXXXV.

1. And after this I saw another dream, and I will show the whole dream to thee, my son.

2. And Enoch lifted up (his voice) and spake to his son Methuselah: 'To thee, my son, will I speak: hear my words--incline thine ear to the dream-vision of thy father.

3. Before I took thy mother Edna, I saw in a vision on my bed, and behold a bull came forth from the earth, and that bull was white; and after it came forth a heifer, and along with this (latter) came forth two bulls, one of them black and the other red.

4. And that black bull gored the red one and pursued him over the earth, and thereupon I could no longer see that red bull.

5. But that black bull grew and that heifer went with him, and I saw that many oxen proceeded from him which resembled and followed him.

6. And that cow, that first one, went from the presence of that first bull in order to seek that red one, but found him not, and lamented with a great lamentation over him and sought him.

7. And I looked till that first bull came to her and quieted her, and from that time onward she cried no more.

8. And after that she bore another white bull, and after him she bore many bulls and black cows.

9. And I saw in my sleep that white bull likewise grow and become a great white bull, and from Him proceeded many white bulls, and they resembled him. And they began to beget many white bulls, which resembled them, one following the other, (even) many.

CHAPTER LXXXVI.
The Fall of the Angels and the Demoralization of Mankind.

1. And again I saw with mine eyes as I slept, and I saw the heaven above, and behold a star fell from heaven, and it arose and eat and pastured amongst those oxen.

2. And after that I saw the large and the black oxen, and behold they all changed their stalls and pastures and their cattle, and began to live with each other.

3. And again I saw in the vision, and looked towards the heaven, and behold I saw many stars descend and cast themselves down from heaven to that first star, and they became bulls amongst those cattle and pastured with them [amongst them].

4. And I looked at them and saw, and behold they all let out their privy members, like horses, and began to cover the cows of the oxen, and they all became pregnant and bare elephants, camels, and asses.

5. And all the oxen feared them and were affrighted at them, and began to bite with their teeth and to devour, and to gore with their horns.

6. And they began, moreover, to devour those oxen; and behold all the children of the earth began to tremble and quake before them and to flee from them.

CHAPTER LXXXVII.
The Advent of the Seven Archangels

1. And again I saw how they began to gore each other and to devour each other, and the earth began to cry aloud.

2. And I raised mine eyes again to heaven, and I saw in the vision, and behold there came forth from heaven beings who were like white men: and four went forth from that place and three with them.

3. And those three that had last come forth grasped me by my hand and took me up, away from the generations of the earth, and raised me up to a lofty place, and showed me a tower raised high above the earth, and all the hills were lower.

4. And one said unto me: 'Remain here till thou seest everything that befalls those elephants, camels, and asses, and the stars and the oxen, and all of them.'

CHAPTER LXXXVIII.
The Punishment of the Fallen Angels by the Archangels.

1. And I saw one of those four who had come forth first, and he seized that first star which had fallen from the heaven, and bound it hand and foot and cast it into an abyss: now that abyss was narrow and deep, and horrible and dark.

2. And one of them drew a sword, and gave it to those elephants and camels and asses: then they began to smite each other, and the whole earth quaked because of them.

3. And as I was beholding in the vision, lo, one of those four who had come forth stoned (them) from heaven, and gathered and took all the great stars whose privy members were like those of horses, and bound them all hand and foot, and cast them in an abyss of the earth.

LXXXIX. 1-9. *The Deluge and the Deliverance of Noah.*

CHAPTER LXXXIX.

1. And one of those four went to that white bull and instructed him in a secret, without his being terrified: he was born a bull and became a man, and built for himself a great vessel and dwelt thereon; and three bulls dwelt with him in that vessel and they were covered in.

2. And again I raised mine eyes towards heaven and saw a lofty roof, with seven water torrents thereon, and those torrents flowed with much water into an enclosure.

3. And I saw again, and behold fountains were opened on the surface of that great enclosure, and that water began to swell and rise upon the surface, and I saw that enclosure till all its surface was covered with water.

4. And the water, the darkness, and mist increased upon it; and as I looked at the height of that water, that water had risen above the height of that enclosure, and was streaming over that enclosure, and it stood upon the earth.

5. And all the cattle of that enclosure were gathered together until I saw how they sank and were swallowed up and perished in that water.

6. But that vessel floated on the water, while all the oxen and elephants and camels and asses sank to the bottom with all the animals, so that I could no longer see them, and they were not able to escape, (but) perished and sank into the depths.

7. And again I saw in the vision till those water torrents were removed from that high roof, and the chasms of the earth were levelled up and other abysses were opened.

8. Then the water began to run down into these, till the earth became visible; but that vessel settled on the earth, and the darkness retired and light appeared.

9. But that white bull which had become a man came out of that vessel, and the three bulls with him, and one of those three was white like that bull, and one of them was red as blood, and one black: and that white bull departed from them.

LXXXIX. 10-27. *From the Death of Noah to the Exodus.*

10. And they began to bring forth beasts of the field and birds, so that there arose different genera: lions, tigers, wolves, dogs, hyenas, wild boars, foxes, squirrels, swine, falcons, vultures, kites, eagles, and ravens; and among them was born a white bull.

11. And they began to bite one another; but that white bull which was born amongst them begat a wild ass and a white bull with it, and the wild asses multiplied.

12. But that bull which was born from him begat a black wild boar and a white sheep; and the former begat many boars, but that sheep begat twelve sheep.

13. And when those twelve sheep had grown, they gave up one of them to the asses, and those asses again gave up that sheep to the wolves, and that sheep grew up among the wolves.

14. And the Lord brought the eleven sheep to live with it and to pasture with it among the wolves: and they multiplied and became many flocks of sheep.

15. And the wolves began to fear them, and they oppressed them until they destroyed their little ones, and they cast their young into a river of much water: but those sheep began to cry aloud on account of their little ones, and to complain unto their Lord.

16. And a sheep which had been saved from the wolves fled and escaped to the wild asses; and I saw the sheep how they lamented and cried, and besought their Lord with all their might, till that Lord of the sheep descended at the voice of the sheep from a lofty abode, and came to them and pastured them. 17. And He called that sheep which had escaped the wolves, and spake with it concerning the wolves that it should admonish them not to touch the shee. And the sheep went to the wolves according to the word of the Lord, and another sheep met it and went with it, and the two went and entered together into the assembly of those wolves, and spake with them and admonished them not to touch the sheep from henceforth.

19. And thereupon I saw the wolves, and how they oppressed the sheep exceedingly with all their power; and the sheep cried aloud.

20. And the Lord came to the sheep and they began to smite those wolves: and the wolves began to make lamentation; but the sheep became quiet and forthwith ceased to cry out.

21. And I saw the sheep till they departed from amongst the wolves; but the eyes of the wolves were blinded, and those wolves departed in pursuit of the sheep with all their power.

22. And the Lord of the sheep went with them, as their leader, and all His sheep followed Him: and his face was dazzling and glorious and terrible to behold.

23. But the wolves began to pursue those sheep till they reached a sea of water.

24. And that sea was divided, and the water stood on this side and on that before their face, and their Lord led them and placed Himself between them and the wolves.

25. And as those wolves did not yet see the sheep, they proceeded into the midst of that sea, and the wolves followed the sheep, and [those wolves] ran after them into that sea.

26. And when they saw the Lord of the sheep, they turned to flee before His face, but that sea gathered itself together, and became as it had been created, and the water swelled and rose till it covered those wolves.

27. And I saw till all the wolves who pursued those sheep perished and were drowned.

LXXXIX. 28-40. *Israel in the Desert, the Giving of the Law, the Entrance into Palestine.*

28. But the sheep escaped from that water and went forth into a wilderness, where there was no water and no grass; and they began to open their eyes and to see; and I saw the Lord of the sheep pasturing them and giving them water and grass, and that sheep going and leading them.

29. And that sheep ascended to the summit of that lofty rock, and the Lord of the sheep sent it to them.

30. And after that I saw the Lord of the sheep who stood before them, and His appearance was great and terrible and majestic, and all those sheep saw Him and were afraid before His face.

31. And they all feared and trembled because of Him, and they cried to that sheep with them [which was amongst them]: "We are not able to stand before our Lord or to behold Him."

32. And that sheep which led them again ascended to the summit of that rock, but the sheep began to be blinded and to wander from the way which he had showed them, but that sheep wot not thereof.

33. And the Lord of the sheep was wrathful exceedingly against them, and that sheep discovered it, and went down from the summit of the rock, and came to the sheep, and found the greatest part of them blinded and fallen away.

34. And when they saw it they feared and trembled at its presence, and desired to return to their folds.

35. And that sheep took other sheep with it, and came to those sheep which had fallen away, and began to slay them; and the sheep feared its presence, and thus that sheep brought back those sheep that had fallen away, and they returned to their folds.

36. And I saw in this vision till that sheep became a man and built a house for the Lord of the sheep, and placed all the sheep in that house.

37. And I saw till this sheep which had met that sheep which led them fell asleep: and I saw till all the great sheep perished and little ones arose in their place, and they came to a pasture, and approached a stream of water.

38. Then that sheep, their leader which had become a man, withdrew from them and fell asleep, and all the sheep sought it and cried over it with a great crying. 39. And I saw till they left off crying for that sheep and crossed that stream of water, and there arose the two sheep as leaders in the place of those which had led them and fallen asleep (lit. "had fallen asleep and led them"). 40. And I saw till the sheep came to a goodly place, and a pleasant and glorious land, and I saw till those sheep were satisfied; and that house stood amongst them in the pleasant land.

LXXXIX. 41-50. *From the Time of the Judges till the Building of the Temple.*

41. And sometimes their eyes were opened, and sometimes blinded, till another sheep arose and led them and brought them all back, and their eyes were opened.

42. And the dogs and the foxes and the wild boars began to devour those sheep till the Lord of the sheep raised up [another sheep] a ram from their midst, which led them.

43. And that ram began to butt on either side those dogs, foxes, and wild boars till he had destroyed them †all†.

44. And that sheep whose eyes were opened saw that ram, which was amongst the sheep, till it †forsook its glory† and began to butt those sheep, and trampled upon them, and behaved itself unseemly.

45. And the Lord of the sheep sent the lamb to another lamb and raised it to being a ram and leader of the sheep instead of that ram which had †forsaken its glory†.

46. And it went to it and spake to it alone, and raised it to being a ram, and made it the prince and leader of the sheep; but during all these things those dogs oppressed the shee.

47. And the first ram pursued that second ram, and that second ram arose and fled before it; and I saw till those dogs pulled down the first ram.

48. And that second ram arose and led the [little] shee. And those sheep grew and multiplied; but all the dogs, and foxes, and wild boars feared and fled before it, and that ram butted and killed the wild beasts, and those wild beasts had no longer any power among the sheep and robbed them no more of ought.

48[b]. And that ram begat many sheep and fell asleep; and a little sheep became ram in its stead, and became prince and leader of those sheep.

50. And that house became great and broad, and it was built for those sheep: (and) a tower lofty and great was built on the house for the Lord of the sheep, and that house was low, but the tower was elevated and lofty, and the Lord of the sheep stood on that tower and they offered a full table before Him.

LXXXIX. 51-67. *The Two Kingdoms of Israel and Judah, to the Destruction of Jerusalem.*

51. And again I saw those sheep that they again erred and went many ways, and forsook that their house, and the Lord of the sheep called some from amongst the sheep and sent them to the sheep, but the sheep began to slay them.

52. And one of them was saved and was not slain, and it sped away and cried aloud over the sheep; and they sought to slay it, but the Lord of the sheep saved it from the sheep, and brought it up to me, and caused it to dwell there.

53. And many other sheep He sent to those sheep to testify unto them and lament over them.

54. And after that I saw that when they forsook the house of the Lord and His tower they fell away entirely, and their eyes were blinded; and I saw the Lord of the sheep how He wrought much slaughter amongst them in their herds until those sheep invited that slaughter and betrayed His place.

55. And He gave them over into the hands of the lions and tigers, and wolves and hyenas, and into the hand of the foxes, and to all the wild beasts, and those wild beasts began to tear in pieces those shee.

56. And I saw that He forsook that their house and their tower and gave them all into the hand of the lions, to tear and devour them, into the hand of all the wild beasts.

57. And I began to cry aloud with all my power, and to appeal to the Lord of the sheep, and to represent to Him in regard to the sheep that they were devoured by all the wild beasts.

58. But He remained unmoved, though He saw it, and rejoiced that they were devoured and swallowed and robbed, and left them to be devoured in the hand of all the beasts.

59. And He called seventy shepherds, and cast those sheep to them that they might pasture them, and He spake to the shepherds and their companions: "Let each individual of you pasture the sheep henceforward, and everything that I shall command you that do ye.

60. And I will deliver them over unto you duly numbered, and tell you which of them are to be destroyed-- and them destroy ye." And He gave over unto them those shee.

61. And He called another and spake unto him: "Observe and mark everything that the shepherds will do to those sheep; for they will destroy more of them than I have commanded them.

62. And every excess and the destruction which will be wrought through the shepherds, record (namely) how many they destroy according to my command, and how many according to their own caprice: record against every individual shepherd all the destruction he effects.

63. And read out before me by number how many they destroy, and how many they deliver over for destruction, that I may have this as a testimony against them, and know every deed of the shepherds, that I may comprehend and see what they do, whether or not they abide by my command which I have commanded them.

64. But they shall not know it, and thou shalt not declare it to them, nor admonish them, but only record against each individual all the destruction which the shepherds effect each in his time and lay it all before me."

65. And I saw till those shepherds pastured in their season, and they began to slay and to destroy more than they were bidden, and they delivered those sheep into the hand of the lions.

66. And the lions and tigers eat and devoured the greater part of those sheep, and the wild boars eat along with them; and they burnt that tower and demolished that house.

67. And I became exceedingly sorrowful over that tower because that house of the sheep was demolished, and afterwards I was unable to see if those sheep entered that house.

LXXXIX. 68-71. *First Period of the Angelic Rulers--from the Destruction of Jerusalem to the Return from the Captivity.*

68. And the shepherds and their associates delivered over those sheep to all the wild beasts, to devour them, and each one of them received in his time a definite number: it was written by the other in a book how many each one of them destroyed of them.

69. And each one slew and destroyed many more than was prescribed; and I began to weep and lament on account of those shee.

70. And thus in the vision I saw that one who wrote, how he wrote down every one that was destroyed by those shepherds, day by day, and carried up and laid down and showed actually the whole book to the Lord of the sheep--(even) everything that they had done, and all that each one of them had made away with, and all that they had given over to destruction.

71. And the book was read before the Lord of the sheep, and He took the book from his hand and read it and sealed it and laid it down.

LXXXIX. 72-77. *Second Period--from the time of Cyrus to that of Alexander the Great.*

72. And forthwith I saw how the shepherds pastured for twelve hours, and behold three of those sheep turned back and came and entered and began to build up all that had fallen down of that house; but the wild boars tried to hinder them, but they were not able.

73. And they began again to build as before, and they reared up that tower, and it was named the high tower; and they began again to place a table before the tower, but all the bread on it was polluted and not pure.

74. And as touching all this the eyes of those sheep were blinded so that they saw not, and (the eyes of) their shepherds likewise; and they delivered them in large numbers to their shepherds for destruction, and they trampled the sheep with their feet and devoured them.

75. And the Lord of the sheep remained unmoved till all the sheep were dispersed over the field and mingled with them (*i.e.* the beasts), and they (*i.e.* the shepherds) did not save them out of the hand of the beasts.

76. And this one who wrote the book carried it up, and showed it and read it before the Lord of the sheep, and implored Him on their account, and besought Him on their account as he showed Him all the doings of the shepherds, and gave testimony before Him against all the shepherds. And he took the actual book and laid it down beside Him and departed.

CHAPTER XC.
1-5. Third Period--from Alexander the Great to the Graeco-Syrian Domination.

1. And I saw till that in this manner thirty-five shepherds undertook the pasturing (of the sheep), and they severally completed their periods as did the first; and others received them into their hands, to pasture them for their period, each shepherd in his own period.

2. And after that I saw in my vision all the birds of heaven coming, the eagles, the vultures, the kites, the ravens; but the eagles led all the birds; and they began to devour those sheep, and to pick out their eyes and to devour their flesh.

3. And the sheep cried out because their flesh was being devoured by the birds, and as for me I looked and lamented in my sleep over that shepherd who pastured the sheep.

4. And I saw until those sheep were devoured by the dogs and eagles and kites, and they left neither flesh nor skin nor sinew remaining on them till only their bones stood there: and their bones too fell to the earth and the sheep became few.

5. And I saw until that twenty-three had undertaken the pasturing and completed in their several periods fifty-eight times.

XC. 6-12. *Fourth Period--from the Graeco-Syrian Domination to the Maccabœan Revolt.*

6. But behold lambs were borne by those white sheep, and they began to open their eyes and to see, and to cry to the sheep.

7. Yea, they cried to them, but they did not hearken to what they said to them, but were exceedingly deaf, and their eyes were very exceedingly blinded.

8. And I saw in the vision how the ravens flew upon those lambs and took one of those lambs, and dashed the sheep in pieces and devoured them.

9. And I saw till horns grew upon those lambs, and the ravens cast down their horns; and I saw till there sprouted a great horn of one of those sheep, and their eyes were opened.

10. And it †looked at† them [and their eyes opened], and it cried to the sheep, and the rams saw it and all ran to it.

11. And notwithstanding all this those eagles and vultures and ravens and kites still kept tearing the sheep and swooping down upon them and devouring them: still the sheep remained silent, but the rams lamented and cried out.

12. And those ravens fought and battled with it and sought to lay low its horn, but they had no power over it.

XC. 13-19. The Last Assault of the Gentiles on the Jews (where vv. 13-15 and 16-18 are doublets).

13. And I saw till the †shepherds and† eagles and those vultures and kites came, and †they cried to the ravens† that they should break the horn of that ram, and they battled and fought with it, and it battled with them and cried that its help might come.

16. All the eagles and vultures and ravens and kites were gathered together, and there came with them all the sheep of the field, yea, they all came together, and helped each other to break that horn of the ram.

14. And I saw till that man, who wrote down the names of the

17. And I saw that man, who wrote the book according to the

shepherds [and] carried up into the presence of the Lord of the sheep [came and helped it and showed it everything: he had come down for the help of that ram].

command of the Lord, till he opened that book concerning the destruction which those twelve last shepherds had wrought, and showed that they had destroyed much more than their predecessors, before the Lord of the sheep.

15. And I saw till the Lord of the sheep came unto them in wrath, and all who saw Him fled, and they all fell †into His shadow† from before His face.

18. And I saw till the Lord of the sheep came unto them and took in His hand the staff of His wrath, and smote the earth, and the earth clave asunder, and all the beasts and all the birds of the heaven fell from among those sheep, and were swallowed up in the earth and it covered them.

19. And I saw till a great sword was given to the sheep, and the sheep proceeded against all the beasts of the field to slay them, and all the beasts and the birds of the heaven fled before their face.

XC. 20-27. *Judgement of the Fallen Angels, the Shepherds, and the Apostates.*

20. And I saw till a throne was erected in the pleasant land, and the Lord of the sheep sat Himself thereon, and the other took the sealed books and opened those books before the Lord of the shee.

21. And the Lord called those men the seven first white ones, and commanded that they should bring before Him, beginning with the first star which led the way, all the stars whose privy members were like those of horses, and they brought them all before Him.

22. And He said to that man who wrote before Him, being one of those seven white ones, and said unto him: "Take those seventy shepherds to whom I delivered the sheep, and who taking them on their own authority slew more than I commanded them."

23. And behold they were all bound, I saw, and they all stood before Him.

24. And the judgement was held first over the stars, and they were judged and found guilty, and went to the place of condemnation, and they were cast into an abyss, full of fire and flaming, and full of pillars of fire.

25. And those seventy shepherds were judged and found guilty, and they were cast into that fiery abyss. 26. And I saw at that time how a like abyss was opened in the midst of the earth, full of fire, and they brought those blinded sheep, and they were all judged and found guilty and cast into this fiery abyss, and they burned; now this abyss was to the right of that house. 27. And I saw those sheep burning †and their bones burning†.

XC. 28-38. *The New Jerusalem, the Conversion of the surviving Gentiles, the Resurrection of the Righteous, the Messiah.*

28. And I stood up to see till they folded up that old house; and carried off all the pillars, and all the beams and ornaments of the house were at the same time folded up with it, and they carried it off and laid it in a place in the south of the land.

29. And I saw till the Lord of the sheep brought a new house greater and loftier than that first, and set it up in the place of the first which had beer folded up: all its pillars were new, and its ornaments were new and larger than those of the first, the old one which He had taken away, and all the sheep were within it.

30. And I saw all the sheep which had been left, and all the beasts on the earth, and all the birds of the heaven, falling down and doing homage to those sheep and making petition to and obeying them in everything.

31. And thereafter those three who were clothed in white and had seized me by my hand [who had taken me up before], and the hand of that ram also seizing hold of me, they took me up and set me down in the midst of those sheep before the judgement took place†.

32. And those sheep were all white, and their wool was abundant and clean.

33. And all that had been destroyed and dispersed, and all the beasts of the field, and all the birds of the heaven, assembled in that house, and the Lord of the sheep rejoiced with great joy because they were all good and had returned to His house.

34. And I saw till they laid down that sword, which had been given to the sheep, and they brought it back into the house, and it was sealed before the presence of the Lord, and all the sheep were invited into that house, but it held them not.

35. And the eyes of them all were opened, and they saw the good, and there was not one among them that did not see. 36. And I saw that that house was large and broad and very full.

37. And I saw that a white bull was born, with large horns and all the beasts of the field and all the birds of the air feared him and made petition to him all the time.

38. And I saw till all their generations were transformed, and they all became white bulls; and the first among them became a lamb, and that lamb became a great animal and had great black horns on its head; and the Lord of the sheep rejoiced over **it** and over all the oxen.

39. And I slept in their midst: and I awoke and saw everything.

40. This is the vision which I saw while I slept, and I awoke and blessed the Lord of righteousness and gave Him glory.

41. Then I wept with a great weeping and my tears stayed not till I could no longer endure it: when I saw, they flowed on account of what I had seen; for everything shall come and be fulfilled, and all the deeds of men in their order were shown to me.

42. On that night I remembered the first dream, and because of it I wept and was troubled--because I had seen that vision.'

THE CONCLUDING SECTION OF THE BOOK.

(XCII-CV.)
XCII. XCI. 1-10. 18-19 *Enoch's Book of Admonition for his Children.*

CHAPTER XCII.

1. The book written by Enoch--[Enoch indeed wrote this complete doctrine of wisdom, (which is) praised of all men and a judge of all the earth] for all my children who shall dwell on the earth. And for the future generations who shall observe uprightness and peace.

2. Let not your spirit be troubled on account of the times;

For the Holy and Great One has appointed days for all things.

3. And the righteous one shall arise from sleep,

[Shall arise] and walk in the paths of righteousness, And all his path and conversation shall be in eternal goodness and grace.

4. He will be gracious to the righteous and give him eternal uprightness,

And He will give him power so that he shall be (endowed) with goodness and righteousness.

And he shall walk in eternal light.

5. And sin shall perish in darkness for ever,

And shall no more be seen from that day for evermore.

CHAPTER XCI.

1-11. 18-19. *Enoch's Admonition to his Children.*

1. 'And now, my son Methuselah, call to me all thy brothers

And gather together to me all the sons of thy mother;

For the word calls me,

And the spirit is poured out upon me,

That I may show you everything

That shall befall you for ever.'

2 And there upon Methuselah went and summoned to him all his brothers and assembled his relatives.

3 And he spake unto all the children of righteousness and said:

'Hear, ye sons of Enoch, all the words of your father,

And hearken aright to the voice of my mouth;

For I exhort you and say unto you, beloved:

Love uprightness and walk therein.

4. And draw not nigh to uprightness with a double heart,

And associate not with those of a double heart,

But walk in righteousness, my sons.

And it shall guide you on good paths,

And righteousness shall be your companion.

5. For I know that violence must increase on the earth,

And a great chastisement be executed on the earth,

And all unrighteousness come to an end:

Yea, it shall be cut off from its roots,

And its whole structure be destroyed.

6. And unrighteousness shall again be consummated on the earth,

And all the deeds of unrighteousness and of violence

And transgression shall prevail in a twofold degree.

7. And when sin and unrighteousness and blasphemy
And violence in all kinds of deeds increase,
And apostasy and transgression and uncleanness increase,
A great chastisement shall come from heaven upon all these,
And the holy Lord will come forth with wrath and chastisement
To execute judgement on earth.

8. In those days violence shall be cut off from its roots,
And the roots of unrighteousness together with deceit,
And they shall be destroyed from under heaven.

9. And all the idols of the heathen shall be abandoned,
And the temples burned with fire,
And they shall remove them from the whole earth,
And they (*i.e.* the heathen) shall be cast into the judgement of fire,
And shall perish in wrath and in grievous judgement for ever.

10. And the righteous shall arise from their sleep,
And wisdom shall arise and be given unto them.

[11. And after that the roots of unrighteousness shall be cut off, and the sinners shall be destroyed by the sword . . . shall be cut off from the blasphemers in every place, and those who plan violence and those who commit blasphemy shall perish by the sword.]

18. And now I tell you, my sons, and show you
The paths of righteousness and the paths of violence.
Yea, I will show them to you again
That ye may know what will come to pass.

19. And now, hearken unto me, my sons,
And walk in the paths of righteousness,
And walk not in the paths of violence;
For all who walk in the paths of unrighteousness shall perish for ever.'

XCIII. XCI. 12-17. *The Apocalypse of Weeks.*

CHAPTER XCIII.

1. And after that Enoch both †gave† and began to recount from the books. And Enoch said:
'Concerning the children of righteousness and concerning the elect of the world,
And concerning the plant of uprightness, I will speak these things,
Yea, I Enoch will declare (them) unto you, my sons:
According to that which appeared to me in the heavenly vision,
And which I have known through the word of the holy angels,
And have learnt from the heavenly tablets.'

3. And Enoch began to recount from the books and said:
'I was born the seventh in the first week,

While judgement and righteousness still endured.

4. And after me there shall arise in the second week great wickedness,

And deceit shall have sprung up;

And in it there shall be the first end.

And in it a man shall be saved;

And after it is ended unrighteousness shall grow up,

And a law shall be made for the sinners.

5. And after that in the third week at its close

A man shall be elected as the plant of righteous judgement,

And his posterity shall become the plant of righteousness for evermore.

6. And after that in the fourth week, at its close,

Visions of the holy and righteous shall be seen,

And a law for all generations and an enclosure shall be made for them.

7. And after that in the fifth week, at its close,

The house of glory and dominion shall be built for ever.

8. And after that in the sixth week all who live in it shall be blinded,

And the hearts of all of them shall godlessly forsake wisdom.

And in it a man shall ascend;

And at its close the house of dominion shall be burnt with fire,

And the whole race of the chosen root shall be dispersed.

9. And after that in the seventh week shall an apostate generation arise,

And many shall be its deeds,

And all its deeds shall be apostate.

10. And at its close shall be elected

The elect righteous of the eternal plant of righteousness,

To receive sevenfold instruction concerning all His creation.

[11. For who is there of all the children of men that is able to hear the voice of the Holy One without being troubled? And who can think His thoughts? and who is there that can behold all the works of heaven? 12. And how should there be one who could behold the heaven, and who is there that could understand the things of heaven and see a soul or a spirit and could tell thereof, or ascend and see all their ends and think them or do like them? 13. And who is there of all men that could know what is the breadth and the length of the earth, and to whom has been shown the measure of all of them? 14. Or is there any one who could discern the length of the heaven and how great is its height, and upon what it is founded, and how great is the number of the stars, and where all the luminaries rest?]

CHAPTER XCI.

12.-17. *The Last Three Weeks.*

12. And after that there shall be another, the eighth week, that of righteousness,

And a sword shall be given to it that a righteous judgement may be executed on the oppressors,

And sinners shall be delivered into the hands of the righteous.

13 And at its close they shall acquire houses through their righteousness,

And a house shall be built for the Great King in glory for evermore,

14d. And all mankind shall look to the path of uprightness.

14a. And after that, in the ninth week, the righteous judgement shall be revealed to the whole world,

b. And all the works of the godless shall vanish from all the earth,

c. And the world shall be written down for destruction.

15. And after this, in the tenth week in the seventh part,

There shall be the great eternal judgement,

In which He will execute vengeance amongst the angels.

16. And the first heaven shall depart and pass away,

And a new heaven shall appear,

And all the powers of the heavens shall give sevenfold light.

17. And after that there will be many weeks without number for ever,

And all shall be in goodness and righteousness,

And sin shall no more be mentioned for ever.

CHAPTER XCIV.

1-5. Admonitions to the Righteous.

1. And now I say unto you, my sons, love righteousness and walk therein;

For the paths of righteousness are worthy of acceptation,

But the paths of unrighteousness shall suddenly be destroyed and vanish.

2. And to certain men of a generation shall the paths of violence and of death be revealed,

And they shall hold themselves afar from them,

And shall not follow them.

3. And now I say unto you the righteous:

Walk not in the paths of wickedness, nor in the paths of death,

And draw not nigh to them, lest ye be destroyed.

4. But seek and choose for yourselves righteousness and an elect life,

And walk in the paths of peace,

And ye shall live and prosper.

5. And hold fast my words in the thoughts of your hearts,

And suffer them not to be effaced from your hearts;

For I know that sinners will tempt men to evilly-entreat wisdom,

So that no place may be found for her,

And no manner of temptation may minish.

XCIV. 6-11. *Woes for the Sinners.*

6. Woe to those who build unrighteousness and oppression

And lay deceit as a foundation;

For they shall be suddenly overthrown,

And they shall have no peace.

7. Woe to those who build their houses with sin;

For from all their foundations shall they be overthrown,

And by the sword shall they fall.

[And those who acquire gold and silver in judgement suddenly shall perish.]

8. Woe to you, ye rich, for ye have trusted in your riches,

And from your riches shall ye depart,

Because ye have not remembered the Most High in the days of your riches.

9. Ye have committed blasphemy and unrighteousness,

And have become ready for the day of slaughter,

And the day of darkness and the day of the great judgement.

10. Thus I speak and declare unto you:

He who hath created you will overthrow you,

And for your fall there shall be no compassion,

And your Creator will rejoice at your destruction.

11. And your righteous ones in those days shall be

A reproach to the sinners and the godless.

CHAPTER XCV.
Enoch's Grief: fresh Woes against the Sinners.

1. Oh that mine eyes were [a cloud of] waters

That I might weep over you,

And pour down my tears as a cloud †of† waters:

That so I might rest from my trouble of heart!

2. †Who has permitted you to practice reproaches and wickedness?

And so judgement shall overtake you, sinners. †

3. Fear not the sinners, ye righteous;

For again will the Lord deliver them into your hands,

That ye may execute judgement upon them according to your desires.

4. Woe to you who fulminate anathemas which cannot be reversed:

Healing shall therefore be far from you because of your sins.

5. Woe to you who requite your neighbour with evil;

For ye shall be requited according to your works.

6. Woe to you, lying witnesses,

And to those who weigh out injustice,

For suddenly shall ye perish.

7. Woe to you, sinners, for ye persecute the righteous;

For ye shall be delivered up and persecuted because of injustice,

And heavy shall its yoke be upon you.

CHAPTER XCVI.
Grounds of Hopefulness for the Righteous: Woes for the Wicked.

1. Be hopeful, ye righteous; for suddenly shall the sinners perish before you,

And ye shall have lordship over them according to your desires.

[2. And in the day of the tribulation of the sinners,

Your children shall mount and rise as eagles,

And higher than the vultures will be your nest,

And ye shall ascend and enter the crevices of the earth,

And the clefts of the rock for ever as coneys before the unrighteous,

And the sirens shall sigh because of you-and weep.]

3. Wherefore fear not, ye that have suffered;

For healing shall be your portion,

And a bright light shall enlighten you,

And the voice of rest ye shall hear from heaven.

4. Woe unto you, ye sinners, for your riches make you appear like the righteous,

But your hearts convict you of being sinners,

And this fact shall be a testimony against you for a memorial of (your) evil deeds.

5. Woe to you who devour the finest of the wheat,

And drink wine in large bowls,

And tread under foot the lowly with your might.

6. Woe to you who drink water from every fountain,

For suddenly shall ye be consumed and wither away,

Because ye have forsaken the fountain of life.

7. Woe to you who work unrighteousness

And deceit and blasphemy:

It shall be a memorial against you for evil.

8. Woe to you, ye mighty,

Who with might oppress the righteous;

For the day of your destruction is coming.

In those days many and good days shall come to the righteous--in the day of your judgement.

CHAPTER XCVII.
The Evils in Store for Sinners and the Possessors of unrighteous Wealth.

1. Believe, ye righteous, that the sinners will become a shame

And perish in the day of unrighteousness.

2. Be it known unto you (ye sinners) that the Most High is mindful of your destruction,

And the angels of heaven rejoice over your destruction.

3. What will ye do, ye sinners,

And whither will ye flee on that day of judgement,

When ye hear the voice of the prayer of the righteous?

4. Yea, ye shall fare like unto them,

Against whom this word shall be a testimony:

"Ye have been companions of sinners."

5. And in those days the prayer of the righteous shall reach unto the Lord,

And for you the days of your judgement shall come.

6. And all the words of your unrighteousness shall be read out before the Great Holy One,

And your faces shall be covered with shame,

And He will reject every work which is grounded on unrighteousness.

7. Woe to you, ye sinners, who live on the mid ocean and on the dry land,

Whose remembrance is evil against you.

8. Woe to you who acquire silver and gold in unrighteousness and say:

"We have become rich with riches and have possessions;

And have acquired everything we have desired.

9. And now let us do what we purposed:

For we have gathered silver,

9^d And many are the husbandmen in our houses."

9^e And our granaries are (brim) full as with water,

10 Yea and like water your lies shall flow away;

For your riches shall not abide

But speedily ascend from you;

For ye have acquired it all in unrighteousness,

And ye shall be given over to a great curse.

CHAPTER XCVIII.
Self-indulgence of Sinners: Sin originated by Man: all Sin recorded in Heaven: Woes for the Sinners.

1. And now I swear unto you, to the wise and to the foolish,

For ye shall have manifold experiences on the earth.

2. For ye men shall put on more adornments than a woman,

And coloured garments more than a virgin:

In royalty and in grandeur and in power,

And in silver and in gold and in purple,

And in splendour and in food they shall be poured out as water.

3. Therefore they shall be wanting in doctrine and wisdom,

And they shall perish thereby together with their possessions;

And with all their glory and their splendour,

And in shame and in slaughter and in great destitution,

Their spirits shall be cast into the furnace of fire.

4. I have sworn unto you, ye sinners, as a mountain has not become a slave,

And a hill does not become the handmaid of a woman,

Even so sin has not been sent upon the earth,

But man of himself has created it,

And under a great curse shall they fall who commit it.

5. And barrenness has not been given to the woman,

But on account of the deeds of her own hands she dies without children.

6. I have sworn unto you, ye sinners, by the Holy Great One,

That all your evil deeds are revealed in the heavens,

And that none of your deeds of oppression are covered and hidden.

7. And do not think in your spirit nor say in your heart that ye do not know and that ye do not see that every sin is every day recorded in heaven in the presence of the Most High.

8. From henceforth ye know that all your oppression wherewith ye oppress is written down every day till the day of your judgement.

9. Woe to you, ye fools, for through your folly shall ye perish: and ye transgress against the wise, and so good hap shall not be your portion.

10. And now, know ye that ye are prepared for the day of destruction: wherefore do not hope to live, ye sinners, but ye shall depart and die; for ye know no ransom; for ye are prepared for the day of the great judgement, for the day of tribulation and great shame for your spirits.

11. Woe to you, ye obstinate of heart, who work wickedness and eat blood:

Whence have ye good things to eat and to drink and to be filled?

From all the good things which the Lord the Most High has placed in abundance on the earth; therefore ye shall have no peace.

12. Woe to you who love the deeds of unrighteousness: wherefore do ye hope for good hap unto yourselves? know that ye shall be delivered into the hands of the righteous, and they shall cut off your necks and slay you, and have no mercy upon you.

13. Woe to you who rejoice in the tribulation of the righteous; for no grave shall be dug for you.

14. Woe to you who set at nought the words of the righteous; for ye shall have no hope of life.

15. Woe to you who write down lying and godless words; for they write down their lies that men may hear them and act godlessly towards (their) neighbour.

16. Therefore they shall have no peace but die a sudden death.

CHAPTER XCIX.
Woes pronounced on the Godless, the Lawbreakers: evil Plight of Sinners in the last Days: further Woes.

1. Woe to you who work godlessness,

And glory in lying and extol them:

Ye shall perish, and no happy life shall be yours.

2. Woe to them who pervert the words of uprightness,

And transgress the eternal law,

And transform themselves into what they were not [into sinners]:

They shall be trodden under foot upon the earth.

3. In those days make ready, ye righteous, to raise your prayers as a memorial,

And place them as a testimony before the angels,

That they may place the sin of the sinners for a memorial before the Most High.

4. In those days the nations shall be stirred up,

And the families of the nations shall arise on the day of destruction.

5. And in those days the destitute shall go forth and carry off their children,

And they shall abandon them, so that their children shall perish through them:

Yea, they shall abandon their children (that are still) sucklings, and not return to them,

And shall have no pity on their beloved ones.

6. And again I swear to you, ye sinners, that sin is prepared for a day of unceasing bloodshed.

7. And they who worship stones, and grave images of gold and silver and wood ⟨and stone⟩ and clay, and those who worship impure spirits and demons, and all kinds of idols not according to knowledge, shall get no manner of help from them.

8. And they shall become godless by reason of the folly of their hearts,

And their eyes shall be blinded through the fear of their hearts

And through visions in their dreams.

9. Through these they shall become godless and fearful;

For they shall have wrought all their work in a lie,

And shall have worshiped a stone:

Therefore in an instant shall they perish.

10. But in those days blessed are all they who accept the words of wisdom, and understand them,

And observe the paths of the Most High, and walk in the path of His righteousness,

And become not godless with the godless;

For they shall be saved.

11. Woe to you who spread evil to your neighbours;

For you shall be slain in Sheol.

12. Woe to you who make deceitful and false measures,

And (to them) who cause bitterness on the earth;

For they shall thereby be utterly consumed.

13. Woe to you who build your houses through the grievous toil of others,

And all their building materials are the bricks and stones of sin;

I tell you ye shall have no peace.

14. Woe to them who reject the measure and eternal heritage of their fathers

And whose souls follow after idols;

For they shall have no rest.

15. Woe to them who work unrighteousness and help oppression,

And slay their neighbours until the day of the great judgement.

16. For He shall cast down your glory,

And bring affliction on your hearts,

And shall arouse His fierce indignation,

And destroy you all with the sword;

And all the holy and righteous shall remember your sins.

CHAPTER C.
The Sinners destroy each other: Judgement of the fallen Angels: the Safety of the Righteous: further Woes for the Sinners.

1. And in those days in one place the fathers together with their sons shall be smitten

And brothers one with another shall fall in death

Till the streams flow with their blood.

2 .For a man shall not withhold his hand from slaying his sons and his sons' sons,

And the sinner shall not withhold his hand from his honoured brother:

From dawn till sunset they shall slay one another.

3. And the horse shall walk up to the breast in the blood of sinners,

And the chariot shall be submerged to its height.

4 In those days the angels shall descend into the secret places

And gather together into one place all those who brought down sin

And the Most High will arise on that day of judgement

To execute great judgement amongst sinners.

5. And over all the righteous and holy He will appoint guardians from amongst the holy angels

To guard them as the apple of an eye,

Until He makes an end of all wickedness and all sin,

And though the righteous sleep a long sleep, they have nought to fear.

6. And (then) the children of the earth shall see the wise in security,

And shall understand all the words of this book,

And recognize that their riches shall not be able to save them

In the overthrow of their sins.

7. Woe to you, Sinners, on the day of strong anguish,

Ye who afflict the righteous and burn them with fire:

Ye shall be requited according to your works.

8. Woe to you, ye obstinate of heart,

Who watch in order to devise wickedness:

Therefore shall fear come upon you

And there shall be none to help you.

9. Woe to you, ye sinners, on account of the words of your mouth,

And on account of the deeds of your hands which your godlessness as wrought,

In blazing flames burning worse than fire shall ye burn.

10 And now, know ye that from the angels He will inquire as to your deeds in heaven, from the sun and from the moon and from the stars in reference to your sins because upon the earth ye execute judgement on the righteous.

11. And He will summon to testify against you every cloud and mist and dew and rain; for they shall all be withheld because of you from descending upon you, and they shall be mindful of your sins.

12. And now give presents to the rain that it be not withheld from descending upon you, nor yet the dew, when it has received gold and silver from you that it may descend.

13. When the hoar-frost and snow with their chilliness, and all the snow-storms with all their plagues fall upon you, in those days ye shall not be able to stand before them.

CHAPTER CI.
Exhortation to the Fear of God: all Nature fears Him, but not the Sinners.

1. Observe the heaven, ye children of heaven, and every work of the Most High, and fear ye Him and work no evil in His presence.

2. If He closes the windows of heaven, and withholds the rain and the dew from descending on the earth on your account, what will ye do then?

3. And if He sends His anger upon you because of your deeds, ye cannot petition Him; for ye spake proud and insolent words against His righteousness: therefore ye shall have no peace.

4. And see ye not the sailors of the ships, how their ships are tossed to and fro by the waves, and are shaken by the winds, and are in sore trouble?

5. And therefore do they fear because all their goodly possessions go upon the sea with them, and they have evil forebodings of heart that the sea will swallow them and they will perish therein.

6. Are not the entire sea and all its waters, and all its movements, the work of the Most High, and has He not set limits to its doings, and confined it throughout by the sand? 7. And at His reproof it is afraid and dries up, and all its fish die and all that is in it; But ye sinners that are on the earth fear Him not.

8. Has He not made the heaven and the earth, and all that is therein? Who has given understanding and wisdom to everything that moves on the earth and in the sea.

9. Do not the sailors of the ships fear the sea? Yet sinners fear not the Most High.

Chapter CII.
Terrors of the Day of Judgement: the adverse Fortunes of the Righteous on the Earth.

1. In those days when He hath brought a grievous fire upon you,

Whither will ye flee, and where will ye find deliverance?

And when He launches forth His Word against you Will you not be affrighted and fear?

2. And all the luminaries shall be affrighted with great fear,

And all the earth shall be affrighted and tremble and be alarmed.

3. And all the †angels shall execute their commands†

And shall seek to hide themselves from the presence of the Great Glory; And the children of earth shall tremble and quake;

And ye sinners shall be cursed for ever, And ye shall have no peace.

4. Fear ye not, ye souls of the righteous,

And be hopeful ye that have died in righteousness.

5. And grieve not if your soul into Sheol has descended in grief,

And that in your life your body fared not according to your goodness,

But wait for the day of the judgement of sinners

And for the day of cursing and chastisement.

6. And yet when ye die the sinners speak over you:

"As we die, so die the righteous,

And what benefit do they reap for their deeds?

7. Behold, even as we, so do they die in grief and darkness,

And what have they more than we?

From henceforth we are equal.

8. And what will they receive and what will they see for ever?

Behold, they too have died,

And henceforth for ever shall they see no light."

9. I tell you, ye sinners, ye are content to eat and drink, and rob and sin, and strip men naked, and acquire wealth and see good days.

10. Have ye seen the righteous how their end falls out, that no manner of violence is found in them till their death?

11. "Nevertheless they perished and became as though they had not been, and their spirits descended into Sheol in tribulation."

CHAPTER CIII.
Different Destinies of the Righteous and the Sinners: fresh Objections of the Sinners.

1. Now, therefore, I swear to you, the righteous, by the glory of the Great and Honoured and 2 Mighty One in dominion, and by His greatness I swear to you:

2. I know a mystery; And have read the heavenly tablets,

And have seen the holy books,

And have found written therein and inscribed regarding them:

3. That all goodness and joy and glory are prepared for them,

And written down for the spirits of those who have died in righteousness,

And that manifold good shall be given to you in recompense for your labours, And that your lot is abundantly beyond the lot of the living.

4. And the spirits of you who have died in righteousness shall live and rejoice,

And their spirits shall not perish, nor their memorial from before the face of the Great One

Unto all the generations of the world: wherefore no longer fear their contumely.

5. Woe to you, ye sinners, when ye have died,

If ye die in the wealth of your sins,

And those who are like you say regarding you:

'Blessed are the sinners: they have seen all their days.

6. And how they have died in prosperity and in wealth,

And have not seen tribulation or murder in their life;

And they have died in honour,

And judgement has not been executed on them during their life."

7. Know ye, that their souls will be made to descend into Sheol

And they shall be wretched in their great tribulation.

8. And into darkness and chains and a burning flame where there is grievous judgement shall your spirits enter;

And the great judgement shall be for all the generations of the world. Woe to you, for ye shall have no peace.

9. Say not in regard to the righteous and good who are in life:

"In our troubled days we have toiled laboriously and experienced every trouble,

And met with much evil and been consumed,

And have become few and our spirit small.

10. And we have been destroyed and have not found any to help us even with a word: We have been tortured [and destroyed], and not hoped to see life from day to day.

11. We hoped to be the head and have become the tail:

We have toiled laboriously and had no satisfaction in our toil;

And we have become the food of the sinners and the unrighteous,

And they have laid their yoke heavily upon us.

12. They have had dominion over us that hated us †and smote us;

And to those that hated us† we have bowed our necks

But they pitied us not.

13. We desired to get away from them that we might escape and be at rest,

But found no place whereunto we should flee and be safe from them.

14. And are complained to the rulers in our tribulation,

And cried out against those who devoured us,

But they did not attend to our cries;

And would not hearken to our voice.

15. And they helped those who robbed us and devoured us and those who made us few; and they concealed their oppression, and they did not remove from us the yoke of those that devoured us and dispersed us and murdered us, and they concealed their murder, and remembered not that they had lifted up their hands against us.

CHAPTER CIV.
Assurances given to the Righteous: Admonitions to Sinners and the Falsifiers of the Words of Uprightness.

1. I swear unto you, that in heaven the angels remember you for good before the glory of the Great One: and your names are written before the glory of the Great One.

2. Be hopeful; for aforetime ye were put to shame through ill and affliction; but now ye shall shine as the lights of heaven, ye shall shine and ye shall be seen, and the portals of heaven shall be opened to you.

3. And in your cry, cry for judgement, and it shall appear to you; for all your tribulation shall be visited on the rulers, and on all who helped those who plundered you.

4. Be hopeful, and cast not away your hopes for ye shall have great joy as the angels of heaven.

5. What shall ye be obliged to do? Ye shall not have to hide on the day of the great judgement and ye shall not be found as sinners, and the eternal judgement shall be far from you for all the generations of the world.

6. And now fear not, ye righteous, when ye see the sinners growing strong and prospering in their ways: be not companions with them, but keep afar from their violence; for ye shall become companions of the hosts of heaven.

7. And, although ye sinners say: "All our sins shall not be searched out and be written down," nevertheless they shall write down all your sins every day.

8. And now I show unto you that light and darkness, day and night, see all your sins.

9. Be not godless in your hearts, and lie not and alter not the words of uprightness, nor charge with lying the words of the Holy Great One, nor take account of your idols; for all your lying and all your godlessness issue not in righteousness but in great sin.

10. And now I know this mystery, that sinners will alter and pervert the words of righteousness in many ways, and will speak wicked words, and lie, and practice great deceits, and write books concerning their words.

11. But when they write down truthfully all my words in their languages, and do not change or minish ought from my words but write them all down truthfully--all that I first testified concerning them.

12. Then, I know another mystery, that books will be given to the righteous and the wise to become a cause of joy and uprightness and much wisdom.

13. And to them shall the books be given, and they shall believe in them and rejoice over them, and then shall all the righteous who have learnt therefrom all the paths of uprightness be recompensed.'

CHAPTER CV.
God and the Messiah to dwell with Man.

1. In those days the Lord bade (them) to summon and testify to the children of earth concerning their wisdom: Show (it) unto them; for ye are their guides, and a recompense over the whole earth.

2. For I and My son will be united with them for ever in the paths of uprightness in their lives; and ye shall have peace: rejoice, ye children of uprightness. Amen.

FRAGMENT OF THE BOOK OF NOAH

(CVI-CVII.)

CHAPTER CVI.

1. And after some days my son Methuselah took a wife for his son Lamech, and she became pregnant by him and bore a son.

2. And his body was white as snow and red as the blooming of a rose, and the hair of his head †and his long locks were white as wool, and his eyes beautiful†. And when he opened his eyes, he lighted up the whole house like the sun, and the whole house was very bright.

3. And thereupon he arose in the hands of the midwife, opened his mouth, and †conversed with† the Lord of righteousness.

4. And his father Lamech was afraid of him and fled, and came to his father Methuselah.

5. And he said unto him: 'I have begotten a strange son, diverse from and unlike man, and resembling the sons of the God of heaven; and his nature is different and he is not like us, and his eyes are as the rays of the sun, and his countenance is glorious.

6. And it seems to me that he is not sprung from me but from the angels, and I fear that in his days a wonder may be wrought on the earth.

7. And now, my father, I am here to petition thee and implore thee that thou mayest go to Enoch, our father, and learn from him the truth, for his dwelling-place is amongst the angels.'

8. And when Methuselah heard the words of his son, he came to me to the ends of the earth; for he had heard that I was there, and he cried aloud, and I heard his voice and I came to him. And 1 said unto him: 'Behold, here am I, my son, wherefore hast thou come to me?'

9. And he answered and said: 'Because of a great cause of anxiety have I come to thee, and because of a disturbing vision have I approached.

10. And now, my father, hear me: unto Lamech my son there hath been born a son, the like of whom there is none, and his nature is not like man's nature, and the colour of his body is whiter than snow and redder than the bloom of a rose, and the hair of his head is whiter than white wool, and his eyes are like the rays of the sun, and he opened his eyes and thereupon lighted up the whole house.

11. And he arose in the hands of the midwife, and opened his mouth and blessed the Lord of heaven.

12. And his father Lamech became afraid and fled to me, and did not believe that he was sprung from him, but that he was in the likeness of the angels of heaven; and behold I have come to thee that thou mayest make known to me the truth.'

13. And I, Enoch, answered and said unto him: 'The Lord will do a new thing on the earth, and this I have already seen in a vision, and make known to thee that in the generation of my father Jared some of the angels of heaven transgressed the word of the Lord.

14. And behold they commit sin and transgress the law, and have united themselves with women and commit sin with them, and have married some of them, and have begot children by them.

15. Yea, there shall come a great destruction over the whole earth, and there shall be a deluge and a great destruction for one year.

16. And this son who has been born unto you shall be left on the earth, and his three children shall be saved with him: when all mankind that are on the earth shall die [he and his sons shall be saved].

17. And they shall produce on the earth giants not according to the spirit, but according to the flesh, and there shall be a great punishment on the earth, and the earth shall be cleansed from all impurity.

18. And now make known to thy son Lamech that he who has been born is in truth his son, and call his name Noah; for he shall be left to you, and he and his sons shall be saved from the destruction, which shall come upon the earth on account of all the sin and all the unrighteousness, which shall be consummated on the earth in his days.

19. And after that there shall be still more unrighteousness than that which was first consummated on the earth; for I know the mysteries of the holy ones; for He, the Lord, has showed me and informed me, and I have read (them) in the heavenly tablets.

CHAPTER CVII.

1. And I saw written on them that generation upon generation shall transgress, till a generation of righteousness arises, and transgression is destroyed and sin passes away from the earth, and all manner of good comes upon it.

2. And now, my son, go and make known to thy son Lamech that this son, which has been born, is in truth his son, and that (this) is no lie.'

3. And when Methuselah had heard the words of his father Enoch--for he had shown to him everything in secret--he returned and showed (them) to him and called the name of that son Noah; for he will comfort the earth after all the destruction.

CHAPTER CVIII.
AN APPENDIX TO THE BOOK OF ENOCH

1. Another book which Enoch wrote for his son Methuselah and for those who will come after him, and keep the law in the last days.

2. Ye who have done good shall wait for those days till an end is made of those who work evil; and an end of the might of the transgressors.

3. And wait ye indeed till sin has passed away, for their names shall be blotted out of the book of life and out of the holy books, and their seed shall be destroyed for ever, and their spirits shall be slain, and they shall cry and make lamentation in a place that is a chaotic wilderness, and in the fire shall they burn; for there is no earth there.

4. And I saw there something like an invisible cloud; for by reason of its depth I could not look over, and I saw a flame of fire blazing brightly, and things like shining mountains circling and sweeping to and fro.

5. And I asked one of the holy angels who was with me and said unto him: 'What is this shining thing? for it is not a heaven but only the flame of a blazing fire, and the voice of weeping and crying and lamentation and strong pain.'

6. And he said unto me: 'This place which thou seest--here are cast the spirits of sinners and blasphemers, and of those who work wickedness, and of those who pervert everything that the Lord hath spoken through the mouth of the prophets--(even) the things that shall be.

7. For some of them are written and inscribed above in the heaven, in order that the angels may read them and know that which shall befall the sinners, and the spirits of the humble, and of those who have afflicted their bodies, and been recompensed by God; and of those who have been put to shame by wicked men:

8. Who love God and loved neither gold nor silver nor any of the good things which are in the world, but gave over their bodies to torture.

9. Who, since they came into being, longed not after earthly food, but regarded everything as a passing breath, and lived accordingly, and the Lord tried them much, and their spirits were found pure so that they should bless His name.

10. And all the blessings destined for them I have recounted in the books. And he hath assigned them their recompense, because they have been found to be such as loved heaven more than their life in the world, and though they were trodden under foot of wicked men, and experienced abuse and reviling from them and were put to shame, yet they blessed Me.

11. And now I will summon the spirits of the good who belong to the generation of light, and I will transform those who were born in darkness, who in the flesh were not recompensed with such honour as their faithfulness deserved.

12. And I will bring forth in shining light those who have loved My holy name, and I will seat each on the throne of his honour.

13. And they shall be resplendent for times without number; for righteousness is the judgement of God; for to the faithful He will give faithfulness in the habitation of upright paths.

14. And they shall see those who were, born in darkness led into darkness, while the righteous shall be resplendent.

15. And the sinners shall cry aloud and see them resplendent, and they indeed will go where days and seasons are prescribed for them.'

THE BOOK OF JASHER

THIS IS THE BOOK OF THE GENERATIONS OF MAN WHOM GOD CREATED UPON THE EARTH ON THE DAY WHEN THE LORD GOD MADE HEAVEN AND EARTH.

Referred to in JOSHUA AND SECOND SAMUEL FAITHFULLY

TRANSLATED FROM THE ORIGINAL HEBREW INTO ENGLISH in a translation based on the original hebrew with the original introductory notes to the english edition.

PUBLISHED BY M. N. NOAH & A. S. GOULD, 1840

Chelsea Square, N. Y,, April 28 1840.

To Messrs. Noah & Gould

GENTLEMEN,

Agreeably to a request made to me yesterday by Mr. Noah, I have sufficiently examined the English version of the Rabbinical work, which heads the title of "the Book of Jasher" , to satisfy myself of its general correctness. I have carefully compared three chapters of the translation with the original, and have no hesitation in saying that in general they give a correct representation of the author's meaning, and as literal as the different idioms of the two languages would allow. In some instances however, it would have been desirable that every word of the Hebrew should have been rendered into English. For instance, in ch. i, v. 2, the translator has omitted the word dust, in mentioning man's formation "from the ground", and in v. 4, the literal version after middle part would be "and he took away one of his ribs and built flesh upon it, and made a woman and brought her to the man." In v. 6 also, the Rabbinical writer does not say "called their names Adam and Eve, "but in the very words of the Hebrew bible, v. 2, "called their name Adam." In ch. xx, v. 4, the version reads thus; "and the servants of Abimelech went to Abimelech, saying", in the original it is "and the servants of Abimelech came and praised Sarah to the kin, saying, &c." In v. 19, the name of Pharaoh is omitted, and occasionally the word "subjects", is substituted for "servants".

It is possible that the translator made use of a copy of some other edition which may have varied in a few words from that examined by me. The points referred to, are, on the whole, unimportant, and do not detract from the general accuracy of the translation.

I am respectfully, Your obt. Serv't

SAMUEL H. TURNER

New York, April 30, 1840.

GENTLEMEN,

I have examined portions of several chapters of the "Book of Jasher" in the original, carefully comparing with it the translation put into my hands by the publishers. The work itself is evidently composed in the purest Rabbinical Hebrew, with a large intermixture of the Biblical idiom, and I consider the translation as a whole, not only as decidedly faithful, but as peculiarly happy in retaining the air of antique simplicity which distinguishes the original, and which constitutes the matchless excellence of our English version of the Hebrew Scriptures. In a few instances I have noticed slight verbal variations from the original, similar to those adverted to by Prof. Turner, as in one case "choice of our sepulchres" for "choice of our land"; but they are of too little moment to detract from the character of general fidelity which I do not hesitate to assign to the translation.

Very respectfully,

Yours, &c, PROF. GEO. BUSH

PREFACE

It is with pleasure that I am able to present to the American public the translation of the Book of Jasher, as referred to in Joshua and Second Samuel, which, after several years' negotiation with the owner and translator of the work in England, I have succeeded in obtaining.

There are many books named in the Old Testament, which are now classed among the missing books, or books supposed to have been lost amidst the many revolutions which have occurred in Judea. These books are not included in the Jewish Canons, and it is questionable whether there are any missing of what were considered as emanating from inspired writers; for, when the works enumerated in the Bible could not be found after the most diligent search, the inference was, that the names applied to other books, or that they were different versions of the same work.

Thus, the Book of the Covenant, [Exodus xxiv. 7.] was a mere collection of the injunctions and institutions delivered by the Almighty to Moses. So it might also be said of the Book of the Law, [Deut. xxxi v. 9.] The Book of the wars of the Lord [Numbers xxi v. 14.] cannot be found, and is everywhere spoken of as one of the missing books. Dr. Lightfoot, in his Chronicles, thinks that Moses refers to a book of his own composing, written by command of God, [Exodus xvii v. 14.] We think, however, that the Book of Judges is the one referred to as the Book of the Wars of the Lord; because, in that book we have all the exploits of the Hebrews detailed at length. We find in Chronicles and Kings a number of books named, which are not to be found. The acts of David the King, written in the Book of Samuel the Seer, also in the Book of Nathan the Prophet, and also in the Book of Gad the Seer; the acts of Solomon are in the Book of Nathan the Prophet, and also in the Book of Abijah the Shulamite; the acts of Rehoboam in the Book of Shemaiah the Prophet; the acts of Jehoshaphat in the Book of Jehu. The journals of the kings of Judah and Israel; the three thousand and five songs, and a treatise on botany and animated nature, by this learned king, are lost; so also are the 'Acts of Manasseh." These works, not having been found by Ezra, could not have been inserted in the Old Testament, and consequently cannot be considered as having been written by divine inspiration. Nevertheless, it would be assuming more than is required or necessary, to say that there were no other books in the time of Ezra, than those considered as divinely inspired. St. Austin says, " The penmen of the Sacred Scripture writ some things as they are, men with historical lore and diligence: other things they writ as prophets, by inspiration from God." We thus have a classification of their labors, both as historians and as prophets. The negligence of the Jews in ancient days, and their constant transition from one country to another, occasioned many losses of the sacred writings. The Book of Deuteronomy was lost for a long time. There were many books rejected by the Canons which are still objects of curiosity, and venerable for their antiquity. The prayer of King Manasseh, Bel and the Dragon, the two Books ofEsdras, the Book of the Maccabees, and the Book of Enoch, recently found and translated from the Ethiopic. The Book of Jasher, referred to in Joshua and Second Samuel, has been long an object of great curiosity. Some of the Hebrew writers contend that it was the lives and acts of Abraham, Isaac, and Jacob, and other patriarchs, who were called Jasherim, the Just. Dr. Lightfoot thinks it is the Book of the Wars of God, and so the reader may think in perusing the various battles it recounts. Grotius calls it a triumphal poem. Josephus says, " That by this book are to be understood certain records kept in some safe place on purpose, giving an account of what happened among the Hebrews from year to year, and called Jasher, or the upright, on account of the fidelity of the annals."

It is known that such have been the curiosity and anxiety to discover this missing book, that several forgeries under that name have appeared from time to time; and the Rev. Mr. Home, in his Introduction to Study of the Scripture, has been at some pains to collect a history of the various fabrications of Jasher; the most remarkable of which was originally published in England, in the year 1751, by a person called Illive, and purported to be a translation from a Hebrew work of that name, found in Persia by Alcuinus. It was republished in Bristol in the year 1829, and a copy is now in my possession. It is a miserable fabrication, occupying but sixty two and a half pages, with copious notes, making out Jasher to be one of the Judges, whereas the translation of the word is the upright, or the upright record. In the same work of Dr. Home, a slight reference is made to the Book of Jasher, written in Rabbinical Hebrew, said to have been discovered in Jerusalem at its capture under Titus, and printed in Venice in 1613. This is the book now translated into English for the first time. Long prior to the destruction of Jerusalem, the Jews had established themselves in various parts of Spain and Italy; they traded to the bay of Gibraltar, as historians affirm, in the earliest periods of history; and Basnage mentions that in Sagunto, a town in Spain, a tombstone was discovered, bearing the following inscription in the Hebrew language: " This is the tomb of Adoniram, an officer of King Solomon, who came to collect the tribute, and died the day," &c. There can be no doubt that Spain, probably France and Italy, were tributary to Solomon. It is, however, certain, that the Jews carried with them into Spain, on their dispersion, an immense number of manuscripts and sacred rolls, where they remained many years, and were, in the eleventh century, placed in their great college at Cordova, and from thence were conveyed to Venice on the first discovery of printing. The printer's Hebrew preface to Jasher shows that it was a painful transcript from a very old and almost illegible Hebrew record, and printed by and with the consent of the Great Consistory of Rabbins at Venice, who alone had the power of publishing such works from the Hebrew records as they deemed authentic. From the Venice edition of Jasher, another edition was many years subsequently published, in Lemberg, in Gallicia. Both editions, in Hebrew, are now in my possession; and the Royal Asiatic Society, having found a copy of Jasher in Calcutta, gave orders to have it translated, which order was countermanded when it was ascertained that considerable progress had been made in England in this translation. The following copy of a letter from the secretary to the translator, shows the estimate which that learned Society placed upon the work.

ROYAL ASIATIC SOCIETY HOUSE.

Grafton St., Bond St., London, Sept. 2, 183 1 .

DEAR SIR:

I am extremely obliged by your having favored me with the sight of Mr. Noah's letter, and in reply to your letter, mention that the Oriental Translation Committee does not consider that it has any claims on your work, and if that ever the Rev. Mr. Adams translates the Book of Jasher, it will not be in the lapse of several years. Hoping that your praiseworthy and valuable labors in that interesting work will soon, in one shape or other, be presented to the public,

I remain, Dear Sir,

Your obliged and ob't Serv't,

Wm. Huttman,

Whatever may have been written and published by commentators, relative to the fabrications of Jasher, I am persuaded they had no reference to this work, although this is the work slightly touched upon by Dr. Home, as the publication in Venice, on the first discovery of printing; but of its origin and history he knew nothing beyond the rumor that it had originally been brought from Jerusalem. There are some events recorded in Jasher, that are found in the Talmud, no doubt copied from Jasher; for although we find in the Talmud, the Mishnah, and Gemarrah, many parables and fanciful tales, to effect moral and religious purposes, yet every thing that we have in Jasher we find recorded in the Bible, with this difference, that in Jasher the occurrences of the Bible are amplified and detailed at length. The celebrated philosopher, Mendelsohn, expresses a high opinion of this work. There are, nevertheless, some events which are recorded in Jasher that may create surprise, particularly a detail of the rape of the Sabines, which, at the first glance, I was disposed to consider as an interpolation; but a little reflection satisfied me that it was an event placed in proper chronological order. Pizron, in his Revolution of Empires, or Antiquities of Nations, says, [page 164,] " It is therefore likely from what I have said, that several of the Titans, in the reign of Uranus, or, at least, in that of Saturn, staying and fixing themselves in that part of Italy which is adjacent to the Tiber and the Appenines, were after ward called Umbrians. If such were the case, as it seems it was, the settlement of the Titans in Italy was made about the time of the calling of Abraham, that is, when he left Chaldea, to go and dwell in the land of Canaan." Page 175, " Now, if all this came to pass, it must have happened about the time Deucalion reigned in Greece, or some years after the deluge that happened under that prince." If as Pizron says, the separation of the Sabines from the Umbrians took place 1500 years before Christ, it will not be far distant from the time at which Jasher places the rape of the Sabine women, in the 91st year of the life of Abraham.

The following is the translator's preface, and with all his admitted learning and ability, he has been unable to do justice to the beauty, grandeur, and alike the simplicity of the original Hebrew. I also subjoin a translation of the Hebrew preface and a translation of the printer's preface, being all the documents in my possession.

Without giving it to the world as a work of Divine inspiration, or assuming the responsibility to say that it is not an inspired book, I have no hesitation in pronouncing it a work of great antiquity and interest, and a work that is entitled, even regarding it as a literary curiosity, to a great circulation among those who take pleasure in studying the Scriptures.

Mordecai Manuel NOAH.

New-York, April, 1839.

TRANSLATOR'S PREFACE

The age in which we live has been, and continues to be, particularly distinguished by a laudable desire in the minds of men, to inquire into the various states of knowledge, and of the arts, as they existed in times anterior to the Christian era; animated with these noble and elevated views, a considerable number of individuals, greatly distinguished for their genius and learning, have in succession turned their attention to the East-to those celebrated countries, in which the arts of civilization and the lights of science first dawned upon, enlightened, and embellished human society. The magnificent and unequalled remains of the arts in Egypt, Babylonia, Assyria, Palestine, and Persia, have, from time to time, been visited and explored; and it has been amidst these fallen monuments of human grandeur, that the adventurous and enlightened traveler has found himself amply rewarded for his laborious and hazardous undertakings; for amidst these wrecks of human greatness, he has succeeded in gathering ample evidence, in confirmation of many of the most important truths recorded in sacred history.

Profane histories have, indeed, conveyed down to us some account of these kingdoms, and of the mighty monarchs who, during a long succession of ages, ruled over them; but the events which they relate are evidently so mixed up with exaggeration, and so adulterated with fable, that, however celebrated their authors might have been, and however fascinating may be the style of their composition, the religious and philosophic student turns from them with dissatisfaction, to the divinely authenticated annals of the Hebrews; because, it is from these alone that he can derive true information concerning the rise, the splendor, the decline, and the real causes of the ruin of those celebrated empires.

In the sacred history we are presented with the only authentic, and, of course, the only valuable information Concerning the origin of the universe,-of men and all other animated creatures-of the gradual increase of the human race-of the flood in the year A. M. 1656, of which mighty event there are existing evidences to the present day; evidences, so universal and so ponderous, that all the ingenuity of the sceptical geologists will never be able to remove them in order to make room for their plausihle hypotheses.

The ever memorable events and transactions recorded in Scripture are with many others of the most interesting nature, comprehended in the Book of Jasher; and they are all arrayed in that style of simple, unadorned majesty and precision, which so particularly distinguishes the genius of the Hebrew language; and this, together with other numerous internal evidences, it is presumed will go far to convince the Hebrew scholar that the book is, with the exception of some doubtful parts, a venerable monument of antiquity; and that, notwithstanding some few additions may have been made to it in comparatively modern times, it still retains sufficient to prove it a copy of the book referred to in Joshua x., and 2v Samuel, ch.i. There are not more than seven or eight words in the whole book that by construction can be derived from the Chaldean language.

The printed Hebrew copy, in the hands of the translator, is without points. During his first perusal of it, some perplexities and doubts rose up in his mind respecting its authenticity; but the more closely he studied it, the more its irresistible evidence satisfied him, that it contained a treasure of information concerning those early times, upon which the histories of other nations are either silent, or cast not a single ray of real light; and hewas more especially delighted to find that the evidence of the whole of its contents went to illustrate and confirm the great and inestimable truths which are recorded in divine history, down to a few years later than the death of Joshua, at which period the book closes.

In this extraordinary book the reader will meet with models of the most sublime virtue, devotion and magnanimity, that cannot fail to raise his admiration, and, at the same time, to excite a generous feeling of emulation to follow the glorious examples set before him.

With these preliminary observations, the translator now respectfully proceeds to lay before the readers a few remarks upon the contents of the book. The tittle "--" is literally, "the upright or correct record," but because the book was not known, it was therefore termed the "Book of Jasher;" this has caused some persons, who are ignorant of the Hebrew language, to suppose that Jasher was the name of a prophet, or of one of the Judges of Israel; an instance of which appears in a publication which came from the press about the middle of the last century, and which purported to have been a translation into English of the Hebrew manuscript of Jasher, found at Gazna in Persia; which translation only was said to have been thence brought by Alcuin. When the translator wrote to the Editor of the London Courier, in November last, he was not aware that the copy of Jasher, announced in the Bristol Gazette as an important discovery, had reference to that fictitious book, which, through the kindness of a friend, he had previously obtained a sight of, and was soon convinced that the whole book was the work of some skeptic in England, in imitation of the language of Scripture, as it was sent forth from the press without the name of printer, bookseller, editor, or publisher; and it is evident that those who were concerned in getting it up, in making Jasher the name of a Judge of Israel were ignorant of the very rudiments of the language from which they pretended to have translated it, as it is well known, even to a tyro in the Hebrew language, that the definite article, is never prefixed to proper names.

The important transactions which are narrated with so remarkable a brevity in the Bible, are, in

Jasher, more circumstantially detailed as in the instance of the murder of Abel by his brother Cain, a particular account is given of the disagreement which preceded it, and of the pretext which Cain sought for the commission of the crime. It appears, also, that when the divine judgment condemned him to wander upon the earth, his wife accompanied him, not to the land of Nod, for no such place is mentioned; but, from this book it appears that the word Nod, in the Scripture, has been given for the participle of the verb "--" "to move or wander about." Jasher has it thus: "--"

ויצא קין בעה ההיא מלפני יהוה מן המקום אשר היה שם ׳ וילך נע
ונדד בארץ קדמת עדן הוא וכל אשר לו

"And at that time Cain went forth from the presence of the Lord, from the place where he was; and he went moving and wandering in the land at the east of Eden, he and all belonging to him."

In the passage respecting the birth of Cain and Abel, three daughters are also mentioned. According to Jasher, the art of writing appears to have been known and practised from the earliest periods; it is stated that Cainan was informed beforehand by God of the intended destruction of mankind by the flood, which he engraved upon tablets of stone, and preserved amongst his treasures.

This book contains a more detailed account of the awful circumstances attending the commencement of the flood, and of the conduct of Noah toward the terrified multitude who had assembled about the ark, when the fatal moment had arrived, and their doom was irrevocably fixed.

A particular delineation of the life and character of Enoch is given, showing, that by his wisdom he reigned over the sons of men, continually instructing them in truth, rightousness, and a knowledge of the Most High.

Jasher informs us, that in the days of Peleg, not only the families of the human race were separated and spread abroad, but that the earth itself was divided; and of both these facts, it may be presumed, there are sufficient existing evidences, even at this day. This book gives, also, a more detailed account of the genealogies of the descendants of Japheth, Shem, and Ham, and of the various parts of the earth which were colonized by them.

Connected with this period of the history is given an account of Nimrod; in which is strikingly depicted the arbitrary and violent character of his conduct and government. The contested point, as to whether Nimrod was the founder of the Assyrian Empire, is here decided. The cause of the dispute amongst commentators proceeded from the word "--" in Gen. chapter x. ver. II, signifying either the name of a man, or the name of the land of Assyria. Jasher has it thus:

ויצא אשור בן שם הוא ובניו ובני ביתו ⁂ ויבנו שם ערים ארבעה

"And Asher, the son of Shem, went forth, he, and his sons, and the children of his household, &c., and they there built four cities."

Jasher clearly elucidates a number of genealogical and chronological difficulties which occur in the Bible; an instance is here adduced of the genealogy of Seir, the Horite, upon which the Bible is silent.

שעיר לא ידענו יחוסו

The learned commentator, Aben Ezra, remarks,

"Seir, his genealogy we do not know;" and the word "--" supposed to come from "--" a noble, but Jasher gives us the descent of Seir, (which accounts for his being called the Horite,) in the following words:

וילך שעיר בן חור בן חוי בן כנען

"And Seir, the son of Hur, the son of Hivi, the son of Canaan, went," &c hence he was called the Horite, from Hur, his father.

The character of Abraham, for piety, true dignity and hospitality, appears to stand unrivaled, but the most affecting and beautiful account in this book, is that of Abraham offering up his son Isaac. The mutual affection of the father and son, and their willing devotion and obedience to the commands of their maker, are so exquisitely described, that the heart of him who can peruse the narrative without being deeply affected, must be callous indeed. The conduct Sarah, as connected with this unexampled and glorious event, was altogether worthy of the wife of Abraham, and the mother of Isaac. At this time Sarah died at Kireath-arba. Her funeral is described as having been magnificent; and it is expressly mentioned, that it was attended by Shem, the son of Noah, Eber his son, king Abimelech, together with Anar, Ashcol and Mamre, and other great people of the land.

In the Bible Sarah is the only woman whose age is given at her death; but it may be interesting to the reader to know that Jasher generally states the ages of the women who are particularly mentioned in the course of the history.

From this book we learn that Noah and Abraham were contemporaries. How beautiful the contemplation of the meeting of these two Patriarchs, the one being a monument of God's mercy, the other having the promise of the favor and grace of God, not only to himself, but to his seed after him. This fact might be proved from Scripture; but from the 32d verse in the 11th chapter of Genesis, most of the Christian commentators have erroneously dated the birth of Abraham 60 years later than it actually took place; as it is generally stated that he was born A. M. 2008, whereas the regular calculation in the Bible leads us to 60 years earlier, viz. 1948. The only cause of this error has been that Abraham's departure from Haran, at the age of 75, is recorded close to the description of the death Terah, at the age of 205, in Gen. ch. xi. v. 32. Although this is the frequent manner of Scripture, to record events out of the regular order of succession (an instance of which we find in Isaac, whose death is recorded Gen. xxxv. 29, when we know from the calculations given us in Scripture, at Isaac's death must have taken place when Joseph was about 29 years old; and the description given in Jasher, of Isaac's coming from Hebron to comfort Jacob upon the loss of Joseph, is beautiful,) it is of great importance, in its making a difference of 60 years in the chronology of the world.

This book gives a particular account of the instruction received by Abraham, Isaac and Jacob, from Shem and Eber, through which they became excellent in piety and wisdom, their tutors in learning having lived to so great an age; and Shem particularly, who, being acquainted with all that was known before the flood, could therefore strengthen his precepts of virtue, the true worship of God, and the necessary dependence upon Him alone, by recording the awful events which he had seen.

The history of Joseph has always been considered one of the most admirable and interesting on record. It is composed in a style of simple and artless eloquence, which touches every feeling heart. A judicious critic has observed, that he considers it a perfect composition. This history, in Jasher, enters more into detail concerning the affairs of Potiphar's wife, Zelicah; Joseph's magnificent procession through the cities of Egypt, on coming into power; the pomp with which he was attended by Pharaoh's chariots, officers, and people, when he went up to meet his father; the affecting scene which then took place, together with other remarkable incidents. This beautiful narrative might justly be entitled, the triumph of virtue and piety; and it is presumed that few can peruse it, unmoved by sentiments of the highest admiration, mixed with the deepest feelings of sympathy. The history of the Israelites during their sojourning in Egypt contains an account of many interesting particulars not noticed in the Bible. Toward the latter end of this period, Balaam, Job, Jannes, and Jambres, appear to have acted their respective parts in some memorable transaction.

This book clears up the reference in 2 Samuel, ch. 1., by showing that David, in the commencement of his beautiful elegy on the death of Saul and Jonathan, revived an injunction given by Jacob in his dying charge to his son Judah, contained in Jasher in these words: אַךְ לְמַד נָא בָנֶיךָ קֶשֶׁת וְכָל כְּלִי מִלְחָמָה

"But teach, I pray thee, thy children the use of the bow, and all instruments of war," &c. This goes far to prove the authenticity of the book, as it beautifully clears up what was always considered obscure.

If commentators upon the holy Scriptures have sought for illustrations in the works of Homer, Pliny, Herodotus, and other profane writers; if they have anxiously caught at glimmerings among the absurdities of Paganism, and the obscurities of Heathen fables, the translator humbly and respectfully hopes that they will now grant a favorable reception to evidence of an entirely opposite character, which is presented in the Book of Jasher.

He does not recommend it to their notice as a work of inspiration, but as a monument of history, comparatively covered with the ivy of the remotest ages; as a work possessing, in its language, all the characteristic simplicity of patriarchal times; and as such, he conceives it peculiarly calculated to illustrate and confirm the sacred truths handed down to us in the Scriptures.

But in making these observations, he is far from offering it as a perfect record. Like all other ancient writings, (except the inspired volume,) it has in some respects suffered from the consuming hand of time; and there is reason to believe that some additions have been made to it. In fine, it contains a history of the lives and memorable transactions of all the illustrious characters recorded in sacred history, from Adam down to the time of the Elders, who immediately succeeded Joshua.

TRANSLATION OF PREFACE TO HEBREW EDITION

THIS BOOK IS THAT WHICH IS CALLED THE UPRIGHT BOOK

IT has at this time been ascertained by us that when the holy city Jerusalem was destroyed by Titus, all the military heads went in to rob and plunder, and that amongst the officers [21] of Titus was one whose name was Sidrus, who went in to search, and found in Jerusalem a house of great extent, and took away all the spoils which he found there; when he wished to go out of the house, he looked at the wall and fancied that he saw treasures there, so he broke down the wall and the building and found a cask full of various books of the Law, the Prophets, and the Hagiographa[22], also books of the kings of Israel, and of the kings of other nations, as well as many other books of Israel, together with the books that the Mishnah adopted and established; many rolls were also lying there; he also found there all sorts of provision and wine in abundance, and discovered an old man sitting there, who was reading in those books. When the officer saw this great sight he was greatly astonished, and said to the old man, why dost thou sit alone in this place, without any person remaining with thee? So the old man answered, for many years past was I aware of this second destruction of Jerusalem, so I built this house and made for myself a balcony [23], and I brought with me these books to read, and I brought also sufficient provision, thinking thereby to save my life[24].

And God caused the old man to find favor in the eyes of the officer, who brought him forth with respect with all his books, and they went from city to city and from country to country until they reached Sevilia; and the officer found that this old man was possessed of wisdom and understanding and acquainted with various kinds of science, upon discovering which he raised and honored him, was constantly in his house and was taught by him all sorts of wisdom, and they built for themselves a lofty and capacious house in the suburbs of Sevilia and placed there all those books.

This house is yet in Sevilia unto this day and they wrote there all the events that would hereafter take place amongst the kings of the world unto the coming of our Messiah. And it came to pass that when God carried us away [25] with a mighty captivity by the hands of the kings of Edom, from city to city and from country to country in bitter anxiety, this book, called " The Generations of Adam" together with other books came into our hands, for they came from that house in Sevilia, and they came afterward to our city Napuli, which city is under the sway of the king of Spain— whose glory may be exalted. And when we saw these books, that they were books of all wisdom, we resolved in our minds to print them like all the books that came to our hands. Now this book is the best and most valuable of all, and of this book twelve copies have reached us, and we searched in them and found them all of one copy, there was no difference, nothing added and nothing deficient, nor any alteration in letters, words or events, for they were all alike as it were of one copy.

Since, therefore, we saw in this book great merit urging us to this resolve, we are determined to print it— and it is found written that this book is called the Book Jasher, because all its transactions are in that order as they had taken place in the world as regards priority and succession, for thou wilt not find in this book any postponement of events that were anterior, or priority of those that were posterior, but every thing is recorded in its place and time.

Thou wilt thus find that it relates the death of such a one at the particular time of the life of another and thus throughout. Owing to this it was called Sepher Hajashar, but it is customary to call it the Generations of Man [26], the reason of which is that they call it by that with which it commences, but the chief name thereof is the book "JASHER" owing to the reasons we have assigned. Now it is found that this book is translated into Greek, entitled "Lo libris de los divitiis" .

It is also found written in the Book of the Asmoneans, which has come down to us, that in the days of Ptolemy king of Egypt, he ordered his servants to go and gather all the books of laws, and all the books of Chronicles which they could find in the world, so that he might become wise through them, and by examining them become acquainted with the subjects and events of the world, and to compile from them a book in all matters of jurisdiction regarding the affairs of life, thereby to exercise pure justice. So they went and collected for him nine hundred and sixty five books and brought to him, when he commanded them to go again and seek to complete the number of a thousand books, and they did so. After this, some of the persecutors of Israel stood up before him and said, O king, why wilt thou trouble thyself in this manner? Send to the Jews in Jerusalem

---

[21] Buxton gives this word "episcopus" which, besides a bishop, means also a lieutenant, overseer, superintendant. See Arach [a dictionary].
[22] Psalms, Proverbs, &c.
[23] "Aksadora" or porch, a Talmudical word derived from the Greek. See Arach.
[24] See same expression in Jeremiah ch. xxxviii, v. 2.
[25] See same expression in Isaiah ch. xxii, v. 17.
[26] The word used in Hebrew is "adam" , which means human as well as Adam.

that they shall bring unto thee the book of their law which was written for them from the mouth of the Lord by their Prophets, from which thou mayest become wise, and regulate all judgments and laws according to thy desire; so the king hearkened to their words, and sent to the Jews upon this matter, who sent to him this book, for they could not give unto him the Book of the Lord, for they said, we cannot give the law of the Lord to a stranger. Now when this book came to the hands of Ptolemy he read it and it pleased him greatly, and he searched therein in his wisdom, and he examined it and found therein what he had desired, and he neglected all the other books which they had collected for him, and he blessed him who had advised him to this thing.

After some time the persecutors of Israel became aware of this, that the Israelites had not sent the Book of the Law to the king, and they came and said unto him, O king, the Israelites have treated thee with contempt, for they did not send to thee the Book of the Law which we had mentioned to thee, but they sent to thee another book which they had in their hands, therefore send to them that they may forward unto thee the book of their law, for from that book thou wilt obtain thy desire much more than from the book which they have sent to thee; so when the king heard their words he became exceedingly wroth against the Israelites, and his anger burned within him until he sent again to them for them to forward to him the Book of the Law. Fearing that they might still continue to scorn him, he acted prudently with them and sent to seventy of their elders and placed them in seventy houses, that each should write the Book of the Law, so that no alteration might be found in them, and the divine spirit rested upon them, and they wrote for him seventy books and they were all of one version, without addition or diminution. At this the king rejoiced greatly and he honored the elders, together with all the Jews, and he sent offerings and gifts to Jerusalem as it is written there. [27] At his death, the Israelites acted cunningly with his son and took from his treasures the Book of the Law, but left this book there and took it not away, in order that every future king might know the wonders of the Lord, blessed be his Name, and that He had chosen Israel from all nations, and that there is no God beside Him.

This book is therefore in Egypt unto this day, and from that time it became circulated throughout the earth, until it reached us in our captivity this day in the city of Napuli, which is under the rule of the king of Spain. Now thou wilt find in this book that some of the kings of Edom, of Chittim and the kings of Africa who were in those days, are mentioned, although it might appear that such was not the aim or intent of this book; but the reason of this was to show to every person obtaining this book the contrast between the wars of Israel and the wars of the Gentiles, for the conquest of Gentile kings one over the other was by accident, which is not so in the conquest of the kings of Israel over the Gentiles, which is by a miracle from our blessed Lord as long as the Israelites trust in his exalted Name.

Now the uses of this book are many, all of which lead us to confidence in God— whose Name be exalted, and to our adherence unto Him and his ways.

The first use is the additional information it affords us upon the subjects of the creation of man and the deluge, recording also the years of the twenty generations and their misdeeds; also at what period they were born, and when they died, by which means our hearts may be inclined to adhere to the Lord, when we see the mighty works which He performed in days of old.

The second use is in the additional account respecting the birth of Abraham and how it was that he cleaved to the Lord, and the transactions that took place between him and Nimrod; and thus also of the account of the builders of the tower of Babel [28], how that the Lord drove them to the four corners of the earth, and how they established the countries and lands called after their names unto this day, by which means we may draw nigh to our Creator. The third use is the explanation it gives us how the patriarchs adhered to the Lord, and of their transactions which convince us of their fear of God. The fourth use is, in what it records of the affairs of Sodom and the iniquities of its people, and in what consisted their sins, as well as their punishment, by which means we may refrain from all evil doings. The fifth use is in the account of the faith of Isaac and Jacob in the Lord, and the prayers and weeping of Sarah at the binding of Isaac for a sacrifice, which is of great use in inclining our hearts to the service of the Lord. The sixth use is in the information it affords us upon the subject of the wars of the sons of Jacob with the people of Shechem and the seven cities of the Amorites. This will rouse our hearts to faith in our God; for how could ten men destroy seven cities if their hearts had not been impressed with faith in the Lord?

The seventh use is, in the information it gives us of all the events that happened to Joseph in Egypt, with Potiphar and his wife and with the king of Egypt, for this will also rouse our hearts to the fear of the Lord, and to remove ourselves from all sin, so that it may be well with us in the latter end.

---

[27] In the Book of the Asmoneans mentioned above.
[28] Called in Hebrew "dor ha-pluggdh" because the earth was then divided.

The eighth use is in the account it furnishes us of what happened to Moses in Cush and in Midian, by which we may understand the wonders of the Lord which He performs for the righteous, and that we may thereby adhere to Him. The ninth use is in its recording what had happened to the Israelites in Egypt, and when the commencement of their servitude took place, and how they served the Egyptians in all manner of hard work, and to what purpose all this tended— how after this God was favorable to them through their trusting in Him, and there is no doubt of this that he who reads the events of Egypt from this book on the nights of the Passover, will receive a great reward, as our Rabbins of blessed memory say, he that is occupied in relating the exit from Egypt is to be praised, in which this book is included, for this is the true narration which ought to be read after the Hagadah, for such person [reading this] may be assured that he will be greatly rewarded; we do so this day in our captivity in the countries of Spain, after having finished reading the Hagadah, we commence reading in this book the whole affair of Egypt, from the Israelites going down to Egypt unto their exit, for in this book a person ought to read. The eleventh [29] use is, that some of the comments of our Rabbins and of other commentators who have explained the law, thou wilt find illustrated in this book, such as the account of the messengers who met Jacob [30], when he came from Mesopotamia after they had gone to Esau, also the account of Gabriel who taught Joseph seventy languages, also the illustration it affords of him [31], who smote Midian in the fields of Moab and the like. The twelfth use is that every man lecturing in public may bring forward in his discourse, subjects from this book, which the commentators have not explained, by which means he may make an impression upon the hearts of his audience. The thirteenth use is, that all merchants and travellers, who have an opportunity to study the law, may read this book and receive their reward, for therein is the reward of the soul as well, as the delight of the body, in the discovery of new matter not recorded in any other book. And by these means will man understand to know the Lord and cleave unto Him.

Now because we have seen the merit of this book, and the great usefulness thereof, we have undertaken to print it without addition or diminution, and from this time we have commenced to print it in a book, that such books may be in the hands of the members of our covenant, the men of our captivity in order that it may be farther circulated throughout every generation, and every city, family and country, so that they may understand the wonders of the Lord which He performed for our ancestors, and his bounties toward them from the days of old, and that He chose us from all nations. May they who devote their hearts to the fear of the Lord, be rendered meritorious by studying therein whilst we confide in the Lord, the God of gods, and depend upon Him and seek salvation and assistance from Him, in this heavenly work, and may He prosper us in the right path, and deliver us from errors, and cleanse us from secret faults, as his anointed said in Psalm ixx. v. 12.: " Who can understand his errors? Cleanse thou me from secret faults." May God teach us the good way and direct us in a prosperous path for the sake of his mercies and kindnesses, and may He graciously fulfill the desires of our hearts, Amen, and so be his will.

THE PRINTER'S PREFACE TO THE HEBREW EDITION OF 1625

THE humble worm, and no man, Joseph, son to my father, the wise and highly respected in Israel, Samuel the little one (Samuel Hakkaton), says, my witness is in heaven and my testimony is on high, the God of gods knows, and Israel knows also, how much fatigue I have undergone, and how much trouble I have taken until I had brought to light the hidden treasures of this book; forever since I was driven from my land, from the metropolis of Israel, the great city of wise men and scribes, the renowned city of Pasia, ever since the Lord, through my great offences, has driven me with a violent captivity, one stumbling after the other, He weakened my strength in the way, the iron entered my soul until I reached the Italian harbor, the royal city Livorno [Leghorn,] which is under the sway of our Lord the most serene Grand Duke Don Ferdinand de Media [Medici Qu?] [32] for neither by day nor by night could I remain silent, I was continually in thought, my soul was humbled in me, and sleep was removed from mine eyes, when I reflected how energetically my father, the crown of my head, strove with his purse and labor to transcribe this book, as was his constant custom from his love of the study of the Law, to lavish money and wealth, principal and interest, for the purchase and the transcribing, for my own use, of books without end, in order that I might obtain wisdom and instruction, to comprehend the words of understanding, as all of the inhabitants of my city can testify and declare; O God remember him favorably to rest in glory with the righteous who are in the garden of Eden, Amen!— for this loss is felt only by me, especially in the transcribing of this book it is holy for praises to the Lord, for there was never seen nor found but one, which the intelligent and pious scribe Jacob, the son of Atiyah, transcribed from a very old

---

[29] The eleventh use. — I cannot see any mention of the tenth use ; this must have been omitted, I think, before the words above, "how after this, God was favourable to them through their trusting in Him."

[30] See the latter part of ch. xxxi.

[31] The obscure passage in Gen. xxxvi v. 35 in the Bible, is cleared up in Jasher ch. Lxii, where it gives a long history of Hadad, the son of Bedad.

[32] Ferdinando de' Medici was Grand Duke of Tuscany from 1587 to 1609. Livorno is a sea port at the western border of the Tuscany region.

manuscript, the letters of which were defaced; and had it not been for the consummate ability of the above mentioned Rabbi, no other person could have made out those letters, nor have transcribed them, from their antiquity and from their having been defaced.

Now my father, of blessed memory, found favor in his eyes, to obtain this book on loan, in order that he might also get one transcribed by the hands of a certain scribe, and in the year 5373 [corresponding with the year 1613], through my great sins, I went out of the pale of my birthplace, and from my father's house, owing to the terrors of famine, pestilence and slaughter. The sword destroyed from without, and within was the terror of pestilence and famine, on account of the battles and contentions which took place between the sons of the old king Maruccus who had died, for each lifted himself up, saying, I will reign, and they devoured the Israelites with open mouth, so that very few remained of them, even a tithe of a tithe; many families and heads of the houses of their fathers were lost and destroyed and became as naught; many books of various kinds, new and old, some in manuscript and others in print, as well as those of modern times, were mostly destroyed by fire, or were torn to pieces, which, together with their owners, lie hid under the ruins to this day. Woe to the eyes that beheld this! Yet may the name of the Lord be blessed for the evil as well as for the good.

Fearing that this book might share the same fate as the others, I daily used the most persevering exertions in sending letters to some particular individuals in the city Argilia, in the city Titu, and in the city Pasia, to such as had been left, humbly beseeching them to search and inquire where might be the place of the glory of this book, and it was sought after and found to be hid in the hands of one of the individuals of the congregation, the wise and highly gifted Moses Chasan; and thanks are due to him, that upon his ascertaining my good intention to print it, and to scatter it throughout all Jewish communities, he did not delay to send it, as he felt a desire for a heavenly reward for this pious act, yea, he sent it to me as a gift, may he receive a blessing from the Lord, and may his reward be perfect. Amen.

Now I, in my humble station, have composed a work entitled r <**>iO m two parts, one part containing some of the scriptural comments which I made with the gracious help of the Lord, and the second part containing fifty lectures which I delivered to a great congregation, besides a later comment containing explanations of parts of the Talmud which I met with in the course of my studies, and which I illustrated according to my humble abilities; now I am revising this work a second time in order to bring it to the press, if heaven spare my life, yet I said to my heart, to thee, O worm, and no man, does the Scripture proclaim " It is time for thee, O Lord, to work, for they have made void thy law" for the printing of this book of Jasher tends to the honor and glory of the Lord, for through it will the hearts of men be directed to cleave to the blessed Lord, and by the means of which they will understand the wonderful works of God, and his bounties toward our ancestors from the days of old, and how He chose us from all nations, as thou wilt see at length in the preface, where in thou wilt perceive enumerated the great many uses, thirteen in number, which induce men to confide in the Lord and to adhere to Him.

I have found another use therein, which is, that many parts of the five books difficult of comprehension, and which the commentators have been unable to reconcile, are, by means of this book, properly understood, as it gives a detail of those parts, wherein the sacred volume is brief in its account, and relates events as they occurred; thou wilt therefore find me lifting up my hand in the margin with the words *V3ffin TDK " The humble editor says" by which will be understood what I have asserted; search and thou will find many things also, which our Rabbies in their works gave in short, are brought forth more fully in this book since it is high time now to act and have a care for the glory of God's name. Since then it is proper for me at present to defer the publication of my above mentioned work until I shall first have brought to light the hidden treasures of this book and to reveal them to the world. I am confident that with the help of the Lord all Israel will exult and rejoice therein.

I have therefore put my trust in the Lord, may He remember me favorably, that I may be enabled in the next year by his help and decree to publish also my aforementioned work.

As for me, my prayer is to Him, who dwells on high, may the Lord God assist me, and send me from on high his peace, favor, and faithfulness to help me, that He may lead me beside the still waters, and conduct me to the paths of righteousness for the sake of his great name, and for the sake of his law. Amen forever and ever.

THE BOOK OF JASHER

CHAPTER 1

1.   And God said, Let us make man in our image, after our likeness, and God created man in his own image.

2.   And God formed man from the ground, and he blew into his nostrils the breath of life, and man became a living soul endowed with speech.

3.   And the Lord said, It is not good for man to be alone; I will make unto him a helpmeet.

4.   And the Lord caused a deep sleep to fall upon Adam, and he slept, and he took away one of his ribs, and he built flesh upon it, and formed it and brought it to Adam, and Adam awoke from his sleep, and behold a woman was standing before him.

5.   And he said, This is a bone of my bones and it shall be called woman, for this has been taken from man; and Adam called her name Eve, for she was the mother of all living.

6.   And God blessed them and called their names Adam and Eve in the day that he created them, and the Lord God said, Be fruitful and multiply and fill the earth.

7.   And the Lord God took Adam and his wife, and he placed them in the garden of Eden to dress it and to keep it; and he commanded them and said unto them, From every tree of the garden you may eat, but from the tree of the knowledge of good and evil you shall not eat, for in the day that you eat thereof you shall surely die.

8.   And when God had blessed and commanded them, he went from them, and Adam and his wife dwelt in the garden according to the command which the Lord had commanded them.

9.   And the serpent, which God had created with them in the earth, came to them to incite them to transgress the command of God which he had commanded them.

10. And the serpent enticed and persuaded the woman to eat from the tree of knowledge, and the woman hearkened to the voice of the serpent, and she transgressed the word of God, and took from the tree of the knowledge of good and evil, and she ate, and she took from it and gave also to her husband and he ate.

11. And Adam and his wife transgressed the command of God which he commanded them, and God knew it, and his anger was kindled against them and he cursed them.

12. And the Lord God drove them that day from the garden of Eden, to till the ground from which they were taken, and they went and dwelt at the east of the garden of Eden; and Adam knew his wife Eve and she bore two sons and three daughters.

13. And she called the name of the first born Cain, saying, I have obtained a man from the Lord, and the name of the other she called Abel, for she said, In vanity we came into the earth, and in vanity we shall be taken from it.

14. And the boys grew up and their father gave them a possession in the land; and Cain was a tiller of the ground, and Abel a keeper of sheep.

15. And it was at the expiration of a few years, that they brought an approximating offering to the Lord, and Cain brought from the fruit of the ground, and Abel brought from the firstlings of his flock from the fat thereof, and God turned and inclined to Abel and his offering, and a fire came down from the Lord from heaven and consumed it.

16. And unto Cain and his offering the Lord did not turn, and he did not incline to it, for he had brought from the inferior fruit of the ground before the Lord, and Cain was jealous against his brother Abel on account of this, and he sought a pretext to slay him.

17. And in some time after, Cain and Abel his brother, went one day into the field to do their work; and they were both in the field, Cain tilling and ploughing his ground, and Abel feeding his flock; and the flock passed that part which Cain had ploughed in the ground, and it sorely grieved Cain on this account.

18. And Cain approached his brother Abel in anger, and he said unto him, What is there between me and thee, that thou comest to dwell and bring thy flock to feed in my land?

19. And Abel answered his brother Cain and said unto him, What is there between me and thee, that thou shalt eat the flesh of my flock and clothe thyself with their wool?

20. And now therefore, put off the wool of my sheep with which thou hast clothed thyself, and recompense me for their fruit and flesh which thou hast eaten, and when thou shalt have done this, I will then go from thy land as thou hast said?

21. And Cain said to his brother Abel, Surely if I slay thee this day, who will require thy blood from me?

22. And Abel answered Cain, saying, Surely God who has made us in the earth, he will avenge my cause, and he will require my blood from thee shouldst thou slay me, for the Lord is the judge and arbiter, and it is he who will requite man according to his evil, and the wicked man according to the wickedness that he may do upon earth.

23. And now, if thou shouldst slay me here, surely God knoweth thy secret views, and will judge thee for the evil which thou didst declare to do unto me this day.

24. And when Cain heard the words which Abel his brother had spoken, behold the anger of Cain was kindled against his brother Abel for declaring this thing.

25. And Cain hastened and rose up, and took the iron part of his ploughing instrument, with which he suddenly smote his brother and he slew him, and Cain spilt the blood of his brother Abel upon the earth, and the blood of Abel streamed upon the earth before the flock.

26. And after this Cain repented having slain his brother, and he was sadly grieved, and he wept over him and it vexed him exceedingly.

27. And Cain rose up and dug a hole in the field, wherein he put his brother's body, and he turned the dust over it.

28. And the Lord knew what Cain had done to his brother, and the Lord appeared to Cain and said unto him, Where is Abel thy brother that was with thee?

29. And Cain dissembled, and said, I do not know, am I my brother's keeper? And the Lord said unto him, What hast thou done? The voice of thy brother's blood crieth unto me from the ground where thou hast slain him.

30. For thou hast slain thy brother and hast dissembled before me, and didst imagine in thy heart that I saw thee not, nor knew all thy actions.

31. But thou didst this thing and didst slay thy brother for naught and because he spoke rightly to thee, and now, therefore, cursed be thou from the ground which opened its mouth to receive thy brother's blood from thy hand, and wherein thou didst bury him.

32. And it shall be when thou shalt till it, it shall no more give thee its strength as in the beginning, for thorns and thistles shall the ground produce, and thou shalt be moving and wandering in the earth until the day of thy death.

33. And at that time Cain went out from the presence of the Lord, from the place where he was, and he went moving and wandering in the land toward the east of Eden, he and all belonging to him.

34. And Cain knew his wife in those days, and she conceived and bare a son, and he called his name Enoch, saying, In that time the Lord began to give him rest and quiet in the earth.

35. And at that time Cain also began to build a city: and he built the city and he called the name of the city Enoch, according to the name of his son; for in those days the Lord had given him rest upon the earth, and he did not move about and wander as in the beginning.

36. And Irad was born to Enoch, and Irad begat Mechuyael and Mechuyael begat Methusael.

CHAPTER 2

1. And it was in the hundred and thirtieth year of the life of Adam upon the earth, that he again knew Eve his wife, and she conceived and bare a son in his likeness and in his image, and she called his name Seth, saying, Because God has appointed me another seed in the place of Abel, for Cain has slain him.

2. And Seth lived one hundred and five years, and he begat a son; and Seth called the name of his son Enosh, saying, Because in that time the sons of men began to multiply, and to afflict their souls and hearts by transgressing and rebelling against God.

3. And it was in the days of Enosh that the sons of men continued to rebel and transgress against God, to increase the anger of the Lord against the sons of men.

4. And the sons of men went and they served other gods, and they forgot the Lord who had created them in the earth: and in those days the sons of men made images of brass and iron, wood and stone, and they bowed down and served them.

5. And every man made his god and they bowed down to them, and the sons of men forsook the Lord all the days of Enosh and his children; and the anger of the Lord was kindled on account of their works and abominations which they did in the earth.

6. And the Lord caused the waters of the river Gihon to overwhelm them, and he destroyed and consumed them, and he destroyed the third part of the earth, and notwithstanding this, the sons of men did not turn from their evil ways, and their hands were yet extended to do evil in the sight of the Lord.

7. And in those days there was neither sowing nor reaping in the earth; and there was no food for the sons of men and the famine was very great in those days.

8. And the seed which they sowed in those days in the ground became thorns, thistles and briers; for from the days of Adam was this declaration concerning the earth, of the curse of God, which he cursed the earth, on account of the sin which Adam sinned before the Lord.

9. And it was when men continued to rebel and transgress against God, and to corrupt their ways, that the earth also became corrupt.

10. And Enosh lived ninety years and he begat Cainan;

11. And Cainan grew up and he was forty years old, and he became wise and had knowledge and skill in all wisdom, and he reigned over all the sons of men, and he led the sons of men to wisdom and knowledge; for Cainan was a very wise man and had understanding in all wisdom, and with his wisdom he ruled over spirits and demons;

12. And Cainan knew by his wisdom that God would destroy the sons of men for having sinned upon earth, and that the Lord would in the latter days bring upon them the waters of the flood.

13. And in those days Cainan wrote upon tablets of stone, what was to take place in time to come, and he put them in his treasures.

14. And Cainan reigned over the whole earth, and he turned some of the sons of men to the service of God.

15. And when Cainan was seventy years old, he begat three sons and two daughters.

16. And these are the names of the children of Cainan; the name of the first born Mahlallel, the second Enan, and the third Mered, and their sisters were Adah and Zillah; these are the five children of Cainan that were born to him.

17. And Lamech, the son of Methusael, became related to Cainan by marriage, and he took his two daughters for his wives, and Adah conceived and bare a son to Lamech, and she called his name Jabal.

18. And she again conceived and bare a son, and called his name Jubal; and Zillah, her sister, was barren in those days and had no offspring.

19. For in those days the sons of men began to trespass against God, and to transgress the commandments which he had commanded to Adam, to be fruitful and multiply in the earth.

20. And some of the sons of men caused their wives to drink a draught that would render them barren, in order that they might retain their figures and whereby their beautiful appearance might not fade.

21. And when the sons of men caused some of their wives to drink, Zillah drank with them.

22. And the child-bearing women appeared abominable in the sight of their husbands as widows, whilst their husbands lived, for to the barren ones only they were attached.

23. And in the end of days and years, when Zillah became old, the Lord opened her womb.

24. And she conceived and bare a son and she called his name Tubal Cain, saying, After I had withered away have I obtained him from the Almighty God.

25. And she conceived again and bare a daughter, and she called her name Naamah, for she said, After I had withered away have I obtained pleasure and delight.

26. And Lamech was old and advanced in years, and his eyes were dim that he could not see, and Tubal Cain, his son, was leading him and it was one day that Lamech went into
the field and Tubal Cain his son was with him, and whilst they were walking in the field, Cain the son of Adam advanced towards them; for Lamech was very old and could not see much, and Tubal Cain his son was very young.

27. And Tubal Cain told his father to draw his bow, and with the arrows he smote Cain, who was yet far off, and he slew him, for he appeared to them to be an animal.

28. And the arrows entered Cain's body although he was distant from them, and he fell to the ground and died.

29. And the Lord requited Cain's evil according to his wickedness, which he had done to his brother Abel, according to the word of the Lord which he had spoken.

30. And it came to pass when Cain had died, that Lamech and Tubal went to see the animal which they had slain, and they saw, and behold Cain their grandfather was fallen dead upon the earth.

31. And Lamech was very much grieved at having done this, and in clapping his hands together he struck his son and caused his death.

32. And the wives of Lamech heard what Lamech had done, and they sought to kill him.

33. And the wives of Lamech hated him from that day, because he slew Cain and Tubal Cain, and the wives of Lamech separated from him, and would not hearken to him in those days.

34. And Lamech came to his wives, and he pressed them to listen to him about this matter.

35. And he said to his wives Adah and Zillah, Hear my voice O wives of Lamech, attend to my words, for now you have imagined and said that I slew a man with my wounds, and a child with my stripes for their having done

no violence, but surely know that I am old and grey-headed, and that my eyes are heavy through age, and I did this thing unknowingly.

36. And the wives of Lamech listened to him in this matter, and they returned to him with the advice of their father Adam, but they bore no children to him from that time, knowing that God's anger was increasing in those days against the sons of men, to destroy them with the waters of the flood for their evil doings.

37. And Mahlallel the son of Cainan lived sixty-five years and he begat Jared; and Jared lived sixty-two years and he begat Enoch.

CHAPTER 3

1. And Enoch lived sixty-five years and he begat Methuselah; and Enoch walked with God after having begot Methuselah, and he served the Lord, and despised the evil ways of men.

2. And the soul of Enoch was wrapped up in the instruction of the Lord, in knowledge and in understanding; and he wisely retired from the sons of men, and secreted himself from them for many days.

3. And it was at the expiration of many years, whilst he was serving the Lord, and praying before him in his house, that an angel of the Lord called to him from Heaven, and he said, Here am I.

4. And he said, Rise, go forth from thy house and from the place where thou dost hide thyself, and appear to the sons of men, in order that thou mayest teach them the way in which they should go and the work which they must accomplish to enter in the ways of God.

5. And Enoch rose up according to the word of the Lord, and went forth from his house, from his place and from the chamber in which he was concealed; and he went to the sons of men and taught them the ways of the Lord, and at that time assembled the sons of men and acquainted them with the instruction of the Lord.

6. And he ordered it to be proclaimed in all places where the sons of men dwelt, saying, Where is the man who wishes to know the ways of the Lord and good works? let him come to Enoch.

7. And all the sons of men then assembled to him, for all who desired this thing went to Enoch, and Enoch reigned over the sons of men according to the word of the Lord, and they came and bowed to him and they heard his word.

8. And the spirit of God was upon Enoch, and he taught all his men the wisdom of God and his ways, and the sons of men served the Lord all the days of Enoch, and they came to hear his wisdom.

9. And all the kings of the sons of men, both first and last, together with their princes and judges, came to Enoch when they heard of his wisdom, and they bowed down to him, and they also required of Enoch to reign over them, to which he consented.

10. And they assembled in all, one hundred and thirty kings and princes, and they made Enoch king over them and they were all under his power and command.

11. And Enoch taught them wisdom, knowledge, and the ways of the Lord; and he made peace amongst them, and peace was throughout the earth during the life of Enoch.

12. And Enoch reigned over the sons of men two hundred and forty-three years, and he did justice and righteousness with all his people, and he led them in the ways of the Lord.

13. And these are the generations of Enoch, Methuselah, Elisha, and Elimelech, three sons; and their sisters were Melca and Nahmah, and Methuselah lived eighty-seven years and he begat Lamech.

14. And it was in the fifty-sixth year of the life of Lamech when Adam died; nine hundred and thirty years old was he at his death, and his two sons, with Enoch and Methuselah his son, buried him with great pomp, as at the burial of kings, in the cave which God had told him.

15. And in that place all the sons of men made a great mourning and weeping on account of Adam; it has therefore become a custom among the sons of men to this day.

16. And Adam died because he ate of the tree of knowledge; he and his children after him, as the Lord God had spoken.

17. And it was in the year of Adam's death which was the two hundred and forty-third year of the reign of Enoch, in that time Enoch resolved to separate himself from the sons of men and to secret himself as at first in order to serve the Lord.

18. And Enoch did so, but did not entirely secret himself from them, but kept away from the sons of men three days and then went to them for one day.

19. And during the three days that he was in his chamber, he prayed to, and praised the Lord his God, and the day on which he went and appeared to his subjects he taught them the ways of the Lord, and all they asked him about the Lord he told them.

20. And he did in this manner for many years, and he afterward concealed himself for six days, and appeared to his people one day in seven; and after that once in a month, and then once in a year, until all the kings, princes and sons of men sought for him, and desired again to see the face of Enoch, and to hear his word; but they could not, as all the sons of men were greatly afraid of Enoch, and they feared to approach him on account of the Godlike awe that was seated upon his countenance; therefore no man could look at him, fearing he might be punished and die.

21. And all the kings and princes resolved to assemble the sons of men, and to come to Enoch, thinking that they might all speak to him at the time when he should come forth amongst them, and they did so.

22. And the day came when Enoch went forth and they all assembled and came to him, and Enoch spoke to them the words of the Lord and he taught them wisdom and knowledge, and they bowed down before him and they said, May the king live! May the king live!

23. And in some time after, when the kings and princes and the sons of men were speaking to Enoch, and Enoch was teaching them the ways of God, behold an angel of the Lord

then called unto Enoch from heaven, and wished to bring him up to heaven to make him reign there over the sons of God, as he had reigned over the sons of men upon earth.

24. When at that time Enoch heard this he went and assembled all the inhabitants of the earth, and taught them wisdom and knowledge and gave them divine instructions, and he said to them, I have been required to ascend into heaven, I therefore do not know the day of my going.

25. And now therefore I will teach you wisdom and knowledge and will give you instruction before I leave you, how to act upon earth whereby you may live; and he did so.

26. And he taught them wisdom and knowledge, and gave them instruction, and he reproved them, and he placed before them statutes and judgments to do upon earth, and he made peace amongst them, and he taught them everlasting life, and dwelt with them some time teaching them all these things.

27. And at that time the sons of men were with Enoch, and Enoch was speaking to them, and they lifted up their eyes and the likeness of a great horse descended from heaven, and the horse paced in the air;

28. And they told Enoch what they had seen, and Enoch said to them, On my account does this horse descend upon earth; the time is come when I must go from you and I shall no more be seen by you.

29. And the horse descended at that time and stood before Enoch, and all the sons of men that were with Enoch saw him.

30. And Enoch then again ordered a voice to be proclaimed, saying, Where is the man who delighteth to know the ways of the Lord his God, let him come this day to Enoch before he is taken from us.

31. And all the sons of men assembled and came to Enoch that day; and all the kings of the earth with their princes and counsellors remained with him that day; and Enoch then taught the sons of men wisdom and knowledge, and gave them divine instruction; and he bade them serve the Lord and walk in his ways all the days of their lives, and he continued to make peace amongst them.

32. And it was after this that he rose up and rode upon the horse; and he went forth and all the sons of men went after him, about eight hundred thousand men; and they went with him one day's journey.

33. And the second day he said to them, Return home to your tents, why will you go? perhaps you may die; and some of them went from him, and those that remained went with him six day's journey; and Enoch said to them every day, Return to your tents, lest you may die; but they were not willing to return, and they went with him.

34. And on the sixth day some of the men remained and clung to him, and they said to him, We will go with thee to the place where thou goest; as the Lord liveth, death only shall separate us.

35. And they urged so much to go with him, that he ceased speaking to them; and they went after him and would not return;

36. And when the kings returned they caused a census to be taken, in order to know the number of remaining men that went with Enoch; and it was upon the seventh day that Enoch ascended into heaven in a whirlwind, with horses and chariots of fire.

37. And on the eighth day all the kings that had been with Enoch sent to bring back the number of men that were with Enoch, in that place from which he ascended into heaven.

38. And all those kings went to the place and they found the earth there filled with snow, and upon the snow were large stones of snow, and one said to the other, Come, let us break through the snow and see, perhaps the men that remained with Enoch are dead, and are now under the stones of snow, and they searched but could not find him, for he had ascended into heaven.

CHAPTER 4

1. And all the days that Enoch lived upon earth, were three hundred and sixty-five years.

2. And when Enoch had ascended into heaven, all the kings of the earth rose and took Methuselah his son and anointed him, and they caused him to reign over them in the place of his father.

3. And Methuselah acted uprightly in the sight of God, as his father Enoch had taught him, and he likewise during the whole of his life taught the sons of men wisdom, knowledge and the fear of God, and he did not turn from the good way either to the right or to the left.

4. But in the latter days of Methuselah, the sons of men turned from the Lord, they corrupted the earth, they robbed and plundered each other, and they rebelled against God and they transgressed, and they corrupted their ways, and would not hearken to the voice of Methuselah, but rebelled against him.

5. And the Lord was exceedingly wroth against them, and the Lord continued to destroy the seed in those days, so that there was neither sowing nor reaping in the earth.

6. For when they sowed the ground in order that they might obtain food for their support, behold, thorns and thistles were produced which they did not sow.

7. And still the sons of men did not turn from their evil ways, and their hands were still extended to do evil in the sight of God, and they provoked the Lord with their evil ways, and the Lord was very wroth, and repented that he had made man.

8. And he thought to destroy and annihilate them and he did so.

9. In those days when Lamech the son of Methuselah was one hundred and sixty years old, Seth the son of Adam died.

10. And all the days that Seth lived, were nine hundred and twelve years, and he died.

11. And Lamech was one hundred and eighty years old when he took Ashmua, the daughter of Elishaa the son of Enoch his uncle, and she conceived.

12. And at that time the sons of men sowed the ground, and a little food was produced, yet the sons of men did not turn from their evil ways, and they trespassed and rebelled against God.

13. And the wife of Lamech conceived and bare him a son at that time, at the revolution of the year.

14. And Methuselah called his name Noah, saying, The earth was in his days at rest and free from corruption, and Lamech his father called his name Menachem, saying, This one shall comfort us in our works and miserable toil in the earth, which God had cursed.

15. And the child grew up and was weaned, and he went in the ways of his father Methuselah, perfect and upright with God.

16. And all the sons of men departed from the ways of the Lord in those days as they multiplied upon the face of the earth with sons and daughters, and they taught one another their evil practices and they continued sinning against the Lord.

17. And every man made unto himself a god, and they robbed and plundered every man his neighbor as well as his relative, and they corrupted the earth, and the earth was filled with violence.

18. And their judges and rulers went to the daughters of men and took their wives by force from their husbands according to their choice, and the sons of men in those days took from the cattle of the earth, the beasts of the field and the fowls of the air, and taught the mixture of animals of one species with the other, in order therewith to provoke the Lord; and God saw the whole earth and it was corrupt, for all flesh had corrupted its ways upon earth, all men and all animals.

19. And the Lord said, I will blot out man that I created from the face of the earth, yea from man to the birds of the air, together with cattle and beasts that are in the field for I repent that I made them.

20. And all men who walked in the ways of the Lord, died in those days, before the Lord brought the evil upon man which he had declared, for this was from the Lord, that they should not see the evil which the Lord spoke of concerning the sons of men.

21. And Noah found grace in the sight of the Lord, and the Lord chose him and his children to raise up seed from them upon the face of the whole earth.

CHAPTER 5

1. And it was in the eighty-fourth year of the life of Noah, that Enoch the son of Seth died, he was nine hundred and five years old at his death.

2. And in the one hundred and seventy ninth year of the life of Noah, Cainan the son of Enosh died, and all the days of Cainan were nine hundred and ten years, and he died.

3. And in the two hundred and thirty fourth year of the life of Noah, Mahlallel the son of Cainan died, and the days of Mahlallel were eight hundred and ninety-five years, and he died.

4. And Jared the son of Mahlallel died in those days, in the three hundred and thirty-sixth year of the life of Noah; and all the days of Jared were nine hundred and sixty-two years, and he died.

5. And all who followed the Lord died in those days, before they saw the evil which God declared to do upon earth.

6. And after the lapse of many years, in the four hundred and eightieth year of the life of Noah, when all those men, who followed the Lord had died away from amongst the sons of men, and only Methuselah was then left, God said unto Noah and Methuselah, saying,

7. Speak ye, and proclaim to the sons of men, saying, Thus saith the Lord, return from your evil ways and forsake your works, and the Lord will repent of the evil that he declared to do to you, so that it shall not come to pass.

8. For thus saith the Lord, Behold I give you a period of one hundred and twenty years; if you will turn to me and forsake your evil ways, then will I also turn away from the evil which I told you, and it shall not exist, saith the Lord.

9. And Noah and Methuselah spoke all the words of the Lord to the sons of men, day after day, constantly speaking to them.

10. But the sons of men would not hearken to them, nor incline their ears to their words, and they were stiffnecked.

11. And the Lord granted them a period of one hundred and twenty years, saying, If they will return, then will God repent of the evil, so as not to destroy the earth.

12. Noah the son of Lamech refrained from taking a wife in those days, to beget children, for he said, Surely now God will destroy the earth, wherefore then shall I beget children?

13. And Noah was a just man, he was perfect in his generation, and the Lord chose him to raise up seed from his seed upon the face of the earth.

14. And the Lord said unto Noah, Take unto thee a wife, and beget children, for I have seen thee righteous before me in this generation.

15. And thou shalt raise up seed, and thy children with thee, in the midst of the earth; and Noah went and took a wife, and he chose Naamah the daughter of Enoch, and she was five hundred and eighty years old.

16. And Noah was four hundred and ninety-eight years old, when he took Naamah for a wife.

17. And Naamah conceived and bare a son, and he called his name Japheth, saying, God has enlarged me in the earth; and she conceived again and bare a son, and he called his name Shem, saying, God has made me a remnant, to raise up seed in the midst of the earth.

18. And Noah was five hundred and two years old when Naamah bare Shem, and the boys grew up and went in the ways of the Lord, in all that Methuselah and Noah their father taught them.

19. And Lamech the father of Noah, died in those days; yet verily he did not go with all his heart in the ways of his father, and he died in the hundred and ninety-fifth year of the life of Noah.

20. And all the days of Lamech were seven hundred and seventy years, and he died.

21. And all the sons of men who knew the Lord, died in that year before the Lord brought evil upon them; for the Lord willed them to die, so as not to behold the evil that God would bring upon their brothers and relatives, as he had so declared to do.

22. In that time, the Lord said to Noah and Methuselah, Stand forth and proclaim to the sons of men all the words that I spoke to you in those days, peradventure they may turn from their evil ways, and I will then repent of the evil and will not bring it.

23. And Noah and Methuselah stood forth, and said in the ears of the sons of men, all that God had spoken concerning them.

24. But the sons of men would not hearken, neither would they incline their ears to all their declarations.

25. And it was after this that the Lord said to Noah, The end of all flesh is come before me, on account of their evil deeds, and behold I will destroy the earth.

26. And do thou take unto thee gopher wood, and go to a certain place and make a large ark, and place it in that spot.

27. And thus shalt thou make it; three hundred cubits its length, fifty cubits broad and thirty cubits high.

28. And thou shalt make unto thee a door, open at its side, and to a cubit thou shalt finish above, and cover it within and without with pitch.

29. And behold I will bring the flood of waters upon the earth, and all flesh be destroyed, from under the heavens all that is upon earth shall perish.

30. And thou and thy household shall go and gather two couple of all living things, male and female, and shall bring them to the ark, to raise up seed from them upon earth.

31. And gather unto thee all food that is eaten by all the animals, that there may be food for thee and for them.

32. And thou shalt choose for thy sons three maidens, from the daughters of men, and they shall be wives to thy sons.

33. And Noah rose up, and he made the ark, in the place where God had commanded him, and Noah did as God had ordered him.

34. In his five hundred and ninety-fifth year Noah commenced to make the ark, and he made the ark in five years, as the Lord had commanded.

35. Then Noah took the three daughters of Eliakim, son of Methuselah, for wives for his sons, as the Lord had commanded Noah.

36. And it was at that time Methuselah the son of Enoch died, nine hundred and sixty years old was he, at his death.

CHAPTER 6

1.   At that time, after the death of Methuselah, the Lord said to Noah, Go thou with thy household into the ark; behold I will gather to thee all the animals of the earth, the beasts of the field and the fowls of the air, and they shall all come and surround the ark.

2.   And thou shalt go and seat thyself by the doors of the ark, and all the beasts, the animals, and the fowls, shall assemble and place themselves before thee, and such of them as shall come and crouch before thee, shalt thou take and deliver into the hands of thy sons, who shall bring them to the ark, and all that will stand before thee thou shalt leave.

3.   And the Lord brought this about on the next day, and animals, beasts and fowls came in great multitudes and surrounded the ark.

4.   And Noah went and seated himself by the door of the ark, and of all flesh that crouched before him, he brought into the ark, and all that stood before him he left upon earth.

5.   And a lioness came, with her two whelps, male and female, and the three crouched before Noah, and the two whelps rose up against the lioness and smote her, and made her flee from her place, and she went away, and they returned to their places, and crouched upon the earth before Noah.

6.   And the lioness ran away, and stood in the place of the lions.

7.   And Noah saw this, and wondered greatly, and he rose and took the two whelps, and brought them into the ark.

8.   And Noah brought into the ark from all living creatures that were upon earth, so that there was none left but which Noah brought into the ark.

9.   Two and two came to Noah into the ark, but from the clean animals, and clean fowls, he brought seven couples, as God had commanded him.

10. And all the animals, and beasts, and fowls, were still there, and they surrounded the ark at every place, and the rain had not descended till seven days after.

11. And on that day, the Lord caused the whole earth to shake, and the sun darkened, and the foundations of the world raged, and the whole earth was moved violently, and the lightning flashed, and the thunder roared, and all the fountains in the earth were broken up, such as was not known to the inhabitants before; and God did this mighty act, in order to terrify the sons of men, that there might be no more evil upon earth.

12. And still the sons of men would not return from their evil ways, and they increased the anger of the Lord at that time, and did not even direct their hearts to all this.

13. And at the end of seven days, in the six hundredth year of the life of Noah, the waters of the flood were upon the earth.

14. And all the fountains of the deep were broken up, and the windows of heaven were opened, and the rain was upon the earth forty days and forty nights.

15. And Noah and his household, and all the living creatures that were with him, came into the ark on account of the waters of the flood, and the Lord shut him in.

16. And all the sons of men that were left upon the earth, became exhausted through evil on account of the rain, for the waters were coming more violently upon the earth, and the animals and beasts were still surrounding the ark.

17. And the sons of men assembled together, about seven hundred thousand men and women, and they came unto Noah to the ark.

18. And they called to Noah, saying, Open for us that we may come to thee in the ark--and wherefore shall we die?

19. And Noah, with a loud voice, answered them from the ark, saying, Have you not all rebelled against the Lord, and said that he does not exist? and therefore the Lord brought upon you this evil, to destroy and cut you off from the face of the earth.

20. Is not this the thing that I spoke to you of one hundred and twenty years back, and you would not hearken to the voice of the Lord, and now do you desire to live upon earth?

21. And they said to Noah, We are ready to return to the Lord; only open for us that we may live and not die.

22. And Noah answered them, saying, Behold now that you see the trouble of your souls, you wish to return to the Lord; why did you not return during these hundred and twenty years, which the Lord granted you as the determined period?

23. But now you come and tell me this on account of the troubles of your souls, now also the Lord will not listen to you, neither will he give ear to you on this day, so that you will not now succeed in your wishes.

24. And the sons of men approached in order to break into the ark, to come in on account of the rain, for they could not bear the rain upon them.

25. And the Lord sent all the beasts and animals that stood round the ark. And the beasts overpowered them and drove them from that place, and every man went his way and they again scattered themselves upon the face of the earth.

26. And the rain was still descending upon the earth, and it descended forty days and forty nights, and the waters prevailed greatly upon the earth; and all flesh that was upon the earth or in the waters died, whether men, animals, beasts, creeping things or birds of the air, and there only remained Noah and those that were with him in the ark.

27. And the waters prevailed and they greatly increased upon the earth, and they lifted up the ark and it was raised from the earth.

28. And the ark floated upon the face of the waters, and it was tossed upon the waters so that all the living creatures within were turned about like pottage in a cauldron.

29. And great anxiety seized all the living creatures that were in the ark, and the ark was like to be broken.

30. And all the living creatures that were in the ark were terrified, and the lions roared, and the oxen lowed, and the wolves howled, and every living creature in the ark spoke and lamented in its own language, so that their voices reached to a great distance, and Noah and his sons cried and wept in their troubles; they were greatly afraid that they had reached the gates of death.

31. And Noah prayed unto the Lord, and cried unto him on account of this, and he said, O Lord help us, for we have no strength to bear this evil that has encompassed us, for the waves of the waters have surrounded us, mischievous torrents have terrified us, the snares of death have come before us; answer us, O Lord, answer us, light up thy countenance toward us and be gracious to us, redeem us and deliver us.

32. And the Lord hearkened to the voice of Noah, and the Lord remembered him.

33. And a wind passed over the earth, and the waters were still and the ark rested.

34. And the fountains of the deep and the windows of heaven were stopped, and the rain from heaven was restrained.

35. And the waters decreased in those days, and the ark rested upon the mountains of Ararat.

36. And Noah then opened the windows of the ark, and Noah still called out to the Lord at that time and he said, O Lord, who didst form the earth and the heavens and all that are therein, bring forth our souls from this confinement, and from the prison wherein thou hast placed us, for I am much wearied with sighing.

37. And the Lord hearkened to the voice of Noah, and said to him, When though shalt have completed a full year thou shalt then go forth.

38. And at the revolution of the year, when a full year was completed to Noah's dwelling in the ark, the waters were dried from off the earth, and Noah put off the covering of the ark.

39. At that time, on the twenty-seventh day of the second month, the earth was dry, but Noah and his sons, and those that were with him, did not go out from the ark until the Lord told them.

40. And the day came that the Lord told them to go out, and they all went out from the ark.

41. And they went and returned every one to his way and to his place, and Noah and his sons dwelt in the land that God had told them, and they served the Lord all their days, and the Lord blessed Noah and his sons on their going out from the ark.

42. And he said to them, Be fruitful and fill all the earth; become strong and increase abundantly in the earth and multiply therein.

CHAPTER 7

1. And these are the names of the sons of Noah: Japheth, Ham and Shem; and children were born to them after the flood, for they had taken wives before the flood.

2. These are the sons of Japheth; Gomer, Magog, Madai, Javan, Tubal, Meshech, and Tiras, seven sons.

3. And the sons of Gomer were Askinaz, Rephath and Tegarmah.

4. And the sons of Magog were Elichanaf and Lubal.

5. And the children of Madai were Achon, Zeelo, Chazoni and Lot.

6. And the sons of Javan were Elisha, Tarshish, Chittim and Dudonim.

7. And the sons of Tubal were Ariphi, Kesed and Taari.

8. And the sons of Meshech were Dedon, Zaron and Shebashni.

9. And the sons of Tiras were Benib, Gera, Lupirion and Gilak; these are the sons of Japheth according to their families, and their numbers in those days were about four hundred and sixty men.

10. And these are the sons of Ham; Cush, Mitzraim, Phut and Canaan, four sons; and the sons of Cush were Seba, Havilah, Sabta, Raama and Satecha, and the sons of Raama were Sheba and Dedan.

11. And the sons of Mitzraim were Lud, Anom and Pathros, Chasloth and Chaphtor.

12. And the sons of Phut were Gebul, Hadan, Benah and Adan.

13. And the sons of Canaan were Zidon, Heth, Amori, Gergashi, Hivi, Arkee, Seni, Arodi, Zimodi and Chamothi.

14. These are the sons of Ham, according to their families, and their numbers in those days were about seven hundred and thirty men.

15. And these are the sons of Shem; Elam, Ashur, Arpachshad, Lud and Aram, five sons; and the sons of Elam were Shushan, Machul and Harmon.

16. And the sons of Ashar were Mirus and Mokil, and the sons of Arpachshad were Shelach, Anar and Ashcol.

17. And the sons of Lud were Pethor and Bizayon, and the sons of Aram were Uz, Chul, Gather and Mash.

18. These are the sons of Shem, according to their families; and their numbers in those days were about three hundred men.

15

19. These are the generations of Shem; Shem begat Arpachshad and Arpachshad begat Shelach, and Shelach begat Eber and to Eber were born two children, the name of one was Peleg, for in his days the sons of men were divided, and in the latter days, the earth was divided.

20. And the name of the second was Yoktan, meaning that in his day the lives of the sons of men were diminished and lessened.

21. These are the sons of Yoktan; Almodad, Shelaf, Chazarmoveth, Yerach, Hadurom, Ozel, Diklah, Obal, Abimael, Sheba, Ophir, Havilah and Jobab; all these are the sons of Yoktan.

22. And Peleg his brother begat Yen, and Yen begat Serug, and Serug begat Nahor and Nahor begat Terah, and Terah was thirty-eight years old, and he begat Haran and Nahor.

23. And Cush the son of Ham, the son of Noah, took a wife in those days in his old age, and she bare a son, and they called his name Nimrod, saying, At that time the sons of men again began to rebel and transgress against God, and the child grew up, and his father loved him exceedingly, for he was the son of his old age.

24. And the garments of skin which God made for Adam and his wife, when they went out of the garden, were given to Cush.

25. For after the death of Adam and his wife, the garments were given to Enoch, the son of Jared, and when Enoch was taken up to God, he gave them to Methuselah, his son.

26. And at the death of Methuselah, Noah took them and brought them to the ark, and they were with him until he went out of the ark.

27. And in their going out, Ham stole those garments from Noah his father, and he took them and hid them from his brothers.

28. And when Ham begat his first born Cush, he gave him the garments in secret, and they were with Cush many days.

29. And Cush also concealed them from his sons and brothers, and when Cush

had begotten Nimrod, he gave him those garments through his love for him, and Nimrod grew up, and when he was twenty years old he put on those garments.

30. And Nimrod became strong when he put on the garments, and God gave him might and strength, and he was a mighty hunter in the earth, yea, he was a mighty hunter in the field, and he hunted the animals and he built altars, and he offered upon them the animals before the Lord.

31. And Nimrod strengthened himself, and he rose up from amongst his brethren, and he fought the battles of his brethren against all their enemies round about.

32. And the Lord delivered all the enemies of his brethren in his hands, and God prospered him from time to time in his battles, and he reigned upon earth.

33. Therefore it became current in those days, when a man ushered forth those that he had trained up for battle, he would say to them, Like God did to Nimrod, who was a mighty hunter in the earth, and who succeeded in the battles that prevailed against his brethren, that he delivered them from the hands of their enemies, so may God strengthen us and deliver us this day.

34. And when Nimrod was forty years old, at that time there was a war between his brethren and the children of Japheth, so that they were in the power of their enemies.

35. And Nimrod went forth at that time, and he assembled all the sons of Cush and their families, about four hundred and sixty men, and he hired also from some of his friends and acquaintances about eighty men, and be gave them their hire, and he went with them to battle, and when he was on the road, Nimrod strengthened the hearts of the people that went with him.

36. And he said to them, Do not fear, neither be alarmed, for all our enemies will be delivered into our hands, and you may do with them as you please.

37. And all the men that went were about five hundred, and they fought against their enemies, and they destroyed them, and subdued them, and Nimrod placed standing officers over them in their respective places.

38. And he took some of their children as security, and they were all servants to Nimrod and to his brethren, and Nimrod and all the people that were with him turned homeward.

39. And when Nimrod had joyfully returned from battle, after having conquered his enemies, all his brethren, together with those who knew him before, assembled to make him king over them, and they placed the regal crown upon his head.

40. And he set over his subjects and people, princes, judges, and rulers, as is the custom amongst kings.

41. And he placed Terah the son of Nahor the prince of his host, and he dignified him and elevated him above all his princes.

42. And whilst he was reigning according to his heart's desire, after having conquered all his enemies around, he advised with his counselors to build a city for his palace, and they did so.

43. And they found a large valley opposite to the east, and they built him a large and extensive city, and Nimrod called the name of the city that he built Shinar, for the Lord had vehemently shaken his enemies and destroyed them.

44. And Nimrod dwelt in Shinar, and he reigned securely, and he fought with his enemies and he subdued them, and he prospered in all his battles, and his kingdom became very great.

45. And all nations and tongues heard of his fame, and they gathered themselves to him, and they bowed down to the earth, and they brought him offerings, and he became their lord and king, and they all dwelt with him in the city at Shinar, and Nimrod reigned in the earth over all the sons of Noah, and they were all under his power and counsel.

46. And all the earth was of one tongue and words of union, but Nimrod did not go in the ways of the Lord, and he was more wicked than all the men that were before him, from the days of the flood until those days.

47. And he made gods of wood and stone, and he bowed down to them, and he rebelled against the Lord, and taught all his subjects and the people of the earth his wicked ways; and Mardon his son was more wicked than his father.

48. And every one that heard of the acts of Mardon the son of Nimrod would say, concerning him, From the wicked goeth forth wickedness; therefore it became a proverb in the whole earth, saying, From the wicked goeth forth wickedness, and it was current in the words of men from that time to this.

49. And Terah the son of Nahor, prince of Nimrod's host, was in those days very great in the sight of the king and his subjects, and the king and princes loved him, and they elevated him very high.

50. And Terah took a wife and her name was Amthelo the daughter of Cornebo; and the wife of Terah conceived and bare him a son in those days.

51. Terah was seventy years old when he begat him, and Terah called the name of his son that was born to him Abram, because the king had raised him in those days, and dignified him above all his princes that were with him.

CHAPTER 8

1. And it was in the night that Abram was born, that all the servants of Terah, and all the wise men of Nimrod, and his conjurors came and ate and drank in the house of Terah, and they rejoiced with him on that night.

2. And when all the wise men and conjurors went out from the house of Terah, they lifted up their eyes toward heaven that night to look at the stars, and they saw, and behold one very large star came from the east and ran in the heavens, and he swallowed up the four stars from the four sides of the heavens.

3. And all the wise men of the king and his conjurors were astonished at the sight, and the sages understood this matter, and they knew its import.

4. And they said to each other, This only betokens the child that has been born to Terah this night, who will grow up and be fruitful, and multiply, and possess all the earth, he and his children for ever, and he and his seed will slay great kings, and inherit their lands.

5. And the wise men and conjurors went home that night, and in the morning all these wise men and conjurors rose up early, and assembled in an appointed house.

6. And they spoke and said to each other, Behold the sight that we saw last night is hidden from the king, it has not been made known to him.

7. And should this thing get known to the king in the latter days, he will say to us, Why have you concealed this matter from me, and then we shall all suffer death; therefore, now let us go and tell the king the sight which we saw, and the interpretation thereof, and we shall then remain clear.

8. And they did so, and they all went to the king and bowed down to him to the ground, and they said, May the king live, may the king live.

9. We heard that a son was born to Terah the son of Nahor, the prince of thy host, and we yesternight came to his house, and we ate and drank and rejoiced with him that night.

10. And when thy servants went out from the house of Terah, to go to our respective homes to abide there for the night, we lifted up our eyes to heaven, and we saw a great star coming from the east, and the same star ran with great speed, and swallowed up four great stars, from the four sides of the heavens.

11. And thy servants were astonished at the sight which we saw, and were greatly terrified, and we made our judgment upon the sight, and knew by our wisdom the proper interpretation thereof, that this thing applies to the child that is born to Terah, who will grow up and multiply greatly, and become powerful, and kill all the kings of the earth, and inherit all their lands, he and his seed forever.

12. And now our lord and king, behold we have truly acquainted thee with what we have seen concerning this child.

13. If it seemeth good to the king to give his father value for this child, we will slay him before he shall grow up and increase in the land, and his evil increase against us, that we and our children perish through his evil.

14. And the king heard their words and they seemed good in his sight, and he sent and called for Terah, and Terah came before the king.

15. And the king said to Terah, I have been told that a son was yesternight born to thee, and after this manner was observed in the heavens at his birth.

16. And now therefore give me the child, that we may slay him before his evil springs up against us, and I will give thee for his value, thy house full of silver and gold.

17. And Terah answered the king and said to him: My Lord and king, I have heard thy words, and thy servant shall do all that his king desireth.

18. But my lord and king, I will tell thee what happened to me yesternight, that I may see what advice the king will give his servant, and then I will answer the king upon what he has just spoken; and the king said, Speak.

19. And Terah said to the king, Ayon, son of Mored, came to me yesternight, saying,

20. Give unto me the great and beautiful horse that the king gave thee, and I will give thee silver and gold, and straw and provender for its value; and I said to him, Wait till I see the king concerning thy words, and behold whatever the king saith, that will I do.

21. And now my lord and king, behold I have made this thing known to thee, and the advice which my king will give unto his servant, that will I follow.

22. And the king heard the words of Terah, and his anger was kindled and he considered him in the light of a fool.

23. And the king answered Terah, and he said to him, Art thou so silly, ignorant, or deficient in understanding, to do this thing, to give thy beautiful horse for silver and gold or even for straw and provender?

24. Art thou so short of silver and gold, that thou shouldst do this thing, because thou canst not obtain straw and provender to feed thy horse? and what is silver and gold to thee, or straw and provender, that thou shouldst give away that fine horse which I gave thee, like which there is none to be had on the whole earth?

25. And the king left off speaking, and Terah answered the king, saying, Like unto this has the king spoken to his servant;

26. I beseech thee, my lord and king, what is this which thou didst say unto me, saying, Give thy son that we may slay him, and I will give thee silver and gold for his value; what shall I do with silver and gold after the death of my son? who shall inherit me? surely then at my death, the silver and gold will return to my king who gave it.

27. And when the king heard the words of Terah, and the parable which he brought concerning the king, it grieved him greatly and he was vexed at this thing, and his anger burned within him.

28. And Terah saw that the anger of the king was kindled against him, and he answered the king, saying, All that I have is in the king's power; whatever the king desireth to do to his servant, that let him do, yea, even my son, he is in the king's power, without value in exchange, he and his two brothers that are older than he.

29. And the king said to Terah, No, but I will purchase thy younger son for a price.

30. And Terah answered the king, saying, I beseech thee my lord and king to let thy servant speak a word before thee, and let the king hear the word of his servant, and Terah said, Let my king give me three days' time till I consider this matter within myself, and consult with my family concerning the words of my king; and he pressed the king greatly to agree to this.

31. And the king hearkened to Terah, and he did so and he gave him three days' time, and Terah went out from the king's presence, and he came home to his family and spoke to them all the words of the king; and the people were greatly afraid.

32. And it was in the third day that the king sent to Terah, saying, Send me thy son for a price as I spoke to thee; and shouldst thou not do this, I will send and slay all thou hast in thy house, so that thou shalt not even have a dog remaining.

33. And Terah hastened, (as the thing was urgent from the king), and he took a child from one of his servants, which his handmaid had born to him that day, and Terah brought the child to the king and received value for him.

34. And the Lord was with Terah in this matter, that Nimrod might not cause Abram's death, and the king took the child from Terah and with all his might dashed his head to the ground, for he thought it had been Abram; and this was concealed from him from that day, and it was forgotten by the king, as it was the will of Providence not to suffer Abram's death.

35. And Terah took Abram his son secretly, together with his mother and nurse, and he concealed them in a cave, and he brought them their provisions monthly.

36. And the Lord was with Abram in the cave and he grew up, and Abram was in the cave ten years, and the king and his princes, soothsayers and sages, thought that the king had killed Abram.

CHAPTER 9

1. And Haran, the son of Terah, Abram's oldest brother, took a wife in those days.

2. Haran was thirty-nine years old when he took her; and the wife of Haran conceived and bare a son, and he called his name Lot.

3. And she conceived again and bare a daughter, and she called her name Milca; and she again conceived and bare a daughter, and she called her name Sarai.

4. Haran was forty-two years old when he begat Sarai, which was in the tenth year of the life of Abram; and in those days Abram and his mother and nurse went out from the cave, as the king and his subjects had forgotten the affair of Abram.

5. And when Abram came out from the cave, he went to Noah and his son Shem, and he remained with them to learn the instruction of the Lord and his ways, and no man knew where Abram was, and Abram served Noah and Shem his son for a long time.

6. And Abram was in Noah's house thirty-nine years, and Abram knew the Lord from three years old, and he went in the ways of the Lord until the day of his death, as Noah and his son Shem had taught him; and all the sons of the earth in those days greatly transgressed against the Lord, and they rebelled against him and they served other gods, and they forgot the Lord who had created them in the earth; and the inhabitants of the earth made unto themselves, at that time, every man his god; gods of wood and stone which could neither speak, hear, nor deliver, and the sons of men served them and they became their gods.

7. And the king and all his servants, and Terah with all his household were then the first of those that served gods of wood and stone.

8. And Terah had twelve gods of large size, made of wood and stone, after the twelve months of the year, and he served each one monthly, and every month Terah would bring his meat offering and drink offering to his gods; thus did Terah all the days.

9. And all that generation were wicked in the sight of the Lord, and they thus made every man his god, but they forsook the Lord who had created them.

10. And there was not a man found in those days in the whole earth, who knew the Lord (for they served each man his own God) except Noah and his household, and all those who were under his counsel knew the Lord in those days.

11. And Abram the son of Terah was waxing great in those days in the house of Noah, and no man knew it, and the Lord was with him.

12. And the Lord gave Abram an understanding heart, and he knew all the works of that generation were vain, and that all their gods were vain and were of no avail.

13. And Abram saw the sun shining upon the earth, and Abram said unto himself Surely now this sun that shines upon the earth is God, and him will I serve.

14. And Abram served the sun in that day and he prayed to him, and when evening came the sun set as usual, and Abram said within himself, Surely this cannot be God?

15. And Abram still continued to speak within himself, Who is he who made the heavens and the earth? who created upon earth? where is he?

16. And night darkened over him, and he lifted up his eyes toward the west, north, south, and east, and he saw that the sun had vanished from the earth, and the day became dark.

17. And Abram saw the stars and moon before him, and he said, Surely this is the God who created the whole earth as well as man, and behold these his servants are gods around him: and Abram served the moon and prayed to it all that night.

18. And in the morning when it was light and the sun shone upon the earth as usual, Abram saw all the things that the Lord God had made upon earth.

19. And Abram said unto himself Surely these are not gods that made the earth and all mankind, but these are the servants of God, and Abram remained in the house of Noah and there knew the Lord and his ways' and he served the Lord all the days of his life, and all that generation forgot the Lord, and served other gods of wood and stone, and rebelled all their days.

20. And king Nimrod reigned securely, and all the earth was under his control, and all the earth was of one tongue and words of union.

21. And all the princes of Nimrod and his great men took counsel together; Phut, Mitzraim, Cush and Canaan with their families, and they said to each other, Come let us build ourselves a city and in it a strong tower, and its top reaching heaven, and we will make ourselves famed, so that we may reign upon the whole world, in order that the evil of our enemies may cease from us, that we may reign mightily over them, and that we may not become scattered over the earth on account of their wars.

22. And they all went before the king, and they told the king these words, and the king agreed with them in this affair, and he did so.

23. And all the families assembled consisting of about six hundred thousand men, and they went to seek an extensive piece of ground to build the city and the tower, and they sought in the whole earth and they found none like one valley at the east of the land of Shinar, about two days' walk, and they journeyed there and they dwelt there.

24. And they began to make bricks and burn fires to build the city and the tower that they had imagined to complete.

25. And the building of the tower was unto them a transgression and a sin, and they began to build it, and whilst they were building against the Lord God of heaven, they imagined in their hearts to war against him and to ascend into heaven.

26. And all these people and all the families divided themselves in three parts; the first said We will ascend into heaven and fight against him; the second said, We will ascend to heaven and place our own gods there and serve them; and the third part said, We will ascend to heaven and smite him with bows and spears; and God knew all their works and all their evil thoughts, and he saw the city and the tower which they were building.

27. And when they were building they built themselves a great city and a very high and strong tower; and on account of its height the mortar and bricks did not reach the builders in their ascent to it, until those who went up had completed a full year, and after that, they reached to the builders and gave them the mortar and the bricks; thus was it done daily.

28. And behold these ascended and others descended the whole day; and if a brick should fall from their hands and get broken, they would all weep over it, and if a man fell and died, none of them would look at him.

29. And the Lord knew their thoughts, and it came to pass when they were building they cast the arrows toward the heavens, and all the arrows fell upon them filled with blood, and when they saw them they said to each other, Surely we have slain all those that are in heaven.

30. For this was from the Lord in order to cause them to err, and in order; to destroy them from off the face of the ground.

31. And they built the tower and the city, and they did this thing daily until many days and years were elapsed.

32. And God said to the seventy angels who stood foremost before him, to those who were near to him, saying, Come let us descend and confuse their tongues, that one man shall not understand the language of his neighbor, and they did so unto them.

33. And from that day following, they forgot each man his neighbor's tongue, and they could not understand to speak in one tongue, and when the builder took from the hands of his neighbor lime or stone which he did not order, the builder would cast it away and throw it upon his neighbor, that he would die.

34. And they did so many days, and they killed many of them in this manner.

35. And the Lord smote the three divisions that were there, and he punished them according to their works and designs; those who said, We will ascend to heaven and serve our gods, became like apes and elephants; and those who said, We will smite the heaven with arrows, the Lord killed them, one man through the hand of his neighbor; and the third division of those who said, We will ascend to heaven and fight against him, the Lord scattered them throughout the earth.

36. And those who were left amongst them, when they knew and understood the evil which was coming upon them, they forsook the building, and they also became scattered upon the face of the whole earth.

37. And they ceased building the city and the tower; therefore he called that place Babel, for there the Lord confounded the Language of the whole earth; behold it was at the east of the land of Shinar.

38. And as to the tower which the sons of men built, the earth opened its mouth and swallowed up one third part thereof, and a fire also descended from heaven and burned another third, and the other third is left to this day, and it is of that part which was aloft, and its circumference is three days' walk.

39. And many of the sons of men died in that tower, a people without number.

CHAPTER 10

1. And Peleg the son of Eber died in those days, in the forty-eighth year of the life of Abram son of Terah, and all the days of Peleg were two hundred and thirty-nine years.

2. And when the Lord had scattered the sons of men on account of their sin at the tower, behold they spread forth into many divisions, and all the sons of men were dispersed into the four corners of the earth.

3. And all the families became each according to its language, its land, or its city.

4. And the sons of men built many cities according to their families, in all the places where they went, and throughout the earth where the Lord had scattered them.

5. And some of them built cities in places from which they were afterward extirpated, and they called these cities after their own names, or the names of their children, or after their particular occurrences.

6. And the sons of Japheth the son of Noah went and built themselves cities in the places where they were scattered, and they called all their cities after their names, and the sons of Japheth were divided upon the face of the earth into many divisions and languages. 7. And these are the sons of Japheth according to their families, Gomer, Magog, Medai, Javan, Tubal, Meshech and Tiras; these are the children of Japheth according to their generations.

8. And the children of Gomer, according to their cities, were the Francum, who dwell in the land of Franza, by the river Franza, by the river Senah.

9. And the children of Rephath are the Bartonim, who dwell in the land of Bartonia by the river Ledah, which empties its waters in the great sea Gihon, that is, oceanus.

10. And the children of Tugarma are ten families, and these are their names: Buzar, Parzunac, Balgar, Elicanum, Ragbib, Tarki, Bid, Zebuc, Ongal and Tilmaz; all these spread and rested in the north and built themselves cities.

11. And they called their cities after their own names, those are they who abide by the rivers Hithlah and Italac unto this day.

12. But the families of Angoli, Balgar and Parzunac, they dwell by the great river Dubnee; and the names of their cities are also according to their own names.

13. And the children of Javan are the Javanim who dwell in the land of Makdonia, and the children of Medaiare are the Orelum that dwell in the land of Curson, and the children of Tubal are those that dwell in the land of Tuskanah by the river Pashiah.

14. And the children of Meshech are the Shibashni and the children of Tiras are Rushash, Cushni, and Ongolis; all these went and built themselves cities; those are the cities that are situate by the sea Jabus by the river Cura, which empties itself in the river Tragan.

15. And the children of Elishah are the Almanim, and they also went and built themselves cities; those are the cities situate between the mountains of Job and Shibathmo; and of them were the people of Lumbardi who dwell opposite the mountains of Job and Shibathmo, and they conquered the land of Italia and remained there unto this day.

16. And the children of Chittim are the Romim who dwell in the valley of Canopia by the river Tibreu.

17. And the children of Dudonim are those who dwell in the cities of the sea Gihon, in the land of Bordna.

18. These are the families of the children of Japheth according to their cities and languages, when they were scattered after the tower, and they called their cities after their names and occurrences; and these are the names of all their cities according to their families, which they built in those days after the tower.

19. And the children of Ham were Cush, Mitzraim, Phut and Canaan according to their generation and cities.

20. All these went and built themselves cities as they found fit places for them, and they called their cities after the names of their fathers Cush, Mitzraim, Phut and Canaan.

21. And the children of Mitzraim are the Ludim, Anamim, Lehabim, Naphtuchim, Pathrusim, Casluchim and Caphturim, seven families.

22. All these dwell by the river Sihor, that is the brook of Egypt, and they built themselves cities and called them after their own names.

23. And the children of Pathros and Casloch intermarried together, and from them went forth the Pelishtim, the Azathim, and the Gerarim, the Githim and the Ekronim, in all five families; these also built themselves cities, and they called their cities after the names of their fathers unto this day.

24. And the children of Canaan also built themselves cities, and they called their cities after their names, eleven cities and others without number.

25. And four men from the family of Ham went to the land of the plain; these are the names of the four men, Sodom, Gomorrah, Admah and Zeboyim.

26. And these men built themselves four cities in the land of the plain, and they called the names of their cities after their own names.

27. And they and their children and all belonging to them dwelt in those cities, and they were fruitful and multiplied greatly and dwelt peaceably.

28. And Seir the son of Hur, son of Hivi, son of Canaan, went and found a valley opposite to Mount Paran, and he built a city there, and he and his seven sons and his household dwelt there, and he called the city which he built Seir, according to his name; that is the land of Seir unto this day.

29. These are the families of the children of Ham, according to their languages and cities, when they were scattered to their countries after the tower.

30. And some of the children of Shem son of Noah, father of all the children of Eber, also went and built themselves cities in the places wherein they were scattered, and they called their cities after their names.

31. And the sons of Shem were Elam, Ashur, Arpachshad, Lud and Aram, and they built themselves cities and called the names of all their cities after their names.

32. And Ashur son of Shem and his children and household went forth at that time, a very large body of them, and they went to a distant land that they found, and they met with a very extensive valley in the land that they went to, and they built themselves four cities, and they called them after their own names and occurrences.

33. And these are the names of the cities which the children of Ashur built, Ninevah, Resen, Calach and Rehobother; and the children of Ashur dwell there unto this day.

34. And the children of Aram also went and built themselves a city, and they called the name of the city Uz after their eldest brother, and they dwell therein; that is the land of Uz to this day.

35. And in the second year after the tower a man from the house of Ashur, whose name was Bela, went from the land of Ninevah to sojourn with his household wherever he could find a place; and they came until opposite the cities of the plain against Sodom, and they dwelt there.

36. And the man rose up and built there a small city, and called its name Bela, after his name; that is the land of Zoar unto this day.

37. And these are the families of the children of Shem according to their language and cities, after they were scattered upon the earth after the tower.

38. And every kingdom, city, and family of the families of the children of Noah built themselves many cities after this.

39. And they established governments in all their cities, in order to be regulated by their orders; so did all the families of the children of Noah forever.

CHAPTER 11

1. And Nimrod son of Cush was still in the land of Shinar, and he reigned over it and dwelt there, and he built cities in the land of Shinar.

2. And these are the names of the four cities which he built, and he called their names after the occurrences that happened to them in the building of the tower.

3. And he called the first Babel, saying, Because the Lord there confounded the language of the whole earth; and the name of the second he called Erech, because from there God dispersed them.

4. And the third he called Eched, saying there was a great battle at that place; and the fourth he called Calnah, because his princes and mighty men were consumed there, and they vexed the Lord, they rebelled and transgressed against him.

5. And when Nimrod had built these cities in the land of Shinar, he placed in them the remainder of his people, his princes and his mighty men that were left in his kingdom.

6. And Nimrod dwelt in Babel, and he there renewed his reign over the rest of his subjects, and he reigned securely, and the subjects and princes of Nimrod called his name Amraphel, saying that at the tower his princes and men fell through his means.

7. And notwithstanding this, Nimrod did not return to the Lord, and he continued in wickedness and teaching wickedness to the sons of men; and Mardon, his son, was worse than his father, and continued to add to the abominations of his father.

8. And he caused the sons of men to sin, therefore it is said, From the wicked goeth forth wickedness.

9. At that time there was war between the families of the children of Ham, as they were dwelling in the cities which they had built.

10. And Chedorlaomer, king of Elam, went away from the families of the children of Ham, and he fought with them and he subdued them, and he went to the five cities of the plain and he fought against them and he subdued them, and they were under his control.

11. And they served him twelve years, and they gave him a yearly tax.

12. At that time died Nahor, son of Serug, in the forty-ninth year of the life of Abram son of Terah.

13. And in the fiftieth year of the life of Abram son of Terah, Abram came forth from the house of Noah, and went to his father's house.

14. And Abram knew the Lord, and he went in his ways and instructions, and the Lord his God was with him.

15. And Terah his father was in those days, still captain of the host of king Nimrod, and he still followed strange gods.

16. And Abram came to his father's house and saw twelve gods standing there in their temples, and the anger of Abram was kindled when he saw these images in his father's house.

17. And Abram said, As the Lord liveth these images shall not remain in my father's house; so shall the Lord who created me do unto me if in three days' time I do not break them all.

18. And Abram went from them, and his anger burned within him. And Abram hastened and went from the chamber to his father's outer court, and he found his father sitting in the court, and all his servants with him, and Abram came and sat before him.

19. And Abram asked his father, saying, Father, tell me where is God who created heaven and earth, and all the sons of men upon earth, and who created thee and me. And Terah answered his son Abram and said, Behold those who created us are all with us in the house.

20. And Abram said to his father, My lord, shew them to me I pray thee; and Terah brought Abram into the chamber of the inner court, and Abram saw, and behold the whole room was full of gods of wood and stone, twelve great images and others less than they without number.

21. And Terah said to his son, Behold these are they which made all thou seest upon earth, and which created me and thee, and all mankind.

22. And Terah bowed down to his gods, and he then went away from them, and Abram, his son, went away with him.

23. And when Abram had gone from them he went to his mother and sat before her, and he said to his mother, Behold, my father has shown me those who made heaven and earth, and all the sons of men.

24. Now, therefore, hasten and fetch a kid from the flock, and make of it savory meat, that I may bring it to my father's gods as an offering for them to eat; perhaps I may thereby become acceptable to them.

25. And his mother did so, and she fetched a kid, and made savory meat thereof, and brought it to Abram, and Abram took the savory meat from his mother and brought it before his father's gods, and he drew nigh to them that they might eat; and Terah his father, did not know of it.

26. And Abram saw on the day when he was sitting amongst them, that they had no voice, no hearing, no motion, and not one of them could stretch forth his hand to eat.

27. And Abram mocked them, and said, Surely the savory meat that I prepared has not pleased them, or perhaps it was too little for them, and for that reason they would not eat; therefore tomorrow I will prepare fresh savory meat, better and more plentiful than this, in order that I may see the result.

28. And it was on the next day that Abram directed his mother concerning the savory meat, and his mother rose and fetched three fine kids from the flock, and she made of them some excellent savory meat, such as her son was fond of, and she gave it to her son Abram; and Terah his father did not know of it.

29. And Abram took the savory meat from his mother, and brought it before his father's gods into the chamber; and he came nigh unto them that they might eat, and he placed it before them, and Abram sat before them all day, thinking perhaps they might eat.

30. And Abram viewed them, and behold they had neither voice nor hearing, nor did one of them stretch forth his hand to the meat to eat.

31. And in the evening of that day in that house Abram was clothed with the spirit of God.

32. And he called out and said, Wo unto my father and this wicked generation, whose hearts are all inclined to vanity, who serve these idols of wood and stone which can neither eat, smell, hear nor speak, who have mouths without speech, eyes without sight, ears without hearing, hands without feeling, and legs which cannot move; like them are those that made them and that trust in them.

33. And when Abram saw all these things his anger was kindled against his father, and he hastened and took a hatchet in his hand, and came unto the chamber of the gods, and he broke all his father's gods.

34. And when he had done breaking the images, he placed the hatchet in the hand of the great god which was there before them, and he went out; and Terah his father came home, for he had heard at the door the sound of the striking of the hatchet; so Terah came into the house to know what this was about.

35. And Terah, having heard the noise of the hatchet in the room of images, ran to the room to the images, and he met Abram going out.

36. And Terah entered the room and found all the idols fallen down and broken, and the hatchet in the hand of the largest, which was not broken, and the savory meat which Abram his son had made was still before them.

37. And when Terah saw this his anger was greatly kindled, and he hastened and went from the room to Abram.

38. And he found Abram his son still sitting in the house; and he said to him, What is this work thou hast done to my gods?

39. And Abram answered Terah his father and he said, Not so my lord, for I brought savory meat before them, and when I came nigh to them with the meat that they might eat, they all at once stretched forth their hands to eat before the great one had put forth his hand to eat.

40. And the large one saw their works that they did before him, and his anger was violently kindled against them, and he went and took the hatchet that was in the house and came to them and broke them all, and behold the hatchet is yet in his hand as thou seest.

41. And Terah's anger was kindled against his son Abram, when he spoke this; and Terah said to Abram his son in his anger, What is this tale that thou hast told? Thou speakest lies to me.

42. Is there in these gods spirit, soul or power to do all thou hast told me? Are they not wood and stone, and have I not myself made them, and canst thou speak such lies, saying that the large god that was with them smote them? It is thou that didst place the hatchet in his hands, and then sayest he smote them all.

43. And Abram answered his father and said to him, And how canst thou then serve these idols in whom there is no power to do any thing? Can those idols in which thou trustest deliver thee? can they hear thy prayers when thou callest upon them? can they deliver thee from the hands of thy enemies, or will they fight thy battles for thee against thy enemies, that thou shouldst serve wood and stone which can neither speak nor hear?

44. And now surely it is not good for thee nor for the sons of men that are connected with thee, to do these things; are you so silly, so foolish or so short of understanding that you will serve wood and stone, and do after this manner?

45. And forget the Lord God who made heaven and earth, and who created you in the earth, and thereby bring a great evil upon your souls in this matter by serving stone and wood?

46. Did not our fathers in days of old sin in this matter, and the Lord God of the universe brought the waters of the flood upon them and destroyed the whole earth?

47. And how can you continue to do this and serve gods of wood and stone, who cannot hear, or speak, or deliver you from oppression, thereby bringing down the anger of the God of the universe upon you?

48. Now therefore my father refrain from this, and bring not evil upon thy soul and the souls of thy household.

49. And Abram hastened and sprang from before his father, and took the hatchet from his father's largest idol, with which Abram broke it and ran away.

50. And Terah, seeing all that Abram had done, hastened to go from his house, and he went to the king and he came before Nimrod and stood before him, and he bowed down to the king; and the king said, What dost thou want?

51. And he said, I beseech thee my lord, to hear me--Now fifty years back a child was born to me, and thus has he done to my gods and thus has he spoken; and now therefore, my lord and king, send for him that he may come before thee, and judge him according to the law, that we may be delivered from his evil.

52. And the king sent three men of his servants, and they went and brought Abram before the king. And Nimrod and all his princes and servants were that day sitting before him, and Terah sat also before them.

53. And the king said to Abram, What is this that thou hast done to thy father and to his gods? And Abram answered the king in the words that he spoke to his father, and he said, The large god that was with them in the house did to them what thou hast heard.

54. And the king said to Abram, Had they power to speak and eat and do as thou hast said? And Abram answered the king, saying, And if there be no power in them why dost thou serve them and cause the sons of men to err through thy follies?

55. Dost thou imagine that they can deliver thee or do anything small or great, that thou shouldst serve them? And why wilt thou not sense the God of the whole universe, who created thee and in whose power it is to kill and keep alive?

56. o foolish, simple, and ignorant king, woe unto thee forever.

57. I thought thou wouldst teach thy servants the upright way, but thou hast not done this, but hast filled the whole earth with thy sins and the sins of thy people who have followed thy ways.

58. Dost thou not know, or hast thou not heard, that this evil which thou doest, our ancestors sinned therein in days of old, and the eternal God brought the waters of the flood upon them and destroyed them all, and also destroyed the whole earth on their account? And wilt thou and thy people rise up now and do like unto this work, in order to bring down the anger of the Lord God of the universe, and to bring evil upon thee and the whole earth?

59. Now therefore put away this evil deed which thou doest, and serve the God of the universe, as thy soul is in his hands, and then it will be well with thee.

60. And if thy wicked heart will not hearken to my words to cause thee to forsake thy evil ways, and to serve the eternal God, then wilt thou die in shame in the latter days, thou, thy people and all who are connected with thee, hearing thy words or walking in thy evil ways.

61. And when Abram had ceased speaking before the king and princes, Abram lifted up his eyes to the heavens, and he said, The Lord seeth all the wicked, and he will judge them.

CHAPTER 12

1. And when the king heard the words of Abram he ordered him to be put into prison; and Abram was ten days in prison.

2. And at the end of those days the king ordered that all the kings, princes and governors of different provinces and the sages should come before him, and they sat before him, and Abram was still in the house of confinement.

3.   And the king said to the princes and sages, Have you heard what Abram, the son of Terah, has done to his father? Thus has he done to him, and I ordered him to be brought before me, and thus has he spoken; his heart did not misgive him, neither did he stir in my presence, and behold now he is confined in the prison.

4.   And therefore decide what judgment is due to this man who reviled the king; who spoke and did all the things that you heard.

5.   And they all answered the king saying, The man who revileth the king should be hanged upon a tree; but having done all the things that he said, and having despised our gods, he must therefore be burned to death, for this is the law in this matter.

6.   If it pleaseth the king to do this, let him order his servants to kindle a fire both night and day in thy brick furnace, and then we will cast this man into it. And the king did so, and he commanded his servants that they should prepare a fire for three days and three nights in the king's furnace, that is in Casdim; and the king ordered them to take Abram from prison and bring him out to be burned.

7.   And all the king's servants, princes, lords, governors, and judges, and all the inhabitants of the land, about nine hundred thousand men, stood opposite the furnace to see Abram.

8.   And all the women and little ones crowded upon the roofs and towers to see what was doing with Abram, and they all stood together at a distance; and there was not a man left that did not come on that day to behold the scene.

9.   And when Abram was come, the conjurors of the king and the sages saw Abram, and they cried out to the king, saying, Our sovereign lord, surely this is the man whom we know to have been the child at whose birth the great star swallowed the four stars, which we declared to the king now fifty years since.

10. And behold now his father has also transgressed thy commands, and mocked thee by bringing thee another child, which thou didst kill.

11. And when the king heard their words, he was exceedingly wroth, and he ordered Terah to be brought before him.

12. And the king said, Hast thou heard what the conjurors have spoken? Now tell me truly, how didst thou; and if thou shalt speak truth thou shalt be acquitted.

13. And seeing that the king's anger was so much kindled, Terah said to the king, My lord and king, thou hast heard the truth, and what the sages have spoken is right. And the king said, How couldst thou do this thing, to transgress my orders and to give me a child that thou didst not beget, and to take value for him?

14. And Terah answered the king, Because my tender feelings were excited for my son, at that time, and I took a son of my handmaid, and I brought him to the king.

15. And the king said Who advised thee to this? Tell me, do not hide aught from me, and then thou shalt not die.

16. And Terah was greatly terrified in the king's presence, and he said to the king, It was Haran my eldest son who advised me to this; and Haran was in those days that Abram was born, two and thirty years old.

17. But Haran did not advise his father to anything, for Terah said this to the king in order to deliver his soul from the king, for he feared greatly; and the king said to Terah, Haran thy son who advised thee to this shall die through fire with Abram; for the sentence of death is upon him for having rebelled against the king's desire in doing this thing.

18. And Haran at that time felt inclined to follow the ways of Abram, but he kept it within himself.

19. And Haran said in his heart, Behold now the king has seized Abram on account of these things which Abram did, and it shall come to pass, that if Abram prevail over the king I will follow him, but if the king prevail I will go after the king.

20. And when Terah had spoken this to the king concerning Haran his son, the king ordered Haran to be seized with Abram.

21. And they brought them both, Abram and Haran his brother, to cast them into the fire; and all the inhabitants of the land and the king's servants and princes and all the women and little ones were there, standing that day over them.

22. And the king's servants took Abram and his brother, and they stripped them of all their clothes excepting their lower garments which were upon them.

23. And they bound their hands and feet with linen cords, and the servants of the king lifted them up and cast them both into the furnace.

24. And the Lord loved Abram and he had compassion over him, and the Lord came down and delivered Abram from the fire and he was not burned.

25. But all the cords with which they bound him were burned, while Abram remained and walked about in the fire.

26. And Haran died when they had cast him into the fire, and he was burned to ashes, for his heart was not perfect with the Lord; and those men who cast him into the fire, the flame of the fire spread over them, and they were burned, and twelve men of them died.

27. And Abram walked in the midst of the fire three days and three nights, and all the servants of the king saw him walking in the fire, and they came and told the king, saying, Behold we have seen Abram walking about in the midst of the fire, and even the lower garments which are upon him are not burned, but the cord with which he was bound is burned.

28. And when the king heard their words his heart fainted and he would not believe them; so he sent other faithful princes to see this matter, and they went and saw it and told it to the king; and the king rose to go and see it, and he saw Abram walking to and fro in the midst of the fire, and he saw Haran's body burned, and the king wondered greatly.

29. And the king ordered Abram to be taken out from the fire; and his servants approached to take him out and they could not, for the fire was round about and the flame ascending toward them from the furnace.

30. And the king's servants fled from it, and the king rebuked them, saying, Make haste and bring Abram out of the fire that you shall not die.

31. And the servants of the king again approached to bring Abram out, and the flames came upon them and burned their faces so that eight of them died.

32. And when the king saw that his servants could not approach the fire lest they should be burned, the king called to Abram, O servant of the God who is in heaven, go forth from amidst the fire and come hither before me; and Abram hearkened to the voice of the king, and he went forth from the fire and came and stood before the king.

33. And when Abram came out the king and all his servants saw Abram coming before the king, with his lower garments upon him, for they were not burned, but the cord with which he was bound was burned.

34. And the king said to Abram, How is it that thou wast not burned in the fire?

35. And Abram said to the king, The God of heaven and earth in whom I trust and who has all in his power, he delivered me from the fire into which thou didst cast me.

36. And Haran the brother of Abram was burned to ashes, and they sought for his body, and they found it consumed.

37. And Haran was eighty-two years old when he died in the fire of Casdim. And the king, princes, and inhabitants of the land, seeing that Abram was delivered from the fire, they came and bowed down to Abram.

38. And Abram said to them, Do not bow down to me, but bow down to the God of the world who made you, and serve him, and go in his ways for it is he who delivered me from out of this fire, and it is he who created the souls and spirits of all men, and formed man in his mother's womb, and brought him forth into the world, and it is he who will deliver those who trust in him from all pain.

39. And this thing seemed very wonderful in the eyes of the king and princes, that Abram was saved from the fire and that Haran was burned; and the king gave Abram many presents and he gave him his two head servants from the king's house; the name of one was Oni and the name of the other was Eliezer.

40. And all the kings, princes and servants gave Abram many gifts of silver and gold and pearl, and the king and his princes sent him away, and he went in peace.

41. And Abram went forth from the king in peace, and many of the king's servants followed him, and about three hundred men joined him.

42. And Abram returned on that day and went to his father's house, he and the men that followed him, and Abram served the Lord his God all the days of his life, and he walked in his ways and followed his law.

43. And from that day forward Abram inclined the hearts of the sons of men to serve the Lord.

44. And at that time Nahor and Abram took unto themselves wives, the daughters of their brother Haran; the wife of Nahor was Milca and the name of Abram's wife was Sarai. And Sarai, wife of Abram, was barren; she had no offspring in those days.

45. And at the expiration of two years from Abram's going out of the fire, that is in the fiftysecond year of his life, behold king Nimrod sat in Babel upon the throne, and the king fell asleep and dreamed that he was standing with his troops and hosts in a valley opposite the king's furnace.

46. And he lifted up his eyes and saw a man in the likeness of Abram coming forth from the furnace, and that he came and stood before the king with his drawn sword, and then sprang to the king with his sword, when the king fled from the man, for he was afraid; and while he was running, the man threw an egg upon the king's head, and the egg became a great river.

47. And the king dreamed that all his troops sank in that river and died, and the king took flight with three men who were before him and he escaped.

48. And the king looked at these men and they were clothed in princely dresses as the garments of kings, and had the appearance and majesty of kings.

49. And while they were running, the river again turned to an egg before the king, and there came forth from the egg a young bird which came before the king, and flew at his head and plucked out the king's eye.

50. And the king was grieved at the sight, and he awoke out of his sleep and his spirit was agitated; and he felt a great terror.

51. And in the morning the king rose from his couch in fear, and he ordered all the wise men and magicians to come before him, when the king related his dream to them.

52. And a wise servant of the king, whose name was Anuki, answered the king, saying, This is nothing else but the evil of Abram and his seed which will spring up against my Lord and king in the latter days.

53. And behold the day will come when Abram and his seed and the children of his household will war with my king, and they will smite all the king's hosts and his troops.

54. And as to what thou hast said concerning three men which thou didst see like unto thyself, and which did escape, this means that only thou wilt escape with three kings from the kings of the earth who will be with thee in battle.

55. And that which thou sawest of the river which turned to an egg as at first, and the young bird plucking out thine eye, this means nothing else but the seed of Abram which will slay the king in latter days.

56. This is my king's dream, and this is its interpretation, and the dream is true, and the interpretation which thy servant has given thee is right.

57. Now therefore my king, surely thou knowest that it is now fifty-two years since thy sages saw this at the birth of Abram, and if my king will suffer Abram to live in the earth it will be to the injury of my lord and king, for all the days that Abram liveth neither thou nor thy kingdom will be established, for this was known formerly at his birth; and why will not my king slay him, that his evil may be kept from thee in latter days?

58. And Nimrod hearkened to the voice of Anuki, and he sent some of his servants in secret to go and seize Abram, and bring him before the king to suffer death.

59. And Eliezer, Abram's servant whom the king had given him, was at that time in the presence of the king, and he heard what Anuki had advised the king, and what the king had said to cause Abram's death.

60. And Eliezer said to Abram, Hasten, rise up and save thy soul, that thou mayest not die through the hands of the king, for thus did he see in a dream concerning thee, and thus did Anuki interpret it, and thus also did Anuki advise the king concerning thee.

61. And Abram hearkened to the voice of Eliezer, and Abram hastened and ran for safety to the house of Noah and his son Shem, and he concealed himself there and found a place of safety; and the king's servants came to Abram's house to seek him, but they could not find him, and they searched through out the country and he was not to be found, and they went and searched in every direction and he was not to be met with.

62. And when the king's servants could not find Abram they returned to the king, but the king's anger against Abram was stilled, as they did not find him, and the king drove from his mind this matter concerning Abram.

63. And Abram was concealed in Noah's house for one month, until the king had forgotten this matter, but Abram was still afraid of the king; and Terah came to see Abram his son secretly in the house of Noah, and Terah was very great in the eyes of the king.

64. And Abram said to his father, Dost thou not know that the king thinketh to slay me, and to annihilate my name from the earth by the advice of his wicked counsellors?

65. Now whom hast thou here and what hast thou in this land? Arise, let us go together to the land of Canaan, that we may be delivered from his hand, lest thou perish also through him in the latter days.

66. Dost thou not know or hast thou not heard, that it is not through love that Nimrod giveth thee all this honor, but it is only for his benefit that he bestoweth all this good upon thee?

67. And if he do unto thee greater good than this, surely these are only vanities of the world, for wealth and riches cannot avail in the day of wrath and anger.

68. Now therefore hearken to my voice, and let us arise and go to the land of Canaan, out of the reach of injury from Nimrod; and serve thou the Lord who created thee in the earth and it will be well with thee; and cast away all the vain things which thou pursuest.

69. And Abram ceased to speak, when Noah and his son Shem answered Terah, saying, True is the word which Abram hath said unto thee.

70. And Terah hearkened to the voice of his son Abram, and Terah did all that Abram said, for this was from the Lord, that the king should not cause Abram's death.

CHAPTER 13

1.   And Terah took his son Abram and his grandson Lot, the son of Haran, and Sarai his daughter-in-law, the wife of his son Abram, and all the souls of his household and went with them from Ur Casdim to go to the land of Canaan. And when they came as far as the land of Haran they remained there, for it was exceedingly good land for pasture, and of sufficient extent for those who accompanied them.

2.   And the people of the land of Haran saw that Abram was good and upright with God and men, and that the Lord his God was with him, and some of the people of the land of Haran came and joined Abram, and he taught them the instruction of the Lord and his ways; and these men remained with Abram in his house and they adhered to him.

3.   And Abram remained in the land three years, and at the expiration of three years the Lord appeared to Abram and said to him; I am the Lord who brought thee forth from Ur Casdim, and delivered thee from the hands of all thine enemies.

4.   And now therefore if thou wilt hearken to my voice and keep my commandments, my statutes and my laws, then will I cause thy enemies to fall before thee, and I will multiply thy seed like the stars of heaven, and I will send my blessing upon all the works of thy hands, and thou shalt lack nothing.

5.   Arise now, take thy wife and all belonging to thee and go to the land of Canaan and remain there, and I will there be unto thee for a God, and I will bless thee. And Abram rose and took his wife and all belonging to him, and he went to the land of Canaan as the Lord had told him; and Abram was fifty years old when he went from Haran.

6.   And Abram came to the land of Canaan and dwelt in the midst of the city, and he there pitched his tent amongst the children of Canaan, inhabitants of the land.

7.   And the Lord appeared to Abram when he came to the land of Canaan, and said to him, This is the land which I gave unto thee and to thy seed after thee forever, and I will make thy seed like the stars of heaven, and I will give unto thy seed for an inheritance all the lands which thou seest.

8.   And Abram built an altar in the place where God had spoken to him, and Abram there called upon the name of the Lord.

9.   At that time, at the end of three years of Abram's dwelling in the land of Canaan, in that year Noah died, which was the fifty-eighth year of the life of Abram; and all the days that Noah lived were nine hundred and fifty years and he died.

10. And Abram dwelt in the land of Canaan, he, his wife, and all belonging to him, and all those that accompanied him, together with those that joined him from the people of the land; but Nahor, Abram's brother, and Terah his father, and Lot the son of Haran and all belonging to them dwelt in Haran.

11. In the fifth year of Abram's dwelling in the land of Canaan the people of Sodom and Gomorrah and all the cities of the plain revolted from the power of Chedorlaomer, king of Elam; for all the kings of the cities of the plain had served Chedorlaomer for twelve years, and given him a yearly tax, but in those days in the thirteenth year, they rebelled against him.

12. And in the tenth year of Abram's dwelling in the land of Canaan there was war between Nimrod king of Shinar and Chedorlaomer king of Elam, and Nimrod came to fight with Chedorlaomer and to subdue him.

13. For Chedorlaomer was at that time one of the princes of the hosts of Nimrod, and when all the people at the tower were dispersed and those that remained were also scattered upon the face of the earth, Chedorlaomer went to the land of Elam and reigned over it and rebelled against his lord.

14. And in those days when Nimrod saw that the cities of the plain had rebelled, he came with pride and anger to war with Chedorlaomer, and Nimrod assembled all his princes and subjects, about seven hundred thousand men, and went against Chedorlaomer, and Chedorlaomer went out to meet him with five thousand men, and they prepared for battle in the valley of Babel which is between Elam and Shinar.

15. And all those kings fought there, and Nimrod and his people were smitten before the people of Chedorlaomer, and there fell from Nimrod's men about six hundred thousand, and Mardon the king's son fell amongst them.

16. And Nimrod fled and returned in shame and disgrace to his land, and he was under subjection to Chedorlaomer for a long time, and Chedorlaomer returned to his land and sent princes of his host to the kings that dwelt around him, to Arioch king of Elasar, and to Tidal king of Goyim, and made a covenant with them, and they were all obedient to his commands.

17. And it was in the fifteenth year of Abram's dwelling in the land of Canaan, which is the seventieth year of the life of Abram, and the Lord appeared to Abram in that year and he said to him, I am the Lord who brought thee out from Ur Casdim to give thee this land for an inheritance.

18. Now therefore walk before me and be perfect and keep my commands, for to thee and to thy seed I will give this land for an inheritance, from the river Mitzraim unto the great river Euphrates.

19. And thou shalt come to thy fathers in peace and in good age, and the fourth generation shall return here in this land and shall inherit it forever; and Abram built an altar, and he called upon the name of the Lord who appeared to him, and he brought up sacrifices upon the altar to the Lord.

20. At that time Abram returned and went to Haran to see his father and mother, and his father's household, and Abram and his wife and all belonging to him returned to Haran,

and Abram dwelt in Haran five years.

21. And many of the people of Haran, about seventy-two men, followed Abram and Abram taught them the instruction of the Lord and his ways, and he taught them to know the Lord.

22. In those days the Lord appeared to Abram in Haran, and he said to him, Behold, I spoke unto thee these twenty years back saying,

23. Go forth from thy land, from thy birth-place and from thy father's house, to the land which I have shown thee to give it to thee and to thy children, for there in that land will I bless thee, and make thee a great nation, and make thy name great, and in thee shall the families of the earth be blessed.

24. Now therefore arise, go forth from this place, thou, thy wife, and all belonging to thee, also every one born in thy house and all the souls thou hast made in Haran, and bring them out with thee from here, and rise to return to the land of Canaan.

25. And Abram arose and took his wife Sarai and all belonging to him and all that were born to him in his house and the souls which they had made in Haran, and they came out to go to the land of Canaan.

26. And Abram went and returned to the land of Canaan, according to the word of the Lord. And Lot the son of his brother Haran went with him, and Abram was seventy-five years old when he went forth from Haran to return to the land of Canaan.

27. And he came to the land of Canaan according to the word of the Lord to Abram, and he pitched his tent and he dwelt in the plain of Mamre, and with him was Lot his brother's son, and all belonging to him.

28. And the Lord again appeared to Abram and said, To thy seed will I give this land; and he there built an altar to the Lord who appeared to him, which is still to this day in the plains of Mamre.

CHAPTER 14

1. In those days there was in the land of Shinar a wise man who had understanding in all wisdom, and of a beautiful appearance, but he was poor and indigent; his name was Rikayon and he was hard set to support himself.

2. And he resolved to go to Egypt, to Oswiris the son of Anom king of Egypt, to show the king his wisdom; for perhaps he might find grace in his sight, to raise him up and give him maintenance; and Rikayon did so.

3. And when Rikayon came to Egypt he asked the inhabitants of Egypt concerning the king, and the inhabitants of Egypt told him the custom of the king of Egypt, for it was then the custom of the king of Egypt that he went from his royal palace and was seen abroad only one day in the year, and after that the king would return to his palace to remain there.

4. And on the day when the king went forth he passed judgment in the land, and every one having a suit came before the king that day to obtain his request.

5. And when Rikayon heard of the custom in Egypt and that he could not come into the presence of the king, he grieved greatly and was very sorrowful.

6. And in the evening Rikayon went out and found a house in ruins, formerly a bake house in Egypt, and he abode there all night in bitterness of soul and pinched with hunger, and sleep was removed from his eyes.

7. And Rikayon considered within himself what he should do in the town until the king made his appearance, and how he might maintain himself there.

8. And he rose in the morning and walked about, and met in his way those who sold vegetables and various sorts of seed with which they supplied the inhabitants.

9. And Rikayon wished to do the same in order to get a maintenance in the city, but he was unacquainted with the custom of the people, and he was like a blind man among them.

10. And he went and obtained vegetables to sell them for his support, and the rabble assembled about him and ridiculed him, and took his vegetables from him and left him nothing.

11. And he rose up from there in bitterness of soul, and went sighing to the bake house in which he had remained all the night before, and he slept there the second night.

12. And on that night again he reasoned within himself how he could save himself from starvation, and he devised a scheme how to act.

13. And he rose up in the morning and acted ingeniously, and went and hired thirty strong men of the rabble, carrying their war instruments in their hands, and he led them to the top of the Egyptian sepulchre, and he placed them there.

14. And he commanded them, saying, Thus saith the king, Strengthen yourselves and be valiant men, and let no man be buried here until two hundred pieces of silver be given, and then he may be buried; and those men did according to the order of Rikayon to the people of Egypt the whole of that year.

15. And in eight months time Rikayon and his men gathered great riches of silver and gold, and Rikayon took a great quantity of horses and other animals, and he hired more men, and he gave them horses and they remained with him.

16. And when the year came round, at the time the king went forth into the town, all the inhabitants of Egypt assembled together to speak to him concerning the work of Rikayon and his men.

17. And the king went forth on the appointed day, and all the Egyptians came before him and cried unto him, saying,

18. May the king live forever. What is this thing thou doest in the town to thy servants, not to suffer a dead body to be buried until so much silver and gold be given? Was there ever the like unto this done in the whole earth, from the days of former kings yea even from the days of Adam, unto this day, that the dead should not be buried only for a set price?

19. We know it to be the custom of kings to take a yearly tax from the living, but thou dost not only do this, but from the dead also thou exactest a tax day by day.

20. Now, O king, we can no more bear this, for the whole city is ruined on this account, and dost thou not know it?

21. And when the king heard all that they had spoken he was very wroth, and his anger burned within him at this affair, for he had known nothing of it.

22. And the king said, Who and where is he that dares to do this wicked thing in my land without my command? Surely you will tell me.

23. And they told him all the works of Rikayon and his men, and the king's anger was aroused, and he ordered Rikayon and his men to be brought before him.

24. And Rikayon took about a thousand children, sons and daughters, and clothed them in silk and embroidery, and he set them upon horses and sent them to the king by means of his men, and he also took a great quantity of silver and gold and precious stones, and a strong and beautiful horse, as a present for the king, with which he came before the king and bowed down to the earth before him; and the king, his servants and all the inhabitants of Egypt wondered at the work of Rikayon, and they saw his riches and the present that he had brought to the king.

25. And it greatly pleased the king and he wondered at it; and when Rikayon sat before him the king asked him concerning all his works, and Rikayon spoke all his words wisely before the king, his servants and all the inhabitants of Egypt.

26. And when the king heard the words of Rikayon and his wisdom, Rikayon found grace in his sight, and he met with grace and kindness from all the servants of the king and from all the inhabitants of Egypt, on account of his wisdom and excellent speeches, and from that time they loved him exceedingly.

27. And the king answered and said to Rikayon, Thy name shall no more be called Rikayon but Pharaoh shall be thy name, since thou didst exact a tax from the dead; and he called his name Pharaoh.

28. And the king and his subjects loved Rikayon for his wisdom, and they consulted with all the inhabitants of Egypt to make him prefect under the king.

29. And all the inhabitants of Egypt and its wise men did so, and it was made a law in Egypt.

30. And they made Rikayon Pharaoh prefect under Oswiris king of Egypt, and Rikayon Pharaoh governed over Egypt, daily administering justice to the whole city, but Oswiris the king would judge the people of the land one day in the year, when he went out to make his appearance.

31. And Rikayon Pharaoh cunningly usurped the government of Egypt, and he exacted a tax from all the inhabitants of Egypt.

32. And all the inhabitants of Egypt greatly loved Rikayon Pharaoh, and they made a decree to call every king that should reign over them and their seed in Egypt, Pharaoh.

33. Therefore all the kings that reigned in Egypt from that time forward were called Pharaoh unto this day.

CHAPTER 15

1.   And in that year there was a heavy famine throughout the land of Canaan, and the inhabitants of the land could not remain on account of the famine for it was very grievous.

2.   And Abram and all belonging to him rose and went down to Egypt on account of the famine, and when they were at the brook Mitzraim they remained there some time to rest from the fatigue of the road.

3.   And Abram and Sarai were walking at the border of the brook Mitzraim, and Abram beheld his wife Sarai that she was very beautiful.

4.   And Abram said to his wife Sarai, Since God has created thee with such a beautiful countenance, I am afraid of the Egyptians lest they should slay me and take thee away, for the fear of God is not in these places.

5.   Surely then thou shalt do this, Say thou art my sister to all that may ask thee, in order that it may be well with me, and that we may live and not be put to death.

6.   And Abram commanded the same to all those that came with him to Egypt on account of the famine; also his nephew Lot he commanded, saying, If the Egyptians ask thee concerning Sarai say she is the sister of Abram.

7.   And yet with all these orders Abram did not put confidence in them, but he took Sarai and placed her in a chest and concealed it amongst their vessels, for Abram was greatly concerned about Sarai on account of the wickedness of the Egyptians.

8.   And Abram and all belonging to him rose up from the brook Mitzraim and came to Egypt; and they had scarcely entered the gates of the city when the guards stood up to them saying, Give tithe to the king from what you have, and then you may come into the town; and Abram and those that were with him did so.

9.   And Abram with the people that were with him came to Egypt, and when they came they brought the chest in which Sarai was concealed and the Egyptians saw the chest.

10. And the king's servants approached Abram, saying, What hast thou here in this chest which we have not seen? Now open thou the chest and give tithe to the king of all that it contains.

11. And Abram said, This chest I will not open, but all you demand upon it I will give. And Pharaoh's officers answered Abram, saying, It is a chest of precious stones, give us the tenth thereof.

12. Abram said, All that you desire I will give, but you must not open the chest.

13. And the king's officers pressed Abram, and they reached the chest and opened it with force, and they saw, and behold a beautiful woman was in the chest.

14. And when the officers of the king beheld Sarai they were struck with admiration at her beauty, and all the princes and servants of Pharaoh assembled to see Sarai, for she was very beautiful. And the king's officers ran and told Pharaoh all that they had seen, and they praised Sarai to the king; and Pharaoh ordered her to be brought, and the woman came before the king.

15. And Pharaoh beheld Sarai and she pleased him exceedingly, and he was struck with her beauty, and the king rejoiced greatly on her account, and made presents to those who brought him the tidings concerning her.

16. And the woman was then brought to Pharaoh's house, and Abram grieved on account of his wife, and he prayed to the Lord to deliver her from the hands of Pharaoh.

17. And Sarai also prayed at that time and said, O Lord God thou didst tell my Lord Abram to go from his land and from his father's house to the land of Canaan, and thou didst promise to do well with him if he would perform thy commands; now behold we have done that which thou didst command us, and we left our land and our families, and we went to a strange land and to a people whom we have not known before.

18. And we came to this land to avoid the famine, and this evil accident has befallen me; now therefore, O Lord God, deliver us and save us from the hand of this oppressor, and do well with me for the sake of thy mercy.

19. And the Lord hearkened to the voice of Sarai, and the Lord sent an angel to deliver Sarai from the power of Pharaoh.

20. And the king came and sat before Sarai and behold an angel of the Lord was standing over them, and he appeared to Sarai and said to her, Do not fear, for the Lord has heard thy prayer.

21. And the king approached Sarai and said to her, What is that man to thee who brought thee hither? and she said, He is my brother.

22. And the king said, It is incumbent upon us to make him great, to elevate him and to do unto him all the good which thou shalt command us; and at that time the king sent to Abram silver and gold and precious stones in abundance, together with cattle, men servants and maid servants; and the king ordered Abram to be brought, and he sat in the court of the king's house, and the king greatly exalted Abram on that night.

23. And the king approached to speak to Sarai, and he reached out his hand to touch her, when the angel smote him heavily, and he was terrified and he refrained from reaching to her.

24. And when the king came near to Sarai, the angel smote him to the ground, and acted thus to him the whole night, and the king was terrified.

25. And the angel on that night smote heavily all the servants of the king, and his whole household, on account of Sarai, and there was a great lamentation that night amongst the people of Pharaoh's house.

26. And Pharaoh, seeing the evil that befell him, said, Surely on account of this woman has this thing happened to me, and he removed himself at some distance from her and spoke pleasing words to her.

27. And the king said to Sarai, Tell me I pray thee concerning the man with whom thou camest here; and Sarai said, This man is my husband, and I said to thee that he was my brother for I was afraid, lest thou shouldst put him to death through wickedness.

28. And the king kept away from Sarai, and the plagues of the angel of the Lord ceased from him and his household; and Pharaoh knew that he was smitten on account of Sarai, and the king was greatly astonished at this.

29. And in the morning the king called for Abram and said to him, What is this thou hast done to me? Why didst thou say, She is my sister, owing to which I took her unto me for a wife, and this heavy plague has therefore come upon me and my household.

30. Now therefore here is thy wife, take her and go from our land lest we all die on her account. And Pharaoh took more cattle, men servants and maid servants, and silver and gold, to give to Abram, and he returned unto him Sarai his wife.

31. And the king took a maiden whom he begat by his concubines, and he gave her to Sarai for a handmaid.

32. And the king said to his daughter, It is better for thee my daughter to be a handmaid in this man's house than to be mistress in my house, after we have beheld the evil that befell us on account of this woman.

33. And Abram arose, and he and all belonging to him went away from Egypt; and Pharaoh ordered some of his men to accompany him and all that went with him.

34. And Abram returned to the land of Canaan, to the place where he had made the altar, where he at first had pitched his tent.

35. And Lot the son of Haran, Abram's brother, had a heavy stock of cattle, flocks and herds and tents, for the Lord was bountiful to them on account of Abram.

36. And when Abram was dwelling in the land the herdsmen of Lot quarrelled with the herdsmen of Abram, for their property was too great for them to remain together in the land, and the land could not bear them on account of their cattle.

37. And when Abram's herdsmen went to feed their flock they would not go into the fields of the people of the land, but the cattle of Lot's herdsmen did otherwise, for they were suffered to feed in the fields of the people of the land.

38. And the people of the land saw this occurrence daily, and they came to Abram and quarrelled with him on account of Lot's herdsmen.

39. And Abram said to Lot, What is this thou art doing to me, to make me despicable to the inhabitants of the land, that thou orderest thy herdsman to feed thy cattle in the fields of other people? Dost thou not know that I am a stranger in this land amongst the children of Canaan, and why wilt thou do this unto me?

40. And Abram quarrelled daily with Lot on account of this, but Lot would not listen to Abram, and he continued to do the same and the inhabitants of the land came and told Abram.

41. And Abram said unto Lot, How long wilt thou be to me for a stumbling block with the inhabitants of the land? Now I beseech thee let there be no more quarrelling between us, for we are kinsmen.

42. But I pray thee separate from me, go and choose a place where thou mayest dwell with thy cattle and all belonging to thee, but Keep thyself at a distance from me, thou and thy household.

43. And be not afraid in going from me, for if any one do an injury to thee, let me know and I will avenge thy cause from him, only remove from me.

44. And when Abram had spoken all these words to Lot, then Lot arose and lifted up his eyes toward the plain of Jordan.

45. And he saw that the whole of this place was well watered, and good for man as well as affording pasture for the cattle.

46. And Lot went from Abram to that place, and he there pitched his tent and he dwelt in Sodom, and they were separated from each other.

47. And Abram dwelt in the plain of Mamre, which is in Hebron, and he pitched his tent there, and Abram remained in that place many years.

CHAPTER 16

1.   At that time Chedorlaomer king of Elam sent to all the neighboring kings, to Nimrod, king of Shinar who was then under his power, and to Tidal, king of Goyim, and to Arioch, king of Elasar, with whom he made a covenant, saying, Come up to me and assist me, that we may smite all the towns of Sodom and its inhabitants, for they have rebelled against me these thirteen years.

2.   And these four kings went up with all their camps, about eight hundred thousand men, and they went as they were, and smote every man they found in their road.

3.   And the five kings of Sodom and Gomorrah, Shinab king of Admah, Shemeber king of Zeboyim, Bera king of Sodom, Bersha king of Gomorrah, and Bela king of Zoar, went out to meet them, and they all joined together in the valley of Siddim.

4.   And these nine kings made war in the valley of Siddim; and the kings of Sodom and Gomorrah were smitten before the kings of Elam.

5.   And the valley of Siddim was full of lime pits and the kings of Elam pursued the kings of Sodom, and the kings of Sodom with their camps fled and fell into the lime pits, and all that remained went to the mountain for safety, and the five kings of Elam came after them and pursued them to the gates of Sodom, and they took all that there was in Sodom.

6.   And they plundered all the cities of Sodom and Gomorrah, and they also took Lot,
Abram's brother's son, and his property, and they seized all the goods of the cities of Sodom, and they went away; and Unic, Abram's servant, who was in the battle, saw this, and told Abram all that the kings had done to the cities of Sodom, and that Lot was taken captive by them.

7.   And Abram heard this, and he rose up with about three hundred and eighteen men that were with him, and he that night pursued these kings and smote them, and they all fell before Abram and his men, and there was none remaining but the four kings who fled, and they went each his own road.

8.   And Abram recovered all the property of Sodom, and he also recovered Lot and his property, his wives and little ones and all belonging to him, so that Lot lacked nothing.

9.   And when he returned from smiting these kings, he and his men passed the valley of Siddim where the kings had made war together.

10. And Bera king of Sodom, and the rest of his men that were with him, went out from the lime pits into which they had fallen, to meet Abram and his men.

11. And Adonizedek king of Jerusalem, the same was Shem, went out with his men to meet Abram and his people, with bread and wine, and they remained together in the valley of Melech.

12. And Adonizedek blessed Abram, and Abram gave him a tenth from all that he had brought from the spoil of his enemies, for Adonizedek was a priest before God.

13. And all the kings of Sodom and Gomorrah who were there, with their servants, approached Abram and begged of him to return them their servants whom he had made captive, and to take unto himself all the property.

14. And Abram answered the kings of Sodom, saying, As the Lord liveth who created heaven and earth, and who redeemed my soul from all affliction, and who delivered me this day from my enemies, and gave them into my hand, I will not take anything belonging to you, that you may not boast tomorrow, saying, Abram became rich from our property that he saved.

15. For the Lord my God in whom I trust said unto me, Thou shalt lack nothing, for I will bless thee in all the works of thy hands.

16. And now therefore behold, here is all belonging to you, take it and go; as the Lord liveth I will not take from you from a living soul down to a shoetie or thread, excepting the expense of the food of those who went out with me to battle, as also the portions of the men who went with me, Anar, Ashcol, and Mamre, they and their men, as well as those also who had remained to watch the baggage, they shall take their portion of the spoil.

17. And the kings of Sodom gave Abram according to all that he had said, and they pressed him to take of whatever he chose, but he would not.

18. And he sent away the kings of Sodom and the remainder of their men, and he gave them orders about Lot, and they went to their respective places.

19. And Lot, his brother's son, he also sent away with his property, and he went with them, and Lot returned to his home, to Sodom, and Abram and his people returned to their home to the plains of Mamre, which is in Hebron.

20. At that time the Lord again appeared to Abram in Hebron, and he said to him, Do not fear, thy reward is very great before me, for I will not leave thee, until I shall have multiplied thee, and blessed thee and made thy seed like the stars in heaven, which cannot be measured nor numbered.

21. And I will give unto thy seed all these lands that thou seest with thine eyes, to them will I give them for an inheritance forever, only be strong and do not fear, walk before me and be perfect.

22. And in the seventy-eighth year of the life of Abram, in that year died Reu, the son of Peleg, and all the days of Reu were two hundred and thirty-nine years, and he died.

23. And Sarai, the daughter of Haran, Abram's wife, was still barren in those days; she did not bear to Abram either son or daughter.

24. And when she saw that she bare no children she took her handmaid Hagar, whom Pharaoh had given her, and she gave her to Abram her husband for a wife.

25. For Hagar learned all the ways of Sarai as Sarai taught her, she was not in any way deficient in following her good ways.

26. And Sarai said to Abram, Behold here is my handmaid Hagar, go to her that she may bring forth upon my knees, that I may also obtain children through her.

27. And at the end of ten years of Abram's dwelling in the land of Canaan, which is the eighty-fifth year of Abram's life, Sarai gave Hagar unto him.

28. And Abram hearkened to the voice of his wife Sarai, and he took his handmaid Hagar and Abram came to her and she conceived.

29. And when Hagar saw that she had conceived she rejoiced greatly, and her mistress was despised in her eyes, and she said within herself, This can only be that I am better before God than Sarai my mistress, for all the days that my mistress has been with my lord, she did not conceive, but me the Lord has caused in so short a time to conceive by him.

30. And when Sarai saw that Hagar had conceived by Abram, Sarai was jealous of her handmaid, and Sarai said within herself, This is surely nothing else but that she must be better than I am.

31. And Sarai said unto Abram, My wrong be upon thee, for at the time when thou didst pray before the Lord for children why didst thou not pray on my account, that the Lord should give me seed from thee?

32. And when I speak to Hagar in thy presence, she despiseth my words, because she has conceived, and thou wilt say nothing to her; may the Lord judge between me and thee for what thou hast done to me.

33. And Abram said to Sarai, Behold thy handmaid is in thy hand, do unto her as it may seem good in thy eyes; and Sarai afflicted her, and Hagar fled from her to the wilderness.

34. And an angel of the Lord found her in the place where she had fled, by a well, and he said to her, Do not fear, for I will multiply thy seed, for thou shalt bear a son and thou shalt call his name Ishmael; now then return to Sarai thy mistress, and submit thyself under her hands.

35. And Hagar called the place of that well Beer-lahai-roi, it is between Kadesh and the wilderness of Bered.

36. And Hagar at that time returned to her master's house, and at the end of days Hagar bare a son to Abram, and Abram called his name Ishmael; and Abram was eighty-six years old when he begat him.

CHAPTER 17

1. And in those days, in the ninety-first year of the life of Abram, the children of Chittim made war with the children of Tubal, for when the Lord had scattered the sons of men upon the face of the earth, the children of Chittim went and embodied themselves in the plain of Canopia, and they built themselves cities there and dwelt by the river Tibreu.

2. And the children of Tubal dwelt in Tuscanah, and their boundaries reached the river
Tibreu, and the children of Tubal built a city in Tuscanan, and they called the name Sabinah, after the name of Sabinah son of Tubal their father, and they dwelt there unto this day.

3. And it was at that time the children of Chittim made war with the children of Tubal, and the children of Tubal were smitten before the children of Chittim, and the children of Chittim caused three hundred and seventy men to fall from the children of Tubal.

4. And at that time the children of Tubal swore to the children of Chittim, saying, You shall not intermarry amongst us, and no man shall give his daughter to any of the sons of Chittim.

5. For all the daughters of Tubal were in those days fair, for no women were then found in the whole earth so fair as the daughters of Tubal.

6. And all who delighted in the beauty of women went to the daughters of Tubal and took wives from them, and the sons of men, kings and princes, who greatly delighted in the beauty of women, took wives in those days from the daughters of Tubal.

7. And at the end of three years after the children of Tubal had sworn to the children of Chittim not to give them their daughters for wives, about twenty men of the children of Chittim went to take some of the daughters of Tubal, but they found none.

8. For the children of Tubal kept their oaths not to intermarry with them, and they would not break their oaths.

9. And in the days of harvest the children of Tubal went into their fields to get in their harvest, when the young men of Chittim assembled and went to the city of Sabinah, and each man took a young woman from the daughters of Tubal, and they came to their cities.

10. And the children of Tubal heard of it and they went to make war with them, and they could not prevail over them, for the mountain was exceedingly high from them, and when they saw they could not prevail over them they returned to their land.

11. And at the revolution of the year the children of Tubal went and hired about ten thousand men from those cities that were near them, and they went to war with the children of Chittim.

12. And the children of Tubal went to war with the children of Chittim, to destroy their land and to distress them, and in this engagement the children of Tubal prevailed over the children of Chittim, and the children of Chittim, seeing that they were greatly distressed, lifted up the children which they had had by the daughters of Tubal, upon the wall which had been built, to be before the eyes of the children of Tubal.

13. And the children of Chittim said to them, Have you come to make war with your own sons and daughters, and have we not been considered your flesh and bones from that time till now?

14. And when the children of Tubal heard this they ceased to make war with the children of Chittim, and they went away.

15. And they returned to their cities, and the children of Chittim at that time assembled and built two cities by the sea, and they called one Purtu and the other Ariza.

16. And Abram the son of Terah was then ninety-nine years old.

17. At that time the Lord appeared to him and he said to him, I will make my covenant between me and thee, and I will greatly multiply thy seed, and this is the covenant which I make between me and thee, that every male child be circumcised, thou and thy seed after thee.

18. At eight days old shall it be circumcised, and this covenant shall be in your flesh for an everlasting covenant.

19. And now therefore thy name shall no more be called Abram but Abraham, and thy wife shall no more be called Sarai but Sarah.

20. For I will bless you both, and I will multiply your seed after you that you shall become a great nation, and kings shall come forth from you.

CHAPTER 18

1. And Abraham rose and did all that God had ordered him, and he took the men of his household and those bought with his money, and he circumcised them as the Lord had commanded him.

2. And there was not one left whom he did not circumcise, and Abraham and his son Ishmael were circumcised in the flesh of their foreskin; thirteen years old was Ishmael when he was circumcised in the flesh of his foreskin.

3. And in the third day Abraham went out of his tent and sat at the door to enjoy the heat of the sun, during the pain of his flesh.

4. And the Lord appeared to him in the plain of Mamre, and sent three of his ministering angels to visit him, and he was sitting at the door of the tent, and he lifted his eyes and saw, and lo three men were coming from a distance, and he rose up and ran to meet them, and he bowed down to them and brought them into his house.

5. And he said to them, If now I have found favor in your sight, turn in and eat a morsel of bread; and he pressed them, and they turned in and he gave them water and they washed their feet, and he placed them under a tree at the door of the tent.

6. And Abraham ran and took a calf, tender and good, and he hastened to kill it, and gave it to his servant Eliezer to dress.

7. And Abraham came to Sarah into the tent, and he said to her, Make ready quickly three measures of fine meal, knead it and make cakes to cover the pot containing the meat, and she did so.

8. And Abraham hastened and brought before them butter and milk, beef and mutton, and gave it before them to eat before the flesh of the calf was sufficiently done, and they did eat.

9. And when they had done eating one of them said to him, I will return to thee according to the time of life, and Sarah thy wife shall have a son.

10. And the men afterward departed and went their ways, to the places to which they were sent.

11. In those days all the people of Sodom and Gomorrah, and of the whole five cities, were exceedingly wicked and sinful against the Lord and they provoked the Lord with their abominations, and they strengthened in aging abominably and scornfully before the Lord, and their wickedness and crimes were in those days great before the Lord.

12. And they had in their land a very extensive valley, about half a day's walk, and in it there were fountains of water and a great deal of herbage surrounding the water.

13. And all the people of Sodom and Gomorrah went there four times in the year, with their wives and children and all belonging to them, and they rejoiced there with timbrels and dances.

14. And in the time of rejoicing they would all rise and lay hold of their neighbor's wives, and some, the virgin daughters of their neighbors, and they enjoyed them, and each man saw his wife and daughter in the hands of his neighbor and did not say a word.

15. And they did so from morning to night, and they afterward returned home each man to his house and each woman to her tent; so they always did four times in the year.

16. Also when a stranger came into their cities and brought goods which he had purchased with a view to dispose of there, the people of these cities would assemble, men, women and children, young and old, and go to the man and take his goods by force, giving a little to each man until there was an end to all the goods of the owner which he had brought into the land.

17. And if the owner of the goods quarreled with them, saying, What is this work which you have done to me, then they would approach to him one by one, and each would show him the little which he took and taunt him, saying, I only took that little which thou didst give me; and when he heard this from them all, he would arise and go from them in sorrow and bitterness of soul, when they would all arise and go after him, and drive him out of the city with great noise and tumult.

18. And there was a man from the country of Elam who was leisurely going on the road, seated upon his ass, which carried a fine mantle of divers colors, and the mantle was bound with a cord upon the ass.

19. And the man was on his journey passing through the street of Sodom when the sun set in the evening, and he remained there in order to abide during the night, but no one would let him into his house; and at that time there was in Sodom a wicked and mischievous man, one skillful to do evil, and his name was Hedad.

20. And he lifted up his eyes and saw the traveler in the street of the city, and he came to him and said, Whence comest thou and whither dost thou go?

21. And the man said to him, I am traveling from Hebron to Elam where I belong, and as I passed the sun set and no one would suffer me to enter his house, though I had bread and water and also straw and provender for my ass, and am short of nothing.

22. And Hedad answered and said to him, All that thou shalt want shall be supplied by me, but in the street thou shalt not abide all night.

23. And Hedad brought him to his house, and he took off the mantle from the ass with the cord, and brought them to his house, and he gave the ass straw and provender whilst the traveler ate and drank in Hedad's house, and he abode there that night.

24. And in the morning the traveler rose up early to continue his journey, when Hedad said to him, Wait, comfort thy heart with a morsel of bread and then go, and the man did so; and he remained with him, and they both ate and drank together during the day, when the man rose up to go.

25. And Hedad said to him, Behold now the day is declining, thou hadst better remain all night that thy heart may be comforted; and he pressed him so that he tarried there all night, and on the second day he rose up early to go away, when Hedad pressed him, saying, Comfort thy heart with a morsel of bread and then go, and he remained and ate with him also the second day, and then the man rose up to continue his journey.

26. And Hedad said to him, Behold now the day is declining, remain with me to comfort thy heart and in the morning rise up early and go thy way.

27. And the man would not remain, but rose and saddled his ass, and whilst he was saddling his ass the wife of Hedad said to her husband, Behold this man has remained with us for two days eating and drinking and he has given us nothing, and now shall he go away from us without giving anything? and Hedad said to her, Be silent.

28. And the man saddled his ass to go, and he asked Hedad to give him the cord and mantle to tie it upon the ass.

29. And Hedad said to him, What sayest thou? And he said to him, That thou my lord shalt give me the cord and the mantle made with divers colors which thou didst conceal with thee in thy house to take care of it.

30. And Hedad answered the man, saying, This is the interpretation of thy dream, the cord which thou didst see, means that thy life will be lengthened out like a cord, and having seen the mantle colored with all sorts of colors, means that thou shalt have a vineyard in which thou wilt plant trees of all fruits.

31. And the traveler answered, saying, Not so my lord, for I was awake when I gave thee the cord and also a mantle woven with different colors, which thou didst take off the ass to put them by for me; and Hedad answered and said, Surely I have told thee the interpretation of thy dream and it is a good dream, and this is the interpretation thereof.

32. Now the sons of men give me four pieces of silver, which is my charge for interpreting dreams, and of thee only I require three pieces of silver.

33. And the man was provoked at the words of Hedad, and he cried bitterly, and he brought Hedad to Serak judge of Sodom.

34. And the man laid his cause before Serak the judge, when Hedad replied, saying, It is not so, but thus the matter stands; and the judge said to the traveler, This man Hedad telleth thee truth, for he is famed in the cities for the accurate interpretation of dreams.

35. And the man cried at the word of the judge, and he said, Not so my Lord, for it was in the day that I gave him the cord and mantle which was upon the ass, in order to put them by in his house; and they both disputed before the judge, the one saying, Thus the matter was, and the other declaring otherwise.

36. And Hedad said to the man, Give me four pieces of silver that I charge for my interpretations of dreams; I will not make any allowance; and give me the expense of the four meals that thou didst eat in my house.

37. And the man said to Hedad, Truly I will pay thee for what I ate in thy house, only give me the cord and mantle which thou didst conceal in thy house.

38. And Hedad replied before the judge and said to the man, Did I not tell thee the interpretation of thy dream? the cord means that thy days shall be prolonged like a cord, and the mantle, that thou wilt have a vineyard in which thou wilt plant all kinds of fruit trees.

39. This is the proper interpretation of thy dream, now give me the four pieces of silver that I require as a compensation, for I will make thee no allowance.

40. And the man cried at the words of Hedad and they both quarreled before the judge, and the judge gave orders to his servants, who drove them rashly from the house.

41. And they went away quarreling from the judge, when the people of Sodom heard them, and they gathered about them and they exclaimed against the stranger, and they drove him rashly from the city.

42. And the man continued his journey upon his ass with bitterness of soul, lamenting and weeping.

43. And whilst he was going along he wept at what had happened to him in the corrupt city of Sodom.

CHAPTER 19

1. And the cities of Sodom had four judges to four cities, and these were their names, Serak in the city of Sodom, Sharkad in Gomorrah, Zabnac in Admah, and Menon in Zeboyim.

2. And Eliezer Abraham's servant applied to them different names, and he converted Serak to Shakra, Sharkad to Shakrura, Zebnac to Kezobim, and Menon to Matzlodin.

3. And by desire of their four judges the people of Sodom and Gomorrah had beds erected in the streets of the cities, and if a man came to these places they laid hold of him and brought him to one of their beds, and by force made him to lie in them.

4. And as he lay down, three men would stand at his head and three at his feet, and measure him by the length of the bed, and if the man was less than the bed these six men would stretch him at each end, and when he cried out to them they would not answer him.

5. And if he was longer than the bed they would draw together the two sides of the bed at each end, until the man had reached the gates of death.

6. And if he continued to cry out to them, they would answer him, saying, Thus shall it be done to a man that cometh into our land.

7. And when men heard all these things that the people of the cities of Sodom did, they refrained from coming there.

8. And when a poor man came to their land they would give him silver and gold, and cause a proclamation in the whole city not to give him a morsel of bread to eat, and if the stranger should remain there some days, and die from hunger, not having been able to obtain a morsel of bread, then at his death all the people of the city would come and take their silver and gold which they had given to him.

9. And those that could recognize the silver or gold which they had given him took it back, and at his death they also stripped him of his garments, and they would fight about them, and he that prevailed over his neighbor took them.

10. They would after that carry him and bury him under some of the shrubs in the deserts; so they did all the days to any one that came to them and died in their land.

11. And in the course of time Sarah sent Eliezer to Sodom, to see Lot and inquire after his welfare.

12. And Eliezer went to Sodom, and he met a man of Sodom fighting with a stranger, and the man of Sodom stripped the poor man of all his clothes and went away.

13. And this poor man cried to Eliezer and supplicated his favor on account of what the man of Sodom had done to him.

14. And he said to him, Why dost thou act thus to the poor man who came to thy land?

15. And the man of Sodom answered Eliezer, saying, Is this man thy brother, or have the people of Sodom made thee a judge this day, that thou speakest about this man?

16. And Eliezer strove with the man of Sodom on account of the poor man, and when Eliezer approached to recover the poor man's clothes from the man of Sodom, he hastened and with a stone smote Eliezer in the forehead.

17. And the blood flowed copiously from Eliezer's forehead, and when the man saw the blood he caught hold of Eliezer, saying, Give me my hire for having rid thee of this bad blood that was in thy forehead, for such is the custom and the law in our land.

18. And Eliezer said to him, Thou hast wounded me and requirest me to pay thee thy hire; and Eliezer would not hearken to the words of the man of Sodom.

19. And the man laid hold of Eliezer and brought him to Shakra the judge of Sodom for judgment.

20. And the man spoke to the judge, saying, I beseech thee my lord, thus has this man done, for I smote him with a stone that the blood flowed from his forehead, and he is unwilling to give me my hire.

21. And the judge said to Eliezer, This man speaketh truth to thee, give him his hire, for this is the custom in our land; and Eliezer heard the words of the judge, and he lifted up a stone and smote the judge, and the stone struck on his forehead, and the blood flowed copiously from the forehead of the judge, and Eliezer said, If this then is the custom in your land give thou unto this man what I should have given him, for this has been thy decision, thou didst decree it.

22. And Eliezer left the man of Sodom with the judge, and he went away.

23. And when the kings of Elam had made war with the kings of Sodom, the kings of Elam captured all the property of Sodom, and they took Lot captive, with his property, and when it was told to Abraham he went and made war with the kings of Elam, and he recovered from their hands all the property of Lot as well as the property of Sodom.

24. At that time the wife of Lot bare him a daughter, and he called her name Paltith, saying, Because God had delivered him and his whole household from the kings of Elam; and Paltith daughter of Lot grew up, and one of the men of Sodom took her for a wife.

25. And a poor man came into the city to seek a maintenance, and he remained in the city some days, and all the people of Sodom caused a proclamation of their custom not to

give this man a morsel of bread to eat, until he dropped dead upon the earth, and they did so.

26. And Paltith the daughter of Lot saw this man lying in the streets starved with hunger, and no one would give him any thing to keep him alive, and he was just upon the point of death.

27. And her soul was filled with pity on account of the man, and she fed him secretly with bread for many days, and the soul of this man was revived.

28. For when she went forth to fetch water she would put the bread in the water pitcher, and when she came to the place where the poor man was, she took the bread from the pitcher and gave it him to eat; so she did many days.

29. And all the people of Sodom and Gomorrah wondered how this man could bear starvation for so many days.

30. And they said to each other, This can only be that he eats and drinks, for no man can bear starvation for so many days or live as this man has, without even his countenance changing; and three men concealed themselves in a place where the poor man was stationed, to know who it was that brought him bread to eat.

31. And Paltith daughter of Lot went forth that day to fetch water, and she put bread into her pitcher of water, and she went to draw water by the poor man's place, and she took out the bread from the pitcher and gave it to the poor man and he ate it.

32. And the three men saw what Paltith did to the poor man, and they said to her, It is thou then who hast supported him, and therefore has he not starved, nor changed in appearance nor died like the rest.

33. And the three men went out of the place in which they were concealed, and they seized Paltith and the bread which was in the poor man's hand.

34. And they took Paltith and brought her before their judges, and they said to them, Thus did she do, and it is she who supplied the poor man with bread, therefore did he not die all this time; now therefore declare to us the punishment due to this woman for having transgressed our law.

35. And the people of Sodom and Gomorrah assembled and kindled a fire in the street of the city, and they took the woman and cast her into the fire and she was burned to ashes.

36. And in the city of Admah there was a woman to whom they did the like.

37. For a traveler came into the city of Admah to abide there all night, with the intention of going home in the morning, and he sat opposite the door of the house of the young woman's father, to remain there, as the sun had set when be had reached that place; and the young woman saw him sitting by the door of the house.

38. And he asked her for a drink of water and she said to him, Who art thou? and he said to her, I was this day going on the road, and reached here when the sun set, so I will abide here all night, and in the morning I will arise early and continue my journey.

39. And the young woman went into the house and fetched the man bread and water to eat and drink.

40. And this affair became known to the people of Admah, and they assembled and brought the young woman before the judges, that they should judge her for this act.

41. And the judge said, The judgment of death must pass upon this woman because she transgressed our law, and this therefore is the decision concerning her.

42. And the people of those cities assembled and brought out the young woman, and anointed her with honey from head to foot, as the judge had decreed, and they placed her before a swarm of bees which were then in their hives, and the bees flew upon her and stung her that her whole body was swelled.

43. And the young woman cried out on account of the bees, but no one took notice of her or pitied her, and her cries ascended to heaven.

44. And the Lord was provoked at this and at all the works of the cities of Sodom, for they had abundance of food, and had tranquility amongst them, and still would not sustain the poor and the needy, and in those days their evil doings and sins became great before the Lord.

45. And the Lord sent for two of the angels that had come to Abraham's house, to destroy Sodom and its cities.

46. And the angels rose up from the door of Abraham's tent, after they had eaten and drunk, and they reached Sodom in the evening, and Lot was then sitting in the gate of Sodom, and when he saw them he rose to meet them, and he bowed down to the ground.

47. And he pressed them greatly and brought them into his house, and he gave them victuals which they ate, and they abode all night in his house.

48. And the angels said to Lot, Arise, go forth from this place, thou and all belonging to thee, lest thou be consumed in the iniquity of this city, for the Lord will destroy this place.

49. And the angels laid hold upon the hand of Lot and upon the hand of his wife, and upon the hands of his children, and all belonging to him, and they brought him forth and set him without the cities.

50. And they said to Lot, Escape for thy life, and he fled and all belonging to him.

51. Then the Lord rained upon Sodom and upon Gomorrah and upon all these cities brimstone and fire from the Lord out of heaven.

52. And he overthrew these cities, all the plain and all the inhabitants of the cities, and that which grew upon the ground; and Ado the wife of Lot looked back to see the destruction of the cities, for her compassion was moved on account of her daughters who remained in Sodom, for they did not go with her.

53. And when she looked back she became a pillar of salt, and it is yet in that place unto this day.

54. And the oxen which stood in that place daily licked up the salt to the extremities of their feet, and in the morning it would spring forth afresh, and they again licked it up unto this day.

55. And Lot and two of his daughters that remained with him fled and escaped to the cave of Adullam, and they remained there for some time.

56. And Abraham rose up early in the morning to see what had been done to the cities of Sodom; and he looked and beheld the smoke of the cities going up like the smoke of a furnace.

57. And Lot and his two daughters remained in the cave, and they made their father drink wine, and they lay with him, for they said there was no man upon earth that could raise up seed from them, for they thought that the whole earth was destroyed.

58. And they both lay with their father, and they conceived and bare sons, and the first born called the name of her son Moab, saying, From my father did I conceive him; he is the father of the Moabites unto this day.

59. And the younger also called her son Benami; he is the father of the children of Ammon unto this day.

60. And after this Lot and his two daughters went away from there, and he dwelt on the other side of the Jordan with his two daughters and their sons, and the sons of Lot grew up, and they went and took themselves wives from the land of Canaan, and they begat children and they were fruitful and multiplied.

CHAPTER 20

1.   And at that time Abraham journeyed from the plain of Mamre, and he went to the land of the Philistines, and he dwelt in Gerar; it was in the twenty-fifth year of Abraham's being in the land of Canaan, and the hundredth year of the life of Abraham, that he came to Gerar in the land of the Philistines.

2.   And when they entered the land he said to Sarah his wife, Say thou art my sister, to any one that shall ask thee, in order that we may escape the evil of the inhabitants of the land.

3.   And as Abraham was dwelling in the land of the Philistines, the servants of Abimelech, king of the Philistines, saw that Sarah was exceedingly beautiful, and they asked Abraham concerning her, and he said, She is my sister.

4.   And the servants of Abimelech went to Abimelech, saying, A man from the land of Canaan is come to dwell in the land, and he has a sister that is exceeding fair.

5.   And Abimelech heard the words of his servants who praised Sarah to him, and Abimelech sent his officers, and they brought Sarah to the king.

6.   And Sarah came to the house of Abimelech, and the king saw that Sarah was beautiful, and she pleased him exceedingly.

7.   And he approached her and said to her, What is that man to thee with whom thou didst come to our land? and Sarah answered and said He is my brother, and we came from the land of Canaan to dwell wherever we could find a place.

8.   And Abimelech said to Sarah, Behold my land is before thee, place thy brother in any part of this land that pleases thee, and it will be our duty to exalt and elevate him above all the people of the land since he is thy brother.

9.   And Abimelech sent for Abraham, and Abraham came to Abimelech.

10. And Abimelech said to Abraham, Behold I have given orders that thou shalt be honored as thou desirest on account of thy sister Sarah.

11. And Abraham went forth from the king, and the king's present followed him.

12. As at evening time, before men lie down to rest, the king was sitting upon his throne, and a deep sleep fell upon him, and he lay upon the throne and slept till morning.

13. And he dreamed that an angel of the Lord came to him with a drawn sword in his hand, and the angel stood over Abimelech, and wished to slay him with the sword, and the king was terrified in his dream, and said to the angel, In what have I sinned against thee

that thou comest to slay me with thy sword?

14. And the angel answered and said to Abimelech, Behold thou diest on account of the woman which thou didst yesternight bring to thy house, for she is a married woman, the wife of Abraham who came to thy house; now therefore return that man his wife, for she is his wife; and shouldst thou not return her, know that thou wilt surely die, thou and all belonging to thee.

15. And on that night there was a great outcry in the land of the Philistines, and the inhabitants of the land saw the figure of a man standing with a drawn sword in his hand, and he smote the inhabitants of the land with the sword, yea he continued to smite them.

16. And the angel of the Lord smote the whole land of the Philistines on that night, and there was a great confusion on that night and on the following morning.

17. And every womb was closed, and all their issues, and the hand of the Lord was upon them on account of Sarah, wife of Abraham, whom Abimelech had taken.

18. And in the morning Abimelech rose with terror and confusion and with a great dread, and he sent and had his servants called in, and he related his dream to them, and the people were greatly afraid.

19. And one man standing amongst the servants of the king answered the king, saying, O sovereign king, restore this woman to her husband, for he is her husband, for the like happened to the king of Egypt when this man came to Egypt.

20. And he said concerning his wife, She is my sister, for such is his manner of doing when he cometh to dwell in the land in which he is a stranger.

21. And Pharaoh sent and took this woman for a wife and the Lord brought upon him grievous plagues until he returned the woman to her husband.

22. Now therefore, O sovereign king, know what happened yesternight to the whole land, for there was a very great consternation and great pain and lamentation, and we know that it was on account of the woman which thou didst take.

23. Now, therefore, restore this woman to her husband, lest it should befall us as it did to Pharaoh king of Egypt and his subjects, and that we may not die; and Abimelech hastened and called and had Sarah called for, and she came before him, and he had Abraham called for, and he came before him.

24. And Abimelech said to them, What is this work you have been doing in saying you are brother and sister, and I took this woman for a wife?

25. And Abraham said, Because I thought I should suffer death on account of my wife; and Abimelech took flocks and herds, and men servants and maid servants, and a thousand pieces of silver, and he gave them to Abraham, and he returned Sarah to him.

26. And Abimelech said to Abraham, Behold the whole land is before thee, dwell in it wherever thou shalt choose.

27. And Abraham and Sarah, his wife, went forth from the king's presence with honor and respect, and they dwelt in the land, even in Gerar.

28. And all the inhabitants of the land of the Philistines and the king's servants were still in pain, through the plague which the angel had inflicted upon them the whole night on account of Sarah.

29. And Abimelech sent for Abraham, saying, Pray now for thy servants to the Lord thy God, that he may put away this mortality from amongst us.

30. And Abraham prayed on account of Abimelech and his subjects, and the Lord heard the prayer of Abraham, and he healed Abimelech and all his subjects.

CHAPTER 21

1. And it was at that time at the end of a year and four months of Abraham's dwelling in the land of the Philistines in Gerar, that God visited Sarah, and the Lord remembered her, and she conceived and bare a son to Abraham.

2. And Abraham called the name of the son which was born to him, which Sarah bare to him, Isaac.

3. And Abraham circumcised his son Isaac at eight days old, as God had commanded Abraham to do unto his seed after him; and Abraham was one hundred, and Sarah ninety years old, when Isaac was born to them.

4. And the child grew up and he was weaned, and Abraham made a great feast upon the day that Isaac was weaned.

5. And Shem and Eber and all the great people of the land, and Abimelech king of the Philistines, and his servants, and Phicol, the captain of his host, came to eat and drink and rejoice at the feast which Abraham made upon the day of his son Isaac's being weaned.

6. Also Terah, the father of Abraham, and Nahor his brother, came from Haran, they and all belonging to them, for they greatly rejoiced on hearing that a son had been born to Sarah.

7. And they came to Abraham, and they ate and drank at the feast which Abraham made upon the day of Isaac's being weaned.

8. And Terah and Nahor rejoiced with Abraham, and they remained with him many days in the land of the Philistines.

9. At that time Serug the son of Reu died, in the first year of the birth of Isaac son of Abraham.

10. And all the days of Serug were two hundred and thirty-nine years, and he died.

11. And Ishmael the son of Abraham was grown up in those days; he was fourteen years old when Sarah bare Isaac to Abraham.

12. And God was with Ishmael the son of Abraham, and he grew up, and he learned to use the bow and became an archer.

13. And when Isaac was five years old he was sitting with Ishmael at the door of the tent.

14. And Ishmael came to Isaac and seated himself opposite to him, and he took the bow and drew it and put the arrow in it, and intended to slay Isaac.

15. And Sarah saw the act which Ishmael desired to do to her son Isaac, and it grieved her exceedingly on account of her son, and she sent for Abraham, and said to him, Cast out this bondwoman and her son, for her son shall not be heir with my son, for thus did he seek to do unto him this day.

16. And Abraham hearkened to the voice of Sarah, and he rose up early in the morning, and he took twelve loaves and a bottle of water which he gave to Hagar, and sent her away with her son, and Hagar went with her son

to the wilderness, and they dwelt in the wilderness of Paran with the inhabitants of the wilderness, and Ishmael was an archer, and he dwelt in the wilderness a long time.

17. And he and his mother afterward went to the land of Egypt, and they dwelt there, and Hagar took a wife for her son from Egypt, and her name was Meribah.

18. And the wife of Ishmael conceived and bare four sons and two daughters, and Ishmael and his mother and his wife and children afterward went and returned to the wilderness.

19. And they made themselves tents in the wilderness, in which they dwelt, and they continued to travel and then to rest monthly and yearly.

20. And God gave Ishmael flocks and herds and tents on account of Abraham his father, and the man increased in cattle.

21. And Ishmael dwelt in deserts and in tents, traveling and resting for a long time, and he did not see the face of his father.

22. And in some time after, Abraham said to Sarah his wife, I will go and see my son Ishmael, for I have a desire to see him, for I have not seen him for a long time.

23. And Abraham rode upon one of his camels to the wilderness to seek his son Ishmael, for he heard that he was dwelling in a tent in the wilderness with all belonging to him.

24. And Abraham went to the wilderness, and he reached the tent of Ishmael about noon, and he asked after Ishmael, and he found the wife of Ishmael sitting in the tent with her children, and Ishmael her husband and his mother were not with them.

25. And Abraham asked the wife of Ishmael, saying, Where has Ishmael gone? and she said, He has gone to the field to hunt, and Abraham was still mounted upon the camel, for he would not get off to the ground as he had sworn to his wife Sarah that he would not get off from the camel.

26. And Abraham said to Ishmael's wife, My daughter, give me a little water that I may drink, for I am fatigued from the journey.

27. And Ishmael's wife answered and said to Abraham, We have neither water nor bread, and she continued sitting in the tent and did not notice Abraham, neither did she ask him who he was.

28. But she was beating her children in the tent, and she was cursing them, and she also cursed her husband Ishmael and reproached him, and Abraham heard the words of Ishmael's wife to her children, and he was very angry and displeased.

29. And Abraham called to the woman to come out to him from the tent, and the woman came and stood opposite to Abraham, for Abraham was still mounted upon the camel.

30. And Abraham said to Ishmael's wife, When thy husband Ishmael returneth home say these words to him,

31. A very old man from the land of the Philistines came hither to seek thee, and thus was his appearance and figure; I did not ask him who he was, and seeing thou wast not here he spoke unto me and said, When Ishmael thy husband returneth tell him thus did this man say, When thou comest home put away this nail of the tent which thou hast placed here, and place another nail in its stead.

32. And Abraham finished his instructions to the woman, and he turned and went off on the camel homeward.

33. And after that Ishmael came from the chase he and his mother, and returned to the tent, and his wife spoke these words to him,

34. A very old man from the land of the Philistines came to seek thee, and thus was his appearance and figure; I did not ask him who he was, and seeing thou wast not at home he said to me, When thy husband cometh home tell him, thus saith the old man, Put away the nail of the tent which thou hast placed here and place another nail in its stead.

35. And Ishmael heard the words of his wife, and he knew that it was his father, and that his wife did not honor him.

36. And Ishmael understood his father's words that he had spoken to his wife, and Ishmael hearkened to the voice of his father, and Ishmael cast off that woman and she went away.

37. And Ishmael afterward went to the land of Canaan, and he took another wife and he brought her to his tent to the place where he then dwelt.

38. And at the end of three years Abraham said, I will go again and see Ishmael my son, for I have not seen him for a long time.

39. And he rode upon his camel and went to the wilderness, and he reached the tent of Ishmael about noon.

40. And he asked after Ishmael, and his wife came out of the tent and she said, He is not here my lord, for he has gone to hunt in the fields, and to feed the camels, and the woman said to Abraham, Turn in my lord into the tent, and eat a morsel of bread, for thy soul must be wearied on account of the journey.

41. And Abraham said to her, I will not stop for I am in haste to continue my journey, but give me a little water to drink, for I have thirst; and the woman hastened and ran into the tent and she brought out water and bread to Abraham, which she placed before him and she urged him to eat, and he ate and drank and his heart was comforted and he blessed his son Ishmael.

42. And he finished his meal and he blessed the Lord, and he said to Ishmael's wife, When Ishmael cometh home say these words to him,

43. A very old man from the land of the Philistines came hither and asked after thee, and thou wast not here; and I brought him out bread and water and he ate and drank and his heart was comforted.

44. And he spoke these words to me: When Ishmael thy husband cometh home, say unto him, The nail of the tent which thou hast is very good, do not put it away from the tent.

45. And Abraham finished commanding the woman, and he rode off to his home to the land of the Philistines; and when Ishmael came to his tent his wife went forth to meet him with joy and a cheerful heart.

46. And she said to him, An old man came here from the land of the Philistines and thus was his appearance, and he asked after thee and thou wast not here, so I brought out bread and water, and he ate and drank and his heart was comforted.

47. And he spoke these words to me, When Ishmael thy husband cometh home say to him, The nail of the tent which thou hast is very good, do not put it away from the tent.

48. And Ishmael knew that it was his father, and that his wife had honored him, and the Lord blessed Ishmael.

CHAPTER 22

1. And Ishmael then rose up and took his wife and his children and his cattle and all belonging to him, and he journeyed from there and he went to his father in the land of the Philistines.

2. And Abraham related to Ishmael his son the transaction with the first wife that Ishmael took, according to what she did.

3. And Ishmael and his children dwelt with Abraham many days in that land, and Abraham dwelt in the land of the Philistines a long time.

4. And the days increased and reached twenty six years, and after that Abraham with his servants and all belonging to him went from the land of the Philistines and removed to a great distance, and they came near to Hebron, and they remained there, and the servants of Abraham dug wells of water, and Abraham and all belonging to him dwelt by the water, and the servants of Abimelech king of the Philistines heard the report that Abraham's servants had dug wells of water in the borders of the land.

5. And they came and quarreled with the servants of Abraham, and they robbed them of the great well which they had dug.

6. And Abimelech king of the Philistines heard of this affair, and he with Phicol the captain of his host and twenty of his men came to Abraham, and Abimelech spoke to Abraham concerning his servants, and Abraham rebuked Abimelech concerning the well of which his servants had robbed him.

7. And Abimelech said to Abraham, As the Lord liveth who created the whole earth, I did not hear of the act which my servants did unto thy servants until this day.

8. And Abraham took seven ewe lambs and gave them to Abimelech, saying, Take these, I pray thee, from my hands that it may be a testimony for me that I dug this well.

9. And Abimelech took the seven ewe lambs which Abraham had given to him, for he had also given him cattle and herds in abundance, and Abimelech swore to Abraham concerning the well, therefore he called that well Beersheba, for there they both swore concerning it.

10. And they both made a covenant in Beersheba, and Abimelech rose up with Phicol the captain of his host and all his men, and they returned to the land of the Philistines, and Abraham and all belonging to him dwelt in Beersheba and he was in that land a long time.

11. And Abraham planted a large grove in Beersheba, and he made to it four gates facing the four sides of the earth, and he planted a vineyard in it, so that if a traveler came to Abraham he entered any gate which was in his road, and remained there and ate and

drank and satisfied himself and then departed.

12. For the house of Abraham was always open to the sons of men that passed and repassed, who came daily to eat and drink in the house of Abraham.

13. And any man who had hunger and came to Abraham's house, Abraham would give him bread that he might eat and drink and be satisfied, and any one that came naked to his house he would clothe with garments as he might

choose, and give him silver and gold and make known to him the Lord who had created him in the earth; this did Abraham all his life.

14. And Abraham and his children and all belonging to him dwelt in Beersheba, and he pitched his tent as far as Hebron.

15. And Abraham's brother Nahor and his father and all belonging to them dwelt in Haran, for they did not come with Abraham to the land of Canaan.

16. And children were born to Nahor which Milca the daughter of Haran, and sister to Sarah, Abraham's wife, bare to him.

17. And these are the names of those that were born to him, Uz, Buz, Kemuel, Kesed, Chazo, Pildash, Tidlaf, and Bethuel, being eight sons, these are the children of Milca which she bare to Nahor, Abraham's brother.

18. And Nahor had a concubine and her name was Reumah, and she also bare to Nahor, Zebach, Gachash, Tachash and Maacha, being four sons.

19. And the children that were born to Nahor were twelve sons besides his daughters, and they also had children born to them in Haran.

20. And the children of Uz the first born of Nahor were Abi, Cheref, Gadin, Melus, and Deborah their sister.

21. And the sons of Buz were Berachel, Naamath, Sheva, and Madonu.

22. And the sons of Kemuel were Aram and Rechob.

23. And the sons of Kesed were Anamlech, Meshai, Benon and Yifi; and the sons of Chazo were Pildash, Mechi and Opher.

24. And the sons of Pildash were Arud, Chamum, Mered and Moloch.

25. And the sons of Tidlaf were Mushan, Cushan and Mutzi.

26. And the children of Bethuel were Sechar, Laban and their sister Rebecca.

27. These are the families of the children of Nahor, that were born to them in Haran; and Aram the son of Kemuel and Rechob his brother went away from Haran, and they found a valley in the land by the river Euphrates.

28. And they built a city there, and they called the name of the city after the name of Pethor the son of Aram, that is Aram Naherayim unto this day.

29. And the children of Kesed also went to dwell where they could find a place, and they went and they found a valley opposite to the land of Shinar, and they dwelt there.

30. And they there built themselves a city, and they called the name at the city Kesed after the name of their father, that is the land Kasdim unto this day, and the Kasdim dwelt in that land and they were fruitful and multiplied exceedingly.

31. And Terah, father of Nahor and Abraham, went and took another wife in his old age, and her name was Pelilah, and she conceived and bare him a son and he called his name Zoba.

32. And Terah lived twenty-five years after he begat Zoba.

33. And Terah died in that year, that is in the thirty-fifth year of the birth of Isaac son of Abraham.

34. And the days of Terah were two hundred and five years, and he was buried in Haran.

35. And Zoba the son of Terah lived thirty years and he begat Aram, Achlis and Merik.

36. And Aram son of Zoba son of Terah, had three wives and he begat twelve sons and three daughters; and the Lord gave to Aram the son of Zoba, riches and possessions, and abundance of cattle, and flocks and herds, and the man increased greatly.

37. And Aram the son of Zoba and his brother and all his household journeyed from Haran, and they went to dwell where they should find a place, for their property was too great to remain in Haran; for they could not stop in Haran together with their brethren the children of Nahor.

38. And Aram the son of Zoba went with his brethren, and they found a valley at a distance toward the eastern country and they dwelt there.

39. And they also built a city there, and they called the name thereof Aram, after the name of their eldest brother; that is Aram Zoba to this day.

40. And Isaac the son of Abraham was growing up in those days, and Abraham his father taught him the way of the Lord to know the Lord, and the Lord was with him.

41. And when Isaac was thirty-seven years old, Ishmael his brother was going about with him in the tent.

42. And Ishmael boasted of himself to Isaac, saying, I was thirteen years old when the Lord spoke to my father to circumcise us, and I did according to the word of the Lord which he spoke to my father, and I gave my soul unto the Lord, and I did not transgress his word which he commanded my father.

43. And Isaac answered Ishmael, saying, Why dost thou boast to me about this, about a little bit of thy flesh which thou didst take from thy body, concerning which the Lord commanded thee?

44. As the Lord liveth, the God of my father Abraham, if the Lord should say unto my father, Take now thy son Isaac and bring him up an offering before me, I would not refrain but I would joyfully accede to it.

45. And the Lord heard the word that Isaac spoke to Ishmael, and it seemed good in the sight of the Lord, and he thought to try Abraham in this matter.

46. And the day arrived when the sons of God came and placed themselves before the Lord, and Satan also came with the sons of God before the Lord.

47. And the Lord said unto Satan, Whence comest thou? and Satan answered the Lord and said, From going to and fro in the earth, and from walking up and down in it.

48. And the Lord said to Satan, What is thy word to me concerning all the children of the earth? and Satan answered the Lord and said, I have seen all the children of the earth who serve thee and remember thee when they require anything from thee.

49. And when thou givest them the thing which they require from thee, they sit at their ease, and forsake thee and they remember thee no more.

50. Hast thou seen Abraham the son of Terah, who at first had no children, and he served thee and erected altars to thee wherever he came, and he brought up offerings upon them, and he proclaimed thy name continually to all the children of the earth.

51. And now that his son Isaac is born to him, he has forsaken thee, he has made a great feast for all the inhabitants of the land, and the Lord he has forgotten.

52. For amidst all that he has done he brought thee no offering; neither burnt offering nor peace offering, neither ox, lamb nor goat of all that he killed on the day that his son was weaned.

53. Even from the time of his son's birth till now, being thirty-seven years, he built no altar before thee, nor brought any offering to thee, for he saw that thou didst give what he requested before thee, and he therefore forsook thee.

54. And the Lord said to Satan, Hast thou thus considered my servant Abraham? for there is none like him upon earth, a perfect and an upright man before me, one that feareth God and avoideth evil; as I live, were I to say unto him, Bring up Isaac thy son before me, he would not withhold him from me, much more if I told him to bring up a burnt offering before me from his flock or herds.

55. And Satan answered the Lord and said, Speak then now unto Abraham as thou hast said, and thou wilt see whether he will not this day transgress and cast aside thy words.

CHAPTER 23

1. At that time the word of the Lord came to Abraham, and he said unto him, Abraham, and he said, Here I am.

2. And he said to him, Take now thy son, thine only son whom thou lovest, even Isaac, and go to the land of Moriah, and offer him there for a burnt offering upon one of the mountains which shall be shown to thee, for there wilt thou see a cloud and the glory of the Lord.

3. And Abraham said within himself, How shall I separate my son Isaac from Sarah his mother, in order to bring him up for a burnt offering before the Lord?

4. And Abraham came into the tent, and he sat before Sarah his wife, and he spoke these words to her,

5. My son Isaac is grown up and he has not for some time studied the service of his God, now tomorrow I will go and bring him to Shem, and Eber his son, and there he will learn the ways of the Lord, for they will teach him to know the Lord as well as to know that when he prayeth continually before the Lord, he will answer him, therefore there he will know the way of serving the Lord his God.

6. And Sarah said, Thou hast spoken well, go my lord and do unto him as thou hast said, but remove him not at a great distance from me, neither let him remain there too long, for my soul is bound within his soul.

7. And Abraham said unto Sarah, My daughter, let us pray to the Lord our God that he may do good with us.

8. And Sarah took her son Isaac and he abode all that night with her, and she kissed and embraced him, and gave him instructions till morning.

9. And she said to him, O my son, how can my soul separate itself from thee? And she still kissed him and embraced him, and she gave Abraham instructions concerning him.

10. And Sarah said to Abraham, O my lord, I pray thee take heed of thy son, and place thine eyes over him, for I have no other son nor daughter but him.

11. O forsake him not. If he be hungry give him bread, and if he be thirsty give him water to drink; do not let him go on foot, neither let him sit in the sun.

12. Neither let him go by himself in the road, neither force him from whatever he may desire, but do unto him as he may say to thee.

13. And Sarah wept bitterly the whole night on account of Isaac, and she gave him instructions till morning.

14. And in the morning Sarah selected a very fine and beautiful garment from those garments which she had in the house, that Abimelech had given to her.

15. And she dressed Isaac her son therewith, and she put a turban upon his head, and she enclosed a precious stone in the top of the turban, and she gave them provision for the road, and they went forth, and Isaac went with his father Abraham, and some of their servants accompanied them to see them off the road.

16. And Sarah went out with them, and she accompanied them upon the road to see them off, and they said to her, Return to the tent.

17. And when Sarah heard the words of her son Isaac she wept bitterly, and Abraham her husband wept with her, and their son wept with them a great weeping; also those who went with them wept greatly.

18. And Sarah caught hold of her son Isaac, and she held him in her arms, and she embraced him and continued to weep with him, and Sarah said, Who knoweth if after this day I shall ever see thee again?

19. And they still wept together, Abraham, Sarah and Isaac, and all those that accompanied them on the road wept with them, and Sarah afterward turned away from her son, weeping bitterly, and all her men servants and maid servants returned with her to the tent.

20. And Abraham went with Isaac his son to bring him up as an offering before the Lord, as He had commanded him.

21. And Abraham took two of his young men with him, Ishmael the son of Hagar and Eliezer his servant, and they went together with them, and whilst they were walking in the road the young men spoke these words to themselves,

22. And Ishmael said to Eliezer, Now my father Abraham is going with Isaac to bring him up for a burnt offering to the Lord, as He commanded him.

23. Now when he returneth he will give unto me all that he possesses, to inherit after him, for I am his first born.

24. And Eliezer answered Ishmael and said, Surely Abraham did cast thee away with thy mother, and swear that thou shouldst not inherit any thing of all he possesses, and to whom will he give all that he has, with all his treasures, but unto me his servant, who has been faithful in his house, who has served him night and day, and has done all that he desired me? to me will he bequeath at his death all that he possesses.

25. And whilst Abraham was proceeding with his son Isaac along the road, Satan came and appeared to Abraham in the figure of a very aged man, humble and of contrite spirit,

and he approached Abraham and said to him, Art thou silly or brutish, that thou goest to do this thing this day to thine only son?

26. For God gave thee a son in thy latter days, in thy old age, and wilt thou go and slaughter him this day because he committed no violence, and wilt thou cause the soul of thine only son to perish from the earth?

27. Dost thou not know and understand that this thing cannot be from the Lord? for the Lord cannot do unto man such evil upon earth to say to him, Go slaughter thy child.

28. And Abraham heard this and knew that it was the word of Satan who endeavored to draw him aside from the way of the Lord, but Abraham would not hearken to the voice of Satan, and Abraham rebuked him so that he went away.

29. And Satan returned and came to Isaac; and he appeared unto Isaac in the figure of a young man comely and well favored.

30. And he approached Isaac and said unto him, Dost thou not know and understand that thy old silly father bringeth thee to the slaughter this day for naught?

31. Now therefore, my son, do not listen nor attend to him, for he is a silly old man, and let not thy precious soul and beautiful figure be lost from the earth.

32. And Isaac heard this, and said unto Abraham, Hast thou heard, my father, that which this man has spoken? even thus has he spoken.

33. And Abraham answered his son Isaac and said to him, Take heed of him and do not listen to his words, nor attend to him, for he is Satan, endeavoring to draw us aside this day from the commands of God.

34. And Abraham still rebuked Satan, and Satan went from them, and seeing he could not prevail over them he hid himself from them, and he went and passed before them in the road; and he transformed himself to a large brook of water in the road, and Abraham and Isaac and his two young men reached that place, and they saw a brook large and powerful as the mighty waters.

35. And they entered the brook and passed through it, and the waters at first reached their legs.

36. And they went deeper in the brook and the waters reached up to their necks, and they were all terrified on account of the water; and whilst they were going over the brook Abraham recognized that place, and he knew that there was no water there before.

37. And Abraham said to his son Isaac, I know this place in which there was no brook nor water, now therefore it is this Satan who does all this to us, to draw us aside this day from the commands of God.

38. And Abraham rebuked him and said unto him, The Lord rebuke thee, O Satan, begone from us for we go by the commands of God.

39. And Satan was terrified at the voice of Abraham, and he went away from them, and the place again became dry land as it was at first.

40. And Abraham went with Isaac toward the place that God had told him.

41. And on the third day Abraham lifted up his eyes and saw the place at a distance which God had told him of.

42. And a pillar of fire appeared to him that reached from the earth to heaven, and a cloud of glory upon the mountain, and the glory of the Lord was seen in the cloud.

43. And Abraham said to Isaac, My son, dost thou see in that mountain, which we perceive at a distance, that which I see upon it?

44. And Isaac answered and said unto his father, I see and lo a pillar of fire and a cloud, and the glory of the Lord is seen upon the cloud.

45. And Abraham knew that his son Isaac was accepted before the Lord for a burnt offering.

46. And Abraham said unto Eliezer and unto Ishmael his son, Do you also see that which we see upon the mountain which is at a distance?

47. And they answered and said, We see nothing more than like the other mountains of the earth. And Abraham knew that they were not accepted before the Lord to go with them, and Abraham said to them, Abide ye here with the ass whilst I and Isaac my son will go to yonder mount and worship there before the Lord and then return to you.

48. And Eliezer and Ishmael remained in that place, as Abraham had commanded.

49. And Abraham took wood for a burnt offering and placed it upon his son Isaac, and he took the fire and the knife, and they both went to that place.

50. And when they were going along Isaac said to his father, Behold, I see here the fire and wood, and where then is the lamb that is to be the burnt offering before the Lord?

51. And Abraham answered his son Isaac, saying, The Lord has made choice of thee my son, to be a perfect burnt offering instead of the lamb.

52. And Isaac said unto his father, I will do all that the Lord spoke to thee with joy and cheerfulness of heart.

53. And Abraham again said unto Isaac his son, Is there in thy heart any thought or counsel concerning this, which is not proper? tell me my son, I pray thee, O my son conceal it not from me.

54. And Isaac answered his father Abraham and said unto him, O my father, as the Lord liveth and as thy soul liveth, there is nothing in my heart to cause me to deviate either to the right or to the left from the word that he has spoken to thee.

55. Neither limb nor muscle has moved or stirred at this, nor is there in my heart any thought or evil counsel concerning this.

56. But I am of joyful and cheerful heart in this matter, and I say, Blessed is the Lord who has this day chosen me to be a burnt offering before Him.

57. And Abraham greatly rejoiced at the words of Isaac, and they went on and came together to that place that the Lord had spoken of.

58. And Abraham approached to build the altar in that place, and Abraham was weeping, and Isaac took stones and mortar until they had finished building the altar.

59. And Abraham took the wood and placed it in order upon the altar which he had built.

60. And he took his son Isaac and bound him in order to place him upon the wood which was upon the altar, to slay him for a burnt offering before the Lord.

61. And Isaac said to his father, Bind me securely and then place me upon the altar lest I should turn and move, and break loose from the force of the knife upon my flesh and thereof profane the burnt offering; and Abraham did so.

62. And Isaac still said to his father, O my father, when thou shalt have slain me and burnt me for an offering, take with thee that which shall remain of my ashes to bring to Sarah my mother, and say to her, This is the sweet smelling savor of Isaac; but do not tell her this if she should sit near a well or upon any high place, lest she should cast her soul after me and die.

63. And Abraham heard the words of Isaac, and he lifted up his voice and wept when Isaac spake these words; and Abraham's tears gushed down upon Isaac his son, and Isaac wept bitterly, and he said to his father, Hasten thou, O my father, and do with me the will of the Lord our God as He has commanded thee.

64. And the hearts of Abraham and Isaac rejoiced at this thing which the Lord had commanded them; but the eye wept bitterly whilst the heart rejoiced.

65. And Abraham bound his son Isaac, and placed him on the altar upon the wood, and Isaac stretched forth his neck upon the altar before his father, and Abraham stretched forth his hand to take the knife to slay his son as a burnt offering before the Lord.

66. At that time the angels of mercy came before the Lord and spake to him concerning Isaac, saying,

67. o Lord, thou art a merciful and compassionate King over all that thou hast created in heaven and in earth, and thou supportest them all; give therefore ransom and redemption instead of thy servant Isaac, and pity and have compassion upon Abraham and Isaac his son, who are this day performing thy commands.

68. Hast thou seen, O Lord, how Isaac the son of Abraham thy servant is bound down to the slaughter like an animal? now therefore let thy pity be roused for them, O Lord.

69. At that time the Lord appeared unto Abraham, and called to him, from heaven, and said unto him, Lay not thine hand upon the lad, neither do thou any thing unto him, for now I know that thou fearest God in performing this act, and in not withholding thy son, thine only son, from me.

70. And Abraham lifted up his eyes and saw, and behold, a ram was caught in a thicket by his horns; that was the ram which the Lord God had created in the earth in the day that he made earth and heaven.

71. For the Lord had prepared this ram from that day, to be a burnt offering instead of Isaac.

72. And this ram was advancing to Abraham when Satan caught hold of him and entangled his horns in the thicket, that he might not advance to Abraham, in order that Abraham might slay his son.

73. And Abraham, seeing the ram advancing to him and Satan withholding him, fetched him and brought him before the altar, and he loosened his son Isaac from his binding, and he put the ram in his stead, and Abraham killed the ram upon the altar, and brought it up as an offering in the place of his son Isaac.

74. And Abraham sprinkled some of the blood of the ram upon the altar, and he exclaimed and said, This is in the place of my son, and may this be considered this day as the blood of my son before the Lord.

75. And all that Abraham did on this occasion by the altar, he would exclaim and say, This is in the room of my son, and may it this day be considered before the Lord in the place of my son; and Abraham finished the whole of the service by the altar, and the service was accepted before the Lord, and was accounted as if it had been Isaac; and the Lord blessed Abraham and his seed on that day.

76. And Satan went to Sarah, and he appeared to her in the figure of an old man very humble and meek, and Abraham was yet engaged in the burnt offering before the Lord.

77. And he said unto her, Dost thou not know all the work that Abraham has made with thine only son this day? for he took Isaac and built an altar, and killed him, and brought him up as a sacrifice upon the altar, and Isaac cried and wept before his father, but he looked not at him, neither did he have compassion over him.

78. And Satan repeated these words, and he went away from her, and Sarah heard all the words of Satan, and she imagined him to be an old man from amongst the sons of men who had been with her son, and had come and told her these things.

79. And Sarah lifted up her voice and wept and cried out bitterly on account of her son; and she threw herself upon the ground and she cast dust upon her head, and she said, O my son, Isaac my son, O that I had this day died instead of thee. And she continued to weep and said, It grieves me for thee, O my son, my son Isaac, O that I had died this day in thy stead.

80. And she still continued to weep, and said, It grieves me for thee after that I have reared thee and have brought thee up; now my joy is turned into mourning over thee, I that had a longing for thee, and cried and prayed to God till I bare thee at ninety years old; and now hast thou served this day for the knife and the fire, to be made an offering.

81. But I console myself with thee, my son, in its being the word of the Lord, for thou didst perform the command of thy God; for who can transgress the word of our God, in whose hands is the soul of every living creature?

82. Thou art just, O Lord our God, for all thy works are good and righteous; for I also am rejoiced with thy word which thou didst command, and whilst mine eye weepeth bitterly my heart rejoiceth.

83. And Sarah laid her head upon the bosom of one of her handmaids, and she became as still as a stone.

84. She afterward rose up and went about making inquiries till she came to Hebron, and she inquired of all those whom she met walking in the road, and no one could tell her what had happened to her son.

85. And she came with her maid servants and men servants to Kireath-arba, which is Hebron, and she asked concerning her Son, and she remained there while she sent some of her servants to seek where Abraham had gone with Isaac; they went to seek him in the house of Shem and Eber, and they could not find him, and they sought throughout the land and he was not there.

86. And behold, Satan came to Sarah in the shape of an old man, and he came and stood before her, and he said unto her, I spoke falsely unto thee, for Abraham did not kill his son and he is not dead; and when she heard the word her joy was so exceedingly violent on account of her son, that her soul went out through joy; she died and was gathered to her people.

87. And when Abraham had finished his service he returned with his son Isaac to his young men, and they rose up and went together to Beersheba, and they came home.

88. And Abraham sought for Sarah, and could not find her, and he made inquiries concerning her, and they said unto him, She went as far as Hebron to seek you both where you had gone, for thus was she informed.

89. And Abraham and Isaac went to her to Hebron, and when they found that she was dead they lifted up their voices and wept bitterly over her; and Isaac fell upon his mother's face and wept over her, and he said, O my mother, my mother, how hast thou left me, and where hast thou gone? O how, how hast thou left me!

90. And Abraham and Isaac wept greatly and all their servants wept with them on account of Sarah, and they mourned over her a great and heavy mourning.

CHAPTER 24

1. And the life of Sarah was one hundred and twenty-seven years, and Sarah died; and Abraham rose up from before his dead to seek a burial place to bury his wife Sarah; and he went and spoke to the children of Heth, the inhabitants of the land, saying,

2. I am a stranger and a sojourner with you in your land; give me a possession of a burial place in your land, that I may bury my dead from before me.

3. And the children of Heth said unto Abraham, behold the land is before thee, in the choice of our sepulchers bury thy dead, for no man shall withhold thee from burying thy dead.

4. And Abraham said unto them, If you are agreeable to this go and entreat for me to Ephron, the son of Zochar, requesting that he may give me the cave of Machpelah, which is in the end of his field, and I will purchase it of him for whatever he desire for it.

5. And Ephron dwelt among the children of Heth, and they went and called for him, and he came before Abraham, and Ephron said unto Abraham, Behold all thou requirest thy servant will do; and Abraham said, No, but I will buy the cave and the field which thou hast for value, In order that it may be for a possession of a burial place for ever.

6. And Ephron answered and said, Behold the field and the cave are before thee, give whatever thou desirest; and Abraham said, Only at full value will I buy it from thy hand, and from the hands of those that go in at the gate of thy city, and from the hand of thy seed for ever.

7. And Ephron and all his brethren heard this, and Abraham weighed to Ephron four hundred shekels of silver in the hands of Ephron and in the hands of all his brethren; and Abraham wrote this transaction, and he wrote it and testified it with four witnesses.

8. And these are the names of the witnesses, Amigal son of Abishna the Hittite, Adichorom son of Ashunach the Hivite, Abdon son of Achiram the Gomerite, Bakdil the son of Abudish the Zidonite.

9. And Abraham took the book of the purchase, and placed it in his treasures, and these are the words that Abraham wrote in the book, namely:

10. That the cave and the field Abraham bought from Ephron the Hittite, and from his seed, and from those that go out of his city, and from their seed for ever, are to be a purchase to Abraham and to his seed and to those that go forth from his loins, for a possession of a burial place for ever; and he put a signet to it and testified it with witnesses.

11. And the field and the cave that was in it and all that place were made sure unto Abraham and unto his seed after him, from the children of Heth; behold it is before Mamre in Hebron, which is in the land of Canaan.

12. And after this Abraham buried his wife Sarah there, and that place and all its boundary became to Abraham and unto his seed for a possession of a burial place.

13. And Abraham buried Sarah with pomp as observed at the interment of kings, and she was buried in very fine and beautiful garments.

14. And at her bier was Shem, his sons Eber and Abimelech, together with Anar, Ashcol and Mamre, and all the grandees of the land followed her bier.

15. And the days of Sarah were one hundred and twenty-seven years and she died, and Abraham made a great and heavy mourning, and he performed the rites of mourning for seven days.

16. And all the inhabitants of the land comforted Abraham and Isaac his son on account of Sarah.

17. And when the days of their mourning passed by Abraham sent away his son Isaac, and he went to the house of Shem and Eber, to learn the ways of the Lord and his instructions, and Abraham remained there three years.

18. At that time Abraham rose up with all his servants, and they went and returned homeward to Beersheba, and Abraham and all his servants remained in Beersheba.

19. And at the revolution of the year Abimelech king of the Philistines died in that year; he was one hundred and ninety-three years old at his death; and Abraham went with his people to the land of the Philistines, and they comforted the whole household and all his servants, and he then turned and went home.

20. And it was after the death of Abimelech that the people of Gerar took Benmalich his son, and he was only twelve years old, and they made him lying in the place of his father.

21. And they called his name Abimelech after the name of his father, for thus was it their custom to do in Gerar, and Abimelech reigned instead of Abimelech his father, and he sat upon his throne.

22. And Lot the son of Haran also died in those days, in the thirty-ninth year of the life of Isaac, and all the days that Lot lived were one hundred and forty years and he died.

23. And these are the children of Lot, that were born to him by his daughters, the name of the first born was Moab, and the name of the second was Benami.

24. And the two sons of Lot went and took themselves wives from the land of Canaan, and they bare children to them, and the children of Moab were Ed, Mayon, Tarsus, and Kanvil, four sons, these are fathers to the children of Moab unto this day.

25. And all the families of the children of Lot went to dwell wherever they should light upon, for they were fruitful and increased abundantly.

26. And they went and built themselves cities in the land where they dwelt, and they called the names of the cities which they built after their own names.

27. And Nahor the son of Terah, brother to Abraham, died in those days in the fortieth year of the life of Isaac, and all the days of Nahor were one hundred and seventy-two years and he died and was buried in Haran.

28. And when Abraham heard that his brother was dead he grieved sadly, and he mourned over his brother many days.

29. And Abraham called for Eliezer his head servant, to give him orders concerning his house, and he came and stood before him.

30. And Abraham said to him, Behold I am old, I do not know the day of my death; for I am advanced in days; now therefore rise up, go forth and do not take a wife for my son from this place and from this land, from the daughters of the Canaanites amongst whom we dwell.

31. But go to my land and to my birthplace, and take from thence a wife for my son, and the Lord God of Heaven and earth who took me from my father's house and brought me to this place, and said unto me, To thy seed will I give this land for an inheritance for ever, he will send his angel before thee and prosper thy way, that thou mayest obtain a wife for my son from my family and from my father's house.

32. And the servant answered his master Abraham and said, Behold I go to thy birthplace and to thy father's house, and take a wife for thy son from there; but if the woman be not willing to follow me to this land, shall I take thy son back to the land of thy birthplace?

33. And Abraham said unto him, Take heed that thou bring not my son hither again, for the Lord before whom I have walked he will send his angel before thee and prosper thy way.

34. And Eliezer did as Abraham ordered him, and Eliezer swore unto Abraham his master upon this matter; and Eliezer rose up and took ten camels of the camels of his master, and ten men from his master's servants with him, and they rose up and went to Haran, the city of Abraham and Nahor, in order to fetch a wife for Isaac the son

of Abraham; and whilst they were gone Abraham sent to the house of Shem and Eber, and they brought from thence his son Isaac.

35. And Isaac came home to his father's house to Beersheba, whilst Eliezer and his men came to Haran; and they stopped in the city by the watering place, and he made his camels to kneel down by the water and they remained there.

36. And Eliezer, Abraham's servant, prayed and said, O God of Abraham my master; send me I pray thee good speed this day and show kindness unto my master, that thou shalt appoint this day a wife for my master's son from his family.

37. And the Lord hearkened to the voice of Eliezer, for the sake of his servant Abraham, and he happened to meet with the daughter of Bethuel, the son of Milcah, the wife of Nahor, brother to Abraham, and Eliezer came to her house.

38. And Eliezer related to them all his concerns, and that he was Abraham's servant, and they greatly rejoiced at him.

39. And they all blessed the Lord who brought this thing about, and they gave him Rebecca, the daughter of Bethuel, for a wife for Isaac.

40. And the young woman was of very comely appearance, she was a virgin, and Rebecca was ten years old in those days.

41. And Bethuel and Laban and his children made a feast on that night, and Eliezer and his men came and ate and drank and rejoiced there on that night.

42. And Eliezer rose up in the morning, he and the men that were with him, and he called to the whole household of Bethuel, saying, Send me away that I may go to my master; and they rose up and sent away Rebecca and her nurse Deborah, the daughter of Uz, and they gave her silver and gold, men servants and maid servants, and they blessed her.

43. And they sent Eliezer away with his men; and the servants took Rebecca, and he went and returned to his master to the land of Canaan.

44. And Isaac took Rebecca and she became his wife, and he brought her into the tent.

45. And Isaac was forty years old when he took Rebecca, the daughter of his uncle Bethuel, for a wife.

CHAPTER 25

1. And it was at that time that Abraham again took a wife in his old age, and her name was Keturah, from the land of Canaan.

2. And she bare unto him Zimran, Jokshan, Medan, Midian, Ishbak and Shuach, being six sons. And the children of Zimran were Abihen, Molich and Narim.

3. And the sons of Jokshan were Sheba and Dedan, and the sons of Medan were Amida, Joab, Gochi, Elisha and Nothach; and the sons of Midian were Ephah, Epher, Chanoch, Abida and Eldaah.

4. And the sons of Ishbak were Makiro, Beyodua and Tator.

5. And the sons of Shuach were Bildad, Mamdad, Munan and Meban; all these are the families of the children of Keturah the Canaanitish woman which she bare unto Abraham the Hebrew.

6. And Abraham sent all these away, and he gave them gifts, and they went away from his son Isaac to dwell wherever they should find a place.

7. And all these went to the mountain at the east, and they built themselves six cities in which they dwelt unto this day.

8. But the children of Sheba and Dedan, children of Jokshan, with their children, did not dwell with their brethren in their cities, and they journeyed and encamped in the countries and wildernesses unto this day.

9. And the children of Midian, son of Abraham, went to the east of the land of Cush, and they there found a large valley in the eastern country, and they remained there and built a city, and they dwelt therein, that is the land of Midian unto this day.

10. And Midian dwelt in the city which he built, he and his five sons and all belonging to him.

11. And these are the names of the sons of Midian according to their names in their cities, Ephah, Epher, Chanoch, Abida and Eldaah.

12. And the sons of Ephah were Methach, Meshar, Avi and Tzanua, and the sons of Epher were Ephron, Zur, Alirun and Medin, and the sons of Chanoch were Reuel, Rekem, Azi, Alyoshub and Alad.

13. And the sons of Abida were Chur, Melud, Kerury, Molchi; and the sons of Eldaah were Miker, and Reba, and Malchiyah and Gabol; these are the names of the Midianites according to their families; and afterward the families of Midian spread throughout the

land of Midian.

14. And these are the generations of Ishmael the son Abraham, whom Hagar, Sarah's handmaid, bare unto Abraham.

15. And Ishmael took a wife from the land of Egypt, and her name was Ribah, the same is Meribah.

16. And Ribah bare unto Ishmael Nebayoth, Kedar, Adbeel, Mibsam and their sister Bosmath.

17. And Ishmael cast away his wife Ribah, and she went from him and returned to Egypt to the house of her father, and she dwelt there, for she had been very bad in the sight of Ishmael, and in the sight of his father Abraham.

18. And Ishmael afterward took a wife from the land of Canaan, and her name was Malchuth, and she bare unto him Nishma, Dumah, Masa, Chadad, Tema, Yetur, Naphish and Kedma.

19. These are the sons of Ishmael, and these are their names, being twelve princes according to their nations; and the families of Ishmael afterward spread forth, and Ishmael took his children and all the property that he had gained, together with the souls of his household and all belonging to him, and they went to dwell where they should find a place.

20. And they went and dwelt near the wilderness of Paran, and their dwelling was from Havilah unto Shur, that is before Egypt as thou comest toward Assyria.

21. And Ishmael and his sons dwelt in the land, and they had children born to them, and they were fruitful and increased abundantly.

22. And these are the names of the sons of Nebayoth the first born of Ishmael; Mend, Send, Mayon; and the sons of Kedar were Alyon, Kezem, Chamad and Eli.

23. And the sons of Adbeel were Chamad and Jabin; and the sons of Mibsam were Obadiah, Ebedmelech and Yeush; these are the families of the children of Ribah the wife of Ishmael.

24. And the sons of Mishma the son of Ishmael were Shamua, Zecaryon and Obed; and the sons of Dumah were Kezed, Eli, Machmad and Amed.

25. And the sons of Masa were Melon, Mula and Ebidadon; and the sons of Chadad were Azur, Minzar and Ebedmelech; and the sons of Tema were Seir, Sadon and Yakol.

26. And the sons of Yetur were Merith, Yaish, Alyo, and Pachoth; and the sons of Naphish were Ebed-Tamed, Abiyasaph and Mir; and the sons of Kedma were Calip, Tachti, and Omir; these were the children of Malchuth the wife of Ishmael according to their families.

27. All these are the families of Ishmael according to their generations, and they dwelt in those lands wherein they had built themselves cities unto this day.

28. And Rebecca the daughter of Bethuel, the wife of Abraham's son Isaac, was barren in those days, she had no offspring; and Isaac dwelt with his father in the land of Canaan; and the Lord was with Isaac; and Arpachshad the son of Shem the son of Noah died in those days, in the forty-eighth year of the life of Isaac, and all the days that Arpachshad lived were four hundred and thirty-eight years, and he died.

CHAPTER 26

1. And in the fifty-ninth year of the life of Isaac the son of Abraham, Rebecca his wife was still barren in those days.

2. And Rebecca said unto Isaac, Truly I have heard, my lord, that thy mother Sarah was barren in her days until my Lord Abraham, thy father, prayed for her and she conceived by him.

3. Now therefore stand up, pray thou also to God and he will hear thy prayer and remember us through his mercies.

4. And Isaac answered his wife Rebecca, saying, Abraham has already prayed for me to God to multiply his seed, now therefore this barrenness must proceed to us from thee.

5. And Rebecca said unto him, But arise now thou also and pray, that the Lord may hear thy prayer and grant me children, and Isaac hearkened to the words of his wife, and Isaac and his wife rose up and went to the land of Moriah to pray there and to seek the Lord, and when they had reached that place Isaac stood up and prayed to the Lord on account of his wife because she was barren.

6. And Isaac said, O Lord God of heaven and earth, whose goodness and mercies fill the earth, thou who didst take my father from his father's house and from his birthplace, and didst bring him unto this land, and didst say unto him, To thy seed will I give the land, and thou didst promise him and didst declare unto him, I will multiply

thy seed as the stars of heaven and as the sand of the sea, now may thy words be verified which thou didst speak unto my father.

7. For thou art the Lord our God, our eyes are toward thee to give us seed of men, as thou didst promise us, for thou art the Lord our God and our eyes are directed toward thee only.

8. And the Lord heard the prayer of Isaac the son of Abraham, and the Lord was entreated of him and Rebecca his wife conceived.

9. And in about seven months after the children struggled together within her, and it pained her greatly that she was wearied on account of them, and she said to all the women who were then in the land, Did such a thing happen to you as it has to me? and they said unto her, No.

10. And she said unto them, Why am I alone in this amongst all the women that were upon earth? and she went to the land of Moriah to seek the Lord on account of this; and she went to Shem and Eber his son to make inquiries of them in this matter, and that they should seek the Lord in this thing respecting her.

11. And she also asked Abraham to seek and inquire of the Lord about all that had befallen her.

12. And they all inquired of the Lord concerning this matter, and they brought her word from the Lord and told her, Two children are in thy womb, and two nations shall rise from them; and one nation shall be stronger than the other, and the greater shall serve the younger.

13. And when her days to be delivered were completed, she knelt down, and behold there were twins in her womb, as the Lord had spoken to her.

14. And the first came out red all over like a hairy garment, and all the people of the land called his name Esau, saying, That this one was made complete from the womb.

15. And after that came his brother, and his hand took hold of Esau's heel, therefore they called his name Jacob.

16. And Isaac, the son of Abraham, was sixty years old when he begat them.

17. And the boys grew up to their fifteenth year, and they came amongst the society of men. Esau was a designing and deceitful man, and an expert hunter in the field, and Jacob was a man perfect and wise, dwelling in tents, feeding flocks and learning the instructions of the Lord and the commands of his father and mother.

18. And Isaac and the children of his household dwelt with his father Abraham in the land of Canaan, as God had commanded them.

19. And Ishmael the son of Abraham went with his children and all belonging to them, and they returned there to the land of Havilah, and they dwelt there.

20. And all the children of Abraham's concubines went to dwell in the land of the east, for Abraham had sent them away from his son, and had given them presents, and they went away.

21. And Abraham gave all that he had to his son Isaac, and he also gave him all his treasures.

22. And he commanded him saying, Dost thou not know and understand the Lord is God in heaven and in earth, and there is no other beside him?

23. And it was he who took me from my father's house, and from my birth place, and gave me all the delights upon earth; who delivered me from the counsel of the wicked, for in him did I trust.

24. And he brought me to this place, and he delivered me from Ur Casdim; and he said unto me, To thy seed will I give all these lands, and they shall inherit them when they keep my commandments, my statutes and my judgments that I have commanded thee, and which I shall command them.

25. Now therefore my son, hearken to my voice, and keep the commandments of the Lord thy God, which I commanded thee, do not turn from the right way either to the right or to the left, in order that it may be well with thee and thy children after thee forever.

26. And remember the wonderful works of the Lord, and his kindness that he has shown toward us, in having delivered us from the hands of our enemies, and the Lord our God caused them to fall into our hands; and now therefore keep all that I have commanded thee, and turn not away from the commandments of thy God, and serve none beside him, in order that it may be well with thee and thy seed after thee.

27. And teach thou thy children and thy seed the instructions of the Lord and his commandments, and teach them the upright way in which they should go, in order that it may be well with them forever.

28. And Isaac answered his father and said unto him, That which my Lord has commanded that will I do, and I will not depart from the commands of the Lord my God, I will keep all that he commanded me; and Abraham blessed his son Isaac, and also his children; and Abraham taught Jacob the instruction of the Lord and his ways.

29. And it was at that time that Abraham died, in the fifteenth year of the life of Jacob and Esau, the sons of Isaac, and all the days of Abraham were one hundred and seventy-five years, and he died and was gathered to his people in good old age, old and satisfied with days, and Isaac and Ishmael his sons buried him.

30. And when the inhabitants of Canaan heard that Abraham was dead, they all came with their kings and princes and all their men to bury Abraham.

31. And all the inhabitants of the land of Haran, and all the families of the house of Abraham, and all the princes and grandees, and the sons of Abraham by the concubines, all came when they heard of Abraham's death, and they requited Abraham's kindness, and comforted Isaac his son, and they buried Abraham in the cave which he bought from Ephron the Hittite and his children, for the possession of a burial place.

32. And all the inhabitants of Canaan, and all those who had known Abraham, wept for Abraham a whole year, and men and women mourned over him.

33. And all the little children, and all the inhabitants of the land wept on account of Abraham, for Abraham had been good to them all, and because he had been upright with God and men.

34. And there arose not a man who feared God like unto Abraham, for he had feared his God from his youth, and had served the Lord, and had gone in all his ways during his life, from his childhood to the day of his death.

35. And the Lord was with him and delivered him from the counsel of Nimrod and his people, and when he made war with the four kings of Elam he conquered them.

36. And he brought all the children of the earth to the service of God, and he taught them the ways of the Lord, and caused them to know the Lord.

37. And he formed a grove and he planted a vineyard therein, and he had always prepared in his tent meat and drink to those that passed through the land, that they might satisfy themselves in his house.

38. And the Lord God delivered the whole earth on account of Abraham.

39. And it was after the death of Abraham that God blessed his son Isaac and his children, and the Lord was with Isaac as he had been with his father Abraham, for Isaac kept all the commandments of the Lord as Abraham his father had commanded him; he did not turn to the right or to the left from the right path which his father had commanded him.

CHAPTER 27

1. And Esau at that time, after the death of Abraham, frequently went in the field to hunt.

2. And Nimrod king of Babel, the same was Amraphel, also frequently went with his mighty men to hunt in the field, and to walk about with his men in the cool of the day.

3. And Nimrod was observing Esau all the days, for a jealousy was formed in the heart of Nimrod against Esau all the days.

4. And on a certain day Esau went in the field to hunt, and he found Nimrod walking in the wilderness with his two men.

5. And all his mighty men and his people were with him in the wilderness, but they removed at a distance from him, and they went from him in different directions to hunt, and Esau concealed himself for Nimrod, and he lurked for him in the wilderness.

6. And Nimrod and his men that were with him did not know him, and Nimrod and his men frequently walked about in the field at the cool of the day, and to know where his men were hunting in the field.

7. And Nimrod and two of his men that were with him came to the place where they were, when Esau started suddenly from his lurking place, and drew his sword, and hastened and ran to Nimrod and cut off his head.

8. And Esau fought a desperate fight with the two men that were with Nimrod, and when they called out to him, Esau turned to them and smote them to death with his sword.

9. And all the mighty men of Nimrod, who had left him to go to the wilderness, heard the cry at a distance, and they knew the voices of those two men, and they ran to know the cause of it, when they found their king and the two men that were with him lying dead in the wilderness.

10. And when Esau saw the mighty men of Nimrod coming at a distance, he fled, and thereby escaped; and Esau took the valuable garments of Nimrod, which Nimrod's father had bequeathed to Nimrod, and with which Nimrod prevailed over the whole land, and he ran and concealed them in his house.

11. And Esau took those garments and ran into the city on account of Nimrod's men, and he came unto his father's house wearied and exhausted from fight, and he was ready to die through grief when he approached his brother Jacob and sat before him.

12. And he said unto his brother Jacob, Behold I shall die this day, and wherefore then do I want the birthright? And Jacob acted wisely with Esau in this matter, and Esau sold his birthright to Jacob, for it was so brought about by the Lord.

13. And Esau's portion in the cave of the field of Machpelah, which Abraham had bought from the children of Heth for the possession of a burial ground, Esau also sold to Jacob, and Jacob bought all this from his brother Esau for value given.

14. And Jacob wrote the whole of this in a book, and he testified the same with witnesses, and he sealed it, and the book remained in the hands of Jacob.

15. And when Nimrod the son of Cush died, his men lifted him up and brought him in consternation, and buried him in his city, and all the days that Nimrod lived were two hundred and fifteen years and he died.

16. And the days that Nimrod reigned upon the people of the land were one hundred and eighty-five years; and Nimrod died by the sword of Esau in shame and contempt, and the seed of Abraham caused his death as he had seen in his dream.

17. And at the death of Nimrod his kingdom became divided into many divisions, and all those parts that Nimrod reigned over were restored to the respective kings of the land, who recovered them after the death of Nimrod, and all the people of the house of Nimrod were for a long time enslaved to all the other kings of the land.

CHAPTER 28

1. And in those days, after the death of Abraham, in that year the Lord brought a heavy famine in the land, and whilst the famine was raging in the land of Canaan, Isaac rose up to go down to Egypt on account of the famine, as his father Abraham had done.

2. And the Lord appeared that night to Isaac and he said to him, Do not go down to Egypt but rise and go to Gerar, to Abimelech king of the Philistines, and remain there till the famine shall cease.

3. And Isaac rose up and went to Gerar, as the Lord commanded him, and he remained there a full year.

4. And when Isaac came to Gerar, the people of the land saw that Rebecca his wife was of a beautiful appearance, and the people of Gerar asked Isaac concerning his wife, and he said, She is my sister, for he was afraid to say she was his wife lest the people of the land should slay him on account of her.

5. And the princes of Abimelech went and praised the woman to the king, but he answered them not, neither did he attend to their words.

6. But he heard them say that Isaac declared her to be his sister, so the king reserved this within himself.

7. And when Isaac had remained three months in the land, Abimelech looked out at the window, and he saw, and behold Isaac was sporting with Rebecca his wife, for Isaac dwelt in the outer house belonging to the king, so that the house of Isaac was opposite the house of the king.

8. And the king said unto Isaac, What is this thou hast done to us in saying of thy wife, She is my sister? how easily might one of the great men of the people have lain with her, and thou wouldst then have brought guilt upon us.

9. And Isaac said unto Abimelech, Because I was afraid lest I die on account of my wife, therefore I said, She is my sister.

10. At that time Abimelech gave orders to all his princes and great men, and they took Isaac and Rebecca his wife and brought them before the king.

11. And the king commanded that they should dress them in princely garments, and make them ride through the streets of the city, and proclaim before them throughout the land, saying, This is the man and this is his wife; whoever toucheth this man or his wife shall surely die. And Isaac returned with his wife to the king's house, and the Lord was with Isaac and he continued to wax great and lacked nothing.

12. And the Lord caused Isaac to find favor in the sight of Abimelech, and in the sight of all his subjects, and Abimelech acted well with Isaac, for Abimelech remembered the oath and the covenant that existed between his father and Abraham.

13. And Abimelech said unto Isaac, Behold the whole earth is before thee; dwell wherever it may seem good in thy sight until thou shalt return to thy land; and Abimelech gave Isaac fields and vineyards and the best part of the land of Gerar, to sow and reap and eat the fruits of the ground until the days of the famine should have passed by.

14. And Isaac sowed in that land, and received a hundred-fold in the same year, and the Lord blessed him.

15. And the man waxed great, and he had possession of flocks and possession of herds and great store of servants.

16. And when the days of the famine had passed away the Lord appeared to Isaac and said unto him, Rise up, go forth from this place and return to thy land, to the land of Canaan; and Isaac rose up and returned to Hebron which is in the land of Canaan, he and all belonging to him as the Lord commanded him.

17. And after this Shelach the son at Arpachshad died in that year, which is the eighteenth year of the lives of Jacob and Esau; and all the days that Shelach lived were four hundred and thirty-three years and he died.

18. At that time Isaac sent his younger son Jacob to the house of Shem and Eber, and he learned the instructions of the Lord, and Jacob remained in the house of Shem and Eber for thirty-two years, and Esau his brother did not go, for he was not willing to go, and he remained in his father's house in the land of Canaan.

19. And Esau was continually hunting in the fields to bring home what he could get, so did Esau all the days.

20. And Esau was a designing and deceitful man, one who hunted after the hearts of men and inveigled them, and Esau was a valiant man in the field, and in the course of time went as usual to hunt; and he came as far as the field of Seir, the same is Edom.

21. And he remained in the land of Seir hunting in the field a year and four months.

22. And Esau there saw in the land of Seir the daughter of a man of Canaan, and her name was Jehudith, the daughter of Beeri, son of Epher, from the families of Heth the son of Canaan.

23. And Esau took her for a wife, and he came unto her; forty years old was Esau when he took her, and he brought her to Hebron, the land of his father's dwelling place, and he dwelt there.

24. And it came to pass in those days, in the hundred and tenth year of the life of Isaac, that is in the fiftieth year of the life of Jacob, in that year died Shem the son of Noah; Shem was six hundred years old at his death.

25. And when Shem died Jacob returned to his father to Hebron which is in the land of Canaan.

26. And in the fifty-sixth year of the life of Jacob, people came from Haran, and Rebecca was told concerning her brother Laban the son of Bethuel.

27. For the wife of Laban was barren in those days, and bare no children, and also all his handmaids bare none to him.

28. And the Lord afterward remembered Adinah the wife of Laban, and she conceived and bare twin daughters, and Laban called the names of his daughters, the name of the elder Leah, and the name of the younger Rachel.

29. And those people came and told these things to Rebecca, and Rebecca rejoiced greatly that the Lord had visited her brother and that he had got children.

CHAPTER 29

1. And Isaac the son of Abraham became old and advanced in days, and his eyes became heavy through age; they were dim and could not see.

2. At that time Isaac called unto Esau his son, saying, Get I pray thee thy weapons, thy quiver and thy bow, rise up and go forth into the field and get me some venison, and make me savory meat and bring it to me, that I may eat in order that I may bless thee before my death, as I have now become old and gray-headed.

3. And Esau did so; and he took his weapon and went forth into the field to hunt for venison, as usual, to bring to his father as he had ordered him, so that he might bless him.

4. And Rebecca heard all the words that Isaac had spoken unto Esau, and she hastened and called her son Jacob, saying, Thus did thy father speak unto thy brother Esau, and thus did I hear, now therefore hasten thou and make that which I shall tell thee.

5. Rise up and go, I pray thee, to the flock and fetch me two fine kids of the goats, and I will get the savory meat for thy father, and thou shalt bring the savory meat that he may eat before thy brother shall have come from the chase, in order that thy father may bless thee.

6. And Jacob hastened and did as his mother had commanded him, and he made the savory meat and brought it before his father before Esau had come from his chase.

7. And Isaac said unto Jacob, Who art thou, my son? And he said, I am thy first born Esau, I have done as thou didst order me, now therefore rise up I pray thee, and eat of my hunt, in order that thy soul may bless me as thou didst speak unto me.

8. And Isaac rose up and he ate and he drank, and his heart was comforted, and he blessed Jacob and Jacob went away from his father; and as soon as Isaac had blessed Jacob and he had gone away from him, behold Esau came from his hunt from the field, and he also made savory meat and brought it to his father to eat thereof and to bless him.

9. And Isaac said unto Esau, And who was he that has taken venison and brought it me before thou camest and whom I did bless? And Esau knew that his brother Jacob had done this, and the anger of Esau was kindled against his brother Jacob that he had acted thus toward him.

10. And Esau said, Is he not rightly called Jacob? for he has supplanted me twice, he took away my birthright and now he has taken away my blessing; and Esau wept greatly; and when Isaac heard the voice of his son Esau weeping, Isaac said unto Esau, What can I do, my son, thy brother came with subtlety and took away thy blessing; and Esau hated his brother Jacob on account of the blessing that his father had given him, and his anger was greatly roused against him.

11. And Jacob was very much afraid of his brother Esau, and he rose up and fled to the house of Eber the son of Shem, and he concealed himself there on account of his brother, and Jacob was sixty-three years old when he went forth from the land of Canaan from Hebron, and Jacob was concealed in Eber's house fourteen years on account of his brother Esau, and he there continued to learn the ways of the Lord and his commandments.

12. And when Esau saw that Jacob had fled and escaped from him, and that Jacob had cunningly obtained the blessing, then Esau grieved exceedingly, and he was also vexed at his father and mother; and he also rose up and took his wife and went away from his father and mother to the land of Seir, and he dwelt there; and Esau saw there a woman from amongst the daughters of Heth whose name was Bosmath, the daughter of Elon the Hittite, and he took her for a wife in addition to his first wife, and Esau called her name Adah, saying the blessing had in that time passed from him.

13. And Esau dwelt in the land of Seir six months without seeing his father and mother, and afterward Esau took his wives and rose up and returned to the land of Canaan, and Esau placed his two wives in his father's house in Hebron.

14. And the wives of Esau vexed and provoked Isaac and Rebecca with their works, for they walked not in the ways of the Lord, but served their father's gods of wood and stone as their father had taught them, and they were more wicked than their father.

15. And they went according to the evil desires of their hearts, and they sacrificed and burnt incense to the Baalim, and Isaac and Rebecca became weary of them.

16. And Rebecca said, I am weary of my life because of the daughters of Heth; if Jacob take a wife of the daughters of Heth, such as these which are of the daughters of the land, what good then is life unto me?

17. And in those days Adah the wife of Esau conceived and bare him a son, and Esau called the name of the son that was born unto him Eliphaz, and Esau was sixty-five years old when she bare him.

18. And Ishmael the son of Abraham died in those days, in the sixty-forth year of the life of Jacob, and all the days that Ishmael lived were one hundred and thirty-seven years and he died.

19. And when Isaac heard that Ishmael was dead he mourned for him, and Isaac lamented over him many days.

20. And at the end of fourteen years of Jacob's residing in the house of Eber, Jacob desired to see his father and mother, and Jacob came to the house of his father and mother to Hebron, and Esau had in those days forgotten what Jacob had done to him in having taken the blessing from him in those days.

21. And when Esau saw Jacob coming to his father and mother he remembered what Jacob had done to him, and he was greatly incensed against him and he sought to slay him.

22. And Isaac the son of Abraham was old and advanced in days, and Esau said, Now my father's time is drawing nigh that he must die, and when he shall die I will slay my brother Jacob.

23. And this was told to Rebecca, and she hastened and sent and called for Jacob her son, and she said unto him, Arise, go and flee to Haran to my brother Laban, and remain there for some time, until thy brother's anger be turned from thee and then shalt thou come back.

24. And Isaac called unto Jacob and said unto him, Take not a wife from the daughters of Canaan, for thus did our father Abraham command us according to the word of the Lord which he had commanded him, saying, Unto thy seed will I give this land; if thy children keep my covenant that I have made with thee, then will I also perform to thy children that which I have spoken unto thee and I will not forsake them.

25. Now therefore my son hearken to my voice, to all that I shall command thee, and refrain from taking a wife from amongst the daughters of Canaan; arise, go to Haran to the house of Bethuel thy mother's father, and take unto thee a wife from there from the daughters of Laban thy mother's brother.

26. Therefore take heed lest thou shouldst forget the Lord thy God and all his ways in the land to which thou goest, and shouldst get connected with the people of the land and pursue vanity and forsake the Lord thy God.

27. But when thou comest to the land serve there the Lord, do not turn to the right or to the left from the way which I commanded thee and which thou didst learn.

28. And may the Almighty God grant thee favor in the sight of the people of the earth, that thou mayest take there a wife according to thy choice; one who is good and upright in the ways of the Lord.

29. And may God give unto thee and thy seed the blessing of thy father Abraham, and make thee fruitful and multiply thee, and mayest thou become a multitude of people in the land whither thou goest, and may God cause

thee to return to this land, the land of thy father's dwelling, with children and with great riches, with joy and with pleasure.

30. And Isaac finished commanding Jacob and blessing him, and he gave him many gifts, together with silver and gold, and he sent him away; and Jacob hearkened to his father and mother; he kissed them and arose and went to Padan-aram; and Jacob was seventyseven years old when he went out from the land of Canaan from Beersheba.

31. And when Jacob went away to go to Haran Esau called unto his son Eliphaz, and secretly spoke unto him, saying, Now hasten, take thy sword in thy hand and pursue Jacob and pass before him in the road, and lurk for him, and slay him with thy sword in

one of the mountains, and take all belonging to him and come back.

32. And Eliphaz the son of Esau was an active man and expert with the bow as his father had taught him, and he was a noted hunter in the field and a valiant man.

33. And Eliphaz did as his father had commanded him, and Eliphaz was at that time thirteen years old, and Eliphaz rose up and went and took ten of his mother's brothers with him and pursued Jacob.

34. And he closely followed Jacob, and he lurked for him in the border of the land of Canaan opposite to the city of Shechem.

35. And Jacob saw Eliphaz and his men pursuing him, and Jacob stood still in the place in which he was going, in order to know what this was, for he did not know the thing; and Eliphaz drew his sword and he went on advancing, he and his men, toward Jacob; and Jacob said unto them, What is to do with you that you have come hither, and what meaneth it that you pursue with your swords.

36. And Eliphaz came near to Jacob and he answered and said unto him, Thus did my father command me, and now therefore I will not deviate from the orders which my father gave me; and when Jacob saw that Esau had spoken to Eliphaz to employ force, Jacob then approached and supplicated Eliphaz and his men, saying to him,

37. Behold all that I have and which my father and mother gave unto me, that take unto thee and go from me, and do not slay me, and may this thing be accounted unto thee a righteousness.

38. And the Lord caused Jacob to find favor in the sight of Eliphaz the son of Esau, and his men, and they hearkened to the voice of Jacob, and they did not put him to death, and Eliphaz and his men took all belonging to Jacob together with the silver and gold that he had brought with him from Beersheba; they left him nothing.

39. And Eliphaz and his men went away from him and they returned to Esau to Beersheba, and they told him all that had occurred to them with Jacob, and they gave him all that they had taken from Jacob.

40. And Esau was indignant at Eliphaz his son, and at his men that were with him, because they had not put Jacob to death.

41. And they answered and said unto Esau, Because Jacob supplicated us in this matter not to slay him, our pity was excited toward him, and we took all belonging to him and brought it unto thee; and Esau took all the silver and gold which Eliphaz had taken from Jacob and he put them by in his house.

42. At that time when Esau saw that Isaac had blessed Jacob, and had commanded him, saying, Thou shalt not take a wife from amongst the daughters of Canaan, and that the daughters of Canaan were bad in the sight of Isaac and Rebecca,

43. Then he went to the house of Ishmael his uncle, and in addition to his older wives he took Machlath the daughter of Ishmael, the sister of Nebayoth, for a wife.

CHAPTER 30

1. And Jacob went forth continuing his road to Haran, and he came as far as mount Moriah, and he tarried there all night near the city of Luz; and the Lord appeared there unto Jacob on that night, and he said unto him, I am the Lord God of Abraham and the God of Isaac thy father; the land upon which thou liest I will give unto thee and thy seed.

2. And behold I am with thee and will keep thee wherever thou goest, and I will multiply thy seed as the stars of Heaven, and I will cause all thine enemies to fall before thee; and when they shall make war with thee they shall not prevail over thee, and I will bring thee again unto this land with joy, with children, and with great riches.

3. And Jacob awoke from his sleep and he rejoiced greatly at the vision which he had seen; and he called the name of that place Bethel.

4. And Jacob rose up from that place quite rejoiced, and when he walked his feet felt light to him for joy, and he went from there to the land of the children of the East, and he returned to Haran and he set by the shepherd's well.

5. And he there found some men; going from Haran to feed their flocks, and Jacob made inquiries of them, and they said, We are from Haran.

6.   And he said unto them, Do you know Laban, the son of Nahor? and they said, We know him, and behold his daughter Rachel is coming along to feed her father's flock.

7.   Whilst he was yet speaking with them, Rachel the daughter of Laban came to feed her father's sheep, for she was a shepherdess.

8.   And when Jacob saw Rachel, the daughter of Laban, his mother's brother, he ran and kissed her, and lifted up his voice and wept.

9.   And Jacob told Rachel that he was the son of Rebecca, her father's sister, and Rachel ran and told her father, and Jacob continued to cry because he had nothing with him to bring to the house of Laban.

10. And when Laban heard that his sister's son Jacob had come, he ran and kissed him and embraced him and brought him into the house and gave him bread, and he ate.

11. And Jacob related to Laban what his brother Esau had done to him, and what his son Eliphaz had done to him in the road.

12. And Jacob resided in Laban's house for one month, and Jacob ate and drank in the house of Laban, and afterward Laban said unto Jacob, Tell me what shall be thy wages, for how canst thou serve me for nought?

13. And Laban had no sons but only daughters, and his other wives and handmaids were still barren in those days; and these are the names of Laban's daughters which his wife Adinah had borne unto him; the name of the elder was Leah and the name of the younger was Rachel; and Leah was tender-eyed, but Rachel was beautiful and well favored, and Jacob loved her.

14. And Jacob said unto Laban, I will serve thee seven years for Rachel thy younger daughter; and Laban consented to this and Jacob served Laban seven years for his daughter Rachel.

15. And in the second year of Jacob's dwelling in Haran, that is in the seventy ninth year of the life of Jacob, in that year died Eber the son of Shem, he was four hundred and sixtyfour years old at his death.

16. And when Jacob heard that Eber was dead he grieved exceedingly, and he lamented and mourned over him many days.

17. And in the third year of Jacob's dwelling in Haran, Bosmath, the daughter of Ishmael, the wife of Esau, bare unto him a son, and Esau called his name Reuel.

18. And in the fourth year of Jacob's residence in the house of Laban, the Lord visited Laban and remembered him on account of Jacob, and sons were born unto him, and his first born was Beor, his second was Alib, and the third was Chorash.

19. And the Lord gave Laban riches and honor, sons and daughters, and the man increased greatly on account of Jacob.

20. And Jacob in those days served Laban in all manner of work, in the house and in the field, and the blessing of the Lord was in all that belonged to Laban in the house and in the field.

21. And in the fifth year died Jehudith, the daughter of Beeri, the wife of Esau, in the land of Canaan, and she had no sons but daughters only.

22. And these are the names of her daughters which she bare to Esau, the name of the elder was Marzith, and the name of the younger was Puith.

23. And when Jehudith died, Esau rose up and went to Seir to hunt in the field, as usual, and Esau dwelt in the land of Seir for a long time.

24. And in the sixth year Esau took for a wife, in addition to his other wives, Ahlibamah, the daughter of Zebeon the Hivite, and Esau brought her to the land of Canaan.

25. And Ahlibamah conceived and bare unto Esau three sons, Yeush, Yaalan, and Korah.

26. And in those days, in the land of Canaan, there was a quarrel between the herdsmen of Esau and the herdsmen of the inhabitants of the land of Canaan, for Esau's cattle and goods were too abundant for him to remain in the land of Canaan, in his father's house, and the land of Canaan could not bear him on account of his cattle.

27. And when Esau saw that his quarreling increased with the inhabitants of the land of Canaan, he rose up and took his wives and his sons and his daughters, and all belonging to him, and the cattle which he possessed, and all his property that he had acquired in the land of Canaan, and he went away from the inhabitants of the land to the land of Seir, and Esau and all belonging to him dwelt in the land of Seir.

28. But from time to time Esau would go and see his father and mother in the land of Canaan, and Esau intermarried with the Horites, and he gave his daughters to the sons of Seir, the Horite.

29. And he gave his elder daughter Marzith to Anah, the son of Zebeon, his wife's brother, and Puith he gave to Azar, the son of Bilhan the Horite; and Esau dwelt in the mountain, he and his children, and they were fruitful and multiplied.

CHAPTER 31

1. And in the seventh year, Jacob's service which he served Laban was completed, and
Jacob said unto Laban, Give me my wife, for the days of my service are fulfilled; and Laban did so, and Laban and Jacob assembled all the people of that place and they made a feast.

2. And in the evening Laban came to the house, and afterward Jacob came there with the people of the feast, and Laban extinguished all the lights that were there in the house.

3. And Jacob said unto Laban, Wherefore dost thou do this thing unto us? and Laban answered, Such is our custom to act in this land.

4. And afterward Laban took his daughter Leah, and he brought her to Jacob, and he came to her and Jacob did not know that she was Leah.

5. And Laban gave his daughter Leah his maid Zilpah for a handmaid.

6. And all the people at the feast knew what Laban had done to Jacob, but they did not tell the thing to Jacob.

7. And all the neighbors came that night to Jacob's house, and they ate and drank and rejoiced, and played before Leah upon timbrels, and with dances, and they responded before Jacob, Heleah, Heleah.

8. And Jacob heard their words but did not understand their meaning, but he thought such might be their custom in this land.

9. And the neighbors spoke these words before Jacob during the night, and all the lights that were in the house Laban had that night extinguished.

10. And in the morning, when daylight appeared, Jacob turned to his wife and he saw, and behold it was Leah that had been lying in his bosom, and Jacob said, Behold now I know what the neighbors said last night, Heleah, they said, and I knew it not.

11. And Jacob called unto Laban, and said unto him, What is this that thou didst unto me?
Surely I served thee for Rachel, and why didst thou deceive me and didst give me Leah?

12. And Laban answered Jacob, saying, Not so is it done in our place to give the younger before the elder now therefore if thou desirest to take her sister likewise, take her unto thee for the service which thou wilt serve me for another seven years.

13. And Jacob did so, and he also took Rachel for a wife, and he served Laban seven years more, and Jacob also came to Rachel, and he loved Rachel more than Leah, and Laban gave her his maid Bilhah for a handmaid.

14. And when the Lord saw that Leah was hated, the Lord opened her womb, and she conceived and bare Jacob four sons in those days.

15. And these are their names, Reuben Simeon, Levi, and Judah, and she afterward left bearing.

16. And at that time Rachel was barren, and she had no offspring, and Rachel envied her sister Leah, and when Rachel saw that she bare no children to Jacob, she took her handmaid Bilhah, and she bare Jacob two sons, Dan and Naphtali.

17. And when Leah saw that she had left bearing, she also took her handmaid Zilpah, and she gave her to Jacob for a wife, and Jacob also came to Zilpah, and she also bare Jacob two sons, Gad and Asher.

18. And Leah again conceived and bare Jacob in those days two sons and one daughter, and these are their names, Issachar, Zebulon, and their sister Dinah.

19. And Rachel was still barren in those days, and Rachel prayed unto the Lord at that time, and she said, O Lord God remember me and visit me, I beseech thee, for now my husband will cast me off, for I have borne him no children.

20. Now O Lord God, hear my supplication before thee, and see my affliction, and give me children like one of the handmaids, that I may no more bear my reproach.

21. And God heard her and opened her womb, and Rachel conceived and bare a son, and she said, The Lord has taken away my reproach, and she called his name Joseph, saying, May the Lord add to me another son; and Jacob was ninety-one years old when she bare him.

22. At that time Jacob's mother, Rebecca, sent her nurse Deborah the daughter of Uz, and two of Isaac's servants unto Jacob.

23. And they came to Jacob to Haran and they said unto him, Rebecca has sent us to thee that thou shalt return to thy father's house to the land of Canaan; and Jacob hearkened unto them in this which his mother had spoken.

24. At that time, the other seven years which Jacob served Laban for Rachel were completed, and it was at the end of fourteen years that he had dwelt in Haran that Jacob said unto Laban, give me my wives and send me away, that I may go to my land, for behold my mother did send unto me from the land at Canaan that I should return to my father's house.

25. And Laban said unto him, Not so I pray thee; if I have found favor in thy sight do not leave me; appoint me thy wages and I will give them, and remain with me.

26. And Jacob said unto him, This is what thou shalt give me for wages, that I shall this day pass through all thy flock and take away from them every lamb that is speckled and spotted and such as are brown amongst the sheep, and amongst the goats, and if thou wilt do this thing for me I will return and feed thy flock and keep them as at first.

27. And Laban did so, and Laban removed from his flock all that Jacob had said and gave them to him.

28. And Jacob placed all that he had removed from Laban's flock in the hands of his sons, and Jacob was feeding the remainder of Laban's flock.

29. And when the servants of Isaac which he had sent unto Jacob saw that Jacob would not then return with them to the land of Canaan to his father, they then went away from him, and they returned home to the land of Canaan.

30. And Deborah remained with Jacob in Haran, and she did not return with the servants of Isaac to the land of Canaan, and Deborah resided with Jacob's wives and children in Haran.

31. And Jacob served Laban six years longer, and when the sheep brought forth, Jacob removed from them such as were speckled and spotted, as he had determined with Laban, and Jacob did so at Laban's for six years, and the man increased abundantly and he had cattle and maid servants and men servants, camels, and asses.

32. And Jacob had two hundred drove of cattle, and his cattle were of large size and of beautiful appearance and were very productive, and all the families of the sons of men desired to get some of the cattle of Jacob, for they were exceedingly prosperous.

33. And many of the sons of men came to procure some of Jacob's flock, and Jacob gave them a sheep for a man servant or a maid servant or for an ass or a camel, or whatever Jacob desired from them they gave him.

34. And Jacob obtained riches and honor and possessions by means of these transactions with the sons of men, and the children of Laban envied him of this honor.

35. And in the course of time he heard the words of Laban's sons, saying, Jacob has taken away all that was our father's, and of that which was our father's has he acquired all this glory.

36. And Jacob beheld the countenance of Laban and of his children, and behold it was not toward him in those days as it had been before.

37. And the Lord appeared to Jacob at the expiration of the six years, and said unto him, Arise, go forth out of this land, and return to the land of thy birthplace and I will be with thee.

38. And Jacob rose up at that time and he mounted his children and wives and all belonging to him upon camels, and he went forth to go to the land of Canaan to his father Isaac.

39. And Laban did not know that Jacob had gone from him, for Laban had been that day sheep-shearing.

40. And Rachel stole her father's images, and she took them and she concealed them upon the camel upon which she sat, and she went on.

41. And this is the manner of the images; in taking a man who is the first born and slaying him and taking the hair off his head, and taking salt and salting the head and anointing it in oil, then taking a small tablet of copper or a tablet of gold and writing the name upon it, and placing the tablet under his tongue, and taking the head with the tablet under the tongue and putting it in the house, and lighting up lights before it and bowing down to it.

42. And at the time when they bow down to it, it speaketh to them in all matters that they ask of it, through the power of the name which is written in it.

43. And some make them in the figures of men, of gold and silver, and go to them in times known to them, and the figures receive the influence of the stars, and tell them future things, and in this manner were the images which Rachel stole from her father.

44. And Rachel stole these images which were her father's, in order that Laban might not know through them where Jacob had gone.

45. And Laban came home and he asked concerning Jacob and his household, and he was not to be found, and Laban sought his images to know where Jacob had gone, and could not find them, and he went to some other images, and he inquired of them and they told him that Jacob had fled from him to his father's, to the land of Canaan.

46. And Laban then rose up and he took his brothers and all his servants, and he went forth and pursued Jacob, and he overtook him in mount Gilead.

47. And Laban said unto Jacob, What is this thou hast done to me to flee and deceive me, and lead my daughters and their children as captives taken by the sword?

48. And thou didst not suffer me to kiss them and send them away with joy, and thou didst steal my gods and didst go away.

49. And Jacob answered Laban, saying, Because I was afraid lest thou wouldst take thy daughters by force from me; and now with whomsoever thou findest thy gods he shall die.

50. And Laban searched for the images and he examined in all Jacob's tents and furniture, but could not find them.

51. And Laban said unto Jacob, We will make a covenant together and it shall be a testimony between me and thee; if thou shalt afflict my daughters, or shalt take other wives besides my daughters, even God shall be a witness between me and thee in this matter.

52. And they took stones and made a heap, and Laban said, This heap is a witness between me and thee, therefore he called the name thereof Gilead.

53. And Jacob and Laban offered sacrifice upon the mount, and they ate there by the heap, and they tarried in the mount all night, and Laban rose up early in the morning, and he wept with his daughters and he kissed them, and he returned unto his place.

54. And he hastened and sent off his son Beor, who was seventeen years old, with Abichorof the son of Uz, the son of Nahor, and with them were ten men.

55. And they hastened and went and passed on the road before Jacob, and they came by another road to the land of Seir.

56. And they came unto Esau and said unto him, Thus saith thy brother and relative, thy mother's brother Laban, the son of Bethuel, saying,

57. Hast thou heard what Jacob thy brother has done unto me, who first came to me naked and bare, and I went to meet him, and brought him to my house with honor, and I made him great, and I gave him my two daughters for wives and also two of my maids.

58. And God blessed him on my account, and he increased abundantly, and had sons, daughters and maid servants.

59. He has also an immense stock of flocks and herds, camels and asses, also silver and gold in abundance; and when he saw that his wealth increased, he left me whilst I went to shear my sheep, and he rose up and fled in secrecy.

60. And he lifted his wives and children upon camels, and he led away all his cattle and property which he acquired in my land, and he lifted up his countenance to go to his father Isaac, to the land of Canaan.

61. And he did not suffer me to kiss my daughters and their children, and he led my daughters as captives taken by the sword, and he also stole my gods and he fled.

62. And now I have left him in the mountain of the brook of Jabuk, him and all belonging to him; he lacketh nothing.

63. If it be thy wish to go to him, go then and there wilt thou find him, and thou canst do unto him as thy soul desireth; and Laban's messengers came and told Esau all these things.

64. And Esau heard all the words of Laban's messengers, and his anger was greatly kindled against Jacob, and he remembered his hatred, and his anger burned within him.

65. And Esau hastened and took his children and servants and the souls of his household, being sixty men, and he went and assembled all the children of Seir the Horite and their people, being three hundred and forty men, and took all this number of four hundred men with drawn swords, and he went unto Jacob to smite him.

66. And Esau divided this number into several parts, and he took the sixty men of his children and servants and the souls of his household as one head, and gave them in care of Eliphaz his eldest son.

67. And the remaining heads he gave to the care of the six sons of Seir the Horite, and he placed every man over his generations and children.

68. And the whole of this camp went as it was, and Esau went amongst them toward Jacob, and he conducted them with speed.

69. And Laban's messengers departed from Esau and went to the land of Canaan, and they came to the house of Rebecca the mother of Jacob and Esau.

70. And they told her saying, Behold thy son Esau has gone against his brother Jacob with four hundred men, for he heard that he was coming, and he is gone to make war with him, and to smite him and to take all that he has.

71. And Rebecca hastened and sent seventy two men from the servants of Isaac to meet Jacob on the road; for she said, Peradventure, Esau may make war in the road when he meets him.

72. And these messengers went on the road to meet Jacob, and they met him in the road of the brook on the opposite side of the brook Jabuk, and Jacob said when he saw them, This camp is destined to me from God, and Jacob called the name of that place Machnayim.

73. And Jacob knew all his father's people, and he kissed them and embraced them and came with them, and Jacob asked them concerning his father and mother, and they said, They were well.

74. And these messengers said unto Jacob, Rebecca thy mother has sent us to thee, saying, I have heard, my son, that thy brother Esau has gone forth against thee on the road with men from the children of Seir the Horite.

75. And therefore, my son, hearken to my voice and see with thy counsel what thou wilt do, and when he cometh up to thee, supplicate him, and do not speak rashly to him, and give him a present from what thou possessest, and from what God has favored thee with.

76. And when he asketh thee concerning thy affairs, conceal nothing from him, perhaps he may turn from his anger against thee and thou wilt thereby save thy soul, thou and all belonging to thee, for it is thy duty to honor him, for he is thy elder brother.

77. And when Jacob heard the words of his mother which the messengers had spoken to him, Jacob lifted up his voice and wept bitterly, and did as his mother then commanded him.

CHAPTER 32

1. And at that time Jacob sent messengers to his brother Esau toward the land of Seir, and he spoke to him words of supplication.

2. And he commanded them, saying, Thus shall ye say to my lord, to Esau, Thus saith thy servant Jacob, Let not my lord imagine that my father's blessing with which he did bless me has proved beneficial to me.

3. For I have been these twenty years with Laban, and he deceived me and changed my wages ten times, as it has all been already told unto my lord.

4. And I served him in his house very laboriously, and God afterward saw my affliction, my labor and the work of my hands, and he caused me to find grace and favor in his sight.

5. And I afterward through God's great mercy and kindness acquired oxen and asses and cattle, and men servants and maid servants.

6. And now I am coming to my land and my home to my father and mother, who are in the land of Canaan; and I have sent to let my lord know all this in order to find favor in the sight of my lord, so that he may not imagine that I have of myself obtained wealth, or that the blessing with which my father blessed me has benefited me.

7. And those messengers went to Esau, and found him on the borders of the land of Edom going toward Jacob, and four hundred men of the children of Seir the Horite were standing with drawn swords.

8. And the messengers of Jacob told Esau all the words that Jacob had spoken to them concerning Esau.

9. And Esau answered them with pride and contempt, and said unto them, Surely I have heard and truly it has been told unto me what Jacob has done to Laban, who exalted him in his house and gave him his daughters for wives, and he begat sons and daughters, and abundantly increased in wealth and riches in Laban's house through his means.

10. And when he saw that his wealth was abundant and his riches great he fled with all belonging to him, from Laban's house, and he led Laban's daughters away from the face of their father, as captives taken by the sword without telling him of it.

11. And not only to Laban has Jacob done thus but also unto me has he done so and has twice supplanted me, and shall I be silent?

12. Now therefore I have this day come with my camps to meet him, and I will do unto him according to the desire of my heart.

13. And the messengers returned and came to Jacob and said unto him, We came to thy brother, to Esau, and we told him all thy words, and thus has he answered us, and behold he cometh to meet thee with four hundred men.

14. Now then know and see what thou shalt do, and pray before God to deliver thee from him.

15. And when he heard the words of his brother which he had spoken to the messengers of Jacob, Jacob was greatly afraid and he was distressed.

16. And Jacob prayed to the Lord his God, and he said, O Lord God of my fathers, Abraham and Isaac, thou didst say unto me when I went away from my father's house, saying,

17. I am the Lord God of thy father Abraham and the God of Isaac, unto thee do I give this land and thy seed after thee, and I will make thy seed as the stars of heaven, and thou shalt spread forth to the four sides of heaven, and in thee and in thy seed shall all the families of the earth be blessed.

18. And thou didst establish thy words, and didst give unto me riches and children and cattle, as the utmost wishes of my heart didst thou give unto thy servant; thou didst give unto me all that I asked from thee, so that I lacked nothing.

19. And thou didst afterward say unto me, Return to thy parents and to thy birth place and I will still do well with thee.

20. And now that I have come, and thou didst deliver me from Laban, I shall fall in the hands of Esau who will slay me, yea, together with the mothers of my children.

21. Now therefore, O Lord God, deliver me, I pray thee, also from the hands of my brother Esau, for I am greatly afraid of him.

22. And if there is no righteousness in me, do it for the sake of Abraham and my father Isaac.

23. For I know that through kindness and mercy have I acquired this wealth; now therefore I beseech thee to deliver me this day with thy kindness and to answer me.

24. And Jacob ceased praying to the Lord, and he divided the people that were with him with the flocks and cattle into two camps, and he gave the half to the care of Damesek, the son of Eliezer, Abraham's servant, for a camp, with his children, and the other half he gave to the care of his brother Elianus the son of Eliezer, to be for a camp with his children.

25. And he commanded them, saying, Keep yourselves at a distance with your camps, and do not come too near each other, and if Esau come to one camp and slay it, the other
camp at a distance from it will escape him.

26. And Jacob tarried there that night, and during the whole night he gave his servants instructions concerning the forces and his children.

27. And the Lord heard the prayer of Jacob on that day, and the Lord then delivered Jacob from the hands of his brother Esau.

28. And the Lord sent three angels of the angels of heaven, and they went before Esau and came to him.

29. And these angels appeared unto Esau and his people as two thousand men, riding upon horses furnished with all sorts of war instruments, and they appeared in the sight of Esau and all his men to be divided into four camps, with four chiefs to them.

30. And one camp went on and they found Esau coming with four hundred men toward his brother Jacob, and this camp ran toward Esau and his people and terrified them, and Esau fell off the horse in alarm, and all his men separated from him in that place, for they were greatly afraid.

31. And the whole of the camp shouted after them when they fled from Esau, and all the warlike men answered, saying,

32. Surely we are the servants of Jacob, who is the servant of God, and who then can stand against us? And Esau said unto them, O then, my lord and brother Jacob is your lord, whom I have not seen for these twenty years, and now that I have this day come to see him, do you treat me in this manner?

33. And the angels answered him saying, As the Lord liveth, were not Jacob of whom thou speaketh thy brother, we had not let one remaining from thee and thy people, but only on account of Jacob we will do nothing to them.

34. And this camp passed from Esau and his men and it went away, and Esau and his men had gone from them about a league when the second camp came toward him with all sorts of weapons, and they also did unto Esau and his men as the first camp had done to them.

35. And when they had left it to go on, behold the third camp came toward him and they were all terrified, and Esau fell off the horse, and the whole camp cried out, and said, Surely we are the servants of Jacob, who is the servant of God, and who can stand against us?

36. And Esau again answered them saying, O then, Jacob my lord and your lord is my brother, and for twenty years I have not seen his countenance and hearing this day that he was coming, I went this day to meet him, and do you treat me in this manner?

37. And they answered him, and said unto him, As the Lord liveth, were not Jacob thy brother as thou didst say, we had not left a remnant from thee and thy men, but on account of Jacob of whom thou speakest being thy brother, we will not meddle with thee or thy men.

38. And the third camp also passed from them, and he still continued his road with his men toward Jacob, when the fourth camp came toward him, and they also did unto him and his men as the others had done.

39. And when Esau beheld the evil which the four angels had done to him and to his men, he became greatly afraid of his brother Jacob, and he went to meet him in peace.

40. And Esau concealed his hatred against Jacob, because he was afraid of his life on account of his brother Jacob, and because he imagined that the four camps that he had lighted upon were Jacob's servants.

41. And Jacob tarried that night with his servants in their camps, and he resolved with his servants to give unto Esau a present from all that he had with him, and from all his property; and Jacob rose up in the morning, he and his men, and they chose from amongst the cattle a present for Esau.

42. And this is the amount of the present which Jacob chose from his flock to give unto his brother Esau: and he selected two hundred and forty head from the flocks, and he selected from the camels and asses thirty each, and of the herds he chose fifty kine.

43. And he put them all in ten droves, and he placed each sort by itself, and he delivered them into the hands of ten of his servants, each drove by itself.

44. And he commanded them, and said unto them, Keep yourselves at a distance from each other, and put a space between the droves, and when Esau and those who are with him shall meet you and ask you, saying, Whose are you, and whither do you go, and to whom belongeth all this before you, you shall say unto them, We are the servants of Jacob, and we come to meet Esau in peace, and behold Jacob cometh behind us.

45. And that which is before us is a present sent from Jacob to his brother Esau.

46. And if they shall say unto you, Why doth he delay behind you, from coming to meet his brother and to see his face, then you shall say unto them, Surely he cometh joyfully behind us to meet his brother, for he said, I will appease him with the present that goeth to him, and after this I will see his face, peradventure he will accept of me.

47. So the whole present passed on in the hands of his servants, and went before him on that day, and he lodged that night with his camps by the border of the brook of Jabuk, and he rose up in the midst of the night, and he took his wives and his maid servants, and all belonging to him, and he that night passed them over the ford Jabuk.

48. And when he passed all belonging to him over the brook, Jacob was left by himself, and a man met him, and he wrestled with him that night until the breaking of the day, and

the hollow of Jacob's thigh was out of joint through wrestling with him.

49. And at the break of day the man left Jacob there, and he blessed him and went away, and Jacob passed the brook at the break of day, and he halted upon his thigh.

50. And the sun rose upon him when he had passed the brook, and he came up to the place of his cattle and children.

51. And they went on till midday, and whilst they were going the present was passing on before them.

52. And Jacob lifted up his eyes and looked, and behold Esau was at a distance, coming along with many men, about four hundred, and Jacob was greatly afraid of his brother.

53. And Jacob hastened and divided his children unto his wives and his handmaids, and his daughter Dinah he put in a chest, and delivered her into the hands of his servants.

54. And he passed before his children and wives to meet his brother, and he bowed down to the ground, yea he bowed down seven times until he approached his brother, and God caused Jacob to find grace and favor in the sight of Esau and his men, for God had heard the prayer of Jacob.

55. And the fear of Jacob and his terror fell upon his brother Esau, for Esau was greatly afraid of Jacob for what the angels of God had done to Esau, and Esau's anger against Jacob was turned into kindness.

56. And when Esau saw Jacob running toward him, he also ran toward him and he embraced him, and he fell upon his neck, and they kissed and they wept.

57. And God put fear and kindness toward Jacob in the hearts of the men that came with Esau, and they also kissed Jacob and embraced him.

58. And also Eliphaz, the son of Esau, with his four brothers, sons of Esau, wept with Jacob, and they kissed him and embraced him, for the fear of Jacob had fallen upon them all.

59. And Esau lifted up his eyes and saw the women with their offspring, the children of Jacob, walking behind Jacob and bowing along the road to Esau.

60. And Esau said unto Jacob, Who are these with thee, my brother? are they thy children or thy servants? and Jacob answered Esau and said, They are my children which God hath graciously given to thy servant.

61. And whilst Jacob was speaking to Esau and his men, Esau beheld the whole camp, and he said unto Jacob, Whence didst thou get the whole of the camp that I met yesternight? and Jacob said, To find favor in the sight of my lord, it is that which God graciously

gave to thy servant.

62. And the present came before Esau, and Jacob pressed Esau, saying, Take I pray thee the present that I have brought to my lord, and Esau said, Wherefore is this my purpose? keep that which thou hast unto thyself.

63. And Jacob said, It is incumbent upon me to give all this, since I have seen thy face, that thou still livest in peace.

64. And Esau refused to take the present, and Jacob said unto him, I beseech thee my lord, if now I have found favor in thy sight, then receive my present at my hand, for I have therefore seen thy face, as though I had seen a god-like face, because thou wast pleased with me.

65. And Esau took the present, and Jacob also gave unto Esau silver and gold and bdellium, for he pressed him so much that he took them.

66. And Esau divided the cattle that were in the camp, and he gave the half to the men who had come with him, for they had come on hire, and the other half he delivered unto the hands of his children.

67. And the silver and gold and bdellium he gave in the hands of Eliphaz his eldest son, and Esau said unto Jacob, Let us remain with thee, and we will go slowly along with thee until thou comest to my place with me, that we may dwell there together.

68. And Jacob answered his brother and said, I would do as my lord speaketh unto me, but my lord knoweth that the children are tender, and the flocks and herds with their young who are with me, go but slowly, for if they went swiftly they would all die, for thou knowest their burdens and their fatigue.

69. Therefore let my lord pass on before his servant, and I will go on slowly for the sake of the children and the flock, until I come to my lord's place to Seir.

70. And Esau said unto Jacob, I will place with thee some of the people that are with me to take care of thee in the road, and to bear thy fatigue and burden, and he said, What needeth it my lord, if I may find grace in thy sight?

71. Behold I will come unto thee to Seir to dwell there together as thou hast spoken, go thou then with thy people for I will follow thee.

72. And Jacob said this to Esau in order to remove Esau and his men from him, so that Jacob might afterward go to his father's house to the land of Canaan.

73. And Esau hearkened to the voice of Jacob, and Esau returned with the four hundred men that were with him on their road to Seir, and Jacob and all belonging to him went that day as far as the extremity of the land of Canaan in its borders, and he remained there some time.

CHAPTER 33

1. And in some time after Jacob went away from the borders of the land, and he came to the land of Shalem, that is the city of Shechem, which is in the land of Canaan, and he rested in front of the city.

2. And he bought a parcel of the field which was there, from the children of Hamor the people of the land, for five shekels.

3. And Jacob there built himself a house, and he pitched his tent there, and he made booths for his cattle, therefore he called the name of that place Succoth.

4. And Jacob remained in Succoth a year and six months.

5. At that time some of the women of the inhabitants of the land went to the city of Shechem to dance and rejoice with the daughters of the people of the city, and when they went forth then Rachel and Leah the wives of Jacob with their families also went to behold the rejoicing of the daughters of the city.

6. And Dinah the daughter of Jacob also went along with them and saw the daughters of the city, and they remained there before these daughters whilst all the people of the city were standing by them to behold their rejoicings, and all the great people of the city were there.

7. And Shechem the son of Hamor, the prince of the land was also standing there to see them.

8. And Shechem beheld Dinah the daughter of Jacob sitting with her mother before the daughters of the city, and the damsel pleased him greatly, and he there asked his friends and his people, saying, Whose daughter is that sitting amongst the women, whom I do not know in this city?

9. And they said unto him, Surely this is the daughter of Jacob the son of Isaac the Hebrew, who has dwelt in this city for some time, and when it was reported that the daughters of the land were going forth to rejoice she went with her mother and maid servants to sit amongst them as thou seest.

10. And Shechem beheld Dinah the daughter of Jacob, and when he looked at her his soul became fixed upon Dinah.

11. And he sent and had her taken by force, and Dinah came to the house of Shechem and he seized her forcibly and lay with her and humbled her, and he loved her exceedingly and placed her in his house.

12. And they came and told the thing unto Jacob, and when Jacob heard that Shechem had defiled his daughter Dinah, Jacob sent twelve of his servants to fetch Dinah from the house of Shechem, and they went and came to the house of Shechem to take away Dinah from there.

13. And when they came Shechem went out to them with his men and drove them from his house, and he would not suffer them to come before Dinah, but Shechem was sitting with Dinah kissing and embracing her before their eyes.

14. And the servants of Jacob came back and told him, saying, When we came, he and his men drove us away, and thus did Shechem do unto Dinah before our eyes.

15. And Jacob knew moreover that Shechem had defiled his daughter, but he said nothing, and his sons were feeding his cattle in the field, and Jacob remained silent till their return.

16. And before his sons came home Jacob sent two maidens from his servants' daughters to take care of Dinah in the house of Shechem, and to remain with her, and Shechem sent three of his friends to his father Hamor the son of Chiddekem, the son of Pered, saying, Get me this damsel for a wife.

17. And Hamor the son of Chiddekem the Hivite came to the house of Shechem his son, and he sat before him, and Hamor said unto his son, Shechem, Is there then no woman amongst the daughters of thy people that thou wilt take an Hebrew woman who is not of thy people?

18. And Shechem said to him, Her only must thou get for me, for she is delightful in my sight; and Hamor did according to the word of his son, for he was greatly beloved by him.

19. And Hamor went forth to Jacob to commune with him concerning this matter, and when he had gone from the house of his son Shechem, before he came to Jacob to speak unto him, behold the sons of Jacob had come from the field, as soon as they heard the thing that Shechem the son of Hamor had done.

20. And the men were very much grieved concerning their sister, and they all came home fired with anger, before the time of gathering in their cattle.

21. And they came and sat before their father and they spoke unto him kindled with wrath, saying, Surely death is due to this man and to his household, because the Lord God of the whole earth commanded Noah and his children that man shall never rob, nor commit adultery; now behold Shechem has both ravaged and committed fornication with our sister, and not one of all the people of the city spoke a word to him.

22. Surely thou knowest and understandest that the judgment of death is due to Shechem, and to his father, and to the whole city on account of the thing which he has done.

23. And whilst they were speaking before their father in this matter, behold Hamor the father of Shechem came to speak to Jacob the words of his son concerning Dinah, and he sat before Jacob and before his sons.

24. And Hamor spoke unto them, saying, The soul of my son Shechem longeth for your daughter; I pray you give her unto him for a wife and intermarry with us; give us your daughters and we will give you our daughters, and you shall dwell with us in our land and we will be as one people in the land.

25. For our land is very extensive, so dwell ye and trade therein and get possessions in it, and do therein as you desire, and no one shall prevent you by saying a word to you.

26. And Hamor ceased speaking unto Jacob and his sons, and behold Shechem his son had come after him, and he sat before them.

27. And Shechem spoke before Jacob and his sons, saying, May I find favor in your sight that you will give me your daughter, and whatever you say unto me that will I do for her.

28. Ask me for abundance of dowry and gift, and I will give it, and whatever you shall say unto me that will I do, and whoever he be that will rebel against your orders, he shall die; only give me the damsel for a wife.

29. And Simeon and Levi answered Hamor and Shechem his son deceitfully, saying, All you have spoken unto us we will do for you.

30. And behold our sister is in your house, but keep away from her until we send to our father Isaac concerning this matter, for we can do nothing without his consent.

31. For he knoweth the ways of our father Abraham, and whatever he sayeth unto us we will tell you, we will conceal nothing from you.

32. And Simeon and Levi spoke this unto Shechem and his father in order to find a pretext, and to seek counsel what was to be done to Shechem and to his city in this matter.

33. And when Shechem and his father heard the words of Simeon and Levi, it seemed good in their sight, and Shechem and his father came forth to go home.

34. And when they had gone, the sons of Jacob said unto their father, saying, Behold, we know that death is due to these wicked ones and to their city, because they transgressed that which God had commanded unto Noah and his children and his seed after them.

35. And also because Shechem did this thing to our sister Dinah in defiling her, for such vileness shall never be done amongst us.

36. Now therefore know and see what you will do, and seek counsel and pretext what is to be done to them, in order to kill all the inhabitants of this city.

37. And Simeon said to them, Here is a proper advice for you: tell them to circumcise every male amongst them as we are circumcised, and if they do not wish to do this, we shall take our daughter from them and go away.

38. And if they consent to do this and will do it, then when they are sunk down with pain, we will attack them with our swords, as upon one who is quiet and peaceable, and we will slay every male person amongst them.

39. And Simeon's advice pleased them, and Simeon and Levi resolved to do unto them as it was proposed.

40. And on the next morning Shechem and Hamor his father came again unto Jacob and his sons, to speak concerning Dinah, and to hear what answer the sons of Jacob would give to their words.

41. And the sons of Jacob spoke deceitfully to them, saying, We told our father Isaac all your words, and your words pleased him.

42. But he spoke unto us, saying, Thus did Abraham his father command him from God the Lord of the whole earth, that any man who is not of his descendants that should wish to take one of his daughters, shall cause every male belonging to him to be circumcised, as we are circumcised, and then we may give him our daughter for a wife.

43. Now we have made known to you all our ways that our father spoke unto us, for we cannot do this of which you spoke unto us, to give our daughter to an uncircumcised man, for it is a disgrace to us.

44. But herein will we consent to you, to give you our daughter, and we will also take unto ourselves your daughters, and will dwell amongst you and be one people as you have spoken, if you will hearken to us, and consent to be like us, to circumcise every male belonging to you, as we are circumcised.

45. And if you will not hearken unto us, to have every male circumcised as we are circumcised, as we have commanded, then we will come to you, and take our daughter from you and go away.

46. And Shechem and his father Hamor heard the words of the sons of Jacob, and the thing pleased them exceedingly, and Shechem and his father Hamor hastened to do the wishes of the sons of Jacob, for Shechem was very fond of Dinah, and his soul was riveted to her.

47. And Shechem and his father Hamor hastened to the gate of the city, and they assembled all the men of their city and spoke unto them the words of the sons of Jacob, saying,

48. We came to these men, the sons of Jacob, and we spoke unto them concerning their daughter, and these men will consent to do according to our wishes, and behold our land is of great extent for them, and they will dwell in it, and trade in it, and we shall be one people; we will take their daughters, and our daughters we will give unto them for wives.

49. But only on this condition will these men consent to do this thing, that every male amongst us be circumcised as they are circumcised, as their God commanded them, and when we shall have done according to their instructions to be circumcised, then will they dwell amongst us, together with their cattle and possessions, and we shall be as one people with them.

50. And when all the men of the city heard the words of Shechem and his father Hamor, then all the men of their city were agreeable to this proposal, and they obeyed to be circumcised, for Shechem and his father Hamor were greatly esteemed by them, being the princes of the land.

51. And on the next day, Shechem and Hamor his father rose up early in the morning, and they assembled all the men of their city into the middle of the city, and they called for the sons of Jacob, who circumcised every male belonging to them on that day and the next.

52. And they circumcised Shechem and Hamor his father, and the five brothers of Shechem, and then every one rose up and went home, for this thing was from the Lord against the city of Shechem, and from the Lord was Simeon's counsel in this matter, in order that the Lord might deliver the city of Shechem into the hands of Jacob's two sons.

CHAPTER 34

1. And the number of all the males that were circumcised, were six hundred and forty-five men, and two hundred and forty-six children.

2. But Chiddekem, son of Pered, the father of Hamor, and his six brothers, would not listen unto Shechem and his father Hamor, and they would not be circumcised, for the proposal of the sons of Jacob was loathsome in their sight, and their anger was greatly roused at this, that the people of the city had not hearkened to them.

3. And in the evening of the second day, they found eight small children who had not been circumcised, for their mothers had concealed them from Shechem and his father Hamor, and from the men of the city.

4. And Shechem and his father Hamor sent to have them brought before them to be circumcised, when Chiddekem and his six brothers sprang at them with their swords, and sought to slay them.

5. And they sought to slay also Shechem and his father Hamor and they sought to slay Dinah with them on account of this matter.

6. And they said unto them, What is this thing that you have done? are there no women amongst the daughters of your brethren the Canaanites, that you wish to take unto yourselves daughters of the Hebrews, whom ye knew not before, and will do this act which your fathers never commanded you?

7. Do you imagine that you will succeed through this act which you have done? and what will you answer in this affair to your brethren the Canaanites, who will come tomorrow and ask you concerning this thing?

8. And if your act shall not appear just and good in their sight, what will you do for your lives, and me for our lives, in your not having hearkened to our voices?

9. And if the inhabitants of the land and all your brethren the children of Ham, shall hear of your act, saying,

10. On account of a Hebrew woman did Shechem and Hamor his father, and all the inhabitants of their city, do that with which they had been unacquainted and which their ancestors never commanded them, where then will you fly or where conceal your shame, all your days before your brethren, the inhabitants of the land of Canaan?

11. Now therefore we cannot bear up against this thing which you have done, neither can we be burdened with this yoke upon us, which our ancestors did not command us.

12. Behold tomorrow we will go and assemble all our brethren, the Canaanitish brethren
who dwell in the land, and we will all come and smite you and all those who trust in you, that there shall not be a remnant left from you or them.

13. And when Hamor and his son Shechem and all the people of the city heard the words of Chiddekem and his brothers, they were terribly afraid of their lives at their words, and they repented of what they had done.

14. And Shechem and his father Hamor answered their father Chiddekem and his brethren, and they said unto them, All the words which you spoke unto us are true.

15. Now do not say, nor imagine in your hearts that on account of the love of the Hebrews we did this thing that our ancestors did not command us.

16. But because we saw that it was not their intention and desire to accede to our wishes concerning their daughter as to our taking her, except on this condition, so we hearkened to their voices and did this act which you saw, in order to obtain our desire from them.

17. And when we shall have obtained our request from them, we will then return to them and do unto them that which you say unto us.

18. We beseech you then to wait and tarry until our flesh shall be healed and we again become strong, and we will then go together against them, and do unto them that which is in your hearts and in ours.

19. And Dinah the daughter of Jacob heard all these words which Chiddekem and his brothers had spoken, and what Hamor and his son Shechem and the people of their city had answered them.

20. And she hastened and sent one of her maidens, that her father had sent to take care of her in the house of Shechem, to Jacob her father and to her brethren, saying:

21. Thus did Chiddekem and his brothers advise concerning you, and thus did Hamor and Shechem and the people of the city answer them.

22. And when Jacob heard these words he was filled with wrath, and he was indignant at them, and his anger was kindled against them.

23. And Simeon and Levi swore and said, As the Lord liveth, the God of the whole earth, by this time tomorrow, there shall not be a remnant left in the whole city.

24. And twenty young men had concealed themselves who were not circumcised, and these young men fought against Simeon and Levi, and Simeon and Levi killed eighteen of them, and two fled from them and escaped to some lime pits that were in the city, and Simeon and Levi sought for them, but could not find them.

25. And Simeon and Levi continued to go about in the city, and they killed all the people of the city at the edge of the sword, and they left none remaining.

26. And there was a great consternation in the midst of the city, and the cry of the people of the city ascended to heaven, and all the women and children cried aloud.

27. And Simeon and Levi slew all the city; they left not a male remaining in the whole city.

28. And they slew Hamor and Shechem his son at the edge of the sword, and they brought away Dinah from the house of Shechem and they went from there.

29. And the sons of Jacob went and returned, and came upon the slain, and spoiled all their property which was in the city and the field.

30. And whilst they were taking the spoil, three hundred men stood up and threw dust at them and struck them with stones, when Simeon turned to them and he slew them all with the edge of the sword, and Simeon turned before Levi, and came into the city.

31. And they took away their sheep and their oxen and their cattle, and also the remainder of the women and little ones, and they led all these away, and they opened a gate and went out and came unto their father Jacob with vigor.

32. And when Jacob saw all that they had done to the city, and saw the spoil that they took from them, Jacob was very angry at them, and Jacob said unto them, What is this that you have done to me? behold I obtained rest amongst the Canaanitish inhabitants of the land, and none of them meddled with me.

33. And now you have done to make me obnoxious to the inhabitants of the land, amongst the Canaanites and the Perizzites, and I am but of a small number, and they will all assemble against me and slay me when they hear of your work with their brethren, and I and my household will be destroyed.

34. And Simeon and Levi and all their brothers with them answered their father Jacob and said unto him, Behold we live in the land, and shall Shechem do this to our sister? why art thou silent at all that Shechem has done? and shall he deal with our sister as with a harlot in the streets?

35. And the number of women whom Simeon and Levi took captives from the city of Shechem, whom they did not slay, was eighty-five who had not known man.

36. And amongst them was a young damsel of beautiful appearance and well favored, whose name was Bunah, and Simeon took her for a wife, and the number of the males which they took captives and did not slay, was forty-seven men, and the rest they slew.

37. And all the young men and women that Simeon and Levi had taken captives from the city of Shechem, were servants to the sons of Jacob and to their children after them, until the day of the sons of Jacob going forth from the land of Egypt.

38. And when Simeon and Levi had gone forth from the city, the two young men that were left, who had concealed themselves in the city, and did not die amongst the people of the city, rose up, and these young men went into the city and walked about in it, and found the city desolate without man, and only women weeping, and these young men cried out and said, Behold, this is the evil which the sons of Jacob the Hebrew did to this city in their having this day destroyed one of the Canaanitish cities, and were not afraid of their lives of all the land of Canaan.

39. And these men left the city and went to the city of Tapnach, and they came there and told the inhabitants of Tapnach all that had befallen them, and all that the sons of Jacob had done to the city of Shechem.

40. And the information reached Jashub king of Tapnach, and he sent men to the city of Shechem to see those young men, for the king did not believe them in this account, saying, How could two men lay waste such a large town as Shechem?

41. And the messengers of Jashub came back and told him, saying, We came unto the city, and it is destroyed, there is not a man there; only weeping women; neither is any flock or cattle there, for all that was in the city the sons of Jacob took away.

42. And Jashub wondered at this, saying, How could two men do this thing, to destroy so large a city, and not one man able to stand against them?

43. For the like has not been from the days of Nimrod, and not even from the remotest time, has the like taken place; and Jashub, king of Tapnach, said to his people, Be courageous and we will go and fight against these Hebrews, and do unto them as they did unto the city, and we will avenge the cause of the people of the city.

44. And Jashub, king of Tapnach, consulted with his counsellors about this matter, and his advisers said unto him, Alone thou wilt not prevail over the Hebrews, for they must be powerful to do this work to the whole city.

45. If two of them laid waste the whole city, and no one stood against them, surely if thou wilt go against them, they will all rise against us and destroy us likewise.

46. But if thou wilt send to all the kings that surround us, and let them come together, then we will go with them and fight against the sons of Jacob; then wilt thou prevail against them.

47. And Jashub heard the words of his counsellors, and their words pleased him and his people, and he did so; and Jashub king of Tapnach sent to all the kings of the Amorites that surrounded Shechem and Tapnach, saying,

48. Go up with me and assist me, and we will smite Jacob the Hebrew and all his sons, and destroy them from the earth, for thus did he do to the city of Shechem, and do you not know of it?

49. And all the kings of the Amorites heard the evil that the sons of Jacob had done to the city of Shechem, and they were greatly astonished at them.

50. And the seven kings of the Amorites assembled with all their armies, about ten thousand men with drawn swords, and they came to fight against the sons of Jacob; and Jacob heard that the kings of the Amorites had assembled to fight against his sons, and Jacob was greatly afraid, and it distressed him.

51. And Jacob exclaimed against Simeon and Levi, saying, What is this act that you did? why have you injured me, to bring against me all the children of Canaan to destroy me and my household? for I was at rest, even I and my household, and you have done this thing to me, and provoked the inhabitants of the land against me by your proceedings.

52. And Judah answered his father, saying, Was it for naught my brothers Simeon and Levi killed all the inhabitants of Shechem? Surely it was because Shechem had humbled our sister, and transgressed the command of our God to Noah and his children, for Shechem took our sister away by force, and committed adultery with her.

53. And Shechem did all this evil and not one of the inhabitants of his city interfered with him, to say, Why wilt thou do this? surely for this my brothers went and smote the city, and the Lord delivered it into their hands, because its inhabitants had transgressed the commands of our God. Is it then for naught that they have done all this?

54. And now why art thou afraid or distressed, and why art thou displeased at my brothers, and why is thine anger kindled against them?

55. Surely our God who delivered into their hand the city of Shechem and its people, he will also deliver into our hands all the Canaanitish kings who are coming against us, and we will do unto them as my brothers did unto Shechem.

56. Now be tranquil about them and cast away thy fears, but trust in the Lord our God, and pray unto him to assist us and deliver us, and deliver our enemies into our hands.

57. And Judah called to one of his father's servants, Go now and see where those kings, who are coming against us, are situated with their armies.

58. And the servant went and looked far off, and went up opposite Mount Sihon, and saw all the camps of the kings standing in the fields, and he returned to Judah and said, Behold the kings are situated in the field with all their camps, a people exceedingly numerous, like unto the sand upon the sea shore.

59. And Judah said unto Simeon and Levi, and unto all his brothers, Strengthen yourselves and be sons of valor, for the Lord our God is with us, do not fear them.

60. Stand forth each man, girt with his weapons of war, his bow and his sword, and we will go and fight against these uncircumcised men; the Lord is our God, He will save us.

61. And they rose up, and each girt on his weapons of war, great and small, eleven sons of Jacob, and all the servants of Jacob with them.

62. And all the servants of Isaac who were with Isaac in Hebron, all came to them equipped in all sorts of war instruments, and the sons of Jacob and their servants, being one hundred and twelve men, went towards these kings, and Jacob also went with them.

63. And the sons of Jacob sent unto their father Isaac the son of Abraham to Hebron, the same is Kireath-arba, saying,

64. Pray we beseech thee for us unto the Lord our God, to protect us from the hands of the Canaanites who are coming against us, and to deliver them into our hands.

65. And Isaac the son of Abraham prayed unto the Lord for his sons, and he said, O Lord God, thou didst promise my father, saying, I will multiply thy seed as the stars of heaven, and thou didst also promise me, and establish thou thy word, now that the kings of Canaan are coming together, to make war with my children because they committed no violence.

66. Now therefore, O Lord God, God of the whole earth, pervert, I pray thee, the counsel of these kings that they may not fight against my sons.

67. And impress the hearts of these kings and their people with the terror of my sons and bring down their pride, and that they may turn away from my sons.

68. And with thy strong hand and outstretched arm deliver my sons and their servants from them, for power and might are in thy hands to do all this.

69. And the sons of Jacob and their servants went toward these kings, and they trusted in the Lord their God, and whilst they were going, Jacob their father also prayed unto the Lord and said, O Lord God, powerful and exalted God, who has reigned from days of old, from thence till now and forever;

70. Thou art He who stirreth up wars and causeth them to cease, in thy hand are power and might to exalt and to bring down; O may my prayer be acceptable before thee that thou mayest turn to me with thy mercies, to impress the hearts of these kings and their people with the terror of my sons, and terrify them and their camps, and with thy great kindness deliver all those that trust in thee, for it is thou who canst bring people under us and reduce nations under our power.

CHAPTER 35

1. And all the kings of the Amorites came and took their stand in the field to consult with their counsellors what was to be done with the sons of Jacob, for they were still afraid of them, saying, Behold, two of them slew the whole of the city of Shechem.

2. And the Lord heard the prayers of Isaac and Jacob, and he filled the hearts of all these kings' advisers with great fear and terror that they unanimously exclaimed,

3. Are you silly this day, or is there no understanding in you, that you will fight with the Hebrews, and why will you take a delight in your own destruction this day?

4. Behold two of them came to the city of Shechem without fear or terror, and they killed all the inhabitants of the city, that no man stood up against them, and how will you be able to fight with them all?

5. Surely you know that their God is exceedingly fond of them, and has done mighty things for them, such as have not been done from days of old, and amongst all the gods of nations, there is none can do like unto his mighty deeds.

6. Surely he delivered their father Abraham, the Hebrew, from the hand of Nimrod, and from the hand of all his people who had many times sought to slay him.

7. He delivered him also from the fire in which king Nimrod had cast him, and his God delivered him from it.

8. And who else can do the like? surely it was Abraham who slew the five kings of Elam, when they had touched his brother's son who in those days dwelt in Sodom.

9. And took his servant that was faithful in his house and a few of his men, and they pursued the kings of Elam in one night and killed them, and restored to his brother's son all his property which they had taken from him.

10. And surely you know the God of these Hebrews is much delighted with them, and they are also delighted with him, for they know that he delivered them from all their enemies.

11. And behold through his love toward his God, Abraham took his only and precious son and intended to bring him up as a burnt offering to his God, and had it not been for God who prevented him from doing this, he would then have done it through his love to his God.

12. And God saw all his works, and swore unto him, and promised him that he would deliver his sons and all his seed from every trouble that would befall them, because he had done this thing, and through his love to his God stifled his compassion for his child.

13. And have you not heard what their God did to Pharaoh king of Egypt, and to Abimelech king of Gerar, through taking Abraham's wife, who said of her, She is my sister, lest they might slay him on account of her, and think of taking her for a wife? and God did unto them and their people all that you heard of.

14. And behold, we ourselves saw with our eyes that Esau, the brother of Jacob, came to him with four hundred men, with the intention of slaying him, for he called to mind that he had taken away from him his father's blessing.

15. And he went to meet him when he came from Syria, to smite the mother with the children, and who delivered him from his hands but his God in whom he trusted? he delivered him from the hand of his brother and also from the hands of his enemies, and surely he again will protect them.

16. Who does not know that it was their God who inspired them with strength to do to the town of Shechem the evil which you heard of?

17. Could it then be with their own strength that two men could destroy such a large city as Shechem had it not been for their God in whom they trusted? he said and did unto them all this to slay the inhabitants of the city in their city.

18. And can you then prevail over them who have come forth together from your city to fight with the whole of them, even if a thousand times as many more should come to your assistance?

19. Surely you know and understand that you do not come to fight with them, but you come to war with their God who made choice of them, and you have therefore all come this day to be destroyed.

20. Now therefore refrain from this evil which you are endeavoring to bring upon yourselves, and it will be better for you not to go to battle with them, although they are but few in numbers, because their God is with them.

21. And when the kings of the Amorites heard all the words of their advisers, their hearts were filled with terror, and they were afraid of the sons of Jacob and would not fight against them.

22. And they inclined their ears to the words of their advisers, and they listened to all their words, and the words of the counsellors greatly pleased the kings, and they did so.

23. And the kings turned and refrained from the sons of Jacob, for they durst not approach them to make war with them, for they were greatly afraid of them, and their hearts melted within them from their fear of them.

24. For this proceeded from the Lord to them, for he heard the prayers of his servants Isaac and Jacob, for they trusted in him; and all these kings returned with their camps on that day, each to his own city, and they did not at that time fight with the sons of Jacob.

25. And the sons of Jacob kept their station that day till evening opposite mount Sihon, and seeing that these kings did not come to fight against them, the sons of Jacob returned home.

CHAPTER 36

1. At that time the Lord appeared unto Jacob saying, Arise, go to Bethel and remain there, and make there an altar to the Lord who appeareth unto thee, who delivered thee and thy sons from affliction.

2. And Jacob rose up with his sons and all belonging to him, and they went and came to Bethel according to the word of the Lord.

3. And Jacob was ninety-nine years old when he went up to Bethel, and Jacob and his sons and all the people that were with him, remained in Bethel in Luz, and he there built an altar to the Lord who appeared unto him, and Jacob and his sons remained in Bethel six months.

4. At that time died Deborah the daughter of Uz, the nurse of Rebecca, who had been with Jacob; and Jacob buried her beneath Bethel under an oak that was there.

5. And Rebecca the daughter of Bethuel, the mother of Jacob, also died at that time in Hebron, the same is Kireath-arba, and she was buried in the cave of Machpelah which Abraham had bought from the children of Heth.

6. And the life of Rebecca was one hundred and thirty-three years, and she died and when Jacob heard that his mother Rebecca was dead he wept bitterly for his mother, and made a great mourning for her, and for Deborah her nurse beneath the oak, and he called the name of that place Allon-bachuth.

7. And Laban the Syrian died in those days, for God smote him because he transgressed the covenant that existed between him and Jacob.

8. And Jacob was a hundred years old when the Lord appeared unto him, and blessed him and called his name Israel, and Rachel the wife of Jacob conceived in those days.

9. And at that time Jacob and all belonging to him journeyed from Bethel to go to his father's house, to Hebron.

10. And whilst they were going on the road, and there was yet but a little way to come to Ephrath, Rachel bare a son and she had hard labor and she died.

11. And Jacob buried her in the way to Ephrath, which is Bethlehem, and he set a pillar upon her grave, which is there unto this day; and the days of Rachel were forty-five years and she died.

12. And Jacob called the name of his son that was born to him, which Rachel bare unto him, Benjamin, for he was born to him in the land on the right hand.

13. And it was after the death of Rachel, that Jacob pitched his tent in the tent of her handmaid Bilhah.

14. And Reuben was jealous for his mother Leah on account of this, and he was filled with anger, and he rose up in his anger and went and entered the tent of Bilhah and he thence removed his father's bed.

15. At that time the portion of birthright, together with the kingly and priestly offices, was removed from the sons of Reuben, for he had profaned his father's bed, and the birthright was given unto Joseph, the kingly office to Judah, and the priesthood unto Levi, because Reuben had defiled his father's bed.

16. And these are the generations of Jacob who were born to him in Padan-aram, and the sons of Jacob were twelve.

17. The sons of Leah were Reuben the first born, and Simeon, Levi, Judah, Issachar, Zebulun, and their sister Dinah; and the sons of Rachel were Joseph and Benjamin.

18. The sons of Zilpah, Leah's handmaid, were Gad and Asher, and the sons of Bilhah, Rachel's handmaid, were Dan and Naphtali; these are the sons of Jacob which were born to him in Padan-aram.

19. And Jacob and his sons and all belonging to him journeyed and came to Mamre, which is Kireath-arba, that is in Hebron, where Abraham and Isaac sojourned, and Jacob with his sons and all belonging to him, dwelt with his father in Hebron.

20. And his brother Esau and his sons, and all belonging to him went to the land of Seir and dwelt there, and had possessions in the land of Seir, and the children of Esau were fruitful and multiplied exceedingly in the land of Seir.

21. And these are the generations of Esau that were born to him in the land of Canaan, and the sons of Esau were five.

22. And Adah bare to Esau his first born Eliphaz, and she also bare to him Reuel, and Ahlibamah bare to him Jeush, Yaalam and Korah.

23. These are the children of Esau who were born to him in the land of Canaan; and the sons of Eliphaz the son of Esau were Teman, Omar, Zepho, Gatam, Kenaz and Amalex, and the sons of Reuel were Nachath, Zerach, Shamah and Mizzah.

24. And the sons of Jeush were Timnah, Alvah, Jetheth; and the sons of Yaalam were Alah, Phinor and Kenaz.

25. And the sons of Korah were Teman, Mibzar, Magdiel and Eram; these are the families of the sons of Esau according to their dukedoms in the land of Seir.

26. And these are the names of the sons of Seir the Horite, inhabitants of the land of Seir, Lotan, Shobal, Zibeon, Anah, Dishan, Ezer and Dishon, being seven sons.

27. And the children of Lotan were Hori, Heman and their sister Timna, that is Timna who came to Jacob and his sons, and they would not give ear to her, and she went and became a concubine to Eliphaz the son of Esau, and she bare to him Amalek.

28. And the sons of Shobal were Alvan, Manahath, Ebal, Shepho, and Onam, and the sons of Zibeon were Ajah, and Anah, this was that Anah who found the Yemim in the wilderness when he fed the asses of Zibeon his father.

29. And whilst he was feeding his father's asses he led them to the wilderness at different times to feed them.

30. And there was a day that he brought them to one of the deserts on the sea shore, opposite the wilderness of the people, and whilst he was feeding them, behold a very heavy storm came from the other side of the sea and rested upon the asses that were feeding there, and they all stood still.

31. And afterward about one hundred and twenty great and terrible animals came out from the wilderness at the other side of the sea, and they all came to the place where the asses were, and they placed themselves there.

32. And those animals, from their middle downward, were in the shape of the children of men, and from their middle upward, some had the likeness of bears, and some the likeness of the keephas, with tails behind them from between their shoulders reaching down to the earth, like the tails of the ducheephath, and these animals came and mounted and rode upon these asses, and led them away, and they went away unto this day.

33. And one of these animals approached Anah and smote him with his tail, and then fled from that place.

34. And when he saw this work he was exceedingly afraid of his life, and he fled and escaped to the city.

35. And he related to his sons and brothers all that had happened to him, and many men went to seek the asses but could not find them, and Anah and his brothers went no more to that place from that day following, for they were greatly afraid of their lives.

36. And the children of Anah the son of Seir, were Dishon and his sister Ahlibamah, and the children of Dishon were Hemdan, Eshban, Ithran and Cheran, and the children of Ezer were Bilhan, Zaavan and Akan, and the children of Dishon were Uz and Aran.

37. These are the families of the children of Seir the Horite, according to their dukedoms in the land of Seir.

38. And Esau and his children dwelt in the land of Seir the Horite, the inhabitant of the land, and they had possessions in it and were fruitful and multiplied exceedingly, and Jacob and his children and all belonging to them, dwelt with their father Isaac in the land of Canaan, as the Lord had commanded Abraham their father.

CHAPTER 37

1. And in the one hundred and fifth year of the life of Jacob, that is the ninth year of Jacob's dwelling with his children in the land of Canaan, he came from Padan-aram.

2. And in those days Jacob journeyed with his children from Hebron, and they went and returned to the city of Shechem, they and all belonging to them, and they dwelt there, for the children of Jacob obtained good and fat pasture land for their cattle in the city of Shechem, the city of Shechem having then been rebuilt, and there were in it about three hundred men and women.

3. And Jacob and his children and all belonging to him dwelt in the part of the field which Jacob had bought from Hamor the father of Shechem, when he came from Padan-aram before Simeon and Levi had smitten the city.

4. And all those kings of the Canaanites and Amorites that surrounded the city of Shechem, heard that the sons of Jacob had again come to Shechem and dwelt there.

5. And they said, Shall the sons of Jacob the Hebrew again come to the city and dwell therein, after that they have smitten its inhabitants and driven them out? shall they now return and also drive out those who are dwelling in the city or slay them?

6. And all the kings of Canaan again assembled, and they came together to make war with Jacob and his sons.

7. And Jashub king of Tapnach sent also to all his neighboring kings, to Elan king of Gaash, and to Ihuri king of Shiloh, and to Parathon king of Chazar, and to Susi king of Sarton, and to Laban king of Bethchoran, and to Shabir king of Othnay-mah, saying,

8. Come up to me and assist me, and let us smite Jacob the Hebrew and his sons, and all belonging to him, for they are again come to Shechem to possess it and to slay its inhabitants as before.

9. And all these kings assembled together and came with all their camps, a people exceedingly plentiful like the sand upon the sea shore, and they were all opposite to Tapnach.

10. And Jashub king of Tapnach went forth to them with all his army, and he encamped with them opposite to Tapnach without the city, and all these kings they divided into seven divisions, being seven camps against the sons of Jacob.

11. And they sent a declaration to Jacob and his son, saying, Come you all forth to us that we may have an interview together in the plain, and revenge the cause of the men of Shechem whom you slew in their city, and you will now again return to the city of Shechem and dwell therein, and slay its inhabitants as before.

12. And the sons of Jacob heard this and their anger was kindled exceedingly at the words of the kings of Canaan, and ten of the sons of Jacob hastened and rose up, and each of them girt on his weapons of war; and there were one hundred and two of their servants with them equipped in battle array.

13. And all these men, the sons of Jacob with their servants, went toward these kings, and Jacob their father was with them, and they all stood upon the heap of Shechem.

14. And Jacob prayed to the Lord for his sons, and he spread forth his hands to the Lord, and he said, O God, thou art an Almighty God, thou art our father, thou didst form us and we are the works of thine hands; I pray thee deliver my sons through thy mercy from the hand of their enemies, who are this day coming to fight with them and save them from their hand, for in thy hand is power and might, to save the few from the many.

15. And give unto my sons, thy servants, strength of heart and might to fight with their enemies, to subdue them, and make their enemies fall before them, and let not my sons and their servants die through the hands of the children of Canaan.

16. But if it seemeth good in thine eyes to take away the lives of my sons and their servants, take them in thy great mercy through the hands of thy ministers, that they may not perish this day by the hands of the kings of the Amorites.

17. And when Jacob ceased praying to the Lord the earth shook from its place, and the sun darkened, and all these kings were terrified and a great consternation seized them.

18. And the Lord hearkened to the prayer of Jacob, and the Lord impressed the hearts of all the kings and their hosts with the terror and awe of the sons of Jacob.

19. For the Lord caused them to hear the voice of chariots, and the voice of mighty horses from the sons of Jacob, and the voice of a great army accompanying them.

20. And these kings were seized with great terror at the sons of Jacob, and whilst they were standing in their quarters, behold the sons of Jacob advanced upon them, with one hundred and twelve men, with a great and tremendous shouting.

21. And when the kings saw the sons of Jacob advancing toward them, they were still more panic struck, and they were inclined to retreat from before the sons of Jacob as at first, and not to fight with them.

22. But they did not retreat, saying, It would be a disgrace to us thus twice to retreat from before the Hebrews.

23. And the sons of Jacob came near and advanced against all these kings and their armies, and they saw, and behold it was a very mighty people, numerous as the sand of the sea.

24. And the sons of Jacob called unto the Lord and said, Help us O Lord, help us and answer us, for we trust in thee, and let us not die by the hands of these uncircumcised men, who this day have come against us.

25. And the sons of Jacob girt on their weapons of war, and they took in their hands each man his shield and his javelin, and they approached to battle.

26. And Judah, the son of Jacob, ran first before his brethren, and ten of his servants with him, and he went toward these kings.

27. And Jashub, king of Tapnach, also came forth first with his army before Judah, and Judah saw Jashub and his army coming toward him, and Judah's wrath was kindled, and his anger burned within him, and he approached to battle in which Judah ventured his life.

28. And Jashub and all his army were advancing toward Judah, and he was riding upon a very strong and powerful horse, and Jashub was a very valiant man, and covered with iron and brass from head to foot.

29. And whilst he was upon the horse, he shot arrows with both hands from before and behind, as was his manner in all his battles, and he never missed the place to which he aimed his arrows.

30. And when Jashub came to fight with Judah, and was darting many arrows against Judah, the Lord bound the hand of Jashub, and all the arrows that he shot rebounded upon his own men.

31. And notwithstanding this, Jashub kept advancing toward Judah, to challenge him with the arrows, but the distance between them was about thirty cubits, and when Judah saw Jashub darting forth his arrows against him, he ran to him with his wrath-excited might.

32. And Judah took up a large stone from the ground, and its weight was sixty shekels, and Judah ran toward Jashub, and with the stone struck him on his shield, that Jashub was stunned with the blow, and fell off from his horse to the ground.

33. And the shield burst asunder out of the hand of Jashub, and through the force of the blow sprang to the distance of about fifteen cubits, and the shield fell before the second camp.

34. And the kings that came with Jashub saw at a distance the strength of Judah, the son of Jacob, and what he had done to Jashub, and they were terribly afraid of Judah.

35. And they assembled near Jashub's camp, seeing his confusion, and Judah drew his sword and smote forty-two men of the camp of Jashub, and the whole of Jashub's camp fled before Judah, and no man stood against him, and they left Jashub and fled from him, and Jashub was still prostrate upon the ground.

36. And Jashub seeing that all the men of his camp had fled from him, hastened and rose up with terror against Judah, and stood upon his legs opposite Judah.

37. And Jashub had a single combat with Judah, placing shield toward shield, and Jashub's men all fled, for they were greatly afraid of Judah.

38. And Jashub took his spear in his hand to strike Judah upon his head, but Judah had quickly placed his shield to his head against Jashub's spear, so that the shield of Judah received the blow from Jashub's spear, and the shield was split in too.

39. And when Judah saw that his shield was split, he hastily drew his sword and smote Jashub at his ankles, and cut off his feet that Jashub fell upon the ground, and the spear fell from his hand.

40. And Judah hastily picked up Jashub's spear, with which he severed his head and cast it next to his feet.

41. And when the sons of Jacob saw what Judah had done to Jashub, they all ran into the ranks of the other kings, and the sons of Jacob fought with the army of Jashub, and the armies of all the kings that were there.

42. And the sons of Jacob caused fifteen thousand of their men to fall, and they smote them as if smiting at gourds, and the rest fled for their lives.

43. And Judah was still standing by the body of Jashub, and stripped Jashub of his coat of mail.

44. And Judah also took off the iron and brass that was about Jashub, and behold nine men of the captains of Jashub came along to fight against Judah.

45. And Judah hastened and took up a stone from the ground, and with it smote one of them upon the head, and his skull was fractured, and the body also fell from the horse to the ground.

46. And the eight captains that remained, seeing the strength of Judah, were greatly afraid and they fled, and Judah with his ten men pursued them, and they overtook them and slew them.

47. And the sons of Jacob were still smiting the armies of the kings, and they slew many of them, but those kings daringly kept their stand with their captains, and did not retreat from their places, and they exclaimed against those of their armies that fled from before the sons of Jacob, but none would listen to them, for they were afraid of their lives lest they should die.

48. And all the sons of Jacob, after having smitten the armies of the kings, returned and came before Judah, and Judah was still slaying the eight captains of Jashub, and stripping off their garments.

49. And Levi saw Elon, king of Gaash, advancing toward him, with his fourteen captains to smite him, but Levi did not know it for certain.

50. And Elon with his captains approached nearer, and Levi looked back and saw that battle was given him in the rear, and Levi ran with twelve of his servants, and they went and slew Elon and his captains with the edge of the sword.

CHAPTER 38

1. And Ihuri king of Shiloh came up to assist Elon, and he approached Jacob, when Jacob drew his bow that was in his hand and with an arrow struck Ihuri which caused his death.

2. And when Ihuri king of Shiloh was dead, the four remaining kings fled from their station with the rest of the captains, and they endeavored to retreat, saying, We have no more strength with the Hebrews after their having killed the three kings and their captains who were more powerful than we are.

3. And when the sons of Jacob saw that the remaining kings had removed from their station, they pursued them, and Jacob also came from the heap of Shechem from the place where he was standing, and they went after the kings and they approached them with their servants.

4. And the kings and the captains with the rest of their armies, seeing that the sons of Jacob approached them, were afraid of their lives and fled till they reached the city of Chazar.

5. And the sons of Jacob pursued them to the gate of the city of Chazar, and they smote a great smiting amongst the kings and their armies, about four thousand men, and whilst they were smiting the army of the kings, Jacob was occupied with his bow confining himself to smiting the kings, and he slew them all.

6. And he slew Parathon king of Chazar at the gate of the city of Chazar, and he afterward smote Susi king of Sarton, and Laban king of Bethchorin, and Shabir king of Machnaymah, and he slew them all with arrows, an arrow to each of them, and they died.

7. And the sons of Jacob seeing that all the kings were dead and that they were broken up and retreating, continued to carry on the battle with the armies of the kings opposite the gate of Chazar, and they still smote about four hundred of their men.

8. And three men of the servants of Jacob fell in that battle, and when Judah saw that three of his servants had died, it grieved him greatly, and his anger burned within him against the Amorites.

9. And all the men that remained of the armies of the kings were greatly afraid of their lives, and they ran and broke the gate of the walls of the city of Chazar, and they all entered the city for safety.

10. And they concealed themselves in the midst of the city of Chazar, for the city of Chazar was very large and extensive, and when all these armies had entered the city, the sons of Jacob ran after them to the city.

11. And four mighty men, experienced in battle, went forth from the city and stood against the entrance of the city, with drawn swords and spears in their hands, and they placed themselves opposite the sons of Jacob, and would not suffer them to enter the city.

12. And Naphtali ran and came between them and with his sword smote two of them, and cut off their heads at one stroke.

13. And he turned to the other two, and behold they had fled, and he pursued them, overtook them, smote them and slew them.

14. And the sons of Jacob came to the city and saw, and behold there was another wall to the city, and they sought for the gate of the wall and could not find it, and Judah sprang upon the top of the wall, and Simeon and Levi followed him, and they all three descended from the wall into the city.

15. And Simeon and Levi slew all the men who ran for safety into the city, and also the inhabitants of the city with their wives and little ones, they slew with the edge of the sword, and the cries of the city ascended up to heaven.

16. And Dan and Naphtali sprang upon the wall to see what caused the noise of lamentation, for the sons of Jacob felt anxious about their brothers, and they heard the inhabitants of the city speaking with weeping and supplications, saying, Take all that we possess in the city and go away, only do not put us to death.

17. And when Judah, Simeon, and Levi had ceased smiting the inhabitants of the city, they ascended the wall and called to Dan and Naphtali, who were upon the wall, and to the rest of their brothers, and Simeon and Levi informed them of the entrance into the city, and all the sons of Jacob came to fetch the spoil.

18. And the sons of Jacob took the spoil of the city of Chazar, the flocks and herds, and the property, and they took all that could be captured, and went away that day from the city.

19. And on the next day the sons of Jacob went to Sarton, for they heard that the men of Sarton who had remained in the city were assembling to fight with them for having slain their king, and Sarton was a very high and fortified city, and it had a deep rampart surrounding the city.

20. And the pillar of the rampart was about fifty cubits and its breadth forty cubits, and there was no place for a man to enter the city on account of the rampart, and the sons of Jacob saw the rampart of the city, and they sought an entrance in it but could not find it.

21. For the entrance to the city was at the rear, and every man that wished to come into the city came by that road and went around the whole city, and he afterwards entered the city.

22. And the sons of Jacob seeing they could not find the way into the city, their anger was kindled greatly, and the inhabitants of the city seeing that the sons of Jacob were
coming to them were greatly afraid of them, for they had heard of their strength and what they had done to Chazar.

23. And the inhabitants of the city of Sarton could not go out toward the sons of Jacob after having assembled in the city to fight against them, lest they might thereby get into the city, but when they saw that they were coming toward them, they were greatly afraid of them, for they had heard of their strength and what they had done to Chazar.

24. So the inhabitants of Sarton speedily took away the bridge of the road of the city, from its place, before the sons of Jacob came, and they brought it into the city.

25. And the sons of Jacob came and sought the way into the city, and could not find it and the inhabitants of the city went up to the top of the wall, and saw, and behold the sons of Jacob were seeking an entrance into the city.

26. And the inhabitants of the city reproached the sons of Jacob from the top of the wall, and they cursed them, and the sons of Jacob heard the reproaches, and they were greatly incensed, and their anger burned within them.

27. And the sons of Jacob were provoked at them, and they all rose and sprang over the rampart with the force of their strength, and through their might passed the forty cubits' breadth of the rampart.

28. And when they had passed the rampart they stood under the wall of the city, and they found all the gates of the city enclosed with iron doors.

29. And the sons of Jacob came near to break open the doors of the gates of the city, and the inhabitants did not let them, for from the top of the wall they were casting stones and arrows upon them.

30. And the number of the people that were upon the wall was about four hundred men, and when the sons of Jacob saw that the men of the city would not let them open the gates of the city, they sprang and ascended the top of the wall, and Judah went up first to the east part of the city.

31. And Gad and Asher went up after him to the west corner of the city, and Simeon and Levi to the north, and Dan and Reuben to the south.

32. And the men who were on the top of the wall, the inhabitants of the city, seeing that the sons of Jacob were coming up to them, they all fled from the wall, descended into the city, and concealed themselves in the midst of the city.

33. And Issachar and Naphtali that remained under the wall approached and broke the gates of the city, and kindled a fire at the gates of the city, that the iron melted, and all the sons of Jacob came into the city, they and all their men, and they fought with the inhabitants of the city of Sarton, and smote them with the edge of the sword, and no man stood up before them.

34. And about two hundred men fled from the city, and they all went and hid themselves in a certain tower in the city, and Judah pursued them to the tower and he broke down the tower, which fell upon the men, and they all died.

35. And the sons of Jacob went up the road of the roof of that tower, and they saw, and behold there was another strong and high tower at a distance in the city, and the top of it reached to heaven, and the sons of Jacob hastened and descended, and went with all their men to that tower, and found it filled with about three hundred men, women and little ones.

36. And the sons of Jacob smote a great smiting amongst those men in the tower and they ran away and fled from them.

37. And Simeon and Levi pursued them, when twelve mighty and valiant men came out to them from the place where they had concealed themselves.

38. And those twelve men maintained a strong battle against Simeon and Levi, and Simeon and Levi could not prevail over them, and those valiant men broke the shields of Simeon and Levi, and one of them struck at Levi's head with his sword, when Levi hastily placed his hand to his head, for he was afraid of the sword, and the sword struck Levi's hand, and it wanted but little to the hand of Levi being cut off.

39. And Levi seized the sword of the valiant man in his hand, and took it forcibly from the man, and with it he struck at the head of the powerful man, and he severed his head.

40. And eleven men approached to fight with Levi, for they saw that one of them was killed, and the sons of Jacob fought, but the sons of Jacob could not prevail over them, for those men were very powerful.

41. And the sons of Jacob seeing that they could not prevail over them, Simeon gave a loud and tremendous shriek, and the eleven powerful men were stunned at the voice of Simeon's shrieking.

42. And Judah at a distance knew the voice of Simeon's shouting, and Naphtali and Judah ran with their shields to Simeon and Levi, and found them fighting with those powerful men, unable to prevail over them as their shields were broken.

43. And Naphtali saw that the shields of Simeon and Levi were broken, and he took two shields from his servants and brought them to Simeon and Levi.

44. And Simeon, Levi and Judah on that day fought all three against the eleven mighty men until the time of sunset, but they could not prevail over them.

45. And this was told unto Jacob, and he was sorely grieved, and he prayed unto the Lord, and he and Naphtali his son went against these mighty men.

46. And Jacob approached and drew his bow, and came nigh unto the mighty men, and slew three of their men with the bow, and the remaining eight turned back, and behold, the war waged against them in the front and rear,

and they were greatly afraid of their lives, and could not stand before the sons of Jacob, and they fled from before them.

47. And in their flight they met Dan and Asher coming toward them, and they suddenly fell upon them, and fought with them, and slew two of them, and Judah and his brothers pursued them, and smote the remainder of them, and slew them.

48. And all the sons of Jacob returned and walked about the city, searching if they could find any men, and they found about twenty young men in a cave in the city, and Gad and Asher smote them all, and Dan and Naphtali lighted upon the rest of the men who had fled and escaped from the second tower, and they smote them all.

49. And the sons of Jacob smote all the inhabitants of the city of Sarton, but the women and little ones they left in the city and did not slay them.

50. And all the inhabitants of the city of Sarton were powerful men, one of them would pursue a thousand, and two of them would not flee from ten thousand of the rest of men.

51. And the sons of Jacob slew all the inhabitants of the city of Sarton with the edge of the sword, that no man stood up against them, and they left the women in the city.

52. And the sons of Jacob took all the spoil of the city, and captured what they desired, and they took flocks and herds and property from the city, and the sons of Jacob did unto Sarton and its inhabitants as they had done to Chazar and its inhabitants, and they turned and went away.

CHAPTER 39

1. And when the sons of Jacob went from the city of Sarton, they had gone about two hundred cubits when they met the inhabitants of Tapnach coming toward them, for they went out to fight with them, because they had smitten the king of Tapnach and all his men.

2. So all that remained in the city of Tapnach came out to fight with the sons of Jacob, and they thought to retake from them the booty and the spoil which they had captured from Chazar and Sarton.

3. And the rest of the men of Tapnach fought with the sons of Jacob in that place, and the sons of Jacob smote them, and they fled before them, and they pursued them to the city of Arbelan, and they all fell before the sons of Jacob.

4. And the sons of Jacob returned and came to Tapnach, to take away the spoil of Tapnach, and when they came to Tapnach they heard that the people of Arbelan had gone out to meet them to save the spoil of their brethren, and the sons of Jacob left ten of their men in Tapnach to plunder the city, and they went out toward the people of Arbelan.

5. And the men of Arbelan went out with their wives to fight with the sons of Jacob, for their wives were experienced in battle, and they went out, about four hundred men and women.

6. And all the sons of Jacob shouted with a loud voice, and they all ran toward the inhabitants of Arbelan, and with a great and tremendous voice.

7. And the inhabitants of Arbelan heard the noise of the shouting of the sons of Jacob, and their roaring like the noise of lions and like the roaring of the sea and its waves.

8. And fear and terror possessed their hearts on account of the sons of Jacob, and they were terribly afraid of them, and they retreated and fled before them into the city, and the sons of Jacob pursued them to the gate of the city, and they came upon them in the city.

9. And the sons of Jacob fought with them in the city, and all their women were engaged in slinging against the sons of Jacob, and the combat was very severe amongst them the whole of that day till evening.

10. And the sons of Jacob could not prevail over them, and the sons of Jacob had almost perished in that battle, and the sons of Jacob cried unto the Lord and greatly gained strength toward evening, and the sons of Jacob smote all the inhabitants of Arbelan by the edge of the sword, men, women and little ones.

11. And also the remainder of the people who had fled from Sarton, the sons of Jacob smote them in Arbelan, and the sons of Jacob did unto Arbelan and Tapnach as they had done to Chazar and Sarton, and when the women saw that all the men were dead, they went upon the roofs of the city and smote the sons of Jacob by showering down stones like rain.

12. And the sons of Jacob hastened and came into the city and seized all the women and smote them with the edge of the sword, and the sons of Jacob captured all the spoil and booty, flocks and herds and cattle.

13. And the sons of Jacob did unto Machnaymah as they had done to Tapnach, to Chazar and to Shiloh, and they turned from there and went away.

14. And on the fifth day the sons of Jacob heard that the people of Gaash had gathered against them to battle, because they had slain their king and their captains, for there had been fourteen captains in the city of Gaash, and the sons of Jacob had slain them all in the first battle.

15. And the sons of Jacob that day girt on their weapons of war, and they marched to battle against the inhabitants of Gaash, and in Gaash there was a strong and mighty people of the people of the Amorites, and Gaash was the strongest and best fortified city of all the cities of the Amorites, and it had three walls.

16. And the sons of Jacob came to Gaash and they found the gates of the city locked, and about five hundred men standing at the top of the outer-most wall, and a people numerous as the sand upon the sea shore were in ambush for the sons of Jacob from without the city at the rear thereof.

17. And the sons of Jacob approached to open the gates of the city, and whilst they were drawing nigh, behold those who were in ambush at the rear of the city came forth from their places and surrounded the sons of Jacob.

18. And the sons of Jacob were enclosed between the people of Gaash, and the battle was both to their front and rear, and all the men that were upon the wall, were casting from the wall upon them, arrows and stones.

19. And Judah, seeing that the men of Gaash were getting too heavy for them, gave a most piercing and tremendous shriek and all the men of Gaash were terrified at the voice of Judah's cry, and men fell from the wall at his powerful shriek, and all those that were from without and within the city were greatly afraid of their lives.

20. And the sons of Jacob still came nigh to break the doors of the city, when the men of Gaash threw stones and arrows upon them from the top of the wall, and made them flee from the gate.

21. And the sons of Jacob returned against the men of Gaash who were with them from without the city, and they smote them terribly, as striking against gourds, and they could not stand against the sons of Jacob, for fright and terror had seized them at the shriek of Judah.

22. And the sons of Jacob slew all those men who were without the city, and the sons of Jacob still drew nigh to effect an entrance into the city, and to fight under the city walls, but they could not for all the inhabitants of Gaash who remained in the city had surrounded the walls of Gaash in every direction, so that the sons of Jacob were unable to approach the city to fight with them.

23. And the sons of Jacob came nigh to one corner to fight under the wall, the inhabitants of Gaash threw arrows and stones upon them like showers of rain, and they fled from under the wall.

24. And the people of Gaash who were upon the wall, seeing that the sons of Jacob could not prevail over them from under the wall, reproached the sons of Jacob in these words, saying,

25. What is the matter with you in the battle that you cannot prevail? can you then do unto the mighty city of Gaash and its inhabitants as you did to the cities of the Amorites that were not so powerful? Surely to those weak ones amongst us you did those things, and slew them in the entrance of the city, for they had no strength when they were terrified at the sound of your shouting.

26. And will you now then be able to fight in this place? Surely here you will all die, and we will avenge the cause of those cities that you have laid waste.

27. And the inhabitants of Gaash greatly reproached the sons of Jacob and reviled them with their gods, and continued to cast arrows and stones upon them from the wall.

28. And Judah and his brothers heard the words of the inhabitants of Gaash and their anger was greatly roused, and Judah was jealous of his God in this matter, and he called out and said, O Lord, help, send help to us and our brothers.

29. And he ran at a distance with all his might, with his drawn sword in his hand, and he sprang from the earth and by dint of his strength, mounted the wall, and his sword fell from his hand.

30. And Judah shouted upon the wall, and all the men that were upon the wall were terrified, and some of them fell from the wall into the city and died, and those who were yet upon the wall, when they saw Judah's strength, they were greatly afraid and fled for their lives into the city for safety.

31. And some were emboldened to fight with Judah upon the wall, and they came nigh to slay him when they saw there was no sword in Judah's hand, and they thought of casting him from the wall to his brothers, and twenty men of the city came up to assist them, and they surrounded Judah and they all shouted over him, and approached him with drawn swords, and they terrified Judah, and Judah cried out to his brothers from the wall.

32. And Jacob and his sons drew the bow from under the wall, and smote three of the men that were upon the top of the wall, and Judah continued to cry and he exclaimed, O Lord help us, O Lord deliver us, and he cried out with a loud voice upon the wall, and the cry was heard at a great distance.

33. And after this cry he again repeated to shout, and all the men who surrounded Judah on the top of the wall were terrified, and they each threw his sword from his hand at the sound of Judah's shouting and his tremor, and fled.

34. And Judah took the swords which had fallen from their hands, and Judah fought with them and slew twenty of their men upon the wall.

35. And about eighty men and women still ascended the wall from the city and they all surrounded Judah, and the Lord impressed the fear of Judah in their hearts, that they were unable to approach him.

36. And Jacob and all who were with him drew the bow from under the wall, and they slew ten men upon the wall, and they fell below the wall, before Jacob and his sons.

37. And the people upon the wall seeing that twenty of their men had fallen, they still ran toward Judah with drawn swords, but they could not approach him for they were greatly terrified at Judah's strength.

38. And one of their mighty men whose name was Arud approached to strike Judah upon the head with his sword, when Judah hastily put his shield to his head, and the sword hit the shield, and it was split in two.

39. And this mighty man after he had struck Judah ran for his life, at the fear of Judah, and his feet slipped upon the wall and he fell amongst the sons of Jacob who were below the wall, and the sons of Jacob smote him and slew him.

40. And Judah's head pained him from the blow of the powerful man, and Judah had nearly died from it.

41. And Judah cried out upon the wall owing to the pain produced by the blow, when Dan heard him, and his anger burned within him, and he also rose up and went at a distance and ran and sprang from the earth and mounted the wall with his wrath-excited strength.

42. And when Dan came upon the wall near unto Judah all the men upon the wall fled, who had stood against Judah, and they went up to the second wall, and they threw arrows and stones upon Dan and Judah from the second wall, and endeavored to drive them from the wall.

43. And the arrows and stones struck Dan and Judah, and they had nearly been killed upon the wall, and wherever Dan and Judah fled from the wall, they were attacked with arrows and stones from the second wall.

44. And Jacob and his sons were still at the entrance of the city below the first wall, and they were not able to draw their bow against the inhabitants of the city, as they could not be seen by them, being upon the second wall.

45. And Dan and Judah when they could no longer bear the stones and arrows that fell upon them from the second wall, they both sprang upon the second wall near the people of the city, and when the people of the city who were upon the second wall saw that Dan and Judah had come to them upon the second wall, they all cried out and descended below between the walls.

46. And Jacob and his sons heard the noise of the shouting from the people of the city, and they were still at the entrance of the city, and they were anxious about Dan and Judah who were not seen by them, they being upon the second wall.

47. And Naphtali went up with his wrath-excited might and sprang upon the first wall to see what caused the noise of shouting which they had heard in the city, and Issachar and Zebulun drew nigh to break the doors of the city, and they opened the gates of the city and came into the city.

48. And Naphtali leaped from the first wall to the second, and came to assist his brothers, and the inhabitants of Gaash who were upon the wall, seeing that Naphtali was the third who had come up to assist his brothers, they all fled and descended into the city, and Jacob and all his sons and all their young men came into the city to them.

49. And Judah and Dan and Naphtali descended from the wall into the city and pursued the inhabitants of the city, and Simeon and Levi were from without the city and knew not that the gate was opened, and they went up from there to the wall and came down to their brothers into the city.

50. And the inhabitants of the city had all descended into the city, and the sons of Jacob came to them in different directions, and the battle waged against them from the front and the rear, and the sons of Jacob smote them terribly, and slew about twenty thousand of them men and women, not one of them could stand up against the sons of Jacob.

51. And the blood flowed plentifully in the city, and it was like a brook of water, and the blood flowed like a brook to the outer part of the city, and reached the desert of Bethchorin.

52. And the people of Bethchorin saw at a distance the blood flowing from the city of Gaash, and about seventy men from amongst them ran to see the blood, and they came to the place where the blood was.

53. And they followed the track of the blood and came to the wall of the city of Gaash, and they saw the blood issue from the city, and they heard the voice of crying from the inhabitants of Gaash, for it ascended unto heaven, and the blood was continuing to flow abundantly like a brook of water.

54. And all the sons of Jacob were still smiting the inhabitants of Gaash, and were engaged in slaying them till evening, about twenty thousand men and women, and the people of Chorin said, Surely this is the work of the Hebrews, for they are still carrying on war in all the cities of the Amorites.

55. And those people hastened and ran to Bethchorin, and each took his weapons of war, and they cried out to all the inhabitants of Bethchorin, who also girt on their weapons of war to go and fight with the sons of Jacob.

56. And when the sons of Jacob had done smiting the inhabitants of Gaash, they walked about the city to strip all the slain, and coming in the innermost part of the city and farther on they met three very powerful men, and there was no sword in their hand.

57. And the sons of Jacob came up to the place where they were, and the powerful men ran away, and one of them had taken Zebulun, who he saw was a young lad and of short stature, and with his might dashed him to the ground.

58. And Jacob ran to him with his sword and Jacob smote him below his loins with the sword, and cut him in two, and the body fell upon Zebulun.

59. And the second one approached and seized Jacob to fell him to the ground, and Jacob turned to him and shouted to him, whilst Simeon and Levi ran and smote him on the hips with the sword and felled him to the ground.

60. And the powerful man rose up from the ground with wrath-excited might, and Judah came to him before he had gained his footing, and struck him upon the head with the sword, and his head was split and he died.

61. And the third powerful man, seeing that his companions were killed, ran from before the sons of Jacob, and the sons of Jacob pursued him in the city; and whilst the powerful man was fleeing he found one of the swords of the inhabitants of the city, and he picked it up and turned to the sons of Jacob and fought them with that sword.

62. And the powerful man ran to Judah to strike him upon the head with the sword, and there was no shield in the hand of Judah; and whilst he was aiming to strike him, Naphtali hastily took his shield and put it to Judah's head, and the sword of the powerful man hit the shield of Naphtali and Judah escaped the sword.

63. And Simeon and Levi ran upon the powerful man with their swords and struck at him forcibly with their swords, and the two swords entered the body of the powerful man and divided it in two, length-wise.

64. And the sons of Jacob smote the three mighty men at that time, together with all the inhabitants of Gaash, and the day was about to decline.

65. And the sons of Jacob walked about Gaash and took all the spoil of the city, even the little ones and women they did not suffer to live, and the sons of Jacob did unto Gaash as they had done to Sarton and Shiloh.

CHAPTER 40

1. And the sons of Jacob led away all the spoil of Gaash, and went out of the city by night.

2. They were going out marching toward the castle of Bethchorin, and the inhabitants of Bethchorin were going to the castle to meet them, and on that night the sons of Jacob fought with the inhabitants of Bethchorin, in the castle of Bethchorin.

3. And all the inhabitants of Bethchorin were mighty men, one of them would not flee from before a thousand men, and they fought on that night upon the castle, and their shouts were heard on that night from afar, and the earth quaked at their shouting.

4. And all the sons of Jacob were afraid of those men, as they were not accustomed to fight in the dark, and they were greatly confounded, and the sons of Jacob cried unto the Lord, saying, Give help to us O Lord, deliver us that we may not die by the hands of these uncircumcised men.

5. And the Lord hearkened to the voice of the sons of Jacob, and the Lord caused great terror and confusion to seize the people of Bethchorin, and they fought amongst themselves the one with the other in the darkness of night, and smote each other in great numbers.

6. And the sons of Jacob, knowing that the Lord had brought a spirit of perverseness amongst those men, and that they fought each man with his neighbor, went forth from among the bands of the people of Bethchorin and went as far as the descent of the castle of Bethchorin, and farther, and they tarried there securely with their young men on that night.

7. And the people of Bethchorin fought the whole night, one man with his brother, and the other with his neighbor, and they cried out in every direction upon the castle, and their cry was heard at a distance, and the whole earth shook at their voice, for they were powerful above all the people of the earth.

8. And all the inhabitants of the cities of the Canaanites, the Hittites, the Amorites, the Hivites and all the kings of Canaan, and also those who were on the other side of the Jordan, heard the noise of the shouting on that night.

9. And they said, Surely these are the battles of the Hebrews who are fighting against the seven cities, who came nigh unto them; and who can stand against those Hebrews?

10. And all the inhabitants of the cities of the Canaanites, and all those who were on the other side of the Jordan, were greatly afraid of the sons of Jacob, for they said, Behold the same will be done to us as was done to those cities, for who can stand against their mighty strength?

11. And the cries of the Chorinites were very great on that night, and continued to increase;
and they smote each other till morning, and numbers of them were killed.

12. And the morning appeared, and all the sons of Jacob rose up at daybreak and went up to the castle, and they smote those who remained of the Chorinites in a terrible manner, and they were all killed in the castle.

13. And the sixth day appeared, and all the inhabitants of Canaan saw at a distance all the people of Bethchorin lying dead in the castle of Bethchorin, and strewed about as the carcasses of lambs and goats.

14. And the sons of Jacob led all the spoil which they had captured from Gaash and went to Bethchorin, and they found the city full of people like the sand of the sea, and they fought with them, and the sons of Jacob smote them there till evening time.

15. And the sons of Jacob did unto Bethchorin as they had done to Gaash and Tapnach, and as they had done to Chazar, to Sarton and to Shiloh.

16. And the sons of Jacob took with them the spoil of Bethchorin and all the spoil of the cities, and on that day they went home to Shechem.

17. And the sons of Jacob came home to the city of Shechem, and they remained without the city, and they then rested there from the war, and tarried there all night.

18. And all their servants together with all the spoil that they had taken from the cities, they left without the city, and they did not enter the city, for they said, Peradventure there may be yet more fighting against us, and they may come to besiege us in Shechem.

19. And Jacob and his sons and their servants remained on that night and the next day in the portion of the field which Jacob had purchased from Hamor for five shekels, and all that they had captured was with them.

20. And all the booty which the sons of Jacob had captured, was in the portion of the field, immense as the sand upon the sea shore.

21. And the inhabitants of the land observed them from afar, and all the inhabitants of the land were afraid of the sons of Jacob who had done this thing, for no king from the days of old had ever done the like.

22. And the seven kings of the Canaanites resolved to make peace with the sons of Jacob, for they were greatly afraid of their lives, on account of the sons of Jacob.

23. And on that day, being the seventh day, Japhia king of Hebron sent secretly to the king of Ai, and to the king of Gibeon, and to the king of Shalem, and to the king of Adulam, and to the king of Lachish, and to the king of Chazar, and to all the Canaanitish kings who were under their subjection, saying,

24. Go up with me, and come to me that we may go to the sons of Jacob, and I will make peace with them, and form a treaty with them, lest all your lands be destroyed by the swords of the sons of Jacob, as they did to Shechem and the cities around it, as you have heard and seen.

25. And when you come to me, do not come with many men, but let every king bring his three head captains, and every captain bring three of his officers.

26. And come all of you to Hebron, and we will go together to the sons of Jacob, and supplicate them that they shall form a treaty of peace with us.

27. And all those kings did as the king of Hebron had sent to them, for they were all under his counsel and command, and all the kings of Canaan assembled to go to the sons of Jacob, to make peace with them; and the sons of Jacob returned and went to the portion of the field that was in Shechem, for they did not put confidence in the kings of the land.

28. And the sons of Jacob returned and remained in the portion of the field ten days, and no one came to make war with them.

29. And when the sons of Jacob saw that there was no appearance of war, they all assembled and went to the city of Shechem, and the sons of Jacob remained in Shechem.

30. And at the expiration of forty days, all the kings of the Amorites assembled from all their places and came to Hebron, to Japhia, king of Hebron.

31. And the number of kings that came to Hebron, to make peace with the sons of Jacob, was twenty-one kings, and the number of captains that came with them was sixty-nine, and their men were one hundred and eighty-nine, and all these kings and their men rested by Mount Hebron.

32. And the king of Hebron went out with his three captains and nine men, and these kings resolved to go to the sons of Jacob to make peace.

33. And they said unto the king of Hebron, Go thou before us with thy men, and speak for us unto the sons of Jacob, and we will come after thee and confirm thy words, and the king of Hebron did so.

34. And the sons of Jacob heard that all the kings of Canaan had gathered together and rested in Hebron, and the sons of Jacob sent four of their servants as spies, saying, Go and spy these kings, and search and examine their men whether they are few or many, and if they are but few in number, number them all and come back.

35. And the servants of Jacob went secretly to these kings, and did as the sons of Jacob had commanded them, and on that day they came back to the sons of Jacob, and said unto them, We came unto those kings, and they are but few in number, and we numbered them all, and behold, they were two hundred and eighty-eight, kings and men.

36. And the sons of Jacob said, They are but few in number, therefore we will not all go out to them; and in the morning the sons of Jacob rose up and chose sixty two of their men, and ten of the sons of Jacob went with them; and they girt on their weapons of war, for they said, They are coming to make war with us, for they knew not that they were coming to make peace with them.

37. And the sons of Jacob went with their servants to the gate of Shechem, toward those kings, and their father Jacob was with them.

38. And when they had come forth, behold, the king of Hebron and his three captains and nine men with him were coming along the road against the sons of Jacob, and the sons of Jacob lifted up their eyes, and saw at a distance Japhia, king of Hebron, with his captains, coming toward them, and the sons of Jacob took their stand at the place of the gate of Shechem, and did not proceed.

39. And the king of Hebron continued to advance, he and his captains, until he came nigh to the sons of Jacob, and he and his captains bowed down to them to the ground, and the king of Hebron sat with his captains before Jacob and his sons.

40. And the sons of Jacob said unto him, What has befallen thee, O king of Hebron? why hast thou come to us this day? what dost thou require from us? and the king of Hebron said unto Jacob, I beseech thee my lord, all the kings of the Canaanites have this day come to make peace with you.

41. And the sons of Jacob heard the words of the king of Hebron, and they would not consent to his proposals, for the sons of Jacob had no faith in him, for they imagined that the king of Hebron had spoken deceitfully to them.

42. And the king of Hebron knew from the words of the sons of Jacob, that they did not believe his words, and the king of Hebron approached nearer to Jacob, and said unto him, I beseech thee, my lord, to be assured that all these kings have come to you on peaceable terms, for they have not come with all their men, neither did they bring their weapons of war with them, for they have come to seek peace from my lord and his sons.

43. And the sons of Jacob answered the king of Hebron, saying, Send thou to all these kings, and if thou speakest truth unto us, let them each come singly before us, and if they come unto us unarmed, we shall then know that they seek peace from us.

44. And Japhia, king of Hebron, sent one of his men to the kings, and they all came before the sons of Jacob, and bowed down to them to the ground, and these kings sat before Jacob and his sons, and they spoke unto them, saying,

45. We have heard all that you did unto the kings of the Amorites with your sword and exceedingly mighty arm, so that no man could stand up before you, and we were afraid of you for the sake of our lives, lest it should befall us as it did to them.

46. So we have come unto you to form a treaty of peace between us, and now therefore contract with us a covenant of peace and truth, that you will not meddle with us, inasmuch as we have not meddled with you.

47. And the sons of Jacob knew that they had really come to seek peace from them, and the sons of Jacob listened to them, and formed a covenant with them.

48. And the sons of Jacob swore unto them that they would not meddle with them, and all the kings of the Canaanites swore also to them, and the sons of Jacob made them tributary from that day forward.

49. And after this all the captains of these kings came with their men before Jacob, with presents in their hands for Jacob and his sons, and they bowed down to him to the ground.

50. And these kings then urged the sons of Jacob and begged of them to return all the spoil they had captured from the seven cities of the Amorites, and the sons of Jacob did so, and they returned all that they had captured, the women, the little ones, the cattle and all the spoil which they had taken, and they sent them off, and they went away each to his city.

51. And all these kings again bowed down to the sons of Jacob, and they sent or brought them many gifts in those days, and the sons of Jacob sent off these kings and their men, and they went peaceably away from them to their cities, and the sons of Jacob also returned to their home, to Shechem.

52. And there was peace from that day forward between the sons of Jacob and the kings of the Canaanites, until the children of Israel came to inherit the land of Canaan.

CHAPTER 41

1. And at the revolution of the year the sons of Jacob journeyed from Shechem, and they came to Hebron, to their father Isaac, and they dwelt there, but their flocks and herds they fed daily in Shechem, for there was there in those days good and fat pasture, and Jacob and his sons and all their household dwelt in the valley of Hebron.

2. And it was in those days, in that year, being the hundred and sixth year of the life of Jacob, in the tenth year of Jacob's coming from Padan-aram, that Leah the wife of Jacob died; she was fifty-one years old when she died in Hebron.

3. And Jacob and his sons buried her in the cave of the field of Machpelah, which is in Hebron, which Abraham had bought from the children of Heth, for the possession of a burial place.

4. And the sons of Jacob dwelt with their father in the valley of Hebron, and all the inhabitants of the land knew their strength and their fame went throughout the land.

5. And Joseph the son of Jacob, and his brother Benjamin, the sons of Rachel, the wife of Jacob, were yet young in those days, and did not go out with their brethren during their battles in all the cities of the Amorites.

6. And when Joseph saw the strength of his brethren, and their greatness, he praised them and extolled them, but he ranked himself greater than them, and extolled himself above them; and Jacob, his father, also loved him more than any of his sons, for he was a son of his old age, and through his love toward him, he made him a coat of many colors.

7. And when Joseph saw that his father loved him more than his brethren, he continued to exalt himself above his brethren, and he brought unto his father evil reports concerning them.

8. And the sons of Jacob seeing the whole of Joseph's conduct toward them, and that their father loved him more than any of them, they hated him and could not speak peaceably to him all the days.

9. And Joseph was seventeen years old, and he was still magnifying himself above his brethren, and thought of raising himself above them.

10. At that time he dreamed a dream, and he came unto his brothers and told them his dream, and he said unto them, I dreamed a dream, and behold we were all binding sheaves in the field, and my sheaf rose and placed itself upon the ground and your sheaves surrounded it and bowed down to it.

11. And his brethren answered him and said unto him, What meaneth this dream that thou didst dream? dost thou imagine in thy heart to reign or rule over us?

12. And he still came, and told the thing to his father Jacob, and Jacob kissed Joseph when he heard these words from his mouth, and Jacob blessed Joseph.

13. And when the sons of Jacob saw that their father had blessed Joseph and had kissed him, and that he loved him exceedingly, they became jealous of him and hated him the more.

14. And after this Joseph dreamed another dream and related the dream to his father in the presence of his brethren, and Joseph said unto his father and brethren, Behold I have again dreamed a dream, and behold the sun and the moon and the eleven stars bowed down to me.

15. And his father heard the words of Joseph and his dream, and seeing that his brethren hated Joseph on account of this matter, Jacob therefore rebuked Joseph before his brethren on account of this thing, saying, What meaneth this dream which thou hast dreamed, and this magnifying thyself before thy brethren who are older than thou art?

16. Dost thou imagine in thy heart that I and thy mother and thy eleven brethren will come and bow down to thee, that thou speakest these things?

17. And his brethren were jealous of him on account of his words and dreams, and they continued to hate him, and Jacob reserved the dreams in his heart.

18. And the sons of Jacob went one day to feed their father's flock in Shechem, for they were still herdsmen in those days; and whilst the sons of Jacob were that day feeding in Shechem they delayed, and the time of gathering in the cattle was passed, and they had not arrived.

19. And Jacob saw that his sons were delayed in Shechem, and Jacob said within himself, Peradventure the people of Shechem have risen up to fight against them, therefore they have delayed coming this day.

20. And Jacob called Joseph his son and commanded him, saying, Behold thy brethren are feeding in Shechem this day, and behold they have not yet come back; go now therefore and see where they are, and bring me word back concerning the welfare of thy brethren and the welfare of the flock.

21. And Jacob sent his son Joseph to the valley of Hebron, and Joseph came for his brothers to Shechem, and could not find them, and Joseph went about the field which was near Shechem, to see where his brothers had turned, and he missed his road in the wilderness, and knew not which way he should go.

22. And an angel of the Lord found him wandering in the road toward the field, and Joseph said unto the angel of the Lord, I seek my brethren; hast thou not heard where they are feeding? and the angel of the Lord said unto Joseph, I saw thy brethren feeding here, and I heard them say they would go to feed in Dothan.

23. And Joseph hearkened to the voice of the angel of the Lord, and he went to his brethren in Dothan and he found them in Dothan feeding the flock.

24. And Joseph advanced to his brethren, and before he had come nigh unto them, they had resolved to slay him.

25. And Simeon said to his brethren, Behold the man of dreams is coming unto us this day, and now therefore come and let us kill him and cast him in one of the pits that are in the wilderness, and when his father shall seek him from us, we will say an evil beast has devoured him.

26. And Reuben heard the words of his brethren concerning Joseph, and he said unto them, You should not do this thing, for how can we look up to our father Jacob? Cast him into this pit to die there, but stretch not forth a hand upon him to spill his blood; and Reuben said this in order to deliver him from their hand, to bring him back to his father.

27. And when Joseph came to his brethren he sat before them, and they rose upon him and seized him and smote him to the earth, and stripped the coat of many colors which he had on.

28. And they took him and cast him into a pit, and in the pit there was no water, but serpents and scorpions. And Joseph was afraid of the serpents and scorpions that were in the pit. And Joseph cried out with a loud voice, and the Lord hid the serpents and scorpions in the sides of the pit, and they did no harm unto Joseph.

29. And Joseph called out from the pit to his brethren, and said unto them, What have I done unto you, and in what have I sinned? why do you not fear the Lord concerning me? am I not of your bones and flesh, and is not Jacob your father, my father? why do you do this thing unto me this day, and how will you be able to look up to our father Jacob?

30. And he continued to cry out and call unto his brethren from the pit, and he said, O Judah, Simeon, and Levi, my brethren, lift me up from the place of darkness in which you have placed me, and come this day to have compassion on me, ye children of the Lord, and sons of Jacob my father. And if I have sinned unto you, are you not the sons of Abraham, Isaac, and Jacob? if they saw an orphan they had compassion over him, or one that was hungry, they gave him bread to eat, or one that was thirsty, they gave him water to drink, or one that was naked, they covered him with garments!

31. And how then will you withhold your pity from your brother, for I am of your flesh and bones, and if I have sinned unto you, surely you will do this on account of my father!

32. And Joseph spoke these words from the pit, and his brethren could not listen to him, nor incline their ears to the words of Joseph, and Joseph was crying and weeping in the pit.

33. And Joseph said, O that my father knew, this day, the act which my brothers have done unto me, and the words which they have this day spoken unto me.

34. And all his brethren heard his cries and weeping in the pit, and his brethren went and removed themselves from the pit, so that they might not hear the cries of Joseph and his weeping in the pit.

CHAPTER 42

1. And they went and sat on the opposite side, about the distance of a bow-shot, and they sat there to eat bread, and whilst they were eating, they held counsel together what was to be done with him, whether to slay him or to bring him back to his father.

2. They were holding the counsel, when they lifted up their eyes, and saw, and behold there was a company of Ishmaelites coming at a distance by the road of Gilead, going down to Egypt.

3. And Judah said unto them, What gain will it be to us if we slay our brother? peradventure God will require him from us; this then is the counsel proposed concerning him, which you shall do unto him: Behold this company of Ishmaelites going down to Egypt,

4. Now therefore, come let us dispose of him to them, and let not our hand be upon him, and they will lead him along with them, and he will be lost amongst the people of the land, and we will not put him to death with our own hands. And the proposal pleased his brethren and they did according to the word of Judah.

5. And whilst they were discoursing about this matter, and before the company of Ishmaelites had come up to them, seven trading men of Midian passed by them, and as they passed they were thirsty, and they lifted up their

eyes and saw the pit in which Joseph was immured, and they looked, and behold every species of bird was upon him.

6. And these Midianites ran to the pit to drink water, for they thought that it contained water, and on coming before the pit they heard the voice of Joseph crying and weeping in the pit, and they looked down into the pit, and they saw and behold there was a youth of comely appearance and well favored.

7. And they called unto him and said, Who art thou and who brought thee hither, and who placed thee in this pit, in the wilderness? and they all assisted to raise up Joseph and they drew him out, and brought him up from the pit, and took him and went away on their journey and passed by his brethren.

8. And these said unto them, Why do you do this, to take our servant from us and to go away? surely we placed this youth in the pit because he rebelled against us, and you come and bring him up and lead him away; now then give us back our servant.

9. And the Midianites answered and said unto the sons of Jacob, Is this your servant, or does this man attend you? peradventure you are all his servants, for he is more comely and well favored than any of you, and why do you all speak falsely unto us?

10. Now therefore we will not listen to your words, nor attend to you, for we found the youth in the pit in the wilderness, and we took him; we will therefore go on.

11. And all the sons of Jacob approached them and rose up to them and said unto them, Give us back our servant, and why will you all die by the edge of the sword? And the Midianites cried out against them, and they drew their swords, and approached to fight with the sons of Jacob.

12. And behold Simeon rose up from his seat against them, and sprang upon the ground and drew his sword and approached the Midianites and he gave a terrible shout before them, so that his shouting was heard at a distance, and the earth shook at Simeon's shouting.

13. And the Midianites were terrified on account of Simeon and the noise of his shouting, and they fell upon their faces, and were excessively alarmed.

14. And Simeon said unto them, Verily I am Simeon, the son of Jacob the Hebrew, who have, only with my brother, destroyed the city of Shechem and the cities of the Amorites; so shall God moreover do unto me, that if all your brethren the people of Midian, and also the kings of Canaan, were to come with you, they could not fight against me.

15. Now therefore give us back the youth whom you have taken, lest I give your flesh to the birds of the skies and the beasts of the earth.

16. And the Midianites were more afraid of Simeon, and they approached the sons of Jacob with terror and fright, and with pathetic words, saying,

17. Surely you have said that the young man is your servant, and that he rebelled against you, and therefore you placed him in the pit; what then will you do with a servant who rebels against his master? Now therefore sell him unto us, and we will give you all that you require for him; and the Lord was pleased to do this in order that the sons of Jacob should not slay their brother.

18. And the Midianites saw that Joseph was of a comely appearance and well-favored; they desired him in their hearts and were urgent to purchase him from his brethren.

19. And the sons of Jacob hearkened to the Midianites and they sold their brother Joseph to them for twenty pieces of silver, and Reuben their brother was not with them, and the Midianites took Joseph and continued their journey to Gilead.

20. They were going along the road, and the Midianites repented of what they had done, in having purchased the young man, and one said to the other, What is this thing that we have done, in taking this youth from the Hebrews, who is of comely appearance and well favored.

21. Perhaps this youth is stolen from the land of the Hebrews, and why then have we done this thing? and if he should be sought for and found in our hands we shall die through him.

22. Now surely hardy and powerful men have sold him to us, the strength of one of whom you saw this day; perhaps they stole him from his land with their might and with their powerful arm, and have therefore sold him to us for the small value which we gave unto them.

23. And whilst they were thus discoursing together, they looked, and behold the company of Ishmaelites which was coming at first, and which the sons of Jacob saw, was advancing toward the Midianites, and the Midianites said to each other, Come let us sell this youth to the company of Ishmaelites who are coming toward us, and we will take for him the little that we gave for him, and we will be delivered from his evil.

24. And they did so, and they reached the Ishmaelites, and the Midianites sold Joseph to the Ishmaelites for twenty pieces of silver which they had given for him to his brethren.

25. And the Midianites went on their road to Gilead, and the Ishmaelites took Joseph and they let him ride upon one of the camels, and they were leading him to Egypt.

26. And Joseph heard that the Ishmaelites were proceeding to Egypt, and Joseph lamented and wept at this thing that he was to be so far removed from the land of Canaan, from his father, and he wept bitterly whilst he was riding upon the camel, and one of their men observed him, and made him go down from the camel and walk on foot, and notwithstanding this Joseph continued to cry and weep, and he said, O my father, my father.

27. And one of the Ishmaelites rose up and smote Joseph upon the cheek, and still he continued to weep; and Joseph was fatigued in the road, and was unable to proceed on account of the bitterness of his soul, and they all smote him and afflicted him in the road, and they terrified him in order that he might cease from weeping.

28. And the Lord saw the ambition of Joseph and his trouble, and the Lord brought down upon those men darkness and confusion, and the hand of every one that smote him became withered.

29. And they said to each other, What is this thing that God has done to us in the road? and they knew not that this befell them on account of Joseph. And the men proceeded on the road, and they passed along the road of Ephrath where Rachel was buried.

30. And Joseph reached his mother's grave, and Joseph hastened and ran to his mother's grave, and fell upon the grave and wept.

31. And Joseph cried aloud upon his mother's grave, and he said, O my mother, my mother, O thou who didst give me birth, awake now, and rise and see thy son, how he has been sold for a slave, and no one to pity him.

32. O rise and see thy son, weep with me on account of my troubles, and see the heart of my brethren.

33. Arouse my mother, arouse, awake from thy sleep for me, and direct thy battles against my brethren. O how have they stripped me of my coat, and sold me already twice for a slave, and separated me from my father, and there is no one to pity me.

34. Arouse and lay thy cause against them before God, and see whom God will justify in the judgment, and whom he will condemn.

35. Rise, O my mother, rise, awake from thy sleep and see my father how his soul is with me this day, and comfort him and ease his heart.

36. And Joseph continued to speak these words, and Joseph cried aloud and wept bitterly upon his mother's grave; and he ceased speaking, and from bitterness of heart he became still as a stone upon the grave.

37. And Joseph heard a voice speaking to him from beneath the ground, which answered him with bitterness of heart, and with a voice of weeping and praying in these words:

38. My son, my son Joseph, I have heard the voice of thy weeping and the voice of thy lamentation; I have seen thy tears; I know thy troubles, my son, and it grieves me for thy sake, and abundant grief is added to my grief.

39. Now therefore my son, Joseph my son, hope to the Lord, and wait for him and do not fear, for the Lord is with thee, he will deliver thee from all trouble.

40. Rise my son, go down unto Egypt with thy masters, and do not fear, for the Lord is with thee, my son. And she continued to speak like unto these words unto Joseph, and she was still.

41. And Joseph heard this, and he wondered greatly at this, and he continued to weep; and after this one of the Ishmaelites observed him crying and weeping upon the grave, and his anger was kindled against him, and he drove him from there, and he smote him and cursed him.

42. And Joseph said unto the men, May I find grace in your sight to take me back to my father's house, and he will give you abundance of riches.

43. And they answered him, saying, Art thou not a slave, and where is thy father? and if thou hadst a father thou wouldst not already twice have been sold for a slave for so little value; and their anger was still roused against him, and they continued to smite him and to chastise him, and Joseph wept bitterly.

44. And the Lord saw Joseph's affliction, and Lord again smote these men, and chastised them, and the Lord caused darkness to envelope them upon the earth, and the lightning flashed and the thunder roared, and the earth shook at the voice of the thunder and of the mighty wind, and the men were terrified and knew not where they should go.

45. And the beasts and camels stood still, and they led them, but they would not go, they smote them, and they crouched upon the ground; and the men said to each other, What is this that God has done to us? what are our transgressions, and what are our sins that this thing has thus befallen us?

46. And one of them answered and said unto them, Perhaps on account of the sin of afflicting this slave has this thing happened this day to us; now therefore implore him strongly to forgive us, and then we shall know on whose

account this evil befalleth us, and if God shall have compassion over us, then we shall know that all this cometh to us on account of the sin of afflicting this slave.

47. And the men did so, and they supplicated Joseph and pressed him to forgive them; and they said, We have sinned to the Lord and to thee, now therefore vouchsafe to request of thy God that he shall put away this death from amongst us, for we have sinned to him.

48. And Joseph did according to their words, and the Lord hearkened to Joseph, and the Lord put away the plague which he had inflicted upon those men on account of Joseph, and the beasts rose up from the ground and they conducted them, and they went on, and the raging storm abated and the earth became tranquilized, and the men proceeded on their journey to go down to Egypt, and the men knew that this evil had befallen them on account of Joseph.

49. And they said to each other, Behold we know that it was on account of his affliction that this evil befell us; now therefore why shall we bring this death upon our souls? Let us hold counsel what to do to this slave.

50. And one answered and said, Surely he told us to bring him back to his father; now therefore come, let us take him back and we will go to the place that he will tell us, and take from his family the price that we gave for him and we will then go away.

51. And one answered again and said, Behold this counsel is very good, but we cannot do so for the way is very far from us, and we cannot go out of our road.

52. And one more answered and said unto them, This is the counsel to be adopted, we will not swerve from it; behold we are this day going to Egypt, and when we shall have come to Egypt, we will sell him there at a high price, and we will be delivered from his evil.

53. And this thing pleased the men and they did so, and they continued their journey to Egypt with Joseph.

CHAPTER 43

1. And when the sons of Jacob had sold their brother Joseph to the Midianites, their hearts were smitten on account of him, and they repented of their acts, and they sought for him to bring him back, but could not find him.

2. And Reuben returned to the pit in which Joseph had been put, in order to lift him out, and restore him to his father, and Reuben stood by the pit, and he heard not a word, and he called out Joseph! Joseph! and no one answered or uttered a word.

3. And Reuben said, Joseph has died through fright, or some serpent has caused his death; and Reuben descended into the pit, and he searched for Joseph and could not find him in the pit, and he came out again.

4. And Reuben tore his garments and he said, The child is not there, and how shall I reconcile my father about him if he be dead? and he went to his brethren and found them grieving on account of Joseph, and counseling together how to reconcile their father about him, and Reuben said unto his brethren, I came to the pit and behold Joseph was not there, what then shall we say unto our father, for my father will only seek the lad from me.

5. And his brethren answered him saying, Thus and thus we did, and our hearts afterward smote us on account of this act, and we now sit to seek a pretext how we shall reconcile our father to it.

6. And Reuben said unto them, What is this you have done to bring down the grey hairs of our father in sorrow to the grave? the thing is not good, that you have done.

7. And Reuben sat with them, and they all rose up and swore to each other not to tell this thing unto Jacob, and they all said, The man who will tell this to our father or his household, or who will report this to any of the children of the land, we will all rise up against him and slay him with the sword.

8. And the sons of Jacob feared each other in this matter, from the youngest to the oldest, and no one spoke a word, and they concealed the thing in their hearts.

9. And they afterward sat down to determine and invent something to say unto their father Jacob concerning all these things.

10. And Issachar said unto them, Here is an advice for you if it seem good in your eyes to do this thing, take the coat which belongeth to Joseph and tear it, and kill a kid of the goats and dip it in its blood.

11. And send it to our father and when he seeth it he will say an evil beast has devoured him, therefore tear ye his coat and behold his blood will be upon his coat, and by your doing this we shall be free of our father's murmurings.

12. And Issachar's advice pleased them, and they hearkened unto him and they did according to the word of Issachar which he had counselled them.

13. And they hastened and took Joseph's coat and tore it, and they killed a kid of the goats and dipped the coat in the blood of the kid, and then trampled it in the dust, and they sent the coat to their father Jacob by the hand of Naphtali, and they commanded him to say these words:

14. We had gathered in the cattle and had come as far as the road to Shechem and farther, when we found this coat upon the road in the wilderness dipped in blood and in dust; now therefore know whether it be thy son's coat or not.

15. And Naphtali went and he came unto his father and he gave him the coat, and he spoke unto him all the words which his brethren had commanded him.

16. And Jacob saw Joseph's coat and he knew it and he fell upon his face to the ground, and became as still as a stone, and he afterward rose up and cried out with a loud and weeping voice and he said, It is the coat of my son Joseph!

17. And Jacob hastened and sent one of his servants to his sons, who went to them and found them coming along the road with the flock.

18. And the sons of Jacob came to their father about evening, and behold their garments were torn and dust was upon their heads, and they found their father crying out and weeping with a loud voice.

19. And Jacob said unto his sons, Tell me truly what evil have you this day suddenly brought upon me? and they answered their father Jacob, saying, We were coming along this day after the flock had been gathered in, and we came as far as the city of Shechem by the road in the wilderness, and we found this coat filled with blood upon the ground, and we knew it and we sent unto thee if thou couldst know it.

20. And Jacob heard the words of his sons and he cried out with a loud voice, and he said, It is the coat of my son, an evil beast has devoured him; Joseph is rent in pieces, for I sent him this day to see whether it was well with you and well with the flocks and to bring me word again from you, and he went as I commanded him, and this has happened to him this day whilst I thought my son was with you.

21. And the sons of Jacob answered and said, He did not come to us, neither have we seen him from the time of our going out from thee until now.

22. And when Jacob heard their words he again cried out aloud, and he rose up and tore his garments, and he put sackcloth upon his loins, and he wept bitterly and he mourned and lifted up his voice in weeping and exclaimed and said these words,

23. Joseph my son, O my son Joseph, I sent thee this day after the welfare of thy brethren, and behold thou hast been torn in pieces; through my hand has this happened to my son.

24. It grieves me for thee Joseph my son, it grieves me for thee; how sweet wast thou to me during life, and now how exceedingly bitter is thy death to me.

25. o that I had died in thy stead Joseph my son, for it grieves me sadly for thee my son, O my son, my son. Joseph my son, where art thou, and where hast thou been drawn? arouse, arouse from thy place, and come and see my grief for thee, O my son Joseph.

26. Come now and number the tears gushing from my eyes down my cheeks, and bring them up before the Lord, that his anger may turn from me.

27. o Joseph my son, how didst thou fall, by the hand of one by whom no one had fallen from the beginning of the world unto this day; for thou hast been put to death by the smiting of an enemy, inflicted with cruelty, but surely I know that this has happened to thee, on account of the multitude of my sins.

28. Arouse now and see how bitter is my trouble for thee my son, although I did not rear thee, nor fashion thee, nor give thee breath and soul, but it was God who formed thee and built thy bones and covered them with flesh, and breathed in thy nostrils the breath of life, and then he gave thee unto me.

29. Now truly God who gave thee unto me, he has taken thee from me, and such then has befallen thee

30. And Jacob continued to speak like unto these words concerning Joseph, and he wept bitterly; he fell to the ground and became still.

31. And all the sons of Jacob seeing their father's trouble, they repented of what they had done, and they also wept bitterly.

32. And Judah rose up and lifted his father's head from the ground, and placed it upon his lap, and he wiped his father's tears from his cheeks, and Judah wept an exceeding great weeping, whilst his father's head was reclining upon his lap, still as a stone.

33. And the sons of Jacob saw their father's trouble, and they lifted up their voices and continued to weep, and Jacob was yet lying upon the ground still as a stone.

34. And all his sons and his servants and his servant's children rose up and stood round him to comfort him, and he refused to be comforted.

35. And the whole household of Jacob rose up and mourned a great mourning on account of Joseph and their father's trouble, and the intelligence reached Isaac, the son of Abraham, the father of Jacob, and he wept bitterly

on account of Joseph, he and all his household, and he went from the place where he dwelt in Hebron, and his men with him, and he comforted Jacob his son, and he refused to be comforted.

36. And after this, Jacob rose up from the ground, and his tears were running down his cheeks, and he said unto his sons, Rise up and take your swords and your bows, and go forth into the field, and seek whether you can find my son's body and bring it unto me that I may bury it.

37. Seek also, I pray you, among the beasts and hunt them, and that which shall come the first before you seize and bring it unto me, perhaps the Lord will this day pity my affliction, and prepare before you that which did tear my son in pieces, and bring it unto me, and I will avenge the cause of my son.

38. And his sons did as their father had commanded them, and they rose up early in the morning, and each took his sword and his bow in his hand, and they went forth into the field to hunt the beasts.

39. And Jacob was still crying aloud and weeping and walking to and fro in the house, and smiting his hands together, saying, Joseph my son, Joseph my son.

40. And the sons of Jacob went into the wilderness to seize the beasts, and behold a wolf came toward them, and they seized him, and brought him unto their father, and they said unto him, This is the first we have found, and we have brought him unto thee as thou didst command us, and thy son's body we could not find.

41. And Jacob took the beast from the hands of his sons, and he cried out with a loud and weeping voice, holding the beast in his hand, and he spoke with a bitter heart unto the beast, Why didst thou devour my son Joseph, and how didst thou have no fear of the God of the earth, or of my trouble for my son Joseph?

42. And thou didst devour my son for naught, because he committed no violence, and didst thereby render me culpable on his account, therefore God will require him that is persecuted.

43. And the Lord opened the mouth of the beast in order to comfort Jacob with its words, and it answered Jacob and spoke these words unto him,

44. As God liveth who created us in the earth, and as thy soul liveth, my lord, I did not see thy son, neither did I tear him to pieces, but from a distant land I also came to seek my son who went from me this day, and I know not whether he be living or dead.

45. And I came this day into the field to seek my son, and your sons found me, and seized me and increased my grief, and have this day brought me before thee, and I have now spoken all my words to thee.

46. And now therefore, O son of man, I am in thy hands, and do unto me this day as it may seem good in thy sight, but by the life of God who created me, I did not see thy son, nor did I tear him to pieces, neither has the flesh of man entered my mouth all the days of my life.

47. And when Jacob heard the words of the beast he was greatly astonished, and sent forth the beast from his hand, and she went her way.

48. And Jacob was still crying aloud and weeping for Joseph day after day, and he mourned for his son many days.

CHAPTER 44

1. And the sons of Ishmael who had bought Joseph from the Midianites, who had bought him from his brethren, went to Egypt with Joseph, and they came upon the borders of Egypt, and when they came near unto Egypt, they met four men of the sons of Medan the son of Abraham, who had gone forth from the land of Egypt on their journey.

2. And the Ishmaelites said unto them, Do you desire to purchase this slave from us? and they said, Deliver him over to us, and they delivered Joseph over to them, and they beheld him, that he was a very comely youth and they purchased him for twenty shekels.

3. And the Ishmaelites continued their journey to Egypt and the Medanim also returned that day to Egypt, and the Medanim said to each other, Behold we have heard that Potiphar, an officer of Pharaoh, captain of the guard, seeketh a good servant who shall stand before him to attend him, and to make him overseer over his house and all belonging to him.

4. Now therefore come let us sell him to him for what we may desire, if he be able to give unto us that which we shall require for him.

5. And these Medanim went and came to the house of Potiphar, and said unto him, We have heard that thou seekest a good servant to attend thee, behold we have a servant that will please thee, if thou canst give unto us that which we may desire, and we will sell him unto thee.

6. And Potiphar said, Bring him before me, and I will see him, and if he please me I will give unto you that which you may require for him.

7. And the Medanim went and brought Joseph and placed him before Potiphar, and he saw him, and he pleased him exceedingly, and Potiphar said unto them, Tell me what you require for this youth?

8. And they said, Four hundred pieces of silver we desire for him, and Potiphar said, I will give it you if you bring me the record of his sale to you, and will tell me his history, for perhaps he may be stolen, for this youth is neither a slave, nor the son of a slave, but I observe in him the appearance of a goodly and handsome person.

9. And the Medanim went and brought unto him the Ishmaelites who had sold him to them, and they told him, saying, He is a slave and we sold him to them.

10. And Potiphar heard the words of the Ishmaelites in his giving the silver unto the Medanim, and the Medanim took the silver and went on their journey, and the Ishmaelites also returned home.

11. And Potiphar took Joseph and brought him to his house that he might serve him, and Joseph found favor in the sight of Potiphar, and he placed confidence in him, and made
   him overseer over his house, and all that belonged to him he delivered over into his hand.

12. And the Lord was with Joseph and he became a prosperous man, and the Lord blessed the house of Potiphar for the sake of Joseph.

13. And Potiphar left all that he had in the hand of Joseph, and Joseph was one that caused things to come in and go out, and everything was regulated by his wish in the house of Potiphar.

14. And Joseph was eighteen years old, a youth with beautiful eyes and of comely appearance, and like unto him was not in the whole land of Egypt.

15. At that time whilst he was in his master's house, going in and out of the house and attending his master, Zelicah, his master's wife, lifted up her eyes toward Joseph and she looked at him, and behold he was a youth comely and well favored.

16. And she coveted his beauty in her heart, and her soul was fixed upon Joseph, and she enticed him day after day, and Zelicah persuaded Joseph daily, but Joseph did not lift up his eyes to behold his master's wife.

17. And Zelicah said unto him, How goodly are thy appearance and form, truly I have looked at all the slaves, and have not seen so beautiful a slave as thou art; and Joseph said unto her, Surely he who created me in my mother's womb created all mankind.

18. And she said unto him, How beautiful are thine eyes, with which thou hast dazzled all the inhabitants of Egypt, men and women; and he said unto her, How beautiful they are whilst we are alive, but shouldst thou behold them in the grave, surely thou wouldst move away from them.

19. And she said unto him, How beautiful and pleasing are all thy words; take now, I pray thee, the harp which is in the house, and play with thy hands and let us hear thy words.

20. And he said unto her, How beautiful and pleasing are my words when I speak the praise of my God and his glory; and she said unto him, How very beautiful is the hair of thy head, behold the golden comb which is in the house, take it I pray thee, and curl the hair of thy head.

21. And he said unto her, How long wilt thou speak these words? cease to utter these words to me, and rise and attend to thy domestic affairs.

22. And she said unto him, There is no one in my house, and there is nothing to attend to but to thy words and to thy wish; yet notwithstanding all this, she could not bring Joseph unto her, neither did he place his eye upon her, but directed his eyes below to the ground.

23. And Zelicah desired Joseph in her heart, that he should lie with her, and at the time that Joseph was sitting in the house doing his work, Zelicah came and sat before him, and she enticed him daily with her discourse to lie with her, or ever to look at her, but Joseph would not hearken to her.

24. And she said unto him, If thou wilt not do according to my words, I will chastise thee with the punishment of death, and put an iron yoke upon thee.

25. And Joseph said unto her, Surely God who created man looseth the fetters of prisoners, and it is he who will deliver me from thy prison and from thy judgment.

26. And when she could not prevail over him, to persuade him, and her soul being still fixed upon him, her desire threw her into a grievous sickness.

27. And all the women of Egypt came to visit her, and they said unto her, Why art thou in this declining state? thou that lackest nothing; surely thy husband is a great and esteemed prince in the sight of the king, shouldst thou lack anything of what thy heart desireth?

28. And Zelicah answered them, saying, This day it shall be made known to you, whence this disorder springs in which you see me, and she commanded her maid servants to prepare food for all the women, and she made a banquet for them, and all the women ate in the house of Zelicah.

29. And she gave them knives to peel the citrons to eat them, and she commanded that they should dress Joseph in costly garments, and that he should appear before them, and Joseph came before their eyes and all the women looked on Joseph, and could not take their eyes from off him, and they all cut their hands with the knives that they had in their hands, and all the citrons that were in their hands were filled with blood.

30. And they knew not what they had done but they continued to look at the beauty of Joseph, and did not turn their eyelids from him.

31. And Zelicah saw what they had done, and she said unto them, What is this work that you have done? behold I gave you citrons to eat and you have all cut your hands.

32. And all the women saw their hands, and behold they were full of blood, and their blood flowed down upon their garments, and they said unto her, this slave in your house has overcome us, and we could not turn our eyelids from him on account of his beauty.

33. And she said unto them, Surely this happened to you in the moment that you looked at him, and you could not contain yourselves from him; how then can I refrain when he is constantly in my house, and I see him day after day going in and out of my house? how then can I keep from declining or even from perishing on account of this?

34. And they said unto her, the words are true, for who can see this beautiful form in the house and refrain from him, and is he not thy slave and attendant in thy house, and why dost thou not tell him that which is in thy heart, and sufferest thy soul to perish through

this matter?

35. And she said unto them, I am daily endeavoring to persuade him, and he will not consent to my wishes, and I promised him everything that is good, and yet I could meet with no return from him; I am therefore in a declining state as you see.

36. And Zelicah became very ill on account of her desire toward Joseph, and she was desperately lovesick on account of him, and all the people of the house of Zelicah and her husband knew nothing of this matter, that Zelicah was ill on account of her love to Joseph.

37. And all the people of her house asked her, saying, Why art thou ill and declining, and lackest nothing? and she said unto them, I know not this thing which is daily increasing upon me.

38. And all the women and her friends came daily to see her, and they spoke with her, and she said unto them, This can only be through the love of Joseph; and they said unto her, Entice him and seize him secretly, perhaps he may hearken to thee, and put off this death from thee.

39. And Zelicah became worse from her love to Joseph, and she continued to decline, till she had scarce strength to stand.

40. And on a certain day Joseph was doing his master's work in the house, and Zelicah came secretly and fell suddenly upon him, and Joseph rose up against her, and he was more powerful than she, and he brought her down to the ground.

41. And Zelicah wept on account of the desire of her heart toward him, and she supplicated him with weeping, and her tears flowed down her cheeks, and she spoke unto him in a voice of supplication and in bitterness of soul, saying,

42. Hast thou ever heard, seen or known of so beautiful a woman as I am, or better than myself, who speak daily unto thee, fall into a decline through love for thee, confer all this honor upon thee, and still thou wilt not hearken to my voice?

43. And if it be through fear of thy master lest he punish thee, as the king liveth no harm shall come to thee from thy master through this thing; now, therefore pray listen to me, and consent for the sake of the honor which I have conferred upon thee, and put off this death from me, and why should I die for thy sake? and she ceased to speak.

44. And Joseph answered her, saying, Refrain from me, and leave this matter to my master; behold my master knoweth not what there is with me in the house, for all that belongeth to him he has delivered into my hand, and how shall I do these things in my master's house?

45. For he hath also greatly honored me in his house, and he hath also made me overseer over his house, and he hath exalted me, and there is no one greater in this house than I

am, and my master hath refrained nothing from me, excepting thee who art his wife, how then canst thou speak these words unto me, and how can I do this great evil and sin to God and to thy husband?

46. Now therefore refrain from me, and speak no more such words as these, for I will not hearken to thy words. But Zelicah would not hearken to Joseph when he spoke these words unto her, but she daily enticed him to listen to her.

47. And it was after this that the brook of Egypt was filled above all its sides, and all the inhabitants of Egypt went forth, and also the king and princes went forth with timbrels and dances, for it was a great rejoicing in Egypt, and a holiday at the time of the inundation of the sea Sihor, and they went there to rejoice all the day.

48. And when the Egyptians went out to the river to rejoice, as was their custom, all the people of the house of Potiphar went with them, but Zelicah would not go with them, for she said, I am indisposed, and she remained alone in the house, and no other person was with her in the house.

49. And she rose up and ascended to her temple in the house, and dressed herself in princely garments, and she placed upon her head precious stones of onyx stones, inlaid with silver and gold, and she beautified her face and skin with all sorts of women's purifying liquids, and she perfumed the temple and the house with cassia and frankincense, and she spread myrrh and aloes, and she afterward sat in the entrance of the temple, in the passage of the house, through which Joseph passed to do his work, and behold Joseph came from the field, and entered the house to do his master's work.

50. And he came to the place through which he had to pass, and he saw all the work of Zelicah, and he turned back.

51. And Zelicah saw Joseph turning back from her, and she called out to him, saying What aileth thee Joseph? come to thy work, and behold I will make room for thee until thou shalt have passed to thy seat.

52. And Joseph returned and came to the house, and passed from thence to the place of his seat, and he sat down to do his master's work as usual and behold Zelicah came to him and stood before him in princely garments, and the scent from her clothes was spread to a distance.

53. And she hastened and caught hold of Joseph and his garments, and she said unto him, As the king liveth if thou wilt not perform my request thou shalt die this day, and she hastened and stretched forth her other hand and drew a sword from beneath her garments, and she placed it upon Joseph's neck, and she said, Rise and perform my request, and if not thou diest this day.

54. And Joseph was afraid of her at her doing this thing, and he rose up to flee from her, and she seized the front of his garments, and in the terror of his flight the garment which Zelicah seized was torn, and Joseph left the garment in the hand of Zelicah, and he fled
and got out, for he was in fear.

55. And when Zelicah saw that Joseph's garment was torn, and that he had left it in her hand, and had fled, she was afraid of her life, lest the report should spread concerning her, and she rose up and acted with cunning, and put off the garments in which she was dressed, and she put on her other garments.

56. And she took Joseph's garment, and she laid it beside her, and she went and seated herself in the place where she had sat in her illness, before the people of her house had gone out to the river, and she called a young lad who was then in the house, and she ordered him to call the people of the house to her.

57. And when she saw them she said unto them with a loud voice and lamentation, See what a Hebrew your master has brought to me in the house, for he came this day to lie with me.

58. For when you had gone out he came to the house, and seeing that there was no person in the house, he came unto me, and caught hold of me, with intent to lie with me.

59. And I seized his garments and tore them and called out against him with a loud voice, and when I had lifted up my voice he was afraid of his life and left his garment before me, and fled.

60. And the people of her house spoke nothing, but their wrath was very much kindled against Joseph, and they went to his master and told him the words of his wile.

61. And Potiphar came home enraged, and his wife cried out to him, saying, What is this thing that thou hast done unto me in bringing a He. brew servant into my house, for he came unto me this day to sport with me; thus did he do unto me this day.

62. And Potiphar heard the words of his wife, and he ordered Joseph to be punished with severe stripes, and they did so to him.

63. And whilst they were smiting him, Joseph called out with a loud voice, and he lifted up his eyes to heaven, and he said, O Lord God, thou knowest that I am innocent of all these things, and why shall I die this day through falsehood, by the hand of these uncircumcised wicked men, whom thou knowest?

64. And whilst Potiphar's men were beating Joseph, he continued to cry out and weep, and there was a child there eleven months old, and the Lord opened the mouth of the child, and he spake these words before Potiphar's men, who were smiting Joseph, saying,

65. What do you want of this man, and why do you do this evil unto him? my mother speaketh falsely and uttereth lies; thus was the transaction.

66. And the child told them accurately all that happened, and all the words of Zelicah to Joseph day after day did he declare unto them.

67. And all the men heard the words of the child and they wondered greatly at the child's words, and the child ceased to speak and became still.

68. And Potiphar was very much ashamed at the words of his son, and he commanded his men not to beat Joseph any more, and the men ceased beating Joseph.

69. And Potiphar took Joseph and ordered him to be brought to justice before the priests, who were judges belonging to the king, in order to judge him concerning this affair.

70. And Potiphar and Joseph came before the priests who were the king's judges, and he said unto them, Decide I pray you, what judgment is due to a servant, for thus has he done.

71. And the priests said unto Joseph, Why didst thou do this thing to thy master? and Joseph answered them, saying, Not so my lords, thus was the matter; and Potiphar said unto Joseph, Surely I entrusted in thy hands all that belonged to me, and I withheld nothing from thee but my wife, and how couldst thou do this evil?

72. And Joseph answered saying, Not so my lord, as the Lord liveth, and as thy soul liveth, my lord, the word which thou didst hear from thy wife is untrue, for thus was the affair this day.

73. A year has elapsed to me since I have been in thy house; hast thou seen any iniquity in me, or any thing which might cause thee to demand my life?

74. And the priests said unto Potiphar, Send, we pray thee, and let them bring before us Joseph's torn garment, and let us see the tear in it, and if it shall be that the tear is in front of the garment, then his face must have been opposite to her and she must have caught hold of him, to come to her, and with deceit did thy wife do all that she has spoken.

75. And they brought Joseph's garment before the priests who were judges, and they saw and behold the tear was in front of Joseph, and all the judging priests knew that she had pressed him, and they said, The judgment of death is not due to this slave for he has done nothing, but his judgment is, that he be placed in the prison house on account of the report, which through him has gone forth against thy wife.

76. And Potiphar heard their words, and he placed him in the prison house, the place where the king's prisoners are confined, and Joseph was in the house of confinement twelve years.

77. And notwithstanding this, his master's wife did not turn from him, and she did not cease from speaking to him day after day to hearken to her, and at the end of three months Zelicah continued going to Joseph to the house of confinement day by day, and she enticed him to hearken to her, and Zelicah said unto Joseph, How long wilt thou remain in this house? but hearken now to my voice, and I will bring thee out of this house.

78. And Joseph answered her, saying, It is better for me to remain in this house than to hearken to thy words, to sin against God; and she said unto him, If thou wilt not perform my wish, I will pluck out thine eyes, add fetters to thy feet, and will deliver thee into the hands of them whom thou didst not know before.

79. And Joseph answered her and said, Behold the God of the whole earth is able to deliver me from all that thou canst do unto me, for he openeth the eyes of the blind, and looseth those that are bound, and preserveth all strangers who are unacquainted with the land.

80. And when Zelicah was unable to persuade Joseph to hearken to her, she left off going to entice him; and Joseph was still confined in the house of confinement. And Jacob the father of Joseph, and all his brethren who were in the land of Canaan still mourned and wept in those days on account of Joseph, for Jacob refused to be comforted for his son Joseph, and Jacob cried aloud, and wept and mourned all those days.

CHAPTER 45

1. And it was at that time in that year, which is the year of Joseph's going down to Egypt after his brothers had sold him, that Reuben the son of Jacob went to Timnah and took unto him for a wife Eliuram, the daughter of Avi the Canaanite, and he came to her.

2. And Eliuram the wife of Reuben conceived and bare him Hanoch, Palu, Chetzron and Carmi, four sons; and Simeon his brother took his sister Dinah for a wife, and she bare unto him Memuel, Yamin, Ohad, Jachin and Zochar, five sons.

3. And he afterward came to Bunah the Canaanitish woman, the same is Bunah whom Simeon took captive from the city of Shechem, and Bunah was before Dinah and attended upon her, and Simeon came to her, and she bare unto him Saul.

4. And Judah went at that time to Adulam, and he came to a man of Adulam, and his name was Hirah, and Judah saw there the daughter of a man from Canaan, and her name was Aliyath, the daughter of Shua, and he took her, and came to her, and Aliyath bare unto Judah, Er, Onan and Shiloh; three sons.

5. And Levi and Issachar went to the land of the east, and they took unto themselves for wives the daughters of Jobab the son of Yoktan, the son of Eber; and Jobab the son of Yoktan had two daughters; the name of the elder was Adinah, and the name of the younger was Aridah.

6. And Levi took Adinah, and Issachar took Aridah, and they came to the land of Canaan, to their father's house, and Adinah bare unto Levi, Gershon, Kehath and Merari; three sons.

7. And Aridah bare unto Issachar Tola, Puvah, Job and Shomron, four sons; and Dan went to the land of Moab and took for a wife Aphlaleth, the daughter of Chamudan the Moabite, and he brought her to the land of Canaan.

8. And Aphlaleth was barren, she had no offspring, and God afterward remembered Aphlaleth the wife of Dan, and she conceived and bare a son, and she called his name Chushim.

9. And Gad and Naphtali went to Haran and took from thence the daughters of Amuram the son of Uz, the son of Nahor, for wives.

10. And these are the names of the daughters of Amuram; the name of the elder was Merimah, and the name of the younger Uzith; and Naphtali took Merimah, and Gad took Uzith; and brought them to the land of Canaan, to their father's house.

11. And Merimah bare unto Naphtali Yachzeel, Guni, Jazer and Shalem, four sons; and

Uzith bare unto Gad Zephion, Chagi, Shuni, Ezbon, Eri, Arodi and Arali, seven sons.

12. And Asher went forth and took Adon the daughter of Aphlal, the son of Hadad, the son of Ishmael, for a wife, and he brought her to the land of Canaan.

13. And Adon the wife of Asher died in those days: she had no offspring; and it was after the death of Adon that Asher went to the other side of the river and took for a wife Hadurah the daughter of Abimael, the son of Eber, the son of Shem.

14. And the young woman was of a comely appearance, and a woman of sense, and she had been the wife of Malkiel the son of Elam, the son of Shem.

15. And Hadurah bare a daughter unto Malkiel, and he called her name Serach, and Malkiel died after this, and Hadurah went and remained in her father's house.

16. And after the death of the wife at Asher he went and took Hadurah for a wife, and brought her to the land of Canaan, and Serach her daughter he also brought with them, and she was three years old, and the damsel was brought up in Jacob's house.

17. And the damsel was of a comely appearance, and she went in the sanctified ways of the children of Jacob; she lacked nothing, and the Lord gave her wisdom and understanding.

18. And Hadurah the wife of Asher conceived and bare unto him Yimnah, Yishvah, Yishvi and Beriah; four sons.

19. And Zebulun went to Midian, and took for a wife Merishah the daughter of Molad, the son of Abida, the son of Midian, and brought her to the land of Canaan.

20. And Merushah bare unto Zebulun Sered, Elon and Yachleel; three sons.

21. And Jacob sent to Aram, the son of Zoba, the son of Terah, and he took for his son Benjamin Mechalia the daughter of Aram, and she came to the land of Canaan to the house of Jacob; and Benjamin was ten years old when he took Mechalia the daughter of Aram for a wife.

22. And Mechalia conceived and bare unto Benjamin Bela, Becher, Ashbel, Gera and Naaman, five sons; and Benjamin went afterward and took for a wife Aribath, the daughter of Shomron, the son of Abraham, in addition to his first wife, and he was eighteen years old; and Aribath bare unto Benjamin Achi, Vosh, Mupim, Chupim, and Ord; five sons.

23. And in those days Judah went to the house of Shem and took Tamar the daughter of Elam, the son of Shem, for a wife for his first born Er.

24. And Er came to his wife Tamar, and she became his wife, and when he came to her he outwardly destroyed his seed, and his work was evil in the sight of the Lord, and the Lord slew him.

25. And it was after the death of Er, Judah's first born, that Judah said unto Onan, go to thy brother's wife and marry her as the next of kin, and raise up seed to thy brother.

26. And Onan took Tamar for a wife and he came to her, and Onan also did like unto the work of his brother, and his work was evil in the sight of the Lord, and he slew him also.

27. And when Onan died, Judah said unto Tamar, Remain in thy father's house until my son Shiloh shall have grown up, and Judah did no more delight in Tamar, to give her unto Shiloh, for he said, Peradventure he will also die like his brothers.

28. And Tamar rose up and went and remained in her father's house, and Tamar was in her father's house for some time.

29. And at the revolution of the year, Aliyath the wife of Judah died; and Judah was comforted for his wife, and after the death of Aliyath, Judah went up with his friend Hirah to Timnah to shear their sheep.

30. And Tamar heard that Judah had gone up to Timnah to shear the sheep, and that Shiloh was grown up, and Judah did not delight in her.

31. And Tamar rose up and put off the garments of her widowhood, and she put a vail upon her, and she entirely covered herself, and she went and sat in the public thoroughfare, which is upon the road to Timnah.

32. And Judah passed and saw her and took her and he came to her, and she conceived by him, and at the time of being delivered, behold, there were twins in her womb, and he called the name of the first Perez, and the name of the second Zarah.

CHAPTER 46

1. In those days Joseph was still confined in the prison house in the land of Egypt.

2. At that time the attendants of Pharaoh were standing before him, the chief of the butlers and the chief of the bakers which belonged to the king of Egypt.

3. And the butler took wine and placed it before the king to drink, and the baker placed bread before the king to eat, and the king drank of the wine and ate of the bread, he and his servants and ministers that ate at the king's table.

4. And whilst they were eating and drinking, the butler and the baker remained there, and Pharaoh's ministers found many flies in the wine, which the butler had brought, and stones of nitre were found in the baker's bread.

5. And the captain of the guard placed Joseph as an attendant on Pharaoh's officers, and Pharaoh's officers were in confinement one year.

6. And at the end of the year, they both dreamed dreams in one night, in the place of confinement where they were, and in the morning Joseph came to them to attend upon them as usual, and he saw them, and behold their countenances were dejected and sad.

7. And Joseph asked them, Why are your countenances sad and dejected this day? and they said unto him, We dreamed a dream, and there is no one to interpret it; and Joseph said unto them, Relate, I pray you, your dream unto me, and God shall give you an answer of peace as you desire.

8. And the butler related his dream unto Joseph, and he said, I saw in my dream, and behold a large vine was before me, and upon that vine I saw three branches, and the vine speedily blossomed and reached a great height, and its clusters were ripened and became grapes.

9. And I took the grapes and pressed them in a cup, and placed it in Pharaoh's hand and he drank; and Joseph said unto him, The three branches that were upon the vine are three days.

10. Yet within three days, the king will order thee to be brought out and he will restore thee to thy office, and thou shalt give the king his wine to drink as at first when thou wast his butler; but let me find favor in thy sight, that thou shalt remember me to Pharaoh when it will be well with thee, and do kindness unto me, and get me brought forth from this prison, for I was stolen away from the land of Canaan and was sold for a slave in this place.

11. And also that which was told thee concerning my master's wife is false, for they placed me in this dungeon for naught; and the butler answered Joseph, saying, If the king deal well with me as at first, as thou last interpreted to me, I will do all that thou desirest, and

get thee brought out of this dungeon.

12. And the baker, seeing that Joseph had accurately interpreted the butler's dream, also approached, and related the whole of his dream to Joseph.

13. And he said unto him, In my dream I saw and behold three white baskets upon my head, and I looked, and behold there were in the upper-most basket all manner of baked meats for Pharaoh, and behold the birds were eating them from off my head.

14. And Joseph said unto him, The three baskets which thou didst see are three days, yet within three days Pharaoh will take off thy head, and hang thee upon a tree, and the birds will eat thy flesh from off thee, as thou sawest in thy dream.

15. In those days the queen was about to be delivered, and upon that day she bare a son unto the king of Egypt, and they proclaimed that the king had gotten his first born son and all the people of Egypt together with the officers and servants of Pharaoh rejoiced greatly.

16. And upon the third day of his birth Pharaoh made a feast for his officers and servants, for the hosts of the land of Zoar and of the land of Egypt.

17. And all the people of Egypt and the servants of Pharaoh came to eat and drink with the king at the feast of his son, and to rejoice at the king's rejoicing.

18. And all the officers of the king and his servants were rejoicing at that time for eight days at the feast, and they made merry with all sorts of musical instruments, with timbrels and with dances in the king's house for eight days.

19. And the butler, to whom Joseph had interpreted his dream, forgot Joseph, and he did not mention him to the king as he had promised, for this thing was from the Lord in order to punish Joseph because he had trusted in man.

20. And Joseph remained after this in the prison house two years, until he had completed twelve years.

CHAPTER 47

1. And Isaac the son of Abraham was still living in those days in the land of Canaan; he was very aged, one hundred and eighty years old, and Esau his son, the brother of Jacob, was in the land of Edom, and he and his sons had possessions in it amongst the children of Seir.

2. And Esau heard that his father's time was drawing nigh to die, and he and his sons and household came unto the land of Canaan, unto his father's house, and Jacob and his sons went forth from the place where they dwelt in Hebron, and they all came to their father Isaac, and they found Esau and his sons in the tent.

3. And Jacob and his sons sat before his father Isaac, and Jacob was still mourning for his son Joseph.

4. And Isaac said unto Jacob, Bring me hither thy sons and I will bless them; and Jacob brought his eleven children before his father Isaac.

5. And Isaac placed his hands upon all the sons of Jacob, and he took hold of them and embraced them, and kissed them one by one, and Isaac blessed them on that day, and he said unto them, May the God of your fathers bless you and increase your seed like the stars of heaven for number.

6. And Isaac also blessed the sons of Esau, saying, May God cause you to be a dread and a terror to all that will behold you, and to all your enemies.

7. And Isaac called Jacob and his sons, and they all came and sat before Isaac, and Isaac said unto Jacob, The Lord God of the whole earth said unto me, Unto thy seed will I give this land for an inheritance if thy children keep my statutes and my ways, and I will perform unto them the oath which I swore unto thy father Abraham.

8. Now therefore my son, teach thy children and thy children's children to fear the Lord, and to go in the good way which will please the Lord thy God, for if you keep the ways of the Lord and his statutes the Lord will also keep unto you his covenant with Abraham, and will do well with you and your seed all the days.

9. And when Isaac had finished commanding Jacob and his children, he gave up the ghost and died, and was gathered unto his people.

10. And Jacob and Esau fell upon the face of their father Isaac, and they wept, and Isaac was one hundred and eighty years old when he died in the land of Canaan, in Hebron, and his sons carried him to the cave of Machpelah, which Abraham had bought from the children of Heth for a possession of a burial place.

11. And all the kings of the land of Canaan went with Jacob and Esau to bury Isaac, and all the kings of Canaan showed Isaac great honor at his death.

12. And the sons of Jacob and the sons of Esau went barefooted round about, walking and lamenting until they reached Kireath-arba.

13. And Jacob and Esau buried their father Isaac in the cave of Machpelah, which is in Kireath-arba in Hebron, and they buried him with very great honor, as at the funeral of kings.

14. And Jacob and his sons, and Esau and his sons, and all the kings of Canaan made a great and heavy mourning, and they buried him and mourned for him many days.

15. And at the death of Isaac, he left his cattle and his possessions and all belonging to him to his sons; and Esau said unto Jacob, Behold I pray thee, all that our father has left we will divide it in two parts, and I will have the choice, and Jacob said, We will do so.

16. And Jacob took all that Isaac had left in the land of Canaan, the cattle and the property, and he placed them in two parts before Esau and his sons, and he said unto Esau, Behold all this is before thee, choose thou unto thyself the half which thou wilt take.

17. And Jacob said unto Esau, Hear thou I pray thee what I will speak unto thee, saying, The Lord God of heaven and earth spoke unto our fathers Abraham and Isaac, saying, Unto thy seed will I give this land for an inheritance forever.

18. Now therefore all that our father has left is before thee, and behold all the land is before thee; choose thou from them what thou desirest.

19. If thou desirest the whole land take it for thee and thy children forever, and I will take this riches, and if thou desirest the riches take it unto thee, and I will take this land for me and for my children to inherit it forever.

20. And Nebayoth, the son of Ishmael, was then in the land with his children, and Esau went on that day and consulted with him, saying.

21. Thus has Jacob spoken unto me, and thus has he answered me, now give thy advice and we will hear.

22. And Nebayoth said, What is this that Jacob hath spoken unto thee? behold all the children of Canaan are dwelling securely in their land, and Jacob sayeth he will inherit it with his seed all the days.

23. Go now therefore and take all thy father's riches and leave Jacob thy brother in the land, as he has spoken.

24. And Esau rose up and returned to Jacob, and did all that Nebayoth the son of Ishmael had advised; and Esau took all the riches that Isaac had left, the souls, the beasts, the cattle and the property, and all the riches; he gave nothing to his brother Jacob; and
Jacob took all the land of Canaan, from the brook of Egypt unto the river Euphrates, and he took it for an everlasting possession, and for his children and for his seed after him forever.

25. Jacob also took from his brother Esau the cave of Machpelah, which is in Hebron, which Abraham had bought from Ephron for a possession of a burial place for him and his seed forever.

26. And Jacob wrote all these things in the book of purchase, and he signed it, and he testified all this with four faithful witnesses.

27. And these are the words which Jacob wrote in the book, saying: The land of Canaan and all the cities of the Hittites, the Hivites, the Jebusites, the Amorites, the Perizzites, and the Gergashites, all the seven nations from the river of Egypt unto the river Euphrates.

28. And the city of Hebron Kireath-arba, and the cave which is in it, the whole did Jacob buy from his brother Esau for value, for a possession and for an inheritance for his seed after him forever.

29. And Jacob took the book of purchase and the signature, the command and the statutes and the revealed book, and he placed them in an earthen vessel in order that they should remain for a long time, and he delivered them into the hands of his children.

30. Esau took all that his father had left him after his death from his brother Jacob, and he took all the property, from man and beast, camel and ass, ox and lamb, silver and gold, stones and bdellium, and all the riches which had belonged to Isaac the son of Abraham; there was nothing left which Esau did not take unto himself, from all that Isaac had left after his death.

31. And Esau took all this, and he and his children went home to the land of Seir the Horite, away from his brother Jacob and his children.

32. And Esau had possessions amongst the children of Seir, and Esau returned not to the land of Canaan from that day forward.

33. And the whole land of Canaan became an inheritance to the children of Israel for an everlasting inheritance, and Esau with all his children inherited the mountain of Seir.

CHAPTER 48

1. In those days, after the death of Isaac, the Lord commanded and caused a famine upon the whole earth.

2. At that time Pharaoh king of Egypt was sitting upon his throne in the land of Egypt, and lay in his bed and dreamed dreams, and Pharaoh saw in his dream that he was standing by the side of the river of Egypt.

3. And whilst he was standing he saw and behold seven fat fleshed and well favored kine came up out of the river.

4. And seven other kine, lean fleshed and ill favored, came up after them, and the seven ill favored ones swallowed up the well favored ones, and still their appearance was ill as at first.

5. And he awoke, and he slept again and he dreamed a second time, and he saw and behold seven ears of corn came up upon one stalk, rank and good, and seven thin ears blasted with the east wind sprang, up after them, and the thin ears swallowed up the full ones, and Pharaoh awoke out of his dream.

6. And in the morning the king remembered his dreams, and his spirit was sadly troubled on account of his dreams, and the king hastened and sent and called for all the magicians of Egypt, and the wise men, and they came and stood before Pharaoh.

7. And the king said unto them, I have dreamed dreams, and there is none to interpret them; and they said unto the king, relate thy dreams to thy servants and let us hear them.

8. And the king related his dreams to them, and they all answered and said with one voice to the king, may the king live forever; and this is the interpretation of thy dreams.

9. The seven good kine which thou didst see denote seven daughters that will be born unto thee in the latter days, and the seven kine which thou sawest come up after them, and swallowed them up, are for a sign that the daughters which will be born unto thee will all die in the life-time of the king.

10. And that which thou didst see in the second dream of seven full good ears of corn coming up upon one stalk, this is their interpretation, that thou wilt build unto thyself in the latter days seven cities throughout the land of Egypt; and that which thou sawest of the seven blasted ears of corn springing up after them and swallowing them up whilst thou didst behold them with thine eyes, is for a sign that the cities which thou wilt build will all be destroyed in the latter days, in the life-time of the king.

11. And when they spoke these words the king did not incline his ear to their words, neither did he fix his heart upon them, for the king knew in his wisdom that they did not give a proper interpretation of the dreams; and when they had finished speaking before the king, the king answered them, saying, What is this thing that you have spoken unto me? surely you have uttered falsehood and spoken lies; therefore now give the proper interpretation of my dreams, that you may not die.

12. And the king commanded after this, and he sent and called again for other wise men, and they came and stood before the king, and the king related his dreams to them, and they all answered him according to the first interpretation, and the king's anger was kindled and he was very wroth, and the king said unto them, Surely you speak lies and utter falsehood in what you have said.

13. And the king commanded that a proclamation should be issued throughout the land of Egypt, saying, It is resolved by the king and his great men, that any wise man who knoweth and understandeth the interpretation of dreams, and will not come this day before the king, shall die.

14. And the man that will declare unto the king the proper interpretation of his dreams, there shall be given unto him all that he will require from the king. And all the wise men of the land of Egypt came before the king, together with all the magicians and sorcerers that were in Egypt and in Goshen, in Rameses, in Tachpanches, in Zoar, and in all the places on the borders of Egypt, and they all stood before the king.

15. And all the nobles and the princes, and the attendants belonging to the king, came together from all the cities of Egypt, and they all sat before the king, and the king related his dreams before the wise men, and the princes, and all that sat before the king were astonished at the vision.

16. And all the wise men who were before the king were greatly divided in their interpretation of his dreams; some of them interpreted them to the king, saying, The seven good kine are seven kings, who from the king's issue will be raised over Egypt.

17. And the seven bad kine are seven princes, who will stand up against them in the latter days and destroy them; and the seven ears of corn are the seven great princes belonging to Egypt, who will fall in the hands of the seven less powerful princes of their enemies, in the wars of our lord the king.

18. And some of them interpreted to the king in this manner, saying, The seven good kine are the strong cities of Egypt, and the seven bad kine are the seven nations of the land of Canaan, who will come against the seven cities of Egypt in the latter days and destroy them.

19. And that which thou sawest in the second dream, of seven good and bad ears of corn, is a sign that the government of Egypt will again return to thy seed as at first.

20. And in his reign the people of the cities of Egypt will turn against the seven cities of Canaan who are stronger than they are, and will destroy them, and the government of Egypt will return to thy seed.

21. And some of them said unto the king, This is the interpretation of thy dreams; the seven good kine are seven queens, whom thou wilt take for wives in the latter days, and the seven bad kine denote that those women will all die in the lifetime of the king.

22. And the seven good and bad ears of corn which thou didst see in the second dream are fourteen children, and it will be in the latter days that they will stand up and fight amongst themselves, and seven of them will smite the seven that are more powerful.

23. And some of them said these words unto the king, saying, The seven good kine denote that seven children will be born to thee, and they will slay seven of thy children's children in the latter days; and the seven good ears of corn which thou didst see in the second dream, are those princes against whom seven other less powerful princes will fight and destroy them in the latter days, and avenge thy children's cause, and the government will again return to thy seed.

24. And the king heard all the words of the wise men of Egypt and their interpretation of his dreams, and none of them pleased the king.

25. And the king knew in his wisdom that they did not altogether speak correctly in all these words, for this was from the Lord to frustrate the words of the wise men of Egypt, in order that Joseph might go forth from the house of confinement, and in order that he should become great in Egypt.

26. And the king saw that none amongst all the wise men and magicians of Egypt spoke correctly to him, and the king's wrath was kindled, and his anger burned within him.

27. And the king commanded that all the wise men and magicians should go out from before him, and they all went out from before the king with shame and disgrace.

28. And the king commanded that a proclamation be sent throughout Egypt to slay all the magicians that were in Egypt, and not one of them should be suffered to live.

29. And the captains of the guards belonging to the king rose up, and each man drew his sword, and they began to smite the magicians of Egypt, and the wise men.

30. And after this Merod, chief butler to the king, came and bowed down before the king and sat before him.

31. And the butler said unto the king, May the king live forever, and his government be exalted in the land.

32. Thou wast angry with thy servant in those days, now two years past, and didst place me in the ward, and I was for some time in the ward, I and the chief of the bakers.

33. And there was with us a Hebrew servant belonging to the captain of the guard, his name was Joseph, for his master had been angry with him and placed him in the house of confinement, and he attended us there.

34. And in some time after when we were in the ward, we dreamed dreams in one night, I and the chief of the bakers; we dreamed, each man according to the interpretation of his dream.

35. And we came in the morning and told them to that servant, and he interpreted to us our dreams, to each man according to his dream, did he correctly interpret.

36. And it came to pass as he interpreted to us, so was the event; there fell not to the ground any of his words.

37. And now therefore my lord and king do not slay the people of Egypt for naught; behold that slave is still confined in the house by the captain of the guard his master, in the house of confinement.

38. If it pleaseth the king let him send for him that he may come before thee and he will make known to thee, the correct interpretation of the dream which thou didst dream.

39. And the king heard the words of the chief butler, and the king ordered that the wise men of Egypt should not be slain.

40. And the king ordered his servants to bring Joseph before him, and the king said unto them, Go to him and do not terrify him lest he be confused and will not know to speak properly.

41. And the servants of the king went to Joseph, and they brought him hastily out of the dungeon, and the king's servants shaved him, and he changed his prison garment and he came before the king.

42. And the king was sitting upon his royal throne in a princely dress girt around with a golden ephod, and the fine gold which was upon it sparkled, and the carbuncle and the ruby and the emerald, together with all the precious stones that were upon the king's head, dazzled the eye, and Joseph wondered greatly at the king.

43. And the throne upon which the king sat was covered with gold and silver, and with onyx stones, and it had seventy steps.

44. And it was their custom throughout the land of Egypt, that every man who came to speak to the king, if he was a prince or one that was estimable in the sight of the king, he ascended to the king's throne as far as the thirty-first step, and the king would descend to the thirty-sixth step, and speak with him.

45. If he was one of the common people, he ascended to the third step, and the king would descend to the fourth and speak to him, and their custom was, moreover, that any man who understood to speak in all the seventy languages, he ascended the seventy steps, and went up and spoke till he reached the king.

46. And any man who could not complete the seventy, he ascended as many steps as the languages which he knew to speak in.

47. And it was customary in those days in Egypt that no one should reign over them, but who understood to speak in the seventy languages.

48. And when Joseph came before the king he bowed down to the ground before the king, and he ascended to the third step, and the king sat upon the fourth step and spoke with Joseph.

49. And the king said unto Joseph, I dreamed a dream, and there is no interpreter to interpret it properly, and I commanded this day that all the magicians of Egypt and the wise men thereof, should come before me, and I related my dreams to them, and no one has properly interpreted them to me.

50. And after this I this day heard concerning thee, that thou art a wise man, and canst correctly interpret every dream that thou hearest.

51. And Joseph answered Pharaoh, saying, Let Pharaoh relate his dreams that he dreamed; surely the interpretations belong to God; and Pharaoh related his dreams to Joseph, the dream of the kine, and the dream of the ears of corn, and the king left off speaking.

52. And Joseph was then clothed with the spirit of God before the king, and he knew all the things that would befall the king from that day forward, and he knew the proper interpretation of the king's dream, and he spoke before the king.

53. And Joseph found favor in the sight of the king, and the king inclined his ears and his heart, and he heard all the words of Joseph. And Joseph said unto the king, Do not imagine that they are two dreams, for it is only one dream, for that which God has chosen to do throughout the land he has shown to the king in his dream, and this is the proper interpretation of thy dream:

54. The seven good kine and ears of corn are seven years, and the seven bad kine and ears of corn are also seven years; it is one dream.

55. Behold the seven years that are coming there will be a great plenty throughout the land, and after that the seven years of famine will follow them, a very grievous famine; and all the plenty will be forgotten from the land, and the famine will consume the inhabitants of the land.

56. The king dreamed one dream, and the dream was therefore repeated unto Pharaoh because the thing is established by God, and God will shortly bring it to pass.

57. Now therefore I will give thee counsel and deliver thy soul and the souls of the inhabitants of the land from the evil of the famine, that thou seek throughout thy kingdom for a man very discreet and wise, who knoweth all the affairs of government,

and appoint him to superintend over the land of Egypt.

58. And let the man whom thou placest over Egypt appoint officers under him, that they gather in all the food of the good years that are coming, and let them lay up corn and deposit it in thy appointed stores.

59. And let them keep that food for the seven years of famine, that it may be found for thee and thy people and thy whole land, and that thou and thy land be not cut off by the famine.

60. Let all the inhabitants of the land be also ordered that they gather in, every man the produce of his field, of all sorts of food, during the seven good years, and that they place it in their stores, that it may be found for them in the days of the famine and that they may live upon it.

61. This is the proper interpretation of thy dream, and this is the counsel given to save thy soul and the souls of all thy subjects.

62. And the king answered and said unto Joseph, Who sayeth and who knoweth that thy words are correct? And he said unto the king, This shall be a sign for thee respecting all my words, that they are true and that my advice is good for thee.

63. Behold thy wife sitteth this day upon the stool of delivery, and she will bear thee a son and thou wilt rejoice with him; when thy child shall have gone forth from his mother's womb, thy first born son that has been born these two years back shall die, and thou wilt be comforted in the child that will be born unto thee this day.

64. And Joseph finished speaking these words to the king, and he bowed down to the king and he went out, and when Joseph had gone out from the king's presence, those signs which Joseph had spoken unto the king came to pass on that day.

65. And the queen bare a son on that day and the king heard the glad tidings about his son, and he rejoiced, and when the reporter had gone forth from the king's presence, the king's servants found the first born son of the king fallen dead upon the ground.

66. And there was great lamentation and noise in the king's house, and the king heard it, and he said, What is the noise and lamentation that I have heard in the house? and they told the king that his first born son had died; then the king knew that all Joseph's words that he had spoken were correct, and the king was consoled for his son by the child that was born to him on that day as Joseph had spoken.

CHAPTER 49

1. After these things the king sent and assembled all his officers and servants, and all the princes and nobles belonging to the king, and they all came before the king.

2. And the king said unto them, Behold you have seen and heard all the words of this Hebrew man, and all the signs which he declared would come to pass, and not any of his words have fallen to the ground.

3. You know that he has given a proper interpretation of the dream, and it will surely come to pass, now therefore take counsel, and know what you will do and how the land will be delivered from the famine.

4. Seek now and see whether the like can be found, in whose heart there is wisdom and knowledge, and I will appoint him over the land.

5. For you have heard what the Hebrew man has advised concerning this to save the land therewith from the famine, and I know that the land will not be delivered from the famine but with the advice of the Hebrew man, him that advised me.

6. And they all answered the king and said, The counsel which the Hebrew has given concerning this is good; now therefore, our lord and king, behold the whole land is in thy hand, do that which seemeth good in thy sight.

7. Him whom thou chooses, and whom thou in thy wisdom knowest to be wise and capable of delivering the land with his wisdom, him shall the king appoint to be under him over the land.

8. And the king said to all the officers: I have thought that since God has made known to the Hebrew man all that he has spoken, there is none so discreet and wise in the whole land as he is; if it seem good in your sight I will place him over the land, for he will save the land with his wisdom.

9. And all the officers answered the king and said, But surely it is written in the laws of Egypt, and it should not be violated, that no man shall reign over Egypt, nor be the second to the king, but one who has knowledge in all the languages of the sons of men.

10. Now therefore our lord and king, behold this Hebrew man can only speak the Hebrew language, and how then can he be over us the second under government, a man who not even knoweth our language?

11. Now we pray thee send for him, and let him come before thee, and prove him in all things, and do as thou see fit.

12. And the king said, It shall be done tomorrow, and the thing that you have spoken is
good; and all the officers came on that day before the king.

13. And on that night the Lord sent one of his ministering angels, and he came into the land of Egypt unto Joseph, and the angel of the Lord stood over Joseph, and behold Joseph was lying in the bed at night in his master's house in the dungeon, for his master had put him back into the dungeon on account of his wife.

14. And the angel roused him from his sleep, and Joseph rose up and stood upon his legs, and behold the angel of the Lord was standing opposite to him; and the angel of the Lord spoke with Joseph, and he taught him all the languages of man in that night, and he called his name Jehoseph.

15. And the angel of the Lord went from him, and Joseph returned and lay upon his bed, and Joseph was astonished at the vision which he saw.

16. And it came to pass in the morning that the king sent for all his officers and servants, and they all came and sat before the king, and the king ordered Joseph to be brought, and the king's servants went and brought Joseph before Pharaoh.

17. And the king came forth and ascended the steps of the throne, and Joseph spoke unto the king in all languages, and Joseph went up to him and spoke unto the king until he arrived before the king in the seventieth step, and he sat before the king.

18. And the king greatly rejoiced on account of Joseph, and all the king's officers rejoiced greatly with the king when they heard all the words of Joseph.

19. And the thing seemed good in the sight of the king and the officers, to appoint Joseph to be second to the king over the whole land of Egypt, and the king spoke to Joseph, saying,

20. Now thou didst give me counsel to appoint a wise man over the land of Egypt, in order with his wisdom to save the land from the famine; now therefore, since God has made all this known to thee, and all the words which thou hast spoken, there is not throughout the land a discreet and wise man like unto thee.

21. And thy name no more shall be called Joseph, but Zaphnath Paaneah shall be thy name; thou shalt be second to me, and according to thy word shall be all the affairs of my government, and at thy word shall my people go out and come in.

22. Also from under thy hand shall my servants and officers receive their salary which is given to them monthly, and to thee shall all the people of the land bow down; only in my throne will I be greater than thou.

23. And the king took off his ring from his hand and put it upon the hand of Joseph, and the king dressed Joseph in a princely garment, and he put a golden crown upon his head, and he put a golden chain upon his neck.

24. And the king commanded his servants, and they made him ride in the second chariot belonging to the king, that went opposite to the king's chariot, and he caused him to ride upon a great and strong horse from the king's horses, and to be conducted through the streets of the land of Egypt.

25. And the king commanded that all those that played upon timbrels, harps and other musical instruments should go forth with Joseph; one thousand timbrels, one thousand mecholoth, and one thousand nebalim went after him.

26. And five thousand men, with drawn swords glittering in their hands, and they went marching and playing before Joseph, and twenty thousand of the great men of the king girt with girdles of skin covered with gold, marched

at the right hand of Joseph, and twenty thousand at his left, and all the women and damsels went upon the roofs or stood in the streets playing and rejoicing at Joseph, and gazed at the appearance of Joseph and at his beauty.

27. And the king's people went before him and behind him, perfuming the road with frankincense and with cassia, and with all sorts of fine perfume, and scattered myrrh and aloes along the road, and twenty men proclaimed these words before him throughout the land in a loud voice:

28. Do you see this man whom the king has chosen to be his second? all the affairs of government shall be regulated by him, and he that transgresses his orders, or that does not bow down before him to the ground, shall die, for he rebels against the king and his second.

29. And when the heralds had ceased proclaiming, all the people of Egypt bowed down to the ground before Joseph and said, May the king live, also may his second live; and all the inhabitants of Egypt bowed down along the road, and when the heralds approached them, they bowed down, and they rejoiced with all sorts of timbrels, mechol and nebal before Joseph.

30. And Joseph upon his horse lifted up his eyes to heaven, and called out and said, He raiseth the poor man from the dust, He lifteth up the needy from the dunghill. O Lord of Hosts, happy is the man who trusteth in thee.

31. And Joseph passed throughout the land of Egypt with Pharaoh's servants and officers, and they showed him the whole land of Egypt and all the king's treasures.

32. And Joseph returned and came on that day before Pharaoh, and the king gave unto Joseph a possession in the land of Egypt, a possession of fields and vineyards, and the king gave unto Joseph three thousand talents of silver and one thousand talents of gold, and onyx stones and bdellium and many gifts.

33. And on the next day the king commanded all the people of Egypt to bring unto Joseph offerings and gifts, and that he that violated the command of the king should die; and they made a high place in the street of the city, and they spread out garments there, and whoever brought anything to Joseph put it into the high place.

34. And all the people of Egypt cast something into the high place, one man a golden earring, and the other rings and ear-rings, and different vessels of gold and silver work, and onyx stones and bdellium did he cast upon the high place; every one gave something of what he possessed.

35. And Joseph took all these and placed them in his treasuries, and all the officers and nobles belonging to the king exalted Joseph, and they gave him many gifts, seeing that the king had chosen him to be his second.

36. And the king sent to Potiphera, the son of Ahiram priest of On, and he took his young daughter Osnath and gave her unto Joseph for a wife.

37. And the damsel was very comely, a virgin, one whom man had not known, and Joseph took her for a wife; and the king said unto Joseph, I am Pharaoh, and beside thee none shall dare to lift up his hand or his foot to regulate my people throughout the land of Egypt.

38. And Joseph was thirty years old when he stood before Pharaoh, and Joseph went out from before the king, and he became the king's second in Egypt.

39. And the king gave Joseph a hundred servants to attend him in his house, and Joseph also sent and purchased many servants and they remained in the house of Joseph.

40. Joseph then built for himself a very magnificent house like unto the houses of kings, before the court of the king's palace, and he made in the house a large temple, very elegant in appearance and convenient for his residence; three years was Joseph in erecting his house.

41. And Joseph made unto himself a very elegant throne of abundance of gold and silver, and he covered it with onyx stones and bdellium, and he made upon it the likeness of the whole land of Egypt, and the likeness of the river of Egypt that watereth the whole land of Egypt; and Joseph sat securely upon his throne in his house and the Lord increased Joseph's wisdom.

42. And all the inhabitants of Egypt and Pharaoh's servants and his princes loved Joseph exceedingly, for this thing was from the Lord to Joseph.

43. And Joseph had an army that made war, going out in hosts and troops to the number of forty thousand six hundred men, capable of bearing arms to assist the king and Joseph against the enemy, besides the king's officers and his servants and inhabitants of Egypt without number.

44. And Joseph gave unto his mighty men, and to all his host, shields and javelins, and caps and coats of mail and stones for slinging.

CHAPTER 50

1.   At that time the children of Tarshish came against the sons of Ishmael, and made war with them, and the children of Tarshish spoiled the Ishmaelites for a long time.

2.   And the children of Ishmael were small in number in those days, and they could not prevail over the children of Tarshish, and they were sorely oppressed.

3.   And the old men of the Ishmaelites sent a record to the king of Egypt, saying, Send I pray thee unto thy servants officers and hosts to help us to fight against the children of Tarshish, for we have been consuming away for a long time.

4.   And Pharaoh sent Joseph with the mighty men and host which were with him, and also his mighty men from the king's house.

5.   And they went to the land of Havilah to the children of Ishmael, to assist them against the children of Tarshish, and the children of Ishmael fought with the children of Tarshish, and Joseph smote the Tarshishites and he subdued all their land, and the children of Ishmael dwell therein unto this day.

6.   And when the land of Tarshish was subdued, all the Tarshishites ran away, and came on the border of their brethren the children of Javan, and Joseph with all his mighty men and host returned to Egypt, not one man of them missing.

7.   And at the revolution of the year, in the second year of Joseph's reigning over Egypt, the Lord gave great plenty throughout the land for seven years as Joseph had spoken, for the Lord blessed all the produce of the earth in those days for seven years, and they ate and were greatly satisfied.

8.   And Joseph at that time had officers under him, and they collected all the food of the good years, and heaped corn year by year, and they placed it in the treasuries of Joseph.

9.   And at any time when they gathered the food Joseph commanded that they should bring the corn in the ears, and also bring with it some of the soil of the field, that it should not spoil.

10. And Joseph did according to this year by year, and he heaped up corn like the sand of the sea for abundance, for his stores were immense and could not be numbered for abundance.

11. And also all the inhabitants of Egypt gathered all sorts of food in their stores in great abundance during the seven good years, but they did not do unto it as Joseph did.

12. And all the food which Joseph and the Egyptians had gathered during the seven years of plenty, was secured for the land in stores for the seven years of famine, for the support

of the whole land.

13. And the inhabitants of Egypt filled each man his store and his concealed place with corn, to be for support during the famine.

14. And Joseph placed all the food that he had gathered in all the cities of Egypt, and he closed all the stores and placed sentinels over them.

15. And Joseph's wife Osnath the daughter of Potiphera bare him two sons, Manasseh and Ephraim, and Joseph was thirty-four years old when he begat them.

16. And the lads grew up and they went in his ways and in his instructions, they did not deviate from the way which their father taught them, either to the right or left.

17. And the Lord was with the lads, and they grew up and had understanding and skill in all wisdom and in all the affairs of government, and all the king's officers and his great men of the inhabitants of Egypt exalted the lads, and they were brought up amongst the king's children.

18. And the seven years of plenty that were throughout the land were at an end, and the seven years of famine came after them as Joseph had spoken, and the famine was throughout the land.

19. And all the people of Egypt saw that the famine had commenced in the land of Egypt, and all the people of Egypt opened their stores of corn for the famine prevailed over them.

20. And they found all the food that was in their stores, full of vermin and not fit to eat, and the famine prevailed throughout the land, and all the inhabitants of Egypt came and cried before Pharaoh, for the famine was heavy upon them.

21. And they said unto Pharaoh, Give food unto thy servants, and wherefore shall we die through hunger before thy eyes, even we and our little ones?

22. And Pharaoh answered them, saying, And wherefore do you cry unto me? did not Joseph command that the corn should be laid up during the seven years of plenty for the years of famine? and wherefore did you not hearken to his voice?

23. And the people of Egypt answered the king, saying, As thy soul liveth, our lord, thy servants have done all that Joseph ordered, for thy servants also gathered in all the produce of their fields during the seven years of plenty and laid it in the stores unto this day.

24. And when the famine prevailed over thy servants we opened our stores, and behold all our produce was filled with vermin and was not fit for food.

25. And when the king heard all that had befallen the inhabitants of Egypt, the king was greatly afraid on account of the famine, and he was much terrified; and the king answered the people of Egypt, saying, Since all this has happened unto you, go unto Joseph, do whatever he shall say unto you, transgress not his commands.

26. And all the people of Egypt went forth and came unto Joseph, and said unto him, Give unto us food, and wherefore shall we die before thee through hunger? for we gathered in our produce during the seven years as thou didst command, and we put it in store, and thus has it befallen us.

27. And when Joseph heard all the words of the people of Egypt and what had befallen them, Joseph opened all his stores of the produce and he sold it unto the people of Egypt.

28. And the famine prevailed throughout the land, and the famine was in all countries, but in the land of Egypt there was produce for sale.

29. And all the inhabitants of Egypt came unto Joseph to buy corn, for the famine prevailed over them, and all their corn was spoiled, and Joseph daily sold it to all the people of Egypt.

30. And all the inhabitants of the land of Canaan and the Philistines, and those beyond the Jordan, and the children of the east and all the cities of the lands far and nigh heard that there was corn in Egypt, and they all came to Egypt to buy corn, for the famine prevailed over them.

31. And Joseph opened the stores of corn and placed officers over them, and they daily stood and sold to all that came.

32. And Joseph knew that his brethren also would come to Egypt to buy corn, for the famine prevailed throughout the earth. And Joseph commanded all his people that they should cause it to be proclaimed throughout the land of Egypt, saying,

33. It is the pleasure of the king, of his second and of their great men, that any person who wishes to buy corn in Egypt shall not send his servants to Egypt to purchase, but his sons, and also any Egyptian or Canaanite, who shall come from any of the stores from buying corn in Egypt, and shall go and sell it throughout the land, he shall die, for no one shall buy but for the support of his household.

34. And any man leading two or three beasts shall die, for a man shall only lead his own beast.

35. And Joseph placed sentinels at the gates of Egypt, and commanded them, saying, Any person who may come to buy corn, suffer him not to enter until his name, and the name of his father, and the name of his father's father be written down, and whatever is written by day, send their names unto me in the evening that I may know their names.

36. And Joseph placed officers throughout the land of Egypt, and he commanded them to do all these things.

37. And Joseph did all these things, and made these statutes, in order that he might know when his brethren should come to Egypt to buy corn; and Joseph's people caused it daily to be proclaimed in Egypt according to these words and statutes which Joseph had commanded.

38. And all the inhabitants of the east and west country, and of all the earth, heard of the statutes and regulations which Joseph had enacted in Egypt, and the inhabitants of the extreme parts of the earth came and they bought corn in Egypt day after day, and then went away.

39. And all the officers of Egypt did as Joseph had commanded, and all that came to Egypt to buy corn, the gate keepers would write their names, and their fathers' names, and daily bring them in the evening before Joseph.

CHAPTER 51

1. And Jacob afterward heard that there was corn in Egypt, and he called unto his sons to go to Egypt to buy corn, for upon them also did the famine prevail, and he called unto his sons, saying,

2. Behold I hear that there is corn in Egypt, and all the people of the earth go there to purchase, now therefore why will you show yourselves satisfied before the whole earth? go you also down to Egypt and buy us a little corn amongst those that come there, that we may not die.

3. And the sons of Jacob hearkened to the voice of their father, and they rose up to go down to Egypt in order to buy corn amongst the rest that came there.

4. And Jacob their father commanded them, saying, When you come into the city do not enter together in one gate, on account of the inhabitants of the land.

5.   And the sons of Jacob went forth and they went to Egypt, and the sons of Jacob did all as their father had commanded them, and Jacob did not send Benjamin, for he said, Lest an accident might befall him on the road like his brother; and ten of Jacob's sons went forth.

6.   And whilst the sons of Jacob were going on the road, they repented of what they had done to Joseph, and they spoke to each other, saying, We know that our brother Joseph went down to Egypt, and now we will seek him where we go, and if we find him we will take him from his master for a ransom, and if not, by force, and we will die for him.

7.   And the sons of Jacob agreed to this thing and strengthened themselves on account of Joseph, to deliver him from the hand of his master, and the sons of Jacob went to Egypt; and when they came near to Egypt they separated from each other, and they came through ten gates of Egypt, and the gate keepers wrote their names on that day, and brought them to Joseph in the evening.

8.   And Joseph read the names from the hand of the gate-keepers of the city, and he found that his brethren had entered at the ten gates of the city, and Joseph at that time commanded that it should be proclaimed throughout the land of Egypt, saying,

9.   Go forth all ye store guards, close all the corn stores and let only one remain open, that those who come may purchase from it.

10. And all the officers of Joseph did so at that time, and they closed all the stores and left only one open.

11. And Joseph gave the written names of his brethren to him that was set over the open store, and he said unto him, Whosoever shall come to thee to buy corn, ask his name, and when men of these names shall come before thee, seize them and send them, and

they did so.

12. And when the sons of Jacob came into the city, they joined together in the city to seek Joseph before they bought themselves corn.

13. And they went to the walls of the harlots, and they sought Joseph in the walls of the harlots for three days, for they thought that Joseph would come in the walls of the harlots, for Joseph was very comely and well favored, and the sons of Jacob sought Joseph for three days, and they could not find him.

14. And the man who was set over the open store sought for those names which Joseph had given him, and he did not find them.

15. And he sent to Joseph, saying, These three days have passed, and those men whose names thou didst give unto me have not come; and Joseph sent servants to seek the men in all Egypt, and to bring them before Joseph.

16. And Joseph's servants went and came into Egypt and could not find them, and went to Goshen and they were not there, and then went to the city of Rameses and could not find them.

17. And Joseph continued to send sixteen servants to seek his brothers, and they went and spread themselves in the four corners of the city, and four of the servants went into the house of the harlots, and they found the ten men there seeking their brother.

18. And those four men took them and brought them before him, and they bowed down to him to the ground, and Joseph was sitting upon his throne in his temple, clothed with princely garments, and upon his head was a large crown of gold, and all the mighty men were sitting around him.

19. And the sons of Jacob saw Joseph, and his figure and comeliness and dignity of countenance seemed wonderful in their eyes, and they again bowed down to him to the ground.

20. And Joseph saw his brethren, and he knew them, but they knew him not, for Joseph was very great in their eyes, therefore they knew him not.

21. And Joseph spoke to them, saying, From whence come ye? and they all answered and said, Thy servants have come from the land of Canaan to buy corn, for the famine prevails throughout the earth, and thy servants heard that there was corn in Egypt, so they have come amongst the other comers to buy corn for their support.

22. And Joseph answered them, saying, If you have come to purchase as you say, why do you come through ten gates of the city? it can only be that you have come to spy through the land.

23. And they all together answered Joseph, and said, Not so my lord, we are right, thy servants are not spies, but we have come to buy corn, for thy servants are all brothers, the sons of one man in the land of Canaan, and our father commanded us, saying, When you come to the city do not enter together at one gate on account of the inhabitants of the land.

24. And Joseph again answered them and said, That is the thing which I spoke unto you, you have come to spy through the land, therefore you all came through ten gates of the city; you have come to see the nakedness of the land.

25. Surely every one that cometh to buy corn goeth his way, and you are already three days in the land, and what do you do in the walls of harlots in which you have been for these three days? surely spies do like unto these things.

26. And they said unto Joseph, Far be it from our lord to speak thus, for we are twelve brothers, the sons of our father Jacob, in the land of Canaan, the son of Isaac, the son of Abraham, the Hebrew, and behold the youngest is with our father this day in the land of Canaan, and one is not, for he was lost from us, and we thought perhaps he might be in this land, so we are seeking him throughout the land, and have come even to the houses of harlots to seek him there.

27. And Joseph said unto them, And have you then sought him throughout the earth, that there only remained Egypt for you to seek him in? And what also should your brother do in the houses of harlots, although he were in Egypt? have you not said, That you are from the sons of Isaac, the son of Abraham, and what shall the sons of Jacob do then in the houses of harlots?

28. And they said unto him, Because we heard that Ishmaelites stole him from us, and it was told unto us that they sold him in Egypt, and thy servant, our brother, is very comely and well favored, so we thought he would surely be in the houses of harlots, therefore thy servants went there to seek him and give ransom for him.

29. And Joseph still answered them, saying, Surely you speak falsely and utter lies, to say of yourselves that you are the sons of Abraham; as Pharaoh liveth you are spies, therefore have you come to the houses of harlots that you should not be known.

30. And Joseph said unto them, And now if you find him, and his master requireth of you a great price, will you give it for him? and they said, It shall be given.

31. And he said unto them, And if his master will not consent to part with him for a great price, what will you do unto him on his account? and they answered him, saying, If he will not give him unto us we will slay him, and take our brother and go away.

32. And Joseph said unto them, That is the thing which I have spoken to you; you are spies, for you are come to slay the inhabitants of the land, for we heard that two of your brethren smote all the inhabitants of Shechem, in the land of Canaan, on account of your sister, and you now come to do the like in Egypt on account of your brother.

33. Only hereby shall I know that you are true men; if you will send home one from amongst you to fetch your youngest brother from your father, and to bring him here unto me, and by doing this thing I will know that you are right.

34. And Joseph called to seventy of his mighty men, and he said unto them, Take these men and bring them into the ward.

35. And the mighty men took the ten men, they laid hold of them and put them into the ward, and they were in the ward three days.

36. And on the third day Joseph had them brought out of the ward, and he said unto them, Do this for yourselves if you be true men, so that you may live, one of your brethren shall be confined in the ward whilst you go and take home the corn for your household to the land of Canaan, and fetch your youngest brother, and bring him here unto me, that I may know that you are true men when you do this thing.

37. And Joseph went out from them and came into the chamber, and wept a great weeping, for his pity was excited for them, and he washed his face, and returned to them again, and he took Simeon from them and ordered him to be bound, but Simeon was not willing to be done so, for he was a very powerful man and they could not bind him.

38. And Joseph called unto his mighty men and seventy valiant men came before him with drawn swords in their hands, and the sons of Jacob were terrified at them.

39. And Joseph said unto them, Seize this man and confine him in prison until his brethren come to him, and Joseph's valiant men hastened and they all laid hold of Simeon to bind him, and Simeon gave a loud and terrible shriek and the cry was heard at a distance.

40. And all the valiant men of Joseph were terrified at the sound of the shriek, that they fell upon their faces, and they were greatly afraid and fled.

41. And all the men that were with Joseph fled, for they were greatly afraid of their lives, and only Joseph and Manasseh his son remained there, and Manassah the son of Joseph saw the strength of Simeon, and he was exceedingly wroth.

42. And Manassah the son of Joseph rose up to Simeon, and Manassah smote Simeon a heavy blow with his fist against the back of his neck, and Simeon was stilled of his rage.

43. And Manassah laid hold of Simeon and he seized him violently and he bound him and brought him into the house of confinement, and all the sons of Jacob were astonished at the act of the youth.

44. And Simeon said unto his brethren, None of you must say that this is the smiting of an Egyptian, but it is the smiting of the house of my father.

45. And after this Joseph ordered him to be called who was set over the storehouse, to fill their sacks with corn as much as they could carry, and to restore every man's money
into his sack, and to give them provision for the road, and thus did he unto them.

46. And Joseph commanded them, saying, Take heed lest you transgress my orders to bring your brother as I have told you, and it shall be when you bring your brother hither unto me, then will I know that you are true men, and you shall traffic in the land, and I will restore unto you your brother, and you shall return in peace to your father.

47. And they all answered and said, According as our lord speaketh so will we do, and they bowed down to him to the ground.

48. And every man lifted his corn upon his ass, and they went out to go to the land of Canaan to their father; and they came to the inn and Levi spread his sack to give provender to his ass, when he saw and behold his money in full weight was still in his sack.

49. And the man was greatly afraid, and he said unto his brethren, My money is restored, and lo, it is even in my sack, and the men were greatly afraid, and they said, What is this that God hath done unto us?

50. And they all said, And where is the Lord's kindness with our fathers, with Abraham, Isaac, end Jacob, that the Lord has this day delivered us into the hands of the king of Egypt to contrive against us?

51. And Judah said unto them, Surely we are guilty sinners before the Lord our God in having sold our brother, our own flesh, and wherefore do you say, Where is the Lord's kindness with our fathers?

52. And Reuben said unto them, Said I not unto you, do not sin against the lad, and you would not listen to me? now God requireth him from us, and how dare you say, Where is the Lord's kindness with our fathers, whilst you have sinned unto the Lord?

53. And they tarried over night in that place, and they rose up early in the morning and laded their asses with their corn, and they led them and went on and came to their father's house in the land of Canaan.

54. And Jacob and his household went out to meet his sons, and Jacob saw and behold their brother Simeon was not with them, and Jacob said unto his sons, Where is your brother Simeon, whom I do not see? and his sons told him all that had befallen them in Egypt.

CHAPTER 52

1.   And they entered their house, and every man opened his sack and they saw and behold every man's bundle of money was there, at which they and their father were greatly terrified.

2.   And Jacob said unto them, What is this that you have done to me? I sent your brother Joseph to inquire after your welfare and you said unto me. A wild beast did devour him.

3.   And Simeon went with you to buy food and you say the king of Egypt hath confined him in prison, and you wish to take Benjamin to cause his death also, and bring down my grey hairs with sorrow to the grave on account of Benjamin and his brother Joseph.

4.   Now therefore my son shall not go down with you, for his brother is dead and he is left alone, and mischief may befall him by the way in which you go, as it befell his brother.

5.   And Reuben said unto his father, Thou shalt slay my two sons if I do not bring thy son and place him before thee; and Jacob said unto his sons, Abide ye here and do not go down to Egypt, for my son shall not go down with you to Egypt, nor die like his brother.

6.   And Judah said unto them, refrain ye from him until the corn is finished, and he will then say, Take down your brother, when he will find his own life and the life of his household in danger from the famine.

7.   And in those days the famine was sore throughout the land, and all the people of the earth went and came to Egypt to buy food, for the famine prevailed greatly amongst them, and the sons of Jacob remained in Canaan a year and two months until their corn was finished.

8.   And it came to pass after their corn was finished, the whole household of Jacob was pinched with hunger, and all the infants of the sons of Jacob came together and they approached Jacob, and they all surrounded him, and they said unto him, Give unto us bread, and wherefore shall we all perish through hunger in thy presence?

9.   Jacob heard the words of his son's children, and he wept a great weeping, and his pity was roused for them, and Jacob called unto his sons and they all came and sat before him.

10. And Jacob said unto them, And have you not seen how your children have been weeping over me this day, saying, Give unto us bread, and there is none? now therefore return and buy for us a little food.

11. And Judah answered and said unto his father, If thou wilt send our brother with us we will go down and buy corn for thee, and if thou wilt not send him then we will not go down, for surely the king of Egypt particularly enjoined us, saying, You shall not see my face unless your brother be with you, for the king of Egypt is a strong and mighty king, and behold if we shall go to him without our brother we shall all be put to death.

12. Dost thou not know and hast thou not heard that this king is very powerful and wise, and there is not like unto him in all the earth? behold we have seen all the kings of the earth and we have not seen one like that king, the king of Egypt; surely amongst all the kings of the earth there is none greater than Abimelech king of the Philistines, yet the king of Egypt is greater and mightier than he, and Abimelech can only be compared to one of his officers.

13. Father, thou hast not seen his palace and his throne, and all his servants standing before him; thou hast not seen that king upon his throne in his pomp and royal appearance, dressed in his kingly robes with a large golden crown upon his head; thou hast not seen the honor and glory which God has given unto him, for there is not like unto him in all the earth.

14. Father, thou hast not seen the wisdom, the understanding and the knowledge which God has given in his heart, nor heard his sweet voice when he spake unto us.

15. We know not, father, who made him acquainted with our names and all that befell us, yet he asked also after thee, saying, Is your father still living, and is it well with him?

16. Thou hast not seen the affairs of the government of Egypt regulated by him, without inquiring of Pharaoh his lord; thou hast not seen the awe and fear which he impressed upon all the Egyptians.

17. And also when we went from him, we threatened to do unto Egypt like unto the rest of the cities of the Amorites, and we were exceedingly wroth against all his words which he spoke concerning us as spies, and now when we shall again come before him his terror will fall upon us all, and not one of us will be able to speak to him either a little or a great thing.

18. Now therefore father, send we pray thee the lad with us, and we will go down and buy thee food for our support, and not die through hunger. And Jacob said, Why have you dealt so ill with me to tell the king you had a brother? what is this thing that you have done unto me?

19. And Judah said unto Jacob his father, Give the lad into my care and we will rise up and go down to Egypt and buy corn, and then return, and it shall be when we return if the lad be not with us, then let me bear thy blame forever.

20. Hast thou seen all our infants weeping over thee through hunger and there is no power in thy hand to satisfy them? now let thy pity be roused for them and send our brother with us and we will go.

21. For how will the Lord's kindness to our ancestors be manifested to thee when thou sayest that the king of Egypt will take away thy son? as the Lord liveth I will not leave him until I bring him and place him before thee; but pray for us unto the Lord, that he

may deal kindly with us, to cause us to be received favorably and kindly before the king of Egypt and his men, for had we not delayed surely now we had returned a second time with thy son.

22. And Jacob said unto his sons, I trust in the Lord God that he may deliver you and give you favor in the sight of the king of Egypt, and in the sight of all his men.

23. Now therefore rise up and go to the man, and take for him in your hands a present from what can be obtained in the land and bring it before him, and may the Almighty God give you mercy before him that he may send Benjamin and Simeon your brethren with you.

24. And all the men rose up, and they took their brother Benjamin, and they took in their hands a large present of the best of the land, and they also took a double portion of silver.

25. And Jacob strictly commanded his sons concerning Benjamin, Saying, Take heed of him in the way in which you are going, and do not separate yourselves from him in the road, neither in Egypt.

26. And Jacob rose up from his sons and spread forth his hands and he prayed unto the Lord on account of his sons, saying, O Lord God of heaven and earth, remember thy covenant with our father Abraham, remember it with my father Isaac and deal kindly with my sons and deliver them not into the hands of the king of Egypt; do it I pray thee O God for the sake of thy mercies and redeem all my children and rescue them from Egyptian power, and send them their two brothers.

27. And all the wives of the sons of Jacob and their children lifted up their eyes to heaven and they all wept before the Lord, and cried unto him to deliver their fathers from the hand of the king of Egypt.

28. And Jacob wrote a record to the king of Egypt and gave it into the hand of Judah and into the hands of his sons for the king of Egypt, saying,

29. From thy servant Jacob, son of Isaac, son of Abraham the Hebrew, the prince of God, to the powerful and wise king, the revealer of secrets, king of Egypt, greeting.

30. Be it known to my lord the king of Egypt, the famine was sore upon us in the land of Canaan, and I sent my sons to thee to buy us a little food from thee for our support.

31. For my sons surrounded me and I being very old cannot see with my eyes, for my eyes have become very heavy through age, as well as with daily weeping for my son, for Joseph who was lost from before me, and I commanded my sons that they should not enter the gates of the city when they came to Egypt, on account of the inhabitants of the land.

32. And I also commanded them to go about Egypt to seek for my son Joseph, perhaps they might find him there, and they did so, and thou didst consider them as spies of the land.

33. Have we not heard concerning thee that thou didst interpret Pharaoh's dream and didst speak truly unto him? how then dost thou not know in thy wisdom whether my sons are spies or not?

34. Now therefore, my lord and king, behold I have sent my son before thee, as thou didst speak unto my sons; I beseech thee to put thy eyes upon him until he is returned to me in peace with his brethren.

35. For dost thou not know, or hast thou not heard that which our God did unto Pharaoh when he took my mother Sarah, and what he did unto Abimelech king of the Philistines on account of her, and also what our father Abraham did unto the nine kings of Elam, how he smote them all with a few men that were with him?

36. And also what my two sons Simeon and Levi did unto the eight cities of the Amorites, how they destroyed them on account of their sister Dinah?

37. And also on account of their brother Benjamin they consoled themselves for the loss of his brother Joseph; what will they then do for him when they see the hand of any people prevailing over them, for his sake?

38. Dost thou not know, O king of Egypt, that the power of God is with us, and that also God ever heareth our prayers and forsaketh us not all the days?

39. And when my sons told me of thy dealings with them, I called not unto the Lord on account of thee, for then thou wouldst have perished with thy men before my son Benjamin came before thee, but I thought that as Simeon my son was in thy house, perhaps thou mightest deal kindly with him, therefore I did not this thing unto thee.

40. Now therefore behold Benjamin my son cometh unto thee with my sons, take heed of him and put thy eyes upon him, and then will God place his eyes over thee and throughout thy kingdom.

41. Now I have told thee all that is in my heart, and behold my sons are coming to thee with their brother, examine the face of the whole earth for their sake and send them back in peace with their brethren.

42. And Jacob gave the record to his sons into the care of Judah to give it unto the king of Egypt.

CHAPTER 53

1. And the sons of Jacob rose up and took Benjamin and the whole of the presents, and they went and came to Egypt and they stood before Joseph.

2. And Joseph beheld his brother Benjamin with them and he saluted them, and these men came to Joseph's house.

3. And Joseph commanded the superintendent of his house to give to his brethren to eat, and he did so unto them.

4. And at noon time Joseph sent for the men to come before him with Benjamin, and the men told the superintendent of Joseph's house concerning the silver that was returned in their sacks, and he said unto them, It will be well with you, fear not, and he brought their brother Simeon unto them.

5. And Simeon said unto his brethren, The lord of the Egyptians has acted very kindly unto me, he did not keep me bound, as you saw with your eyes, for when you went out from the city he let me free and dealt kindly with me in his house.

6. And Judah took Benjamin by the hand, and they came before Joseph, and they bowed down to him to the ground.

7. And the men gave the present unto Joseph and they all sat before him, and Joseph said unto them, Is it well with you, is it well with your children, is it well with your aged father? and they said, It is well, and Judah took the record which Jacob had sent and gave it into the hand of Joseph.

8. And Joseph read the letter and knew his father's writing, and he wished to weep and he went into an inner room and he wept a great weeping; and he went out.

9. And he lifted up his eyes and beheld his brother Benjamin, and he said, Is this your brother of whom you spoke unto me? And Benjamin approached Joseph, and Joseph placed his hand upon his head and he said unto him, May God be gracious unto thee my son.

10. And when Joseph saw his brother, the son of his mother, he again wished to weep, and he entered the chamber, and he wept there, and he washed his face, and went out and refrained from weeping, and he said, Prepare food.

11. And Joseph had a cup from which he drank, and it was of silver beautifully inlaid with onyx stones and bdellium, and Joseph struck the cup in the sight of his brethren whilst they were sitting to eat with him.

12. And Joseph said unto the men, I know by this cup that Reuben the first born, Simeon
and Levi and Judah, Issachar and Zebulun are children from one mother, seat yourselves to eat according to your births.

13. And he also placed the others according to their births, and he said, I know that this your youngest brother has no brother, and I, like him, have no brother, he shall therefore sit down to eat with me.

14. And Benjamin went up before Joseph and sat upon the throne, and the men beheld the acts of Joseph, and they were astonished at them; and the men ate and drank at that time with Joseph, and he then gave presents unto them, and Joseph gave one gift unto Benjamin, and Manasseh and Ephraim saw the acts of their father, and they also gave presents unto him, and Osnath gave him one present, and they were five presents in the hand of Benjamin.

15. And Joseph brought them out wine to drink, and they would not drink, and they said, From the day on which Joseph was lost we have not drunk wine, nor eaten any delicacies.

16. And Joseph swore unto them, and he pressed them hard, and they drank plentifully with him on that day, and Joseph afterward turned to his brother Benjamin to speak with him, and Benjamin was still sitting upon the throne before Joseph.

17. And Joseph said unto him, Hast thou begotten any children? and he said, Thy servant has ten sons, and these are their names, Bela, Becher, Ashbal, Gera, Naaman, Achi, Rosh, Mupim, Chupim, and Ord, and I called their names after my brother whom I have not seen.

18. And he ordered them to bring before him his map of the stars, whereby Joseph knew all the times, and Joseph said unto Benjamin, I have heard that the Hebrews are acquainted with all wisdom, dost thou know anything of this?

19. And Benjamin said, Thy servant is knowing also in all the wisdom which my father taught me, and Joseph said unto Benjamin, Look now at this instrument and understand where thy brother Joseph is in Egypt, who you said went down to Egypt.

20. And Benjamin beheld that instrument with the map of the stars of heaven, and he was wise and looked therein to know where his brother was, and Benjamin divided the whole land of Egypt into four divisions, and he found that he who was sitting upon the throne before him was his brother Joseph, and Benjamin wondered greatly, and when Joseph saw that his brother Benjamin was so much astonished, he said unto Benjamin, What hast thou seen, and why art thou astonished?

21. And Benjamin said unto Joseph, I can see by this that Joseph my brother sitteth here with me upon the throne, and Joseph said unto him, I am Joseph thy brother, reveal not this thing unto thy brethren; behold I will send thee with them when they go away, and I will command them to be brought back again into the city, and I will take thee away from them.

22. And if they dare their lives and fight for thee, then shall I know that they have repented of what they did unto me, and I will make myself known to them, and if they forsake thee when I take thee, then shalt thou remain with me, and I will wrangle with them, and they shall go away, and I will not become known to them.

23. At that time Joseph commanded his officer to fill their sacks with food, and to put each man's money into his sack, and to put the cup in the sack of Benjamin, and to give them provision for the road, and they did so unto them.

24. And on the next day the men rose up early in the morning, and they loaded their asses with their corn, and they went forth with Benjamin, and they went to the land of Canaan with their brother Benjamin.

25. They had not gone far from Egypt when Joseph commanded him that was set over his house, saying, Rise, pursue these men before they get too far from Egypt, and say unto them, Why have you stolen my master's cup?

26. And Joseph's officer rose up and he reached them, and he spoke unto them all the words of Joseph; and when they heard this thing they became exceedingly wroth, and they said, He with whom thy master's cup shall be found shall die, and we will also become slaves.

27. And they hastened and each man brought down his sack from his ass, and they looked in their bags and the cup was found in Benjamin's bag, and they all tore their garments and they returned to the city, and they smote Benjamin in the road, continually smiting him until he came into the city, and they stood before Joseph.

28. And Judah's anger was kindled, and he said, This man has only brought me back to destroy Egypt this day.

29. And the men came to Joseph's house, and they found Joseph sitting upon his throne, and all the mighty men standing at his right and left.

30. And Joseph said unto them, What is this act that you have done, that you took away my silver cup and went away? but I know that you took my cup in order to know thereby in what part of the land your brother was.

31. And Judah said, What shall we say to our lord, what shall we speak and how shall we justify ourselves, God has this day found the iniquity of all thy servants, therefore has he done this thing to us this day.

32. And Joseph rose up and caught hold of Benjamin and took him from his brethren with violence, and he came to the house and locked the door at them, and Joseph commanded him that was set over his house that he should say unto them, Thus saith the king, Go in peace to your father, behold I have taken the man in whose hand my cup was found.

CHAPTER 54

1. And when Judah saw the dealings of Joseph with them, Judah approached him and broke open the door, and came with his brethren before Joseph.

2. And Judah said unto Joseph, Let it not seem grievous in the sight of my lord, may thy servant I pray thee speak a word before thee? and Joseph said unto him, Speak.

3. And Judah spoke before Joseph, and his brethren were there standing before them; and Judah said unto Joseph, Surely when we first came to our lord to buy food, thou didst consider us as spies of the land, and we brought Benjamin before thee, and thou still makest sport of us this day.

4. Now therefore let the king hear my words, and send I pray thee our brother that he may go along with us to our father, lest thy soul perish this day with all the souls of the inhabitants of Egypt.

5. Dost thou not know what two of my brethren, Simeon and Levi, did unto the city of Shechem, and unto seven cities of the Amorites, on account of our sister Dinah, and also what they would do for the sake of their brother Benjamin?

6. And I with my strength, who am greater and mightier than both of them, come this day upon thee and thy land if thou art unwilling to send our brother.

7. Hast thou not heard what our God who made choice of us did unto Pharaoh on account of Sarah our mother, whom he took away from our father, that he smote him and his household with heavy plagues, that even unto this day the Egyptians relate this wonder to each other? so will our God do unto thee on account of Benjamin whom thou hast this day taken from his father, and on account of the evils which thou this day heapest over us in thy land; for our God will remember his covenant with our father Abraham and bring evil upon thee, because thou hast grieved the soul of our father this day.

8. Now therefore hear my words that I have this day spoken unto thee, and send our brother that he may go away lest thou and the people of thy land die by the sword, for you cannot all prevail over me.

9. And Joseph answered Judah, saying, Why hast thou opened wide thy mouth and why dost thou boast over us, saying, Strength is with thee? as Pharaoh liveth, if I command all my valiant men to fight with you, surely thou and these thy brethren would sink in the mire.

10. And Judah said unto Joseph, Surely it becometh thee and thy people to fear me; as the Lord liveth if I once draw my sword I shall not sheathe it again until I shall this day have slain all Egypt, and I will commence with thee and finish with Pharaoh thy master.

11. And Joseph answered and said unto him, Surely strength belongeth not alone to thee; I
am stronger and mightier than thou, surely if thou drawest thy sword I will put it to thy neck and the necks of all thy brethren.

12. And Judah said unto him, Surely if I this day open my mouth against thee I would swallow thee up that thou be destroyed from off the earth and perish this day from thy kingdom. And Joseph said, Surely if thou openest thy mouth I have power and might to close thy mouth with a stone until thou shalt not be able to utter a word; see how many stones are before us, truly I can take a stone, and force it into thy mouth and break thy jaws.

13. And Judah said, God is witness between us, that we have not hitherto desired to battle with thee, only give us our brother and we will go from thee; and Joseph answered and said, As Pharaoh liveth, if all the kings of Canaan came together with you, you should not take him from my hand.

14. Now therefore go your way to your father, and your brother shall be unto me for a slave, for he has robbed the king's house. And Judah said, What is it to thee or to the character of the king, surely the king sendeth forth from his house, throughout the land, silver and gold either in gifts or expenses, and thou still talkest about thy cup which thou didst place in our brother's bag and sayest that he has stolen it from thee?

15. God forbid that our brother Benjamin or any of the seed of Abraham should do this thing to steal from thee, or from any one else, whether king, prince, or any man.

16. Now therefore cease this accusation lest the whole earth hear thy words, saying, For a little silver the king of Egypt wrangled with the men, and he accused them and took their brother for a slave.

17. And Joseph answered and said, Take unto you this cup and go from me and leave your brother for a slave, for it is the judgment of a thief to be a slave.

18. And Judah said, Why art thou not ashamed of thy words, to leave our brother and to take thy cup? Surely if thou givest us thy cup, or a thousand times as much, we will not leave our brother for the silver which is found in the hand of any man, that we will not die over him.

19. And Joseph answered, And why did you forsake your brother and sell him for twenty pieces of silver unto this day, and why then will you not do the same to this your brother?

20. And Judah said, the Lord is witness between me and thee that we desire not thy battles; now therefore give us our brother and we will go from thee without quarreling.

21. And Joseph answered and said, If all the kings of the land should assemble they will not be able to take your brother from my hand; and Judah said, What shall we say unto our father, when he seeth that our brother cometh not with us, and will grieve over him?

22. And Joseph answered and said, This is the thing which you shall tell unto your father, saying, The rope has gone after the bucket.

23. And Judah said, Surely thou art a king, and why speakest thou these things, giving a false judgment? woe unto the king who is like unto thee.

24. And Joseph answered and said, There is no false judgment in the word that I spoke on account of your brother Joseph, for all of you sold him to the Midianites for twenty pieces of silver, and you all denied it to your father and said unto him, An evil beast has devoured him, Joseph has been torn to pieces.

25. And Judah said, Behold the fire of Shem burneth in my heart, now I will burn all your land with fire; and Joseph answered and said, Surely thy sister-in-law Tamar, who killed your sons, extinguished the fire of Shechem.

26. And Judah said, If I pluck out a single hair from my flesh, I will fill all Egypt with its blood.

27. And Joseph answered and said, Such is your custom to do as you did to your brother whom you sold, and you dipped his coat in blood and brought it to your father in order that he might say an evil beast devoured him and here is his blood.

28. And when Judah heard this thing he was exceedingly wroth and his anger burned within him, and there was before him in that place a stone, the weight of which was about four hundred shekels, and Judah's anger was kindled and he took the stone in one hand and cast it to the heavens and caught it with his left hand.

29. And he placed it afterward under his legs, and he sat upon it with all his strength and the stone was turned into dust from the force of Judah.

30. And Joseph saw the act of Judah and he was very much afraid, but he commanded Manassah his son and he also did with another stone like unto the act of Judah, and Judah said unto his brethren, Let not any of you say, this man is an Egyptian, but by his doing this thing he is of our father's family.

31. And Joseph said, Not to you only is strength given, for we are also powerful men, and why will you boast over us all? and Judah said unto Joseph, Send I pray thee our brother and ruin not thy country this day.

32. And Joseph answered and said unto them, Go and tell your father, an evil beast hath devoured him as you said concerning your brother Joseph.

33. And Judah spoke to his brother Naphtali, and he said unto him, Make haste, go now and number all the streets of Egypt and come and tell me; and Simeon said unto him, Let not this thing be a trouble to thee; now I will go to the mount and take up one large stone from the mount and level it at every one in Egypt, and kill all that are in it.

34. And Joseph heard all these words that his brethren spoke before him, and they did not know that Joseph understood them, for they imagined that he knew not to speak Hebrew.

35. And Joseph was greatly afraid at the words of his brethren lest they should destroy Egypt, and he commanded his son Manasseh, saying, Go now make haste and gather unto me all the inhabitants of Egypt, and all the valiant men together, and let them come to me now upon horseback and on foot and with all sorts of musical instruments, and Manasseh went and did so.

36. And Naphtali went as Judah had commanded him, for Naphtali was lightfooted as one of the swift stags, and he would go upon the ears of corn and they would not break under him.

37. And he went and numbered all the streets of Egypt, and found them to be twelve, and he came hastily and told Judah, and Judah said unto his brethren, Hasten you and put on every man his sword upon his loins and we will come over Egypt, and smite them all, and let not a remnant remain.

38. And Judah said, Behold, I will destroy three of the streets with my strength, and you shall each destroy one street; and when Judah was speaking this thing, behold the inhabitants of Egypt and all the mighty men came toward them with all sorts of musical instruments and with loud shouting.

39. And their number was five hundred cavalry and ten thousand infantry, and four hundred men who could fight without sword or spear, only with their hands and strength.

40. And all the mighty men came with great storming and shouting, and they all surrounded the sons of Jacob and terrified them, and the ground quaked at the sound of their shouting.

41. And when the sons of Jacob saw these troops they were greatly afraid of their lives, and Joseph did so in order to terrify the sons of Jacob to become tranquilized.

42. And Judah, seeing some of his brethren terrified, said unto them, Why are you afraid whilst the grace of God is with us? and when Judah saw all the people of Egypt surrounding them at the command of Joseph to terrify them, only Joseph commanded them, saying, Do not touch any of them.

43. Then Judah hastened and drew his sword, and uttered a loud and bitter scream, and he smote with his sword, and he sprang upon the ground and he still continued to shout against all the people.

44. And when he did this thing the Lord caused the terror of Judah and his brethren to fall upon the valiant men and all the people that surrounded them.

45. And they all fled at the sound of the shouting, and they were terrified and fell one upon the other, and many of them died as they fell, and they all fled from before Judah and
his brethren and from before Joseph.

46. And whilst they were fleeing, Judah and his brethren pursued them unto the house of Pharaoh, and they all escaped, and Judah again sat before Joseph and roared at him like a lion, and gave a great and tremendous shriek at him.

47. And the shriek was heard at a distance, and all the inhabitants of Succoth heard it, and all Egypt quaked at the sound of the shriek, and also the walls of Egypt and of the land of Goshen fell in from the shaking of the earth, and Pharaoh also fell from his throne upon the ground, and also all the pregnant women of Egypt and Goshen miscarried when they heard the noise of the shaking, for they were terribly afraid.

48. And Pharaoh sent word, saying, What is this thing that has this day happened in the land of Egypt? and they came and told him all the things from beginning to end, and Pharaoh was alarmed and he wondered and was greatly afraid.

49. And his fright increased when he heard all these things, and he sent unto Joseph, saying, Thou hast brought unto me the Hebrews to destroy all Egypt; what wilt thou do with that thievish slave? send him away and let him go with his brethren, and let us not perish through their evil, even we, you and all Egypt.

50. And if thou desirest not to do this thing, cast off from thee all my valuable things, and go with them to their land, if thou delightest in it, for they will this day destroy my whole country and slay all my people; even all the women of Egypt have miscarried through their screams; see what they have done merely by their shouting and speaking, moreover if they fight with the sword, they will destroy the land; now therefore choose that which thou desirest, whether me or the Hebrews, whether Egypt or the land of the Hebrews.

51. And they came and told Joseph all the words of Pharaoh that he had said concerning him, and Joseph was greatly afraid at the words of Pharaoh and Judah and his brethren were still standing before Joseph indignant and enraged, and all the sons of Jacob roared at Joseph, like the roaring of the sea and its waves.

52. And Joseph was greatly afraid of his brethren and on account of Pharaoh, and Joseph sought a pretext to make himself known unto his brethren, lest they should destroy all Egypt.

53. And Joseph commanded his son Manasseh, and Manasseh went and approached Judah, and placed his hand upon his shoulder, and the anger of Judah was stilled.

54. And Judah said unto his brethren, Let no one of you say that this is the act of an Egyptian youth for this is the work of my father's house.

55. And Joseph seeing and knowing that Judah's anger was stilled, he approached to speak unto Judah in the language of mildness.

56. And Joseph said unto Judah, Surely you speak truth and have this day verified your assertions concerning your strength, and may your God who delighteth in you, increase your welfare; but tell me truly why from amongst all thy brethren dost thou wrangle with me on account of the lad, as none of them have spoken one word to me concerning him.

57. And Judah answered Joseph, saying, Surely thou must know that I was security for the lad to his father, saying, If I brought him not unto him I should bear his blame forever.

58. Therefore have I approached thee from amongst all my brethren, for I saw that thou wast unwilling to suffer him to go from thee; now therefore may I find grace in thy sight that thou shalt send him to go with us, and behold I will remain as a substitute for him, to serve thee in whatever thou desirest, for wheresoever thou shalt send me I will go to serve thee with great energy.

59. Send me now to a mighty king who has rebelled against thee, and thou shalt know what I will do unto him and unto his land; although he may have cavalry and infantry or an exceeding mighty people, I will slay them all and bring the king's head before thee.

60. Dost thou not know or hast thou not heard that our father Abraham with his servant Eliezer smote all the kings of Elam with their hosts in one night, they left not one remaining? and ever since that day our father's strength was given unto us for an inheritance, for us and our seed forever.

61. And Joseph answered and said, You speak truth, and falsehood is not in your mouth, for it was also told unto us that the Hebrews have power and that the Lord their God delighteth much in them, and who then can stand before them?

62. However, on this condition will I send your brother, if you will bring before me his brother the son of his mother, of whom you said that he had gone from you down to Egypt; and it shall come to pass when you bring unto me his brother I will take him in his stead, because not one of you was security for him to your father, and when he shall come unto me, I will then send with you his brother for whom you have been security.

63. And Judah's anger was kindled against Joseph when he spoke this thing, and his eyes dropped blood with anger, and he said unto his brethren, How doth this man this day seek his own destruction and that of all Egypt!

64. And Simeon answered Joseph, saying, Did we not tell thee at first that we knew not the particular spot to which he went, and whether he be dead or alive, and wherefore speaketh my lord like unto these things?

65. And Joseph observing the countenance of Judah discerned that his anger began to kindle when he spoke unto him, saying, Bring unto me your other brother instead of this brother.

66. And Joseph said unto his brethren, Surely you said that your brother was either dead or lost, now if I should call him this day and he should come before you, would you give him unto me instead of his brother?

67. And Joseph began to speak and call out, Joseph, Joseph, come this day before me, and appear to thy brethren and sit before them.

68. And when Joseph spoke this thing before them, they looked each a different way to see from whence Joseph would come before them.

69. And Joseph observed all their acts, and said unto them, Why do you look here and there? I am Joseph whom you sold to Egypt, now therefore let it not grieve you that you sold me, for as a support during the famine did God send me before you.

70. And his brethren were terrified at him when they heard the words of Joseph, and Judah was exceedingly terrified at him.

71. And when Benjamin heard the words of Joseph he was before them in the inner part of the house, and Benjamin ran unto Joseph his brother, and embraced him and fell upon his neck, and they wept.

72. And when Joseph's brethren saw that Benjamin had fallen upon his brother's neck and wept with him, they also fell upon Joseph and embraced him, and they wept a great weeping with Joseph.

73. And the voice was heard in the house of Joseph that they were Joseph's brethren, and it pleased Pharaoh exceedingly, for he was afraid of them lest they should destroy Egypt.

74. And Pharaoh sent his servants unto Joseph to congratulate him concerning his brethren who had come to him, and all the captains of the armies and troops that were in Egypt came to rejoice with Joseph, and all Egypt rejoiced greatly about Joseph's brethren.

75. And Pharaoh sent his servants to Joseph, saying, Tell thy brethren to fetch all belonging to them and let them come unto me, and I will place them in the best part of the land of Egypt, and they did so.

76. And Joseph commanded him that was set over his house to bring out to his brethren gifts and garments, and he brought out to them many garments being robes of royalty and many gifts, and Joseph divided them amongst his brethren.

77. And he gave unto each of his brethren a change of garments of gold and silver, and three hundred pieces of silver, and Joseph commanded them all to be dressed in these garments, and to be brought before Pharaoh.

78. And Pharaoh seeing that all Joseph's brethren were valiant men, and of beautiful appearance, he greatly rejoiced.

79. And they afterward went out from the presence of Pharaoh to go to the land of Canaan, to their father, and their brother Benjamin was with them.

80. And Joseph rose up and gave unto them eleven chariots from Pharaoh, and Joseph gave unto them his chariot, upon which he rode on the day of his being crowned in Egypt, to fetch his father to Egypt; and Joseph sent to all his brothers' children, garments according to their numbers, and a hundred pieces of silver to each of them, and he also sent garments to the wives of his brethren from the garments of the king's wives, and he sent them.

81. And he gave unto each of his brethren ten men to go with them to the land of Canaan to serve them, to serve their children and all belonging to them in coming to Egypt.

82. And Joseph sent by the hand of his brother Benjamin ten suits of garments for his ten sons, a portion above the rest of the children of the sons of Jacob.

83. And he sent to each fifty pieces of silver, and ten chariots on the account of Pharaoh, and he sent to his father ten asses laden with all the luxuries of Egypt, and ten she asses laden with corn and bread and nourishment for his father, and to all that were with him as provisions for the road.

84. And he sent to his sister Dinah garments of silver and gold, and frankincense and myrrh, and aloes and women's ornaments in great plenty, and he sent the same from the wives of Pharaoh to the wives of Benjamin.

85. And he gave unto all his brethren, also to their wives, all sorts of onyx stones and bdellium, and from all the valuable things amongst the great people of Egypt, nothing of all the costly things was left but what Joseph sent of to his father's household.

86. And he sent his brethren away, and they went, and he sent his brother Benjamin with them.

87. And Joseph went out with them to accompany them on the road unto the borders of Egypt, and he commanded them concerning his father and his household, to come to Egypt.

88. And he said unto them, Do not quarrel on the road, for this thing was from the Lord to keep a great people from starvation, for there will be yet five years of famine in the land.

89. And he commanded them, saying, When you come unto the land of Canaan, do not come suddenly before my father in this affair, but act in your wisdom.

90. And Joseph ceased to command them, and he turned and went back to Egypt, and the sons of Jacob went to the land of Canaan with joy and cheerfulness to their father Jacob.

91. And they came unto the borders of the land, and they said to each other, What shall we do in this matter before our father, for if we come suddenly to him and tell him the

matter, he will be greatly alarmed at our words and will not believe us.

92. And they went along until they came nigh unto their houses, and they found Serach, the daughter of Asher, going forth to meet them, and the damsel was very good and subtle, and knew how to play upon the harp.

93. And they called unto her and she came before them, and she kissed them, and they took her and gave unto her a harp, saying, Go now before our father, and sit before him, and strike upon the harp, and speak these words.

94. And they commanded her to go to their house, and she took the harp and hastened before them, and she came and sat near Jacob.

95. And she played well and sang, and uttered in the sweetness of her words, Joseph my uncle is living, and he ruleth throughout the land of Egypt, and is not dead.

96. And she continued to repeat and utter these words, and Jacob heard her words and they were agreeable to him.

97. He listened whilst she repeated them twice and thrice, and joy entered the heart of Jacob at the sweetness of her words, and the spirit of God was upon him, and he knew all her words to be true.

98. And Jacob blessed Serach when she spoke these words before him, and he said unto her, My daughter, may death never prevail over thee, for thou hast revived my spirit; only speak yet before me as thou hast spoken, for thou hast gladdened me with all thy words.

99. And she continued to sing these words, and Jacob listened and it pleased him, and he rejoiced, and the spirit of God was upon him.

100. Whilst he was yet speaking with her, behold his sons came to him with horses and chariots and royal garments and servants running before them.

101. And Jacob rose up to meet them, and saw his sons dressed in royal garments and he saw all the treasures that Joseph had sent to them.

102. And they said unto him, Be informed that our brother Joseph is living, and it is he who ruleth throughout the land of Egypt, and it is he who spoke unto us as we told thee.

103. And Jacob heard all the words of his sons, and his heart palpitated at their words, for he could not believe them until he saw all that Joseph had given them and what he had sent him, and all the signs which Joseph had spoken unto them.

104.   And they opened out before him, and showed him all that Joseph had sent, they gave unto each what Joseph had sent him, and he knew that they had spoken the truth, and he rejoiced exceedingly an account of his son.

105.   And Jacob said, It is enough for me that my son Joseph is still living, I will go and see him before I die.

106.   And his sons told him all that had befallen them, and Jacob said, I will go down to Egypt to see my son and his offspring.

107.   And Jacob rose up and put on the garments which Joseph had sent him, and after he had washed, and shaved his hair, he put upon his head the turban which Joseph had sent him.

108.   And all the people of Jacob's house and their wives put on the garments which Joseph had sent to them, and they greatly rejoiced at Joseph that he was still living and that he was ruling in Egypt,

109.   And all the inhabitants of Canaan heard of this thing, and they came and rejoiced much with Jacob that he was still living.

110.   And Jacob made a feast for them for three days, and all the kings of Canaan and nobles of the land ate and drank and rejoiced in the house of Jacob.

CHAPTER 55

1. And it came to pass after this that Jacob said, I will go and see my son in Egypt and will then come back to the land of Canaan of which God had spoken unto Abraham, for I cannot leave the land of my birth-place.

2. Behold the word of the Lord came unto him, saying, Go down to Egypt with all thy household and remain there, fear not to go down to Egypt for I will there make thee a great nation.

3. And Jacob said within himself, I will go and see my son whether the fear of his God is yet in his heart amidst all the inhabitants of Egypt.

4. And the Lord said unto Jacob, Fear not about Joseph, for he still retaineth his integrity to serve me, as will seem good in thy sight, and Jacob rejoiced exceedingly concerning his son.

5. At that time Jacob commanded his sons and household to go to Egypt according to the word of the Lord unto him, and Jacob rose up with his sons and all his household, and he went out from the land of Canaan from Beersheba, with joy and gladness of heart, and they went to the land of Egypt.

6. And it came to pass when they came near Egypt, Jacob sent Judah before him to Joseph that he might show him a situation in Egypt, and Judah did according to the word of his father, and he hastened and ran and came to Joseph, and they assigned for them a place in the land of Goshen for all his household, and Judah returned and came along the road to his father.

7. And Joseph harnessed the chariot, and he assembled all his mighty men and his servants and all the officers of Egypt in order to go and meet his father Jacob, and Joseph's mandate was proclaimed in Egypt, saying, All that do not go to meet Jacob shall die.

8. And on the next day Joseph went forth with all Egypt a great and mighty host, all dressed in garments of fine linen and purple and with instruments of silver and gold and with their instruments of war with them.

9. And they all went to meet Jacob with all sorts of musical instruments, with drums and timbrels, strewing myrrh and aloes all along the road, and they all went after this fashion, and the earth shook at their shouting.

10. And all the women of Egypt went upon the roofs of Egypt and upon the walls to meet Jacob, and upon the head of Joseph was Pharaoh's regal crown, for Pharaoh had sent it unto him to put on at the time of his going to meet his father.

11. And when Joseph came within fifty cubits of his father, he alighted from the chariot and he walked toward his father, and when all the officers of Egypt and her nobles saw that Joseph had gone on foot toward his father, they also alighted and walked on foot toward Jacob.

12. And when Jacob approached the camp of Joseph, Jacob observed the camp that was coming toward him with Joseph, and it gratified him and Jacob was astonished at it.

13. And Jacob said unto Judah, Who is that man whom I see in the camp of Egypt dressed in kingly robes with a very red garment upon him and a royal crown upon his head, who has alighted from his chariot and is coming toward us? and Judah answered his father, saying, He is thy son Joseph the king; and Jacob rejoiced in seeing the glory of his son.

14. And Joseph came nigh unto his father and he bowed to his father, and all the men of the camp bowed to the ground with him before Jacob.

15. And behold Jacob ran and hastened to his son Joseph and fell upon his neck and kissed him, and they wept, and Joseph also embraced his father and kissed him, and they wept and all the people of Egypt wept with them.

16. And Jacob said unto Joseph, Now I will die cheerfully after I have seen thy face, that thou art still living and with glory.

17. And the sons of Jacob and their wives and their children and their servants, and all the household of Jacob wept exceedingly with Joseph, and they kissed him and wept greatly with him.

18. And Joseph and all his people returned afterward home to Egypt, and Jacob and his sons and all the children of his household came with Joseph to Egypt, and Joseph placed them in the best part of Egypt, in the land of Goshen.

19. And Joseph said unto his father and unto his brethren, I will go up and tell Pharaoh, saying, My brethren and my father's household and all belonging to them have come unto me, and behold they are in the land of Goshen.

20. And Joseph did so and took from his brethren Reuben, Issachar Zebulun and his brother Benjamin and he placed them before Pharaoh.

21. And Joseph spoke unto Pharaoh, saying, My brethren and my father's household and all belonging to them, together with their flocks and cattle have come unto me from the land of Canaan, to sojourn in Egypt; for the famine was sore upon them.

22. And Pharaoh said unto Joseph, Place thy father and brethren in the best part of the land, withhold not from them all that is good, and cause them to eat of the fat of the land.

23. And Joseph answered, saying, Behold I have stationed them in the land of Goshen, for they are shepherds, therefore let them remain in Goshen to feed their flocks apart from the Egyptians.

24. And Pharaoh said unto Joseph, Do with thy brethren all that they shall say unto thee; and the sons of Jacob bowed down to Pharaoh, and they went forth from him in peace, and Joseph afterward brought his father before Pharaoh.

25. And Jacob came and bowed down to Pharaoh, and Jacob blessed Pharaoh, and he then went out; and Jacob and all his sons, and all his household dwelt in the land of Goshen.

26. In the second year, that is in the hundred and thirtieth year of the life of Jacob, Joseph maintained his father and his brethren, and all his father's household, with bread according to their little ones, all the days of the famine; they lacked nothing.

27. And Joseph gave unto them the best part of the whole land; the best of Egypt had they all the days of Joseph; and Joseph also gave unto them and unto the whole of his father's household, clothes and garments year by year; and the sons of Jacob remained securely in Egypt all the days of their brother.

28. And Jacob always ate at Joseph's table, Jacob and his sons did not leave Joseph's table day or night, besides what Jacob's children consumed in their houses.

29. And all Egypt ate bread during the days of the famine from the house of Joseph, for all the Egyptians sold all belonging to them on account of the famine.

30. And Joseph purchased all the lands and fields of Egypt for bread on the account of Pharaoh, and Joseph supplied all Egypt with bread all the days of the famine, and Joseph collected all the silver and gold that came unto him for the corn which they bought throughout the land, and he accumulated much gold and silver, besides an immense quantity of onyx stones, bdellium and valuable garments which they brought unto Joseph from every part of the land when their money was spent.

31. And Joseph took all the silver and gold that came into his hand, about seventy two talents of gold and silver, and also onyx stones and bdellium in great abundance, and Joseph went and concealed them in four parts, and he concealed one part in the wilderness near the Red sea, and one part by the river Perath, and the third and fourth part he concealed in the desert opposite to the wilderness of Persia and Media.

32. And he took part of the gold and silver that was left, and gave it unto all his brothers and unto all his father's household, and unto all the women of his father's household, and the rest he brought to the house of Pharaoh, about twenty talents of gold and silver.

33. And Joseph gave all the gold and silver that was left unto Pharaoh, and Pharaoh placed it in the treasury, and the days of the famine ceased after that in the land, and they sowed and reaped in the whole land, and they obtained their usual quantity year by year; they lacked nothing.

34. And Joseph dwelt securely in Egypt, and the whole land was under his advice, and his father and all his brethren dwelt in the land of Goshen and took possession of it.

35. And Joseph was very aged, advanced in days, and his two sons, Ephraim and Manasseh, remained constantly in the house of Jacob, together with the children of the sons of Jacob their brethren, to learn the ways of the Lord and his law.

36. And Jacob and his sons dwelt in the land of Egypt in the land of Goshen, and they took possession in it, and they were fruitful and multiplied in it.

CHAPTER 56

1.   And Jacob lived in the land of Egypt seventeen years, and the days of Jacob, and the years of his life were a hundred and forty seven years.

2.   At that time Jacob was attacked with that illness of which he died and he sent and called for his son Joseph from Egypt, and Joseph his son came from Egypt and Joseph came unto his father.

3.   And Jacob said unto Joseph and unto his sons, Behold I die, and the God of your ancestors will visit you, and bring you back to the land, which the Lord sware to give unto you and unto your children after you, now therefore when I am dead, bury me in the cave which is in Machpelah in Hebron in the land of Canaan, near my ancestors.

4.   And Jacob made his sons swear to bury him in Machpelah, in Hebron, and his sons swore unto him concerning this thing.

5.   And he commanded them, saying, Serve the Lord your God, for he who delivered your fathers will also deliver you from all trouble.

6.   And Jacob said, Call all your children unto me, and all the children of Jacob's sons came and sat before him, and Jacob blessed them, and he said unto them, The Lord God of your fathers shall grant you a thousand times as much and bless you, and may he give you the blessing of your father Abraham; and all the children of Jacob's sons went forth on that day after he had blessed them.

7.   And on the next day Jacob again called for his sons, and they all assembled and came to him and sat before him, and Jacob on that day blessed his sons before his death, each man did he bless according to his blessing; behold it is written in the book of the law of the Lord appertaining to Israel.

8.   And Jacob said unto Judah, I know my son that thou art a mighty man for thy brethren; reign over them, and thy sons shall reign over their sons forever.

9.   Only teach thy sons the bow and all the weapons of war, in order that they may fight the battles of their brother who will rule over his enemies.

10. And Jacob again commanded his sons on that day, saying, Behold I shall be this day gathered unto my people; carry me up from Egypt, and bury me in the cave of Machpelah as I have commanded you.

11. Howbeit take heed I pray you that none of your sons carry me, only yourselves, and this is the manner you shall do unto me, when you carry my body to go with it to the land of Canaan to bury me,

12. Judah, Issachar and Zebulun shall carry my bier at the eastern side; Reuben, Simeon and Gad at the south, Ephraim, Manasseh and Benjamin at the west, Dan, Asher and Naphtali at the north.

13. Let not Levi carry with you, for he and his sons will carry the ark of the covenant of the Lord with the Israelites in the camp, neither let Joseph my son carry, for as a king so let his glory be; howbeit, Ephraim and Manasseh shall be in their stead.

14. Thus shall you do unto me when you carry me away; do not neglect any thing of all that I command you; and it shall come to pass when you do this unto me, that the Lord will remember you favorably and your children after you forever.

15. And you my sons, honor each his brother and his relative, and command your children and your children's children after you to serve the Lord God of your ancestors all the days.

16. In order that you may prolong your days in the land, you and your children and your children's children for ever, when you do what is good and upright in the sight of the Lord your God, to go in all his ways.

17. And thou, Joseph my son, forgive I pray thee the prongs of thy brethren and all their misdeeds in the injury that they heaped upon thee, for God intended it for thine and thy children's benefit.

18. And O my son leave not thy brethren to the inhabitants of Egypt, neither hurt their feelings, for behold I consign them to the hand of God and in thy hand to guard them from the Egyptians; and the sons of Jacob answered their father saying, O, our father, all that thou hast commanded us, so will we do; may God only be with us.

19. And Jacob said unto his sons, So may God be with you when you keep all his ways; turn not from his ways either to the right or the left in performing what is good and upright in his sight.

20. For I know that many and grievous troubles will befall you in the latter days in the land, yea your children and children's children, only serve the Lord and he will save you from all trouble.

21. And it shall come to pass when you shall go after God to serve him and will teach your children after you, and your children's children, to know the Lord, then will the Lord raise up unto you and your children a servant from amongst your children, and the Lord will deliver you through his hand from all affliction, and bring you out of Egypt and bring you back to the land of your fathers to inherit it securely.

22. And Jacob ceased commanding his sons, and he drew his feet into the bed, he died and was gathered to his people.

23. And Joseph fell upon his father and he cried out and wept over him and he kissed him, and he called out in a bitter voice, and he said, O my father, my father.

24. And his son's wives and all his household came and fell upon Jacob, and they wept over him, and cried in a very loud voice concerning Jacob.

25. And all the sons of Jacob rose up together, and they tore their garments, and they all put sackcloth upon their loins, and they fell upon their faces, and they cast dust upon their heads toward the heavens.

26. And the thing was told unto Osnath Joseph's wife, and she rose up and put on a sack and she with all the Egyptian women with her came and mourned and wept for Jacob.

27. And also all the people of Egypt who knew Jacob came all on that day when they heard this thing, and all Egypt wept for many days.

28. And also from the land of Canaan did the women come unto Egypt when they heard that Jacob was dead, and they wept for him in Egypt for seventy days.

29. And it came to pass after this that Joseph commanded his servants the doctors to embalm his father with myrrh and frankincense and all manner of incense and perfume, and the doctors embalmed Jacob as Joseph had commanded them.

30. And all the people of Egypt and the elders and all the inhabitants of the land of Goshen wept and mourned over Jacob, and all his sons and the children of his household lamented and mourned over their father Jacob many days.

31. And after the days of his weeping had passed away, at the end of seventy days, Joseph said unto Pharaoh, I will go up and bury my father in the land of Canaan as he made me swear, and then I will return.

32. And Pharaoh sent Joseph, saying, Go up and bury thy father as he said, and as he made thee swear; and Joseph rose up with all his brethren to go to the land of Canaan to bury their father Jacob as he had commanded them.

33. And Pharaoh commanded that it should be proclaimed throughout Egypt, saying, Whoever goeth not up with Joseph and his brethren to the land of Canaan to bury Jacob, shall die.

34. And all Egypt heard of Pharaoh's proclamation, and they all rose up together, and all the servants of Pharaoh, and the elders of his house, and all the elders of the land of Egypt went up with Joseph, and all the officers and nobles of Pharaoh went up as the servants of Joseph, and they went to bury Jacob in the land of Canaan.

35. And the sons of Jacob carried the bier upon which he lay; according to all that their father commanded them, so did his sons unto him.

36. And the bier was of pure gold, and it was inlaid round about with onyx stones and bdellium; and the covering of the bier was gold woven work, joined with threads, and over them were hooks of onyx stones and bdellium.

37. And Joseph placed upon the head of his father Jacob a large golden crown, and he put a golden scepter in his hand, and they surrounded the bier as was the custom of kings during their lives.

38. And all the troops of Egypt went before him in this array, at first all the mighty men of
Pharaoh, and the mighty men of Joseph, and after them the rest of the inhabitants of Egypt, and they were all girded with swords and equipped with coats of mail, and the trappings of war were upon them.

39. And all the weepers and mourners went at a distance opposite to the bier, going and weeping and lamenting, and the rest of the people went after the bier.

40. And Joseph and his household went together near the bier barefooted and weeping, and the rest of Joseph's servants went around him; each man had his ornaments upon him, and they were all armed with their weapons of war.

41. And fifty of Jacob's servants went in front of the bier, and they strewed along the road myrrh and aloes, and all manner of perfume, and all the sons of Jacob that carried the bier walked upon the perfumery, and the servants of Jacob went before them strewing the perfume along the road.

42. And Joseph went up with a heavy camp, and they did after this manner every day until they reached the land of Canaan, and they came to the threshing floor of Atad, which was on the other side of Jordan, and they mourned an exceeding great and heavy mourning in that place.

43. And all the kings of Canaan heard of this thing and they all went forth, each man from his house, thirty-one kings of Canaan, and they all came with their men to mourn and weep over Jacob.

44. And all these kings beheld Jacob's bier, and behold Joseph's crown was upon it, and they also put their crowns upon the bier, and encircled it with crowns.

45. And all these kings made in that place a great and heavy mourning with the sons of Jacob and Egypt over Jacob, for all the kings of Canaan knew the valor of Jacob and his sons.

46. And the report reached Esau, saying, Jacob died in Egypt, and his sons and all Egypt are conveying him to the land of Canaan to bury him.

47. And Esau heard this thing, and he was dwelling in mount Seir, and he rose up with his sons and all his people and all his household, a people exceedingly great, and they came to mourn and weep over Jacob.

48. And it came to pass, when Esau came he mourned for his brother Jacob, and all Egypt and all Canaan again rose up and mourned a great mourning with Esau over Jacob in that place

49. And Joseph and his brethren brought their father Jacob from that place, and they went to Hebron to bury Jacob in the cave by his fathers.

50. And they came unto Kireath-arba, to the cave, and as they came Esau stood with his sons against Joseph and his brethren as a hindrance in the cave, saying, Jacob shall not be buried therein, for it belongeth to us and to our father.

51. And Joseph and his brethren heard the words of Esau's sons, and they were exceedingly wroth, and Joseph approached unto Esau, saying, What is this thing which they have spoken? surely my father Jacob bought it from thee for great riches after the death of Isaac, now five and twenty years ago, and also all the land of Canaan he bought from thee and from thy sons, and thy seed after thee.

52. And Jacob bought it for his sons and his seed after him for an inheritance for ever, and why speakest thou these things this day?

53. And Esau answered, saying, Thou speakest falsely and utterest lies, for I sold not anything belonging to me in all this land, as thou sayest, neither did my brother Jacob buy aught belonging to me in this land.

54. And Esau spoke these things in order to deceive Joseph with his words, for Esau knew that Joseph was not present in those days when Esau sold all belonging to him in the land of Canaan to Jacob.

55. And Joseph said unto Esau, Surely my father inserted these things with thee in the record of purchase, and testified the record with witnesses, and behold it is with us in Egypt.

56. And Esau answered, saying unto him, Bring the record, all that thou wilt find in the record, so will we do.

57. And Joseph called unto Naphtali his brother, and he said, Hasten quickly, stay not, and run I pray thee to Egypt and bring all the records; the record of the purchase, the sealed record and the open record, and also all the first records in which all the transactions of the birth-right are written, fetch thou.

58. And thou shalt bring them unto us hither, that we may know from them all the words of Esau and his sons which they spoke this day.

59. And Naphtali hearkened to the voice of Joseph and he hastened and ran to go down to Egypt, and Naphtali was lighter on foot than any of the stags that were upon the wilderness, for he would go upon ears of corn without crushing them.

60. And when Esau saw that Naphtali had gone to fetch the records, he and his sons increased their resistance against the cave, and Esau and all his people rose up against Joseph and his brethren to battle.

61. And all the sons of Jacob and the people of Egypt fought with Esau and his men, and the sons of Esau and his people were smitten before the sons of Jacob, and the sons of Jacob slew of Esau's people forty men.

62. And Chushim the son of Dan, the son of Jacob, was at that time with Jacob's sons, but he was about a hundred cubits distant from the place of battle, for he remained with the children of Jacob's sons by Jacob's bier to guard it.

63. And Chushim was dumb and deaf, still he understood the voice of consternation amongst men.

64. And he asked, saying, Why do you not bury the dead, and what is this great consternation? and they answered him the words of Esau and his sons; and he ran to Esau in the midst of the battle, and he slew Esau with a sword, and he cut off his head, and it sprang to a distance, and Esau fell amongst the people of the battle.

65. And when Chushim did this thing the sons of Jacob prevailed over the sons of Esau, and the sons of Jacob buried their father Jacob by force in the cave, and the sons of Esau beheld it.

66. And Jacob was buried in Hebron, in the cave of Machpelah which Abraham had bought from the sons of Heth for the possession of a burial place, and he was buried in very costly garments.

67. And no king had such honor paid him as Joseph paid unto his father at his death, for he buried him with great honor like unto the burial of kings.

68. And Joseph and his brethren made a mourning of seven days for their father.

CHAPTER 57

1.   And it was after this that the sons of Esau waged war with the sons of Jacob, and the sons of Esau fought with the sons of Jacob in Hebron, and Esau was still lying dead, and not buried.

2.   And the battle was heavy between them, and the sons of Esau were smitten before the sons of Jacob, and the sons of Jacob slew of the sons of Esau eighty men, and not one died of the people of the sons of Jacob; and the hand of Joseph prevailed over all the people of the sons of Esau, and he took Zepho, the son of Eliphaz, the son of Esau, and fifty of his men captive, and he bound them with chains of iron, and gave them into the hand of his servants to bring them to Egypt.

3.   And it came to pass when the sons of Jacob had taken Zepho and his people captive, all those that remained were greatly afraid of their lives from the house of Esau, lest they should also be taken captive, and they all fled with Eliphaz the son of Esau and his people, with Esau's body, and they went on their road to Mount Seir.

4.   And they came unto Mount Seir and they buried Esau in Seir, but they had not brought his head with them to Seir, for it was buried in that place where the battle had been in Hebron.

5.   And it came to pass when the sons of Esau had fled from before the sons of Jacob, the sons of Jacob pursued them unto the borders of Seir, but they did not slay a single man from amongst them when they pursued them, for Esau's body which they carried with them excited their confusion, so they fled and the sons of Jacob turned back from them and came up to the place where their brethren were in Hebron, and they remained there on that day, and on the next day until they rested from the battle.

6.   And it came to pass on the third day they assembled all the sons of Seir the Horite, and they assembled all the children of the east, a multitude of people like the sand of the sea, and they went and came down to Egypt to fight with Joseph and his brethren, in order to deliver their brethren.

7.   And Joseph and all the sons of Jacob heard that the sons of Esau and the children of the east had come upon them to battle in order to deliver their brethren.

8.   And Joseph and his brethren and the strong men of Egypt went forth and fought in the city of Rameses, and Joseph and his brethren dealt out a tremendous blow amongst the sons of Esau and the children of the east.

9.   And they slew of them six hundred thousand men, and they slew amongst them all the mighty men of the children of Seir the Horite; there were only a few of them left, and they slew also a great many of the children of the east, and of the children of Esau; and Eliphaz the son of Esau, and the children of the east all fled before Joseph and his brethren.

10. And Joseph and his brethren pursued them until they came unto Succoth, and they yet slew of them in Succoth thirty men, and the rest escaped and they fled each to his city.

11. And Joseph and his brethren and the mighty men of Egypt turned back from them with joy and cheerfulness of heart, for they had smitten all their enemies.

12. And Zepho the son of Eliphaz and his men were still slaves in Egypt to the sons of Jacob, and their pains increased.

13. And when the sons of Esau and the sons of Seir returned to their land, the sons of Seir saw that they had all fallen into the hands of the sons of Jacob, and the people of Egypt, on account of the battle of the sons of Esau.

14. And the sons of Seir said unto the sons of Esau, You have seen andtherefore you know that this camp was on your account, and not one mighty man or an adept in war remaineth.

15. Now therefore go forth from our land, go from us to the land of Canaan to the land of the dwelling of your fathers; wherefore shall your children inherit the effects of our children in latter days?

16. And the children of Esau would not listen to the children of Seir, and the children of Seir considered to make war with them.

17. And the children of Esau sent secretly to Angeas king of Africa, the same is Dinhabah, saying,

18. Send unto us some of thy men and let them come unto us, and we will fight together with the children of Seir the Horite, for they have resolved to fight with us to drive us away from the land.

19. And Angeas king of Dinhabah did so, for he was in those days friendly to the children of Esau, and Angeas sent five hundred valiant infantry to the children of Esau, and eight hundred cavalry.

20. And the children of Seir sent unto the children of the east and unto the children of Midian, saying, You have seen what the children of Esau have done unto us, upon whose account we are almost all destroyed, in their battle with the sons of Jacob.

21. Now therefore come unto us and assist us, and we will fight them together, and we will drive them from the land and be avenged of the cause of our brethren who died for their sakes in their battle with their brethren the sons of Jacob.

22. And all the children of the east listened to the children of Seir, and they came unto them about eight hundred men with drawn swords, and the children of Esau fought with the children of Seir at that time in the wilderness of Paran.

23. And the children of Seir prevailed then over the sons of Esau, and the children of Seir slew on that day of the children of Esau in that battle about two hundred men of the people of Angeas king of Dinhabah.

24. And on the second day the children of Esau came again to fight a second time with the children of Seir, and the battle was sore upon the children of Esau this second time, and it troubled them greatly on account of the children of Seir.

25. And when the children of Esau saw that the children of Seir were more powerful than they were, some men of the children of Esau turned and assisted the children of Seir their enemies.

26. And there fell yet of the people of the children of Esau in the second battle fifty-eight men of the people at Angeas king of Dinhabah.

27. And on the third day the children of Esau heard that some of their brethren had turned from them to fight against them in the second battle; and the children of Esau mourned when they heard this thing.

28. And they said, What shall we do unto our brethren who turned from us to assist the children of Seir our enemies? and the children of Esau again sent to Angeas king of Dinhabah, saying,

29. Send unto us again other men that with them we may fight with the children of Seir, for they have already twice been heavier than we were.

30. And Angeas again sent to the children of Esau about six hundred valiant men, and they came to assist the children of Esau.

31. And in ten days' time the children of Esau again waged war with the children of Seir in the wilderness of Paran, and the battle was very severe upon the children of Seir, and the children of Esau prevailed at this time over the children of Seir, and the children of Seir were smitten before the children of Esau, and the children of Esau slew from them about two thousand men.

32. And all the mighty men of the children of Seir died in this battle, and there only remained their young children that were left in their cities.

33. And all Midian and the children of the east betook themselves to flight from the battle, and they left the children of Seir and fled when they saw that the battle was severe upon them, and the children of Esau pursued all the children of the east until they reached their land.

34. And the children of Esau slew yet of them about two hundred and fifty men and from the people of the children of Esau there fell in that battle about thirty men, but this evil came upon them through their brethren turning from them to assist the children of Seir
the Horite, and the children of Esau again heard of the evil doings of their brethren, and they again mourned on account of this thing.

35. And it came to pass after the battle, the children of Esau turned back and came home unto Seir, and the children of Esau slew those who had remained in the land of the children of Seir; they slew also their wives and little ones, they left not a soul alive except fifty young lads and damsels whom they suffered to live, and the children of Esau did not put them to death, and the lads became their slaves, and the damsels they took for wives.

36. And the children of Esau dwelt in Seir in the place of the children of Seir, and they inherited their land and took possession of it.

37. And the children of Esau took all belonging in the land to the children of Seir, also their flocks, their bullocks and their goods, and all belonging to the children of Seir, did the children of Esau take, and the children of Esau dwelt in Seir in the place of the children of Seir unto this day, and the children of Esau divided the land into divisions to the five sons of Esau, according to their families.

38. And it came to pass in those days, that the children of Esau resolved to crown a king over them in the land of which they became possessed. And they said to each other, Not so, for he shall reign over us in our land, and we shall be under his counsel and he shall fight our battles, against our enemies, and they did so.

39. And all the children of Esau swore, saying, That none of their brethren should ever reign over them, but a strange man who is not of their brethren, for the souls of all the children of Esau were embittered every man against his son, brother and friend, on account of the evil they sustained from their brethren when they fought with the children of Seir.

40. Therefore the sons of Esau swore, saying, From that day forward they would not choose a king from their brethren, but one from a strange land unto this day.

41. And there was a man there from the people of Angeas king of Dinhabah; his name was Bela the son of Beor, who was a very valiant man, beautiful and comely and wise in all wisdom, and a man of sense and counsel; and there was none of the people of Angeas like unto him.

42. And all the children of Esau took him and anointed him and they crowned him for a king, and they bowed down to him, and they said unto him, May the king live, may the king live.

43. And they spread out the sheet, and they brought him each man earrings of gold and silver or rings or bracelets, and they made him very rich in silver and in gold, in onyx stones and bdellium, and they made him a royal throne, and they placed a regal crown upon his head, and they built a palace for him and he dwelt therein, and he became king over all the children of Esau.

44. And the people of Angeas took their hire for their battle from the children of Esau, and they went and returned at that time to their master in Dinhabah.

45. And Bela reigned over the children of Esau thirty years, and the children of Esau dwelt in the land instead of the children of Seir, and they dwelt securely in their stead unto this day.

CHAPTER 58

1. And it came to pass in the thirty-second year of the Israelites going down to Egypt, that is in the seventy-first year of the life of Joseph, in that year died Pharaoh king of Egypt, and Magron his son reigned in his stead.

2. And Pharaoh commanded Joseph before his death to be a father to his son, Magron, and that Magron should be under the care of Joseph and under his counsel.

3. And all Egypt consented to this thing that Joseph should be king over them, for all the Egyptians loved Joseph as of heretofore, only Magron the son of Pharaoh sat upon, his father's throne, and he became king in those days in his father's stead.

4. Magron was forty-one years old when he began to reign, and forty years he reigned in Egypt, and all Egypt called his name Pharaoh after the name of his father, as it was their custom to do in Egypt to every king that reigned over them.

5. And it came to pass when Pharaoh reigned in his father's stead, he placed the laws of Egypt and all the affairs of government in the hand of Joseph, as his father had commanded him.

6. And Joseph became king over Egypt, for he superintended over all Egypt, and all Egypt was under his care and under his counsel, for all Egypt inclined to Joseph after the death of Pharaoh, and they loved him exceedingly to reign over them.

7. But there were some people amongst them, who did not like him, saying, No stranger shall reign over us; still the whole government of Egypt devolved in those days upon Joseph, after the death of Pharaoh, he being the regulator, doing as he liked throughout the land without any one interfering.

8. And all Egypt was under the care of Joseph, and Joseph made war with all his surrounding enemies, and he subdued them; also all the land and all the Philistines, unto the borders of Canaan, did Joseph subdue, and they were all under his power and they gave a yearly tax unto Joseph.

9. And Pharaoh king of Egypt sat upon his throne in his father's stead, but he was under the control and counsel of Joseph, as he was at first under the control of his father.

10. Neither did he reign but in the land of Egypt only, under the counsel of Joseph, but Joseph reigned over the whole country at that time, from Egypt unto the great river Perath.

11. And Joseph was successful in all his ways, and the Lord was with him, and the Lord gave Joseph additional wisdom, and honor, and glory, and love toward him in the hearts of the Egyptians and throughout the land, and Joseph reigned over the whole country forty years.

12. And all the countries of the Philistines and Canaan and Zidon, and on the other side of Jordan, brought presents unto Joseph all his days, and the whole country was in the hand of Joseph, and they brought unto him a yearly tribute as it was regulated, for Joseph had fought against all his surrounding enemies and subdued them, and the whole country was in the hand of Joseph, and Joseph sat securely upon his throne in Egypt.

13. And also all his brethren the sons of Jacob dwelt securely in the land, all the days of Joseph, and they were fruitful and multiplied exceedingly in the land, and they served the Lord all their days, as their father Jacob had commanded them.

14. And it came to pass at the end of many days and years, when the children of Esau were dwelling quietly in their land with Bela their king, that the children of Esau were fruitful and multiplied in the land, and they resolved to go and fight with the sons of Jacob and all Egypt, and to deliver their brother Zepho, the son of Eliphaz, and his men, for they were yet in those days slaves to Joseph.

15. And the children of Esau sent unto all the children of the east, and they made peace with them, and all the children of the east came unto them to go with the children of Esau to Egypt to battle.

16. And there came also unto them of the people of Angeas, king of Dinhabah, and they also sent unto the children of Ishmael and they also came unto them.

17. And all this people assembled and came unto Seir to assist the children of Esau in their battle, and this camp was very large and heavy with people, numerous as the sand of the sea, about eight hundred thousand men, infantry and cavalry, and all these troops went down to Egypt to fight with the sons of Jacob, and they encamped by Rameses.

18. And Joseph went forth with his brethren with the mighty men of Egypt, about six hundred men, and they fought with them in the land of Rameses; and the sons of Jacob at that time again fought with the children of Esau, in the fiftieth year of the sons of Jacob going down to Egypt, that is the thirtieth year of the reign of Bela over the children of Esau in Seir.

19. And the Lord gave all the mighty men of Esau and the children of the east into the hand of Joseph and his brethren, and the people of the children of Esau and the children of the east were smitten before Joseph.

20. And of the people of Esau and the children of the east that were slain, there fell before the sons of Jacob about two hundred thousand men, and their king Bela the son of Beor fell with them in the battle, and when the children of Esau saw that their king had fallen in battle and was dead, their hands became weak in the combat.

21. And Joseph and his brethren and all Egypt were still smiting the people of the house of Esau, and all Esau's people were afraid of the sons of Jacob and fled from before them.

22. And Joseph and his brethren and all Egypt pursued them a day's journey, and they slew yet from them about three hundred men, continuing to smite them in the road; and they afterward turned back from them.

23. And Joseph and all his brethren returned to Egypt, not one man was missing from them, but of the Egyptians there fell twelve men.

24. And when Joseph returned to Egypt he ordered Zepho and his men to be additionally bound, and they bound them in irons and they increased their grief.

25. And all the people of the children of Esau, and the children of the east, returned in shame each unto his city, for all the mighty men that were with them had fallen in battle.

26. And when the children of Esau saw that their king had died in battle they hastened and took a man from the people of the children of the east; his name was Jobab the son of Zarach, from the land of Botzrah, and they caused him to reign over them instead of Bela their king.

27. And Jobab sat upon the throne of Bela as king in his stead, and Jobab reigned in Edom over all the children of Esau ten years, and the children of Esau went no more to fight with the sons of Jacob from that day forward, for the sons of Esau knew the valor of the sons of Jacob, and they were greatly afraid of them.

28. But from that day forward the children of Esau hated the sons of Jacob, and the hatred and enmity were very strong between them all the days, unto this day.

29. And it came to pass after this, at the end of ten years, Jobab, the son of Zarach, from Botzrah, died, and the children of Esau took a man whose name was Chusham, from the land of Teman, and they made him king over them instead of Jobab, and Chusham reigned in Edom over all the children of Esau for twenty years.

30. And Joseph, king of Egypt, and his brethren, and all the children of Israel dwelt securely in Egypt in those days, together with all the children of Joseph and his brethren, having no hindrance or evil accident and the land of Egypt was at that time at rest from war in the days of Joseph and his brethren.

CHAPTER 59

1. And these are the names of the sons of Israel who dwelt in Egypt, who had come with Jacob, all the sons of Jacob came unto Egypt, every man with his household.

2. The children of Leah were Reuben, Simeon, Levi, Judah, Issachar and Zebulun, and their sister Dinah.

3. And the sons of Rachel were Joseph and Benjamin.

4. And the sons of Zilpah, the handmaid of Leah, were Gad and Asher.

5. And the sons of Bilhah, the handmaid of Rachel, were Dan and Naphtali.

6. And these were their offspring that were born unto them in the land of Canaan, before they came unto Egypt with their father Jacob.

7. The sons of Reuben were Chanoch, Pallu, Chetzron and Carmi.

8. And the sons of Simeon were Jemuel, Jamin, Ohad, Jachin, Zochar and Saul, the son of the Canaanitish woman.

9. And the children of Levi were Gershon, Kehath and Merari, and their sister Jochebed, who was born unto them in their going down to Egypt.

10. And the sons of Judah were Er, Onan, Shelah, Perez and Zarach.

11. And Er and Onan died in the land of Canaan; and the sons of Perez were Chezron and Chamul.

12. And the sons of Issachar were Tola, Puvah, Job and Shomron.

13. And the sons of Zebulun were Sered, Elon and Jachleel, and the son of Dan was Chushim.

14. And the sons of Naphtali were Jachzeel, Guni, Jetzer and Shilam.

15. And the sons of Gad were Ziphion, Chaggi, Shuni, Ezbon, Eri, Arodi and Areli.

16. And the children of Asher were Jimnah, Jishvah, Jishvi, Beriah and their sister Serach; and the sons of Beriah were Cheber and Malchiel.

17. And the sons of Benjamin were Bela, Becher, Ashbel, Gera, Naaman, Achi, Rosh, Mupim, Chupim and Ord.

18. And the sons of Joseph, that were born unto him in Egypt, were Manasseh and Ephraim.

19. And all the souls that went forth from the loins of Jacob, were seventy souls; these are they who came with Jacob their father unto Egypt to dwell there: and Joseph and all his brethren dwelt securely in Egypt, and they ate of the best of Egypt all the days of the life of Joseph.

20. And Joseph lived in the land of Egypt ninety-three years, and Joseph reigned over all Egypt eighty years.

21. And when the days of Joseph drew nigh that he should die, he sent and called for his brethren and all his father's household, and they all came together and sat before him.

22. And Joseph said unto his brethren and unto the whole of his father's household, Behold I die, and God will surely visit you and bring you up from this land to the land which he swore to your fathers to give unto them.

23. And it shall be when God shall visit you to bring you up from here to the land of your fathers, then bring up my bones with you from here.

24. And Joseph made the sons of Israel to swear for their seed after them, saying, God will surely visit you and you shall bring up my bones with you from here.

25. And it came to pass after this that Joseph died in that year, the seventy-first year of the Israelites going down to Egypt.

26. And Joseph was one hundred and ten years old when he died in the land of Egypt, and all his brethren and all his servants rose up and they embalmed Joseph, as was their custom, and his brethren and all Egypt mourned over him for seventy days.

27. And they put Joseph in a coffin filled with spices and all sorts of perfume, and they buried him by the side of the river, that is Sihor, and his sons and all his brethren, and the whole of his father's household made a seven day's mourning for him.

28. And it came to pass after the death of Joseph, all the Egyptians began in those days to rule over the children of Israel, and Pharaoh, king of Egypt, who reigned in his father's stead, took all the laws of Egypt and conducted the whole government of Egypt under his counsel, and he reigned securely over his people.

CHAPTER 60

1. And when the year came round, being the seventy-second year from the Israelites going down to Egypt, after the death of Joseph, Zepho, the son of Eliphaz, the son of Esau, fled from Egypt, he and his men, and they went away.

2. And he came to Africa, which is Dinhabah, to Angeas king of Africa, and Angeas received them with great honor, and he made Zepho the captain of his host.

3. And Zepho found favor in the sight of Angeas and in the sight of his people, and Zepho was captain of the host to Angeas king of Africa for many days.

4. And Zepho enticed Angeas king of Africa to collect all his army to go and fight with the Egyptians, and with the sons of Jacob, and to avenge of them the cause of his brethren.

5. But Angeas would not listen to Zepho to do this thing, for Angeas knew the strength of the sons of Jacob, and what they had done to his army in their warfare with the children of Esau.

6. And Zepho was in those days very great in the sight of Angeas and in the sight of all his people, and he continually enticed them to make war against Egypt, but they would not.

7. And it came to pass in those days there was in the land of Chittim a man in the city of Puzimna, whose name was Uzu, and he became degenerately deified by the children of Chittim, and the man died and had no son, only one daughter whose name was Jania.

8. And the damsel was exceedingly beautiful, comely and intelligent, there was none seen like unto her for beauty and wisdom throughout the land.

9. And the people of Angeas king of Africa saw her and they came and praised her unto him, and Angeas sent to the children of Chittim, and he requested to take her unto himself for a wife, and the people of Chittim consented to give her unto him for a wife.

10. And when the messengers of Angeas were going forth from the land of Chittim to take their journey, behold the messengers of Turnus king of Bibentu came unto Chittim, for Turnus king of Bibentu also sent his messengers to request Jania for him, to take unto himself for a wife, for all his men had also praised her to him, therefore he sent all his servants unto her.

11. And the servants of Turnus came to Chittim, and they asked for Jania, to be taken unto Turnus their king for a wife.

12. And the people of Chittim said unto them, We cannot give her, because Angeas king of Africa desired her to take her unto him for a wife before you came, and that we should give her unto him, and now therefore we cannot do this thing to deprive Angeas of the damsel in order to give her unto Turnus.

13. For we are greatly afraid of Angeas lest he come in battle against us and destroy us, and Turnus your master will not be able to deliver us from his hand.

14. And when the messengers of Turnus heard all the words of the children of Chittim, they turned back to their master and told him all the words of the children of Chittim.

15. And the children of Chittim sent a memorial to Angeas, saying, Behold Turnus has sent for Jania to take her unto him for a wife, and thus have we answered him; and we heard that he has collected his whole army to go to war against thee, and he intends to pass by the road of Sardunia to fight against thy brother Lucus, and after that he will come to fight against thee.

16. And Angeas heard the words of the children of Chittim which they sent to him in the record, and his anger was kindled and he rose up and assembled his whole army and came through the islands of the sea, the road to Sardunia, unto his brother Lucus king of Sardunia.

17. And Niblos, the son of Lucus, heard that his uncle Angeas was coming, and he went out to meet him with a heavy army, and he kissed him and embraced him, and Niblos said unto Angeas, When thou askest my father after his welfare, when I shall go with thee to fight with Turnus, ask of him to make me captain of his host, and Angeas did so, and he came unto his brother and his brother came to meet him, and he asked him after his welfare.

18. And Angeas asked his brother Lucus after his welfare, and to make his son Niblos captain of his host, and Lucus did so, and Angeas and his brother Lucus rose up and they went toward Turnus to battle, and there was with them a great army and a heavy people.

19. And he came in ships, and they came into the province of Ashtorash, and behold Turnus came toward them, for he went forth to Sardunia, and intended to destroy it and afterward to pass on from there to Angeas to fight with him.

20. And Angeas and Lucus his brother met Turnus in the valley of Canopia, and the battle was strong and mighty between them in that place.

21. And the battle was severe upon Lucus king of Sardunia, and all his army fell, and Niblos his son fell also in that battle.

22. And his uncle Angeas commanded his servants and they made a golden coffin for Niblos and they put him into it, and Angeas again waged battle toward Turnus, and Angeas was stronger than he, and he slew him, and he smote all his people with the edge of the sword, and Angeas avenged the cause of Niblos his brother's son and the cause of the army of his brother Lucus.

23. And when Turnus died, the hands of those that survived the battle became weak, and they fled from before Angeas and Lucus his brother.

24. And Angeas and his brother Lucus pursued them unto the highroad, which is between Alphanu and Romah, and they slew the whole army of Turnus with the edge of the sword.

25. And Lucus king of Sardunia commanded his servants that they should make a coffin of brass, and that they should place therein the body of his son Niblos, and they buried him in that place.

26. And they built upon it a high tower there upon the highroad, and they called its name after the name of Niblos unto this day, and they also buried Turnus king of Bibentu there in that place with Niblos.

27. And behold upon the highroad between Alphanu and Romah the grave of Niblos is on one side and the grave of Turnus on the other, and a pavement between them unto this day.

28. And when Niblos was buried, Lucus his father returned with his army to his land Sardunia, and Angeas his brother king of Africa went with his people unto the city of Bibentu, that is the city of Turnus.

29. And the inhabitants of Bibentu heard of his fame and they were greatly afraid of him, and they went forth to meet him with weeping and supplication, and the inhabitants of Bibentu entreated of Angeas not to slay them nor destroy their city; and he did so, for Bibentu was in those days reckoned as one of the cities of the children of Chittim; therefore he did not destroy the city.

30. But from that day forward the troops of the king of Africa would go to Chittim to spoil and plunder it, and whenever they went, Zepho the captain of the host of Angeas would go with them.

31. And it was after this that Angeas turned with his army and they came to the city of Puzimna, and Angeas took thence Jania the daughter of Uzu for a wife and brought her unto his city unto Africa.

CHAPTER 61

1. And it came to pass at that time Pharaoh king of Egypt commanded all his people to make for him a strong palace in Egypt.

2. And he also commanded the sons of Jacob to assist the Egyptians in the building, and the Egyptians made a beautiful and elegant palace for a royal habitation, and he dwelt therein and he renewed his government and he reigned securely.

3. And Zebulun the son of Jacob died in that year, that is the seventy-second year of the going down of the Israelites to Egypt, and Zebulun died a hundred and fourteen years old, and was put into a coffin and given into the hands of his children.

4. And in the seventy-fifth year died his brother Simeon, he was a hundred and twenty years old at his death, and he was also put into a coffin and given into the hands of his children.

5. And Zepho the son of Eliphaz the son of Esau, captain of the host to Angeas king of Dinhabah, was still daily enticing Angeas to prepare for battle to fight with the sons of Jacob in Egypt, and Angeas was unwilling to do this thing, for his servants had related to him all the might of the sons of Jacob, what they had done unto them in their battle with the children of Esau.

6. And Zepho was in those days daily enticing Angeas to fight with the sons of Jacob in those days.

7. And after some time Angeas hearkened to the words of Zepho and consented to him to fight with the sons of Jacob in Egypt, and Angeas got all his people in order, a people numerous as the sand which is upon the sea shore, and he formed his resolution to go to Egypt to battle.

8. And amongst the servants of Angeas was a youth fifteen years old, Balaam the son of Beor was his name and the youth was very wise and understood the art of witchcraft.

9. And Angeas said unto Balaam, Conjure for us, I pray thee, with the witchcraft, that we may know who will prevail in this battle to which we are now proceeding.

10. And Balaam ordered that they should bring him wax, and he made thereof the likeness of chariots and horsemen representing the army of Angeas and the army of Egypt, and he put them in the cunningly prepared waters that he had for that purpose, and he took in his hand the boughs of myrtle trees, and he exercised his cunning, and he joined them over the water, and there appeared unto him in the water the resembling images of the hosts of Angeas falling before the resembling images of the Egyptians and the sons of Jacob.

11. And Balaam told this thing to Angeas, and Angeas despaired and did not arm himself to go down to Egypt to battle, and he remained in his city.

12. And when Zepho the son of Eliphaz saw that Angeas despaired of going forth to battle with the Egyptians, Zepho fled from Angeas from Africa, and he went and came unto Chittim.

13. And all the people of Chittim received him with great honor, and they hired him to fight their battles all the days, and Zepho became exceedingly rich in those days, and the troops of the king of Africa still spread themselves in those days, and the children of Chittim assembled and went to Mount Cuptizia on account of the troops of Angeas king of Africa, who were advancing upon them.

14. And it was one day that Zepho lost a young heifer, and he went to seek it, and he heard it lowing round about the mountain.

15. And Zepho went and he saw and behold there was a large cave at the bottom of the mountain, and there was a great stone there at the entrance of the cave, and Zepho split the stone and he came into the cave and he looked and behold, a large animal was devouring the ox; from the middle upward it resembled a man, and from the middle downward it resembled an animal, and Zepho rose up against the animal and slew it with his swords.

16. And the inhabitants of Chittim heard of this thing, and they rejoiced exceedingly, and they said, What shall we do unto this man who has slain this animal that devoured our cattle?

17. And they all assembled to consecrate one day in the year to him, and they called the name thereof Zepho after his name, and they brought unto him drink offerings year after year on that day, and they brought unto him gifts.

18. At that time Jania the daughter of Uzu wife of king Angeas became ill, and her illness was heavily felt by Angeas and his officers, and Angeas said unto his wise men, What shall I do to Jania and how shall I heal her from

her illness? And his wise men said unto him, Because the air of our country is not like the air of the land of Chittim, and our water is not like their water, therefore from this has the queen become ill.

19. For through the change of air and water she became ill, and also because in her country she drank only the water which came from Purmah, which her ancestors had brought up with bridges.

20. And Angeas commanded his servants, and they brought unto him in vessels of the waters of Purmah belonging to Chittim, and they weighed those waters with all the waters of the land of Africa, and they found those waters lighter than the waters of Africa.

21. And Angeas saw this thing, and he commanded all his officers to assemble the hewers of stone in thousands and tens of thousands, and they hewed stone without number, and

the builders came and they built an exceedingly strong bridge, and they conveyed the spring of water from the land of Chittim unto Africa, and those waters were for Jania the queen and for all her concerns, to drink from and to bake, wash and bathe therewith, and also to water therewith all seed from which food can be obtained, and all fruit of the ground.

22. And the king commanded that they should bring of the soil of Chittim in large ships, and they also brought stones to build therewith, and the builders built palaces for Jania the queen, and the queen became healed of her illness.

23. And at the revolution of the year the troops of Africa continued coming to the land of Chittim to plunder as usual, and Zepho son of Eliphaz heard their report, and he gave orders concerning them and he fought with them, and they fled before him, and he delivered the land of Chittim from them.

24. And the children of Chittim saw the valor of Zepho, and the children of Chittim resolved and they made Zepho king over them, and he became king over them, and whilst he reigned they went to subdue the children of Tubal, and all the surrounding islands.

25. And their king Zepho went at their head and they made war with Tubal and the islands, and they subdued them, and when they returned from the battle they renewed his government for him, and they built for him a very large palace for his royal habitation and seat, and they made a large throne for him, and Zepho reigned over the whole land of Chittim and over the land of Italia fifty years.

CHAPTER 62

1. In that year, being the seventy-ninth year of the Israelites going down to Egypt, died Reuben the son of Jacob, in the land of Egypt; Reuben was a hundred and twenty-five years old when he died, and they put him into a coffin, and he was given into the hands of his children.

2. And in the eightieth year died his brother Dan; he was a hundred and twenty years at his death, and he was also put into a coffin and given into the hands of his children.

3. And in that year died Chusham king of Edom, and after him reigned Hadad the son of Bedad, for thirty-five years; and in the eighty-first year died Issachar the son of Jacob, in Egypt, and Issachar was a hundred and twenty-two years old at his death, and he was put into a coffin in Egypt, and given into the hands of his children.

4. And in the eighty-second year died Asher his brother, he was a hundred and twentythree years old at his death, and he was placed in a coffin in Egypt, and given into the hands of his children.

5. And in the eighty-third year died Gad, he was a hundred and twenty-five years old at his death, and he was put into a coffin in Egypt, and given into the hands of his children.

6. And it came to pass in the eighty-fourth year, that is the fiftieth year of the reign of Hadad, son of Bedad, king of Edom, that Hadad assembled all the children of Esau, and he got his whole army in readiness, about four hundred thousand men, and he directed his way to the land of Moab, and he went to fight with Moab and to make them tributary to him.

7. And the children of Moab heard this thing, and they were very much afraid, and they sent to the children of Midian to assist them in fighting with Hadad, son of Bedad, king of Edom.

8. And Hadad came unto the land of Moab, and Moab and the children of Midian went out to meet him, and they placed themselves in battle array against him in the field of Moab.

9. And Hadad fought with Moab, and there fell of the children of Moab and the children of Midian many slain ones, about two hundred thousand men.

10. And the battle was very severe upon Moab, and when the children of Moab saw that the battle was sore upon them, they weakened their hands and turned their backs, and left the children of Midian to carry on the battle.

11. And the children of Midian knew not the intentions of Moab, but they strengthened themselves in battle and fought with Hadad and all his host, and all Midian fell before him.

12. And Hadad smote all Midian with a heavy smiting, and he slew them with the edge of the sword, he left none remaining of those who came to assist Moab.

13. And when all the children of Midian had perished in battle, and the children at Moab had escaped, Hadad made all Moab at that time tributary to him, and they became under his hand, and they gave a yearly tax as it was ordered, and Hadad turned and went back to his land.

14. And at the revolution of the year, when the rest of the people of Midian that were in the land heard that all their brethren had fallen in battle with Hadad for the sake of Moab, because the children of Moab had turned their backs in battle and left Midian to fight, then five of the princes of Midian resolved with the rest of their brethren who remained in their land, to fight with Moab to avenge the cause of their brethren.

15. And the children of Midian sent to all their brethren the children of the east, and all their brethren, all the children of Keturah came to assist Midian to fight with Moab.

16. And the children of Moab heard this thing, and they were greatly afraid that all the children of the east had assembled together against them for battle, and they the children of Moab sent a memorial to the land of Edom to Hadad the son of Bedad, saying,

17. Come now unto us and assist us and we will smite Midian, for they all assembled together and have come against us with all their brethren the children of the east to battle, to avenge the cause of Midian that fell in battle.

18. And Hadad, son of Bedad, king of Edom, went forth with his whole army and went to the land of Moab to fight with Midian, and Midian and the children of the east fought with Moab in the field of Moab, and the battle was very fierce between them.

19. And Hadad smote all the children of Midian and the children of the east with the edge of the sword, and Hadad at that time delivered Moab from the hand of Midian, and those that remained of Midian and of the children of the east fled before Hadad and his army, and Hadad pursued them to their land, and smote them with a very heavy slaughter, and the slain fell in the road.

20. And Hadad delivered Moab from the hand of Midian, for all the children of Midian had fallen by the edge of the sword, and Hadad turned and went back to his land.

21. And from that day forth, the children of Midian hated the children of Moab, because they had fallen in battle for their sake, and there was a great and mighty enmity between them all the days.

22. And all that were found of Midian in the road of the land of Moab perished by the sword of Moab, and all that were found of Moab in the road of the land of Midian, perished by the sword of Midian; thus did Midian unto Moab and Moab unto Midian for many days.

23. And it came to pass at that time that Judah the son of Jacob died in Egypt, in the eightysixth year of Jacob's going down to Egypt, and Judah was a hundred and twenty-nine years old at his death, and they embalmed him and put him into a coffin, and he was given into the hands of his children.

24. And in the eighty-ninth year died Naphtali, he was a hundred and thirty-two years old, and he was put into a coffin and given into the hands of his children.

25. And it came to pass in the ninety-first year of the Israelites going down to Egypt, that is in the thirtieth year of the reign of Zepho the son of Eliphaz, the son of Esau, over the children of Chittim, the children of Africa came upon the children of Chittim to plunder them as usual, but they had not come upon them for these thirteen years.

26. And they came to them in that year, and Zepho the son of Eliphaz went out to them with some of his men and smote them desperately, and the troops of Africa fled from before Zepho and the slain fell before him, and Zepho and his men pursued them, going on and smiting them until they were near unto Africa.

27. And Angeas king of Africa heard the thing which Zepho had done, and it vexed him exceedingly, and Angeas was afraid of Zepho all the days.

CHAPTER 63

1. And in the ninety-third year died Levi, the son of Jacob, in Egypt, and Levi was a hundred and thirty-seven years old when he died, and they put him into a coffin and he was given into the hands of his children.

2. And it came to pass after the death of Levi, when all Egypt saw that the sons of Jacob the brethren of Joseph were dead, all the Egyptians began to afflict the children of Jacob, and to embitter their lives from that day unto the day of their going forth from Egypt, and they took from their hands all the vineyards and fields which Joseph had given unto them, and all the elegant houses in which the people of Israel lived, and all the fat of Egypt, the Egyptians took all from the sons of Jacob in those days.

3. And the hand of all Egypt became more grievous in those days against the children of Israel, and the Egyptians injured the Israelites until the children of Israel were wearied of their lives on account of the Egyptians.

4. And it came to pass in those days, in the hundred and second year of Israel's going down to Egypt, that Pharaoh king of Egypt died, and Melol his son reigned in his stead, and all the mighty men of Egypt and all that generation which knew Joseph and his brethren died in those days.

5. And another generation rose up in their stead, which had not known the sons of Jacob and all the good which they had done to them, and all their might in Egypt.

6. Therefore all Egypt began from that day forth to embitter the lives of the sons of Jacob, and to afflict them with all manner of hard labor, because they had not known their ancestors who had delivered them in the days of the famine.

7. And this was also from the Lord, for the children of Israel, to benefit them in their latter days, in order that all the children of Israel might know the Lord their God.

8. And in order to know the signs and mighty wonders which the Lord would do in Egypt on account of his people Israel, in order that the children of Israel might fear the Lord God of their ancestors, and walk in all his ways, they and their seed after them all the days.

9. Melol was twenty years old when he began to reign, and he reigned ninety-four years, and all Egypt called his name Pharaoh after the name of his father, as it was their custom to do to every king who reigned over them in Egypt.

10. At that time all the troops of Angeas king of Africa went forth to spread along the land of Chittim as usual for plunder.

11. And Zepho the son of Eliphaz the son of Esau heard their report, and he went forth to meet them with his army, and he fought them there in the road.

12. And Zepho smote the troops of the king of Africa with the edge of the sword, and left none remaining of them, and not even one returned to his master in Africa.

13. And Angeas heard of this which Zepho the son of Eliphaz had done to all his troops, that he had destroyed them, and Angeas assembled all his troops, all the men of the land of Africa, a people numerous like the sand by the sea shore.

14. And Angeas sent to Lucus his brother, saying, Come to me with all thy men and help me to smite Zepho and all the children of Chittim who have destroyed my men, and Lucus came with his whole army, a very great force, to assist Angeas his brother to fight with Zepho and the children of Chittim.

15. And Zepho and the children of Chittim heard this thing, and they were greatly afraid and a great terror fell upon their hearts.

16. And Zepho also sent a letter to the land of Edom to Hadad the son of Bedad king of Edom and to all the children of Esau, saying,

17. I have heard that Angeas king of Africa is coming to us with his brother for battle against us, and we are greatly afraid of him, for his army is very great, particularly as he comes against us with his brother and his army likewise.

18. Now therefore come you also up with me and help me, and we will fight together against Angeas and his brother Lucus, and you will save us out of their hands, but if not, know ye that we shall all die.

19. And the children of Esau sent a letter to the children of Chittim and to Zepho their king, saying, We cannot fight against Angeas and his people for a covenant of peace has been between us these many years, from the days of Bela the first king, and from the days of Joseph the son of Jacob king of Egypt, with whom we fought on the other side of Jordan when he buried his father.

20. And when Zepho heard the words of his brethren the children of Esau he refrained from them, and Zepho was greatly afraid of Angeas.

21. And Angeas and Lucus his brother arrayed all their forces, about eight hundred thousand men, against the children of Chittim.

22. And all the children of Chittim said unto Zepho, Pray for us to the God of thy ancestors, peradventure he may deliver us from the hand of Angeas and his army, for we have heard that he is a great God and that he delivers all who trust in him.

23. And Zepho heard their words, and Zepho sought the Lord and he said,

24. o Lord God of Abraham and Isaac my ancestors, this day I know that thou art a true God, and all the gods of the nations are vain and useless.

25. Remember now this day unto me thy covenant with Abraham our father, which our ancestors related unto us, and do graciously with me this day for the sake of Abraham and Isaac our fathers, and save me and the children of Chittim from the hand of the king of Africa who comes against us for battle.

26. And the Lord hearkened to the voice of Zepho, and he had regard for him on account of Abraham and Isaac, and the Lord delivered Zepho and the children of Chittim from the hand of Angeas and his people.

27. And Zepho fought Angeas king of Africa and all his people on that day, and the Lord gave all the people of Angeas into the hands of the children of Chittim.

28. And the battle was severe upon Angeas, and Zepho smote all the men of Angeas and Lucus his brother, with the edge of the sword, and there fell from them unto the evening of that day about four hundred thousand men.

29. And when Angeas saw that all his men perished, he sent a letter to all the inhabitants of Africa to come to him, to assist him in the battle, and he wrote in the letter, saying, All who are found in Africa let them come unto me from ten years old and upward; let them all come unto me, and behold if he comes not he shall die, and all that he has, with his whole household, the king will take.

30. And all the rest of the inhabitants of Africa were terrified at the words of Angeas, and there went out of the city about three hundred thousand men and boys, from ten years upward, and they came to Angeas.

31. And at the end of ten days Angeas renewed the battle against Zepho and the children of Chittim, and the battle was very great and strong between them.

32. And from the army of Angeas and Lucus, Zepho sent many of the wounded unto his hand, about two thousand men, and Sosiphtar the captain of the host of Angeas fell in that battle.

33. And when Sosiphtar had fallen, the African troops turned their backs to flee, and they fled, and Angeas and Lucus his brother were with them.

34. And Zepho and the children of Chittim pursued them, and they smote them still heavily on the road, about two hundred men, and they pursued Azdrubal the son of Angeas who had fled with his father, and they smote twenty of his men in the road, and Azdrubal escaped from the children of Chittim, and they did not slay him.

35. And Angeas and Lucus his brother fled with the rest of their men, and they escaped and came into Africa with terror and consternation, and Angeas feared all the days lest Zepho the son of Eliphaz should go to war with him.

CHAPTER 64

1. And Balaam the son of Beor was at that time with Angeas in the battle, and when he saw that Zepho prevailed over Angeas, he fled from there and came to Chittim.

2. And Zepho and the children of Chittim received him with great honor, for Zepho knew Balaam's wisdom, and Zepho gave unto Balaam many gifts and he remained with him.

3. And when Zepho had returned from the war, he commanded all the children of Chittim to be numbered who had gone into battle with him, and behold not one was missed.

4. And Zepho rejoiced at this thing, and he renewed his kingdom, and he made a feast to all his subjects.

5. But Zepho remembered not the Lord and considered not that the Lord had helped him in battle, and that he had delivered him and his people from the hand of the king of Africa, but still walked in the ways of the children of Chittim and the wicked children of Esau, to serve other gods which his brethren the children of Esau had taught him; it is therefore said, From the wicked goes forth wickedness.

6. And Zepho reigned over all the children of Chittim securely, but knew not the Lord who had delivered him and all his people from the hand of the king of Africa; and the troops of Africa came no more to Chittim to plunder as usual, for they knew of the power of Zepho who had smitten them all at the edge of the sword, so Angeas was afraid of Zepho the son of Eliphaz, and of the children of Chittim all the days.

7. At that time when Zepho had returned from the war, and when Zepho had seen how he prevailed over all the people of Africa and had smitten them in battle at the edge of the sword, then Zepho advised with the children of Chittim, to go to Egypt to fight with the sons of Jacob and with Pharaoh king of Egypt.

8. For Zepho heard that the mighty men of Egypt were dead and that Joseph and his brethren the sons at Jacob were dead, and that all their children the children of Israel remained in Egypt.

9. And Zepho considered to go to fight against them and all Egypt, to avenge the cause of his brethren the children of Esau, whom Joseph with his brethren and all Egypt had smitten in the land of Canaan, when they went up to bury Jacob in Hebron.

10. And Zepho sent messengers to Hadad, son of Bedad, king of Edom, and to all his brethren the children of Esau, saying,

11. Did you not say that you would not fight against the king of Africa for he is a member of your covenant? behold I fought with him and smote him and all his people.

12. Now therefore I have resolved to fight against Egypt and the children of Jacob who are there, and I will be revenged of them for what Joseph, his brethren and ancestors did to us in the land of Canaan when they went up to bury their father in Hebron.

13. Now then if you are willing to come to me to assist me in fighting against them and Egypt, then shall we avenge the cause of our brethren.

14. And the children of Esau hearkened to the words of Zepho, and the children of Esau gathered themselves together, a very great people, and they went to assist Zepho and the children of Chittim in battle.

15. And Zepho sent to all the children of the east and to all the children of Ishmael with words like unto these, and they gathered themselves and came to the assistance of Zepho and the children of Chittim in the war upon Egypt.

16. And all these kings, the king of Edom and the children of the east, and all the children of Ishmael, and Zepho the king of Chittim went forth and arrayed all their hosts in Hebron.

17. And the camp was very heavy, extending in length a distance of three days' journey, a people numerous as the sand upon the sea shore which can not be counted.

18. And all these kings and their hosts went down and came against all Egypt in battle, and encamped together in the valley of Pathros.

19. And all Egypt heard their report, and they also gathered themselves together, all the people of the land of Egypt, and of all the cities belonging to Egypt, about three hundred thousand men.

20. And the men of Egypt sent also to the children of Israel who were in those days in the land of Goshen, to come to them in order to go and fight with these kings.

21. And the men of Israel assembled and were about one hundred and fifty men, and they went into battle to assist the Egyptians.

22. And the men of Israel and of Egypt went forth, about three hundred thousand men and one hundred and fifty men, and they went toward these kings to battle, and they placed themselves from without the land of Goshen opposite Pathros.

23. And the Egyptians believed not in Israel to go with them in their camps together for battle, for all the Egyptians said, Perhaps the children of Israel will deliver us into the hand of the children of Esau and Ishmael, for they are their brethren.

24. And all the Egyptians said unto the children of Israel, Remain you here together in your stand and we will go and fight against the children of Esau and Ishmael, and if these kings should prevail over us, then come you altogether upon them and assist us, and the children of Israel did so.

25. And Zepho the son of Eliphaz the son of Esau king of Chittim, and Hadad the son of Bedad king of Edom, and all their camps, and all the children of the east, and children of Ishmael, a people numerous as sand, encamped together in the valley of Pathros opposite Tachpanches.

26. And Balaam the son of Beor the Syrian was there in the camp of Zepho, for he came with the children of Chittim to the battle, and Balaam was a man highly honored in the eyes of Zepho and his men.

27. And Zepho said unto Balaam, Try by divination for us that we may know who will prevail in the battle, we or the Egyptians.

28. And Balaam rose up and tried the art of divination, and he was skillful in the knowledge of it, but he was confused and the work was destroyed in his hand.

29. And he tried it again but it did not succeed, and Balaam despaired of it and left it and did not complete it, for this was from the Lord, in order to cause Zepho and his people to fall into the hand of the children of Israel, who had trusted in the Lord, the God of their ancestors, in their war.

30. And Zepho and Hadad put their forces in battle array, and all the Egyptians went alone against them, about three hundred thousand men, and not one man of Israel was with them.

31. And all the Egyptians fought with these kings opposite Pathros and Tachpanches, and the battle was severe against the Egyptians.

32. And the kings were stronger than the Egyptians in that battle, and about one hundred and eighty men of Egypt fell on that day, and about thirty men of the forces of the kings, and all the men of Egypt fled from before the kings, so the children of Esau and Ishmael pursued the Egyptians, continuing to smite them unto the place where was the camp of the children of Israel.

33. And all the Egyptians cried unto the children of Israel, saying, Hasten to us and assist us and save us from the hand of Esau, Ishmael and the children of Chittim.

34. And the hundred and fifty men of the children of Israel ran from their station to the camps of these kings, and the children of Israel cried unto the Lord their God to deliver them.

35. And the Lord hearkened to Israel, and the Lord gave all the men of the kings into their hand, and the children of Israel fought against these kings, and the children of Israel smote about four thousand of the kings' men.

36. And the Lord threw a great consternation in the camp of the kings, so that the fear of the children of Israel fell upon them.

37. And all the hosts of the kings fled from before the children of Israel and the children of Israel pursued them continuing to smite them unto the borders of the land of Cush.

38. And the children of Israel slew of them in the road yet two thousand men, and of the children of Israel not one fell.

39. And when the Egyptians saw that the children of Israel had fought with such few men with the kings, and that the battle was so very severe against them,

40. All the Egyptians were greatly afraid of their lives on account of the strong battle, and all Egypt fled, every man hiding himself from the arrayed forces, and they hid themselves in the road, and they left the Israelites to fight.

41. And the children of Israel inflicted a terrible blow upon the kings' men, and they returned from them after they had driven them to the border of the land of Cush.

42. And all Israel knew the thing which the men of Egypt had done to them, that they had fled from them in battle, and had left them to fight alone.

43. So the children of Israel also acted with cunning, and as the children of Israel returned from battle, they found some of the Egyptians in the road and smote them there.

44. And whilst they slew them, they said unto them these words:

45. Wherefore did you go from us and leave us, being a few people, to fight against these kings who had a great people to smite us, that you might thereby deliver your own souls?

46. And of some which the Israelites met on the road, they the children of Israel spoke to each other, saying, Smite, smite, for he is an Ishmaelite, or an Edomite, or from the children of Chittim, and they stood over him and slew him, and they knew that he was an Egyptian.

47. And the children of Israel did these things cunningly against the Egyptians, because they had deserted them in battle and had fled from them.

48. And the children of Israel slew of the men of Egypt in the road in this manner, about two hundred men.

49. And all the men of Egypt saw the evil which the children of Israel had done to them, so all Egypt feared greatly the children of Israel, for they had seen their great power, and that not one man of them had fallen.

50. So all the children of Israel returned with joy on their road to Goshen, and the rest of Egypt returned each man to his place.

CHAPTER 65

1. And it came to pass after these things, that all the counsellors of Pharaoh, king of Egypt, and all the elders of Egypt assembled and came before the king and bowed down to the ground, and they sat before him.

2. And the counsellors and elders of Egypt spoke unto the king, saying,

3. Behold the people of the children of Israel is greater and mightier than we are, and thou knowest all the evil which they did to us in the road when we returned from battle.

4. And thou hast also seen their strong power, for this power is unto them from their fathers, for but a few men stood up against a people numerous as the sand, and smote them at the edge of the sword, and of themselves not one has fallen, so that if they had been numerous they would then have utterly destroyed them.

5. Now therefore give us counsel what to do with them, until we gradually destroy them from amongst us, lest they become too numerous for us in the land.

6. For if the children of Israel should increase in the land, they will become an obstacle to us, and if any war should happen to take place, they with their great strength will join our enemy against us, and fight against us, destroy us from the land and go away from it.

7. So the king answered the elders of Egypt and said unto them, This is the plan advised against Israel, from which we will not depart,

8. Behold in the land are Pithom and Rameses, cities unfortified against battle, it behooves you and us to build them, and to fortify them.

9. Now therefore go you also and act cunningly toward them, and proclaim a voice in Egypt and in Goshen at the command of the king, saying,

10. All ye men of Egypt, Goshen, Pathros and all their inhabitants! the king has commanded us to build Pithom and Rameses, and to fortify them for battle; who amongst you of all Egypt, of the children of Israel and of all the

inhabitants of the cities, are willing to build with us, shall each have his wages given to him daily at the king's order; so go you first and do cunningly, and gather yourselves and come to Pithom and Rameses to build.

11. And whilst you are building, cause a proclamation of this kind to be made throughout Egypt every day at the command of the king.

12. And when some of the children of Israel shall come to build with you, you shall give them their wages daily for a few days.

13. And after they shall have built with you for their daily hire, drag yourselves away from them daily one by one in secret, and then you shall rise up and become their taskmasters and officers, and you shall leave them afterward to build without wages, and should they refuse, then force them with all your might to build.

14. And if you do this it will be well with us to strengthen our land against the children of Israel, for on account of the fatigue of the building and the work, the children of Israel will decrease, because you will deprive them from their wives day by day.

15. And all the elders of Egypt heard the counsel of the king, and the counsel seemed good in their eyes and in the eyes of the servants of Pharaoh, and in the eyes of all Egypt, and they did according to the word of the king.

16. And all the servants went away from the king, and they caused a proclamation to be made in all Egypt, in Tachpanches and in Goshen, and in all the cities which surrounded Egypt, saying,

17. You have seen what the children of Esau and Ishmael did to us, who came to war against us and wished to destroy us.

18. Now therefore the king commanded us to fortify the land, to build the cities Pithom and Rameses, and to fortify them for battle, if they should again come against us.

19. Whosoever of you from all Egypt and from the children of Israel will come to build with us, he shall have his daily wages given by the king, as his command is unto us.

20. And when Egypt and all the children of Israel heard all that the servants of Pharaoh had spoken, there came from the Egyptians, and the children of Israel to build with the servants of Pharaoh, Pithom and Rameses, but none of the children of Levi came with their brethren to build.

21. And all the servants of Pharaoh and his princes came at first with deceit to build with all Israel as daily hired laborers, and they gave to Israel their daily hire at the beginning.

22. And the servants of Pharaoh built with all Israel, and were employed in that work with Israel for a month.

23. And at the end of the month, all the servants of Pharaoh began to withdraw secretly from the people of Israel daily.

24. And Israel went on with the work at that time, but they then received their daily hire, because some of the men of Egypt were yet carrying on the work with Israel at that time; therefore the Egyptians gave Israel their hire in those days, in order that they, the Egyptians their fellow-workmen, might also take the pay for their labor.

25. And at the end of a year and four months all the Egyptians had withdrawn from the children of Israel, so that the children of Israel were left alone engaged in the work.

26. And after all the Egyptians had withdrawn from the children of Israel they returned and became oppressors and officers over them, and some of them stood over the children of Israel as task masters, to receive from them all that they gave them for the pay of their labor.

27. And the Egyptians did in this manner to the children of Israel day by day, in order to afflict in their work.

28. And all the children of Israel were alone engaged in the labor, and the Egyptians refrained from giving any pay to the children of Israel from that time forward.

29. And when some of the men of Israel refused to work on account of the wages not being given to them, then the exactors and the servants of Pharaoh oppressed them and smote them with heavy blows, and made them return by force, to labor with their brethren; thus did all the Egyptians unto the children of Israel all the days.

30. And all the children of Israel were greatly afraid of the Egyptians in this matter, and all the children of Israel returned and worked alone without pay.

31. And the children of Israel built Pithom and Rameses, and all the children of Israel did the work, some making bricks, and some building, and the children of Israel built and fortified all the land of Egypt and its walls, and the children of Israel were engaged in work for many years, until the time came when the Lord remembered them and brought them out of Egypt.

32. But the children of Levi were not employed in the work with their brethren of Israel, from the beginning unto the day of their going forth from Egypt.

33. For all the children of Levi knew that the Egyptians had spoken all these words with deceit to the Israelites, therefore the children of Levi refrained from approaching to the work with their brethren.

34. And the Egyptians did not direct their attention to make the children of Levi work afterward, since they had not been with their brethren at the beginning, therefore the Egyptians left them alone.

35. And the hands of the men of Egypt were directed with continued severity against the children of Israel in that work, and the Egyptians made the children of Israel work with rigor.

36. And the Egyptians embittered the lives of the children of Israel with hard work, in mortar and bricks, and also in all manner of work in the field.

37. And the children of Israel called Melol the king of Egypt "Meror, king of Egypt," because in his days the Egyptians had embittered their lives with all manner of work.

38. And all the work wherein the Egyptians made the children of Israel labor, they exacted with rigor, in order to afflict the children of Israel, but the more they afflicted them, the more they increased and grew, and the Egyptians were grieved because of the children of Israel.

CHAPTER 66

1. At that time died Hadad the son of Bedad king of Edom, and Samlah from Mesrekah, from the country of the children of the east, reigned in his place.

2. In the thirteenth year of the reign of Pharaoh king of Egypt, which was the hundred and twenty-fifth year of the Israelites going down into Egypt, Samlah had reigned over Edom eighteen years.

3. And when he reigned, he drew forth his hosts to go and fight against Zepho the son of Eliphaz and the children of Chittim, because they had made war against Angeas king of Africa, and they destroyed his whole army.

4. But he did not engage with him, for the children of Esau prevented him, saying, He was their brother, so Samlah listened to the voice of the children of Esau, and turned back with all his forces to the land of Edom, and did not proceed to fight against Zepho the son of Eliphaz.

5. And Pharaoh king of Egypt heard this thing, saying, Samlah king of Edom has resolved to fight the children of Chittim, and afterward he will come to fight against Egypt.

6. And when the Egyptians heard this matter, they increased the labor upon the children of Israel, lest the Israelites should do unto them as they did unto them in their war with the children of Esau in the days of Hadad.

7. So the Egyptians said unto the children of Israel, Hasten and do your work, and finish your task, and strengthen the land, lest the children of Esau your brethren should come to fight against us, for on your account will they come against us.

8. And the children of Israel did the work of the men of Egypt day by day, and the Egyptians afflicted the children of Israel in order to lessen them in the land.

9. But as the Egyptians increased the labor upon the children of Israel, so did the children of Israel increase and multiply, and all Egypt was filled with the children of Israel.

10. And in the hundred and twenty-fifth year of Israel's going down into Egypt, all the Egyptians saw that their counsel did not succeed against Israel, but that they increased and grew, and the land of Egypt and the land of Goshen were filled with the children of Israel.

11. So all the elders of Egypt and its wise men came before the king and bowed down to him and sat before him.

12. And all the elders of Egypt and the wise men thereof said unto the king, May the king live forever; thou didst counsel us the counsel against the children of Israel, and we did unto them according to the word of the king.

13. But in proportion to the increase of the labor so do they increase and grow in the land, and behold the whole country is filled with them.

14. Now therefore our lord and king, the eyes of all Egypt are upon thee to give them advice with thy wisdom, by which they may prevail over Israel to destroy them, or to diminish them from the land; and the king answered them saying, Give you counsel in this matter that we may know what to do unto them.

15. And an officer, one of the king's counsellors, whose name was Job, from Mesopotamia, in the land of Uz, answered the king, saying,

16. If it please the king, let him hear the counsel of his servant; and the king said unto him, Speak.

17. And Job spoke before the king, the princes, and before all the elders of Egypt, saying,

18. Behold the counsel of the king which he advised formerly respecting the labor of the children of Israel is very good, and you must not remove from them that labor forever.

19. But this is the advice counselled by which you may lessen them, if it seems good to the king to afflict them.

20. Behold we have feared war for a long time, and we said, When Israel becomes fruitful in the land, they will drive us from the land if a war should take place.

21. If it please the king, let a royal decree go forth, and let it be written in the laws of Egypt which shall not be revoked, that every male child born to the Israelites, his blood shall be spilled upon the ground.

22. And by your doing this, when all the male children of Israel shall have died, the evil of their wars will cease; let the king do so and send for all the Hebrew midwives and order them in this matter to execute it; so the thing pleased the king and the princes, and the king did according to the word of Job.

23. And the king sent for the Hebrew midwives to be called, of which the name of one was Shephrah, and the name of the other Puah.

24. And the midwives came before the king, and stood in his presence.

25. And the king said unto them, When you do the office of a midwife to the Hebrew women, and see them upon the stools, if it be a son, then you shall kill him, but if it be a daughter, then she shall live.

26. But if you will not do this thing, then will I burn you up and all your houses with fire.

27. But the midwives feared God and did not hearken to the king of Egypt nor to his words, and when the Hebrew women brought forth to the midwife son or daughter, then did the midwife do all that was necessary to the child and let it live; thus did the midwives all the days.

28. And this thing was told to the king, and he sent and called for the midwives and he said to them, Why have you done this thing and have saved the children alive?

29. And the midwives answered and spoke together before the king, saying,

30. Let not the king think that the Hebrew women are as the Egyptian women, for all the children of Israel are hale, and before the midwife comes to them they are delivered, and as for us thy handmaids, for many days no Hebrew woman has brought forth upon us, for all the Hebrew women are their own midwives, because they are hale.

31. And Pharaoh heard their words and believed them in this matter, and the midwives went away from the king, and God dealt well with them, and the people multiplied and waxed exceedingly.

CHAPTER 67

1. There was a man in the land of Egypt of the seed of Levi, whose name was Amram, the son of Kehath, the son of Levi, the son of Israel.

2. And this man went and took a wife, namely Jochebed the daughter of Levi his father's sister, and she was one hundred and twenty-six years old, and he came unto her.

3. And the woman conceived and bare a daughter, and she called her name Miriam, because in those days the Egyptians had embittered the lives of the children of Israel.

4. And she conceived again and bare a son and she called his name Aaron, for in the days of her conception, Pharaoh began to spill the blood of the male children of Israel.

5. In those days died Zepho the son of Eliphaz, son of Esau, king of Chittim, and Janeas reigned in his stead.

6. And the time that Zepho reigned over the children of Chittim was fifty years, and he died and was buried in the city of Nabna in the land of Chittim.

7. And Janeas, one of the mighty men of the children of Chittim, reigned after him and he reigned fifty years.

8. And it was after the death of the king of Chittim that Balaam the son of Beor fled from the land of Chittim, and he went and came to Egypt to Pharaoh king of Egypt.

9. And Pharaoh received him with great honor, for he had heard of his wisdom, and he gave him presents and made him for a counsellor, and aggrandized him.

10. And Balaam dwelt in Egypt, in honor with all the nobles of the king, and the nobles exalted him, because they all coveted to learn his wisdom.

11. And in the hundred and thirtieth year of Israel's going down to Egypt, Pharaoh dreamed that he was sitting upon his kingly throne, and lifted up his eyes and saw an old man standing before him, and there were scales in the hands of the old man, such scales as are used by merchants.

12. And the old man took the scales and hung them before Pharaoh.

13. And the old man took all the elders of Egypt and all its nobles and great men, and he tied them together and put them in one scale.

14. And he took a milk kid and put it into the other scale, and the kid preponderated over all.

15. And Pharaoh was astonished at this dreadful vision, why the kid should preponderate over all, and Pharaoh awoke and behold it was a dream.

16. And Pharaoh rose up early in the morning and called all his servants and related to them the dream, and the men were greatly afraid.

17. And the king said to all his wise men, Interpret I pray you the dream which I dreamed, that I may know it.

18. And Balaam the son of Beor answered the king and said unto him, This means nothing else but a great evil that will spring up against Egypt in the latter days.

19. For a son will be born to Israel who will destroy all Egypt and its inhabitants, and bring forth the Israelites from Egypt with a mighty hand.

20. Now therefore, O king, take counsel upon this matter, that you may destroy the hope of the children of Israel and their expectation, before this evil arise against Egypt.

21. And the king said unto Balaam, And what shall we do unto Israel? surely after a certain manner did we at first counsel against them and could not prevail over them.

22. Now therefore give you also advice against them by which we may prevail over them.

23. And Balaam answered the king, saying, Send now and call thy two counsellors, and we will see what their advice is upon this matter and afterward thy servant will speak.

24. And the king sent and called his two counsellors Reuel the Midianite and Job the Uzite, and they came and sat before the king.

25. And the king said to them, Behold you have both heard the dream which I have dreamed, and the interpretation thereof; now therefore give counsel and know and see what is to be done to the children of Israel, whereby we may prevail over them, before their evil shall spring up against us.

26. And Reuel the Midianite answered the king and said, May the king live, may the king live forever.

27. If it seem good to the king, let him desist from the Hebrews and leave them, and let him not stretch forth his hand against them.

28. For these are they whom the Lord chose in days of old, and took as the lot of his inheritance from amongst all the nations of the earth and the kings of the earth; and who is there that stretched his hand against them with impunity, of whom their God was not avenged?

29. Surely thou knowest that when Abraham went down to Egypt, Pharaoh, the former king of Egypt, saw Sarah his wife, and took her for a wife, because Abraham said, She is my sister, for he was afraid, lest the men of Egypt should slay him on account of his wife.

30. And when the king of Egypt had taken Sarah then God smote him and his household with heavy plagues, until he restored unto Abraham his wife Sarah, then was he healed.

31. And Abimelech the Gerarite, king of the Philistines, God punished on account of Sarah wife of Abraham, in stopping up every womb from man to beast.

32. When their God came to Abimelech in the dream of night and terrified him in order that he might restore to Abraham Sarah whom he had taken, and afterward all the people of Gerar were punished on account of Sarah, and Abraham prayed to his God for them, and he was entreated of him, and he healed them.

33. And Abimelech feared all this evil that came upon him and his people, and he returned to Abraham his wife Sarah, and gave him with her many gifts.

34. He did so also to Isaac when he had driven him from Gerar, and God had done wonderful things to him, that all the water courses of Gerar were dried up, and their productive trees did not bring forth.

35. Until Abimelech of Gerar, and Ahuzzath one of his friends, and Pichol the captain of his host, went to him and they bent and bowed down before him to the ground.

36. And they requested of him to supplicate for them, and he prayed to the Lord for them, and the Lord was entreated of him and he healed them.

37. Jacob also, the plain man, was delivered through his integrity from the hand of his brother Esau, and the hand of Laban the Syrian his mother's brother, who had sought his life; likewise from the hand of all the kings of Canaan who had come together against him and his children to destroy them, and the Lord delivered them out of their hands, that they turned upon them and smote them, for who had ever stretched forth his hand against them with impunity?

38. Surely Pharaoh the former, thy father's father, raised Joseph the son of Jacob above all the princes of the land of Egypt, when he saw his wisdom, for through his wisdom he rescued all the inhabitants of the land from the famine.

39. After which he ordered Jacob and his children to come down to Egypt, in order that through their virtue, the land of Egypt and the land of Goshen might be delivered from the famine.

40. Now therefore if it seem good in thine eyes, cease from destroying the children of Israel, but if it be not thy will that they shall dwell in Egypt, send them forth from here, that they may go to the land of Canaan, the land where their ancestors sojourned.

41. And when Pharaoh heard the words of Jethro he was very angry with him, so that he rose with shame from the king's presence, and went to Midian, his land, and took Joseph's stick with him.

42. And the king said to Job the Uzite, What sayest thou Job, and what is thy advice respecting the Hebrews?

43. So Job said to the king, Behold all the inhabitants of the land are in thy power, let the king do as it seems good in his eyes.

44. And the king said unto Balaam, What dost thou say, Balaam, speak thy word that we may hear it.

45. And Balaam said to the king, Of all that the king has counselled against the Hebrews will they be delivered, and the king will not be able to prevail over them with any counsel.

46. For if thou thinkest to lessen them by the flaming fire, thou canst not prevail over them, for surely their God delivered Abraham their father from Ur of the Chaldeans; and if thou thinkest to destroy them with a sword, surely Isaac their father was delivered from it, and a ram was placed in his stead.

47. And if with hard and rigorous labor thou thinkest to lessen them, thou wilt not prevail even in this, for their father Jacob served Laban in all manner of hard work, and prospered.

48. Now therefore, O King, hear my words, for this is the counsel which is counselled against them, by which thou wilt prevail over them, and from which thou shouldst not depart.

49. If it please the king let him order all their children which shall be born from this day forward, to be thrown into the water, for by this canst thou wipe away their name, for none of them, nor of their fathers, were tried in this manner.

50. And the king heard the words of Balaam, and the thing pleased the king and the princes, and the king did according to the word of Balaam.

51. And the king ordered a proclamation to be issued and a law to be made throughout the land of Egypt, saying, Every male child born to the Hebrews from this day forward shall be thrown into the water.

52. And Pharaoh called unto all his servants, saying, Go now and seek throughout the land of Goshen where the children of Israel are, and see that every son born to the Hebrews shall be cast into the river, but every daughter you shall let live.

53. And when the children of Israel heard this thing which Pharaoh had commanded, to cast their male children into the river, some of the people separated from their wives and
others adhered to them.

54. And from that day forward, when the time of delivery arrived to those women of Israel who had remained with their husbands, they went to the field to bring forth there, and they brought forth in the field, and left their children upon the field and returned home.

55. And the Lord who had sworn to their ancestors to multiply them, sent one of his ministering angels which are in heaven to wash each child in water, to anoint and swathe it and to put into its hands two smooth stones from one of which it sucked milk and from the other honey, and he caused its hair to grow to its knees, by which it might cover itself; to comfort it and to cleave to it, through his compassion for it.

56. And when God had compassion over them and had desired to multiply them upon the face of the land, he ordered his earth to receive them to be preserved therein till the time of their growing up, after which the earth opened its mouth and vomited them forth and they sprouted forth from the city like the herb of the earth, and the grass of the forest, and they returned each to his family and to his father's house, and they remained with them.

57. And the babes of the children of Israel were upon the earth like the herb of the field, through God's grace to them.

58. And when all the Egyptians saw this thing, they went forth, each to his field with his yoke of oxen and his ploughshare, and they ploughed it up as one ploughs the earth at seed time.

59. And when they ploughed they were unable to hurt the infants of the children of Israel, so the people increased and waxed exceedingly.

60. And Pharaoh ordered his officers daily to go to Goshen to seek for the babes of the children of Israel.

61. And when they had sought and found one, they took it from its mother's bosom by force, and threw it into the river, but the female child they left with its mother; thus did the Egyptians do to the Israelites all the days.

CHAPTER 68

1. And it was at that time the spirit of God was upon Miriam the daughter of Amram the sister of Aaron, and she went forth and prophesied about the house, saying, Behold a son will be born unto us from my father and mother this time, and he will save Israel from the hands of Egypt.

2. And when Amram heard the words of his daughter, he went and took his wife back to the house, after he had driven her away at the time when Pharaoh ordered every male child of the house of Jacob to be thrown into the water.

3. So Amram took Jochebed his wife, three years after he had driven her away, and he came to her and she conceived.

4. And at the end of seven months from her conception she brought forth a son, and the whole house was filled with great light as of the light of the sun and moon at the time of their shining.

5. And when the woman saw the child that it was good and pleasing to the sight, she hid it for three months in an inner room.

6. In those days the Egyptians conspired to destroy all the Hebrews there.

7. And the Egyptian women went to Goshen where the children of Israel were, and they carried their young ones upon their shoulders, their babes who could not yet speak.

8. And in those days, when the women of the children of Israel brought forth, each woman had hidden her son from before the Egyptians, that the Egyptians might not know of their bringing forth, and might not destroy them from the land.

9. And the Egyptian women came to Goshen and their children who could not speak were upon their shoulders, and when an Egyptian woman came into the house of a Hebrew woman her babe began to cry.

10. And when it cried the child that was in the inner room answered it, so the Egyptian women went and told it at the house of Pharaoh.

11. And Pharaoh sent his officers to take the children and slay them; thus did the Egyptians to the Hebrew women all the days.

12. And it was at that time, about three months from Jochebed's concealment of her son, that the thing was known in Pharaoh's house.

13. And the woman hastened to take away her son before the officers came, and she took for him an ark of bulrushes, and daubed it with slime and with pitch, and put the child therein, and she laid it in the flags by the river's brink.

14. And his sister Miriam stood afar off to know what would be done to him, and what would become of her words.

15. And God sent forth at that time a terrible heat in the land of Egypt, which burned up the flesh of man like the sun in his circuit, and it greatly oppressed the Egyptians.

16. And all the Egyptians went down to bathe in the river, on account of the consuming heat which burned up their flesh.

17. And Bathia, the daughter of Pharaoh, went also to bathe in the river, owing to the consuming heat, and her maidens walked at the river side, and all the women of Egypt as well.

18. And Bathia lifted up her eyes to the river, and she saw the ark upon the water, and sent her maid to fetch it.

19. And she opened it and saw the child, and behold the babe wept, and she had compassion on him, and she said, This is one of the Hebrew children.

20. And all the women of Egypt walking on the river side desired to give him suck, but he would not suck, for this thing was from the Lord, in order to restore him to his mother's breast.

21. And Miriam his sister was at that time amongst the Egyptian women at the river side, and she saw this thing and she said to Pharaoh's daughter, Shall I go and fetch a nurse of the Hebrew women, that she may nurse the child for thee?

22. And Pharaoh's daughter said to her, Go, and the young woman went and called the child's mother.

23. And Pharaoh's daughter said to Jochebed, Take this child away and suckle it for me, and I will pay thee thy wages, two bits of silver daily; and the woman took the child and nursed it.

24. And at the end of two years, when the child grew up, she brought him to the daughter of Pharaoh, and he was unto her as a son, and she called his name Moses, for she said, Because I drew him out of the water.

25. And Amram his father called his name Chabar, for he said, It was for him that he associated with his wife whom he had turned away.

26. And Jochebed his mother called his name Jekuthiel, Because, she said, I have hoped for him to the Almighty, and God restored him unto me.

27. And Miriam his sister called him Jered, for she descended after him to the river to know what his end would be.

28. And Aaron his brother called his name Abi Zanuch, saying, My father left my mother and returned to her on his account.

29. And Kehath the father of Amram called his name Abigdor, because on his account did God repair the breach of the house of Jacob, that they could no longer throw their male children into the water.

30. And their nurse called him Abi Socho, saying, In his tabernacle was he hidden for three months, on account of the children of Ham.

31. And all Israel called his name Shemaiah, son of Nethanel, for they said, In his days has God heard their cries and rescued them from their oppressors.

32. And Moses was in Pharaoh's house, and was unto Bathia, Pharaoh's daughter, as a son, and Moses grew up amongst the king's children.

CHAPTER 69

1.   And the king of Edom died in those days, in the eighteenth year of his reign, and was buried in his temple which he had built for himself as his royal residence in the land of
Edom.

2.   And the children of Esau sent to Pethor, which is upon the river, and they fetched from there a young man of beautiful eyes and comely aspect, whose name was Saul, and they made him king over them in the place of Samlah.

3.   And Saul reigned over all the children of Esau in the land of Edom for forty years.

4.   And when Pharaoh king of Egypt saw that the counsel which Balaam had advised respecting the children of Israel did not succeed, but that still they were fruitful, multiplied and increased throughout the land of Egypt,

5.   Then Pharaoh commanded in those days that a proclamation should be issued throughout Egypt to the children of Israel, saying, No man shall diminish any thing of his daily labor.

6.   And the man who shall be found deficient in his labor which he performs daily, whether in mortar or in bricks, then his youngest son shall be put in their place.

7.   And the labor of Egypt strengthened upon the children of Israel in those days, and behold if one brick was deficient in any man's daily labor, the Egyptians took his youngest boy by force from his mother, and put him into the building in the place of the brick which his father had left wanting.

8.   And the men of Egypt did so to all the children of Israel day by day, all the days for a long period.

9.   But the tribe of Levi did not at that time work with the Israelites their brethren, from the beginning, for the children of Levi knew the cunning of the Egyptians which they exercised at first toward the Israelites.

CHAPTER 70

1.   And in the third year from the birth of Moses, Pharaoh was sitting at a banquet, when Alparanith the queen was sitting at his right and Bathia at his left, and the lad Moses was lying upon her bosom, and Balaam the son of Beor with his two sons, and all the princes of the kingdom were sitting at table in the king's presence.

2.   And the lad stretched forth his hand upon the king's head, and took the crown from the king's head and placed it on his own head.

3.   And when the king and princes saw the work which the boy had done, the king and princes were terrified, and one man to his neighbor expressed astonishment.

4.   And the king said unto the princes who were before him at table, What speak you and what say you, O ye princes, in this matter, and what is to be the judgment against the boy on account of this act?

5.   And Balaam the son of Beor the magician answered before the king and princes, and he said, Remember now, O my lord and king, the dream which thou didst dream many days since, and that which thy servant interpreted unto thee.

6.   Now therefore this is a child from the Hebrew children, in whom is the spirit of God, and let not my lord the king imagine that this youngster did this thing without knowledge.

7.   For he is a Hebrew boy, and wisdom and understanding are with him, although he is yet a child, and with wisdom has he done this and chosen unto himself the kingdom of Egypt.

8. For this is the manner of all the Hebrews to deceive kings and their nobles, to do all these things cunningly, in order to make the kings of the earth and their men tremble.

9. Surely thou knowest that Abraham their father acted thus, who deceived the army of Nimrod king of Babel, and Abimelech king of Gerar, and that he possessed himself of the land of the children of Heth and all the kingdoms of Canaan.

10. And that he descended into Egypt and said of Sarah his wife, she is my sister, in order to mislead Egypt and her king.

11. His son Isaac also did so when he went to Gerar and dwelt there, and his strength prevailed over the army of Abimelech king of the Philistines.

12. He also thought of making the kingdom of the Philistines stumble, in saying that Rebecca his wife was his sister.

13. Jacob also dealt treacherously with his brother, and took from his hand his birthright and his blessing.

14. He went then to Padan-aram to the house of Laban his mother's brother, and cunningly obtained from him his daughter, his cattle, and all belonging to him, and fled away and returned to the land of Canaan to his father.

15. His sons sold their brother Joseph, who went down into Egypt and became a slave, and was placed in the prison house for twelve years.

16. Until the former Pharaoh dreamed dreams, and withdrew him from the prison house, and magnified him above all the princes in Egypt on account of his interpreting his dreams to him.

17. And when God caused a famine throughout the land he sent for and brought his father and all his brothers, and the whole of his father's household, and supported them without price or reward, and bought the Egyptians for slaves.

18. Now therefore my lord king behold this child has risen up in their stead in Egypt, to do according to their deeds and to trifle with every king, prince and judge.

19. If it please the king, let us now spill his blood upon the ground, lest he grow up and take away the government from thy hand, and the hope of Egypt perish after he shall have reigned.

20. And Balaam said to the king, Let us moreover call for all the judges of Egypt and the wise men thereof, and let us know if the judgment of death is due to this boy as thou didst say, and then we will slay him.

21. And Pharaoh sent and called for all the wise men of Egypt and they came before the king, and an angel of the Lord came amongst them, and he was like one of the wise men of Egypt.

22. And the king said to the wise men, Surely you have heard what this Hebrew boy who is in the house has done, and thus has Balaam judged in the matter.

23. Now judge you also and see what is due to the boy for the act he has committed.

24. And the angel, who seemed like one of the wise men of Pharaoh, answered and said as follows, before all the wise men of Egypt and before the king and the princes:

25. If it please the king let the king send for men who shall bring before him an onyx stone and a coal of fire, and place them before the child, and if the child shall stretch forth his hand and take the onyx stone, then shall we know that with wisdom has the youth done all that he has done, and we must slay him.

26. But if he stretch forth his hand upon the coal, then shall we know that it was not with knowledge that he did this thing, and he shall live.

27. And the thing seemed good in the eyes of the king and the princes, so the king did according to the word of the angel of the Lord.

28. And the king ordered the onyx stone and coal to be brought and placed before Moses.

29. And they placed the boy before them, and the lad endeavored to stretch forth his hand to the onyx stone, but the angel of the Lord took his hand and placed it upon the coal, and the coal became extinguished in his hand, and he lifted it up and put it into his mouth, and burned part of his lips and part of his tongue, and he became heavy in mouth and tongue.

30. And when the king and princes saw this, they knew that Moses had not acted with wisdom in taking off the crown from the king's head.

31. So the king and princes refrained from slaying the child, so Moses remained in Pharaoh's house, growing up, and the Lord was with him.

32. And whilst the boy was in the king's house, he was robed in purple and he grew amongst the children of the king.

33. And when Moses grew up in the king's house, Bathia the daughter of Pharaoh considered him as a son, and all the household of Pharaoh honored him, and all the men of Egypt were afraid of him.

34. And he daily went forth and came into the land of Goshen, where his brethren the children of Israel were, and Moses saw them daily in shortness of breath and hard labor.

35. And Moses asked them, saying, Wherefore is this labor meted out unto you day by day?

36. And they told him all that had befallen them, and all the injunctions which Pharaoh had put upon them before his birth.

37. And they told him all the counsels which Balaam the son of Beor had counselled against them, and what he had also counselled against him in order to slay him when he had taken the king's crown from off his head.

38. And when Moses heard these things his anger was kindled against Balaam, and he sought to kill him, and he was in ambush for him day by day.

39. And Balaam was afraid of Moses, and he and his two sons rose up and went forth from Egypt, and they fled and delivered their souls and betook themselves to the land of Cush to Kikianus, king of Cush.

40. And Moses was in the king's house going out and coming in, the Lord gave him favor in the eyes of Pharaoh, and in the eyes of all his servants, and in the eyes of all the people of Egypt, and they loved Moses exceedingly.

41. And the day arrived when Moses went to Goshen to see his brethren, that he saw the children of Israel in their burdens and hard labor, and Moses was grieved on their account.

42. And Moses returned to Egypt and came to the house of Pharaoh, and came before the king, and Moses bowed down before the king.

43. And Moses said unto Pharaoh, I pray thee my lord, I have come to seek a small request from thee, turn not away my face empty; and Pharaoh said unto him, Speak.

44. And Moses said unto Pharaoh, Let there be given unto thy servants the children of Israel who are in Goshen, one day to rest therein from their labor.

45. And the king answered Moses and said, Behold I have lifted up thy face in this thing to grant thy request.

46. And Pharaoh ordered a proclamation to be issued throughout Egypt and Goshen, saying,

47. To you, all the children of Israel, thus says the king, for six days you shall do your work and labor, but on the seventh day you shall rest, and shall not preform any work, thus shall you do all the days, as the king and Moses the son of Bathia have commanded.

48. And Moses rejoiced at this thing which the king had granted to him, and all the children of Israel did as Moses ordered them.

49. For this thing was from the Lord to the children of Israel, for the Lord had begun to remember the children of Israel to save them for the sake of their fathers.

50. And the Lord was with Moses and his fame went throughout Egypt.

51. And Moses became great in the eyes of all the Egyptians, and in the eyes of all the children of Israel, seeking good for his people Israel and speaking words of peace regarding them to the king.

CHAPTER 71

1. And when Moses was eighteen years old, he desired to see his father and mother and he went to them to Goshen, and when Moses had come near Goshen, he came to the place where the children of Israel were engaged in work, and he observed their burdens, and he saw an Egyptian smiting one of his Hebrew brethren.

2. And when the man who was beaten saw Moses he ran to him for help, for the man Moses was greatly respected in the house of Pharaoh, and he said to him, My lord attend to me, this Egyptian came to my house in the night, bound me, and came to my wife in my presence, and now he seeks to take my life away.

3. And when Moses heard this wicked thing, his anger was kindled against the Egyptian, and he turned this way and the other, and when he saw there was no man there he smote the Egyptian and hid him in the sand, and delivered the Hebrew from the hand of him that smote him.

4. And the Hebrew went to his house, and Moses returned to his home, and went forth and came back to the king's house.

5. And when the man had returned home, he thought of repudiating his wife, for it was not right in the house of Jacob, for any man to come to his wife after she had been defiled.

6. And the woman went and told her brothers, and the woman's brothers sought to slay him, and he fled to his house and escaped.

7. And on the second day Moses went forth to his brethren, and saw, and behold two men were quarreling, and he said to the wicked one, Why dost thou smite thy neighbor?

8. And he answered him and said to him, Who has set thee for a prince and judge over us? dost thou think to slay me as thou didst slay the Egyptian? and Moses was afraid and he said, Surely the thing is known?

9. And Pharaoh heard of this affair, and he ordered Moses to be slain, so God sent his angel, and he appeared unto Pharaoh in the likeness of a captain of the guard.

10. And the angel of the Lord took the sword from the hand of the captain of the guard, and took his head off with it, for the likeness of the captain of the guard was turned into the likeness of Moses.

11. And the angel of the Lord took hold of the right hand of Moses, and brought him forth from Egypt, and placed him from without the borders of Egypt, a distance of forty days' journey.

12. And Aaron his brother alone remained in the land of Egypt, and he prophesied to the children of Israel, saying,

13. Thus says the Lord God of your ancestors, Throw away, each man, the abominations of his eyes, and do not defile yourselves with the idols of Egypt.

14. And the children of Israel rebelled and would not hearken to Aaron at that time.

15. And the Lord thought to destroy them, were it not that the Lord remembered the covenant which he had made with Abraham, Isaac and Jacob.

16. In those days the hand of Pharaoh continued to be severe against the children of Israel, and he crushed and oppressed them until the time when God sent forth his word and took notice of them.

CHAPTER 72

1. And it was in those days that there was a great war between the children of Cush and the children of the east and Aram, and they rebelled against the king of Cush in whose hands they were.

2. So Kikianus king of Cush went forth with all the children of Cush, a people numerous as the sand, and he went to fight against Aram and the children of the east, to bring them under subjection.

3. And when Kikianus went out, he left Balaam the magician, with his two sons, to guard the city, and the lowest sort of the people of the land.

4. So Kikianus went forth to Aram and the children of the east, and he fought against them and smote them, and they all fell down wounded before Kikianus and his people.

5. And he took many of them captives and he brought them under subjection as at first, and he encamped upon their land to take tribute from them as usual.

6. And Balaam the son of Beor, when the king of Cush had left him to guard the city and the poor of the city, he rose up and advised with the people of the land to rebel against king Kikianus, not to let him enter the city when he should come home.

7. And the people of the land hearkened to him, and they swore to him and made him king over them, and his two sons for captains of the army.

8. So they rose up and raised the walls of the city at the two corners, and they built an exceeding strong building.

9. And at the third corner they dug ditches without number, between the city and the river which surrounded the whole land of Cush, and they made the waters of the river burst forth there.

10. At the fourth corner they collected numerous serpents by their incantations and enchantments, and they fortified the city and dwelt therein, and no one went out or in before them.

11. And Kikianus fought against Aram and the children of the east and he subdued them as before, and they gave him their usual tribute, and he went and returned to his land.

12. And when Kikianus the king of Cush approached his city and all the captains of the forces with him, they lifted up their eyes and saw that the walls of the city were built up and greatly elevated, so the men were astonished at this.

13. And they said one to the other, It is because they saw that we were delayed, in battle,

and were greatly afraid of us, therefore have they done this thing and raised the city walls and fortified them so that the kings of Canaan might not come in battle against them.

14. So the king and the troops approached the city door and they looked up and behold, all the gates of the city were closed, and they called out to the sentinels, saying, Open unto us, that we may enter the city.

15. But the sentinels refused to open to them by the order of Balaam the magician, their king, they suffered them not to enter their city.

16. So they raised a battle with them opposite the city gate, and one hundred and thirty men of the army at Kikianus fell on that day.

17. And on the next day they continued to fight and they fought at the side of the river; they endeavored to pass but were not able, so some of them sank in the pits and died.

18. So the king ordered them to cut down trees to make rafts, upon which they might pass to them, and they did so.

19. And when they came to the place of the ditches, the waters revolved by mills, and two hundred men upon ten rafts were drowned.

20. And on the third day they came to fight at the side where the serpents were, but they could not approach there, for the serpents slew of them one hundred and seventy men, and they ceased fighting against Cush, and they besieged Cush for nine years, no person came out or in.

21. At that time that the war and the siege were against Cush, Moses fled from Egypt from Pharaoh who sought to kill him for having slain the Egyptian.

22. And Moses was eighteen years old when he fled from Egypt from the presence of Pharaoh, and he fled and escaped to the camp of Kikianus, which at that time was besieging Cush.

23. And Moses was nine years in the camp of Kikianus king of Cush, all the time that they were besieging Cush, and Moses went out and came in with them.

24. And the king and princes and all the fighting men loved Moses, for he was great and worthy, his stature was like a noble lion, his face was like the sun, and his strength was like that of a lion, and he was counsellor to the king.

25. And at the end of nine years, Kikianus was seized with a mortal disease, and his illness prevailed over him, and he died on the seventh day.

26. So his servants embalmed him and carried him and buried him opposite the city gate to the north of the land of Egypt.

27. And they built over him an elegant strong and high building, and they placed great stones below.

28. And the king's scribes engraved upon those stones all the might of their king Kikianus, and all his battles which he had fought, behold they are written there at this day.

29. Now after the death of Kikianus king of Cush it grieved his men and troops greatly on account of the war.

30. So they said one to the other, Give us counsel what we are to do at this time, as we have resided in the wilderness nine years away from our homes.

31. If we say we will fight against the city many of us will fall wounded or killed, and if we remain here in the siege we shall also die.

32. For now all the kings of Aram and of the children of the east will hear that our king is dead, and they will attack us suddenly in a hostile manner, and they will fight against us and leave no remnant of us.

33. Now therefore let us go and make a king over us, and let us remain in the siege until the city is delivered up to us.

34. And they wished to choose on that day a man for king from the army of Kikianus, and they found no object of their choice like Moses to reign over them.

35. And they hastened and stripped off each man his garments and cast them upon the ground, and they made a great heap and placed Moses thereon.

36. And they rose up and blew with trumpets and called out before him, and said, May the king live, may the king live!

37. And all the people and nobles swore unto him to give him for a wife Adoniah the queen, the Cushite, wife of Kikianus, and they made Moses king over them on that day.

38. And all the people of Cush issued a proclamation on that day, saying, Every man must give something to Moses of what is in his possession.

39. And they spread out a sheet upon the heap, and every man cast into it something of what he had, one a gold earring and the other a coin.

40. Also of onyx stones, bdellium, pearls and marble did the children of Cush cast unto Moses upon the heap, also silver and gold in great abundance.

41. And Moses took all the silver and gold, all the vessels, and the bdellium and onyx stones, which all the children of Cush had given to him, and he placed them amongst his treasures.

42. And Moses reigned over the children of Cush on that day, in the place of Kikianus king of Cush.

CHAPTER 73

1. In the fifty-fifth year of the reign of Pharaoh king of Egypt, that is in the hundred and fifty-seventh year of the Israelites going down into Egypt, reigned Moses in Cush.

2. Moses was twenty-seven years old when he began to reign over Cush, and forty years did he reign.

3. And the Lord granted Moses favor and grace in the eyes of all the children of Cush, and the children of Cush loved him exceedingly, so Moses was favored by the Lord and by men.

4. And in the seventh day of his reign, all the children of Cush assembled and came before Moses and bowed down to him to the ground.

5. And all the children spoke together in the presence of the king, saying, Give us counsel that we may see what is to be done to this city.

6. For it is now nine years that we have been besieging round about the city, and have not seen our children and our wives.

7. So the king answered them, saying, If you will hearken to my voice in all that I shall command you, then will the Lord give the city into our hands and we shall subdue it.

8. For if we fight with them as in the former battle which we had with them before the death of Kikianus, many of us will fall down wounded as before.

9. Now therefore behold here is counsel for you in this matter; if you will hearken to my voice, then will the city be delivered into our hands.

10. So all the forces answered the king, saying, All that our lord shall command that will we do.

11. And Moses said unto them, Pass through and proclaim a voice in the whole camp unto all the people, saying,

12. Thus says the king, Go into the forest and bring with you of the young ones of the stork, each man a young one in his hand.

13. And any person transgressing the word of the king, who shall not bring his young one, he shall die, and the king will take all belonging to him.

14. And when you shall bring them they shall be in your keeping, you shall rear them until they grow up, and you shall teach them to dart upon, as is the way of the young ones of the hawk.

15. So all the children of Cush heard the words of Moses, and they rose up and caused a proclamation to be issued throughout the camp, saying,

16. Unto you, all the children of Cush, the king's order is, that you go all together to the forest, and catch there the young storks each man his young one in his hand, and you shall bring them home.

17. And any person violating the order of the king shall die, and the king will take all that belongs to him.

18. And all the people did so, and they went out to the wood and they climbed the fir trees and caught, each man a young one in his hand, all the young of the storks, and they brought them into the desert and reared them by order of the king, and they taught them to dart upon, similar to the young hawks.

19. And after the young storks were reared, the king ordered them to be hungered for three days, and all the people did so.

20. And on the third day, the king said unto them, strengthen yourselves and become valiant men, and put on each man his armor and gird on his sword upon him, and ride each man his horse and take each his young stork in his hand.

21. And we will rise up and fight against the city at the place where the serpents are; and all the people did as the king had ordered.

22. And they took each man his young one in his hand, and they went away, and when they came to the place of the serpents the king said to them, Send forth each man his young stork upon the serpents.

23. And they sent forth each man his young stork at the king's order, and the young storks ran upon the serpents and they devoured them all and destroyed them out of that place.

24. And when the king and people had seen that all the serpents were destroyed in that place, all the people set up a great shout.

25. And they approached and fought against the city and took it and subdued it, and they entered the city.

26. And there died on that day one thousand and one hundred men of the people of the city, all that inhabited the city, but of the people besieging not one died.

27. So all the children of Cush went each to his home, to his wife and children and to all belonging to him.

28. And Balaam the magician, when he saw that the city was taken, he opened the gate and he and his two sons and eight brothers fled and returned to Egypt to Pharaoh king of Egypt.

29. They are the sorcerers and magicians who are mentioned in the book of the law, standing against Moses when the Lord brought the plagues upon Egypt.

30. So Moses took the city by his wisdom, and the children of Cush placed him on the throne instead of Kikianus king of Cush.

31. And they placed the royal crown upon his head, and they gave him for a wife Adoniah the Cushite queen, wife of Kikianus.

32. And Moses feared the Lord God of his fathers, so that he came not to her, nor did he turn his eyes to her.

33. For Moses remembered how Abraham had made his servant Eliezer swear, saying unto him, Thou shalt not take a woman from the daughters of Canaan for my son Isaac.

34. Also what Isaac did when Jacob had fled from his brother, when he commanded him, saying, Thou shalt not take a wife from the daughters of Canaan, nor make alliance with any of the children of Ham.

35. For the Lord our God gave Ham the son of Noah, and his children and all his seed, as slaves to the children of Shem and to the children of Japheth, and unto their seed after them for slaves, forever.

36. Therefore Moses turned not his heart nor his eyes to the wife of Kikianus all the days that he reigned over Cush.

37. And Moses feared the Lord his God all his life, and Moses walked before the Lord in truth, with all his heart and soul, he turned not from the right way all the days of his life; he declined not from the way either to the right or to the left, in which Abraham, Isaac and Jacob had walked.

38. And Moses strengthened himself in the kingdom of the children of Cush, and he guided the children of Cush with his usual wisdom, and Moses prospered in his kingdom.

39. And at that time Aram and the children of the east heard that Kikianus king of Cush had died, so Aram and the children of the east rebelled against Cush in those days.

40. And Moses gathered all the children of Cush, a people very mighty, about thirty thousand men, and he went forth to fight with Aram and the children of the east.

41. And they went at first to the children of the east, and when the children of the east heard their report, they went to meet them, and engaged in battle with them.

42. And the war was severe against the children of the east, so the Lord gave all the children of the east into the hand of Moses, and about three hundred men fell down slain.

43. And all the children of the east turned back and retreated, so Moses and the children of Cush followed them and subdued them, and put a tax upon them, as was their custom.

44. So Moses and all the people with him passed from there to the land of Aram for battle.

45. And the people of Aram also went to meet them, and they fought against them, and the Lord delivered them into the hand of Moses, and many of the men of Aram fell down wounded.

46. And Aram also were subdued by Moses and the people of Cush, and also gave their usual tax.

47. And Moses brought Aram and the children of the east under subjection to the children of Cush, and Moses and all the people who were with him, turned to the land of Cush.

48. And Moses strengthened himself in the kingdom of the children of Cush, and the Lord was with him, and all the children of Cush were afraid of him.

CHAPTER 74

1. In the end of years died Saul king of Edom, and Baal Chanan the son of Achbor reigned in his place.

2. In the sixteenth year of the reign of Moses over Cush, Baal Chanan the son of Achbor reigned in the land of Edom over all the children of Edom for thirty-eight years.

3. In his days Moab rebelled against the power of Edom, having been under Edom since the days of Hadad the son of Bedad, who smote them and Midian, and brought Moab under subjection to Edom.

4. And when Baal Chanan the son of Achbor reigned over Edom, all the children of Moab withdrew their allegiance from Edom.

5. And Angeas king of Africa died in those days, and Azdrubal his son reigned in his stead.

6. And in those days died Janeas king of the children of Chittim, and they buried him in his temple which he had built for himself in the plain of Canopia for a residence, and Latinus reigned in his stead.

7. In the twenty-second year of the reign of Moses over the children of Cush, Latinus reigned over the children of Chittim forty-five years.

8. And he also built for himself a great and mighty tower, and he built therein an elegant temple for his residence, to conduct his government, as was the custom.

9. In the third year of his reign he caused a proclamation to be made to all his skilful men, who made many ships for him.

10. And Latinus assembled all his forces, and they came in ships, and went therein to fight with Azdrubal son of Angeas king of Africa, and they came to Africa and engaged in battle with Azdrubal and his army.

11. And Latinus prevailed over Azdrubal, and Latinus took from Azdrubal the aqueduct which his father had brought from the children of Chittim, when he took Janiah the daughter of Uzi for a wife, so Latinus overthrew the bridge of the aqueduct, and smote the whole army of Azdrubal a severe blow.

12. And the remaining strong men of Azdrubal strengthened themselves, and their hearts were filled with envy, and they courted death, and again engaged in battle with Latinus king of Chittim.

13. And the battle was severe upon all the men of Africa, and they all fell wounded before Latinus and his people, and Azdrubal the king also fell in that battle.

14. And the king Azdrubal had a very beautiful daughter, whose name was Ushpezena, and all the men of Africa embroidered her likeness on their garments, on account of her great beauty and comely appearance.

15. And the men of Latinus saw Ushpezena, the daughter of Azdrubal, and praised her unto Latinus their king.

16. And Latinus ordered her to be brought to him, and Latinus took Ushpezena for a wife, and he turned back on his way to Chittim.

17. And it was after the death of Azdrubal son of Angeas, when Latinus had turned back to his land from the battle, that all the inhabitants of Africa rose up and took Anibal the son of Angeas, the younger brother of Azdrubal, and made him king instead at his brother over the whole land at Africa.

18. And when he reigned, he resolved to go to Chittim to fight with the children of Chittim, to avenge the cause of Azdrubal his brother, and the cause of the inhabitants of Africa, and he did so.

19. And he made many ships, and he came therein with his whole army, and he went to Chittim.

20. So Anibal fought with the children of Chittim, and the children of Chittim fell wounded before Anibal and his army, and Anibal avenged his brother's cause.

21. And Anibal continued the war for eighteen years with the children of Chittim, and Anibal dwelt in the land of Chittim and encamped there for a long time.

22. And Anibal smote the children of Chittim very severely, and he slew their great men and princes, and of the rest of the people he smote about eighty thousand men.

23. And at the end of days and years, Anibal returned to his land of Africa, and he reigned securely in the place of Azdrubal his brother.

CHAPTER 75

1. At that time, in the hundred and eightieth year of the Israelites going down into Egypt, there went forth from Egypt valiant men, thirty thousand on foot, from the children of Israel, who were all of the tribe of Joseph, of the children of Ephraim the son of Joseph.

2. For they said the period was completed which the Lord had appointed to the children of Israel in the times of old, which he had spoken to Abraham.

3. And these men girded themselves, and they put each man his sword at his side, and every man his armor upon him, and they trusted to their strength, and they went out together from Egypt with a mighty hand.

4. But they brought no provision for the road, only silver and gold, not even bread for that day did they bring in their hands, for they thought of getting their provision for pay from the Philistines, and if not they would take it by force.

5. And these men were very mighty and valiant men, one man could pursue a thousand and two could rout ten thousand, so they trusted to their strength and went together as they were.

6. And they directed their course toward the land of Gath, and they went down and found the shepherds of Gath feeding the cattle of the children of Gath.

7. And they said to the shepherds, Give us some of the sheep for pay, that we may eat, for we are hungry, for we have eaten no bread this day.

8. And the shepherds said, Are they our sheep or cattle that we should give them to you even for pay? so the children of Ephraim approached to take them by force.

9. And the shepherds of Gath shouted over them that their cry was heard at a distance, so all the children of Gath went out to them.

10. And when the children of Gath saw the evil doings of the children of Ephraim, they returned and assembled the men of Gath, and they put on each man his armor, and came forth to the children of Ephraim for battle.

11. And they engaged with them in the valley of Gath, and the battle was severe, and they smote from each other a great many on that day.

12. And on the second day the children of Gath sent to all the cities of the Philistines that they should come to their help, saying,

13. Come up unto us and help us, that we may smite the children of Ephraim who have come forth from Egypt to take our cattle, and to fight against us without cause.

14. Now the souls of the children of Ephraim were exhausted with hunger and thirst, for they had eaten no bread for three days. And forty thousand men went forth from the cities of the Philistines to the assistance of the men of Gath.

15. And these men were engaged in battle with the children of Ephraim, and the Lord delivered the children of Ephraim into the hands of the Philistines.

16. And they smote all the children of Ephraim, all who had gone forth from Egypt, none were remaining but ten men who had run away from the engagement.

17. For this evil was from the Lord against the children of Ephraim, for they transgressed the word of the Lord in going forth from Egypt, before the period had arrived which the Lord in the days of old had appointed to Israel.

18. And of the Philistines also there fell a great many, about twenty thousand men, and their brethren carried them and buried them in their cities.

19. And the slain of the children of Ephraim remained forsaken in the valley of Gath for many days and years, and were not brought to burial, and the valley was filled with men's bones.

20. And the men who had escaped from the battle came to Egypt, and told all the children of Israel all that had befallen them.

21. And their father Ephraim mourned over them for many days, and his brethren came to console him.

22. And he came unto his wife and she bare a son, and he called his name Beriah, for she was unfortunate in his house.

CHAPTER 76

1. And Moses the son of Amram was still king in the land of Cush in those days, and he prospered in his kingdom, and he conducted the government of the children of Cush in justice, in righteousness, and integrity.

2. And all the children of Cush loved Moses all the days that he reigned over them, and all the inhabitants of the land of Cush were greatly afraid of him.

3. And in the fortieth year of the reign of Moses over Cush, Moses was sitting on the royal throne whilst Adoniah the queen was before him, and all the nobles were sitting around him.

4. And Adoniah the queen said before the king and the princes, What is this thing which you, the children of Cush, have done for this long time?

5. Surely you know that for forty years that this man has reigned over Cush he has not approached me, nor has he served the gods of the children of Cush.

6. Now therefore hear, O ye children of Cush, and let this man no more reign over you as he is not of our flesh.

7. Behold Menacrus my son is grown up, let him reign over you, for it is better for you to serve the son of your lord, than to serve a stranger, slave of the king of Egypt.

8. And all the people and nobles of the children of Cush heard the words which Adoniah the queen had spoken in their ears.

9. And all the people were preparing until the evening, and in the morning they rose up early and made Menacrus, son of Kikianus, king over them.

10. And all the children of Cush were afraid to stretch forth their hand against Moses, for the Lord was with Moses, and the children of Cush remembered the oath which they swore unto Moses, therefore they did no harm to him.

11. But the children of Cush gave many presents to Moses, and sent him from them with great honor.

12. So Moses went forth from the land of Cush, and went home and ceased to reign over Cush, and Moses was sixty-six years old when he went out of the land of Cush, for the thing was from the Lord, for the period had arrived which he had appointed in the days of old, to bring forth Israel from the affliction of the children of Ham.

13. So Moses went to Midian, for he was afraid to return to Egypt on account of Pharaoh, and he went and sat at a well of water in Midian.

14. And the seven daughters of Reuel the Midianite went out to feed their father's flock.

15. And they came to the well and drew water to water their father's flock.

16. So the shepherds of Midian came and drove them away, and Moses rose up and helped them and watered the flock.

17. And they came home to their father Reuel, and told him what Moses did for them.

18. And they said, An Egyptian man has delivered us from the hands of the shepherds, he drew up water for us and watered the flock.

19. And Reuel said to his daughters, And where is he? wherefore have you left the man?

20. And Reuel sent for him and fetched him and brought him home, and he ate bread with him.

21. And Moses related to Reuel that he had fled from Egypt and that he reigned forty years over Cush, and that they afterward had taken the government from him, and had sent him away in peace with honor and with presents.

22. And when Reuel had heard the words of Moses, Reuel said within himself, I will put this man into the prison house, whereby I shall conciliate the children of Cush, for he has fled from them.

23. And they took and put him into the prison house, and Moses was in prison ten years, and whilst Moses was in the prison house, Zipporah the daughter of Reuel took pity over him, and supported him with bread and water all the time.

24. And all the children of Israel were yet in the land of Egypt serving the Egyptians in all manner of hard work, and the hand of Egypt continued in severity over the children of Israel in those days.

25. At that time the Lord smote Pharaoh king of Egypt, and he afflicted with the plague of leprosy from the sole of his foot to the crown of his head; owing to the cruel treatment of the children of Israel was this plague at that time from the Lord upon Pharaoh king of Egypt.

26. For the Lord had hearkened to the prayer of his people the children of Israel, and their cry reached him on account of their hard work.

27. Still his anger did not turn from them, and the hand of Pharaoh was still stretched out against the children of Israel, and Pharaoh hardened his neck before the Lord, and he increased his yoke over the children of Israel, and embittered their lives with all manner of hard work.

28. And when the Lord had inflicted the plague upon Pharaoh king of Egypt, he asked his wise men and sorcerers to cure him.

29. And his wise men and sorcerers said unto him, That if the blood of little children were put into the wounds he would be healed.

30. And Pharaoh hearkened to them, and sent his ministers to Goshen to the children of Israel to take their little children.

31. And Pharaoh's ministers went and took the infants of the children of Israel from the bosoms of their mothers by force, and they brought them to Pharaoh daily, a child each day, and the physicians killed them and applied them to the plague; thus did they all the days.

32. And the number of the children which Pharaoh slew was three hundred and seventy-five.

33. But the Lord hearkened not to the physicians of the king of Egypt, and the plague went on increasing mightily.

34. And Pharaoh was ten years afflicted with that plague, still the heart of Pharaoh was more hardened against the children of Israel.

35. And at the end of ten years the Lord continued to afflict Pharaoh with destructive plagues.

36. And the Lord smote him with a bad tumor and sickness at the stomach, and that plague turned to a severe boil.

37. At that time the two ministers of Pharaoh came from the land of Goshen where all the children of Israel were, and went to the house of Pharaoh and said to him, We have seen the children of Israel slacken in their work and negligent in their labor.

38. And when Pharaoh heard the words of his ministers, his anger was kindled against the children of Israel exceedingly, for he was greatly grieved at his bodily pain.

39. And he answered and said, Now that the children of Israel know that I am ill, they turn and scoff at us, now therefore harness my chariot for me, and I will betake myself to Goshen and will see the scoff of the children of Israel with which they are deriding me; so his servants harnessed the chariot for him.

40. And they took and made him ride upon a horse, for he was not able to ride of himself;

41. And he took with him ten horsemen and ten footmen, and went to the children of Israel to Goshen.

42. And when they had come to the border of Egypt, the king's horse passed into a narrow place, elevated in the hollow part of the vineyard, fenced on both sides, the low, plain country being on the other side.

43. And the horses ran rapidly in that place and pressed each other, and the other horses pressed the king's horse.

44. And the king's horse fell into the low plain whilst the king was riding upon it, and when he fell the chariot turned over the king's face and the horse lay upon the king, and the king cried out, for his flesh was very sore.

45. And the flesh of the king was torn from him, and his bones were broken and he could not ride, for this thing was from the Lord to him, for the Lord had heard the cries of his people the children of Israel and their affliction.

46. And his servants carried him upon their shoulders, a little at a time, and they brought him back to Egypt, and the horsemen who were with him came also back to Egypt.

47. And they placed him in his bed, and the king knew that his end was come to die, so Aparanith the queen his wife came and cried before the king, and the king wept a great weeping with her.

48. And all his nobles and servants came on that day and saw the king in that affliction, and wept a great weeping with him.

49. And the princes of the king and all his counselors advised the king to cause one to reign in his stead in the land, whomsoever he should choose from his sons.

50. And the king had three sons and two daughters which Aparanith the queen his wife had borne to him, besides the king's children of concubines.

51. And these were their names, the firstborn Othri, the second Adikam, and the third Morion, and their sisters, the name of the elder Bathia and of the other Acuzi.

52. And Othri the first born of the king was an idiot, precipitate and hurried in his words.

53. But Adikam was a cunning and wise man and knowing in all the wisdom of Egypt, but of unseemly aspect, thick in flesh, and very short in stature; his height was one cubit.

54. And when the king saw Adikam his son intelligent and wise in all things, the king resolved that he should be king in his stead after his death.

55. And he took for him a wife Gedudah daughter of Abilot, and he was ten years old, and she bare unto him four sons.

56. And he afterward went and took three wives and begat eight sons and three daughters.

57. And the disorder greatly prevailed over the king, and his flesh stank like the flesh of a carcass cast upon the field in summer time, during the heat of the sun.

58. And when the king saw that his sickness had greatly strengthened itself over him, he ordered his son Adikam to be brought to him, and they made him king over the land in his place.

59. And at the end of three years, the king died, in shame, disgrace, and disgust, and his servants carried him and buried him in the sepulcher of the kings of Egypt in Zoan Mizraim.

60. But they embalmed him not as was usual with kings, for his flesh was putrid, and they could not approach to embalm him on account of the stench, so they buried him in haste.

61. For this evil was from the Lord to him, for the Lord had requited him evil for the evil which in his days he had done to Israel.

62. And he died with terror and with shame, and his son Adikam reigned in his place.<

CHAPTER 77

1. Adikam was twenty years old when he reigned over Egypt, he reigned four years.

2. In the two hundred and sixth year of Israel's going down to Egypt did Adikam reign over Egypt, but he continued not so long in his reign over Egypt as his fathers had continued their reigns.

3. For Melol his father reigned ninety-four years in Egypt, but he was ten years sick and died, for he had been wicked before the Lord.

4. And all the Egyptians called the name of Adikam Pharaoh like the name of his fathers, as was their custom to do in Egypt.

5. And all the wise men of Pharaoh called the name of Adikam Ahuz, for short is called Ahuz in the Egyptian language.

6. And Adikam was exceedingly ugly, and he was a cubit and a span and he had a great beard which reached to the soles of his feet.

7.   And Pharaoh sat upon his father's throne to reign over Egypt, and he conducted the government of Egypt in his wisdom.

8.   And whilst he reigned he exceeded his father and all the preceding kings in wickedness, and he increased his yoke over the children of Israel.

9.   And he went with his servants to Goshen to the children of Israel, and he strengthened the labor over them and he said unto them, Complete your work, each day's task, and let not your hands slacken from our work from this day forward as you did in the days of my father.

10. And he placed officers over them from amongst the children of Israel, and over these officers he placed taskmasters from amongst his servants.

11. And he placed over them a measure of bricks for them to do according to that number, day by day, and he turned back and went to Egypt.

12. At that time the task-masters of Pharaoh ordered the officers of the children of Israel according to the command of Pharaoh, saying,

13. Thus says Pharaoh, Do your work each day, and finish your task, and observe the daily measure of bricks; diminish not anything.

14. And it shall come to pass that if you are deficient in your daily bricks, I will put your young children in their stead.

15. And the task-masters of Egypt did so in those days as Pharaoh had ordered them.

16. And whenever any deficiency was found in the children of Israel's measure of their daily bricks, the task-masters of Pharaoh would go to the wives of the children of Israel and take infants of the children of Israel to the number of bricks deficient, they would take them by force from their mother's laps, and put them in the building instead of the bricks;

17. Whilst their fathers and mothers were crying over them and weeping when they heard the weeping voices of their infants in the wall of the building.

18. And the task-masters prevailed over Israel, that the Israelites should place their children in the building, so that a man placed his son in the wall and put mortar over him, whilst his eyes wept over him, and his tears ran down upon his child.

19. And the task-masters of Egypt did so to the babes of Israel for many days, and no one pitied or had compassion over the babes of the children of Israel.

20. And the number of all the children killed in the building was two hundred and seventy, some whom they had built upon instead of the bricks which had been left deficient by their fathers, and some whom they had drawn out dead from the building.

21. And the labor imposed upon the children of Israel in the days of Adikam exceeded in hardship that which they performed in the days of his father.

22. And the children of Israel sighed every day on account of their heavy work, for they had said to themselves, Behold when Pharaoh shall die, his son will rise up and lighten our work!

23. But they increased the latter work more than the former, and the children of Israel sighed at this and their cry ascended to God on account of their labor.

24. And God heard the voice of the children of Israel and their cry, in those days, and God remembered to them his covenant which he had made with Abraham, Isaac and Jacob.

25. And God saw the burden of the children of Israel, and their heavy work in those days, and he determined to deliver them.

26. And Moses the son of Amram was still confined in the dungeon in those days, in the house of Reuel the Midianite, and Zipporah the daughter of Reuel did support him with food secretly day by day.

27. And Moses was confined in the dungeon in the house of Reuel for ten years.

28. And at the end of ten years which was the first year of the reign of Pharaoh over Egypt, in the place of his father,

29. Zipporah said to her father Reuel, No person inquires or seeks after the Hebrew man, whom thou didst bind in prison now ten years.

30. Now therefore, if it seem good in thy sight, let us send and see whether he is living or dead, but her father knew not that she had supported him.

31. And Reuel her father answered and said to her, Has ever such a thing happened that a man should be shut up in a prison without food for ten years, and that he should live?

32. And Zipporah answered her father, saying, Surely thou hast heard that the God of the Hebrews is great and awful, and does wonders for them at all times.

33. He it was who delivered Abraham from Ur of the Chaldeans, and Isaac from the sword of his father, and Jacob from the angel of the Lord who wrestled with him at the ford of Jabbuk.

34. Also with this man has he done many things, he delivered him from the river in Egypt and from the sword of Pharaoh, and from the children of Cush, so also can he deliver him from famine and make him live.

35. And the thing seemed good in the sight of Reuel, and he did according to the word of his daughter, and sent to the dungeon to ascertain what became of Moses.

36. And he saw, and behold the man Moses was living in the dungeon, standing upon his feet, praising and praying to the God of his ancestors.

37. And Reuel commanded Moses to be brought out of the dungeon, so they shaved him and he changed his prison garments and ate bread.

38. And afterward Moses went into the garden of Reuel which was behind the house, and he there prayed to the Lord his God, who had done mighty wonders for him.

39. And it was that whilst he prayed he looked opposite to him, and behold a sapphire stick was placed in the ground, which was planted in the midst of the garden.

40. And he approached the stick and he looked, and behold the name of the Lord God of hosts was engraved thereon, written and developed upon the stick.

41. And he read it and stretched forth his hand and he plucked it like a forest tree from the thicket, and the stick was in his hand.

42. And this is the stick with which all the works of our God were performed, after he had created heaven and earth, and all the host of them, seas, rivers and all their fishes.

43. And when God had driven Adam from the garden of Eden, he took the stick in his hand and went and tilled the ground from which he was taken.

44. And the stick came down to Noah and was given to Shem and his descendants, until it came into the hand of Abraham the Hebrew.

45. And when Abraham had given all he had to his son Isaac, he also gave to him this stick.

46. And when Jacob had fled to Padan-aram, he took it into his hand, and when he returned to his father he had not left it behind him.

47. Also when he went down to Egypt he took it into his hand and gave it to Joseph, one portion above his brethren, for Jacob had taken it by force from his brother Esau.

48. And after the death of Joseph, the nobles of Egypt came into the house of Joseph, and the stick came into the hand of Reuel the Midianite, and when he went out of Egypt, he took it in his hand and planted it in his garden.

49. And all the mighty men of the Kinites tried to pluck it when they endeavored to get Zipporah his daughter, but they were unsuccessful.

50. So that stick remained planted in the garden of Reuel, until he came who had a right to it and took it.

51. And when Reuel saw the stick in the hand of Moses, he wondered at it, and he gave him his daughter Zipporah for a wife.

CHAPTER 78

1. At that time died Baal Channan son of Achbor, king of Edom, and was buried in his house in the land of Edom.

2. And after his death the children of Esau sent to the land of Edom, and took from there a man who was in Edom, whose name was Hadad, and they made him king over them in the place of Baal Channan, their king.

3. And Hadad reigned over the children of Edom forty-eight years.

4. And when he reigned he resolved to fight against the children of Moab, to bring them under the power of the children of Esau as they were before, but he was not able, because the children of Moab heard this thing, and they rose up and hastened to elect a king over them from amongst their brethren.

5. And they afterward gathered together a great people, and sent to the children of Ammon their brethren for help to fight against Hadad king of Edom.

6. And Hadad heard the thing which the children of Moab had done, and was greatly afraid of them, and refrained from fighting against them.

7. In those days Moses, the son of Amram, in Midian, took Zipporah, the daughter of Reuel the Midianite, for a wife.

8. And Zipporah walked in the ways of the daughters of Jacob, she was nothing short of the righteousness of Sarah, Rebecca, Rachel and Leah.

9. And Zipporah conceived and bare a son and he called his name Gershom, for he said, I was a stranger in a foreign land; but he circumcised not his foreskin, at the command of Reuel his father-in-law.

10. And she conceived again and bare a son, but circumcised his foreskin, and called his name Eliezer, for Moses said, Because the God of my fathers was my help, and delivered me from the sword of Pharaoh.

11. And Pharaoh king of Egypt greatly increased the labor of the children of Israel in those days, and continued to make his yoke heavier upon the children of Israel.

12. And he ordered a proclamation to be made in Egypt, saying, Give no more straw to the people to make bricks with, let them go and gather themselves straw as they can find it.

13. Also the tale of bricks which they shall make let them give each day, and diminish nothing from them, for they are idle in their work.

14. And the children of Israel heard this, and they mourned and sighed, and they cried unto the Lord on account of the bitterness of their souls.

15. And the Lord heard the cries of the children of Israel, and saw the oppression with which the Egyptians oppressed them.

16. And the Lord was jealous of his people and his inheritance, and heard their voice, and he resolved to take them out of the affliction of Egypt, to give them the land of Canaan for a possession.

CHAPTER 79

1. And in those days Moses was feeding the flock of Reuel the Midianite his father-in-law, beyond the wilderness of Sin, and the stick which he took from his father-in-law was in his hand.

2. And it came to pass one day that a kid of goats strayed from the flock, and Moses pursued it and it came to the mountain of God to Horeb.

3. And when he came to Horeb, the Lord appeared there unto him in the bush, and he found the bush burning with fire, but the fire had no power over the bush to consume it.

4. And Moses was greatly astonished at this sight, wherefore the bush was not consumed, and he approached to see this mighty thing, and the Lord called unto Moses out of the fire and commanded him to go down to Egypt, to Pharaoh king of Egypt, to send the children of Israel from his service.

5. And the Lord said unto Moses, Go, return to Egypt, for all those men who sought thy life are dead, and thou shalt speak unto Pharaoh to send forth the children of Israel from his land.

6. And the Lord showed him to do signs and wonders in Egypt before the eyes of Pharaoh and the eyes of his subjects, in order that they might believe that the Lord had sent him.

7. And Moses hearkened to all that the Lord had commanded him, and he returned to his father-in-law and told him the thing, and Reuel said to him, Go in peace.

8. And Moses rose up to go to Egypt, and he took his wife and sons with him, and he was at an inn in the road, and an angel of God came down, and sought an occasion against him.

9. And he wished to kill him on account of his first born son, because he had not circumcised him, and had transgressed the covenant which the Lord had made with Abraham.

10. For Moses had hearkened to the words of his father-in-law which he had spoken to him, not to circumcise his first born son, therefore he circumcised him not.

11. And Zipporah saw the angel of the Lord seeking an occasion against Moses, and she knew that this thing was owing to his not having circumcised her son Gershom.

12. And Zipporah hastened and took of the sharp rock stones that were there, and she circumcised her son, and delivered her husband and her son from the hand of the angel of the Lord.

13. And Aaron the son of Amram, the brother of Moses, was in Egypt walking at the river side on that day.

14. And the Lord appeared to him in that place, and he said to him, Go now toward Moses in the wilderness, and he went and met him in the mountain of God, and he kissed him.

15. And Aaron lifted up his eyes, and saw Zipporah the wife of Moses and her children, and he said unto Moses, Who are these unto thee?

16. And Moses said unto him, They are my wife and sons, which God gave to me in Midian; and the thing grieved Aaron on account of the woman and her children.

17. And Aaron said to Moses, Send away the woman and her children that they may go to her father's house, and Moses hearkened to the words of Aaron, and did so.

18. And Zipporah returned with her children, and they went to the house of Reuel, and remained there until the time arrived when the Lord had visited his people, and brought them forth from Egypt from the hand at Pharaoh.

19. And Moses and Aaron came to Egypt to the community of the children of Israel, and they spoke to them all the words of the Lord, and the people rejoiced an exceeding great rejoicing.

20. And Moses and Aaron rose up early on the next day, and they went to the house of Pharaoh, and they took in their hands the stick of God.

21. And when they came to the king's gate, two young lions were confined there with iron instruments, and no person went out or came in from before them, unless those whom the king ordered to come, when the conjurors came and withdrew the lions by their incantations, and this brought them to the king.

22. And Moses hastened and lifted up the stick upon the lions, and he loosed them, and Moses and Aaron came into the king's house.

23. The lions also came with them in joy, and they followed them and rejoiced as a dog rejoices over his master when he comes from the field.

24. And when Pharaoh saw this thing he was astonished at it, and he was greatly terrified at the report, for their appearance was like the appearance of the children of God.

25. And Pharaoh said to Moses, What do you require? and they answered him, saying, The Lord God of the Hebrews has sent us to thee, to say, Send forth my people that they may serve me.

26. And when Pharaoh heard their words he was greatly terrified before them, and he said to them, Go today and come back to me tomorrow, and they did according to the word

of the king.

27. And when they had gone Pharaoh sent for Balaam the magician and to Jannes and Jambres his sons, and to all the magicians and conjurors and counsellors which belonged to the king, and they all came and sat before the king.

28. And the king told them all the words which Moses and his brother Aaron had spoken to him, and the magicians said to the king, But how came the men to thee, on account of the lions which were confined at the gate?

29. And the king said, Because they lifted up their rod against the lions and loosed them, and came to me, and the lions also rejoiced at them as a dog rejoices to meet his master.

30. And Balaam the son of Beor the magician answered the king, saying, These are none else than magicians like ourselves.

31. Now therefore send for them, and let them come and we will try them, and the king did so.

32. And in the morning Pharaoh sent for Moses and Aaron to come before the king, and they took the rod of God, and came to the king and spoke to him, saying,

33. Thus said the Lord God of the Hebrews, Send my people that they may serve me.

34. And the king said to them, But who will believe you that you are the messengers of God and that you come to me by his order?

35. Now therefore give a wonder or sign in this matter, and then the words which you speak will be believed.

36. And Aaron hastened and threw the rod out of his hand before Pharaoh and before his servants, and the rod turned into a serpent.

37. And the sorcerers saw this and they cast each man his rod upon the ground and they became serpents.

38. And the serpent of Aaron's rod lifted up its head and opened its mouth to swallow the rods of the magicians.

39. And Balaam the magician answered and said, This thing has been from the days of old, that a serpent should swallow its fellow, and that living things devour each other.

40. Now therefore restore it to a rod as it was at first, and we will also restore our rods as they were at first, and if thy rod shall swallow our rods, then shall we know that the spirit of God is in thee, and if not, thou art only an artificer like unto ourselves.

41. And Aaron hastened and stretched forth his hand and caught hold of the serpent's tail and it became a rod in his hand, and the sorcerers did the like with their rods, and they got hold, each man of the tail of his serpent, and they became rods as at first.

42. And when they were restored to rods, the rod of Aaron swallowed up their rods.

43. And when the king saw this thing, he ordered the book of records that related to the kings of Egypt, to be brought, and they brought the book of records, the chronicles of the kings of Egypt, in which all the idols of Egypt were inscribed, for they thought of finding therein the name of Jehovah, but they found it not.

44. And Pharaoh said to Moses and Aaron, Behold I have not found the name of your God written in this book, and his name I know not.

45. And the counsellors and wise men answered the king, We have heard that the God of the Hebrews is a son of the wise, the son of ancient kings.

46. And Pharaoh turned to Moses and Aaron and said to them, I know not the Lord whom you have declared, neither will I send his people.

47. And they answered and said to the king, The Lord God of Gods is his name, and he proclaimed his name over us from the days of our ancestors, and sent us, saying, Go to Pharaoh and say unto him, Send my people that they may serve me.

48. Now therefore send us, that we may take a journey for three days in the wilderness, and there may sacrifice to him, for from the days of our going down to Egypt, he has not taken from our hands either burnt offering, oblation or sacrifice, and if thou wilt not send us, his anger will be kindled against thee, and he will smite Egypt either with the plague or with the sword.

49. And Pharaoh said to them, Tell me now his power and his might; and they said to him, He created the heaven and the earth, the seas and all their fishes, he formed the light, created the darkness, caused rain upon the earth and watered it, and made the herbage and grass to sprout, he created man and beast and the animals of the forest, the birds of the air and the fish of the sea, and by his mouth they live and die.

50. Surely he created thee in thy mother's womb, and put into thee the breath of life, and reared thee and placed thee upon the royal throne of Egypt, and he will take thy breath and soul from thee, and return thee to the ground whence thou wast taken.

51. And the anger of the king was kindled at their words, and he said to them, But who amongst all the Gods of nations can do this? my river is mine own, and I have made it for myself.

52. And he drove them from him, and he ordered the labor upon Israel to be more severe than it was yesterday and before.

53. And Moses and Aaron went out from the king's presence, and they saw the children of Israel in an evil condition for the task-masters had made their labor exceedingly heavy.

54. And Moses returned to the Lord and said, Why hast thou ill treated thy people? for since I came to speak to Pharaoh what thou didst send me for, he has exceedingly ill used the children of Israel.

55. And the Lord said to Moses, Behold thou wilt see that with an outstretched hand and heavy plagues, Pharaoh will send the children of Israel from his land.

56. And Moses and Aaron dwelt amongst their brethren the children of Israel in Egypt.

57. And as for the children of Israel the Egyptians embittered their lives, with the heavy work which they imposed upon them.

CHAPTER 80

1. And at the end of two years, the Lord again sent Moses to Pharaoh to bring forth the children of Israel, and to send them out of the land of Egypt.

2. And Moses went and came to the house of Pharaoh, and he spoke to him the words of the Lord who had sent him, but Pharaoh would not hearken to the voice of the Lord, and God roused his might in Egypt upon Pharaoh and his subjects, and God smote Pharaoh and his people with very great and sore plagues.

3. And the Lord sent by the hand of Aaron and turned all the waters of Egypt into blood, with all their streams and rivers.

4. And when an Egyptian came to drink and draw water, he looked into his pitcher, and behold all the water was turned into blood; and when he came to drink from his cup the water in the cup became blood.

5. And when a woman kneaded her dough and cooked her victuals, their appearance was turned to that of blood.

6. And the Lord sent again and caused all their waters to bring forth frogs, and all the frogs came into the houses of the Egyptians.

7. And when the Egyptians drank, their bellies were filled with frogs and they danced in their bellies as they dance when in the river.

8. And all their drinking water and cooking water turned to frogs, also when they lay in their beds their perspiration bred frogs.

9. Notwithstanding all this the anger of the Lord did not turn from them, and his hand was stretched out against all the Egyptians to smite them with every heavy plague.

10. And he sent and smote their dust to lice, and the lice became in Egypt to the height of two cubits upon the earth.

11. The lice were also very numerous, in the flesh of man and beast, in all the inhabitants of Egypt, also upon the king and queen the Lord sent the lice, and it grieved Egypt exceedingly on account of the lice.

12. Notwithstanding this, the anger of the Lord did not turn away, and his hand was still stretched out over Egypt.

13. And the Lord sent all kinds of beasts of the field into Egypt, and they came and destroyed all Egypt, man and beast, and trees, and all things that were in Egypt.

14. And the Lord sent fiery serpents, scorpions, mice, weasels, toads, together with others creeping in dust.

15. Flies, hornets, fleas, bugs and gnats, each swarm according to its kind.

16. And all reptiles and winged animals according to their kind came to Egypt and grieved the Egyptians exceedingly.

17. And the fleas and flies came into the eyes and ears of the Egyptians.

18. And the hornet came upon them and drove them away, and they removed from it into their inner rooms, and it pursued them.

19. And when the Egyptians hid themselves on account of the swarm of animals, they locked their doors after them, and God ordered the Sulanuth which was in the sea, to come up and go into Egypt.

20. And she had long arms, ten cubits in length of the cubit of a man.

21. And she went upon the roofs and uncovered the raftering and flooring and cut them, and stretched forth her arm into the house and removed the lock and the bolt, and opened the houses of Egypt.

22. Afterward came the swarm of animals into the houses of Egypt, and the swarm of animals destroyed the Egyptians, and it grieved them exceedingly.

23. Notwithstanding this the anger of the Lord did not turn away from the Egyptians, and his hand was yet stretched forth against them.

24. And God sent the pestilence, and the pestilence pervaded Egypt, in the horses and asses, and in the camels, in herds of oxen and sheep and in man.

25. And when the Egyptians rose up early in the morning to take their cattle to pasture they found all their cattle dead.

26. And there remained of the cattle of the Egyptians only one in ten, and of the cattle belonging to Israel in Goshen not one died.

27. And God sent a burning inflammation in the flesh of the Egyptians, which burst their skins, and it became a severe itch in all the Egyptians from the soles of their feet to the crowns of their heads.

28. And many boils were in their flesh, that their flesh wasted away until they became rotten and putrid.

29. Notwithstanding this the anger of the Lord did not turn away, and his hand was still stretched out over all Egypt.

30. And the Lord sent a very heavy hail, which smote their vines and broke their fruit trees and dried them up that they fell upon them.

31. Also every green herb became dry and perished, for a mingling fire descended amidst the hail, therefore the hail and the fire consumed all things.

32. Also men and beasts that were found abroad perished of the flames of fire and of the hail, and all the young lions were exhausted.

33. And the Lord sent and brought numerous locusts into Egypt, the Chasel, Salom, Chargol, and Chagole, locusts each of its kind, which devoured all that the hail had left remaining.

34. Then the Egyptians rejoiced at the locusts, although they consumed the produce of the field, and they caught them in abundance and salted them for food.

35. And the Lord turned a mighty wind of the sea which took away all the locusts, even those that were salted, and thrust them into the Red Sea; not one locust remained within the boundaries of Egypt.

36. And God sent darkness upon Egypt, that the whole land of Egypt and Pathros became dark for three days, so that a man could not see his hand when he lifted it to his mouth.

37. At that time died many of the people of Israel who had rebelled against the Lord and who would not hearken to Moses and Aaron, and believed not in them that God had sent them.

38. And who had said, We will not go forth from Egypt lest we perish with hunger in a desolate wilderness, and who would not hearken to the voice of Moses.

39. And the Lord plagued them in the three days of darkness, and the Israelites buried them in those days, without the Egyptians knowing of them or rejoicing over them.

40. And the darkness was very great in Egypt for three days, and any person who was standing when the darkness came, remained standing in his place, and he that was sitting remained sitting, and he that was lying continued lying in the same state, and he that was walking remained sitting upon the ground in the same spot; and this thing happened to all the Egyptians, until the darkness had passed away.

41. And the days of darkness passed away, and the Lord sent Moses and Aaron to the children of Israel, saying, Celebrate your feast and make your Passover, for behold I come in the midst of the night amongst all the Egyptians, and I will smite all their first born, from the first born of a man to the first born of a beast, and when I see your Passover, I will pass over you.

42. And the children of Israel did according to all that the Lord had commanded Moses and Aaron, thus did they in that night.

43. And it came to pass in the middle of the night, that the Lord went forth in the midst of Egypt, and smote all the first born of the Egyptians, from the first born of man to the first born of beast.

44. And Pharaoh rose up in the night, he and all his servants and all the Egyptians, and there was a great cry throughout Egypt in that night, for there was not a house in which there was not a corpse.

45. Also the likenesses of the first born of Egypt, which were carved in the walls at their houses, were destroyed and fell to the ground.

46. Even the bones of their first born who had died before this and whom they had buried in their houses, were raked up by the dogs of Egypt on that night and dragged before the Egyptians and cast before them.

47. And all the Egyptians saw this evil which had suddenly come upon them, and all the Egyptians cried out with a loud voice.

48. And all the families of Egypt wept upon that night, each man for his son and each man for his daughter, being the first born, and the tumult of Egypt was heard at a distance on that night.

49. And Bathia the daughter of Pharaoh went forth with the king on that night to seek Moses and Aaron in their houses, and they found them in their houses, eating and drinking and rejoicing with all Israel.

50. And Bathia said to Moses, Is this the reward for the good which I have done to thee, who have reared thee and stretched thee out, and thou hast brought this evil upon me and my father's house?

51. And Moses said to her, Surely ten plagues did the Lord bring upon Egypt; did any evil accrue to thee from any of them? did one of them affect thee? and she said, No.

52. And Moses said to her, Although thou art the first born to thy mother, thou shalt not die, and no evil shall reach thee in the midst of Egypt.

53. And she said, What advantage is it to me, when I see the king, my brother, and all his household and subjects in this evil, whose first born perish with all the first born of Egypt?

54. And Moses said to her, Surely thy brother and his household, and subjects, the families of Egypt, would not hearken to the words of the Lord, therefore did this evil come upon them.

55. And Pharaoh king of Egypt approached Moses and Aaron, and some of the children of Israel who were with them in that place, and he prayed to them, saying,

56. Rise up and take your brethren, all the children of Israel who are in the land, with their sheep and oxen, and all belonging to them, they shall leave nothing remaining, only pray for me to the Lord your God.

57. And Moses said to Pharaoh, Behold though thou art thy mother's first born, yet fear not, for thou wilt not die, for the Lord has commanded that thou shalt live, in order to show thee his great might and strong stretched out arm.

58. And Pharaoh ordered the children of Israel to be sent away, and all the Egyptians strengthened themselves to send them, for they said, We are all perishing.

59. And all the Egyptians sent the Israelites forth, with great riches, sheep and oxen and precious things, according to the oath of the Lord between him and our Father Abraham.

60. And the children of Israel delayed going forth at night, and when the Egyptians came to them to bring them out, they said to them, Are we thieves, that we should go forth at night?

61. And the children of Israel asked of the Egyptians, vessels of silver, and vessels of gold, and garments, and the children of Israel stripped the Egyptians.

62. And Moses hastened and rose up and went to the river of Egypt, and brought up from thence the coffin of Joseph and took it with him.

63. The children of Israel also brought up, each man his father's coffin with him, and each man the coffins of his tribe.

CHAPTER 81

1. And the children of Israel journeyed from Rameses to Succoth, about six hundred thousand men on foot, besides the little ones and their wives.

2. Also a mixed multitude went up with them, and flocks and herds, even much cattle.

3. And the sojourning of the children of Israel, who dwelt in the land of Egypt in hard labor, was two hundred and ten years.

4. And at the end of two hundred and ten years, the Lord brought forth the children of Israel from Egypt with a strong hand.

5. And the children of Israel traveled from Egypt and from Goshen and from Rameses, and encamped in Succoth on the fifteenth day of the first month.

6. And the Egyptians buried all their first born whom the Lord had smitten, and all the Egyptians buried their slain for three days.

7. And the children of Israel traveled from Succoth and encamped in Ethom, at the end of the wilderness.

8. And on the third day after the Egyptians had buried their first born, many men rose up from Egypt and went after Israel to make them return to Egypt, for they repented that they had sent the Israelites away from their servitude.

9. And one man said to his neighbor, Surely Moses and Aaron spoke to Pharaoh, saying, We will go a three days' journey in the wilderness and sacrifice to the Lord our God.

10. Now therefore let us rise up early in the morning and cause them to return, and it shall be that if they return with us to Egypt to their masters, then shall we know that there is faith in them, but if they will not return, then will we fight with them, and make them come back with great power and a strong hand.

11. And all the nobles of Pharaoh rose up in the morning, and with them about seven hundred thousand men, and they went forth from Egypt on that day, and came to the place where the children of Israel were.

12. And all the Egyptians saw and behold Moses and Aaron and all the children of Israel were sitting before Pi-hahiroth, eating and drinking and celebrating the feast of the Lord.

13. And all the Egyptians said to the children of Israel, Surely you said, We will go a journey for three days in the wilderness and sacrifice to our God and return.

14. Now therefore this day makes five days since you went, why do you not return to your masters?

15. And Moses and Aaron answered them, saying, Because the Lord our God has testified in us, saying, You shall no more return to Egypt, but we will betake ourselves to a land flowing with milk and honey, as the Lord our God had sworn to our ancestors to give to us.

16. And when the nobles of Egypt saw that the children of Israel did not hearken to them, to return to Egypt, they girded themselves to fight with Israel.

17. And the Lord strengthened the hearts of the children of Israel over the Egyptians, that they gave them a severe beating, and the battle was sore upon the Egyptians, and all the Egyptians fled from before the children of Israel, for many of them perished by the hand of Israel.

18. And the nobles of Pharaoh went to Egypt and told Pharaoh, saying, The children of Israel have fled, and will no more return to Egypt, and in this manner did Moses and Aaron speak to us.

19. And Pharaoh heard this thing, and his heart and the hearts of all his subjects were turned against Israel, and they repented that they had sent Israel; and all the Egyptians advised Pharaoh to pursue the children of Israel to make them come back to their burdens.

20. And they said each man to his brother, What is this which we have done, that we have sent Israel from our servitude?

21. And the Lord strengthened the hearts of all the Egyptians to pursue the Israelites, for the Lord desired to overthrow the Egyptians in the Red Sea.

22. And Pharaoh rose up and harnessed his chariot, and he ordered all the Egyptians to assemble, not one man was left excepting the little ones and the women.

23. And all the Egyptians went forth with Pharaoh to pursue the children of Israel, and the camp of Egypt was an exceedingly large and heavy camp, about ten hundred thousand men.

24. And the whole of this camp went and pursued the children of Israel to bring them back to Egypt, and they reached them encamping by the Red Sea.

25. And the children of Israel lifted up their eyes, and beheld all the Egyptians pursuing them, and the children of Israel were greatly terrified at them, and the children of Israel cried to the Lord.

26. And on account of the Egyptians, the children of Israel divided themselves into four divisions, and they were divided in their opinions, for they were afraid of the Egyptians, and Moses spoke to each of them.

27. The first division was of the children of Reuben, Simeon, and Issachar, and they resolved to cast themselves into the sea, for they were exceedingly afraid of the Egyptians.

28. And Moses said to them, Fear not, stand still and see the salvation of the Lord which He will effect this day for you.

29. The second division was of the children of Zebulun, Benjamin and Naphtali, and they resolved to go back to Egypt with the Egyptians.

30. And Moses said to them, Fear not, for as you have seen the Egyptians this day, so shall you see them no more for ever.

31. The third division was of the children of Judah and Joseph, and they resolved to go to meet the Egyptians to fight with them.

32. And Moses said to them, Stand in your places, for the Lord will fight for you, and you shall remain silent.

33. And the fourth division was of the children of Levi, Gad, and Asher, and they resolved to go into the midst of the Egyptians to confound them, and Moses said to them, Remain in your stations and fear not, only call unto the Lord that he may save you out of their hands.

34. After this Moses rose up from amidst the people, and he prayed to the Lord and said,

35. O Lord God of the whole earth, save now thy people whom thou didst bring forth from Egypt, and let not the Egyptians boast that power and might are theirs.

36. So the Lord said to Moses, Why dost thou cry unto me? speak to the children of Israel that they shall proceed, and do thou stretch out thy rod upon the sea and divide it, and the children of Israel shall pass through it.

37. And Moses did so, and he lifted up his rod upon the sea and divided it.

38. And the waters of the sea were divided into twelve parts, and the children of Israel passed through on foot, with shoes, as a man would pass through a prepared road.

39. And the Lord manifested to the children of Israel his wonders in Egypt and in the sea by the hand of Moses and Aaron.

40. And when the children of Israel had entered the sea, the Egyptians came after them, and the waters of the sea resumed upon them, and they all sank in the water, and not one man was left excepting Pharaoh, who gave thanks to the Lord and believed in him, therefore the Lord did not cause him to perish at that time with the Egyptians.

41. And the Lord ordered an angel to take him from amongst the Egyptians, who cast him upon the land of Ninevah and he reigned over it for a long time.

42. And on that day the Lord saved Israel from the hand of Egypt, and all the children of Israel saw that the Egyptians had perished, and they beheld the great hand of the Lord, in what he had performed in Egypt and in the sea.

43. Then sang Moses and the children of Israel this song unto the Lord, on the day when the Lord caused the Egyptians to fall before them.

44. And all Israel sang in concert, saying, I will sing to the Lord for He is greatly exalted, the horse and his rider has he cast into the sea; behold it is written in the book of the law of God.

45. After this the children of Israel proceeded on their journey, and encamped in Marah, and the Lord gave to the children of Israel statutes and judgments in that place in Marah, and the Lord commanded the children of Israel to walk in all his ways and to serve him.

46. And they journeyed from Marah and came to Elim, and in Elim were twelve springs of water and seventy date trees, and the children encamped there by the waters.

47. And they journeyed from Elim and came to the wilderness of Sin, on the fifteenth day of the second month after their departure from Egypt.

48. At that time the Lord gave the manna to the children of Israel to eat, and the Lord caused food to rain from heaven for the children of Israel day by day.

49. And the children of Israel ate the manna for forty years, all the days that they were in the wilderness, until they came to the land of Canaan to possess it.

50. And they proceeded from the wilderness of Sin and encamped in Alush.

51. And they proceeded from Alush and encamped in Rephidim.

52. And when the children of Israel were in Rephidim, Amalek the son of Eliphaz, the son of Esau, the brother of Zepho, came to fight with Israel.

53. And he brought with him eight hundred and one thousand men, magicians and conjurers, and he prepared for battle with Israel in Rephidim.

54. And they carried on a great and severe battle against Israel, and the Lord delivered Amalek and his people into the hands of Moses and the children of Israel, and into the hand of Joshua, the son of Nun, the Ephrathite, the servant of Moses.

55. And the children of Israel smote Amalek and his people at the edge of the sword, but
the battle was very sore upon the children of Israel.

56. And the Lord said to Moses, Write this thing as a memorial for thee in a book, and place it in the hand of Joshua, the son of Nun, thy servant, and thou shalt command the children of Israel, saying, When thou shalt come to the land of Canaan, thou shalt utterly efface the remembrance of Amalek from under heaven.

57. And Moses did so, and he took the book and wrote upon it these words, saying,

58. Remember what Amalek has done to thee in the road when thou wentest forth from Egypt.

59. Who met thee in the road and smote thy rear, even those that were feeble behind thee when thou wast faint and weary.

60. Therefore it shall be when the Lord thy God shall have given thee rest from all thine enemies round about in the land which the Lord thy God giveth thee for an inheritance, to possess it, that thou shalt blot out the remembrance of Amalek from under heaven, thou shalt not forget it.

61. And the king who shall have pity on Amalek, or upon his memory or upon his seed, behold I will require it of him, and I will cut him off from amongst his people.

62. And Moses wrote all these things in a book, and he enjoined the children of Israel respecting all these matters.

CHAPTER 82

1. And the children of Israel proceeded from Rephidim and they encamped in the wilderness of Sinai, in the third month from their going forth from Egypt.

2. At that time came Reuel the Midianite, the father-in-law of Moses, with Zipporah his daughter and her two sons, for he had heard of the wonders of the Lord which he had done to Israel, that he had delivered them from the hand of Egypt.

3. And Reuel came to Moses to the wilderness where he was encamped, where was the mountain of God.

4. And Moses went forth to meet his father-in-law with great honor, and all Israel was with him.

5. And Reuel and his children remained amongst the Israelites for many days, and Reuel knew the Lord from that day forward.

6. And in the third month from the children of Israel's departure from Egypt, on the sixth day thereof, the Lord gave to Israel the ten commandments on Mount Sinai.

7. And all Israel heard all these commandments, and all Israel rejoiced exceedingly in the Lord on that day.

8. And the glory of the Lord rested upon Mount Sinai, and he called to Moses, and Moses came in the midst of a cloud and ascended the mountain.

9. And Moses was upon the mount forty days and forty nights; he ate no bread and drank no water, and the Lord instructed him in the statutes and judgments in order to teach the children of Israel.

10. And the Lord wrote the ten commandments which he had commanded the children of Israel upon two tablets of stone, which he gave to Moses to command the children of Israel.

11. And at the end of forty days and forty nights, when the Lord had finished speaking to Moses on Mount Sinai, then the Lord gave to Moses the tablets of stone, written with the finger of God.

12. And when the children of Israel saw that Moses tarried to come down from the mount, they gathered round Aaron, and said, As for this man Moses we know not what has become of him.

13. Now therefore rise up, make unto us a god who shall go before us, so that thou shalt not die.

14. And Aaron was greatly afraid of the people, and he ordered them to bring him gold and he made it into a molten calf for the people.

15. And the Lord said to Moses, before he had come down from the mount, Get thee down, for thy people whom thou didst bring forth from Egypt have corrupted themselves.

16. They have made to themselves a molten calf, and have bowed down to it, now therefore leave me, that I may consume them from off the earth, for they are a stiffnecked people.

17. And Moses besought the countenance of the Lord, and he prayed to the Lord for the people on account of the calf which they had made, and he afterward descended from the mount and in his hands were the two tablets of stone, which God had given him to command the Israelites.

18. And when Moses approached the camp and saw the calf which the people had made, the anger of Moses was kindled and he broke the tablets under the mount.

19. And Moses came to the camp and he took the calf and burned it with fire, and ground it till it became fine dust, and strewed it upon the water and gave it to the Israelites to drink.

20. And there died of the people by the swords of each other about three thousand men who had made the calf.

21. And on the morrow Moses said to the people, I will go up to the Lord, peradventure I may make atonement for your sins which you have sinned to the Lord.

22. And Moses again went up to the Lord, and he remained with the Lord forty days and forty nights.

23. And during the forty days did Moses entreat the Lord in behalf of the children of Israel, and the Lord hearkened to the prayer of Moses, and the Lord was entreated of him in behalf of Israel.

24. Then spake the Lord to Moses to hew two stone tablets and to bring them up to the Lord, who would write upon them the ten commandments.

25. Now Moses did so, and he came down and hewed the two tablets and went up to Mount Sinai to the Lord, and the Lord wrote the ten commandments upon the tablets.

26. And Moses remained yet with the Lord forty days and forty nights, and the Lord instructed him in statutes and judgments to impart to Israel.

27. And the Lord commanded him respecting the children of Israel that they should make a sanctuary for the Lord, that his name might rest therein, and the Lord showed him the likeness of the sanctuary and the likeness of all its vessels.

28. And at the end of the forty days, Moses came down from the mount and the two tablets were in his hand.

29. And Moses came to the children of Israel and spoke to them all the words of the Lord, and he taught them laws, statutes and judgments which the Lord had taught him.

30. And Moses told the children of Israel the word of the Lord, that a sanctuary should be made for him, to dwell amongst the children of Israel.

31. And the people rejoiced greatly at all the good which the Lord had spoken to them, through Moses, and they said, We will do all that the Lord has spoken to thee.

32. And the people rose up like one man and they made generous offerings to the sanctuary of the Lord, and each man brought the offering of the Lord for the work of the sanctuary, and for all its service.

33. And all the children of Israel brought each man of all that was found in his possession for the work of the sanctuary of the Lord, gold, silver and brass, and every thing that was serviceable for the sanctuary.

34. And all the wise men who were practiced in work came and made the sanctuary of the Lord, according to all that the Lord had commanded, every man in the work in which he had been practiced; and all the wise men in heart made the sanctuary, and its furniture and all the vessels for the holy service, as the Lord had commanded Moses.

35. And the work of the sanctuary of the tabernacle was completed at the end of five months, and the children of Israel did all that the Lord had commanded Moses.

36. And they brought the sanctuary and all its furniture to Moses; like unto the representation which the Lord had shown to Moses, so did the children of Israel.

37. And Moses saw the work, and behold they did it as the Lord had commanded him, so Moses blessed them.

CHAPTER 83

1. And in the twelfth month, in the twenty-third day of the month, Moses took Aaron and his sons, and he dressed them in their garments, and anointed them and did unto them as the Lord had commanded him, and Moses brought up all the offerings which the Lord had on that day commanded him.

2. Moses afterward took Aaron and his sons and said to them, For seven days shall you remain at the door of the tabernacle, for thus am I commanded.

3. And Aaron and his sons did all that the Lord had commanded them through Moses, and they remained for seven days at the door of the tabernacle.

4. And on the eighth day, being the first day of the first month, in the second year from the Israelites' departure from Egypt, Moses erected the sanctuary, and Moses put up all the furniture of the tabernacle and all the furniture of the sanctuary, and he did all that the Lord had commanded him.

5.   And Moses called to Aaron and his sons, and they brought the burnt offering and the sin offering for themselves and the children of Israel, as the Lord had commanded Moses.

6.   On that day the two sons of Aaron, Nadab and Abihu, took strange fire and brought it before the Lord who had not commanded them, and a fire went forth from before the Lord, and consumed them, and they died before the Lord on that day.

7.   Then on the day when Moses had completed to erect the sanctuary, the princes of the children of Israel began to bring their offerings before the Lord for the dedication of the altar.

8.   And they brought up their offerings each prince for one day, a prince each day for twelve days.

9.   And all the offerings which they brought, each man in his day, one silver charger weighing one hundred and thirty shekels, one silver bowl of seventy shekels after the shekel of the sanctuary, both of them full of fine flour, mingled with oil for a meat offering.

10. One spoon, weighing ten shekels of gold, full of incense.

11. One young bullock, one ram, one lamb of the first year for a burnt offering.

12. And one kid of the goats for a sin offering.

13. And for a sacrifice of peace offering, two oxen, five rams, five he-goats, five lambs of a year old.

14. Thus did the twelve princes of Israel day by day, each man in his day.

15. And it was after this, in the thirteenth day of the month, that Moses commanded the children of Israel to observe the Passover.

16. And the children of Israel kept the Passover in its season in the fourteenth day of the month, as the Lord had commanded Moses, so did the children of Israel.

17. And in the second month, on the first day thereof, the Lord spoke unto Moses, saying,

18. Number the heads of all the males of the children of Israel from twenty years old and upward, thou and thy brother Aaron and the twelve princes of Israel.

19. And Moses did so, and Aaron came with the twelve princes of Israel, and they numbered the children of Israel in the wilderness of Sinai.

20. And the numbers of the children of Israel by the houses of their fathers, from twenty years old and upward, were six hundred and three thousand, five hundred and fifty.

21. But the children of Levi were not numbered amongst their brethren the children of Israel.

22. And the number of all the males of the children of Israel from one month old and upward, was twenty-two thousand, two hundred and seventy-three.

23. And the number of the children of Levi from one month old and above, was twenty-two thousand.

24. And Moses placed the priests and the Levites each man to his service and to his burden to serve the sanctuary of the tabernacle, as the Lord had commanded Moses.

25. And on the twentieth day of the month, the cloud was taken away from the tabernacle of testimony.

26. At that time the children of Israel continued their journey from the wilderness of Sinai, and they took a journey of three days, and the cloud rested upon the wilderness of Paran; there the anger of the Lord was kindled against Israel, for they had provoked the Lord in asking him for meat, that they might eat.

27. And the Lord hearkened to their voice, and gave them meat which they ate for one month.

28. But after this the anger of the Lord was kindled against them, and he smote them with a great slaughter, and they were buried there in that place.

29. And the children of Israel called that place Kebroth Hattaavah, because there they buried the people that lusted flesh.

30. And they departed from Kebroth Hattaavah and pitched in Hazeroth, which is in the wilderness of Paran.

31. And whilst the children of Israel were in Hazeroth, the anger of the Lord was kindled against Miriam on account of Moses, and she became leprous, white as snow.

32. And she was confined without the camp for seven days, until she had been received again after her leprosy.

33. The children of Israel afterward departed from Hazeroth, and pitched in the end of the wilderness of Paran.

34. At that time, the Lord spoke to Moses to send twelve men from the children of Israel, one man to a tribe, to go and explore the land of Canaan.

35. And Moses sent the twelve men, and they came to the land of Canaan to search and examine it, and they explored the whole land from the wilderness of Sin to Rechob as thou comest to Chamoth.

36. And at the end of forty days they came to Moses and Aaron, and they brought him word as it was in their hearts, and ten of the men brought up an evil report to the children of Israel, of the land which they had explored, saying, It is better for us to return to Egypt than to go to this land, a land that consumes its inhabitants.

37. But Joshua the son of Nun, and Caleb the son of Jephuneh, who were of those that explored the land, said, The land is exceedingly good.

38. If the Lord delight in us, then he will bring us to this land and give it to us, for it is a land flowing with milk and honey.

39. But the children of Israel would not hearken to them, and they hearkened to the words of the ten men who had brought up an evil report of the land.

40. And the Lord heard the murmurings of the children of Israel and he was angry and swore, saying,

41. Surely not one man of this wicked generation shall see the land from twenty years old and upward excepting Caleb the son of Jephuneh and Joshua the son of Nun.

42. But surely this wicked generation shall perish in this wilderness, and their children shall come to the land and they shall possess it; so the anger of the Lord was kindled against Israel, and he made them wander in the wilderness for forty years until the end of that wicked generation, because they did not follow the Lord.

43. And the people dwelt in the wilderness of Paran a long time, and they afterward proceeded to the wilderness by the way of the Red Sea.

CHAPTER 84

1. At that time Korah the son of Jetzer the son of Kehath the son of Levi, took many men of the children of Israel, and they rose up and quarreled with Moses and Aaron and the whole congregation.

2. And the Lord was angry with them, and the earth opened its mouth, and swallowed them up, with their houses and all belonging to them, and all the men belonging to Korah.

3. And after this God made the people go round by the way of Mount Seir for a long time.

4. At that time the Lord said unto Moses, Provoke not a war against the children of Esau, for I will not give to you of any thing belonging to them, as much as the sole of the foot could tread upon, for I have given Mount Seir for an inheritance to Esau.

5. Therefore did the children of Esau fight against the children of Seir in former times, and the Lord had delivered the children of Seir into the hands of the children of Esau, and destroyed them from before them, and the children of Esau dwelt in their stead unto this day.

6. Therefore the Lord said to the children of Israel, Fight not against the children of Esau your brethren, for nothing in their land belongs to you, but you may buy food of them for money and eat it, and you may buy water of them for money and drink it.

7. And the children of Israel did according to the word of the Lord.

8. And the children of Israel went about the wilderness, going round by the way of Mount Sinai for a long time, and touched not the children of Esau, and they continued in that district for nineteen years.

9. At that time died Latinus king of the children of Chittim, in the forty-fifth year of his reign, which is the fourteenth year of the children of Israel's departure from Egypt.

10. And they buried him in his place which he had built for himself in the land of Chittim, and Abimnas reigned in his place for thirty-eight years.

11. And the children of Israel passed the boundary of the children of Esau in those days, at the end of nineteen years, and they came and passed the road of the wilderness of Moab.

12. And the Lord said to Moses, besiege not Moab, and do not fight against them, for I will give you nothing of their land.

13. And the children of Israel passed the road of the wilderness of Moab for nineteen years, and they did not fight against them.

14. And in the thirty-sixth year of the children of Israel's departing from Egypt the Lord smote the heart of Sihon, king of the Amorites, and he waged war, and went forth to fight against the children of Moab.

15. And Sihon sent messengers to Beor the son of Janeas, the son of Balaam, counsellor to the king of Egypt, and to Balaam his son, to curse Moab, in order that it might be delivered into the hand of Sihon.

16. And the messengers went and brought Beor the son of Janeas, and Balaam his son, from Pethor in Mesopotamia, so Beor and Balaam his son came to the city of Sihon and they cursed Moab and their king in the presence of Sihon king of the Amorites.

17. So Sihon went out with his whole army, and he went to Moab and fought against them, and he subdued them, and the Lord delivered them into his hands, and Sihon slew the king of Moab.

18. And Sihon took all the cities of Moab in the battle; he also took Heshbon from them, for Heshbon was one of the cities of Moab, and Sihon placed his princes and his nobles in Heshbon, and Heshbon belonged to Sihon in those days.

19. Therefore the parable speakers Beor and Balaam his son uttered these words, saying, Come unto Heshbon, the city of Sihon will be built and established.

20. Woe unto thee Moab! thou art lost, O people of Kemosh! behold it is written upon the book of the law of God.

21. And when Sihon had conquered Moab, he placed guards in the cities which he had taken from Moab, and a considerable number of the children of Moab fell in battle into the hand of Sihon, and he made a great capture of them, sons and daughters, and he slew their king; so Sihon turned back to his own land.

22. And Sihon gave numerous presents of silver and gold to Beor and Balaam his son, and he dismissed them, and they went to Mesopotamia to their home and country.

23. At that time all the children of Israel passed from the road of the wilderness of Moab, and returned and surrounded the wilderness of Edom.

24. So the whole congregation came to the wilderness of Sin in the first month of the fortieth year from their departure from Egypt, and the children of Israel dwelt there in Kadesh, of the wilderness of Sin, and Miriam died there and she was buried there.

25. At that time Moses sent messengers to Hadad king of Edom, saying, Thus says thy brother Israel, Let me pass I pray thee through thy land, we will not pass through field or vineyard, we will not drink the water of the well; we will walk in the king's road.

26. And Edom said to him, Thou shalt not pass through my country, and Edom went forth
to meet the children of Israel with a mighty people.

27. And the children of Esau refused to let the children of Israel pass through their land, so the Israelites removed from them and fought not against them.

28. For before this the Lord had commanded the children of Israel, saying, You shall not fight against the children of Esau, therefore the Israelites removed from them and did not fight against them.

29. So the children of Israel departed from Kadesh, and all the people came to Mount Hor.

30. At that time the Lord said to Moses, Tell thy brother Aaron that he shall die there, for he shall not come to the land which I have given to the children of Israel.

31. And Aaron went up, at the command of the Lord, to Mount Hor, in the fortieth year, in the fifth month, in the first day of the month.

32. And Aaron was one hundred and twenty-three years old when he died in Mount Hor

CHAPTER 85

1. And king Arad the Canaanite, who dwelt in the south, heard that the Israelites had come by the way of the spies, and he arranged his forces to fight against the Israelites.

2. And the children of Israel were greatly afraid of him, for he had a great and heavy army, so the children of Israel resolved to return to Egypt.

3. And the children of Israel turned back about the distance of three days' journey unto Maserath Beni Jaakon, for they were greatly afraid on account of the king Arad.

4. And the children of Israel would not get back to their places, so they remained in Beni Jaakon for thirty days.

5. And when the children of Levi saw that the children of Israel would not turn back, they were jealous for the sake of the Lord, and they rose up and fought against the Israelites their brethren, and slew of them a great body, and forced them to turn back to their place, Mount Hor.

6. And when they returned, king Arad was still arranging his host for battle against the Israelites.

7. And Israel vowed a vow, saying, If thou wilt deliver this people into my hand, then I will utterly destroy their cities.

8. And the Lord hearkened to the voice of Israel, and he delivered the Canaanites into their hand, and he utterly destroyed them and their cities, and he called the name of the place Hormah.

9. And the children of Israel journeyed from Mount Hor and pitched in Oboth, and they journeyed from Oboth and they pitched at Ije-abarim, in the border of Moab.

10. And the children of Israel sent to Moab, saying, Let us pass now through thy land into our place, but the children of Moab would not suffer the children of Israel to pass through their land, for the children of Moab were greatly afraid lest the children of Israel should do unto them as Sihon king of the Amorites had done to them, who had taken their land and had slain many of them.

11. Therefore Moab would not suffer the Israelites to pass through his land, and the Lord commanded the children of Israel, saying, That they should not fight against Moab, so the Israelites removed from Moab.

12. And the children of Israel journeyed from the border of Moab, and they came to the other side of Arnon, the border of Moab, between Moab and the Amorites, and they pitched in the border of Sihon, king of the Amorites, in the wilderness of Kedemoth.

13. And the children of Israel sent messengers to Sihon, king of the Amorites, saying,

14. Let us pass through thy land, we will not turn into the fields or into the vineyards, we will go along by the king's highway until we shall have passed thy border, but Sihon would not suffer the Israelites to pass.

15. So Sihon collected all the people of the Amorites and went forth into the wilderness to meet the children of Israel, and he fought against Israel in Jahaz.

16. And the Lord delivered Sihon king of the Amorites into the hand of the children of Israel, and Israel smote all the people of Sihon with the edge of the sword and avenged the cause of Moab.

17. And the children of Israel took possession of the land of Sihon from Aram unto Jabuk, unto the children of Ammon, and they took all the spoil of the cities.

18. And Israel took all these cities, and Israel dwelt in all the cities of the Amorites.

19. And all the children of Israel resolved to fight against the children of Ammon, to take their land also.

20. So the Lord said to the children of Israel, Do not besiege the children of Ammon, neither stir up battle against them, for I will give nothing to you of their land, and the children of Israel hearkened to the word of the Lord, and did not fight against the children of Ammon.

21. And the children of Israel turned and went up by the way of Bashan to the land of Og, king of Bashan, and Og the king of Bashan went out to meet the Israelites in battle, and he had with him many valiant men, and a very strong force from the people of the Amorites.

22. And Og king of Bashan was a very powerful man, but Naaron his son was exceedingly powerful, even stronger than he was.

23. And Og said in his heart, Behold now the whole camp of Israel takes up a space of three parsa, now will I smite them at once without sword or spear.

24. And Og went up Mount Jahaz, and took therefrom one large stone, the length of which was three parsa, and he placed it on his head, and resolved to throw it upon the camp of the children of Israel, to smite all the Israelites with that stone.

25. And the angel of the Lord came and pierced the stone upon the head of Og, and the stone fell upon the neck of Og that Og fell to the earth on account of the weight of the stone upon his neck.

26. At that time the Lord said to the children of Israel, Be not afraid of him, for I have given him and all his people and all his land into your hand, and you shall do to him as you did to Sihon.

27. And Moses went down to him with a small number of the children of Israel, and Moses smote Og with a stick at the ankles of his feet and slew him.

28. The children of Israel afterward pursued the children of Og and all his people, and they beat and destroyed them till there was no remnant left of them.

29. Moses afterward sent some of the children of Israel to spy out Jaazer, for Jaazer was a very famous city.

30. And the spies went to Jaazer and explored it, and the spies trusted in the Lord, and they fought against the men of Jaazer.

31. And these men took Jaazer and its villages, and the Lord delivered them into their hand, and they drove out the Amorites who had been there.

32. And the children of Israel took the land of the two kings of the Amorites, sixty cities which were on the other side of Jordan, from the brook of Arnon unto Mount Herman.

33. And the children of Israel journeyed and came into the plain of Moab which is on this side of Jordan, by Jericho.

34. And the children of Moab heard all the evil which the children of Israel had done to the two kings of the Amorites, to Sihon and Og, so all the men of Moab were greatly afraid of the Israelites.

35. And the elders of Moab said, Behold the two kings of the Amorites, Sihon and Og, who were more powerful than all the kings of the earth, could not stand against the children of Israel, how then can we stand before them?

36. Surely they sent us a message before now to pass through our land on their way, and we would not suffer them, now they will turn upon us with their heavy swords and destroy us; and Moab was distressed on account of the children of Israel, and they were greatly afraid of them, and they counselled together what was to be done to the children of Israel.

37. And the elders of Moab resolved and took one of their men, Balak the son of Zippor the Moabite, and made him king over them at that time, and Balak was a very wise man.

38. And the elders of Moab rose up and sent to the children of Midian to make peace with them, for a great battle and enmity had been in those days between Moab and Midian, from the days of Hadad the son of Bedad king of Edom, who smote Midian in the field of Moab, unto these days.

39. And the children of Moab sent to the children of Midian, and they made peace with them, and the elders of Midian came to the land of Moab to make peace in behalf of the children of Midian.

40. And the elders of Moab counselled with the elders of Midian what to do in order to save their lives from Israel.

41. And all the children of Moab said to the elders of Midian, Now therefore the children of Israel lick up all that are round about us, as the ox licks up the grass of the field, for thus did they do to the two kings of the Amorites who are stronger than we are.

42. And the elders of Midian said to Moab, We have heard that at the time when Sihon king of the Amorites fought against you, when he prevailed over you and took your land, he had sent to Beor the son of Janeas and to Balaam his son from Mesopotamia, and they came and cursed you; therefore did the hand of Sihon prevail over you, that he took your land.

43. Now therefore send you also to Balaam his son, for he still remains in his land, and give him his hire, that he may come and curse all the people of whom you are afraid; so the elders of Moab heard this thing, and it pleased them to send to Balaam the son of Beor.

44. So Balak the son of Zippor king of Moab sent messengers to Balaam, saying,

45. Behold there is a people come out from Egypt, behold they cover the face of the earth, and they abide over against me.

46. Now therefore come and curse this people for me, for they are too mighty for me, peradventure I shall prevail to fight against them, and drive them out, for I heard that he whom thou blessest is blessed, and whom thou cursest is cursed.

47. So the messengers of Balak went to Balaam and brought Balaam to curse the people to fight against Moab.

48. And Balaam came to Balak to curse Israel, and the Lord said to Balaam, Curse not this people for it is blessed.

49. And Balak urged Balaam day by day to curse Israel, but Balaam hearkened not to Balak on account of the word of the Lord which he had spoken to Balaam.

50. And when Balak saw that Balaam would not accede to his wish, he rose up and went home, and Balaam also returned to his land and he went from there to Midian.

51. And the children of Israel journeyed from the plain of Moab, and pitched by Jordan from Beth-jesimoth even unto Abel-shittim, at the end of the plains of Moab.

52. And when the children of Israel abode in the plain of Shittim, they began to commit whoredom with the daughters of Moab.

53. And the children of Israel approached Moab, and the children of Moab pitched their tents opposite to the camp of the children of Israel.

54. And the children of Moab were afraid of the children of Israel, and the children of Moab took all their daughters and their wives of beautiful aspect and comely appearance, and dressed them in gold and silver and costly garments.

55. And the children of Moab seated those women at the door of their tents, in order that the children of Israel might see them and turn to them, and not fight against Moab.

56. And all the children of Moab did this thing to the children of Israel, and every man placed his wife and daughter at the door of his tent, and all the children of Israel saw the act of the children of Moab, and the children of Israel turned to the daughters of Moab and coveted them, and they went to them.

57. And it came to pass that when a Hebrew came to the door of the tent of Moab, and saw a daughter of Moab and desired her in his heart, and spoke with her at the door of the tent that which he desired, whilst they were speaking together the men of the tent would come out and speak to the Hebrew like unto these words:

58. Surely you know that we are brethren, we are all the descendants of Lot and the descendants of Abraham his brother, wherefore then will you not remain with us, and wherefore will you not eat our bread and our sacrifice?

59. And when the children of Moab had thus overwhelmed him with their speeches, and enticed him by their flattering words, they seated him in the tent and cooked and sacrificed for him, and he ate of their sacrifice and of their bread.

60. They then gave him wine and he drank and became intoxicated, and they placed before him a beautiful damsel, and he did with her as he liked, for he knew not what he was doing, as he had drunk plentifully of wine.

61. Thus did the children of Moab to Israel in that place, in the plain of Shittim, and the anger of the Lord was kindled against Israel on account of this matter, and he sent a pestilence amongst them, and there died of the Israelites twenty-four thousand men.

62. Now there was a man of the children of Simeon whose name was Zimri, the son of Salu, who connected himself with the Midianite Cosbi, the daughter of Zur, king of Midian, in the sight of all the children of Israel.

63. And Phineas the son of Elazer, the son of Aaron the priest, saw this wicked thing which Zimri had done, and he took a spear and rose up and went after them, and pierced them both and slew them, and the pestilence ceased from the children of Israel.

CHAPTER 86

1. At that time after the pestilence, the Lord said to Moses, and to Elazer the son of Aaron the priest, saying,

2. Number the heads of the whole community of the children of Israel, from twenty years old and upward, all that went forth in the army.

3. And Moses and Elazer numbered the children of Israel after their families, and the number of all Israel was seven hundred thousand, seven hundred and thirty.

4. And the number of the children of Levi, from one month old and upward, was twentythree thousand, and amongst these there was not a man of those numbered by Moses and Aaron in the wilderness of Sinai.

5. For the Lord had told them that they would die in the wilderness, so they all died, and not one had been left of them excepting Caleb the son of Jephuneh, and Joshua the son of Nun.

6. And it was after this that the Lord said to Moses, Say unto the children of Israel to avenge upon Midian the cause of their brethren the children of Israel.

7. And Moses did so, and the children of Israel chose from amongst them twelve thousand men, being one thousand to a tribe, and they went to Midian.

8. And the children of Israel warred against Midian, and they slew every male, also the five princes of Midian, and Balaam the son of Beor did they slay with the sword.

9. And the children of Israel took the wives of Midian captive, with their little ones and their cattle, and all belonging to them.

10. And they took all the spoil and all the prey, and they brought it to Moses and to Elazer to the plains of Moab.

11. And Moses and Elazer and all the princes of the congregation went forth to meet them with joy.

12. And they divided all the spoil of Midian, and the children of Israel had been revenged upon Midian for the cause of their brethren the children of Israel.

CHAPTER 87

1. At that time the Lord said to Moses, Behold thy days are approaching to an end, take now Joshua the son of Nun thy servant and place him in the tabernacle, and I will command him, and Moses did so.

2. And the Lord appeared in the tabernacle in a pillar of cloud, and the pillar of cloud stood at the entrance of the tabernacle.

3. And the Lord commanded Joshua the son of Nun and said unto him, Be strong and courageous, for thou shalt bring the children of Israel to the land which I swore to give them, and I will be with thee.

4. And Moses said to Joshua, Be strong and courageous, for thou wilt make the children of Israel inherit the land, and the Lord will be with thee, he will not leave thee nor forsake thee, be not afraid nor disheartened.

5. And Moses called to all the children of Israel and said to them, You have seen all the good which the Lord your God has done for you in the wilderness.

6. Now therefore observe all the words of this law, and walk in the way of the Lord your God, turn not from the way which the Lord has commanded you, either to the right or to the left.

7. And Moses taught the children of Israel statutes and judgments and laws to do in the land as the Lord had commanded him.

8. And he taught them the way of the Lord and his laws; behold they are written upon the book of the law of God which he gave to the children of Israel by the hand of Moses.

9. And Moses finished commanding the children of Israel, and the Lord said to him, saying, Go up to the Mount Abarim and die there, and be gathered unto thy people as Aaron thy brother was gathered.

10. And Moses went up as the Lord had commanded him, and he died there in the land of Moab by the order of the Lord, in the fortieth year from the Israelites going forth from the land of Egypt.

11. And the children of Israel wept for Moses in the plains of Moab for thirty days, and the days of weeping and mourning for Moses were completed.

CHAPTER 88

1. And it was after the death of Moses that the Lord said to Joshua the son of Nun, saying,

2. Rise up and pass the Jordan to the land which I have given to the children of Israel, and thou shalt make the children of Israel inherit the land.

3. Every place upon which the sole of your feet shall tread shall belong to you, from the wilderness of Lebanon unto the great river the river of Perath shall be your boundary.

4. No man shall stand up against thee all the days of thy life; as I was with Moses, so will I be with thee, only be strong and of good courage to observe all the law which Moses commanded thee, turn not from the way either to the right or to the left, in order that thou mayest prosper in all that thou doest.

5. And Joshua commanded the officers of Israel, saying, Pass through the camp and command the people, saying, Prepare for yourselves provisions, for in three days more you will pass the Jordan to possess the land.

6. And the officers of the children of Israel did so, and they commanded the people and they did all that Joshua had commanded.

7. And Joshua sent two men to spy out the land of Jericho, and the men went and spied out Jericho.

8. And at the end of seven days they came to Joshua in the camp and said to him, The Lord has delivered the whole land into our hand, and the inhabitants thereof are melted with fear because of us.

9. And it came to pass after that, that Joshua rose up in the morning and all Israel with him, and they journeyed from Shittim, and Joshua and all Israel with him passed the Jordan; and Joshua was eighty-two years old when he passed the Jordan with Israel.

10. And the people went up from Jordan on the tenth day of the first month, and they encamped in Gilgal at the eastern corner of Jericho.

11. And the children of Israel kept the Passover in Gilgal, in the plains of Jericho, on the fourteenth day at the month, as it is written in the law of Moses.

12. And the manna ceased at that time on the morrow of the Passover, and there was no more manna for the children of Israel, and they ate of the produce of the land of Canaan.

13. And Jericho was entirely closed against the children of Israel, no one came out or went in.

14. And it was in the second month, on the first day of the month, that the Lord said to Joshua, Rise up, behold I have given Jericho into thy hand with all the people thereof; and all your fighting men shall go round the city, once each day, thus shall you do for six days.

15. And the priests shall blow upon trumpets, and when you shall hear the sound of the trumpet, all the people shall give a great shouting, that the walls of the city shall fall down; all the people shall go up every man against his opponent.

16. And Joshua did so according to all that the Lord had commanded him.

17. And on the seventh day they went round the city seven times, and the priests blew upon trumpets.

18. And at the seventh round, Joshua said to the people, Shout, for the Lord has delivered the whole city into our hands.

19. Only the city and all that it contains shall be accursed to the Lord, and keep yourselves from the accursed thing, lest you make the camp of Israel accursed and trouble it.

20. But all the silver and gold and brass and iron shall be consecrated to the Lord, they shall come into the treasury of the Lord.

21. And the people blew upon trumpets and made a great shouting, and the walls of Jericho fell down, and all the people went up, every man straight before him, and they took the city and utterly destroyed all that was in it, both man and woman, young and old, ox and sheep and ass, with the edge of the sword.

22. And they burned the whole city with fire; only the vessels of silver and gold, and brass and iron, they put into the treasury of the Lord.

23. And Joshua swore at that time, saying, Cursed be the man who builds Jericho; he shall lay the foundation thereof in his first-born, and in his youngest son shall he set up the gates thereof.

24. And Achan the son of Carmi, the son of Zabdi, the son of Zerah, son of Judah, dealt treacherously in the accursed thing, and he took of the accursed thing and hid it in the tent, and the anger of the Lord was kindled against Israel.

25. And it was after this when the children of Israel had returned from burning Jericho, Joshua sent men to spy out also Ai, and to fight against it.

26. And the men went up and spied out Ai, and they returned and said, Let not all the people go up with thee to Ai, only let about three thousand men go up and smite the city, for the men thereof are but few.

27. And Joshua did so, and there went up with him of the children of Israel about three thousand men, and they fought against the men of Ai.

28. And the battle was severe against Israel, and the men of Ai smote thirty-six men of Israel, and the children of Israel fled from before the men of Ai.

29. And when Joshua saw this thing, he tore his garments and fell upon his face to the ground before the Lord, he, with the elders of Israel, and they put dust upon their heads.

30. And Joshua said, Why O Lord didst thou bring this people over the Jordan? what shall I say after the Israelites have turned their backs against their enemies?

31. Now therefore all the Canaanites, inhabitants of the land, will hear this thing, and surround us and cut off our name.

32. And the Lord said to Joshua, Why dost thou fall upon thy face? rise, get thee off, for the Israelites have sinned, and taken of the accursed thing; I will no more be with them unless they destroy the accursed thing from amongst them.

33. And Joshua rose up and assembled the people, and brought the Urim by the order of the Lord, and the tribe of Judah was taken, and Achan the son of Carmi was taken.

34. And Joshua said to Achan, Tell me my son, what hast thou done, and Achan said, I saw amongst the spoil a goodly garment of Shinar and two hundred shekels of silver, and a wedge of gold of fifty shekels weight; I coveted them and took them, and behold they are all hid in the earth in the midst of the tent.

35. And Joshua sent men who went and took them from the tent of Achan, and they brought them to Joshua.

36. And Joshua took Achan and these utensils, and his sons and daughters and all belonging to him, and they brought them into the valley of Achor.

37. And Joshua burned them there with fire, and all the Israelites stoned Achan with stones, and they raised over him a heap of stones, therefore did he call that place the valley of Achor, so the Lord's anger was appeased, and Joshua afterward came to the city and fought against it.

38. And the Lord said to Joshua, Fear not, neither be thou dismayed, behold I have given into thy hand Ai, her king and her people, and thou shalt do unto them as thou didst to Jericho and her king, only the spoil thereof and the cattle thereof shall you take for a prey for yourselves; lay an ambush for the city behind it.

39. So Joshua did according to the word of the Lord, and he chose from amongst the sons of war thirty thousand valiant men, and he sent them, and they lay in ambush for the city.

40. And he commanded them, saying, When you shall see us we will flee before them with cunning, and they will pursue us, you shall then rise out of the ambush and take the city, and they did so.

41. And Joshua fought, and the men of the city went out toward Israel, not knowing that they were lying in ambush for them behind the city.

42. And Joshua and all the Israelites feigned themselves wearied out before them, and they fled by the way of the wilderness with cunning.

43. And the men of Ai gathered all the people who were in the city to pursue the Israelites, and they went out and were drawn away from the city, not one remained, and they left the city open and pursued the Israelites.

44. And those who were lying in ambush rose up out of their places, and hastened to come to the city and took it and set it on fire, and the men of Ai turned back, and behold the smoke of the city ascended to the skies, and they had no means of retreating either one way or the other.

45. And all the men of Ai were in the midst of Israel, some on this side and some on that side, and they smote them so that not one of them remained.

46. And the children of Israel took Melosh king of Ai alive, and they brought him to Joshua, and Joshua hanged him on a tree and he died.

47. And the children of Israel returned to the city after having burned it, and they smote all those that were in it with the edge of the sword.

48. And the number of those that had fallen of the men of Ai, both man and woman, was twelve thousand; only the cattle and the spoil of the city they took to themselves, according to the word of the Lord to Joshua.

49. And all the kings on this side Jordan, all the kings of Canaan, heard of the evil which the children of Israel had done to Jericho and to Ai, and they gathered themselves together to fight against Israel.

50. Only the inhabitants of Gibeon were greatly afraid of fighting against the Israelites lest they should perish, so they acted cunningly, and they came to Joshua and to all Israel, and said unto them, We have come from a distant land, now therefore make a covenant with us.

51. And the inhabitants of Gibeon over-reached the children of Israel, and the children of Israel made a covenant with them, and they made peace with them, and the princes of the congregation swore unto them, but afterward the children of Israel knew that they were neighbors to them and were dwelling amongst them.

52. But the children of Israel slew them not; for they had sworn to them by the Lord, and they became hewers of wood and drawers of water.

53. And Joshua said to them, Why did you deceive me, to do this thing to us? and they answered him, saying, Because it was told to thy servants all that you had done to all the kings of the Amorites, and we were greatly afraid of our lives, and we did this thing.

54. And Joshua appointed them on that day to hew wood and to draw water, and he divided them for slaves to all the tribes of Israel.

55. And when Adonizedek king of Jerusalem heard all that the children of Israel had done to Jericho and to Ai, he sent to Hoham king of Hebron and to Piram king at Jarmuth, and to Japhia king of Lachish and to Deber king of Eglon, saying,

56. Come up to me and help me, that we may smite the children of Israel and the inhabitants of Gibeon who have made peace with the children of Israel.

57. And they gathered themselves together and the five kings of the Amorites went up with all their camps, a mighty people numerous as the sand of the sea shore.

58. And all these kings came and encamped before Gibeon, and they began to fight against the inhabitants of Gibeon, and all the men of Gibeon sent to Joshua, saying, Come up quickly to us and help us, for all the kings of the Amorites have gathered together to fight against us.

59. And Joshua and all the fighting people went up from Gilgal, and Joshua came suddenly to them, and smote these five kings with a great slaughter.

60. And the Lord confounded them before the children at Israel, who smote them with a terrible slaughter in Gibeon, and pursued them along the way that goes up to Beth Horon unto Makkedah, and they fled from before the children of Israel.

61. And whilst they were fleeing, the Lord sent upon them hailstones from heaven, and more of them died by the hailstones, than by the slaughter of the children of Israel.

62. And the children of Israel pursued them, and they still smote them in the road, going on and smiting them.

63. And when they were smiting, the day was declining toward evening, and Joshua said in the sight of all the people, Sun, stand thou still upon Gibeon, and thou moon in the valley of Ajalon, until the nation shall have revenged itself upon its enemies.

64. And the Lord hearkened to the voice of Joshua, and the sun stood still in the midst of the heavens, and it stood still six and thirty moments, and the moon also stood still and hastened not to go down a whole day.

65. And there was no day like that, before it or after it, that the Lord hearkened to the voice of a man, for the Lord fought for Israel.

CHAPTER 89

1. Then spoke Joshua this song, on the day that the Lord had given the Amorites into the hand of Joshua and the children of Israel, and he said in the sight of all Israel,

2. Thou hast done mighty things, O Lord, thou hast performed great deeds; who is like unto thee? my lips shall sing to thy name.

3. My goodness and my fortress, my high tower, I will sing a new song unto thee, with thanksgiving will I sing to thee, thou art the strength of my salvation.

4. All the kings of the earth shall praise thee, the princes of the world shall sing to thee, the children of Israel shall rejoice in thy salvation, they shall sing and praise thy power.

5. To thee, O Lord, did we confide; we said thou art our God, for thou wast our shelter and strong tower against our enemies.

6. To thee we cried and were not ashamed, in thee we trusted and were delivered; when we cried unto thee, thou didst hear our voice, thou didst deliver our souls from the sword, thou didst show unto us thy grace, thou didst give unto us thy salvation, thou didst rejoice our hearts with thy strength.

7.   Thou didst go forth for our salvation, with thine arm thou didst redeem thy people; thou didst answer us from the heavens of thy holiness, thou didst save us from ten thousands of people.

8.   The sun and moon stood still in heaven, and thou didst stand in thy wrath against our oppressors and didst command thy judgments over them.

9.   All the princes of the earth stood up, the kings of the nations had gathered themselves together, they were not moved at thy presence, they desired thy battles.

10. Thou didst rise against them in thine anger, and didst bring down thy wrath upon them; thou didst destroy them in thine anger, and cut them off in thine heart.

11. Nations have been consumed with thy fury, kingdoms have declined because of thy wrath, thou didst wound kings in the day of thine anger.

12. Thou didst pour out thy fury upon them, thy wrathful anger took hold of them; thou didst turn their iniquity upon them, and didst cut them off in their wickedness.

13. They did spread a trap, they fell therein, in the net they hid, their foot was caught.

14. Thine hand was ready for all thine enemies who said, Through their sword they possessed the land, through their arm they dwelt in the city; thou didst fill their faces with shame, thou didst bring their horns down to the ground, thou didst terrify them in thy wrath, and didst destroy them in thine anger.

15. The earth trembled and shook at the sound of thy storm over them, thou didst not withhold their souls from death, and didst bring down their lives to the grave.

16. Thou didst pursue them in thy storm, thou didst consume them in thy whirlwind, thou didst turn their rain into hail, they fell in deep pits so that they could not rise.

17. Their carcasses were like rubbish cast out in the middle of the streets.

18. They were consumed and destroyed in thine anger, thou didst save thy people with thy might.

19. Therefore our hearts rejoice in thee, our souls exalt in thy salvation.

20. Our tongues shall relate thy might, we will sing and praise thy wondrous works.

21. For thou didst save us from our enemies, thou didst deliver us from those who rose up against us, thou didst destroy them from before us and depress them beneath our feet.

22. Thus shall all thine enemies perish O Lord, and the wicked shall be like chaff driven by the wind, and thy beloved shall be like trees planted by the waters.

23. So Joshua and all Israel with him returned to the camp in Gilgal, after having smitten all the kings, so that not a remnant was left of them.

24. And the five kings fled alone on foot from battle, and hid themselves in a cave, and Joshua sought for them in the field of battle, and did not find them.

25. And it was afterward told to Joshua, saying, The kings are found and behold they are hidden in a cave.

26. And Joshua said, Appoint men to be at the mouth of the cave, to guard them, lest they take themselves away; and the children of Israel did so.

27. And Joshua called to all Israel and said to the officers of battle, Place your feet upon the necks of these kings, and Joshua said, So shall the Lord do to all your enemies.

28. And Joshua commanded afterward that they should slay the kings and cast them into the cave, and to put great stones at the mouth of the cave.

29. And Joshua went afterward with all the people that were with him on that day to Makkedah, and he smote it with the edge of the sword.

30. And he utterly destroyed the souls and all belonging to the city, and he did to the king and people thereof as he had done to Jericho.

31. And he passed from there to Libnah and he fought against it, and the Lord delivered it into his hand, and Joshua smote it with the edge of the sword, and all the souls thereof, and he did to it and to the king thereof as he had done to Jericho.

32. And from there he passed on to Lachish to fight against it, and Horam king of Gaza went up to assist the men of Lachish, and Joshua smote him and his people until there was none left to him.

33. And Joshua took Lachish and all the people thereof, and he did to it as he had done to Libnah.

34. And Joshua passed from there to Eglon, and he took that also, and he smote it and all the people thereof with the edge of the sword.

35. And from there he passed to Hebron and fought against it and took it and utterly destroyed it, and he returned from there with all Israel to Debir and fought against it and smote it with the edge of the sword.

36. And he destroyed every soul in it, he left none remaining, and he did to it and the king thereof as he had done to Jericho.

37. And Joshua smote all the kings of the Amorites from Kadesh-barnea to Azah, and he took their country at once, for the Lord had fought for Israel.

38. And Joshua with all Israel came to the camp to Gilgal.

39. When at that time Jabin king of Chazor heard all that Joshua had done to the kings of the Amorites, Jabin sent to Jobat king of Midian, and to Laban king of Shimron, to Jephal king of Achshaph, and to all the kings of the Amorites, saying,

40. Come quickly to us and help us, that we may smite the children of Israel, before they come upon us and do unto us as they have done to the other kings of the Amorites.

41. And all these kings hearkened to the words of Jabin, king of Chazor, and they went forth with all their camps, seventeen kings, and their people were as numerous as the sand on the sea shore, together with horses and chariots innumerable, and they came and pitched together at the waters of Merom, and they were met together to fight against Israel.

42. And the Lord said to Joshua, Fear them not, for tomorrow about this time I will deliver them up all slain before you, thou shalt hough their horses and burn their chariots with fire.

43. And Joshua with all the men of war came suddenly upon them and smote them, and they fell into their hands, for the Lord had delivered them into the hands of the children of Israel.

44. So the children of Israel pursued all these kings with their camps, and smote them until there was none left of them, and Joshua did to them as the Lord had spoken to him.

45. And Joshua returned at that time to Chazor and smote it with the sword and destroyed every soul in it and burned it with fire, and from Chazor, Joshua passed to Shimron and smote it and utterly destroyed it.

46. From there he passed to Achshaph and he did to it as he had done to Shimron.

47. From there he passed to Adulam and he smote all the people in it, and he did to Adulam as he had done to Achshaph and to Shimron.

48. And he passed from them to all the cities of the kings which he had smitten, and he smote all the people that were left of them and he utterly destroyed them.

49. Only their booty and cattle the Israelites took to themselves as a prey, but every human being they smote, they suffered not a soul to live.

50. As the Lord had commanded Moses so did Joshua and all Israel, they failed not in anything.

51. So Joshua and all the children of Israel smote the whole land of Canaan as the Lord had commanded them, and smote all their kings, being thirty and one kings, and the children of Israel took their whole country.

52. Besides the kingdoms of Sihon and Og which are on the other side Jordan, of which Moses had smitten many cities, and Moses gave them to the Reubenites and the Gadites and to half the tribe of Manasseh.

53. And Joshua smote all the kings that were on this side Jordan to the west, and gave them for an inheritance to the nine tribes and to the half tribe of Israel.

54. For five years did Joshua carry on the war with these kings, and he gave their cities to the Israelites, and the land became tranquil from battle throughout the cities of the Amorites and the Canaanites.

CHAPTER 90

1. At that time in the fifth year after the children of Israel had passed over Jordan, after the children of Israel had rested from their war with the Canaanites, at that time great and severe battles arose between Edom and the children of Chittim, and the children of Chittim fought against Edom.

2. And Abianus king of Chittim went forth in that year, that is in the thirty-first year of his reign, and a great force with him of the mighty men of the children of Chittim, and he went to Seir to fight against the children of Esau.

3. And Hadad the king of Edom heard of his report, and he went forth to meet him with a heavy people and strong force, and engaged in battle with him in the field of Edom.

4. And the hand of Chittim prevailed over the children of Esau, and the children of Chittim slew of the children of Esau, two and twenty thousand men, and all the children of Esau fled from before them.

5. And the children of Chittim pursued them and they reached Hadad king of Edom, who was running before them and they caught him alive, and brought him to Abianus king of Chittim.

6. And Abianus ordered him to be slain, and Hadad king of Edom died in the forty-eighth year of his reign.

7. And the children of Chittim continued their pursuit of Edom, and they smote them with a great slaughter and Edom became subject to the children of Chittim.

8. And the children of Chittim ruled over Edom, and Edom became under the hand of the children of Chittim and became one kingdom from that day.

9. And from that time they could no more lift up their heads, and their kingdom became one with the children of Chittim.

10. And Abianus placed officers in Edom and all the children of Edom became subject and tributary to Abianus, and Abianus turned back to his own land, Chittim.

11. And when he returned he renewed his government and built for himself a spacious and fortified palace for a royal residence, and reigned securely over the children of Chittim and over Edom.

12. In those days, after the children of Israel had driven away all the Canaanites and the Amorites, Joshua was old and advanced in years.

13. And the Lord said to Joshua, Thou art old, advanced in life, and a great part of the land remains to be possessed.

14. Now therefore divide this land for an inheritance to the nine tribes and to the half tribe of Manasseh, and Joshua rose up and did as the Lord had spoken to him.

15. And he divided the whole land to the tribes of Israel as an inheritance according to their divisions.

16. But to the tribe at Levi he gave no inheritance, the offerings of the Lord are their inheritance as the Lord had spoken of them by the hand of Moses.

17. And Joshua gave Mount Hebron to Caleb the son of Jephuneh, one portion above his brethren, as the Lord had spoken through Moses.

18. Therefore Hebron became an inheritance to Caleb and his children unto this day.

19. And Joshua divided the whole land by lots to all Israel for an inheritance, as the Lord had commanded him.

20. And the children of Israel gave cities to the Levites from their own inheritance, and suburbs for their cattle, and property, as the Lord had commanded Moses so did the children of Israel, and they divided the land by lot whether great or small.

21. And they went to inherit the land according to their boundaries, and the children of Israel gave to Joshua the son of Nun an inheritance amongst them.

22. By the word of the Lord did they give to him the city which he required, Timnathserach in Mount Ephraim, and he built the city and dwelt therein.

23. These are the inheritances which Elazer the priest and Joshua the son of Nun and the heads of the fathers of the tribes portioned out to the children of Israel by lot in Shiloh, before the Lord, at the door of the tabernacle, and they left off dividing the land.

24. And the Lord gave the land to the Israelites, and they possessed it as the Lord had spoken to them, and as the Lord had sworn to their ancestors.

25. And the Lord gave to the Israelites rest from all their enemies around them, and no man stood up against them, and the Lord delivered all their enemies into their hands, and not one thing failed of all the good which the Lord had spoken to the children of Israel, yea the Lord performed every thing.

26. And Joshua called to all the children of Israel and he blessed them, and commanded them to serve the Lord, and he afterward sent them away, and they went each man to his city, and each man to his inheritance.

27. And the children of Israel served the Lord all the days of Joshua, and the Lord gave them rest from all around them, and they dwelt securely in their cities.

28. And it came to pass in those days, that Abianus king of Chittim died, in the thirty-eighth year of his reign, that is the seventh year of his reign over Edom, and they buried him in his place which he had built for himself, and Latinus reigned in his stead fifty years.

29. And during his reign he brought forth an army, and he went and fought against the inhabitants of Britannia and Kernania, the children of Elisha son of Javan, and he prevailed over them and made them tributary.

30. He then heard that Edom had revolted from under the hand of Chittim, and Latinus went to them and smote them and subdued them, and placed them under the hand of the children of Chittim, and Edom became one kingdom with the children of Chittim all the days.

31. And for many years there was no king in Edom, and their government was with the children of Chittim and their king.

32. And it was in the twenty-sixth year after the children of Israel had passed the Jordan, that is the sixty-sixth year after the children of Israel had departed from Egypt, that Joshua was old, advanced in years, being one hundred and eight years old in those days.

33. And Joshua called to all Israel, to their elders, their judges and officers, after the Lord had given to all the Israelites rest from all their enemies round about, and Joshua said to the elders of Israel, and to their judges, Behold I am old, advanced in years, and you have seen what the Lord has done to all the nations whom he has driven away from before you, for it is the Lord who has fought for you.

34. Now therefore strengthen yourselves to keep and to do all the words of the law of Moses, not to deviate from it to the right or to the left, and not to come amongst those nations who are left in the land; neither shall you make mention of the name of their gods, but you shall cleave to the Lord your God, as you have done to this day.

35. And Joshua greatly exhorted the children of Israel to serve the Lord all their days.

36. And all the Israelites said, We will serve the Lord our God all our days, we and our children, and our children's children, and our seed for ever.

37. And Joshua made a covenant with the people on that day, and he sent away the children of Israel, and they went each man to his inheritance and to his city.

38. And it was in those days, when the children of Israel were dwelling securely in their cities, that they buried the coffins of the tribes of their ancestors, which they had brought up from Egypt, each man in the inheritance of his children, the twelve sons of Jacob did the children of Israel bury, each man in the possession of his children.

39. And these are the names of the cities wherein they buried the twelve sons of Jacob, whom the children of Israel had brought up from Egypt.

40. And they buried Reuben and Gad on this side Jordan, in Romia, which Moses had given to their children.

41. And Simeon and Levi they buried in the city Mauda, which he had given to the children of Simeon, and the suburb of the city was for the children of Levi.

42. And Judah they buried in the city of Benjamin opposite Bethlehem.

43. And the bones of Issachar and Zebulun they buried in Zidon, in the portion which fell to their children.

44. And Dan was buried in the city of his children in Eshtael, and Naphtali and Asher they buried in Kadesh-naphtali, each man in his place which he had given to his children.

45. And the bones of Joseph they buried in Shechem, in the part of the field which Jacob had purchased from Hamor, and which became to Joseph for an inheritance.

46. And they buried Benjamin in Jerusalem opposite the Jebusite, which was given to the children of Benjamin; the children of Israel buried their fathers each man in the city of his children.

47. And at the end of two years, Joshua the son of Nun died, one hundred and ten years old, and the time which Joshua judged Israel was twenty-eight years, and Israel served the Lord all the days of his life.

48. And the other affairs of Joshua and his battles and his reproofs with which he reproved Israel, and all which he had commanded them, and the names of the cities which the children of Israel possessed in his days, behold they are written in the book of the words of Joshua to the children of Israel, and in the book of the wars of the Lord, which Moses and Joshua and the children of Israel had written.

49. And the children of Israel buried Joshua in the border of his inheritance, in Timnathserach, which was given to him in Mount Ephraim.

50. And Elazer the son of Aaron died in those days, and they buried him in a hill belonging to Phineas his son, which was given him in Mount Ephraim.

CHAPTER 91

1. At that time, after the death of Joshua, the children of the Canaanites were still in the land, and the Israelites resolved to drive them out.

2. And the children of Israel asked of the Lord, saying, Who shall first go up for us to the Canaanites to fight against them? and the Lord said, Judah shall go up.

3. And the children of Judah said to Simeon, Go up with us into our lot, and we will fight against the Canaanites and we likewise will go up with you, in your lot, so the children of Simeon went with the children of Judah.

4. And the children of Judah went up and fought against the Canaanites, so the Lord delivered the Canaanites into the hands of the children of Judah, and they smote them in Bezek, ten thousand men.

5. And they fought with Adonibezek in Bezek, and he fled from before them, and they pursued him and caught him, and they took hold of him and cut off his thumbs and great toes.

6. And Adonibezek said, Three score and ten kings having their thumbs and great toes cut off, gathered their meat under my table, as I have done, so God has requited me, and they brought him to Jerusalem and he died there.

7. And the children of Simeon went with the children of Judah, and they smote the Canaanites with the edge of the sword.

8. And the Lord was with the children of Judah, and they possessed the mountain, and the children of Joseph went up to Bethel, the same is Luz, and the Lord was with them.

9. And the children of Joseph spied out Bethel, and the watchmen saw a man going forth from the city, and they caught him and said unto him, Show us now the entrance of the city and we will show kindness to thee.

10. And that man showed them the entrance of the city, and the children of Joseph came and smote the City with the edge of the sword.

11. And the man with his family they sent away, and he went to the Hittites and he built a city, and he called the name thereof Luz, so all the Israelites dwelt in their cities, and the children at Israel dwelt in their cities, and the children of Israel served the Lord all the days of Joshua, and all the days of the elders, who had lengthened their days after Joshua, and saw the great work of the Lord, which he had performed for Israel.

12. And the elders judged Israel after the death of Joshua for seventeen years.

13. And all the elders also fought the battles of Israel against the Canaanites and the Lord drove the Canaanites from before the children of Israel, in order to place the Israelites in their land.

14. And he accomplished all the words which he had spoken to Abraham, Isaac, and Jacob, and the oath which he had sworn, to give to them and to their children, the land of the Canaanites.

15. And the Lord gave to the children of Israel the whole land of Canaan, as he had sworn to their ancestors, and the Lord gave them rest from those around them, and the children of Israel dwelt securely in their cities.

16. Blessed be the Lord for ever, amen, and amen.

17. Strengthen yourselves, and let the hearts of all you that trust in the Lord be of good courage.
THE END

THE BOOK OF JUBILEES

OR

THE LITTLE GENESIS

TRANSLATED FROM THE ETHIOPIC TEXT

BY

R. H. CHARLES, D.LITT., D.D.

CANON OF WESTMINSTER; FELLOW OF MERTON COLLEGE;

EDITORS' PREFACE

THE object of this series of translations is primarily to furnish students with short, cheap, and handy text-books, which, it is hoped, will facilitate the study of the particular texts in class under competent teachers. But it is also hoped that the volumes will be acceptable to the general reader who may be interested in the subjects with which they deal. It has been thought advisable, as a general rule, to restrict the notes and comments to a small compass; more especially as, in most cases, excellent works of a more elaborate character are available. Indeed, it is much to be desired that these translations may have the effect of inducing readers to study the larger works.

Our principal aim, in a word, is to make some difficult texts, important for the study of Christian origins, more generally accessible in faithful and scholarly translations.

In most cases these texts are not available in a cheap and handy form. In one or two cases texts have been included of books which are available in the official Apocrypha; but in every such case reasons exist for putting forth these texts in a new translation, with an Introduction, in this series.

We desire to express our thanks to Canon Charles and Messrs. A. and C. Black, for their permission to reprint here the translation of *The Book of Jubilees*, published in 1902.

W. O. E.

INTRODUCTION

SHORT ACCOUNT OF THE BOOK

THE Book of Jubilees, or, as it is sometimes called, "the little Genesis," purports to be a revelation given by God to Moses through the medium of an angel (" the Angel of the Presence," i. 27), and containing a history, divided up into jubilee-periods of fortynine years, from the creation to the coming of Moses. Though the actual narrative of events is only carried down to the birth and early career of Moses, its author envisages the events of a later time, and in particular certain events of special interest at the time when he wrote, which was probably in the latter years of the second century B.C., perhaps in the reign of the Maccabean prince John Hyrcanus. Though distinguished from the Pentateuch proper ("the first Law," vi. 22), it presupposes and supplements the latter. The actual narrative embraces material contained in the whole of Genesis and part of Exodus. But the legal regulations given presuppose other parts of the Pentateuch, especially the so-called "Priest's Code" (P), and certain details in the narrative are probably intended to apply to events that occurred in the author's own time (the latter years of the second century B.C.). The author himself seems to have contemplated the speedy inauguration of the Messianic Age, and in this respect his point of view is similar to that of the Apocalyptic writers. But his work, though it contains one or two passages of an apocalyptic character, is quite unlike the typical apocalypses. It is largely narrative based upon the historical narratives in Genesis and Exodus, interspersed with legends, and emphasizing certain legal practices (such as the strict observance of the Sabbath, circumcision, etc.), and laying much stress upon their eternal obligation. But his main object was to inculcate a reform in the regulation of the calendar and festivals, in place of the intercalated lunar calendar, which he condemns in the strongest language. He proposes to substitute for this a solar calendar consisting of 12 months and containing 364 days. The result of such a system is to make all festivals, except the Day of Atonement, fall on a Sunday; the author also fixes the date of the Feast of Weeks (Pentecost) on Sivan 15th (in place of the traditional Sivan 6th). He obviously believes that the prevailing system has produced grave consequences in religious practice. The proper observance of the feasts, which had been prescribed by divine authority, is, according to his view, rendered impossible so long as the right principles for regulating the calendar are ignored. These principles are justified from the written Law, and are represented as having been ordained in heaven. To what party or tendency in Judaism did the author belong? Various answers have been given to this question, which will be fully discussed below. It is very difficult to believe, as Dr. Charles contends, that the author was a Pharisee, for the positions he advocates are in many respects fundamentally opposed to later Pharisaic practice. In particular, how can any member of the Pharisaic party, which from its beginning championed popular religious custom, have advocated a solar calendar? More can be said for the view that the author was a member of the Hasidim or "pious" (who must not be confounded with the Pharisees), while in a recent important discussion Leszynsky has made out a strong, if not quite convincing, case for Sadducean authorship. The Book has sometimes been styled a Midrash, but such a descriptive term needs some qualification. It claims to be a revelation, and not a mere exposition of Genesis and Exodus. At the same time, there is a certain Midrashic tendency observable in the way the author rewrites the older narratives, which reminds one of the work of the Chronicler as compared with the earlier canonical books which he remodelled. But *Jubilees* is not at all like the typical Midrash of the later Rabbinical period; it is more independent, and resembles rather such works as the "*Chronicles of Jerahmeel*," or the earlier (narrative) part of the "Apocalypse of Abraham."

The Book, which was probably composed in Hebrew, is divided into fifty chapters, and appears to be complete.

TITLES

The Book was known under various titles, most of them in Greek as referred to in later Greek writers. The most important are "Jubilees" (= τ ωβηλα α or) and "the little Genesis" (= λεπτ; and variants). Both of these seem to go back to Hebrew originals, and there would thus appear to have been two authoritative Hebrew titles of the original Hebrew work, viz. *ha-yôbĕlîm* (or *sēfer hâ-yôbĕlôth*), and *Berēshîth zûtā*. In the latter the epithet "little" [33]refers not to the extent of the work, but to its relatively inferior position as compared with the

---

[33] Applied also to certain minor midrashîm ("midrash zûtā," etc.)

canonical Genesis. It is also noteworthy that a clear reference to our Book is made in the recently recovered fragments of a "Zadokite Work." [34]The passage runs as follows (xx. 1):

And as for the exact statement of their Periods to put Israel in remembrance in regard to all these, behold it is treated accurately in the Book of the Divisions of the Seasons according to their jubilees and their Weeks.

This is remarkably like the opening words of the Prologue of our Book: *This is the history of the division* p. x *of the days . . . of the events of the years according to their (year-) weeks, according to their jubilees. . . .* Cf. also the colophon at the end of the Book:

Herewith is completed the account of the division of the days.

Other titles of our Book are: *The Apocalypse of Moses* (Syncellus); *The Testament of Moses* (the Catena of Nicephorus); *The Book of Adam's Daughters* (perhaps applied only to a portion of *Jubilees*); *The Life of Adam* (perhaps an amplified excerpt of our Book).

VERSIONS AND ORIGINAL LANGUAGE

The complete text of the Book is extant in an Ethiopic Version, which is also the most accurate that has survived. Four MSS. of it are known, and are preserved in European Libraries, the two most important in the National Library in Paris and in the British Museum respectively. A critical edition of the text, based on all the known MSS., has been published by Dr. Charles (Oxford, 1895), which was preceded by an important one by Dillmann (published 1859). Fragments of a Greek, Latin and (possibly) a Syriac version are also extant. The fragments of the Greek version are contained in numerous citations in Justin Martyr, Origen, Diodorus of Antioch, Isidore of Alexandria, Epiphanius, Syncellus and other writers. The Latin version, of -which about one-fourth has been preserved, is very valuable for the criticism of the text. The fragments that have survived were first published by Ceriani (in his *Monumenta Sacra el Profana*, 1861), and have been edited by Rönsch (1874), and more recently by Charles (in his edition of the Ethiopic text referred to above). What may possibly be a fragment of a Syriac Version of our Book is contained in a British Museum MS.

(Add. 12154, fol. 180) entitled "Names of the Wives of the Patriarchs according to the Hebrew Book called Jubilees." But whether this p. xi is really part of a complete version is very doubtful (see Charles, *op. cit.*, Appendix iii.).

It is generally agreed that both the Ethiopic and Latin versions were translated from the Greek which, it may be inferred from the large number of quotations scattered about in different writers over a wide period, must have been widely diffused. The fact that a Greek text underlies these versions is clear from such phenomena as the presence, in the Ethiopic, of transliterations of Greek words (*e. g.* λιου, "of the sun," in xxxiv. 11); proper names are transliterated as they appear in Greek, not in Hebrew; and certain textual corruptions can only be explained by reference to an underlying Greek text. Similar phenomena characterize the Latin version. Thus in xxxviii. 12, "timoris" = δειλίας, which is corrupt for δουλείας; and sometimes the Greek has been misunderstood, as *e. g.* in xxxviii. 13, "honorem" = τιμ ν, which should have been rendered by "tributum."

It is more difficult to determine whether a Semitic original underlies the Greek, and, if that be the case, whether the original Semitic text was Hebrew or Aramaic. It must be admitted that in a number of passages where the text of the canonical Genesis is cited the Ethiopic agrees with the LXX against all other authorities (see Charles' *Jubilees*, p. xxxiv). But these cases are not, on the whole, either numerous or important. [35]On the other hand, the Ethiopic often agrees with the LXX, supported by other authorities (especially the Samaritan text and version) against the Masoretic Hebrew text, and there are other variations in the textual phenomena. From a survey of these phenomena Charles deduces the conclusion, no doubt rightly, that "our book attests an independent form of the Hebrew text of the Pentateuch. . . . Our book represents *some form of the Hebrew text of the Pentateuch midway between the forms presupposed by the LXX and the Syriac.*" [36]

It agrees with the LXX, or with combinations into which the LXX enters, more often than with any other authority or group of authorities. On the other hand, it is often independent of the LXX, and in a considerable number of cases attests readings, with the support of MT and Sam., against the LXX, and manifestly superior to the latter. It is noteworthy that it never agrees with M against all the other authorities. These phenomena

---

[34] First published by Schechter in 1910 (Cambridge Press).

[35] They *may* be due to assimilation in the Greek Version with the LXX.

[36] *Jubilees*, p. xxxviii

suggest that the composition of *Jubilees* is to be assigned to "some period between 250 B.C. (LXX version of the Pentateuch) and A.D. 100 [when M was finally fixed], and at a time nearer the earlier date than the latter."[37]

A number of considerations may be adduced which suggest that the original language of *Jubilees* was Hebrew. Thus mistranslations of Hebrew words occur, *e. g.* in xliii. 11, the word rendered (as corrected) "I pray thee," is, in the Ethiopic, "in me"--a confusion of the Hebrew *bî* = δέομαι (Gen. xliv. 18) with the Hebrew word (spelt in exactly the same way) which = "in me;" there are also numerous Hebraisms surviving in the Ethiopic and Latin versions, [38] as well as paronomasiae based upon Hebrew words. [39] It is noteworthy, also, that the author lays special stress upon the sacred character of Hebrew, which was originally the language of creation (cf. xii. 25-26; xliii. 15). Moreover, he represents his work as having emanated from Moses, and a genuinely Mosaic work would naturally be written in Hebrew. Finally, certain parts of *Jubilees*, or of something remarkably like *Jubilees*, have survived in Hebrew form in certain Hebrew books, especially the *Chronicles of Jerahmeel*, and the Midrash Tadshe. It is not improbable, also, that a Hebrew form of *Jubilees* was known to the compiler of the *Pir e de R. Eliezer* (see Friedlander's Introduction to the latter book, p. xxii). The only ground for suggesting that the Semitic p. xiii original may have been Aramaic rather than Hebrew is the presence of certain Aramaizing forms of proper names (*e. g. Filistin*, with the termination *n* instead of *m*) in the Latin version. But in all these cases the Ethiopic transliteration has *m* (not *n*), and it seems probable that the Aramaizing forms in these cases are due to the Latin translator, who there is other ground for supposing was a Palestinian Jew. We may, therefore, safely conclude that the original language of our Book was Hebrew.

AFFINITIES WITH OTHER LITERATURE

Though there is no reason to doubt the essential unity of our Book (that is to say, that it was composed and written in its present form by one author), it is equally clear that this writer incorporated earlier traditions and legends into his work. Thus he refers explicitly to Noachic writings (xxi. 10; cf. x. 13), and has apparently incorporated two considerable sections of a "Book of Noah" in vii. 20-39 and x. 1-15. It is well-known that this Noachic Book was also one of the sources of the Book of Enoch, 1 Enoch, vi.-xi., ix., lxv.-lxix. 25, and cvi.-cvii. being probably derived from it. There is reason, also, to believe that the author of *Jubilees* was acquainted with some form of the Book of Enoch (1 Enoch). According to Charles the parts of 1 Enoch with which our author was acquainted are 1 Enoch vi-xvi., xxiii.-xxxvi. and lxxii.-xc. He seems clearly to refer to the last section in iv. 17:

And he [Enoch] was the first among men that are born on earth who learnt writing and knowledge and wisdom and who wrote down the signs of heaven according to the order of their months in a book, that men might know the seasons of the years according to the order of their separate months.

Here the Enoch-book referred to forms a description of 1 Enoch lxxii.-lxxxii. ("the Book of the courses of the Heavenly Luminaries "), while iv. 19 (*And what was and what will be he saw in a vision of his sleep, as it will happen to the children of men throughout their generations until the day of judgement; he saw and understood everything, and wrote his testimony, and placed the testimony on earth for all the children of men and for their generations*) forms an exact description of the "Dream-Visions" in 1 Enoch lxxxiii.-xc. [40]There are also a number of parallels with the *Testaments of the XII Patriarchs*, but these are not sufficient to show dependence on either side; the phenomena rather suggest that both writers are using common sources: Cf. xviii. 9; xxx. 2-6, 18, 25; xxxi. 3-4, 13, 15, 16; xxxii. 1, 8; xxxiii. 1, 2, 4; xxxiv. 1-9; xxxvii.-xxxviii.; xli. 8-14, 24-25, xlvi. 6-9.

It has already been mentioned that a knowledge of our Book seems to be presupposed in some of the later Jewish literature. Thus the *Chronicles of Jerahmeel*, a late compilation written in Hebrew, contains much material common to *Jubilees*; at times it reproduces the actual words of the text of the latter. Another late Jewish work, the Midrash *Tadshe*, contains passages which are largely identical with portions of the text of our Book. This Midrash was compiled in its present form by Moses haDarshan in the eleventh century A.D., but is

---

[37] *Op. cit.*, p. xxxix.

[38] Cf. *e. g.* xxii. 10, "eligere in te" = Heb. *bāhar bĕ*.

[39] See Charles, *op. cit.*, p. xxxiii for details.

[40] For further parallels see Charles, Jubilees, pp. lxviii ff.

based upon a much earlier work by R. Pinchas b. Jair (end of second century, A.D.), who utilized materials from our Book.

Besides the above, our Book appears to have been known to the compiler of the Samaritan Chronicle (twelfth century, A.D.), and also to the compiler of the *Pirke de R. Eliezer* (finally redacted in the ninth century A.D.). In fact, in both cases there is implicit a certain amount of polemic (especially in calendar-matters) against the positions advocated in *Jubilees*. But besides this, there is a remarkable parallelism in subject-matter between our Book and the *Pirke de R. Eliezer*, to which Friedlander calls attention. He points out that both "are alike in being practically Midrashic paraphrases and expansions of the narratives contained in the Book of Genesis and part of the Book of Exodus. . . . Both books deal with the Calendar . . . and in this respect they recall the Books of Enoch." Both "have chapters setting forth the story of the Creation (*Ma'aseh Bereshith*). . . . The past is recalled and the future revealed. The nature of God, angels and man is unfolded. We read of sin and grace, repentance and atonement, good and evil, life and death, Paradise and Gehenna, Satan and Messiah." [41]

Numerous references to *Jubilees* occur in Christian literature (patristic period and later), where long extracts from the Book are often cited, and by name. These have been collected by Charles (*op. cit.*, pp. lxxvii ff.), who also cites a number of parallels between our Book and the New Testament. But these are somewhat vague, and are hardly sufficient to establish any real or direct connexion.

THE SPECIAL AIMS AND GENERAL CHARACTER OF THE BOOK

It is obvious that *Jubilees* is dominated by certain interests and antipathies. It is to a large extent polemical in character, and its author desires at once to protest against certain tendencies which, in his view, threaten true religion, and to inculcate certain reforms. Incidentally it commends certain religious practices, and endeavours to invest them with enhanced sanctions. In the forefront, as its name ("the Book of Jubilees") suggests [42] stands the question of the Calendar. It is all important in the author's view that the divinely ordained principle according to which history is divided up by year-weeks (*i. e.* periods of 7 years) and jubilees (*i. e.* periods of 7 X 7 years) is recognized (Cf. i. 26 f.). Accordingly, he gives a history from Creation to Moses, in which the sequence of events is recorded and dated exactly by jubilee-periods, or portions of such. This leads up to a final section in which the law respecting jubilees and sabbatical years is solemnly enjoined. The writer's aim seems to have been nothing less than a reformation of the Jewish Calendar. The prevailing system has led to the nation "forgetting" new moons, festivals, and sabbaths (and (?) jubilees); [43] in other words, it has produced grave irregularities in the observance of matters which were of divine obligation.

A cardinal feature of the writer's system is the jubilee-period, which consists of 7 X 7 (*i. e.* 49) years. Here we are confronted with a difficulty. The passage in Lev. (xxv. 814) which ordains the observance of the jubilee-year expressly identifies this, in the present form of the text, with the fiftieth year (Lev. xxv. 10 and 11). But it is incredible that the author of our Book would deliberately have violated the express injunctions of the Pentateuch on such a matter, and we are driven to conclude that he had a text before him in which the word "fiftieth" was absent. [44] The wording of verses 8 and 9 is ambiguous, and allows of the explanation that the jubilee-year was the forty-ninth and not the fiftieth. It is quite possible that in verses 10 and 11 "fiftieth" has been added to the text, in the interests of the rival explanation that ultimately prevailed, for, as has been pointed out already, our Book presupposes a text of the Pentateuch that is independent of and earlier than M.T. This explanation suffers from the difficulty that the LXX and other ancient versions (including the Samaritan text) support the currently received reading. But it is not improbable that on such a matter the influence of Orthodox views may have operated to bring their text of the verses into harmony with the currently accepted theory. [45]

But more revolutionary is the writer's advocacy of a solar calendar. In ii. 9 he says, "God appointed the sun to be a great sign upon the earth for days and for sabbaths, and for feasts and for years and for jubilees and for

---

[41] *Op. cit.*, p. xxii.

[42] This is obscured by such titles as "the little Genesis," "the Apocalypse of Moses," etc.

[43] vi. 34; cf. i. 10.

[44] So Leszynsky, *Die Sadduzäer*, pp. 156 ff.

[45] It should be noted that the Talmud (T.B., *Ned.*, 61a) refers to the view (held by R. Jehuda) that the jubilee-period was forty-nine years.

all seasons of the years." In Gen. i. 14 this function is assigned to the sun *and the moon*; but in our Book the moon is deliberately excluded. The writer objected fiercely to the traditional calendar which was based upon the changes of the moon, and was adjusted to the solar year by means of intercalation. How can his apparent violation of the express wording of Scripture be explained? His answer would probably have been that the solar year of 364 days (cf. vi. 32) was actually the system implied in the Pentateuch. It has been pointed out by Bacon [46]that in the P sections of the Flood-narrative in Genesis a year of 364 days is pre-supposed. It is said that the Flood began on the 17th day of the second month, and ended on the 27th day of the second month the following year, *i. e.* reckoning by the ordinary lunar months, 12 months (= 12 X 29½ days) or 354 days + 10 days (to make up the solar year), or 364 days in all, this completing the one whole year which, according to the Babylonian source, was the length of the Flood's duration. Thus the author of *Jubilees* had a dogmatic basis within the text of the Pentateuch itself for his view that the true year was a solar one of 364 days. He may very well have believed that whatever may be the exact significance of Gen. i. 14, it could not override this fact. It is interesting to notice that this tradition of a solar year of 364 days should be implicit in the P sections of Genesis. There are strong reasons for believing that the author of *Jubilees* was a priest, and, as such, may have been acquainted in some special way with this priestly tradition. There are, however, difficulties in connexion with the reckoning of such a solar year. It is obvious that a year of 12 months, each of which contains 30 days, will only yield a total of 360 days. It has been supposed that our author overcame this difficulty by inserting one intercalary day at the beginning of each quarter. Thus each three months would contain 31 + 30 + 30 (= 91) days. But this solution will not harmonize with the date assigned by our author to the Feast of Weeks, which is the "middle" of the third month (xvi. 13). Scholars are agreed that the 15th of Sivan is meant. Now the Feast of Weeks was to be celebrated on the fiftieth day, counting from the "morrow" after the Sabbath of Passover (Lev. xxiii. 15 f.) . The Pharisees, as is well known, interpreted "Sabbath" here to be the first day of the Feast (Nisan 15th), whatever the day of the week on which it fell, and reckoned from Nisan 16th, which would bring the Feast of Weeks to Sivan 6th. Another view, with which our Book agrees, interpreted "sabbath" as = "week" (as in fact it has this meaning throughout the rest of the verse). Then render: *And ye shall count unto you from the morrow after the (festival) week, from the day that ye bring the wave-sheaf, seven complete weeks shall there be, until the morrow after the seventh week ye shall number fifty days*: the festival-week would be Nisan 15-21, and its "morrow" Nisan 22; reckoning 28 days to the month, this would leave 6 days in Nisan + 28 days in Iyar + 15 in Sivan = 49 +Nisan 22 = 50 (lays. This seems to have been the reckoning of our author. Moreover, since the year he advocates contains 364 days, the festivals would always fall upon the same day of the week, and as Nisan 1st the first day of Creation fell, according to his scheme, on the first day of the week, *i. e.* Sunday, it must always fall on that day; thus Nisan 14th and 21st would always fall on a Sabbath, while Nisan 22nd and Sivan 15th would always fall on a Sunday. To make the Feast of Weeks fall on the 1st day of the week was a Sadducean practice, and one that it is inconceivable that any Pharisee can ever have sanctioned or tolerated. It will be noticed, however, that the view of our author, according to which the Feast of Weeks falls on Sivan 15th, implies a reckoning of 28 days to the months Nisan and Iyar. How is this to be reconciled with a solar year of 12 months? Eppstein supposes that our author used two reckonings, one for the civil year of 12 months, 8 of 30, and 4 of 31 days, and an ecclesiastical year of 13 months each containing 28 days. But it is difficult to believe that the writer used two systems side by side. A better solution would be that he added a week to every third month, which would make each 3 months consist of 28 + 28 + 35 days (total 91 days), or 4 + 4 + 5 weeks. It is evident that his calendar-system is based upon the number 7; thus each month consists of 4 X 7 (or 5 X 7) days, while the year consists of 52 X 7 days, the year-week of 7 years, and the jubilee of 7 X 7 years. On this reckoning the Feast of Weeks would still fall on the 15th of Sivan, but the 15th would not strictly be the "middle" of that month, which, *ex hypothesi*, consisted of 35 days. It might, however, be used loosely for such a date. Perhaps, too, the author desired to avoid specifying more particularly this date, because current Sadducean practice (based upon 4 different length of days assigned to the months) would not quite harmonize with it. [47]With regard to the Passover, it is noticeable that our author interprets the phrase "between the two evenings" (at which time the Passover lamb was to be slain, cf. Exod. xii. 6; Lev. xxiii. 5) to mean the third part of the day (xlix. 10); *i. e.* assuming the day to contain 12 hours, we may fix the third part as from 2 to 6 p.m. This, again, contradicts

---

[46] In *Hebraica*, vol. viii. (1891-2), cited by Charles on vi. 32.

[47] Thus the Abyssinian Jews (*Falashas*), maintaining old practice, reckon the 50 days from Nisan 21, as our author does, but fix Sivan 12 as the date for the Feast of Weeks, as they use alternate months of 30 and 29 days. It should be noted that the author of 1 Enoch lxxii.-lxxxii. also advocates a year of 364 days.

Pharisaic practice. Notable, too, is the mention of wine in connexion with the Passover: *All Israel* [*i. e.* in Egypt] *was eating the flesh of the Paschal lamb and drinking the wine* (xlix. 6). Now this was a Pharisaic custom in later times, and has no basis, apparently, in the canonical account in Exodus. In view, however, of the fact that our author usually follows the prescriptions of Scripture with scrupulous care, the question arises whether he did not, in fact, derive this from the Pentateuch. Leszyrisky suggests [48]that the word rendered "bitter herbs" in Exod. xii. 8 ("with bitter herbs shall they eat it") was interpreted by our author to mean "wine"--the word simply means "bitter," or "what is poisonous," and a cognate form is used in connexion with wine in Deut. xxxii. 32. It is certainly curious that our author makes no mention of "bitter herbs" in connexion with the Egyptian Passover.

The Feast of Tabernacles, too, as described in our Book (xvi. 10-31), has certain peculiar features. In particular, the specifically Pharisaic custom of pouring water on the altar [49]at the Feast is not mentioned or recognized. Now as early as the time of Alexander Jannæus (102-76 B.C.) the Pharisees tried to enforce the adoption of this custom upon the Sadducean priest-king, who, to show his contempt, allowed the water, which should have been poured solemnly on the altar, to run over his feet. The protest that ensued was followed later by a massacre of Pharisees. It is difficult to believe that our author, a few years earlier, if he was himself a Pharisee, could have been ignorant of this custom, which was based upon old popular tradition. His silence concerning it is much more probably deliberate. The custom was objectionable, from the Sadducean standpoint, because it had no basis in the written Law. The custom of wearing wreaths upon the head which is here prescribed (xvi. 30) is also unknown to tradition; nor has it, apparently, any Scriptural basis, unless it was inferred as an act of rejoicing, from the words "and ye shall rejoice before the Lord your God seven days" (Lev. xxiii. 40), taken in conjunction with the command (in the preceding clause) to take "branches of palm trees, and boughs of thick trees, and willows of the brook." Wearing a wreath of palm-leaves may have been regarded as one of the ways in which this command was to be fulfilled.

Even more striking are the sections which give directions about the observance of the Sabbath (l. 1-13; cf. ii. 29-30). These directions are very severe. The following actions are prohibited on the Sabbath under penalty of death: travelling by land or sea, buying or selling, drawing water, carrying burdens out of the house, killing or striking, snaring beasts, birds or fish, fasting or making war, marital intercourse. The last prescription is in direct opposition to Pharisaic practice, as is also the severe penalty imposed for non-observance of the various prescriptions. It is interesting to notice that these agree with the practice still maintained by the Falashas, Samaritans, and Karaite Jews. Probably this rigid view of sabbath-observance was cherished in specially pious priestly circles at the time when our author wrote. In this connexion it may be noted that our Book, in its interpretation of the law about the fruit of newly-planted trees given in Lev. xix. 23-24, agrees with the view of the Samaritans and Karaite Jews in directing that the first fruits of the fruit of the fourth year should be offered on the altar, and what remained given to the priests. According to Pharisaic practice what remained was to be eaten by the owners within the walls of Jerusalem.

Another point in which *Jubilees* upholds a view which is certainly not Pharisaic is on the question of the law of retribution, the so-called *lex talionis*. It is well known that while the Sadducees insisted on the strict letter of the Law, "an eye for an eye, and a tooth for a tooth," the Pharisees strove to mitigate its harshness by the substitution (except in the case of murder) of compensating money-payments. Moreover, the Mishna directs that where the death-penalty is inflicted it is to be carried out by the sword (cf. *Sanhedrin* ix. i: "These are to be beheaded"). Our Book, however, seems to wage a polemic against such views in no uncertain language:

Take no gifts for the blood of man, [50] *lest it be shed with impunity, without judgement; for it is the blood that is shed that causes the earth to sin, and the earth cannot be cleansed from the blood of man save by the blood of him who shed it. And take no present or gift for the blood of man; blood for blood* (xxi. 19 f.).

In iv. 31 f. the circumstances of Cain's death are described: *his house fell upon him and he died in the midst of his house; for with a stone he had killed Abel, and by a stone was he killed in righteous judgement. For this reason it was ordained on the heavenly tables: "With the instrument with which a man kills his neighbour, with the same shall he be killed; after the manner that he wounded him, in like manner shall they deal with him."*

---

[48] *Op. cit.*, pp. 207 ff.

[49] Cf. *R.W.S.*², p. 401 f.

[50] This would be allowed in certain cases of homicide (not deliberate murder) by the Rabbinical Law.

It is true that a school of Pharisees (the School of Shammai) still, to some extent, upheld, in theory at any rate, the severer and older view. But this does not alter the fact that it was a distinctive tenet of the Sadducees; and it is difficult to believe that any Pharisee can, at any time, have used such unqualified language as that employed in the extracts given above. [51]

At this point we may well ask what was the author's attitude towards the belief in a future life? At the time when he wrote the doctrine of the resurrection of the body had become well established in certain Jewish circles. In the Book of Daniel it had received classical expression. It was a cherished belief of the Pharisaic party. Now our Book does not in any way accept such a belief. The one passage in which the language employed might, at first sight, suggest a hint of such a belief is a sentence describing the happiness of the righteous in the age of felicity which is to dawn:

And at that time the Lord will heal His servants, And they will rise up and see great peace, And drive out their adversaries (xxiii. 30).

But here there is probably no reference to the idea of a resurrection. As Charles points out, the words "shall rise up" have here "apparently no reference to the resurrection, and mean merely that when God heals His servants (cf. Rev. xxii. 2) they become strong." The clause in the preceding verse, *all their days will be days of blessing and healing* (cf. also i. 29) renders "this view the most probable." On the other hand, the opening words of xxiii. 31

And their bones will rest in the earth, And their spirits will have much joy, though they are susceptible of another interpretation, may point to a belief that the righteous dead are destined to enjoy a blessed immortality. But it is to be noticed that no emphasis is laid on the idea; and in any case no countenance is given to the doctrine of resurrection. This attitude accords with the Sadducean position. What the Sadducees maintained was that the resurrection doctrine could not be proved from the Pentateuch. They did not assert that the personality was annihilated at death, or deny the doctrine of immortality--indeed, it is by no means impossible that some sections of the Sadducean party accepted this doctrine; but in general their position towards this question--apart from that of the bodily resurrection--was cautious and reserved. And this certainly seems to be the attitude of our author. It should be noted that Sheol is represented--somewhat vaguely and in poetical passages--as a place of punishment for the wicked (vii. 29; xxii. 22; xxiv. 31). This looks like the converse of the idea that the righteous dead are destined to enjoy a blessed immortality. In this connexion a word may be said about the angelology and demonology of our Book. These are in a fairly advanced stage, and imply much the same development as is to be seen in 1 Enoch and the *Testaments of the XII Patriarchs*. There are three classes of angels, two of a superior order, the angels of the presence, and the angels of sanctification (Cf. ii. 2, 18), and, besides these, a numerous inferior order who presided over natural phenomena (ii. 2). It is noteworthy that the two superior orders are represented as observing the Sabbath, and as fulfilling the prescriptions of the Law regarding circumcision, etc.; they even observe in heaven the great festivals, such as the Feast of Weeks (vi. 18). [52]

Various activities are assigned to the angels in connexion with mankind throughout our Book. [53]

Over against the angelic orders there stands a well-organized demonic kingdom, presided over by "the prince of the Mastêmâ" (cf. xvii. 16; xlviii. 2; xviii. 9, 12, etc.). [54] Among the Satanic beings that appear in our Book is Beliar (i. 20).

What is the attitude of our author towards the Messianic Hope? The hope for the coming of the Messianic King who should spring from the old Royal House of David was always cherished among the masses of the people, and in times of unusual stress was apt to flame up in vivid expression. The Pharisees, who themselves sprang from the ranks of the people, were naturally influenced by this tradition, and gave literary expression to it in the *Psalms of Solomon* (70-40 B.C.?). But at the time when our author wrote the desire for a Messianic King of the House of David was probably only latent. A period of national prosperity came in during the reign

---

[51] Cf., however, xlviii, 14 note.

[52] Besides the above there were the seventy angelic patrons of the nations (xv. 31 and note) and the guardian angels of individuals (xxxv. 17).

[53] For details see Charles, *op. cit.*, p. lvii f.

[54] This is the right form of the expression (not "prince Mastêmâ"): "Mastêmâ" in derivation and meaning = "Satan" (cf. x. 8 note).

of John Hyrcanus, and the people generally were well content. It is not to be supposed, however, that the popular hope had completely died away. It was merely quiescent. On the other hand, there was a party, which no doubt had its seat in the priesthood, and may represent the old Sadducean party, that claimed for the priesthood not only sacerdotal but also ruling functions: Levi's descendants are not only to be priests, but also the civil rulers of the nation, and this view receives expression in our Book (cf. xxxi. 15). Now it is well known that the Pharisees objected to the double office being exercised by one person, and when Alexander Jannæus assumed the title of "king" this feeling broke out into open hostility. At a somewhat later time a Pharisaic author in the *Psalms of Solomon*, looking back upon the terrible events that followed the breakup of the Hasmonean dynasty, evidently regards the bloody chastisement which the Jews had to endure at that time from the hands of the Romans as the punishment inflicted on the people for having acquiesced in the usurpation by the Hasmoneans of the royal dignity which had been reserved for the Messianic prince of the House of David. Especially significant in this connexion is the promise recounted in our Book of Levi (xxxii. i): *And he abode that night at Bethel, and Levi dreamed that they had ordained and made him the Priest of the Most High God, him and his sons for ever.* This, originally the title of the priest-king Melchizedek (Gen. xiv. 18), was revived by the Maccabean princely High Priests, and there is some evidence that in certain (?

Sadducean) quarters it was expected that the Messiah would spring from the tribe of Levi, and even from the priestly ruling Maccabean house. The one possible reference to the hope of a Messiah from Judah in our Book occurs in the blessing of Judah, xxxi. 18:

A prince shall thou be, thou and one of thy sons over the sons of Jacob;

Here Judah is addressed, and is singled out for special honour by the side of Levi. This was only natural, as the Jews derived their name from the tribe of Judah, who may be regarded as a sort of symbol of the nation generally. But who is meant by "one of thy sons"? Some would see in this a reference to the expected Messiah, but if this be so it is very vague. It is much more likely that the historic David is meant. The priestly author is significantly silent about a Davidic Messiah. Any Messiah he may have hoped for would, according to his view, spring from the tribe of Levi. He does not accept the view that the Davidic dynasty is of eternal duration, even ideally. May he not, too, have been thinking, in the address to Judah, of Judas Maccabæus? ₁ Judas by his warlike exploits had shed a new glory on the name "Judah." But Judas himself belonged to the priestly family of the Hasmoneans, and it would be easy for our author to see in him the embodiment of the glories of the tribe of Judah, without diminishing the claims of the priestly tribe to civil as well as sacerdotal primacy.

In the same context (xxxi. 20) two lines occur in the address to Judah which run as follows:

And when thou sittest on the throne of the honour of thy righteousness, There will be great peace for all the seed of the sons of the beloved.

The exact meaning of these words is not clear. They can hardly refer to the expected Messiah from David's House, because in that case the context would demand the use of the third person, whereas the second person is employed and Judah is being addressed. Leszynsky suggests that here in the Hebrew original there may be an allusion to the Sadducees, suggested by a word-play in the Hebrew word for "righteousness" (*sedek*). But even so the sentence is not clear. Is our author still thinking of Judas Maccabæus? If so, he may mean "and when thou (Judas), in the person of thy High-Priestly successors, sittest as Priest-king on thy Sadducean throne of honour." It must be admitted that this is not very convincing, and the sentence remains obscure and uncertain in meaning. But of the high position assigned by our author to the tribe of Levi there can be no doubt. The lofty position of HighPriest and civil ruler is assigned to Levi as a reward for the destruction of Shechem (cf. xxx. 17-23; xxxii. 1-3). As Kohler says: "The Levites are represented as the keepers of the sacred books and of the secret lore entrusted to them by the saints from of yore (xlv. 16; cf. x. 14). This indicates that the priests and Levites still included among themselves, as in the days of the author of the Book of Chronicles, the men of learning, the masters of the schools, and that these positions were not filled by men from among the people, as was the case in the time of Shammai and Hillel." Other features of our Book entirely accord with this. For instance, the glorification of the Patriarchs in which our author loves to indulge is the development of a tendency already marked in the Priestly Sections of the Hexateuch. ₁ In *Jubilees* they become saints of the Law. Incidents which might reflect discredit upon them (such as that described in Gen. xii. 11-13) are omitted. Abram is represented as having known the true God from his youth (xi. 16-17; xii. i ff.). Jacob is "a model of filial affection and obedience." A noticeable feature is also the insistence upon the unique position of Israel among the nations, and its rigid separation from the latter. Circumcision is a sign of Israel's elect position (xv. 26) and a privilege which they enjoy in common with the two chief orders of angels (xv. 27). This is also true of the Sabbath, which the same angelic orders observe with Israel. It is needless to add that our author glorifies the Law, which is of heavenly origin and everlasting validity. This is his estimate of the Law in its narrow sense, *i. e.* the Pentateuch. It is by this criterion that he measures everything. It is true that *Jubilees* contains incidents and amplifications which are not to be found in the written Torah. But the author is careful to base everything that is of legal obligation upon the letter of the Law itself. Anything that he allows himself to introduce by way of amplification or addition serves merely to enhance the obligation of the written precept.

Finally, his eschatology is essentially that of one who is primarily interested in the Law. In xxiii. 12-31, he introduces an apocalyptic passage which gives a history of the Maccabean times from the persecution of Antiochus Epiphanes to the Messianic Kingdom, the advent of which is just at hand. A dark picture is drawn of the inroads of Hellenism, and of its disintegrating effects upon the observance of. the Law and the covenant (xxiii. 16-20); the warlike efforts of the Maccabees to reclaim the Hellenizers to Judaism are then described (xxiii. 20-22), and the cry of the nation for deliverance from its calamities (xxiii. 23-25). Then follows a passage (xxiii. 26-32) in which, as a consequence of Israel's renewed study of the Law, a happier period follows. The Messianic Kingdom is to be "brought about gradually by the progressive spiritual development of man and a corresponding transformation of nature." Its members are "to attain to the full limit of 1000 years in happiness and peace." Prof. Charles [1] adds: "The writer of *Jubilees*, we can hardly doubt thought that the era of the Messianic Kingdom had already set in."

The important point to notice about this picture is that the dawn of the happier Age is brought about by renewed study and observance of the Law:

And in those days the children will begin to study the laws,

And to seek the commandments,

And to return to the Path of righteousness (xxiii. 26).

The result is a gradual transformation of men and their environment. There is no catastrophe. It is doubtful whether the author clearly envisages a final judgement, though there may be an allusion to such, in rather vague language, in xxiii. 30 f. The tone throughout is priestly, and it can hardly be doubted that the author was a priest.

AUTHORSHIP AND DATE

According to Charles, the author was not only a priest but a Pharisee "of the straitest sect." We have already seen that many of the positions advocated in the Book are essentially un-Pharisaic in character. Such a fundamentally Pharisaic doctrine as the resurrection of the body, is not accepted, and it is more than doubtful whether the author looked for the advent of a Davidic Messiah. Moreover, it is difficult to conceive any Pharisee at any time advocating the adoption of a solar calendar. Then, again, though there were, of course, Pharisaic priests in later times, when the influence of Pharisaism had become all-powerful, it would certainly be remarkable to find in the second century B.C. so priestly a writer as our author a member of the Pharisaic party. For that party arose from the ranks of the people. It was essentially a lay movement, and it championed popular religious, as opposed to priestly, tradition. All this has been instinctively felt by the Jewish scholars [55] who have discussed the problems connected with the authorship and general character of our Book. By these scholars our Book has been variously ascribed to Essene (Jellinek, 1855), Samaritan (Beer, 1856-7), Hellenist (Frankel, 1856), and Jewish-Christian (Singer, 1898) authorship. None of these views is entirely satisfactory. None can be said for the view that the author belonged to the party--if party it can be called--of the Hasidim ("Assideans" or "Hasideans") who are referred to in I Maccabees. [56]

These "pious" members of the Jewish community were devoted adherents of the Law, and banded themselves together to resist the Hellenizers even unto death. They must not be confounded with the Pharisees, who may, however, have been influenced by them. There is nothing to show that the earlier Hasidim accepted popular religious tradition which had no basis in the written Law. Indeed, the reverse is probable. We know that, in spite of their anti-Hellenism, they scrupled to oppose the legitimate High Priest, even when he was on the Greek side. On the other hand, it is doubtful whether they would have countenanced the claim that the priests should exercise civil rule, while, as we have seen, the author of *Jubilees* distinctly takes up this position,

---

[55] With the distinguished exception of Dr. K. Kohler (in *JE*, s.v. *Jubilees*), who accepts Charles's view, though he suggests that the book may reflect early Hasidæan practice.

[56] Cf. 1 Macc. vii.

and appears to have been an admirer of the Maccabean Priest-Princes--at any rate, of John Hyrcanus [57]and Simon Maccabæus. Still there is a certain affinity between our author and the Hasidim, and if he was not actually a "Hasid," he may very well have been in sympathy with members of that party in fundamental religious positions. Recently Leszyrisky, [58]has maintained the thesis that *Jubilees* was written by a Sadducean author, and, it must be admitted, makes out a strong case. Unfortunately, scholars are not yet agreed as to the real character and position of the Sadducean party, but of recent years there has been a growing consensus of opinion that the party had a real religious basis. It was not, as it is sometimes represented to have been, a mere political party of worldly opportunists who used religious questions as a stick to beat the Pharisees, who represented true religion, while the real interests of their opponents were to safeguard their privileged position and wealth. If such books as Sirach are really, in any sense, Sadducean, and if we weigh the evidence of Josephus impartially, we may conclude that the real Sadducees represented the conservative tradition of the old scribal schools which grew up under priestly influence. The Sadducees stood for the written Law of Moses against the oral tradition, derived from popular religious elements, represented by the Pharisees. What could not be proved from the Law they refused to accept. Their essential objection to the new doctrine of the resurrection of the body was that it could not be proved from the Law. They stood for priestly privilege against the democratic tendencies of the Pharisees, who wished to bring in the laity as much as possible. It was natural that this party should be strong among the priests, and especially among families connected with the High Priesthood. The best members of it were, no doubt, pious devotees of the Law. This is not to say that worldly-minded members of the party did not exist. No doubt there were such, and some such men may have found it convenient to attach themselves to the Sadducean party. There were also worldly and hypocritical adherents in the ranks of the Pharisees. But in neither case is it just to estimate the essential character of the party from such elements. The persistence of the Sadducean party for so long a time within Judaism suggests that it possessed elements of real vitality and vigour. No doubt, also, it was divided into sections--one such is known to us as the sect of the Bœthusians. In view of its long continuance as an active party, and its significance in the history of Judaism, it must have stood for something more than mere negations. While it rejected the resurrection doctrine, the hope of a Davidic Messiah, and the Pharisaic oral tradition, it upheld the sole binding force of the written Torah, and emphasized priestly privilege. Judged by these criteria, our author may well have been a pious Sadducean priest. It is not necessary, of course, to suppose that all the positions upheld in our Book were commonly accepted by the Sadducean party. Our author had views of his own, particularly regarding the calendar--which at the time when he wrote seems to have been a burning subject of debate--which would not necessarily have commended themselves to the party generally. It is to be noted that the positions he upholds on other matters often agree with those of the Samaritans and Falashas and Karaite Jews, who are well-known to represent old Sadducean views on various points.

On one point of detail the Ethiopic text of our Book does uphold a specifically Pharisaic view. In xvi. 18, Israel is spoken of as destined to become *a kingdom and Priests and a holy nation*. This is an echo of Exod. xix. 6, but there the Hebrew text has *a kingdom of priests* ("And ye shall be unto me a kingdom of priests and an holy nation"). Now the alteration yielded by the text of our Book here reflects the Pharisaic exegesis of this passage; the same alteration appears also in Rev. v. 10 (cf. i. 6). The Pharisees were anxious to separate the kingdom from the priesthood, and expounded

Exod. xix. 6 in this way, as the Jewish Targums attest. But the original text of our Book can hardly have been under any such influence. Such an exegesis would contradict the express claims made for the priesthood elsewhere in the Book. The

Latin version, which has "a kingdom of priests" (as in the original Hebrew text in Exod. xix. 6), is no doubt right. Probably the Ethiopic scribe was influenced by the form of the text in Rev. v. 10, and introduced it here.

We may sum up by saying that the author was undoubtedly a pious priest, a devoted adherent of the Law, and an upholder of priestly tradition; he was certainly not a Pharisee, but has affinities with the Hasidim or "pious" of early Maccabean times; not improbably he was a Sadducean priest. The exact date of the composition of *Jubilees* cannot be fixed with absolute certainty, but no doubt, as Charles has argued, it falls some time within the reigns of Simon Maccabæus or John Hyrcanus, the flourishing period of the Hasmonean rule. This, at any rate, may be inferred from the historical sketch embodied in the apocalyptic passage, xxiii. 12-31, and is

---

[57] It is true that John Hyrcanus favoured the Pharisees, according to Josephus (*Ant.*, xiii. 10, 5), who even speaks of him as their "disciple." But this probably means no more than that he adopted a conciliatory attitude towards them. He also had intimate friends among the Sadducees (Josephus, Ant., xiii. 10, 6).

[58] *Die Sadduzäer* (1912), pp. 179-236.

reinforced by a number of other considerations. The date to which the various phenomena point is some time in the last half of the second century B.C.

BIBLIOGRAPHY

The important edition of the Ethiopic text by Charles has already been referred to, as well as his English translation of the Book with Introduction and Notes (1902). This translation has also been reprinted (with an Introduction and Notes) in the Oxford *Corpus* (vol. ii. Pseudepigrapha, 1913) and is reproduced in the pages that follow.

The most recent, and in many respects the most important, discussion of *Jubilees* is contained in Leszynsky's *Die Sadduzäer* (Berlin, 1912), pp. 179-236. Leszynsky's arguments have been referred to fully above. Kohler's article in *JE*, vol. vii. ("Jubilees Book of") is interesting and useful. Of earlier works the following are important:

Jellinek, *Ueber das Büch der Jubiläen* (1855);

Beer, *Das Büch der Jubiläen und sein Verhältniss zu den Midraschim*, (Leipzig, 18,56); also *Noch ein Wort über das Bitch der Jubiläen* (1857)

Frankel in *Monatsschrift* (1856);

Singer, *Das Büch der Jubiläen oder die Leptogenesis* (Stuhlweissenburg, 1898).

There is a good discussion in Schürer *GJV.*, iii. 371-384, with full Bibliography.

SHORT TITLES, ABBREVIATIONS AND BRACKETS USED IN THIS EDITION

1 Enoch = The Ethiopic Book of Enoch.

2 Enoch = The Slavonic Book of Enoch.

Ap. Bar. The Syriac Apocalypse of Baruch.

Pire de R. Eliezer is cited according to the edition (English translation and Notes) of G. Friedlander (London, 1916).

MT = Masoretic text.

Sam. = Samaritan version, and Hebrew text in Samaritan characters when both agree.

Syr. = the Syriac version of the Old Testament.

Vulg. = Vulgate.

( ) Words or letters so enclosed are supplied by the editor from some other source.

[ ] Words so enclosed are interpolated.

† † Words so enclosed are corrupt.

Charles's *Jubilees* = *The Book of Jubilees translated from the Ethiopic Text*, by R. H. Charles, D.D. (London, 1902).

JE = Jewish Encyclopædia.

RWS[2] = *Religion and Worship of the Synagogue* (1911).

THE BOOK OF JUBILEES

Prologue

THIS is the history of the division of the days [59]of the law and of the testimony, of the events of the years, of [60]their (year) weeks, of their jubilees throughout all the years of the world, [61]as the Lord spake to Moses on Mount Sinai when he went up to receive the tables of the law and of the commandment, according to the voice of God as He said unto him, "Go up to the top of the Mount."[62]

God's Revelation to Moses on Mount Sinai

(i. 1-26: cf. Ex. xxiv. 15-18).

1. And it came to pass in the first year of the exodus (2450 A.M. (A.M. = Anno Mundi)) of the children of Israel out of Egypt, in the third month, on the sixteenth day of the month, that God spake to Moses, saying: "Come up to Me on the Mount, and I will give thee two tables of stone of the law and of the commandment, which I have written, that thou mayst teach them." [63]2. And Moses went up into the mount of God, and the glory of the Lord abode on Mount Sinai, and a cloud overshadowed it six days. 3. And He called to Moses on the seventh day out of the midst of the cloud, and the appearance of the glory of the Lord was like a flaming fire on the top of the Mount. 4. And Moses was on the Mount forty days and forty nights, and God taught him the earlier and the later history [64]of the division of all the days of the law and of the testimony. 5. And He said: "Incline thine heart to every word which I shall speak to thee on this Mount, and write them[65] in a book in order that their generations may see how I have not forsaken them for all the evil which they have wrought in transgressing the covenant which I establish between Me and thee for their generations this day on Mount Sinai. 6. And thus it will come to pass when all these things come upon them, [66]that they will recognize that I am more righteous than they in all their judgments and in all their actions, and they will recognize that I have been truly with them. 7. And do thou write for thyself [67]all these words which I declare unto thee this day, for I know their rebellion and their stiff neck, [68]before I bring them into the land of which I sware to their fathers, to Abraham and to Isaac and to Jacob, saying: "Unto your seed will I give a land flowing with milk and honey. 8. And they will eat and be satisfied, and they will turn to strange gods, to (gods) which cannot deliver them from aught of their tribulation: "and this witness shall be heard for a witness against them. [69]9. For they will forget all My commandments, (even) all that I command them, and they will walk after the Gentiles, and after their uncleanness, and after their shame, and will serve their gods, and these will prove unto them an offence and a

---

[59] The Prologue sums up the contents of the Book as at once a *history* and a *chronological system based upon the number seven.*

[60] *i. e.* according to (their year-weeks): a year-week = seven years (cf. Lev. xxv. 8 f.).

[61] The writer apparently intended to write a history from Creation to the establishment of the Messianic Kingdom.

[62] Cf. Exod. xxiv. 12

[63] Cf. Exod. xxiv. 12.

[64] Cf. i. 26. According to the Jewish Midrash, also, God showed Moses "all the generations that should arise," as well as "all the minutiæ of the Law" (*Shemoth rabb.* xl.; Megilla 19*b*).

[65] Cf. Exod. xxxiv. 27.

[66] Cf. Deut. xxx. 1.

[67] Cf. i. 27.

[68] Cf. Deut. xxxi. 27

[69] Cf. Deut. xxxi. 20.

tribulation and an affliction and a snare. [70]10. And many will perish and they will be taken captive, [71]and will fall into the hands of the enemy, because they have forsaken My ordinances and My commandments, and the festivals of My covenant, and My sabbaths, and My holy place[72] which I have hallowed for Myself in their midst, and My tabernacle,[73]and My sanctuary, which I have hallowed for Myself in the midst of the land, that I should set My name upon it, and that it should dwell (there). 11. And they [74]will make to themselves high places and groves and graven images, [75]and they will worship, each his own (graven image), so as to go astray, and they will sacrifice their children to demons, [76]and to all the works of the error of their hearts. 12. And I will send witnesses unto them, that I may witness against them, but they will not hear, [77]and will slay [78]the witnesses also, and they will persecute those who seek the law, and they will abrogate and change everything so as to work evil before My eyes. 13. And I shall hide My face from them, and I shall deliver them into the hand of the Gentiles for captivity, and for a prey, and for devouring, [79]and I shall remove them from the midst of the land, and I shall scatter [80]them amongst the Gentiles. 14. And they will forget all My law and all My commandments and all My judgments, and will go astray as to new moons, and sabbaths, and festivals, and jubilees, and ordinances. 15. And after this they will turn to Me[81] from amongst the Gentiles with all their heart and with all their soul and with all their strength, and I shall gather them from amongst all the Gentiles, [82]and they will seek Me, so that I shall be found of them, when they seek Me with all their heart and with all their soul. 16. And I shall disclose to them abounding peace with righteousness, and I shall †remove them the plant of uprightness†, [83]with all My heart and with all My soul, [84]and they will be for a blessing and not for a curse, [85]and they will be the head and not the tail. [86]17. And I shall build My sanctuary [87]in their midst, and I shall

---

[70] Cf. Exod. xxiii. 33

[71] N. Israel is referred to.

[72] *i. e.* the Temple in Jerusalem

[73] The Tabernacle is apparently thought of as still in existence (in Jerusalem) during the time of the monarchy.

[74] *i. e.* Judah.

[75] Cf. 2 Chron. xxxiii. 3 ff.

[76] Cf. 2 Chron. xxviii. 3, xxxiii. 6.

[77] Cf. 2 Chron. xxiv. 19.

[78] Cf. Matt. xxiii. 34.

[79] Cf. 2 Kings xxi. 14.

[80] Cf. Deut. iv. 27, xxviii. 64.

[81] Cf. Deut. iv. 30.

[82] Cf. Jer. xxix. 14.

[83] The obelized words are corrupt. Charles suggests reading "And I will plant them the plant of uprightness in the land."

[84] Cf. Jer. xxxii. 41.

[85] Cf. Zech. viii. 13.

[86] Cf. Deut. xxviii. 13.

[87] *i. e.* the second Temple

dwell with them, and I shall be their God and they will be My people [88]in truth and righteousness. 18. And I shall not forsake them nor fail them; [89]for I am the Lord their God." 19. And Moses fell on his face and prayed and said, "O Lord my God, do not forsake Thy people and Thy inheritance, [90]so that they should wander in the error of their hearts, and do not deliver them into the hands of their enemies, the Gentiles, lest they should rule over them and cause them to sin against Thee. 20. Let Thy mercy, O Lord, be lifted up upon Thy people, and create in them an upright spirit, [91]and let not the spirit of Beliar [92]rule over them to accuse them before Thee, and to ensnare them from all the paths of righteousness, so that they may perish from before Thy face. 21. But they are Thy people and Thy inheritance, which Thou hast delivered with Thy great power [93]from the hands of the Egyptians: create in them a clean heart and a holy Spirit, [94]and let them not be ensnared in their sins from henceforth until eternity." 22. And the Lord said unto Moses: "I know their contrariness and their thoughts and their stiffneckedness, [95]and they will not be obedient till they confess their own sin and the sin of their fathers. [96]23. And after this they will turn to Me in all uprightness and with all (their) heart and with all (their) soul, and I shall circumcise the foreskin of their heart [97]and the foreskin of the heart of their seed, and I shall create in them a holy spirit, and I shall cleanse them so that they shall not turn away from Me from that day unto eternity. 24. And their souls will cleave to Me and to all My commandments, and they will fulfil My commandments, and I shall be their Father and they will be My children. 25. And they will all be called children of the living God, [98]and every angel and every spirit will know, yea, they will know that these are My children, and that I am their Father in uprightness and righteousness, and that I love them. 26. And do thou write down for thyself all these words [99]which I declare unto thee on this mountain, the first and the last, which shall come to pass in all the divisions of the days in the law and in the testimony and in the weeks and the jubilees unto eternity, until I descend and dwell with them [100]throughout eternity."

God commands the Angel to write (i. 27-29).

---

[88] Cf. Lev. xxvi. 12 and often

[89] Cf. Deut. xxxi. 6.

[90] Cf. Deut. ix. 26.

[91] Cf. Ps. li. 10.

[92] Beliar (Belial) is here, as in the *Ascension of Isaiah* (see Introduction to that work), a Satanic being, apparently "the prince of the devils."

[93] Cf. Deut. ix. 29

[94] Cf. Ps. li. 10 (and ver. 20 above).

[95] Cf. Deut. xxxi. 27.

[96] Cf. Lev. xxvi. 40.

[97] Cf. Deut. x. 16, xxx. 6.

[98] Cf. Hos. i. 10.

[99] Viz. those contained in our Book (the *Book of Jubilees*) as distinguished from the Book of the First Law (vi. 22 = the Pentateuch), which was written by the angel himself.

[100] viz. in the perfect theocracy inaugurated by the Messianic Kingdom.

27. And He said to the angel of the presence: [101]"Write[102] for Moses from the beginning of creation till My sanctuary has been built among them for all eternity. 28. [103]And the Lord will appear to the eyes of all, [104]and all will know that I am the God of Israel and the Father of all the children of Jacob, [105]and King on Mount Zion [106]for all eternity. And Zion and Jerusalem will be holy." 29. And the angel of the presence who went before the camp of Israel [107]took the tables of the divisions of the years[108]from the time of the creation--of the law and of the testimony of the weeks, of the jubilees, according to the individual years, according to all the number of the jubilees [according to the individual years], from the day of the [new] creation †when† the heavens [109]and the earth shall be renewed and all their creation according to the powers of the heaven, and according to all the creation of the earth, until the sanctuary of the Lord shall be made in Jerusalem [110]on Mount Zion, and all the luminaries be renewed for healing [111]and for peace and for blessing for all the elect of Israel, and that thus it may be from that day and unto all the days of the earth.

The Angel dictates to Moses the Primæval History: the Creation of the World and Institution of the Sabbath (ii. 1-33; cf. Gen. i.-ii. 3).

II. And the angel of the presence spake to Moses according to the word of the Lord, saying: Write the complete history of the creation, how in six days the Lord God finished all His works and all that He created, and kept Sabbath on the seventh day and hallowed it for all ages, and appointed it as a sign for all His works. 2. [112]For on the first day He created the heavens which are above and the earth and the waters and all the spirits which serve before Him--the angels [113]of the presence, and the angels of sanctification, [114]and the angels [of

---

[101] Cf. Isa. lxiii. 9; *Test. XII. Patr., Judah 25: probably Michael is meant. Note that the medium of communication is an angel, and cf. Gal. iii. 19 (" The Law . . . ordained through angels"). Later Judaism rejected this idea.*

[102] *i. e. not the Pentateuch, "but a history up to the Messianic Kingdom" (Charles, in Oxford Corpus).*

[103] *Read this ver. after ver. 25.*

[104] *Cf. Rev. i. 7 (in the final theophany).*

[105] *Cf. i. 24; Jer. xxxi. i.*

[106] *Cf. Isa. xxiv. 23.*

[107] *Cf. Exod. xiv. 19.*

[108] *From these the angel dictates to Moses (who writes) the Book of Jubilees.*

[109] *Text corrupt. Read "from the day of creation, till the heavens."*

[110] *i. e. in the Messianic Kingdom.*

[111] *Cf. Rev. xxii. 2*

[112] 2-3 record the creations of the first day, seven in number, viz. heaven, earth, the waters, spirits, the abysses, darkness, light. According to *Pire de R. Eliezer* iii., "eight things were created on the first day: namely, heaven, earth, the light, darkness, Tohu (chaos), Bohu (void), wind (or spirit), water." Perhaps *Tohu* and *Bohu* here = *abysses.*

[113] According to our Book the angels were created on the first day, and this probably represents the view of earlier Judaism. This was opposed by later Judaism, which objected to the idea that angels assisted in the work of creation on the days following the first. *Pirke de R. Eliezer* placed the creation of angels in the *second* day; some Rabbis on the *fifth* (cf. *Gen. rabb.* i. 5).

[114] Cf. ii. 18, xv. 27, xxxi. 14. These are the two chief orders of angels. The "angels of sanctification" sing praises to God.

the spirit of fire and the angels] of the spirit of the winds, [115]and the angels of the spirit of the clouds, and of darkness, and of snow and of hail and of hoar frost, [116]and the angels of the voices [117]and of the thunder and of the lightning, [118]and the angels of the spirits of cold and of heat, and of winter and of spring and of autumn and of summer, [119]and of all the spirits of His creatures which are in the heavens and on the earth, (He created) the abysses and the darkness, eventide (and night), and the light, dawn and day, which He hath prepared in the knowledge of His heart. 3. And thereupon we saw His works, and praised Him, and lauded before Him on account of all His works; for seven great works did He create on the first day. 4. And on the second day [120]He created the firmament in the midst of the waters, and the waters were divided on that day-half of them went up above and half of them went down below the firmament (that was) in the midst over the face of the whole earth. And this was the only work (God) created on the second day. 5. And on the third day [121]He commanded the waters to pass from off the face of the whole earth into one place, and the dry land to appear. 6. And the waters did so as He commanded them, and they retired from off the face of the earth into one place outside of this firmament, and the dry land appeared. 7. And on that day He created for them all the seas according to their separate gathering places, and all the rivers, and the gatherings of the waters in the mountains and on all the earth, and all the lakes, and all the dew of the earth, and the seed which is sown, and all sprouting things, and fruit-bearing trees, and trees of the wood, and the garden of Eden, in Eden, and all (plants after their kind). These four great works God created on the third day. 8. And on the fourth day[122] He created the sun and the moon and the stars, and set them in the firmament of the heaven, to give light upon all the earth, and to rule over the day and the night, and divide the light from the darkness. 9. And God appointed the sun [123]to be a great sign on the earth for days and for sabbaths and for months and for feasts and for years and for sabbaths of years and for jubilees and for all seasons of the years. 10. And it divideth the light from the darkness [and] for prosperity, that all things may prosper which shoot and grow on the earth. These three kinds He made on the fourth day. 11. And on the fifth day [124]He created great sea monsters in the depths of the waters, for these were the first things of flesh that were created by His hands, the fish and everything that moves in the waters, and everything that flies, the birds and all their kind. 12. And the sun rose above them to prosper (them), and above everything that was on the earth, everything that shoots out of the earth, and all fruit-bearing trees, and all flesh. These three kinds He created on the fifth day. 13. And on the sixth day[125] He created all the animals of the earth, and all cattle, and everything that moves on the earth. 14. And after all this He created man, a man and a woman created He them, and gave him dominion over all that is upon the earth, and in the seas, and over everything that flies, and over beasts and over cattle, and over everything that moves

---

[115] The various classes of angels that follow constitute the third or lowest order. They preside over the elements and natural phenomena; cf. 1 Enoch lx. 12-21, lxxv., lxxx.; 2 Enoch xix. 1-4, For the "angels of the winds," cf. Rev. vii. 1 f.; 1 Enoch xviii. 1-5, xxxiv.-xxxvi., lxxvi.

[116] Cf. x Enoch lx. 17-18.

[117] Cf. Rev. iv. .5, xi. 19, xvi. 18.

[118] Cf. 1 Enoch IX. 13-15

[119] Cf. 1 Enoch lxxxii. 13-20.

[120] Cf. Gen. i. 6-7; 2, Enoch xxvi.-xxvii. According to *Pirke de R. Eliezer* iv. the following were created on the second day: the firmament, angels, fire for flesh and blood, and the fire of Gehinnom.

[121] Cf. Gen. i. 9-13 (dry land, seas, herbage, fruit trees = 3 works). Our Book adds a fourth, the Garden of Eden (so also the Midrash *Bereshith rabb.* xv.; 2 Enoch xxx. i). Another view was that Paradise (? the Heavenly Paradise) was created before the world; cf. 4 Ezra iii. 6 (note).

[122] Cf. Gen. i. 14-19; 2 Enoch xxx. 2-6

[123] Note the intentional omission of the moon. The writer objected to a calendar based upon the changes of the moon.

[124] Cf. Gen. i. 20-23; 2 Enoch xxx. 7; 4 Ezra vi. 47 ff. According to our Book the three works of the fifth day were the great sea-monsters, fish and birds; according to *Pirke de R. Eliezer* ix. birds, fish and locusts.

[125] Cf. Gen. i. 24-28; 2 Enoch xxx. 8 f.

on the earth, and over the whole earth, and over all this He gave him dominion. And these four kinds He created on the sixth day. 15. And there were altogether two and twenty kinds. [126]16. And He finished all His work on the sixth [127]day--all that is in the heavens and on the earth, and in the seas and in the abysses, and in the light and in the darkness, and in everything. 17. And He gave us a great sign, the Sabbath day, [128]that we should work six days, but keep Sabbath on the seventh day from all work.

18. And all the angels of the presence, and all the angels of sanctification, these two great classes-He hath hidden us to keep the Sabbath with Him [129]in heaven and on earth. 19. And He said unto us: "Behold, I will separate unto Myself [130]a people from among all the peoples, and these will keep the Sabbath day, and I will sanctify them unto Myself as My people, and will bless them; as I have sanctified the Sabbath day and do sanctify (it) unto Myself, even so shall I bless them, and they will be My people and I shall be their God. 20 . And I have chosen the seed of Jacob [131]from amongst all that I have seen, and have written him down as My firstborn son, [132]and have sanctified him unto Myself for ever and ever; and I will teach them the Sabbath day, that they may keep Sabbath thereon from all work." 21. And thus He created therein a sign [133]in accordance with which they should keep Sabbath with us [134]on the seventh day, to eat and to drink, and to bless Him [135]who hath created all things as He hath blessed and sanctified unto Himself a peculiar people [136]above all peoples, and that they should keep Sabbath together with us. 22. And He caused His commands to ascend as a sweet savour [137]acceptable before Him all the days. . . . 23. There (were) two and twenty heads of mankind from Adam to Jacob, and two and twenty kinds of work were made [138]until the seventh day; this [139]is blessed and holy; and the former [140]also is blessed and holy; and this one serves with that one for sanctification and blessing. 24. And to this (Jacob and his seed) it was granted that they should always be the blessed and holy ones of the first testimony and law, even as He had sanctified and blessed the Sabbath day on the seventh day. 25. He created heaven and earth and everything that He created in six days, and God made the seventh day holy, for all His

---

[126] Cf. ii. 23 (below).

[127] This is possibly the right reading of Gen. ii. 2*a* (so Sam. text, LXX, Syr.). It implies a severer view of Sabbath observance. The Masoretic text has "seventh."

[128] Cf. Exod. xxxi. 13.

[129] The two chief orders of angels observe the Sabbath with God (and Israel). The third order and the Gentiles are denied this privilege.

[130] Cf. 1 Kings viii. 53.

[131] Cf. Isa. xli. 8 (" Jacob whom I have chosen "), xliv. 1, 2.

[132] Cf. Exod. iv. 22; Ps. lxxxix. 27.

[133] For the Sabbath day as a sign between God and Israel, cf. Exod. xxxi 13, 17; Ezek.xx.12

[134] *i. e.* with God and the superior angels

[135] The Sabbath is to be a delight

[136] Cf. Deut. vii. 6.

[137] Cf. 2 Cor. ii. 15; Eph. v. 2

[138] It is probable that at end of 22 above there is a lacuna in the text (indicated by the dotted line). Charles restores the missing words as follows: *As there were two and twenty letters, and two and twenty (sacred) books* [viz. in the Old Testament], *and two and twenty heads of mankind from Adam to Jacob, so there were made two and twenty kinds of work*, etc.

[139] viz. the Sabbath.

[140] viz. Jacob.

works; therefore He commanded on its behalf that, whoever doth any work thereon shall die, [141]and that he who defileth it shall surely die. 26. Wherefore do thou command the children of Israel to observe this day that they may keep it holy [142]and not do thereon any work, and not to defile it, as it is holier than all other days.[143] 27. And whoever profaneth it shall surely die, and whoever doeth thereon any work shall surely die eternally, that the children of Israel may observe this day throughout their generations, and not be rooted out of the land; for it is a holy day and a blessed day. 28. And every one who observeth it and keepeth Sabbath thereon from all his work, will be holy and blessed throughout all days like unto us. 29. Declare and say to the children of Israel the law of this day both that they should keep Sabbath thereon, and that they should not forsake it in the error of their hearts; (and) that it is not lawful to do any work thereon which is unseemly, to do thereon their own pleasure, [144]and that they should not prepare thereon anything to be eaten or drunk. [145]†and (that it is not lawful) to draw water, or bring in or take out thereon through their gates any burden,† [146]which they had not prepared for themselves on the sixth day [147]in their dwellings. 30. And they shall not bring in nor take out from house to house [148]on that day; for that day is more holy and blessed than any jubilee day of the jubilees: on this we kept Sabbath in the heavens before it was made known to any flesh to keep Sabbath thereon on the earth. 31. And the Creator of all things blessed it,[149] but He did not sanctify all peoples and nations to keep Sabbath thereon, but Israel alone: them alone He permitted to eat and drink and to keep Sabbath thereon on the earth. 32. And the Creator of all things blessed this day which He had created for a blessing and a sanctification and a glory above all days. 33. This law and testimony was given to the children of Israel as a law for ever unto their generations. [150]

Paradise and the Fall (iii. 1-35; cf. Gen. ii. 4-iii .).

III. And on the six days of the second week we brought, according to the word of God, unto Adam all the beasts, and all the cattle, and all the birds, and everything that moveth on the earth, and everything that moveth in the water, according to their kinds, and according to their types: the beasts on the first day; the cattle on the second day; the birds on the third day; and all that which moveth on the earth on the fourth day; and that which moveth in the water on the fifth day. 2. And Adam named them all by their respective names, and as he called them, so was their name (Gen. ii.19). 3. And on these five days Adam saw all these, male and female, according to every kind that was on the earth, but he was alone and found no helpmeet for him. (Gen. ii.20)4 . And the Lord said unto us: "It is not good that the man should be alone: let us make a helpmeet for him." [151]5. And the Lord our God caused a deep sleep to fall upon him, and he slept, and He took for the woman one rib from amongst his ribs, and this rib was the origin of the woman from amongst his ribs, and He built up the flesh in its stead, and built the woman. 6. And He awaked Adam out of his sleep and on awaking he rose on the sixth day, and He brought her to him, and he knew her, and said unto her: "This is now bone of my bones and flesh

---

[141] Cf. Exod. xxxi. 14, 15, xxxv. 2; Num. xv. 32 f.

[142] Cf. Exod. xx. 8.

[143] Cf. ii. 30.

[144] Cf. Isa. lviii. 13.

[145] Deduced from Exod. xvi. 23, 25

[146] The obelized words should either be omitted or read *after their own pleasure* above. For the law about "bringing in or taking out . . . any burden" on the Sabbath, cf. ii. 30, l. 8; Jer. xvii. 21 f.; Neh. xiii. 19; John v. 10.

[147] This is in accordance with Rabbinic law which forbids anything being eaten on the Sabbath unless it had been prepared beforehand for that purpose on a week-day.

[148] This was relaxed later by the Rabbinic law of *erub*, which was based on Exod. xvi. 29. See *JE.* v. 203 f. (s.v. Erub).

[149] *i.e.* Israel

[150] Cf. Exod. xxvii, 21, etc., for the phrase.

[151] Cf. Gen. ii. 21-23. According to the Talmud, Adam was originally (as first created, Gen. i. 27) hermaphroditic.

of my flesh; she will be called [my] wife; because she was taken from her husband." [152]7. Therefore shall man and wife be one, and therefore shall a man leave his father and his mother, and cleave unto his wife, and they shall be one flesh. (Gen. ii. 24) 8. In the first week was Adam created, and the rib--his wife: in the second week He showed her unto him: and for this reason the commandment was given to keep in their defilement, for a male seven days, and for a female twice seven days. [153]9. And after Adam had completed forty days in the land where he had been created, we brought him into the Garden of Eden to till and keep it, but his wife they brought in on the eightieth day, and after this she entered into the Garden of Eden. 10. And for this reason the commandment is written on the heavenly tables [154]in regard to her that giveth birth: "if she beareth a male, she shall remain in her uncleanness seven days according to the first week of days, and thirty and three days shall she remain in the blood of her purifying, and she shall not touch any hallowed thing, nor enter into the sanctuary, until she accomplisheth these days which (are enjoined) in the case of a male child. 11. But in the case of a female child she shall remain in her uncleanness two weeks of days, according to the first two weeks, and sixty-six days in the blood of her purification, and they will be in all eighty days." 12. And when she had completed these eighty days we brought her into the Garden of Eden, for it is holier than all the earth besides, and every tree that is planted in it is holy. 13. Therefore, there was ordained regarding her who beareth a male or a female child the statute of those days that she should touch no hallowed thing, nor enter into the sanctuary until these days for the male or female child are accomplished. 14. This is the law and testimony which was written down for Israel, in order that they should observe (it) all the days. 15. And in the first week of the first jubilee, (1-7 A.M.) Adam and his wife were in the Garden of Eden for seven [155]years tilling and keeping it, and we gave him work and we instructed him to do everything that is suitable for tillage. [156]16. And he tilled (the garden), and was naked and knew it not, and was not ashamed, (Gen. ii. 25) and he protected the garden from the birds and beasts and cattle, and gathered its fruit, and ate, and put aside the residue for himself and for his wife [and put aside that which was being kept]. [157]17. [158]And after the completion of the seven years, which he had completed there, seven years exactly, and in the second month, on the seventeenth day (of the month), (8 A.M.) the serpent came and approached the woman, and the serpent said to the woman, "Hath God commanded you, saying, Ye shall not eat of every tree of the garden?" 18. And she said to it, "Of all the fruit of the trees of the garden God hath said unto us, Eat; but of the fruit of the tree which is in the midst of the garden God hath said unto us, Ye shall not eat thereof, neither shall ye touch it, lest ye die." 19. And the serpent said unto the woman, "Ye shall not surely die: for God doth know that on the day ye shall eat thereof, your eyes will be opened, and ye will be as gods, and ye will know good and evil." 20. And the woman saw the tree that it was agreeable and pleasant to the eye, and that its fruit was good for food, and she took thereof and ate. 21. And when she had first covered her shame with fig-leaves, she gave thereof to Adam and he ate, and his eyes were opened, and he saw that he was naked. 22. And he took fig-leaves and sewed (them) together, and made an apron for himself, and covered his shame. 32. And God cursed the serpent, and was wroth with it for ever. . . .

---

[152] Cf. Gen. ii. 21-23. According to the Talmud, Adam was originally (as first created, Gen. i. 27) hermaphroditic.

[153] For these laws cf. Lev. xii. 2-5, according to which in the one case the mother was not to enter the sanctuary till the lapse of forty days, in the other eighty days. The reason for this is given in the following section (9), according to the author of *Jubilees*. This peculiar idea recurs elsewhere (Philo, *Book of Adam and Eve*), but not in Rabbinic literature, except for some slight traces. See Charles, *ad loc.*

[154] Cf. 1 Enoch lxxxi. 1, 2, xciii. 2, ciii. 2; the expression also occurs in *Test. XII. Patriarchs.* In our Book the *heavenly tables* are conceived of as the divine statute book of which the Mosaic Law is the earthly reproduction; but they also contain records of events and predictions. The underlying idea is predestinarian.

[155] According to *Ber. rabba* xviii., *Sanh.* 38b, Adam was only six hours in the Garden; cf. *Pirke de R. Eliezer* xviii. (Adam entered the garden at the seventh hour and was driven forth at twilight, *i. e.* the twelfth hour on Friday the eve of the Sabbath).

[156] Agriculture is a divine institution. Here the instruction is given by angels; contrast Isa. xxviii. 26-29. See also 4 Ezra vi. 42. *Test. XII. Patr.* Issachar iii.

[157] The bracketed words are a dittograph

[158] For 17-22 cf. Gen. iii. 1-7.

[159]24. And He was wroth with the woman, because she hearkened to the voice of the serpent, and did eat; and He said unto her: (Gen. iii.) I shall greatly multiply thy sorrow and thy pains in sorrow thou shalt bring forth children, and thy return [160]shall be unto thy husband, and he will rule over thee." 25. And to Adam also He said, "Because thou hast hearkened unto the voice of thy wife, and hast eaten of the tree of which I commanded thee that thou shouldst not eat thereof, cursed be the ground for thy sake: thorns and thistles shall it bring forth to thee, and thou shalt eat thy bread in the sweat of thy face, till thou returnest to the earth from whence thou wast taken; for earth thou art, and unto earth shalt thou return." 26. And He made for them coats of skin, and clothed them, and sent them forth from the Garden of Eden. (Gen. ii. 17-19, 21, 24) 27. And on that day on which Adam went forth from the garden, he offered as a sweet savour an offering, frankincense, galbanum, and stacte, and spices [161]in the morning with the rising of the sun from the day when he covered his shame. 28. And on that day was closed the mouth of all beasts, and of cattle, and of birds, and of whatever walketh, and of whatever moveth, so that they could no longer speak: [162]for they had all spoken one with another with one lip and with one tongue. 29. And He sent out of the Garden of Eden all flesh that was in the Garden of Eden, and all flesh was scattered according to its kinds, and according to its types unto the places which had been created for them. 30. And to Adam alone did He give (the wherewithal) to cover his shame, of all the beasts and cattle. 31. On this account, it is prescribed on the heavenly tables as touching all those who know the judgment of the law, that they should cover their shame, and should not uncover themselves as the Gentiles uncover themselves.[163]32. And on the new moon of the fourth month, Adam and his wife went forth from the Garden of Eden, and they dwelt in the land of 'Eldâ, [164]in the land of their creation. 33. And Adam called the name of his wife Eve. 34. And they had no son till the first jubilee, and after this he knew her. 35.

Now he tilled the land as he had been instructed in the Garden of Eden. [165]

Cain and Abel (iv. 1-12; cf. Gen. iv.).

IV. And in the third week in the second jubilee she gave birth to Cain, and in the fourth she gave birth (64-70 A.M.) to Abel, and in the fifth she gave birth to her daughter (71-77 A.M.)'Âwân. [166]2. And in the first (year) of the third jubilee, (78-84 A.M.) Cain slew Abel because (God) accepted the sacrifice of Abel, (99-105 A.M.) and did not accept the offering of Cain. 3. And he slew him in the field: and his blood cried from the ground to heaven, complaining because he had slain him. [167]4. And the Lord reproved Cain because of Abel, because he had slain him, and he made him a fugitive on the earth because of the blood of his brother, and he cursed him upon the earth. [168] 5. And on this account it is written on the heavenly tables, "Cursed is he who smiteth his neighbour treacherously, and let all who have seen and heard say, So be it; and the man who hath seen and not

---

[159] Charles suspects a lacuna here. It may have contained a statement to the effect that the serpent's four feet, which it is supposed to have originally possessed, were cut off. Cf. Targ. Ps.-Jon. on Gen. iii. 14, and Josephus, *Ant.* i. 1, 4.

[160] So LXX and Syr. (ποστραφ σου), MT, "thy desire."

[161] *i. e.* the incense-offering of Exod. xxx. 34

[162] For this belief cf. Josephus, *Ant.* i. 1, 4. The idea underlying the text here is that up to this time both men and animals spoke Hebrew, which was the universal language till the building of the Tower of Babel.

[163] A protest against the Greek custom of exposing the person in public athletic sports; cf. 1 Macc. i. 13 f.; 2 Macc. iv. 9-14; Josephus, *Ant.* xii. 5, 1.

[164] Charles suggests that 'Eldâ may be a corruption of the Hebrew word meaning "nativity" (land of "nativity").

[165] Cf. iii. 15

[166] *i.e.* "iniquity" (Heb. *'āwen*). Another daughter, 'Azûrâ (= "well guarded"), was born later. Cain married 'Âwân and Seth 'Azûrâ. There is great divergence as to these names in later writers . According to *Pirke de R. Eliezer*, Cain's wife was his twin-sister (xxi.).

[167] Cf. Gen. iv. 4, 5, 8, 10.

[168] Cf. Gen. iv. 11-12.

declared (it), let him be accursed as the other." [169]And for this reason we announce when we come before the Lord our God all the sin which is committed in heaven and on earth, and in light and in darkness, and everywhere. 7. And Adam and his wife mourned for Abel four weeks of years, and in the fourth year (99- of the fifth week they became joyful, and Adam knew his wife again, and she bare him a son, and he [170]called his name Seth; for he said "God hath raised up a second seed unto us on the earth instead of Abel; for Cain slew him." [171]8. And in the sixth week (134-140 A.M.) he begat his daughter 'Azûrâ. 9. And Cain took 'Âwân his sister to be his wife and she bare him Enoch [172]at the close of the fourth jubilee (190-196 A.M.). And in the first year of the first week of the fifth jubilee (197 A.M.), houses were built on the earth, and Cain built a city, and called its name after the name of his son Enoch. 10. And Adam knew Eve his wife and she bare yet nine sons. [173]11. And in the fifth week of the fifth jubilee (225-231 A.M.) Seth took 'Azûrâ his sister to be his wife, and in the fourth (year of the sixth week) (235 A.M.) she bare him Enos. (Gen. iv. 26) 12. He [174]began to call on the name of the Lord on the earth.

The Patriarchs from Adam to Noah (cf. Gen. v.); Life of Enoch; Death of Adam and Gain (iv. 13-33).

13.[175]And in the seventh jubilee in the third week (309-315 A.M.) Enos took Nôâm his sister to be his wife, and she bare him a son in the third year of the fifth week (325 A.M.), and he called his name Kenan. 14. And at the close of the eighth jubilee (386-392 A.M.) Kenan took Mûalêlêth [176]his sister to be his wife, and she bare him a son in the ninth jubilee, (395 A.M.) in the first week in the third year of this week, (449-455 A.M.) and he called his name Mahalalel. 15. And in the second week of the tenth jubilee Mahalalel took unto him to wife Dînâh, the daughter of Barâkî'êl the daughter of his father's brother, and she bare him a son in the third week in the sixth year (461 A.M.), and he called his name Jared; (Gen. v. 15) for in his days the angels of the Lord descended on p. 53 the earth, [177]those who are named the Watchers,[178] that they should instruct the children of men, [179]and that they should do judgment and uprightness on the earth. 16. And in the eleventh jubilee (512-518 A.M.) Jared took to himself a wife, and her name was Bâraka, the daughter of Râsûjâl, a daughter of his father's brother, in the fourth week of this jubilee, and she bare him a son in the fifth week, in the fourth year of the jubilee, and

---

[169] Cf. Deut. xxvii. 24.

[170] So Sam.; but MT "she." In our Book it is generally the father who names the child.

[171] Cf. Gen. iv. 25.

[172] Cf. Gen. iv. 17.

[173] Pseudo-Philo, *Bibl. Antiq.*, gives the names of these nine sons.

[174] So LXX and Vulg.; but MT "then it was begun (men began)."

[175] For 13-14 cf. Gen. v. 9, 12.

[176] A fem. form = "she who praises God."

[177] This last line looks like a quotation from 1 Enoch vi. 6 ("who descended in the days of Jared"). Note the play in Hebrew on the name *Jared* (*yāred*) and "descended" (Heb. *yārĕdû*). The myth of the descent of the angels was based on Gen. vi. 1-4, but was rejected by the Rabbis, who rendered "sons of God" (*i. e.* angels) "sons of the judges."

[178] This name is given to angels in Dan. iv. 13, 17, 23; in 1 Enoch it is applied especially to the fallen angels (cf. 1 Enoch i. 5, x. 9, 15 and often).

[179] This statement is interesting. It describes what was probably the original commission by God to the angelic watchers, who, however, fell when they descended to the earth. According to 1 Enoch, Enoch acquired his supernatural knowledge from the instruction of angels.

he called his name Enoch. [180]17. And he [181]was the first among men that are born on earth who learnt writing and knowledge and wisdom [182]and who wrote down the signs of heaven according to the order of their months in a book, [183]that men might know the seasons of the years according to the order of their separate months. 18. And he was the first to write a testimony, and he testified to the sons of men among the generations of the earth, and recounted the weeks of the jubilees, and made known to them the days of the years, [184]and set in order the months and recounted the Sabbaths of the years as we made (them) known to him. 19. And what was and what will be he saw in a vision [185]of his sleep, as it will happen to the children of men throughout their generations until the day of judgment; he[186] saw and understood everything, and wrote his testimony, and placed the testimony on earth for all the children of men and for their generations. 20. And in the twelfth jubilee (582-588 A.M.), in the seventh week thereof, he took to himself a wife, and her name was Ednî, [187]the daughter of Dânêl, the daughter of his father's brother, and in the sixth year in this week (587 AM.) she bare him a son and he called his name Methuselah. [188]21. And he was moreover with the angels of God these six jubilees of years, and they showed him everything which is on earth [189]and in the heavens, the rule of the sun, and he wrote down everything. 22. And he testified to the Watchers, who had sinned with the daughters of men; for these had begun to unite themselves, so as to be defiled, with the daughters of men, and Enoch testified against (them) all. 23. And he was taken from amongst the children of men, and we conducted him into the Garden of Eden [190]in majesty and honour, and behold there he writeth down the condemnation and judgment of the world, and all the wickedness of the children of men. [191]24. And on account of it (God) brought the waters of the flood [192]upon all the land of Eden; for there he was set as a sign and that he should testify against all the children of men, that he should recount all the deeds of the generations until the day of condemnation. [193]25. And he burnt the incense of the sanctuary, (even) sweet spices, [194]acceptable before the Lord on the Mount. 26. For the Lord hath four places [195]on the earth, the Garden of Eden, and the Mount of

---

[180] Cf. Gen. v. 18.

[181] The passage that follows about Enoch (17-23) implies knowledge on the part of the author of Enochic writings. Charles infers that these were 1 Enoch vi-xvi., xxiii.-xxxvi., and lxxii.-xc.

[182] Cf. the phrase "Scribe of righteousness" applied to Enoch in 1 Enoch xii. 4, xv . 1.

[183] Probably a reference to 1 Enoch lxxii.-lxxxii. ("The Book of the courses of the Heavenly Luminaries ").

[184] There is nothing in 1 or 2 Enoch about "jubilees," etc. This statement is probably due solely to the author of *Jubilees*, who wished to invest the institution with a spurious antiquity.

[185] The reference is probably to the "Dream-Visions" (1 Enoch lxxxiii.-xc.).

[186] *i. e.* Enoch. The writings of Enoch are mentioned elsewhere (1 Enoch, *Test. XII. Patriarchs*).

[187] *Edna* in 1 Enoch lxxxv. 3

[188] Cf. Gen. V. 21.

[189] 1 Enoch xxiii.-xxxvi.

[190] Cf. 1 Enoch lxx. 1-3

[191] Cf. 1 Enoch xii. 3 f., xiv. i. The title ("Scribe of the Knowledge of the Most High") is conferred upon Ezra in 4 Ezra xiv. 50 (Syriac text).

[192] Cf. 2 Enoch xxxiv. 3

[193] Cf. x. 17

[194] Cf. Exod. xxx. 7

[195] Three of these places are connected with critical events in the history of the world; Eden (with Adam), Sinai (with Moses), Zion (with David).

the East, [196]and this mountain on which thou art this day, Mount Sinai, and Mount Zion (which) will be sanctified in the new creation for a sanctification of the earth; through it will the earth be sanctified from all (its) guilt and its uncleanness throughout the generations of the world. [197]27. And in the fourteenth (652 AM) jubilee Methuselah took unto himself a wife, Ednâ the daughter of 'Âzrîâl, the daughter of his father's brother, in the third week, in the first year of this week, and he begat a son and called his name Lamech.[198] 28. And in the fifteenth jubilee in the third week (701-707 A.M.) Lamech took to himself a wife, and her name was Bêtênôs the daughter of Bârâkî'îl, the daughter of his father's brother, and in this week she bare him a son and he called his name Noah, saying, "This one will comfort me for my trouble and all my work, and for the ground which the Lord hath cursed." [199]29. And at the close of the nineteenth jubilee, in the seventh week in the sixth year thereof, (930 A.M.) Adam died, and all his sons buried him in the land of his creation, [200]and he was the first to be buried[201] in the earth. 30. And he lacked seventy years of one thousand years; for one thousand years are as one day in the testimony of the heavens and therefore was it written concerning the tree of knowledge: "On the day that ye eat thereof ye will die." [202]For this reason he did not complete the years of this day; for he died during it. 31. At the close of this jubilee Cain was killed after him in the same year; for his house fell upon him and he died in the midst of his house, and he was killed by its stones, for with a stone he had killed Abel, and by a stone was he killed in righteous judgment. 32. For this reason it was ordained on the heavenly tables: "With the instrument with which a man killeth his neighbour with the same shall he be killed; after the manner that he wounded him, in like manner shall they deal with him." [203]33. And in the twenty-fifth jubilee (1205 A.M.) Noah took to himself a wife, and her name was 'Ĕmzârâ, the daughter of Râkê'êl, the daughter of his father's brother, in the first year in the fifth week (1207 A.M.): and in the third year thereof she bare him Shem, in the fifth year thereof (1209 A.M.) she bare him Ham, and in the first year in the sixth week (1212 A.M.) she bare him Japheth. [204]

The Fall of the Angels and their Punishment; the Deluge foretold (v. 1-20; cf. Gen. vi. 1-12).

V. And it came to pass when the children of men began to multiply on the face of the earth and daughters were born unto them, that the angels of God [205]saw them on a certain year of this jubilee, that they were beautiful to look upon; and they took themselves wives of all whom they chose, and they bare unto them sons and they were giants. (*Giants, i. e.* "Nephilim.")

---

[196] The exact identification is uncertain; possibly the mount above Eden, where the Scthites live, is meant. Other suggestions are Mt. Ephraim, which would imply a Samaritan authorship, and Lubar, on Ararat, which would connect well with the history of Noah.

[197] Cf. i. 29

[198] Cf. Gen. v. 25

[199] Cf. Gen. v. 29.

[200] Cf. iii. 32

[201] This implies the view that Abel's body was not buried before Adam's. According to *Pirke de R. Eliezer* (xxi.), Adam was at first uncertain what to do, but then buried Abel's corpse.

[202] Cf. Gen. ii. 14. Notice that "day" here is interpreted as = 1000 years--a belief early current among Jews and Christians (cf. *Ber. rabba* xix. on Gen. iii. 8), 2 Pet. iii. 8. Justin Martyr, *Trypho.* lxxxi; cf. also *Pirke de R. Eliezer* xviii.

[203] The *lex talionis*; cf. Exod. xxi. 24 ("eye for eye, tooth for tooth"); Lev. xxiv. 19. Similar examples are given in 2 Macc. v. 19 f., xv. 32 f. The rigorous application of this "law" was upheld by the Sadducees, as against the Pharisees.

[204] Cf. Gen. V. 22. Note that Shem is represented as the eldest; cf. Gen. x. 21 (R.V.).

[205] This is the LXX rendering of Gen, vi. 2 (R.V. "sons of God"). and represents the older Jewish exegesis, which was later given up.

2. And lawlessness increased on the earth and all flesh corrupted its way, [206]alike men and cattle and beasts and birds and everything that walketh on the earth-all of them corrupted their ways and their orders, and they began to devour [207]each other, and lawlessness increased on the earth and every imagination of the thoughts of all men (was) thus evil continually. [208]3. And God looked upon the earth, and behold it was corrupt, and all flesh had corrupted its orders, and all that were upon the earth [209]had wrought all manner of evil before His eyes. 4. And He said: "I shall destroy man and all flesh upon the face of the earth which I have created." 5. But Noah found grace before the eyes of the Lord. [210]6. And against the angels whom He had sent upon the earth, He was exceedingly wroth, and He gave commandment to root them out of all their dominion, and He bade us to bind them in the depths of the earth, and behold they are bound in the midst of them, and are (kept) separate. 7. And against their sons went forth a command from before His face that they should be smitten with the sword, and be removed from under heaven. 8. And He said "Thy spirit will not always abide [211]on man; for they also are flesh and their days shall be one hundred and twenty years." 9. And He sent His sword into their midst that each should slay his neighbour, and they began to slay each other till they all fell by the sword and were destroyed from the earth. 10. And their fathers were witnesses (of their destruction), and after this they were bound in the depths of the earth for ever, until the day of the great condemnation [212]when judgment is executed on all those who have corrupted their ways and their works before the Lord. 11. And He †destroyed† all from their places, and there †was† not left one of them whom He judged not according to all their wickedness. 12. And He †made† for all His works a new and righteous nature, [213]so that they should not sin in their whole nature for ever, but should be all righteous each in his kind alway. 13. And the judgment of all is ordained and written on the heavenly tables in righteousness--even (the judgment of) all who depart from the path which is ordained for them to walk in; and if they walk not therein judgment is written down for every creature and for every kind. 14. And there is nothing in heaven or on earth, or in light or in darkness, or in Sheol or in the depth, or in the place of darkness (which is not judged); and all their judgments are ordained and written and engraved. 15. In regard to all He will judge, the great according to his greatness, and the small according to his smallness, and each according to his way. 16. And He is not one who will regard the person (of any), nor is He one who will receive gifts, if He saith that He will execute judgment on each: if one gave everything that is on the earth, He will not regard the gifts or the person (of any), nor accept anything at his hands, for He is a righteous judge. [214][17. And of the children of Israel it hath been written and ordained: If they turn to Him in righteousness, He will forgive all their transgressions and pardon all their sins. 18. It is written and ordained that He will show mercy to all who turn from all their guilt once each year.] [215]19. And as for all those who corrupted their ways and their thoughts before the flood, no man's person was accepted save that of Noah alone; for his person was accepted in behalf of his sons, whom (God) saved from the waters of the flood on his account; for his heart was righteous in all his ways, according as it was commanded regarding him, and he had not departed from aught that was ordained for him. 20. And the Lord said that He would destroy everything

---

[206] Cf. Gen. vi. 12.

[207] Cf. 1 Enoch vii. 5.

[208] Cf. Gen. vi. .5.

[209] Cf. Gen. vi. 12.

[210] Cf. Gen. vi. 7, 8.

[211] Cf. Gen. vi. 3, R.V. marg.

[212] Cf. 1 Enoch x. 12.

[213] 10-12, as Charles has shown, describe the *final* judgment. The tenses must be altered from past to future. Render: "until the day of the great condemnation, when judgment *shall be* executed. . . .
And He *shall* destroy . . . and there *shall not* be left one of them whom He *shall* not have judged. . . . And He *shall* make," etc.

[214] Cf. xl. 8; Deut. x. 17; 2 Chron. xix. 7.

[215] The bracketed clauses have been either transposed here or interpolated from xxxiv. 18-19. The reference is to the Day of Atonement which takes place on the 10th of the 7th month. For "once each year," cf. Heb. ix. 7.

which was upon the earth, both men and cattle, and beasts, and fowls of the air, and that which moveth on the earth. [216]

The Building of the Ark; the Flood (v. 21-32; cf. Gen. vi. 13-viii. 19).

21. And He commanded Noah to make him an ark, that he might save himself from the waters of the flood. [217] 22. And Noah made the ark in all respects as He commanded him, in the twenty-seventh jubilee of years, in the fifth week in the fifth year (on the new moon of the first month). 23. And he entered in the sixth (year) thereof (1307 A.M.), in the second month, on the new moon of the second month, till the sixteenth (1308 A.M.); and he entered, and all that we brought to him, into the ark, and the Lord closed [218] it from without on the seventeenth [219]evening. 24. And the Lord opened seven flood-gates [220]of heaven, And the mouths of the fountains of the great deep, seven mouths in number.

25. And the flood-gates began to pour down water from the heaven forty days and forty nights, And the fountains of the deep also sent up waters, until the whole world was full of water. 26. And the waters increased upon the earth Fifteen cubits did the waters rise above all the high mountains, And the ark was lift up above the earth, And it moved upon the face of the waters.[221]

27. And the water prevailed on the face of the earth five months-one hundred and fifty days. [222]28. And the ark went and rested on the top of Lûbâr, one of the mountains of Ararat. [223]29. And (on the new moon) in the fourth month the fountains of the great deep were closed and the flood-gates of heaven were restrained; and on the new moon of the seventh month all the mouths of the abysses of the earth were opened, and the water began to descend into the deep below. [224]30. And on the new moon of the tenth month (1309 A.M.) the tops of the mountains were seen, and on the new moon of the first month the earth became visible. [225]31. And the waters disappeared from above the earth in the fifth week in the seventh year thereof, and on the seventeenth [226]day in the second month the earth was dry. 32. And on the twenty-seventh thereof he opened the ark, and sent forth from it beasts, and cattle, and birds, and every moving thing.[227]

Noah's Sacrifice; God's Covenant with him (cf. Gen. viii. 20-ix. 17). Instructions to Moses about eating of Blood, the Feast of Weeks, etc., and Division of the Year (vi. 1-38).

---

[216] Cf. Gen. vi. 7

[217] Cf. Gen. vi. 14.

[218] Cf. Gen. vii. 16.

[219] Cf. Gen. vii. 11.

[220] Cf. 1 Enoch lxxxix. 2. Note the recurrence of the number seven in these connexions.

[221] For 24-26 cf. Gen. vii. 11, 12, 18, 20.

[222] Cf. Gen. vii. 24, viii. 3

[223] Cf. Gen. viii. 4. Lubar is mentioned again in vii. 1, 17.

[224] Cf. Gen. viii. 2; 1 Enoch lxxxix. 7.

[225] Cf. Gen. viii. 5, 13.

[226] According to Gen. viii. 14 it was the 27th day of the month.

[227] Cf. Gen. viii. 19.

V1. And on the new moon of the third month he went forth from the ark, and built an altar on that mountain. [228]2. And he made atonement for the earth, [229]and took a kid and made atonement by its blood for all the guilt of the earth; for everything that had been on it had been destroyed, save those that were in the ark with Noah. 3. And he placed the fat thereof on the altar, and he took an ox, and a goat, and a sheep and kids, and salt, and a turtle-dove, and the young of a dove, and placed a burnt sacrifice on the altar, and poured thereon an offering mingled with oil, and sprinkled wine and strewed frankincense over everything, and caused a goodly savour to arise, acceptable before the Lord. [230]4. And the Lord smelt the goodly savour, [231]and He made a covenant with him that there should not be any more a flood to destroy the earth;[232] that all the days of the earth seed-time and harvest should never cease; cold and heat, and summer and winter, and day and night should not change their order, nor cease for ever. [233]5. "And you, increase ye and multiply upon the earth, and become many upon it, and be a blessing upon it. [234]The fear of you and the dread of you I shall inspire in everything that is on earth and in the sea. [235]6. And behold I have given unto you all beasts, and all winged things, and everything that moveth on the earth, and the fish in the waters, and all things for food; as the green herbs, I have given you all things to eat. [236]7. But flesh, with the life thereof, with the blood, ye shall not eat; for the life of all flesh is in the blood, lest your blood of your lives be required. At the hand of every man, at the hand of every (beast), shall I require the blood of man. [237]8. Whoso sheddeth man's blood by man shall his blood be shed; for in the image of God made He man. [238]9. And you, increase ye, and multiply on the earth." 10. And Noah and his sons swore that they would not eat any blood that was in any flesh, and he made a covenant before the Lord God for ever throughout all the generations of the earth in this month. 11. On this account He spake to thee [239]that thou shouldst make a covenant with the children of Israel in this month upon the mountain with an oath, and that thou shouldst sprinkle blood [240]upon them because of all the words of the covenant, which the Lord made with them for ever. 12. And this testimony is written concerning you that you should observe it continually, so that you should not eat on any day any blood of beasts or birds or cattle during all the days of the earth, and the man who eateth the blood of beast or of cattle or of birds during all the days of the earth, he and his seed shall be rooted out of the land. 13. And do thou command the children of Israel to eat no blood, so that their names and their seed may be before the Lord our God continually. [241]14. And for this law there is no limit of days, for it is for ever. They shall observe it throughout their generations, so that they may continue supplicating on your

---

[228] Cf. Gen. viii. 20. The mountain is Lubar.

[229] The earth needed expiation and cleansing for the vices and crimes that had polluted it.

[230] The sacrifice is elaborated here to accord with the developed ritual of a later age; cf. Exod. xxix. 40; Lev. ii. 2-5, 15.

[231] Gen. viii. 21

[232] Cf. Gen. ix. 11.

[233] Cf. Gen. viii. 22.

[234] Cf. Gen. ix. 7.

[235] Cf. Gen. ix. 2.

[236] Cf. Gen. ix. 2, 3.

[237] Cf. Gen. ix. 4, 5.

[238] Cf. Gen. ix. 6.

[239] *i. e.* Moses.

[240] The proper use of blood in the daily sacrifice is here referred to; cf. 14 below.

[241] For 12-13 cf. Lev. xvii. 10, 12, 14; Deut. xii. 23.

behalf with blood before the altar; [242]every day and at the time of morning and evening they shall seek forgiveness [243]on your behalf perpetually before the Lord that they may keep it and not be rooted out. 15 And He gave to Noah [244]and his sons a sign that there should not again be a flood on the earth. 16. He set His bow in the cloud for a sign of the eternal covenant that there should not again be a flood on the earth to destroy it all the days of the earth. [245]17. For this reason it is ordained and written on the heavenly tables, that they should celebrate the feast of weeks [246]in this month once a year, to renew the covenant every year. 18. And this whole festival was celebrated in heaven from the day of creation till the days of Noah-twenty-six jubilees and five weeks of years: and Noah and his sons observed it for seven jubilees and one week of years, till the day of Noah's death (1309-1659 A.M.), and from the day of Noah's death his sons did away with (it) until the days of Abraham, and they ate blood.[247] 19. But Abraham observed it, and Isaac and Jacob and his children observed it up to thy days, and in thy days the children of Israel forgot it until ye celebrated it anew on this mountain. 20. And do thou command the children of Israel to observe this festival in all their generations for a commandment unto them: one day [248]in the year in this month they shall celebrate the festival. 21. For it is the feast of weeks and the feast of first-fruits: [249]this feast is twofold and of a double nature: [250]according to what is written and engraven concerning it celebrate it. 22. For I have written in the book of the first law, [251]in that which I have written for thee, that thou shouldst celebrate it in its season, one day [252]in the year, and I explained to thee its sacrifices that the children of Israel should remember and should celebrate it throughout their generations in this month, one day in every year. 23. And on the new moon of the first month, and on the new moon of the fourth month, and on the new moon of the seventh month, and on the new moon of the tenth month are the days of remembrance, and the days of the seasons in the four divisions of the year. [253]These are written and ordained as a testimony for ever. 24. And Noah ordained them for himself as feasts for the generations for ever, so that they have become thereby a memorial unto him. 25. And on the new moon of the first month he was bidden to make for himself an ark, and on that (day) the earth became dry and he opened (the ark) and saw the earth. 26. And on the new moon of the fourth month the mouths of the depths of the abysses beneath were closed. And on the new moon of the seventh month all the mouths of the abysses of the earth were opened, and the waters began to descend into them.[254] 27. And on the new moon of the tenth month the tops of the

---

[242] Cf. Lev. xvii. ii.

[243] Cf. Num. xxviii. 3-8. -Note that in our text here 11-14 deal with the Mosaic development of the covenant with Noah.

[244] The text here returns to Noah.

[245] Cf. Gen. ix. 13-15.

[246] The "Feast of Weeks" (cf. Exod. xxxiv. 22) is here only connected with Noah's covenant, the establishment of which it is supposed to commemorate. Later Judaism associated it with the giving of the Law on Sinai. It was celebrated, according to our Book, on the 15th day of the 3rd month.

[247] Notice that the non-observance of the Feast signalizes the breaking of the covenant-condition about eating blood.

[248] Or "the first day" (of the week). See 22 below.

[249] It is called "the day of first-fruits" in Num. xxviii. 26.

[250] "Of a double nature" in that (?) it commemorates the covenant with Noah, and also has an agricultural character.

[251] *i. e.* the Pentateuch

[252] Or "the first day" (of the week) = Sunday. Consequently, Pentecost would always fall on the same day of the week, Sunday. This accords with the Sadducean view.

[253] According to Lev. xxiii. 24 only the 1st day of the 7th month was a "day of memorial." The "four days" here mentioned correspond to the four intercalary days "which are not reckoned in the reckoning of the year" mentioned in 1 Enoch lxxv. 1. They introduce the four quarters of the year and apparently, according to the scheme of 1 Enoch and our Book, were intended to be added to the 360 days (= 12 x 30), which made up the solar year (360 + 4 days).

[254] Cf. 1 Enoch lxxxix. 7, 8.

mountains were seen, and Noah was glad. [255]28. And on this account he ordained them for himself as feasts for a memorial for ever, and thus are they ordained. 29. And they placed them on the heavenly tables, each had thirteen weeks; from one to another (passed) their memorial, from the first to the second, and from the second to the third, and from the third to the fourth. 30. And all the days of the commandment will be two and fifty weeks of days, and (these will make) the entire year complete. [256]31. Thus it is engraven and ordained on the heavenly tables. And there is no neglecting (this commandment) for a single -year or from year to year. 32. And command thou the children of Israel that they observe the years according to this reckoning-three hundred and sixty-four days, and (these) will constitute a complete year, and they will not disturb its time from its days and from its feasts; for everything will fall out in them according to their testimony, and they will not leave out any day nor disturb any feasts. [257]33. But if they do neglect and do not observe them according to His commandment, then they will disturb all their seasons, and the years will be dislodged from this (order), [and they will disturb the seasons and the years will be dislodged] [258]and they will neglect their ordinances. 34. And all the children of Israel will forget, and will not find the path of the years, and will forget the new moons, and seasons, and sabbaths, and they will go wrong as to all the order of the years. [259]35. For I know and from henceforth shall I declare it unto thee, and it is not of my own devising; for the book (lieth) written before me, and on the heavenly tables the division of days is ordained, lest they forget the feasts of the covenant and walk according to the feasts of the Gentiles after their error and after their ignorance. 36. For there will be those who will assuredly make observations of the moon--now (it) disturbeth the seasons and cometh in from year to year ten days too soon. [260]37. For this reason the years will come upon them when they will disturb (the order), and make an abominable (day) the day of testimony, and an unclean day a feast day, and they will confound all the days, the holy with the unclean, and the unclean day with the holy; for they will go wrong as to the months and sabbaths and feasts and jubilees. 38. For this reason I command and testify to thee that thou mayest testify to them; for after thy death thy children will disturb (them), so that they will not make the year three hundred and sixty-four days only, and for this reason they will go wrong as to the new moons [261]and seasons and sabbaths and festivals, and they will eat all kinds of blood with all kinds of flesh.

Noah offers Sacrifice; the Cursing of Canaan (cf. Gen. ix. 20-28): Noah's Sons and Grandsons (cf. Gen. x.) and their Cities. Noah's Admonitions (vii. 1-39).

VII. And in the seventh week in the first year thereof, in this jubilee, (1317 A.M.) Noah planted vines on the mountain on which the ark had rested, named Lûbâr, [262]one of the Ararat Mountains, and they produced fruit in the fourth year, (1320 A.M.), [263]and he guarded their fruit, and gathered it in this year in the seventh month. 2. And he made wine therefrom and put it into a vessel, and kept it until the fifth year, until the first day (1321 A.M.), on the new moon of the first month. 3. And he celebrated with joy the day of this feast, and he made a burnt sacrifice unto the Lord, one young ox and one ram, and seven sheep, each a year old, and a kid of the

---

[255] Cf. Gen. viii. 5.

[256] If the year consists of 52 weeks (= 4 X 13 weeks), how can it be divided into 12 months of 30 days each, which is the reckoning implied throughout the Book? For the solutions proposed see Charles's discussion, *ad loc.*

[257] The effect of a solar year reckoned at 364 days would be that the festivals would always be celebrated on the same day of the week. Nisan 14 would always fall on a Sabbath, Nisan 22 (when the wave sheaf was to be offered) on a Sunday, and the Feast of Weeks, Sivan 15, on a Sunday. There is some reason to suppose that this conception of a solar year of 364 days has a dogmatic basis. See Introd., p. xvii.

[258] The bracketed words are a dittograph.

[259] For 33-34 cf. 1 Enoch lxxxii. 4-6.

[260] A lunar year consists of 354 days. Our author wages a polemic against the use of the moon for determining the seasons and feasts. But a lunar year was accepted by the Pharisees.

[261] Render (for "new moons") "beginnings of the months."

[262] Cf. v. 28

[263] Cf. Lev. xix. 23-25 (fruit of trees not to be touched during the first three years after planting).

goats, that he might make atonement thereby for himself and his sons. [264]4. And he prepared the kid first, and placed some of its blood on the flesh that was on the altar which he had made, and all the p. 67 fat he laid on the altar where he made the burnt sacrifice, and the ox and the ram and the sheep, and he laid all their flesh upon the altar. 5. And he placed all their offerings mingled with oil upon it, and afterwards he sprinkled wine on the fire which he had previously made on the altar, and he placed incense on the altar and caused a sweet savour to ascend acceptable before the Lord his God. 6. And he rejoiced and drank of this wine, he and his children with joy. 7. And it was evening, and he went into his tent, and being drunken he lay down and slept, and was uncovered in his tent as he slept. [265]8. And Ham saw Noah his father naked, and went forth and told his two brethren without. 9. And Shem took his garment and arose, he and Japheth, and they placed the garment on their shoulders and went backward and covered the shame of their father, and their faces were backward. [266]10. And Noah awoke from his sleep and knew all that his younger son had done unto him, and he cursed his son and said: "Cursed be Canaan; an enslaved servant shall he be unto his brethren." [267]11. And he blessed Shem, and said: "Blessed be the Lord God of Shem, and Canaan shall be his servant. 12. God shall enlarge Japheth, and God shall dwell in the dwelling of Shem, and Canaan shall be his servant." [268]13. And Ham knew that his father had cursed his younger son, and he was displeased that he had cursed his son, and he parted from his father, he and his sons with him, Cush and Mizraim and Put and Canaan. [269]14. And he built for himself a city and called its name after the name of his wife Nê'êlâtamâ'ûk. 15. And Japheth saw it, and became envious of his brother, and he too built for himself a city, and he called its name after the name of his wife 'Adâtanêsês. 16. And Shem dwelt with his father Noah, and he built a city close to his father on the mountain, and he too called its name p. 68 after the name of his wife Sêdêqêtêlĕbâb. [270]17. And behold these three cities are near Mount Lûbâr; Sêdêqêtêlĕbâb fronting the mountain on its east; and Na'êlâtamâ'ûk on the south; 'Adatanêsês towards the west. 18. And these are the sons of Shem: Elam, and Asshur, and Arpachshad--this (son) was born two years after the flood--and Lud, and Aram. [271]19. The sons of Japheth: Gomer and Magog and Madai and Javan, Tubal and Meshech and Tiras: these are the sons of Noah.[272] 20. [273]And in the twenty-eighth jubilee (1324-1372 A.M.) Noah began to enjoin upon his sons' sons the ordinances and commandments, and all the judgments that he knew, and he exhorted his sons to observe righteousness, and to cover the shame [274]of their flesh, and to bless their Creator, and honour father and mother, and love their neighbour, and guard their souls from fornication and uncleanness and all iniquity. 21. For owing to these three things [275]came the flood upon the earth, namely, owing to the fornication wherein the Watchers against the law of their ordinances went a

---

[264] Cf. Num. xxix. 2, 5.

[265] For 6-7 cf. Gen. ix. 21.

[266] For 8-9 cf. Gen. ix. 22-23

[267] Cf. Gen. ix. 24-25.

[268] For 11-12 cf. Gen. ix. 26-27.

[269] Cf. Gen. x. 6.

[270] "righteousness of the heart."

[271] Cf. Gen. x. 22

[272] Cf. Gen. x. 2

[273] From here to the end of the chapter there is incorporated a fragment of the lost Book of Noah

[274] Cf. iii. 31.

[275] viz. fornication, uncleanness and all iniquity. According to Maimonides (Kings, 89) Adam received six commandments against (1) idolatry; (2) blasphemy; (3) murder; (4) incest; (5) stealing; (6) perverting justice. These were enjoined by Noah, who added a seventh, prohibiting the eating of flesh with blood.

whoring after the daughters of men, and took themselves wives of all which they chose: [276]and they made the beginning of uncleanness. 22. And they begat sons the Nâphîdîm, [277]and †they were all unlike†, [278]and they devoured one another: and the Giants slew the Nâphîl, and the Nâphîl slew the Eljô, and the Eljô mankind, and one man another. 23. And every one sold himself [279]to work iniquity and to shed much blood, [280]and the earth was filled with iniquity. [281]24. And after this they sinned against the beasts and birds, and all that moveth and walketh on the earth: [282]and much blood was shed on the earth, and every imagination and desire of men imagined vanity and evil continually. [283]25. And the Lord destroyed everything from off the face of the earth; [284]because of the wickedness of their deeds, and because of the blood which they had shed in the midst of the earth He destroyed everything. 26. "And we were left, I [285]and you, my sons, and everything that entered with us into the ark, and behold I see your works before me that ye do not walk in righteousness; for in the path of destruction ye have begun to walk, and ye are parting one from another, and are envious one of another, and (so it cometh) that ye are not in harmony, my sons, each with his brother. 27. For I see, and behold the demons have begun (their) seductions against you and against your children, and now I fear on your behalf, that after my death ye will shed the blood of men upon the earth, and that ye, too, will be destroyed from the face of the earth. [286]28. For whoso sheddeth man's blood, and whoso eateth the blood of any flesh, will all be destroyed from the earth. [287]

29. And there will not be left any man that eateth blood.

Or that sheddeth the blood of man on the earth,

Nor will there be left to him any seed or descendants living under heaven;

For into Sheol will they go,

And into the place of condemnation will they descend.

And into the darkness of the deep will they all be removed by a violent death.[288]

30. There shall be no blood seen upon you of all the blood there shall be all the days in which ye have killed any beasts or cattle or whatever flieth upon the earth, and work ye a good work to your souls by covering that which hath been shed [289]on the face of the earth. 31. And ye shall not be like him who eateth with blood, but

---

[276] Cf. Gen. vi. 2; 1 Enoch vii

[277] *i. e.* the Nephilim

[278] Text probably corrupt

[279] Cf. 1 Kings xxi. 20 (phrase).

[280] Cf. 1 Enoch ix. i.

[281] Cf. Gen. vi. ii; 1 Enoch ix. 9.

[282] Cf. 1 Enoch vii. 5.

[283] Cf. Gen. vi. 5.

[284] Cf. Gen. vi. 7, vii. 4

[285] Noah is the speaker here and to the end of the chapter

[286] Cf. x. 1 (x. 1-15 is another excerpt from the Noah apocalypse).

[287] Cf. Gen. ix. 4, 6; Lev. vii. 27.

[288] Cf. xxii. 22; 1 Enoch ciii. 7, 8.

[289] Cf. Lev. xvii. 113; Ezek. xxiv. 7 (here the precept is carried back to Noah).

guard yourselves that none may eat blood before you: [290]cover the blood, for thus have I been commanded to testify to you and your children, together with all flesh.

32. And suffer not the soul to be eaten with the flesh, that your blood, which is your life, may not be required at the hand of any flesh that sheddeth (it) on the earth. [291]33. For the earth will not be clean from the blood which hath been shed upon it; [292]for (only) through the blood of him that shed it [293]will the earth be purified throughout all its generations. 34. And now, my children, hearken: work judgment and righteousness that ye may be planted in righteousness [294]over the face of the whole earth, and your glory lifted up before my God, who saved me from the waters of the flood. [295]35. And behold, ye will go and build for yourselves cities, and plant in them all the plants that are upon the earth, and moreover all fruit-bearing trees. 36. For three years the fruit of everything that is eaten will not be gathered: and in the fourth year its fruit will be accounted holy [and they will offer the first-fruits], [296] acceptable before the Most High God, who created heaven and earth and all things. Let them offer in abundance the first of the wine and oil (as) first-fruits on the altar of the Lord, who receiveth it, and what is left let the servants of the house of the Lord [297]eat before the altar which receiveth (it). 37. And in the fifth year [298]make ye the release so that ye release it [299]in righteousness and uprightness, and ye shall be righteous, and all that you plant will prosper. 38. For thus did Enoch, the father of your father command Methuselah, his son, and Methuselah his son Lamech, and Lamech commanded me all the things which his fathers commanded him. 39. And I also will give you commandment, my sons, as Enoch commanded his son in the first jubilees: whilst still living, the seventh [300]in his generation, he commanded and testified to his son and to his sons' sons until the day of his death."

Genealogy of the Descendants of Shem: Noah and his Sons divide the Earth (viii. 130; cf. Gen. x.).

VIII. In the twenty-ninth jubilee, in the first week, (1373 A. M.) in the beginning thereof Arpachshad took to himself a wife and her name was Râsû'ĕjâ, [the daughter of Sûsân,] the daughter of Elam, and she bare him a son in the third year in this week, (1375 A. M.) and he called his name Kâinâm. [301]2. And the son grew, and his father taught him writing, and he went to seek for himself a place where he might seize for himself a city. 3. And he found a writing which former (generations) had carved on the rock, and he read what was thereon, and he transcribed it and sinned owing to it; for it contained the teaching of the Watchers in accordance with

---

[290] One of the seven Noachic laws (binding on all men) was the prohibition of eating flesh with the blood. Cf. note on 21 above.

[291] Cf. Gen. ix. 4; Lev. xvii. 10, 11, 14.

[292] Cf. vi. 2.

[293] Cf. Num. xxxv. 33.

[294] A frequent metaphor in the O.T. Israel is "the plant of righteousness" (1 Enoch x. 16, etc.).

[295] Cf. 2 Pet. ii. 5

[296] These words, if genuine, direct that in the fourth year only the first-fruits (not all the fruit) are to be offered to God. Cf. Lev. xix. 23-24.

[297] i. e. the priests. Later Judaism directed that the rest of the fruit should be eaten by the owners within the walls of Jerusalem. The view of the text is supported by the Samaritans, the Karaite Jews and Ibn Ezra.

[298] Charles suspects a lacuna in the text here.

[299] Or render "(In the seventh year) ye will let it (the land) rest and lie fallow" (Charles).

[300] Cf. 1 Enoch lx. 8, xciii. 3; Jude 14.

[301] This name occurs in the LXX of Gen. xi. 13, but not in the MT or other Versions. It also occurs in the genealogy in Luke iii. 36.

which they used to observe the omens of the sun and moon and stars in all the signs of heaven. [302]4. And he wrote it down and said nothing regarding it; for he was afraid to speak to Noah about it lest he should be angry with him on account of it. 5. And in the thirtieth jubilee, in the second week, (1429 A.M.) in the first year thereof, he took to himself a wife, and her name was Mêlkâ, the daughter of Madai, the son of Japheth, and in the fourth year (1432 A.M.) he begat a son, and called his name Shelah; [303]for he said: "Truly I have been sent."[304] 6. [And in the fourth year he was born], and Shelah grew up and took to himself a wife, and her name was Mû'ak, the daughter of Kêsêd, his father's brother, in the one and thirtieth jubilee, in the fifth week, in the first year thereof. (1499 A.M.) 7. And she bare him a son in the fifth year thereof (1503 A.M.), and he called his name Eber: and he took unto himself a wife, and her name was 'Azûrâd [305]the daughter of Nêbrôd, in the thirty-second jubilee, in the seventh week, in the third year thereof. (1564 A.M.) 8. And in the sixth year thereof, (1567 A.M.) she bare him a son, and he called his name Peleg; for in the days when he was born the children of Noah began to divide the earth amongst themselves: for this reason he called his name Peleg. [306]9. And they divided (it) secretly [307]amongst themselves, p. 73 and told it to Noah. 10. And it came to pass in the beginning of the thirty-third jubilee that they divided the earth into three parts, for Shem and Ham and Japheth, according to the inheritance of each, in the first year in the first week, (1569 A.M.) when one of us, [308]who had been sent, was with them. 11. And he called his sons, and they drew nigh to him, they and their children, and he divided the earth into the lots, which his three sons were to take in possession, and they reached forth their hands, and took the writing out of the bosom of Noah, their father. 12. And there came forth on the writing as Shem's lot [309]the middle of the earth [310]which he should take as an inheritance for himself and for his sons for the generations of eternity, from the middle of the mountain range of Râfâ, [311]from the mouth of the water from the river Tînâ. [312]and his portion goeth towards the west through the midst of this river, and it extendeth till it reacheth the water of the abysses, out of which this river goeth forth and poureth its waters into the sea Mê'at, [313]and this river floweth into the great sea. And all that is towards the north is Japheth's, and all that is towards the south belongeth to Shem. 13. And it extendeth till it reacheth Kârâsô: [314]this is in the bosom of the tongue [315]which looketh towards the south. 14. And his portion extendeth along the great sea, and it extendeth in a

---

[302] Cf. Josephus, *Ant.* i. 2, 3, who assigns this wisdom not to the Watchers, but to the children of Seth.

[303] Cf. Gen. X. 24

[304] A paronomasia is implied in the original Hebrew here

[305] Read *'Azûrâ*

[306] There is a play (in the original Hebrew) on the meaning of the name *Peleg* here.

[307] The secret division of the earth is followed by an authoritative one by Noah, and made binding on his descendants. Canaan is included in Shem's lot. Hence, the Israelite conquest later is justified. 'Noah's division of the earth is alluded to in *Pirke de R. Eliezer* xxiii. (end).

[308] *i. e.* one of the angels

[309] For the countries included in Shem's lot, See 21, ix. 2-6, 13*b*. According to Epiphanius it extended from Persia and Bactria to India, to Rhinocurura (between Egypt and Palestine).

[310] According to Ezek. xxxviii. 12 (1 Enoch xxvi. i) Palestine was the "navel" of the earth.

[311] Probably the Rhipaean mountains (identified sometimes with the Ural mountains).

[312] *i. e.* the river Tanais or Don.

[313] *i. e.* the Maeotis or Sea of Azov.

[314] *i. e.* (?) the Rhinocurura (= "the torrent of Egypt") on the confines of Egypt and Palestine (Charles); cf. Isa. xxvii. 12.

[315] *i. e.* either promontory of land, or bay

straight line till it reacheth the west of the tongue which looketh towards the south; [316]for this sea is named the tongue of the Egyptian Sea. [317]15. And it turneth from here towards the south towards the mouth of the great sea [318]on the shore of (its) waters, and it extendeth to the west to 'Afrâ [319]and it extendeth till it reacheth the waters of the river Gihon, and to the south of the waters of Gihon, (*The Nile) to the banks of this river. 16. And it extendeth towards the east, till it reacheth the Garden of Eden, to the south thereof, [to the south] and from the east of the whole land of Eden and of the whole cast, it turneth to the †east,† [320]and proceedeth till it reacheth the east of the mountain named Râfâ, and it descendeth to the bank of the mouth of the river Tînâ. 17. This portion came forth by lot for Shem and his sons, that they should possess it for ever unto his generations for evermore. 18. And Noah rejoiced that this portion came forth for Shem and for his sons, and he remembered all that he had spoken with his mouth in prophecy; for he had said:

Blessed be the Lord God of Shem,

And may the Lord dwell in the dwelling of Shem."[321]

19. And he knew that the Garden of Eden is the holy of holies, and the dwelling of the Lord, and Mount Sinai the centre of the desert, and Mount Zion--the centre of the navel of the earth: these three [322]were created as holy places facing each other. 20. And he blessed the God of gods, who had put the word of the Lord into his mouth, and the Lord for evermore. 21. And he knew that a blessed portion and a blessing had come to Shem and his sons unto the generations for ever--the whole land of Eden and the whole land of the Red Sea, and the whole land of the east, and India, and on the Red Sea and the mountains thereof, and all the land of Bashan, and all the land of Lebanon and the islands of Kaftûr, [323]and all the mountains of Sanîr [324]and 'Amânâ, [325]and the mountains of Asshur in the north, and all the land of Elam, Asshur, and Bâbêl, and Sûsân and Mâ'ĕdâi [326]and all the mountains of Ararat, and all the region beyond the sea, which is beyond the mountains of Asshur towards the north, a blessed and spacious land, and all that is in it is very good. 22. [327]And for Ham came forth the second portion, beyond the Gihon towards the south to the right [328]of the Garden, and it extendeth towards the south and it extendeth to all the mountains of fire, [329]and it extendeth towards the west to the sea of 'Atêl

---

[316] . e. (?) the promontory on which Mt. Sindi is situated.

[317] I i. e. the Gulf of Akaba; cf. Isa. xi. 15.

[318] the northern waters of the Red Sea.

[319] i. e. Africa in the restricted sense of the Roman province which included Egypt and the other northern parts of Africa bordering the Mediterranean.

[320] Read west.

[321] Cf. vii. 11.

[322] These three holy places fall within Shem's lot

[323] ? Crete. The ancient Versions identify Caphtor with Cappadocia.

[324] i. e. Senir (Deut. iii. 9; Ezek. xxvii. 5) = Hermon.

[325] ? Mt. Amanus in N. Syria.

[326] i. e. Media; cf. x. 35.

[327] 22-24 give details of Ham's portion, which includes all Africa and certain parts of Asia.

[328] i. e. to the south.

[329] Cf. 1 Enoch xviii. 6-9, xxiv. 1-3.

330and it extendeth towards the west till it reacheth the sea of Mâ'ûk 331that (sea) into which †everything which is not destroyed descendeth†. 33223. And it goeth forth towards the north to the limits of Gâdîr,333 and it goeth forth to the coast of the waters of the sea to the waters of the great sea till it draweth near to the river Gihon, and goeth along the river Gihon till it reacheth the right of the Garden of Eden. 24. And this is the land which came forth for Ham as the portion which he was to occupy for ever for himself and his sons unto their generations for ever. 25. 334And for Japheth came forth the third portion beyond 335the river Tînâ 336to the north of the outflow of its waters, and it extendeth north-easterly to the whole region of Gog 337and to all the country east thereof. 26. And it extendeth northerly to the north, and it extendeth to the mountains of Qêlt 338towards the north, and towards the sea of Mâ'ûk, and it goeth forth to the east of Gâdîr as far as the region of the waters of the sea. 27. And it extendeth until it approacheth the west of Fârâ 339and it returneth towards 'Afêrâg, 340and it extendeth easterly to the waters of the sea of Mê'at. 34128. And it extendeth to the region of the river Tînâ in a northeasterly direction until it approacheth the boundary of its waters towards the mountain Râfâ, 342and it turneth round towards the north. 29. This is the land which came forth for Japheth and his sons as the portion of his inheritance which he should possess for himself and his sons, for their generations for ever; five great islands, 343and a great land in the north. 30. But it is cold, and the land of Ham is hot, and the land of Shem is neither hot nor cold, but it is of blended cold and heat.

Subdivision of the Three Portions amongst the Grandchildren: Oath taken by Noah's Sons (ix. 1-15; cf. Gen. x. partly).

IX. And Ham divided amongst his sons, and the first portion came forth for Cush 344towards the east, and to the west of him for Mizraim, 345 and to the west of him for Put, 346and to the west of him [and to the west

---

330 *i. e.* the Atlantic.

331 ? The great ocean stream in the extreme west.

332 The text may be corrupt. Render, perhaps, "if anything descends into it, it perishes" (Charles).

333 *i. e.* Cadiz.

334 25-29*a* Japheth's portion (N. Asia, Europe, five great islands); cf. ix. 7-13.

335 Japheth's portion is elaborately described in Josephus, *Ant.* i. 6, 1.

336 *i. e.* the river Don.

337 In N. Asia. Josephus identifies Gog with the Scythians.

338 *Qêlt* = probably the Celts.

339 ? Africa.

340 ? Phrygia.

341 *i. e.* the Sea of Azov (see viii. 12 above).

342 ? the Ural mountains (Cf. viii. 12 above).

343 Including, probably, Cyprus, Sicily, Sardinia, Corsica.

344 Ethiopia

345 *i. e.* Egypt.

346 *i. e.* the Atlantic. For Canaan's portion (from Libya to the Atlantic) Cf. x. 28-29.

thereof] [347] on the sea for Canaan.[348] 2. And Sherri also divided amongst his sons, and the first portion came forth for Elam and his sons, to the east of the river Tigris till it approacheth the east, the whole land of India, and on the Red Sea on its coast, and the waters of Dêdân, and all the mountains of Mebrî and 'Êlâ, and all the land of Sûsân and all that is on the side of Pharnâk [349]to the Red Sea and the river Tînâ. 3. And for Asshur came forth the second portion, all the land of Asshur and Nineveh and Shinar and to the border of India, and it ascendeth and skirteth the river. 4. And for Arpachshad came forth the third portion, all the land of the region of the Chaldees to the east of the Euphrates, bordering on the Red Sea, and all the waters of the desert close to the tongue of the sea which looketh towards Egypt, all the land of Lebanon and Sanîr and 'Amânâ [350] to the border of the Euphrates. 5. And for Aram [351]there came forth the fourth portion, all the land of Mesopotamia between the Tigris and the Euphrates to the north of the Chaldees to the border of the mountains of Asshur and the land of 'Arârâ. [352]6. And there came forth for Lud [353]the fifth portion, the mountains of Asshur and all appertaining to them till it reacheth the Great Sea, and till it reacheth the east of Asshur his brother. 7. And Japheth also divided the land of his inheritance amongst his sons. 8. And the first portion came forth for Gomer to the east from the north side to the river Tînâ; and in the north there came forth for Magog all the inner portions of the north until it reacheth to the sea of Mê'at. 9 And for Madai came forth as his portion that he should possess from the west of his two brothers to the islands, [354]and to the coasts of the islands. 10. And for Javan [355]came forth the fourth portion every island [356]and the islands which are towards the border of Lud. 11. And for Tubal [357]there came forth the fifth portion in the midst of the tongue which approacheth towards the border of the portion of Lud to the second tongue, to the region beyond the second tongue unto the third tongue. [358]12. And for Meshech came forth the sixth portion, all the region beyond the third tongue[359] till it approacheth the east of Gâdîr. [360]13. And for Tiras [361]there came forth the seventh portion, four great islands [362]in the midst of the sea, which reach to the portion of Ham [and the islands of Kamâtûrî

---

[347] *i. e.* Libya (west of Egypt).

[348] For 1 cf. Gen. x. 6.

[349] ? Pharnacia on the coast of Pontus (Charles).

[350] Cf. viii. 21.

[351] *i. e.* the Syrians.

[352] Ararat; Cf. viii. 21.

[353] According to Josephus the descendants of Lud were the Lydians.

[354] Including (?) Britain and Ireland.

[355] *i.e.* properly Ionia (so Isa. lxvi. 19; Ezek. xxvii. 13): but in Daniel (Viii. 21, X. 20, xi. 2) it = the Græco-Macedonian Empire. Here it seems to embrace all the islands off the coast of Asia Minor.

[356] ? coastland.

[357] Tubal's portion apparently extends from Thrace to Italy.

[358] The three tongues of land may be Thrace, Greece and Italy.

[359] *i. e.* probably Italy.

[360] *i. e.* Cadiz.

[361] The descendants of Tiras may have been the Tyrseni, a branch of the Pelasgians.

[362] Cf. viii. 29.

came out by lot for the sons of Arpachshad as his inheritance]. [363]14. And thus the sons of Noah divided unto their sons in the presence of Noah their father, and he bound them all by an oath, imprecating a curse on every one that sought to seize the portion which had not fallen (to him) by his lot. 15. And they all said, "So be it; so be it," for themselves and their sons for ever throughout their generations till the day of judgment, on which the Lord God shall judge them with a sword and with fire, for all the unclean wickedness of their errors, wherewith they have filled the earth with transgression and uncleanness and fornication and sin.

Noah's Sons led astray by Evil Spirits; Noah's Prayer; Mastêmâ; Death of Noah (x. 1-17; cf. Gen. ix. 28).

X. [364]And in the third week of this jubilee the unclean demons [365]began to lead astray †the children of†[366] the sons of Noah; and to make to err and destroy them. 2. And the sons of Noah came to Noah their father, and they told him concerning the demons which were, leading astray and blinding and slaying his sons' sons. 3. And he prayed before the Lord his God, and said:

God of the spirits of all flesh, [367]who hast shown mercy unto me,

And hast saved me and my sons from the waters of the flood,

And hast not caused me to perish as Thou didst the sons of perdition;[368]

For Thy grace hath been great towards me,

And great hath been Thy mercy to my soul;

Let Thy grace be lift up upon my sons, And let not wicked spirits rule over them Lest they should destroy them from the earth.

4. But do Thou bless me and my sons, that we may increase and multiply and replenish the earth. 5. And Thou knowest how Thy Watchers, the fathers of these spirits, acted in my day: and as for these spirits which are living, imprison them and hold them fast in the place of condemnation, and let them not bring destruction on the sons of thy servant, my God; for these are malignant, and created in order to destroy. 6. And let them not rule over the spirits of the living; for Thou alone canst exercise dominion over them. And let them not have power over the sons of the righteous from henceforth and for evermore." 7. And the Lord our God bade us to bind all. [369]8. And the chief of the spirits, Mastêmâ, [370]came and said: "Lord, Creator, let some of them remain before me, and let them hearken to my voice, and do all that I shall say unto them; for if some of them are not left to me, I shall not be able to execute the power of my will on the sons of men; for these are for corruption and leading astray before my judgment, for great is the wickedness of the sons of men." 9. And He said: "Let the tenth part of them remain before him, and let nine parts descend into the place of condemnation." [371]10.

---

[363] The bracketed words are probably an interpolation (Charles). Arpachsad was a son of Shem.

[364] Here we have (in x. 1-15) another fragment of the lost Apocalypse of Noah (as in vii. 20-39). The Hebrew original of 1-2 and 9-14 of this section is extant.

[365] *i. e.* the spirits which issued from the children of the angels and the daughters of men.

[366] Omit *the children of.*

[367] Cf. Num. xvi. 22, xxvii. 16.

[368] Cf. 2 Thess. ii. 3.

[369] Cf. 1 Enoch x. 4, 12.

[370] The word apparently = *matîm* (Hif. part of *â am*), "to be adverse," "inimical"; the Heb. noun masēmâ = "animosity," in Hos. ix. 7, 8. Thus the word = Satan ("adversary"). As a proper name it is practically confined to the Jubilees-literature. The evil spirits under the guidance of Mastêmâ tempt, accuse and destroy men.

[371] Only one-tenth are permitted to act freely against mankind till the Day of judgment; but in 1 Enoch xv.-xvi. all the demons are allowed to do this.

And one of us [372]He commanded that we should teach Noah all their medicines; for He knew that they would not walk in uprightness, nor strive in righteousness. 11. And we did according to all His words: all the malignant evil ones we bound in the place of condemnation, and a tenth part of them we left that they might be subject before Satan [373]on the earth. 12. And we explained to Noah all the medicines of their diseases, together with their seductions, how he might heal them with herbs of the earth. 13. And Noah wrote down all things in a book as we instructed him concerning every kind of medicine. Thus the evil spirits were precluded from (hurting) the sons of Noah. 14. And he gave all that he had written to Shem, his eldest son; for he loved him exceedingly above all his sons. 15. And Noah slept with his fathers, and was buried on Mount Lûbâr in the land of Ararat. 16. Nine hundred and fifty years he completed in his life, nineteen jubilees and two

1659 weeks and five years. 17. And in his life on earth he excelled the children of men save A.M. Enoch because of the righteousness, wherein he was perfect. For Enoch's office was ordained for a testimony to the generations of the world, [374]so that he should recount all the deeds of generation unto generation, till the day of judgment.

The Tower of Babel and the Confusion of Tongues (x. 18-27; cf. Gen. xi. 1-9).

18. And in the three and thirtieth jubilee, in the first year in the second week, Peleg took to himself a wife, whose name was Lômnâ the daughter of Sînâ'ar, and she bare him a son in the fourth year of this week, and he called his name Reu; [375]for he said: "Behold the children of men have become evil [376]through the wicked purpose of building for themselves a city and a tower in the land of Shinar." 19. For they departed from the land of Ararat eastward to Shinar; for in his days they built the city and the tower, saying, "Go to, let us ascend thereby into heaven." [377]20. And they began to build, and in the fourth week they made brick with fire, and the bricks served them for stone, and the clay [378]with which they cemented them together was asphalt which cometh out of the sea, and out of the fountains of water in the land of Shinar. 21. And they built it: forty and three years were they building it (1645-1688 A.M.); its breadth was 203 bricks, and the height (of a brick) was the third of one; its height amounted to 5433 cubits and 2 palms, and (the extent of one wall was) thirteen stades (and of the other thirty stades). 22. And the Lord our God said unto us: "Behold, they are one people, and (this) they begin to do, and now nothing will be withholden from them. Go to, let us go down and confound their language, that they may not understand one another's speech, [379]and they may be dispersed into cities and nations, and one purpose will no longer abide with them till the day of judgment." 23. And the Lord descended, and we descended with Him to see the city and the tower which the children of men had built. 24. And He confounded their language, and they no longer understood one another's speech, and they ceased then to build the city and the tower. 25. For this reason the whole land of Shinar is called Babel, because the Lord did there confound all the language of the children of men, and from thence they were dispersed [380]into their

---

[372] The angel Raphael is referred to, as is shown by the Hebrew Book of Noah. For Raphael in this connection cf. Tobit iii. 17, xii. 14, 15.

[373] Thus Satan and Mastêmâ are identical.

[374] Cf. iv. 24

[375] Cf. Gen. xi. 18.

[376] There is a play on the name Reu in Hebrew here (*re'û . . . rā'û*).

[377] Cf. Gen. xi. 4

[378] Cf. Gen. xi. 3.

[379] Cf. Gen. xi. 6 f.

[380] Cf. Gen. xi. 9.

cities, each according to his language and his nation. 381 26. And the Lord sent a mighty wind 382against the tower and overthrew it upon the earth, and behold it was between Asshur and Babylon in the land of Shinar, and they called its name "Overthrow." 383 27. In the fourth week in the first year (1688 A.M.) in the beginning thereof in the four and thirtieth jubilee, were they dispersed from the land of Shinar.

The Children of Noah enter their Districts Canaan seizes Palestine wrongfully; Madai receives Media (x. 28-36)

28. And Ham and his sons went into the land which he was to occupy, which he acquired as his portion in the land of the south. 384 29. And Canaan saw the land of Lebanon to the river of Egypt that it was very good, and he went not into the land of his inheritance to the west (that is to) the sea, 385and he dwelt in the land of Lebanon, eastward and westward from the border of Jordan and from the border of the sea. 386 30. And Ham, his father, and Cush and Mizraim, his brothers, said unto him: "Thou hast settled in a land which. is not thine, and which did not fall to us by lot: do not do so; for if thou dost do so, thou and thy sons will fall in the land and (be) accursed through sedition; for by sedition ye have settled, and by sedition will thy children fall, and thou shalt be rooted out for ever. 31. Dwell not in the dwelling of Shem; for to Shem and to his sons did it come by their lot. 32. Cursed art thou, and cursed shalt thou be beyond all the sons of Noah, by the curse 387by which we bound ourselves by an oath in the presence of the holy judge, 388and in the presence of Noah our father." 33. But he did not hearken unto them, and dwelt in the land of Lebanon from Hamath389 to the entering of Egypt, 390he and his sons until this day. 34. And for this reason that land is named Canaan. 35. And Japheth and his sons went towards the sea and dwelt in the land of their portion, and Madai saw the land of the sea and it did not please him, and he begged a (portion) from Elam and Asshur and Arpachshad, his wife's brother, and he dwelt in the land of Media, near to his wife's brother until this day. 36. And he called his dwelling-place, and the dwelling-place of his sons, Media, after the name of their father Madai.

The History of the Patriarchs from Reu to Abraham (cf. Gen. xi, 20-30); the Corruption of the Human Race (xi. 1-15).

XI. And in the thirty-fifth jubilee, in the third week, in the first year thereof, (1681 A.M.) Reu took to himself a wife, and her name was 'Ôrâ, the daughter of 'Ûr, the son of Kêsêd, and she bare him a son, and he called his name Sêrô , 391in the seventh year of this week in this jubilee. (1687 A.M.) 2. 392And the sons of Noah began

---

381 According to Jewish tradition seventy nations (under seventy patron angels) were thus created.

382 An old tradition; cf. *Sibyll. Oracles* iii. 98-103; Josephus, *Ant.* i. 4, 3.

383 A play on the preceding verb (" overthrew "). But its real name was Babel.

384 "South" should be "north" here: N. Africa is meant.

385 *i. e.* N.-W. Africa (his true inheritance).

386 Canaan wrongfully seized Palestine, which belonged by right to Arpachshad.

387 Cf. ix, 14, 15.

388 *i. e.* the angel who was present at the lot (viii. 10).

389 Hamath marked the northern boundary of Israel.

390 The extreme south.

391 Cf. Gen. xi. 20 f. (MT. has *Serug* for *Sêrô*).

392 In 2-6 the corruption of mankind is ascribed to the period of Serug.

to war on each other, to take captive and to slay each other, and to shed the blood of men on the earth, and to eat blood, and to build strong cities, and walls, and towers, and individuals (began) to exalt themselves above the nation, [393]and to found the beginnings of kingdoms, and to go to war people against people, and nation against nation, and city against city, and all (began) to do evil, and to acquire arms, and to teach their sons war, and they began to capture cities, and to sell male and female slaves. 3. And 'Ûr, the son of Kêsêd, [394]built the city of 'Arâ [395]of the Chaldees, and called its name after his own name and the name of his father. 4. And they made for themselves molten images, and they worshipped each the idol, the molten image which they had made for themselves, and they began to make graven images and unclean simulacra, and malignant spirits assisted and seduced (them) into committing transgression and uncleanness. 5. And the prince Mastêmâ exerted himself to do all this, and he sent forth other spirits, those which were put under his hand, to do all manner of wrong and sin, and all manner of transgression, to corrupt and destroy, and to shed blood upon the earth.[396]6. For this reason he called the name of Sêrô, Serug, for every one turned to do all manner of sin and transgression. 7. And he grew up, and dwelt in Ur of the Chaldees, near to the father of his wife's mother, and he worshipped idols, and he took to himself a wife in the thirty-sixth jubilee, in the fifth week, in the first year thereof, (1744 A.M.) and her name was Mêlkâ, [397]the daughter of Kâbêr, the daughter of his father's brother. 8. And she bare him Nahor, in the first year of this week, and he grew and dwelt in Ur of the Chaldees, and his father taught him the researches of the Chaldees to divine and augur, according to the signs of heaven. 9. And in the thirty-seventh jubilee, in the sixth week, in the first year thereof (1800 A.M.) , he took to himself a wife, and her name was 'Îjâskâ, [398]the daughter of Nêstâg of the Chaldees. 10. And she bare him Terah[399] in the seventh year of this week. (1806 A.M.) 11. And the prince Mastêmâ sent ravens and birds to devour the seed which was sown in the land, in order to destroy the land, and rob the children of men of their labours. Before they could plough in the seed, the ravens picked (it) from the surface of the ground. 12. And for this reason he called his name Terah, because the ravens and the birds reduced them to destitution and devoured their seed. [400]13. And the years began to be barren, owing to the birds, and they devoured all the fruit of the trees from the trees: it was only with great effort that they could save a little of all the fruit of the earth in their days. 14. And in this thirty-ninth jubilee, in the second week in the first year, (1870 A.M.) Terah took to himself a wife, and her name was 'Êdnâ, [401]the daughter of 'Abrâm[402] the daughter of his father's sister. 15. And in the seventh year of this week (1876 A.M.) she bare him a son, and he called his name Abram, by the name of the father of his mother; for he had died before his daughter had conceived a son.[403]

Abram's Knowledge of God and wonderful Deeds (xi. 16-24).

---

[393] A note of hostility to monarchy.

[394] The place name *Ur Kasdîm* ("Ur of the Chaldees") is here transformed into the names of two persons, after whom the city is named.

[395] *i. e.* Ur.

[396] Cf. 1 Enoch xvi.

[397] In Gen. xi. 29 Milcah is the name of the wife of Nahor, Abram's brother.

[398] = Iscah (cf. Gen. xi. 29; but there she is daughter of Haran).

[399] Cf. Gen. xi. 24.

[400] Apparently some play on the name Terah is involved in the original Hebrew; but the explanation is uncertain.

[401] According to the Talmud (*Baba bathra* 91a) her name was Amthelai, daughter of Karnebo.

[402] *i. e.* the grandfather of the Biblical Abram.

[403] it was customary to name a child after a grandfather. Here the child's name apparently perpetuates the memory of a grandfather who had died before the child was conceived.

16. And the child began to understand the errors of the earth that all went astray after graven images and after uncleanness, and his father taught him writing, and he was two weeks of years old, (1890 A.M.) and he separated himself from his father [404]that he might not worship idols with him. 17. And he began to pray to the Creator of all things that He might save him from the errors of the children of men, and that his portion should not fall into error after uncleanness and vileness. 18. And the seed time came for the sowing of seed upon the land, and they all went forth together to protect their seed against the ravens, and Abram went forth with those that went, and the child was a lad of fourteen years. 19. And a cloud of ravens came to devour the seed, and Abram ran to meet them before they settled on the ground, and cried to them before they settled on the ground to devour the seed, and said, "Descend not: return to the place whence ye came," and they proceeded to turn back. 20. And he caused the clouds of ravens to turn back that day seventy times, and of all the ravens throughout all the land where Abram was there settled there not so much as one. 21. And all who were with him throughout all the land saw him cry out, and all the ravens turn back, and his name became great in all the land of the Chaldees. 22. And there came to him this year all those that wished to sow, and he went with them until the time of sowing ceased: and they sowed their land, and that year they brought enough grain home and ate and were satisfied. 23. And in the first year of the fifth week (1891 A.M.) Abram taught those who made implements for oxen, the artificers in wood, and they made a vessel above the ground, facing the frame of the plough, [405]in order to put the seed thereon, and the seed fell down therefrom upon the share of the plough, and was hidden in the earth, and they no longer feared the ravens. 24. And after this manner they made (vessels) above the ground on all the frames of the ploughs, and they sowed and tilled all the land, according as Abram commanded them, and they no longer feared the birds.

Abram seeks to convert Terah from Idolatry; the Family of Terah (cf. Gen. xi. 27-30). Abram burns the Idols. Death of Haran (cf. Gen. xi. 28) (xii. 1-14).

XII. And it came to pass in the sixth week, in the seventh year thereof, (1904 A.M.)that Abram said to Terah his father, saying, A.M. "Father!" And he said, "Behold, here am I, my son." 2. And he said,

"What help and profit have we from those idols which thou dost worship, And before which thou dost bow thyself?[406]

3. For there is no spirit in them,[407]

For they are dumb forms, and a misleading of the heart. Worship them not:

4.Worship the God of heaven,

Who causeth the rain and the dew to descend on the earth,[408]

And doeth everything upon the earth,

And hath created everything by His word, [409]And all life is from before His face.

5. Why do ye worship things that have no spirit in them? For they are the work of (men's) hands,[410]

---

[404] This is the theme of much later Jewish legend. See especially the first part of the *Apocalypse of Abraham*, an edition of which appears in this series. Cf. xii. 1-14 below.

[405] An improved method of sowing by means of a seed-scatterer attached to the plough (Arab. *bûk*) is here described. This marked an advance on the primitive method of scattering the seed by hand, and its invention is ascribed to Abraham. In Rabbinical tradition Noah is the inventor of the plough and kindred instruments. Cf. Krauss, *Talmudische Archäologie*, ii. 553 (note 151).

[406] In 1-14 we have an early form of the legend of Abram's protest against idolatry. This section has remarkable parallels, both in thought and expression, with chaps. i.-viii. of the Apocalypse of Abraham. In the later (Rabbinic) forms of the legend Abram's birth excites the alarm of Nimrod, who endeavours to destroy him in a furnace of fire.

[407] Cf. Ps. cxxxv. 17.

[408] Cf. XX. 9; Jer. xiv. 22.

[409] Cf. Ps. xxxiii. 6: Heb. xi. 3; 2 Pet. iii. 5; 4 Ezra vi. 38.

[410] Cf. Jer. x. 3, 9.

And on your shoulders do ye bear them,[411]

And ye have no help from them,

But they are a great cause of shame to those who make them, And a misleading of the heart to those who worship them: Worship them not."

6. And his father said unto him, "I also know it, my son, but what shall I do with a people who have made me to serve before them? 7. And if I tell them the truth, they will slay me; for their soul cleaveth to them to worship them and honour them. Keep silent, [412]my son, lest they slay thee." 8. And these words he spake to his two brothers, and they were angry with him and he kept silent. 9. And in the fortieth jubilee, in the second week, in the seventh year thereof (1925 A.M.), Abram took to himself a wife, and her name was Sarai, the daughter of his father, and she became his wife. [413]10. And Haran, his brother, took to himself a wife in the third year of the third week, (1932 A.M.), and she bare him a son in the seventh year of this week and he called his name Lot. 11. And Nahor, his brother, took to himself a wife. [414]12. And in the sixtieth year of the life of Abram, that is, in the fourth week, in the fourth year thereof, (1936 A.M.), Abram arose by night, and burned the house of the idols, and he burned all that was in the house, and no man knew it. 13. And they arose in the night and sought to save their gods from the midst of the fire. 14. And Haran hasted to save them, but the fire flamed over him, and he was burnt in the fire, and he died in Ur of the Chaldees before Terah his father, and they buried him in Ur of the Chaldees. [415]

The Family of Terah in Haran; Abram's Experiences there; his Journey to Canaan (xii. 15-31; cf. Gen. xi, 31-xii. 3).

15. And Terah went forth from Ur of the Chaldees, he and his sons, to go into the land of Lebanon and into the land of Canaan, and he dwelt in the land of Haran, and Abram, dwelt with Terah his father in Haran two weeks of years. [416]16. And in the sixth week, in the fifth year thereof, Abram sat up throughout the night on the new moon of the seventh month to observe the stars from the evening to the morning, in order to see what would be the character of the year with regard to the rains, and he was alone as he sat and observed. 17. And a word came into his heart and he said: "All the signs of the stars, and the signs of the moon and of the sun are all in the hand of the Lord. Why do I search (them) out?

18. If He desireth, He causeth it to rain, morning and evening;

And if He desireth, He withholdeth it, And all things are in His hand."

19. And he prayed that night and said

"My God, God Most High, Thou alone art my God, And Thee and Thy dominion have I chosen.

And Thou hast created all things,

And all things that are are the work of Thy hands.

20.Deliver me from the hands of evil spirits who have sway over the thoughts of men's hearts, And let them not lead me astray from Thee, my God. And stablish Thou me and my seed for ever, That we go not astray from henceforth and for evermore." 21. And he said Shall I return unto Ur of the Chaldees who seek my face that I may return to them, or am I to remain here in this place? The right path before Thee prosper it in the hands of Thy servant that he may fulfil (it) and that I may not walk in the deceitfulness of my heart, O my God." 22. And he made an end of speaking and praying, and behold the word of the Lord was sent to him through me, saying:

---

[411] Cf. Isa. xlvi. 7; Jer. x. 5; Assumpt. Moses, viii. 4.

[412] In *Ap. Abraham* Terah is indignant with Abraham for deriding the idols.

[413] Cf. Gen. xx. 12, according to which Sarah was Abraham's half-sister. According to Rabbinic tradition marriage with half-sisters on the father's side was permitted to the descendants of Noah. In Lev. xviii. 9, 11, xx. 17, marriage with a sister or half-sister is strictly forbidden.

[414] According to Gen. xi. 29, Milcah.

[415] In *Ap. Abraham*, viii. the fire descends from heaven and burns the house and all in it (including Terah). Only Abraham, escapes.

[416] Cf. Gen. xi. 31.

"Get thee up from thy country, and from thy kindred and from the house of thy father unto a land which I shall show thee, and I shall make thee a great and numerous nation. (1951 A.M.)

23. And I shall bless thee

And I shall make thy name great,

And thou wilt be blessed in the earth,

And in thee will all families of the earth be blessed,

And I shall bless them that bless thee,

And curse them that curse thee.[417]

24. And I shall be a God to thee and thy son, and to thy son's son, and to all thy seed: fear not, from henceforth and unto all generations of the earth I am thy God." 25. And the Lord God said: "Open his mouth and his ears, that he may hear and speak with his mouth, with the language which hath been revealed"; [418]for it had ceased from the mouths of all the children of men from the day of the overthrow (of Babel). 26. And I [419]opened his mouth, and his ears and his lips, and I began to speak with him in Hebrew in the tongue of the creation. 27. And he took the books of his fathers, and these were written in Hebrew and he transcribed them, and he began from henceforth to study them, and I made known to him that which he could not (understand), and he studied them during the six rainy months. [420]28. And it came to pass in the seventh year of the sixth week (1953 A.M.) that he spoke to his father, and informed him that he would leave Haran to go into the land of Canaan to see it and return to him. 29. And Terah his father said unto him; "Go in peace: May the eternal God make thy path straight,

And the Lord [(be) with thee, and] protect thee from all evil,

And grant unto thee grace, mercy and favour before those who see thee, And may none of the children of men have power over thee to harm thee; Go in peace.

30. And if thou seest a land pleasant to thy eyes to dwell in, then arise and take me to thee and take Lot with thee, the son of Haran thy brother, as thine own son: the Lord be with thee. 31. And Nahor thy brother leave with me till thou returnest in peace, and we go with thee all together."

Abram with Lot in Canaan and Egypt (cf. Gen. xii. 4-20). Abram separates from Lot (cf. Gen. xiii. 11-18) (xiii. 1-21).

XIII. And Abram journeyed from Haran, and he took Sarai, his wife, and Lot his brother Haran's son, to the land of Canaan, and he came into †Asshur†, [421]and proceeded to Shechem, and dwelt near a lofty oak. [422]2. And he saw, and, behold, the land was very pleasant from the entering of Hamath to the lofty oak. [423]And the Lord said to him: "To thee and to thy seed will I give this land." 4. And he built an altar there, and he offered thereon a burnt sacrifice to the Lord, who had appeared to him. 5. And he removed from thence unto the mountain . . . 3 Bethel on the west and Ai on the east, and pitched his tent there. [424]6. And he saw and behold, the land was very wide and good, and everything grew thereon--vines and figs and pomegranates, oaks and ilexes, and terebinths and oil trees, and cedars and cypresses and date trees, and all trees of the field, and there was water on the mountains. 7. And he blessed the Lord who had led him out of Ur of the Chaldees, and had

---

[417] Cf. Gen. xii. 1-3 (cf. Acts vii. 3).

[418] *i. e.* the sacred language, Hebrew, knowledge of which had been lost since the overthrow of Babel. According to another tradition Heber alone retained knowledge of Hebrew because he had taken no part in the building of the Tower.

[419] The angel is the speaker.

[420] *i. e.* the winter.

[421] Corrupt. Read probably *Canaan.*

[422] For 1 cf. Gen. xii. 5-6. For "lofty oak" (so LXX) NIT has "oak of Moreh."

[423] Supply (?) "to the east of Bethel with" (Charles).

[424] For 3-5 cf. Gen. xii. 7, 8.

brought him to this land. 8. And it came to pass in the first year, in the seventh week, on the new moon of the first month, (1954 A.M.), that he built an altar on this mountain, and called on the name of the Lord: "Thou, the eternal God, art my God." [425]9. And he offered on the altar a burnt sacrifice unto the Lord that He should be with him and not forsake him all the days of his life. 10. And he removed from thence and went towards the south,[426] and he came to Hebron, and Hebron was built at, that time, and he dwelt there two years, and he went (thence) into the land of the south, to Bealoth [427]and there was a famine in the land. 11. And Abram went into Egypt[428] in the third year of the week, (1956 A.M.) and he dwelt in Egypt five years before his wife was torn away from him.

12. NOW Tanais [429]in Egypt was at that time built--seven years after Hebron. [430]11 And it came to pass when Pharaoh seized Sarai, the wife of Abram, that the Lord plagued Pharaoh and his house with great plagues because of Sarai, Abram's wife. 14. And Abram was very glorious by reason of possessions in sheep, and cattle, and asses, and horses, and camels, and menservants, and maidservants, and in silver and gold exceedingly. And Lot also, his brother's son, was wealthy. 15. And Pharaoh gave back Sarai, the wife of Abram, and he sent him out of the land of Egypt, [431]and he journeyed to the place where he had pitched his tent at the beginning, to the place of the altar, with Ai on the east, and Bethel on the west, and he blessed the Lord his God who had brought him back in peace. [432]16. And it came to pass in the forty-first jubilee, in the third year of the first week, that he returned to this place and offered thereon a burnt sacrifice, and called on A.M. the name of the Lord, and said: "Thou, the most high God, art my God for ever and ever." [433]17. And in the fourth year of this week Lot parted from him, and Lot dwelt in Sodom, and the men of Sodom were A.M. sinners exceedingly. [434]18. And it grieved him in his heart that his brother's son had parted from him; for he had no children. 19. [435]In that year when Lot was taken captive, the Lord said unto Abram, after that Lot had parted from him, in the fourth year of this week: "Lift up thine eyes from the place where thou art dwelling, northward and southward, and westward and eastward. 20. For all the land which thou seest I shall give to thee and to thy seed for ever, and I shall make thy seed as the sand of the sea: [436]though a man may number the dust of the earth, yet thy seed shall not be numbered. [437]21. Arise, walk (through the land) in the length of it and the breadth of it, and see it all; for to thy seed shall I give it." And Abram went to Hebron, and dwelt there.

The Campaign of Chedorlaomer (xiii. 22-29; cf. Gen. xiv)

---

[425] Cf. Gen. xii. 8.

[426] Cf. Gen. xii. 9.

[427] A town in S. Judah (Josh. XV. 24)

[428] Cf. Gen. xii. 10

[429] *i. e.* Zoan.

[430] Cf. Num. xiii. 22.

[431] For 13-15a cf. Gen. xii. 15-20 (note that Gen. xii. 18 is omitted).

[432] Cf. Gen. xiii. 3-4.

[433] Cf. 8 above.

[434] Cf. Gen. xiii. 11, 13.

[435] For 19-21 cf. Gen. xiii. 14-18.

[436] Cf. Gen. xxii. 17 (Gen. xiii. 16 has as the dust of the earth").

[437] "So that if a man can number then shall thy seed also be numbered" (Gen. xiii. 16).

22. And in this year came Chedorlaomer, king of Elam, and Amraphel, king of Shinar, and Arioch, king of Sêllâsar[438] and Têrgâl, [439]king of nations, and slew the king of Gomorrah, and the king of Sodom fled, and many fell through wounds in the vale of Siddim, by the Salt Sea. 23. And they took captive Sodom and Adam [440]and Zeboim, and they took captive Lot also, the son of Abram's brother, and all his possessions, and they went to Dan. [441]24. And one who had escaped came and told Abram that his brother's son had been taken captive and (Abram) armed [442]his household servants. 25 . . . . for Abram, and for his seed, a tenth of the first-fruits to the Lord, [443]and the Lord ordained it as an ordinance for ever that they should give it to the priests who served before Him, that they should possess it for ever. [444]26. And to this law there is no limit of days; for He hath ordained it for the generations for ever that they should give to the Lord the tenth of everything, of the seed and of the wine and of the oil and of the cattle and of the sheep. 27. And He gave (it) unto His priests to eat and to drink with joy before Him. 28. And the king of Sodom came to him and bowed himself before him, and said: "Our Lord Abram, give unto us the souls which thou hast rescued, but let the booty be thine." 29. And Abram said unto him: "I lift up my hands to the Most High God, that from a thread to a shoe-latchet I shall not take aught that is thine, lest thou shouldst say I have made Abram rich; save only what the young men have eaten, and the portion of the men who went with me--Aner, Eschol, and Mamre. These will take their portion."[445]

God's Covenant with Abram (xiv. 1-20; cf. Gen. xv.).

XIV.[446]After these things, in the fourth year of this week, on the new moon of the third month, the word of the Lord came to Abram in a dream, saying: "Fear not, Abram; I am thy defender, and thy reward will be exceeding great." 2. And he said: "Lord, Lord, what wilt thou give me, seeing I go hence childless, and the son of Mâsêq, [447]the son of my handmaid, is the Dammasek Eliezer: he will be my heir, and to me thou hast given no seed." 3. And He said unto him: "This (man) will not be thy heir, but one that will come out of thine own bowels; he will be thine heir." 4. And He brought him forth abroad, and said unto him: "Look toward heaven and number the stars, if thou art able to number them." 5. And he looked toward heaven, and beheld the stars. And He said unto him: "So shall thy seed be." 6. And he believed in the Lord, and it was counted to him for righteousness. 7. And He said unto him: "I am the Lord that brought thee out of Ur of the Chaldees, to give thee the land of the Canaanites to possess it for ever; and I shall be God unto thee and to thy seed after thee." [448]8. And he said: "Lord, Lord, whereby shall I know that I shall inherit (it)?" 9. And he said unto him: "Take Me an heifer of three years, and a goat of three years, and a sheep of three years, and a turtle-dove, and a pigeon."[449] 10. And he took all these in the middle of the month; and he dwelt at the oak of Mamre, which is

---

[438] MT *Ellasar*

[439] MT *Tidal* (for form here cf. LXX Θαργάλ).

[440] *i. e.* Admah.

[441] Cf. Gen. xiv. 14.

[442] R.V. "led forth"; the rendering "armed" has the support of the Targum Onkelos.

[443] Charles suspects a lacuna at the beginning of 25. It no doubt contained an account of the pursuit of the kings and told of Melchizedek (cf. Gen. xiv. 15-20). That Abraham should have given tithes to Melchizedek (who was uncircumcised) was a difficulty to later Jews (cf. Justin, Trypho xix.). One way of overcoming it was to identify Melchizedek with Shem.

[444] The law about tithes is made to apply for the Levitical priesthood; cf. xxxii. 15.

[445] For 28-29 cf. Gen. xiv. 21-24.

[446] For 1-6 cf. Gen. xv. 1-6.

[447] Wrongly taken as a proper name (cf. RX.). So LXX.

[448] Cf. Gen. xv. 7.

[449] For 8-9 cf. Gen. xv. 8-9.

near Hebron.[450] 11. And he built there an altar, and sacrificed all these; and he poured their blood upon the altar, and divided them in the midst, and laid them over against each other; but the birds divided he not. 12. And birds came down upon the pieces, and Abram drove them away, and did not suffer the birds to touch them. [451]13. And it came to pass, when the sun had set, that an ecstasy fell upon Abram, and lo! an horror of great darkness fell upon him, and it was said unto Abram: "Know of a surety that thy seed shall be a stranger in a land (that is) not theirs, and they will bring them into bondage, and afflict them four hundred years. [452]14. And the nation also to whom they will be in bondage shall I judge, and after that they will come forth thence with much substance. 15. And thou wilt go to thy fathers in peace, and be buried in a good old age. 16. But in the fourth generation [453]they will return hither; for the iniquity of the Amorites is not yet full."[454] 17. And he awoke from his sleep, and he arose, and the sun had set; and there was a flame, and behold! a furnace was smoking, and a flame of fire passed between the pieces. 18. And on that day the Lord made a covenant with Abram, saying: "To thy seed will I give this land, from the river of Egypt unto the great river, the river Euphrates, the Kenites, the Kenizzites, the Kadmonites, the Perizzites, and the Rephaim, the Phakorites, [455]and the Hivites, [456]and the Amorites, and the Canaanites, and the Girgashites, and the Jebusites." [457]19. And the day passed, and Abram offered the pieces, and the birds, and their fruit-offerings, and their drink-offerings, and the fire devoured them. 20. And on that day [458]we made a covenant with Abram, according as we had covenanted with Noah in this month; [459]and Abram renewed the festival and ordinance for himself for ever.

The Birth of Ishmael (xiv. 21-24; cf. Gen. xvi. 1-4. 11).

21. And Abram rejoiced, and made all these things known to Sarai his wife; and he believed that he would have seed, but she did not bear. 22. And Sarai advised her husband Abram, and said unto him: "Go in unto Hagar, my Egyptian maid: it may be that I shall build up seed unto thee by her." 23. And Abram hearkened unto the voice of Sarai his wife, and said unto her, "Do (so)." And Sarai took Hagar, her maid, the Egyptian, and gave her to Abram, her husband, to be his wife. 24. And he went in unto her, and she conceived and bare him a son, and he called his name Ishmael, in the fifth year of this week; and this was the eighty-sixth year in the life of Abram.

The Feast of First-fruits Circumcision instituted. The Promise of Isaac's Birth. Circumcision ordained for all Israel (xv. 1-34; cf. Gen. xvii.).

---

[450] Cf. Gen. xiv. 13

[451] For 11-12 cf. Gen. xv. 10-11.

[452] Cf. Gen. xv. 13, but Exod. xii. 40 gives the number 430. Tradition assumes that the number includes the sojourn of the Patriarchs in Canaan. Our text reckons the period from the birth of Isaac (when Abraham was 100 years old). St. Paul (Gal. iii. 16-17) reckons 430 years from the announcement. According to Targ. Ps.-Jon. on Exod. xii. 40 f., the odd 30 years cover the period between the announcement and Isaac's birth.

[453] A generation=100 years. Isaac was born when Abraham was 100 years old (Gen.xxi.5)

[454] For 13-16 cf. Gen. xv. 12-16.

[455] Absent from NIT (which inserts "Hittite" before "Perizite").

[456] So LXX and Sam. here (Gen. XV. 20); but MT, Syr. and Vulg. omit.

[457] For 17-18 cf. Gen. xv. 17-21.

[458] *i. e.* the 15th of Sivan.

[459] Probably, according to our author, on the same day of the month.

XV. And in the fifth year of the †fourth† [460]week of this jubilee, in the third month, in the middle of the month, [461]Abram celebrated the feast of the first-fruits [462]of the grain harvest. 2. And he offered new offerings on the altar, the first-fruits of the produce, unto the Lord, an heifer and a goat and a sheep on the altar as a burnt sacrifice unto the Lord; their fruit-offerings and their drink-offerings he offered upon the altar with frankincense. [463]3. And the Lord appeared to Abram, and said unto him: "I am God Almighty; approve thyself before Me and be thou perfect. 4. And I will make My covenant between Me and thee, and I will multiply thee exceedingly." [464]5. [465]And Abram fell on his face, and God talked with him, and said:

6. "Behold My ordinance is with thee,
And thou wilt be the father of many nations.

7. Neither will thy name any more be called Abram,
But thy name from henceforth, even for ever, shall be Abraham. For the
father of many nations have I made thee.

8. And I shall make thee very great, And I shall make thee into nations, And kings will come forth from thee.

9. And I shall establish My covenant between Me and thee, and thy seed after thee, throughout their generations, for an eternal covenant, so that I may be a God unto thee, and to thy seed after thee. 10. (And I shall give to thee and to thy seed after thee) [466]the land where thou hast been a sojourner, the land of Canaan, that thou mayst possess it for ever, and I shall be their God." 11. [467]And the Lord said unto Abraham: "And as for thee, do thou keep My Covenant, thou and thy seed after thee, and circumcise ye every male among you, and circumcise your foreskins, and it will be a token of an eternal covenant between Me and you. 12. And the child on the eighth day [468]ye will circumcise, every male throughout your generations, him that is born in the house, or whom ye have bought with money from any stranger, whom ye have acquired who is not of thy seed. 13. He that is born in thy house will surely be circumcised, and those whom thou hast bought with money will be circumcised, and My covenant will be in your flesh for an eternal ordinance. 14. [469]And the uncircumcised male who is not circumcised in the flesh of his foreskin on the eighth day, [470]that soul will be cut off from his people, for he hath broken My covenant." 15. [471]And God said unto Abraham: "As for Sarai thy wife, her name will no more be called Sarai, but Sarah will be her name. 16. And I shall bless her, and give thee a son by her, and I shall bless him, [472]and he will become a nation, and kings of nations will proceed from him." 17. And Abraham fell on his face, and rejoiced, and said in his heart: "Shall a son be born to him that is a hundred years

---

[460] Read "third."

[461] *i. e.* the 15th of Sivan.

[462] *i. e.* the Feast of Weeks. The Pharisees celebrated this feast not on Sivan 15th, but on Sivan 6th. See further Introduction.

[463] Cf. xiv. 9. The offerings prescribed for this festival in Lev. xxiii. 118-20 are different.

[464] For 3-4 cf. Gen. xvii. 1 f.

[465] For 5-10 cf. Gen. xvii. 3-8.

[466] The bracketed words (lost through homoioteleuton) are restored from Gen. xvii. 8.

[467] For 11-13 cf. Gen. xvii. 9-13.

[468] MT has "and the child of eight days." Our text here may be a deliberate alteration.

[469] For 14 cf. Gen. xvii. 14

[470] The words *on the eighth day* are absent from the text of Gen. xvii. 14, in MT, Syr. and Vulg., but are attested by the LXX and Sam. The strict rule about the eighth day was later relaxed among the Jews, but is still practised by the Samaritans.

[471] For 15-22 cf. Gen. xvii. 15-22

[472] So LXX, Sam., Syr. and Vulg. of Gen. xvii. 22. But MT makes the text refer to Sarah ("yea, I will bless her, [and she shall be a mother of nations: kings of peoples shall be of her]," R.V.).

old, and shall Sarah, who is ninety years old, bring forth?" 18. And Abraham said unto God: "O that Ishmael might live before thee!" 19. And God said: "Yea, and Sarah also will bear thee a son, and thou wilt call his name Isaac, and I shall establish My covenant with him, an everlasting covenant, and for his seed after him. 20. And as for Ishmael also have I heard thee, and behold I shall bless him, and make him great, and multiply him exceedingly, and he will beget twelve princes, and I shall make him a great nation. 21. But My covenant shall I establish with Isaac, whom Sarah will bear to thee, in these days, in the next year." 22. And He left off speaking with him, and God went up from Abraham. 23. [473]And Abraham did according as God had said unto him, and he took Ishmael his son, and all that were born in his house, and whom he had bought with his money, every male in his house, and circumcised the flesh of their foreskin. 24. And on the selfsame day[474] was Abraham circumcised, and all the men of his house, (and those born in the house), and all those, whom he had bought with money from the children of the stranger, were circumcised with him. 25. This law is for all the generations for ever, and there is no circumcision of the days, [475]and no omission of one day out of the eight days; [476]for it is an eternal ordinance, ordained and written on the heavenly tables. 26. And every one that is born, the flesh of whose foreskin is not circumcised on [477]the eighth day, belongeth not to the children of the covenant which the Lord made with Abraham, but to the children of destruction; nor is there, moreover, any sign on him that he is the Lord's, but (he is destined) to be destroyed and slain from the earth, and to be rooted out of the earth, for he hath broken the covenant of the Lord our God. 27. For all the angels of the presence and all the angels of sanctification[478] have been so created [479]from the day of their creation, and before the angels of the presence and the angels of sanctification He hath sanctified Israel, that they should be with Him and with His holy angels. 28. And do thou command the children of Israel and let them observe the sign of this covenant for their generations as an eternal ordinance, and they will not be rooted out of the land. 29. For the command is ordained for a covenant, that they should observe it for ever among all the children of Israel. 30. For Ishmael and his sons and his brothers and Esau, the Lord did not cause to approach Him, and he chose them not because they are the children of Abraham, because He knew them, but He chose Israel to be His people. 31. And He sanctified it, and gathered it from amongst all the children of men[480]; for there are many nations and many peoples, and all are His, and over all hath He placed spirits in authority to lead them astray[481] from Him. 32. But over Israel He did not appoint any angel or spirit, for He alone is their ruler, and He will preserve them and require them at the hand of His angels and His spirits, and at the hand of all His powers in order that He may preserve them and bless them, and that they may be His and He may be theirs from henceforth for ever. 33. And now I announce unto thee that the children of Israel will not keep true to this ordinance, and they will not circumcise their sons according to all this law; for in the flesh of their circumcision they will omit this circumcision of their sons, and all of them, sons of Beliar, [482]will leave their sons uncircumcised as they were

---

[473] For 23-24 cf. Gen. xvii. 23-27.

[474] *i. e.* the 15th of Sivan.

[475] *i. e.?* of the days preceding the eighth day.

[476] Only on the eighth day is the rite to be performed.

[477] Ethiop. MSS. and Lat. have "till."

[478] The two highest orders of angels, who share with Israel the privilege of observing the Sabbath (cf. ii. 18-21), and of being circumcised.

[479] *i. e.* have been created circumcised.

[480] Israel is God's portion; cf. Deut. xxxii. 8-9 in the LXX form of which "angels" is read instead of "children of Israel"; cf. also Ecclus. xvii. 17. The "seventy nations of the earth were placed under the dominion of seventy angels"; but in Dan. x. 13, 20, 21, xii. 1, Michael is referred to as Israel's angel-prince.

[481] This describes the result, not the original purpose of their appointment.

[482] In i. 20 (see note). Beliar is clearly a Satanic being. This meaning may possibly be present in the use of the expression here. "Sons of Belial" is common in the O.T. (cf. *e.g.* 1 Sam. ii. 12).

born.[483]34. And there will be great wrath from the Lord against the children of Israel, because they have forsaken His covenant and turned aside from His word, and provoked and blasphemed, inasmuch as they do not observe the ordinance of this law; for they have treated their members like the Gentiles, so that they may be removed and rooted out of the land. And there will no more be pardon or forgiveness unto them [so that there should be forgiveness and pardon] for all the sin of this eternal error.

Angelic Visitation of Abraham in Hebron; Promise of Isaac's Birth repeated. The Destruction of Sodom and Lot's Deliverance (xvi. 1-9; cf. Gen. xviii.-xix.).

XVI. And on the new moon of the fourth month we [484]appeared unto Abraham, at the oak of Mamre, and we talked with him, and we announced to him that a son would be given to him by Sarah his wife. [485]2. And Sarah laughed, for she heard that we had spoken these words with Abraham, and we admonished her, and she became afraid, and denied that she had laughed on account of the words.[486] 3. And we told her the name of her son, as his name is ordained and written in the heavenly tables (*i.e.*) Isaac. 4. And (that) when we returned to her at a set time, she would have conceived a son. 5. And in this month the Lord executed his judgments on Sodom, and Gomorrah, and Zeboim,[487] and all the region of the Jordan, and He burned them with fire and brimstone, and destroyed them until this day, even as [lo] I have declared unto thee all their works, that they are wicked and sinners exceedingly, and that they defile themselves and commit fornication in their flesh, and work uncleanness on the earth. [488]6. And, in like manner, God will execute judgment on the places where they have done according to the uncleanness of the Sodomites, like unto the judgment of Sodom. 7. But Lot we saved; for God remembered Abraham, and sent him out from the midst of the overthrow. 8. And he and his daughters committed sin upon the earth, such as had not been on the earth since the days of Adam till his time; for the man lay with his daughters. [489]9. And, behold, it was commanded and engraven concerning all his seed, on the heavenly tables, to remove them and root them out, and to execute judgment upon them like the judgment of Sodom, and to leave no seed of the man on earth on the day of condemnation.

Abraham at Beersheba. Birth and Circumcision of Isaac (cf. Gen. xxi. 1-4). Institution of the Feast of Tabernacles (xvi. 10-31).

10. And in this month Abraham moved from Hebron, and departed and dwelt between Kadesh and Shur in the mountains[490] of Gerar. 11. And in the middle of the fifth month he moved from thence, and dwelt at the Well of the Oath. [491]12. [492]And in the middle of the sixth month the Lord visited Sarah and did unto her as He had spoken, and she conceived. 13. And she bare a son in the third month, (1980 A.M.) and in the middle of the month,[493] at the time of which the Lord had spoken to Abraham, on the festival of the first-fruits of the harvest,

---

[483] Apparently such apostasy was widely spread when our author wrote.

[484] *i. e.* the angels.

[485] For 1 cf. Gen. xviii. i, 10 (vers. 2-9 omitted).

[486] Cf. Gen. xviii. 10, 12, 15.

[487] Cf. Gen. xiv. 2, 8.

[488] For 5 cf. Gen. xix. 24

[489] For 7-8 cf. Gen. xix. 29, 311 ff.

[490] Or "territories."

[491] *i. e.* Beersheba; cf. Gen. xxi. 31.

[492] For 12-14 cf. Gen. xxi. 1-4.

[493] *i. e.* the 15th of Sivan.

[494]Isaac was born. 14. And Abraham circumcised his son on the eighth day: he was the first that was circumcised according to the covenant which is ordained for ever. 15. And in the sixth year of the †fourth† [495]week we came to Abraham, to the Well of the Oath, and we appeared unto him [as we had told Sarah that we should return to her, and she would have conceived a son. 16. And we returned in the seventh month, and found Sarah with child before us] [496]and we blessed him, and we announced to him all the things which had been decreed concerning him, that he should not die till he should beget six sons more, [497]and should see (them) before he died; but (that) in Isaac should his name and seed be called: [498]17. And (that) all the seed of his sons should be Gentiles, and be reckoned with the Gentiles; but from the sons of Isaac one should become a holy seed, and should not be reckoned among the Gentiles. [499]18. For he should become the portion of the Most High, [500]and all his seed had fallen into the possession of God, that it should be unto the Lord a people for (His) possession[501] above all nations and that it should become a kingdom and priests and a holy nation. [502]19. And we went our way, and we announced to Sarah all that we had told him, and they both rejoiced with exceeding great joy. 20. And he built there an altar to the Lord who had delivered him, and who was making him rejoice in the land of his sojourning, and he celebrated a festival of joy in this month seven days, [503]near the altar which he had built at the Well of the Oath. 21. And he built booths for himself and for his servants on this festival, and he was the first to celebrate the feast of tabernacles on the earth. 22. And during these seven days he brought each day to the altar a burnt-offering to the Lord, two oxen, [504]two rams, seven sheep, [505]one he-goat, for a sin-offering, that he might atone thereby for himself and for his seed. 23. And, as a thank-offering, seven rams, seven kids, seven sheep, and seven he-goats, and their fruit-offerings and their drink-offerings;[506] and he burnt all the fat thereof on the altar, a chosen offering unto the Lord for a sweet smelling savour. 24. And morning and evening he burnt fragrant substances,[507] frankincense and galbanum, and stacte, and nard, and myrrh, and spice, and costum; all these seven he offered, crushed, mixed together in equal parts (and) pure. 25. And he celebrated this feast during seven days, rejoicing with all his heart and with all his soul, he and all those who were in his house; and there was no stranger with him, nor any that was uncircumcised. 26. And he blessed his Creator who had created him in his generation, for He had created him according to His good pleasure; for He knew

---

[494] *i. e.* Pentecost.

[495] Read "third" as in xv. 1 (Charles).

[496] The bracketed words are an incorrect gloss, according to Charles, and should be omitted.

[497] Six sons by Keturah (Gen. xxv. 2).

[498] Cf. Gen. xxi. 12

[499] All Abraham's descendants, except Jacob and his seed, were to be reckoned among the Gentiles.

[500] Cf. xv. 31 f.

[501] Cf. Deut. vii. 6; Exod. xix. 5.

[502] Cf. Exod. xix. 6 (MT has "a kingdom of priests"); cf. Rev. v. 10, i. 6, which agree with our text substantially, and this may be the original sense. See Introduction, p. xxxii

[503] In 20-31 we have an account of the Feast of Tabernacles which is marked by peculiar features

[504] According to Num. xxix. 13-33 thirteen bullocks were sacrificed the first day, and this number was diminished by one each day following.

[505] In Num. xxix. 13 fourteen he-lambs.

[506] Cf. 2 Chron. xxix. .21.

[507] Cf. Exod. xxx. 34; Ecclus. xxiv. 15.

and perceived that from him would arise the plant of righteousness [508]for the eternal generations, and from him a holy seed, so that it should become like Him who had made all things.

27. And he blessed and rejoiced, and he called the name of this festival the festival of the Lord, a joy acceptable to the Most High God. 28. And we blessed him for ever, and all his seed after him throughout all the generations of the earth, because he celebrated this festival in its season, according to the testimony of the heavenly tables. 29. For this reason it is ordained on the heavenly tables concerning Israel, that they shall celebrate the feast of tabernacles seven days with joy, in the seventh month, acceptable before the Lord--a statute for ever throughout their generations every year. [509]30. And to this there is no limit of days; for it is ordained for ever regarding Israel that they should celebrate it and dwell in booths, and set wreaths upon their heads, [510]and take leafy boughs, and willows from the brook.[511] 31. And Abraham took branches of palm trees, and the fruit of goodly trees, and every day going round the altar with the branches seven times[512] [a day] in the morning, he praised and gave thanks to his God for all things in joy.

The Expulsion of Hagar and Ishmael (xvii. 1-14; cf. Gen. xxi. 8-21).

XVII. And in the first year of the †fifth† [513]week Isaac was weaned in this jubilee, and Abraham made a great banquet in the third month, (1982 A.M.) on the day his son Isaac was weaned. [514]2. And Ishmael, the son of Hagar, the Egyptian, was before the face of Abraham, his father, in his place, and Abraham rejoiced and blessed God because he had seen his sons 3. And had not died childless. [515] And he remembered the words which He had spoken to him on the day on which Lot had parted from him, and he rejoiced because the Lord had given him seed upon the earth to inherit the earth, and he blessed with all his mouth the Creator of all things. [516]4.[517] And Sarah saw Ishmael playing and dancing [518]and Abraham rejoicing with great joy, and she became jealous of Ishmael and said to Abraham, "Cast out this bondwoman and her son; for the son of this bondwoman will not be heir with my son, Isaac." 5. And the thing was grievous in Abraham's sight, because of his maidservant and because of his son, that he should drive them from him. 6. And God said to Abraham "Let it not be grievous in thy sight, because of the child and because of the bondwoman; in all that Sarah hath said unto thee, hearken to her words and do (them); for in Isaac shall thy name and seed be called. 7. But as for the son of this bondwoman I will make him a great [519]nation, because he is of thy seed." 8. And Abraham rose up early in the morning and took bread and a bottle of water, and placed them on the shoulders of Hagar and the child, and sent her away. 9. And she departed and wandered in the wilderness of Beersheba, and the water in the bottle was spent, and the child thirsted, and was not able to go on, and fell down. 10. And his mother took

---

[508] Cf. xxi. 24; 1 Enoch x. 16, xciii. 5, 10.

[509] Cf. Lev. xxiii. 41.

[510] This custom in connection with Tabernacles seems to be unknown to tradition; cf., however, Wisdom ii. 7 f.; Josephus, *Ant.* xix. 9, 1. Bridegrooms wore wreaths, but the custom was later abolished. See further Introduction, p. xx f

[511] Cf. Lev. xxiii. 40.

[512] According to later Jewish tradition it was only on the seventh day that the worshippers went round the altar seven times.

[513] Read "fourth" (Charles).

[514] Cf. Gen. xxi. 8

[515] Cf. xvi. 16.

[516] Cf. xiii. 19 ff.

[517] For 4-13 cf. Gen. xxi. 9-21.

[518] Possibly *and dancing* is corrupt for *with Isaac*, which is read in LXX and Vulg.; cf. Gen. xxi.

[519] LXX, Sam., Syr. and Vulg. of Gen. xxi. 13, have *great*; but MT omits.

him and cast him under an olive tree, [520]and went and sat her down over against him, at the distance of a bow-shot; for she said, "Let me not see the death of my child," and as she sat she wept. 11. And an angel of God, one of the holy ones, said unto her, "Why weepest thou, Hagar? Arise, take the child, and hold him in thine hand; for God hath heard thy voice, and hath seen the child." 12. And she[521] opened her eyes, and she saw a well of water, and she went and filled her bottle with water, and she gave her child to drink, and she arose and went towards the wilderness of Paran. 13. And the child grew and became an archer, and God was with him; and his mother took him a wife from among the daughters of Egypt. 14. And she bare him a son, and he called his name Nebaioth; [522]for she said, "The Lord was nigh to me when I called upon him."

Mastêmâ proposes to God that Abraham shall be put to the Proof (xvi. 15-18).

15. And it came to pass in the seventh week, in the first year thereof, in the first month in this jubilee, (2003 A.M.) [523]on the twelfth of this month, there were voices in heaven regarding Abraham, that he was faithful in all that He told him, and that he loved the Lord, and that in every affliction he was faithful. 16. And the prince Mastêmâ[524] came and said before God, "Behold, Abraham loveth Isaac his son, and he delighteth in him above all things else; bid him offer him as a burnt-offering on the altar, and Thou wilt see if he will do this command, and Thou wilt know if he is faithful in everything wherein Thou dost try him." 17. And the Lord knew that Abraham was faithful in all his afflictions; for He had tried him through his country and with famine, and had tried him with the wealth of kings, and had tried him again through his wife, when she was torn (from him), and with circumcision, and had tried him through Ishmael and Hagar, his maid-servant, when he sent them away. 18. And in everything wherein He had tried him, he was found faithful, and his soul was not impatient, and he was not slow to act; for he was faithful and a lover of the Lord.

The Sacrifice of Isaac: Abraham returns to Beersheba (xviii. 1-19; Cf. Gen. xxii. 119).

XVIII. And God said to him, "Abraham, Abraham"; and he said, "Behold, (here) am I." [525] And He said, "Take thy beloved [526]son whom thou lovest, (even) Isaac, and go unto the high country, [527]and offer him on one of the mountains which I will point out unto thee." 3. And he rose early in the morning and saddled his ass, and took his two young men with him, and Isaac his son, and clave the wood of the burnt-offering, and he went to the place on the third day, and he saw the place afar off. 4. And he came to a well of water, and he said to his young men, "Abide ye here with the ass, and I and the lad shall go (yonder), and when we have worshipped we shall come again to you." 5. And he took the wood of the burnt-offering and laid it on Isaac his son, and he took in his hand the fire and the knife, and they went both of them together to that place. 6. And Isaac said to his father, "Father"; and he said, "Here am I, my son." And he said unto him, "Behold the fire, and the knife, and the wood; but where is the sheep for the burnt offering, father?" 7. And he said, "God will provide for himself

---

[520] LXX (Gen. xxi. 15) "under a fir tree"; MT "under one of the shrubs."

[521] Read (?) "He" (God).

[522] Cf. Gen. xxv. 13.

[523] According to the chronology of our Book (Cf. xvi. 12 with this passage) Isaac was twenty three years old when he was offered up; according to the Seder Olam he was thirty-seven.

[524] In Gen. xxii. 1 it is God Himself who directly proves Abraham.

[525] Seven of the traditional ten trials of Abraham are here mentioned: (1) Departure from his country; (2) famine; (3) the wealth of kings; (4) seizure of his wife; (5) circumcision; (6) and (7) expulsion of Hagar and Ishmael [(8) is the unfruitfulness of Sarah; (9) the sacrifice of Isaac, and (10) the burial of Sarah; Cf. xiv. 21 and xix. 3, 8]. Slightly different enumerations occur elsewhere (*e. g. Pirke de R. Eliezer*, xxvi.-xxx.).

[526] So LXX (Gen. xxii. 2): MT *only* (son).

[527] So LXX; but NIT "the land of Moriah."

a sheep for a burnt-offering, my son." And he drew near to the place of the mount of God. [528]8. And he built an altar, and he placed the wood on the altar, and bound Isaac his son, and placed him on the wood which was upon the altar, and stretched forth his hand to take the knife to slay Isaac his son. 9. And I stood before him, and before the prince of the Mastêmâ,[529] and the Lord said, "Bid him not to lay his hand on the lad, nor to do anything to him, for I have shown that he feareth the Lord." 10. And I called to him from heaven, and said unto him: "Abraham, Abraham"; and he was terrified and said: "Behold, (here) am I." 11. And I said unto him: "Lay not thy hand upon the lad, neither do thou anything to him; for now I have shown that thou fearest the Lord, and hast not withheld thy son, thy first-born son, from me." 12. And the prince of the Mastêmâ was put to shame; and Abraham lifted up his eyes and looked, and, behold, a single ram caught [530]. . . by his horns, and Abraham went and took the ram and offered it for a burnt-offering in the stead of his son. 13. And Abraham called that place "The Lord hath seen," so that it is said "(in the mount) the Lord hath seen": [531]that is Mount Sion. 14. And the Lord called Abraham by his name a second time from heaven, as he caused us to appear to speak to him in the name of the Lord.

15. And He said: "By Myself have I sworn, saith the Lord,

Because thou hast done this thing,

And hast not withheld thy son, thy beloved [532]son, from Me,

That in blessing I shall bless thee

And in multiplying I shall multiply thy seed

As the stars of heaven,

And as the sand which is on the seashore.

And thy seed will inherit the cities [533]of its enemies,

16. And in thy seed will all nations of the earth be blessed;

Because thou hast obeyed My voice,

And I have shown to all that thou art faithful unto Me in all that I have said unto thee: Go in peace."[534]

17. And Abraham went to his young men, and they arose and went together to Beersheba, and Abraham dwelt by the Well of the Oath. 18. And he celebrated this festival every year, seven days with joy, and he called it the festival of the Lord according to the seven days during which he went and returned in peace. 19. And accordingly hath it been ordained and written on the heavenly tables regarding Israel and its seed that they should observe this festival seven days with the joy of festival.

The Death and Burial of Sarah (xix. 1-9; cf. Gen. xxiii.).

XIX. And in the first year of the first week in the forty-second jubilee (2010 A.M.), Abraham returned and dwelt opposite Hebron, that is Kirjath Arba, two weeks of years. 2. And in the first year of the †third† [535]week of this jubilee the days of the life of Sarah were accomplished, and she died in Hebron. 3. And Abraham went to mourn over her and bury her, and we tried him [to see] if his spirit were patient and he were not indignant

---

[528] Instead of the words *of the mount of God*, MT (Gen. xxii. 9) reads, *which God hath told him of*.

[529] Here (cf., also, xviii. 12, xlvii. 9, 12, 15), Mastêmâ is the name given to the whole class of evil spirits, or Satans; elsewhere of the prince of these himself.

[530] ? add *in a thicket*.

[531] Syr. and Vulg. render (Gen. xxii. 14) "will see," "seeth." MT "it shall be seen" (provided).

[532] MT "thine only" (Gen. xxii. 16).

[533] So Sam., version, LXX: MT "gate" (Gen. xxii. 17).

[534] Cf. 1 Sam. i. 17.

[535] Read "second" (Charles).

in the words of his mouth; and he was found patient in this, and was not disturbed. [536]4. For in patience of spirit he conversed with the children of Heth, to the intent that they should give him a place in which to bury his dead. 5. And the Lord gave him grace before all who saw him, and he besought in gentleness the sons of Heth, and they gave him the land of the double cave [537]over against Mamre, that is Hebron, for four hundred pieces of silver. 6. And they besought him, saying, "We shall give it to thee for nothing"; but he would not take it from their hands for nothing, for he gave the price of the place, the money in full, and he bowed down before them twice; and after this he buried his dead in the double cave. 7. And all the days of the life of Sarah were one hundred and twenty-seven years, that is, two jubilees and four weeks and one year: these are the days of the years of the life of Sarah. 8. This is the tenth [538] trial wherewith Abraham was tried, and he was found faithful, patient in spirit. 9. And he said not a single word regarding the rumour in the land how that God had said that He would give it to him and to his seed after him, and he begged a place there to bury his dead; for he was found faithful, and was recorded on the heavenly tables as the friend of God.[539]

Marriage of Isaac and second Marriage of Abraham (cf. Gen. xxiv. 15, xxv. 1-4); the Birth of Esau and Jacob (cf. Gen. xxv. 19 ff.) (xix. 10-14).

10. And in the fourth year thereof (2020 A.M.) he took a wife for his son Isaac and her name was Rebecca [the daughter of Bethuel, the son of Nahor, the A.M. brother of Abraham] [540]the sister of Laban and daughter of Bethuel; and Bethuel was the son of Mêlcâ, who was the wife of Nahor, the brother of Abraham. 11. And Abraham took to himself a third wife, and her name was Keturah, from among the daughters of his household servants, for Hagar had died before Sarah. [541]12. And she bare him six sons, Zimram, and Jokshan, and Medan, and Midian, and Ishbak, and Shuah, in the two weeks of years. 13. And in the sixth week, in the second year thereof, (2046 A.M.) Rebecca bare to Isaac two sons, Jacob and Esau, and Jacob was a smooth and upright [542]man, and Esau was fierce, a man of the field, and hairy, and Jacob dwelt in tents. 14. And the youths grew, and Jacob learned to write; [543]but Esau did not learn, for he was a man of the field and a hunter, and he learnt war, and all his deeds were fierce.

---

[536] This is the tenth trial of Abraham; cf. xvii. 17 note.

[537] *i. e.* the cave of Machpelah (LXX, τ σπ λαιον τ διπλο ν).

[538] This is the tenth trial of Abraham; cf. xvii. 17 note.

[539] A traditional title of Abraham. It goes back to Isa. xli. 8; cf. Jas. ii. 23, *T.B. Men.* 53*b*.

[540] The bracketed words a dittograph.

[541] This explains why Abraham did not take Hagar back. The later tradition (cf. *e. g. Pirke de R. Eliezer* xxx.) identifies Hagar with Keturah.

[542] Cf. Gen. xxv. 27 (where "plain" = lit. "upright"), and Gen. xxvii. 11 (combined here).

[543] According to the Targums the "tents" were academies. Jacob is represented as a lifelong student of the Torah (cf. *Ber. rabba* lxiii; *Pirke de R. Eliezer* xxxii.).

Abraham loves Jacob and blesses him (xix. 15-31).

15. And Abraham loved Jacob, but Isaac loved Esau. 16. And Abraham saw the deeds of Esau, and he knew that in Jacob [544]should his name and seed be called; and he called Rebecca and gave commandment regarding Jacob, for he knew that she (too) loved Jacob much more than Esau. 17. And he said unto her: "My daughter, watch over my son Jacob, For he shall be in my stead on the earth, And for a blessing in the midst of the children of men, And for the glory of the whole seed of Shem. 18. For I know that the Lord will choose him to be a people for possession unto Himself, above all peoples that are upon the face of the earth.[545]

19. And behold, Isaac my son loveth Esau more than Jacob, but I see that thou truly lovest Jacob.

20. Add still further to thy kindness to him,

And let thine eyes be upon him in love;

For he will be a blessing unto us on the earth from henceforth unto all generations of the earth.

21. Let thy hands be strong

And let thy heart rejoice in thy son Jacob;

For I have loved him far beyond all my sons.

He will be blessed for ever,

And his seed will fill the whole earth.

22. If a man can number the sand of the earth,

His seed also will be numbered.[546]

23. And all the blessings wherewith the Lord hath blessed me and my seed shall belong to Jacob and his seed alway. 24. And in his seed shall my name be blessed, and the name of my fathers, Shem, and

Noah, and Enoch, and Mahalalel, and Enos, and Seth, and Adam.[547]25. And these shall serve

To lay the foundations of the heaven,

And to strengthen the earth,

And to renew all the luminaries which are in the firmament."

26. And he called Jacob before the eyes of Rebecca his mother, and kissed him, and blessed him, and said: 27. "Jacob, my beloved son, whom my soul loveth, may God bless thee from above the firmament, and may He give thee all the blessings wherewith He blessed Adam, and Enoch, and Noah, and Shem; and all the things of which He told me, and all the things which He promised to give me, may He cause to cleave to thee and to thy seed for ever, according to the days of heaven above the earth. [548]28. And the spirits of Mastêmâ shall not rule over thee or over thy seed[549] to turn thee from the Lord, who is thy God from henceforth for ever. 29. And may the Lord God be a father to thee and thou the first-born son, and to the people alway. Go in peace, my son." 30. And they both went forth together from Abraham. 31. And Rebecca loved Jacob, with all her heart and with all her soul, very much more than Esau; but Isaac loved Esau much more than Jacob.

Abraham's Last Words to his Children and Grandchildren (xx. i-ii).

---

[544] Jacob was to be the founder of the chosen nation; cf. ii. 20.

[545] Cf. Deut. vii. 6.

[546] Cf. Gen. xiii. 16 (cf. also xiii. 20 of our Book).

[547] Notice that Methuselah is omitted, and Adam is reckoned among the saints (with Noah and Enoch).

[548] Cf. xxii. 13.

[549] As over the Gentiles.

XX. And in the forty-second jubilee, in the first year of the †seventh† [550]week, (2052 A.M.) Abraham called Ishmael, and his twelve sons, [551]and Isaac and (?2045 A.M.) his two sons, and the six sons of Keturah, and their sons. 2. And he commanded them that they should observe the way of the Lord; that they should work righteousness, and love each his neighbour, and act on this manner amongst all men; that they should each so walk with regard to them as to do judgment and righteousness on the earth. 3. That they should circumcise their sons, [552]according to the covenant which He had made with them, and not deviate to the right hand or the left of all the paths which the Lord had commanded us; and that we should keep ourselves from all fornication and uncleanness, [and renounce from amongst us all fornication and uncleanness]. [553]4. And if any woman or maid commit fornication amongst you, burn her with fire, [554]and let them not commit fornication with her after their eyes and their heart; and let them not take to themselves wives from the daughters of Canaan; for the seed of Canaan will be rooted out of the land. 5. And he told them of the judgment of the giants, and the judgment of the Sodomites, how they had been judged on account of their wickedness, and had died on account of their fornication, and uncleanness, and mutual corruption through fornication. [555]

6."And guard yourselves from all fornication and uncleanness,

And from all pollution of sin,

Lest ye make our name a curse,

And your whole life a hissing, [556]

And all your sons be destroyed by the sword,

And ye become accursed like Sodom,

And all your remnant as the sons of Gomorrah.

7. I implore you, my sons, love the God of heaven,

And cleave ye to all His commandments. p. 117

And walk not after their idols, and after their uncleannesses,

8.[557]And make not for yourselves molten or graven gods;[558]

For they are vanity,

And there is no spirit in them;

For they are work of (men's) hands,

And all who trust in them, trust in nothing.

Serve them not, nor worship them,[559]

9. But serve ye the Most High God, and worship Him continually:

---

[550] Probably corrupt for "sixth" (Charles).

[551] Cf. Gen. xxv. 13-15.

[552] Circumcision, according to our author, is binding upon Ishmael's and Keturah's descendants (cf. Gen. xvii. 9f.). 'Notice the omission of Esau's descendants. According to *Pirke de R. Eliezer* xxix., Esau, though he had been circumcised, "despised circumcision" (his birthright).

[553] Bracketed as a dittograph

[554] According to the Law only the adulterous priest's daughter was to be burned with fire; others were to be stoned (cf. Lev. xxi. 9, xx. 10).

[555] Cf. vii. 21 (note).

[556] Cf. Isa. lxv. 15; Jer. xxix. 18.

[557] For 8 cf. xii. 5, xxii. 18.

[558] Cf. Deut. xxvii. 15.

[559] Cf. Exod. xx. 5.

And hope for His countenance always,

And work uprightness and righteousness before Him,

That He may have pleasure in you and grant you His mercy,

And send rain [560]upon you morning and evening,

And bless all your works which ye have wrought upon the earth, And bless thy bread and thy water,[561]

And bless the fruit of thy womb and the fruit of thy land,

And the herds of thy cattle, and the flocks of thy sheep.[562]

10. And ye will be for a blessing [563]on the earth,

And all nations of the earth will desire you,

And bless your sons in my name,

That they may be blessed as I am."

11. And he gave to Ishmael and to his sons, and to the sons of Keturah, gifts, and sent them away from Isaac his son, and he gave everything to Isaac his son.[564]

The Dwelling-places of the Ishmaelites and of the Sons of Keturah (xx. 12-13).

12. And Ishmael and his sons, and the sons of Keturah and their sons, went together and dwelt from Paran to the entering in of Babylon in all the land which is towards the East facing the desert. 13. And these mingled with each other, and their name was called Arabs, and Ishmaelites.

Abraham's Last Words to Isaac (xxi. 1-25).

XXI. And in the sixth year of the †seventh† [565]week of this jubilee (2057 A.M. (?2050)) Abraham called Isaac his son, [566]and commanded him, saying: "I am become old, and. know not the day of my death, [567]and am full of my days. [568]2. And behold, I am one hundred and seventy-five years old, [569]and throughout all the days of my life I have remembered the Lord, and sought with all my heart to do His will, and to walk uprightly in all His ways. 3. My soul hath hated idols, (and I have despised those that served them, and I have given my heart and spirit) [570]that I might observe to do the will of Him who created me. 4. For He is the living God, and He is holy and faithful, and He is righteous beyond all, and there is with Him no accepting of (men's) persons and

---

[560] Cf. xii. 4, 18.

[561] Cf. Exod. xxiii. 25.

[562] Cf. Deut. vii. 13.

[563] Cf. Gen. xii. 2.

[564] Cf. Gen. xxv. 5-6.

[565] Read "sixth" (Charles).

[566] The rest of this chapter purports to give Abraham's directions to Isaac regarding certain kinds of sacrifice. It has a remarkable parallel in *Test. XII Patriarchs*, Levi ix., where Isaac instructs Levi in the law of the priesthood, of sacrifices, etc. The latter is much shorter than our chapter, but hardly more original. The two books may have used a common source.

[567] In Gen. xxvii. 2 these words are uttered by Isaac.

[568] Cf. Gen. xxv. 8, where LXX, Sam., Vulg. read "full of days," but MT omits "days."

[569] Cf. Gen. xxv. 7.

[570] The bracketed words are supplied from the Latin.

no accepting of gifts;[571] for God is righteous, and executeth judgment on all those who transgress His commandments and despise His covenant. 5. And do thou, my son, observe His commandments and His ordinances and His judgments, and walk not after the abominations and after the graven images and after the molten images. 6. And eat no blood at all of animals or cattle, or of any bird which flieth in the heaven. [572]7. [573]And if thou dost slay a victim as an acceptable peace-offering, slay ye it, and pour out its blood upon the altar, and all the fat of the offering offer on the altar with fine flour (and the meat-offering) mingled with oil, [574]with its drink-offering--offer them all together on the altar of burnt-offering; it is a sweet savour before the Lord. [575]8. And thou wilt offer the fat of the sacrifice of thank-offerings on the fire which is upon the altar, and the fat which is on the belly, and all the fat on the inwards and the two kidneys, and all the fat that is upon them, and upon the loins and liver thou shalt remove together with the kidneys. [576]9. And offer all these for a sweet savour acceptable before the Lord, with its meat-offering and with its drink-offering, for a sweet savour, the bread [577]of the offering unto the Lord, 10. And eat its meat on that day and on the second day, and let not the sun on the second day go down upon it till it is eaten, and let nothing be left over for the third day; for it is not acceptable [for it is not approved][578] and let it no longer be eaten, and all who eat thereof will bring sin upon themselves; for thus I have found it written in the books of my forefathers, and in the words of Enoch, and in the words of Noah. [579]11. And on all thy oblations thou shalt strew salt, and let not the salt of the covenant be lacking in all thy oblations before the Lord. [580]12. And as regards the wood of the sacrifices, beware lest thou bring (other) wood for the altar in addition to these: [581]cypress, dêfrân, [582]sagâd, pine, fir, cedar, savin, palm, olive, myrrh, laurel, and citron, juniper, and balsam. 13. And of these kinds of wood lay upon the altar under the sacrifice, such as have been tested as to their appearance, and do not lay (thereon) any split or dark wood, (but) hard and clean, without fault, a sound and new growth; and do not lay (thereon) old wood, [for its fragrance is gone] for there is no longer fragrance in it as before. [583]14. Besides these kinds of wood there is none other that thou shalt place (on the altar), for the fragrance is dispersed, and the smell of its fragrance goeth not up to heaven. 15. Observe this commandment and do it, my son, that thou mayst be upright in all thy deeds. 16. And at all times be clean in thy body, and wash thyself with water before thou approachest to offer on the altar, and wash thy hands and thy feet before thou drawest near to the altar; and when thou art done sacrificing, wash again thy hands and thy feet. [584]17. And let no blood appear upon you nor upon your clothes;

---

[571] Cf. Deut. x. 17.

[572] Cf. vii. 28 (note).

[573] For 7-9 cf. the summary in *Test. XII Patr.* Levi ix. 7.

[574] Cf. Lev. ii. 4.

[575] For 7 cf. Lev. iii. 7-10.

[576] Cf. Lev. iii. 9-10.

[577] "Or food"; cf. Lev. iii. 11.

[578] Bracketed words a dittograph

[579] No trace of such halakic rules exists in the Books of Enoch or the fragments of the Noah apocalypse that are extant. The statement in the text seems to be original to the author of *Jubilees*.

[580] Cf. Lev. ii. 13; *Test. Levi* ix. 14.

[581] In *Test. Levi* ix. 12 "twelve" evergreen trees are mentioned; here fourteen, and this number is probably correct.

[582] Probably a kind of fir.

[583] This may be the old halaka; the Mishna has no trace of it. The Mishna (*Tamid* ii. 3) allows all kinds of wood except that of the olive and vine; cf., also, *Sifra* on Lev. i. 8.

[584] Cf. Exod. xxx. 19-21; cf. *Test. Levi* ix. ii.

be on thy guard, my son, against blood, be on thy guard exceedingly; cover it with dust. [585]18. And do not eat any blood, for it is the soul; eat no blood whatever. [586]19. And take no gifts for the blood of man, lest it be shed with impunity, without judgment; for it is the blood that is shed that causeth the earth to sin, and the earth cannot be cleansed from the blood of man save by the blood of him who shed it. [587]20. And take no present or gift for the blood of man: blood for blood, that thou mayest be accepted before the Lord, the Most High God; for He is the defence of the good: and that thou mayest be preserved from all evil, and that He may save thee from every kind of death..

21. I see, my son, That all the works of the children of men are sin and wickedness, And all their deeds are uncleanness and an abomination and a pollution, And there is no righteousness with them.

22. Beware, lest thou shouldest walk in their ways

And tread in their paths,

And sin a sin unto death [588]before the Most High God.

Else He will [hide His face from thee,

And] [589]give thee back into the hands [590]of thy transgression,

And root thee out of the land, and thy seed likewise from under heaven, And thy name and thy seed will perish from the whole earth.

23. Turn away from all their deeds and all their uncleanness, And observe the ordinance of the Most High God, And do His will and be upright in all things.

24. And He will bless thee in all thy deeds,

And will raise up from thee the plant of righteousness [591]through all the earth, throughout all generations of the earth,

And my name and thy name will not be forgotten under heaven for ever.

25. Go, my son, in peace.

May the Most High God, my God and thy God, strengthen thee to do His will,

And may He bless all thy seed and the residue of thy seed for the generations for ever, with all righteous blessings,

That thou mayest be a blessing on all the earth."[592]

26. And he went out from him rejoicing.

Isaac, Ishmael and Jacob join in Festival with Abraham for the Last Time. Abraham's Prayer (xxii. 1-9)

---

[585] Cf. Lev. xvii. 13.

[586] Cf. Lev. xvii. 14; Deut. xii. 23.

[587] Cf. vii. 33; Num. xxxv. 33.

[588] Cf. xxxiii. 18.

[589] Bracketed by Charles as an interpolation.

[590] *i. e.* into the power of.

[591] Cf. xvi. 26.

[592] Cf. xx. 10.

XXII. And it came to pass in the †first† [593]week in the †forty-fourth† [594]jubilee, in the †second† year, that is, the year in which Abraham died, that Isaac and Ishmael came from the Well of the Oath to celebrate the feast of weeks--that is, the feast of the first-fruits of the harvest--to Abraham, their father, and Abraham rejoiced because his two sons had come. 2. For Isaac had many possessions in Beersheba, and Isaac was wont to go and see his possessions and to return to his father. 3. And in those days Ishmael came to see his father, and they both came together, and Isaac offered a sacrifice for a burnt-offering, and presented it on the altar of his father which he had made in Hebron. 4. And he offered a thank-offering and made a feast of joy before Ishmael, his brother: and Rebecca made new cakes from the new grain, and gave them to Jacob, her son, to take them to Abraham, his father, from the first-fruits of the land, that he might eat and bless the Creator of all things before he died. 5. And Isaac, too,!sent by the hand of Jacob to Abraham a best thank-offering, that he might eat and drink. 6. And he ate and drank, and blessed the Most High God,

Who hath created heaven and earth,
Who hath made all the fat things of the earth,
And given them to the children of men
That they might eat and drink and bless their Creator.

7. "And now I give thanks unto Thee, my God, because Thou hast caused me to see this day: behold, I am one hundred three score and fifteen years, an old man and full of days, [595]and all my days have been unto me peace. 8. The sword of the adversary [596]hath not overcome me in all that Thou hast given me and my children all the days of my life until this day. 9. My God, may Thy mercy and Thy peace be upon Thy servant, and upon the seed of his sons, that they may be to Thee a chosen nation and an inheritance [597]from amongst all the nations of the earth from henceforth unto all the days of the generations of the earth, unto all the ages."

Abraham's Last Words to and Blessings of Jacob (xxii. 10-30).

10. And he called Jacob and said My son Jacob, may the God of all [598]bless thee and strengthen thee to do righteousness, and His will before Him, and may He choose thee and thy seed that ye may become a people for His inheritance according to His will alway. And do thou, my son, Jacob, draw near and kiss me."

11. And he drew near and kissed him, and he said:

"Blessed be my son Jacob

And all the sons of God Most High, unto all the ages:

May God give unto thee a seed of righteousness;

And some of thy sons may He sanctify in the midst of the whole earth; May nations serve thee,

And all the nations bow themselves before thy seed.[599]

12. Be strong in the presence of men,

And exercise authority over all the seed of Seth. [600]Then thy ways and the ways of thy sons will be justified, So that they shall become a holy nation.

13. May the Most High God give thee all the blessings

Wherewith he hath blessed me

---

[593] Read "sixth" (Charles).

[594] Read "forty-second" (Charles).

[595] Cf. xxi. 1.

[596] Cf. Jer. vi. 25.

[597] Israel is God's inheritance; cf. Deut. iv. 20.

[598] *i. e.* of the universe; this idea often recurs in our author.

[599] Verbally from Gen. xxvii. 29 (Isaac's blessing of Jacob).

[600] *i. e.* all mankind (Charles).

And wherewith He blessed Noah and Adam;[601]

May they rest on the sacred head of thy seed from generation to generation for ever.

14. And may He cleanse thee from all unrighteousness and impurity,

That thou mayest be forgiven all (thy) transgressions; (and) thy sins of ignorance. And may He strengthen thee, And bless thee.

And mayest thou inherit the whole earth,

15. And may He renew His covenant with thee,

That thou mayest be to Him a nation for His inheritance [602]for all the ages,

And that He may be to thee and to thy seed a God in truth and righteousness throughout all the days of the earth.

16. And do thou, my son Jacob, remember my words, And observe the commandments of Abraham, thy father:

Separate thyself from the nations,

And eat not with them: [603]

And do not according to their works,

And become not their associate;

For their works are unclean,

And all their ways are a pollution and an abomination and uncleanness.

17. They offer their sacrifices to the dead,[604]

And they worship evil spirits,[605]

And they eat over the graves,[606]

And all their works are vanity and nothingness. 18. They have no heart to understand

And their eyes do not see what their works are,

And how they err in saying to a piece of wood: 'Thou art my God,'

And to a stone: 'Thou art my Lord and thou art my deliverer.' [607][And they have no heart.][608]

And as for thee, my son Jacob,

May the Most High God help thee

And the God of heaven bless thee

And remove thee from their uncleanness and from all their error.

Be thou ware, my son Jacob, of taking a wife from any seed of the daughters of Canaan;

For all his seed is to be rooted out of the earth. [609]

---

[601] Cf. xix. 27.

[602] Cf. xxii, 9.

[603] A strict observance of the dietary laws would make this practically impossible; cf. Dan. i. 8; Matt. ix. 11. The question was one of crucial importance in the early Maccabean period; cf. *e. g.* 1 Macc. i. 62.

[604] Cf. Deut. xxvi. 14; Ecclus. xxx. 18, 19, etc.

[605] Cf. 1 Cor. x. 20 (1 Enoch xix. i).

[606] *i.e.* Partake of the sacrifices offered to the dead; cf. Deut. xxvi. 14 (according to one interpretation).

[607] Cf. Jer. ii. 27.

[608] Bracketed words a dittograph.

[609] Cf. Gen. xxviii. i; *Test. Levi* ix. 10.

21. For, owing to the transgression of Ham, [610]Canaan erred, [611]

And all his seed will be destroyed from off the earth and all the residue thereof, And none springing from him will be saved on the day of judgment.

22. And as for all the worshippers of idols and the profane

[612](*b*) There will be no hope for them in the land of the living;

(*e*) And there will be no remembrance of them on the earth;

For they will descend into Sheol,

And into the place of condemnation will they go, [613]As the children of Sodom were taken away from the earth So will all those who worship idols be taken away.

23. Fear not, my son Jacob,

And be not dismayed, O son of Abraham:

May the Most High God preserve thee from destruction, And from all the paths of error may He deliver thee.

24. This house have I built for myself that I might put my name upon it in the earth: [it is given to thee and to thy seed for ever], [614]and it will be named the house of Abraham; it is given to thee and to thy seed for ever; for thou wilt build my house [615]and establish my name before God for ever: thy seed and thy name will stand throughout all generations of the earth."

25. And he ceased commanding [616]him and blessing him. 26: And the two lay together on one bed, and Jacob slept in the bosom of Abraham, his father's father and he kissed him seven times, and his affection and his heart rejoiced over him. 27. [617]And he blessed him with all his heart and said: "The Most High God, the God of all, and Creator of all, who brought me forth from Ur of the Chaldees, that He might give me this land to inherit [618]it for ever, and that I might establish a holy seed-blessed be the Most High for ever." 28. And he blessed Jacob and said: "My son, over whom with all my heart and my affection I rejoice, may Thy grace and Thy mercy be lift up [619]upon him and upon his seed alway. 29. And do not forsake him, nor set him at nought from henceforth unto the days of eternity, and may Thine eyes be opened upon him and upon his seed, [620]that Thou mayest preserve him, and bless him, and mayest sanctify him as a nation for Thine inheritance; 30. And bless him with all Thy blessings from henceforth unto all the days of eternity, and renew Thy covenant and Thy grace with him and with his seed according to all Thy good pleasure unto all the generations of the earth."

The Death and Burial of Abraham (xxiii. 1-8; cf. Gen. xxv. 7-10).

---

[610] Cf. vii. 8.

[611] Canaan wrongfully seized Palestine; cf. x. 29-34.

[612] The four following lines have been transposed by Charles for the sake of parallelism.

[613] Cf. vii. 29.

[614] Bracketed words a dittograph.

[615] "House" throughout this passage = "family."

[616] *i. e.* giving the last commands; cf. Gen. xlix. 33 and often.

[617] Charles suspects 27 may be an interpolation.

[618] Cf. Gen. xv. 7; Neh. ix. 7.

[619] Cf. Num. vi. 26.

[620] Cf. 1 Kings viii. 29, 52; Dan. ix. 18.

XXIII. And he placed two fingers of Jacob on his eyes, [621]and he blessed the God of gods, and he covered his face and stretched out his feet [622]and slept the sleep of eternity,[623] and was gathered to his fathers. 2. And notwithstanding all this Jacob was lying in his bosom, and knew not that Abraham, his father's father, was dead. 3. And Jacob awoke from his sleep, and behold Abraham was cold as ice, and he said: "Father, father!"; but there was none that spake, and he knew that he was dead. 4. And he arose from his bosom and ran and told Rebecca, his mother; and Rebecca went to Isaac in the night and told him; and they went together, and Jacob with them, and a lamp was in his hand, and when they had gone in they found Abraham lying dead. 5. And Isaac fell on the face of his father, and wept and kissed him. [624]6. And the voices were heard in the house of Abraham, and Ishmael his son arose, and went to Abraham his father, and wept over Abraham his father, he and all the house of Abraham, and they wept with a great weeping. 7. And his sons Isaac and Ishmael buried him in the double cave, [625]near Sarah his wife, and they wept for him forty days, all the men of his house, and Isaac and Ishmael, and all their sons, and all the sons of Keturah in their places, and the days of weeping for Abraham were ended. 8. And he lived three jubilees and four weeks of years, one hundred and seventy-five years, and completed the days of his life, being old and full of days.

The decreasing Years and increasing Corruption of Mankind (xxiii. 9-17).

9. For the days of the forefathers, of their life, were nineteen jubilees; and after the Flood they began to grow less than nineteen jubilees, and to decrease in jubilees, and to grow old quickly, and to be full of their days by reason of manifold tribulation and the wickedness of their ways, with the exception of Abraham. [626]10. For Abraham was perfect in all his deeds with the Lord, and well-pleasing in righteousness all the days of his life; and behold, he did not complete four jubilees in his life, when he had grown old by reason of the wickedness [627]and was full of his days. 11. And all the generations which will arise from this time until the day of the great judgment will grow old quickly, before they complete two jubilees, and their knowledge will forsake them by reason of their old age [and all their knowledge will vanish away]. [628]12. And in those days, if a man live a jubilee and a half of years, they will say regarding him: "He hath lived long, and the greater part of his days are pain and sorrow and tribulation, [629]and there is no peace: 13. For calamity followeth on calamity, and wound on wound, and tribulation on tribulation, and evil tidings on evil tidings, and illness on illness, and all evil judgments such as these, one with another, illness and overthrow, and snow and frost and ice, and fever, and chills, and torpor, and famine, and death, and sword, and captivity, and all kinds of calamities and pains." [630]14. And all these will come on an evil generation, which transgresseth on the earth: their works are uncleanness and fornication, and pollution and abominations. [631]15. Then they will say: "The days of the forefathers were many (even), unto a thousand years, and were good; but, behold, the days of our life, if a man hath lived many,

---

[621] Cf. Gen. xlvi. 4. The closing of the eyes (by the eldest son) should strictly only be done after death, according to Jewish tradition.

[622] Cf. Gen. xlix. 33 (of the death of Jacob).

[623] Cf. Jer. li. 39, 57.

[624] Cf. Gen. l. 1.

[625] *i. e.* Machpelah; cf. Gen. xxv. 9.

[626] ? Man's years grow less as mankind grows more corrupt; cf. for a similar idea 4 Ezra v. 5055.

[627] Even Abraham grew prematurely old owing to the universal wickedness.

[628] Bracketed words a dittograph.

[629] Cf. Ps. xc. 10.

[630] ? a picture of contemporary misfortunes (200 B.C. and following years).

[631] Cf. vii. 21, xx. 5, xxii. 16.

are three score years and ten, and, if he is strong, four score years, and those evil[632]and there is no peace in the days of this evil generation."

16. And in that generation the sons will convict their fathers and their elders of sin and unrighteousness, [633]and of the words of their mouth and the great wickednesses which they perpetrate, and concerning their forsaking the covenant [634]which the Lord made between them and Him, that they should observe and do all His commandments and His ordinances and all His laws, without departing either to the right hand or to the left. [635]17. For all have done evil, [636]and every mouth speaketh iniquity [637]and all their works are an uncleanness and an abomination, and all their ways are pollution, uncleanness and destruction.

The Messianic Woes (xxiii. 18-25).

[Eschatological partly.]

18. Behold the earth will be destroyed on account of all their works, and there will be no seed of the vine, and no oil; for their works are altogether faithless, and they will all perish together, beasts and cattle and birds, and all the fish of the sea, [638]on account of the children of men. 19. And they will strive one with another, the young with the old, and the old with the young, the poor with the rich, and the lowly with the great, and the beggar with the prince,[639] on account of the law and the covenant; [640]for they have forgotten commandment, and covenant, and feasts, and months, and Sabbaths, and jubilees, and all judgments. 20. And they will stand (with bows and) swords and war to turn them back into the way; [641]but they will not return until much blood hath been shed on the earth, one by another. [642]21. And those who have escaped will not return from their wickedness to the way of righteousness, but they will all exalt themselves to deceit and wealth, that they may each take all that is his neighbour's, and they will name the great name, but not in truth and not in righteousness, and they will defile the holy of holies with their uncleanness and the corruption of their pollution. [643]22. And a great punishment will befall the deeds of this generation from the Lord, and He will give them over to the sword and to judgment and to captivity, and to be plundered and devoured. 23. And He will wake up against them the sinners of the Gentiles, who have neither mercy nor compassion, and who will respect the person of none, neither old nor young, nor any one, for they are more wicked and strong to do evil than all the children of men.

And they will use violence against Israel and transgression against Jacob,

And much blood will be shed upon the earth,

---

[632] Cf. Ps. xc. 10.

[633] ? the protest of the Hasidim ("the pious") against the Hellenizers; cf. 1 Macc. ii. 42 ff.

[634] Cf. 1 Macc. i. 15.

[635] Cf. 1 Macc. ii. 21 f. (Deut. v. 31-32, xxviii. 14).

[636] Cf. 1 Macc. i. 52-53.

[637] Cf. 1 Macc. ii, 6.

[638] Cf. 4 Ezra v. 7 (Ezek. xxxviii. 20).

[639] Internecine strife is a standing feature in such eschatological passages; cf. 4 Ezra vi. 24; Matt. xxiv. 10; *Ap. Bar.*, lxx. 3-4.

[640] Here the writer passes to a description of what is happening in his own time.

[641] "Way" here = the true path of religion; cf. Isa. xxx. 21 Acts ix. 2, etc.

[642] The conflicts between the early Maccabeans (at the head of the national party in Judah) and the Hellenizers seem to be referred to.

[643] Probably the machinations of the Hellenizing party under the High Priest Alcimus are referred to; cf. 1 Macc. ix. 54.

And there will be none to gather and none to bury. [644]

24.In those days they will cry aloud,

And call and pray that they may be saved from the hand of the sinners, the Gentiles; [645]But none will be saved.

25.And the heads of the children will be white with grey hair, [646]

And a child of three weeks will appear old like a man of one hundred years, And their stature will be destroyed by tribulation and oppression.

Renewed Study of the Law followed by a Renewal of Mankind. The Messianic Kingdom and the Blessedness of the Righteous (xxiii. 26-32; cf. Isa. lxv. 17 ff.

[Eschatological.]

26. And in those days the children will begin to study the laws,

And to seek the commandments,

And to return to the path of righteousness.

27. And the days will begin to grow many and increase amongst those children of men,

Till their days draw nigh to one thousand years,[647]

And to a greater number of years than (before) was the number of the days.

28. And there will be no old man

Nor one who is not satisfied with his days,

For all will be (as) children and youths.[648]

29. And all their days they will complete and live in peace and in joy,[649]And there will be no Satan [650]nor any evil destroyer;

For all their days will be days of blessing and healing, [651]

30. And at that time the Lord will heal His servants,

And they will rise up [652]and see [653]great peace, And drive out their adversaries.

And the righteous will see and be thankful,

And rejoice with joy for ever and ever,

And will see all their judgments and all their curses on their enemies.

---

[644] The sufferings of the nation up to (but not including) Simon's High Priesthood (142-135 B.C.) may be referred to. For the last line cf. Jer. viii. 2.

[645] Cf. Gal. ii. 15.

[646] Cf. *Sibylline Oracles*, ii. 155 ("children with grey hair on their temples born")--one of the signs of the coming in of the Messianic age.

[647] The span of life originally designed for mankind. Adam fell short of this because of his sin.

[648] Cf. Isa. lxv. 20

[649] Cf. Isa. lxv. 14.

[650] Cf. *Assumpt. Moses* x. 1

[651] Cf. i. 29.

[652] Probably there is no reference here to a resurrection. Apparently the Messianic kingdom depicted is a temporary one. The eschatology harmonizes with that of 1 Enoch xci.-civ.

[653] *i.e.* enjoy.

31. And their bones will rest in the earth,

And their spirits will have much joy, [654]

And they will know that it is the Lord who executeth judgment,

And showeth mercy to hundreds and thousands and to all that love Him. [655]

32. And do thou, Moses, write down these words; for thus are they written, and they record (them) on the heavenly tables for a testimony for the generations for ever.

Isaac at the Well of Vision: Esau sells his Birthright (xxiv. 1-7; cf. Gen. xxv. 11, 2934).

XXIV. And it came to pass after the death of Abraham, that the Lord blessed Isaac his son, and he arose from Hebron and went and dwelt at the Well of the Vision [656]in the first year of the third week of this jubilee, seven years. (2073 A.M.) 2. And in the first year of the fourth week (2080 A.M a famine began in the land, besides the first famine, which had been in the days of Abraham. [657]3. And Jacob sod lentil pottage, and Esau came from the field hungry. And he said to Jacob his brother: "Give me of this red pottage."[658] And Jacob said to him: "Sell to me thy [primogeniture, this] birthright and I will give thee bread, and also some of this lentil pottage." 4. And Esau said in his heart: "I shall die; of what profit to me is this birthright?" And he said to Jacob: "I give it to thee." 5. And Jacob said "Swear to me, this day," and he sware unto him. 6. And Jacob gave his brother Esau bread and pottage, and he ate till he was satisfied, and Esau despised his birthright; for this reason was Esau's name called Edom,[659] on account of the red pottage which Jacob gave him for his birthright. 7. And Jacob became the elder, and Esau was brought down from his dignity.

Isaac's Sojourn in Gerar and Dealings with Abimelech (xxiv. 8-27; cf. Gen. xxvi.).

8. And the famine was over the land, and Isaac departed to go down into Egypt in the second year of this week, and went to the king of the Philistines to Gerar, unto Abimelech. 9. [660]And the Lord appeared unto him and said unto him: "Go not down into Egypt; dwell in the land that I shall tell thee of, and sojourn in this land, and I shall be with thee and bless thee. 10. For to thee and to thy seed shall I give all this land, and I shall establish My oath which I sware unto Abraham thy father, and I shall multiply thy seed as the stars of heaven, and shall give unto thy seed all this land. 11. And in thy seed will all the nations of the earth be blessed, because thy father obeyed My voice, and kept My charge and My commandments, and My laws, and My ordinances, and My covenant; and now obey My voice and dwell in this land."

12. And he dwelt in Gerar three weeks of years. (2080-2101 A.M.) 13. And Abimelech charged concerning A.M.) him, and concerning all that was his, saying: "Any man that shall touch him or aught that is his shall surely die." [661]14. And Isaac waxed strong among the Philistines, and he got many possessions, oxen and sheep and camels and asses and a great household. 15. And he sowed in the land of the Philistines and brought in a hundred-fold, and Isaac became exceedingly great, and the Philistines envied him. 16. Now all the wells which the servants of Abraham had dug during the life of Abraham, the Philistines had stopped them after the death of Abraham, and filled them with earth. 17. And Abimelech said unto Isaac: "Go from us, for thou art much

---

[654] *i.e.* they will enjoy a blessed immortality (with no bodily resurrection); cf. 1 Enoch ciii. 3-4.

[655] Cf. 4 Ezra vii. 132 ff.

[656] *i.e. Beer-lahai-roi* ("the well of the Living One that seeth me"); Gen. xxv. iii.

[657] Cf. Gen. xxvi. 11.

[658] Cf. Gen. xxv. 30.

[659] *Edom* = "red."

[660] For 9-12 cf. Gen. xxvi. 2-6.

[661] Cf. Gen. xxvi. ii. Notice that no reference is made in our text to Isaac's deception about Rebecca.

mightier than we"; and Isaac departed thence in the first year of the seventh week, (2101 A.M.) and sojourned in the valleys of Gerar. 18. And they digged again the wells of water which the servants of Abraham, his father, had digged, and which the Philistines had closed after the death of Abraham his father, and he called their names as Abraham his father had named them. 19. And the servants of Isaac dug a well in the valley, and found living water, and the shepherds of Gerar strove with the shepherds of Isaac, saying: "The water is ours "; and Isaac called the name of the well "Perversity," [662]because they had been perverse with us. 20. And they dug a second well, and they strove for that also, and he called its name "Enmity."[663]And he arose from thence and they digged another well, and for that they strove not, and he called the name of it "Room," [664]and Isaac said: "Now the Lord hath made room for us, and we have increased in the land." 21. And he went up from thence to the Well of the Oath[665] in the first year of the first week in the forty-fourth jubilee. 22. And the Lord appeared to him that night, on the new moon of the first month, (2108 A.M.) and said unto him: "I am the God of Abraham thy father; fear not, for I am with thee, and shall bless thee and shall surely multiply thy seed as the sand of the earth, for the sake of Abraham my servant." 23. And he built an altar there, which Abraham his father had first built, and he called upon the name of the Lord, and he offered sacrifice to the God of Abraham his father. 24. And they digged a well and they found living water. 25. And the servants of Isaac digged another well and did not [666]find water, and they went and told Isaac that they had not found water, and Isaac said: "I have sworn this day to the Philistines and this thing hath been announced to us." 26. And he called the name of that place the "Well of the Oath"; for there he had sworn to Abimelech and Ahuzzath his friend and Phicol the prefect of his host. [667]27. And Isaac knew that day that under constraint he had sworn to them to make peace with them.

Isaac curses the Philistines (xxiv. 28-33).

28. And Isaac on that day cursed the Philistines [668]and said: "Cursed be the Philistines unto the day of wrath and indignation from the midst of all nations; may God make them a derision and a curse and an object of wrath and indignation in the hands of the sinners the Gentiles and in the hands of the Kittim. [669]

29. And whoever escapeth the sword of the enemy and the Kittim, may the righteous nation [670]root out in judgment from under heaven; for they will be the enemies and foes of my children throughout their generations upon the earth.

30. And no remnant will be left to them,

Nor one that will be saved on the day of the wrath of judgment;

For for destruction and rooting out and expulsion from the earth is the whole seed of the Philistines (reserved),

And there will no longer be left for these Caphtorim [671]a name or a seed on the earth.

---

[662] = Esek; cf. Gen. xxvi. 20.

[663] = Sinai; cf. Gen. xxvi. 21.

[664] = Rehoboth; cf. Gen. xxvi. 22.

[665] *i. e.* Beersheba.

[666] In Gen. xxvi. 32 the MT does not read *not*; but LXX agrees with our text in so reading. It is implied here that their failure to find water was due to the covenant made with Abimelech.

[667] Cf. Geri. xxvi. 31, 33.

[668] The text reflects the bitter feeling towards the Philistines existing among the Jews in Maccabean times. The Philistine cities were either destroyed or captured by the Maccabees.

[669] *i. e.* the Macedonians; cf. 1 Macc. i. 1, viii. 5.

[670] *i. e.* Judah under the Maccabees.

[671] The Philistines came originally from Caphtor according to Amos ix. 7 (Deut. ii. 23; Jer. xlvii. 4).

31. [672]For though he ascend unto heaven,

Thence will he be brought down,

And though he make himself strong on earth,

Thence will he be dragged forth,

And though he hide himself amongst the nations,

Even from thence will he be rooted out;

And though he descend into Sheol, There also will his condemnation be great, And there also he will have no peace.

32. And if he go into captivity,

By the hands of those that seek his life will they slay him on the way, And neither name nor seed will be left to him on all the earth;

For into eternal malediction will he depart."

33. And thus is it written and engraved concerning him on the heavenly tables, to do unto him on the day of judgment, so that he may be rooted out of the earth.

Rebecca admonishes Jacob not to marry a Canaanitish Woman. Rebecca's Blessing
(xxv. 1-23; cf. Gen. xxviii. 1-4). [673]

XXV. And in the second year of this week in this jubilee, (2109 A.M), Rebecca called Jacob her son, and spake unto him, saying: "My son, do not take thee a wife of the daughters of Canaan, as Esau, thy brother, who took him two wives of the daughters of Canaan, [674]and they have embittered my soul [675]with all their unclean deeds: for all their deeds are fornication and lust, and there is no righteousness with them, for (their deeds) are evil. 2. And I, my son, love thee exceedingly, and my heart and my affection bless thee every hour of the day and watch of the night. 3. And now, my son, hearken to my voice, and do the will of thy mother, and do not take thee a wife of the daughters of this land, but only of the house of my father, and of my father's kindred. Thou wilt take thee a wife of the house of my father, and the Most High God will bless thee, and thy children will be a righteous generation and a holy seed." 4. And then spake Jacob to Rebecca, his mother, and said unto her: "Behold, mother, I am nine weeks [676]of years old, and I neither know nor have I touched any woman, nor have I betrothed myself to any, nor even think of taking me a wife of the daughters of Canaan. 5. For I remember, mother, the words of Abraham, our father, for he commanded me not to take a wife of the daughters of Canaan, but to take me a wife from the seed of my father's house and from my kindred. 6. I have heard before that daughters have been born to Laban, thy brother, and I have set my heart on them to take a wife from amongst them. 7. And for this reason I have guarded myself in my spirit against sinning or being corrupted in all my ways throughout all the days of my life; for with regard to lust and fornication, Abraham, my father, gave me many commands. [677]8. And, despite all that he hath commanded me, these two and twenty years my brother hath striven with me, and spoken frequently to me and said: 'My brother, take to wife a sister of my two wives'; but I refuse to do as he hath done. 9. I swear before thee, mother, that all the days of my life I will not take me a wife from the daughters of the seed of Canaan, and I will not act wickedly as my brother hath done. 19. Fear not, mother; be assured that I shall do thy will and walk in uprightness, and not corrupt my ways for ever." 11. And thereupon she lifted up her face to heaven and extended the fingers of her hands, and opened her mouth and blessed the Most High God, who had created the heaven and the earth, and she gave Him thanks and

---

[672] The basis of 31-32 seems to be Amos ix. 2-4.

[673] With this section also compare xxvii. of our Book.

[674] Cf. Gen. xxvi. 34.

[675] Cf. Gen. xxvii. 46, xxvi. 35.

[676] *i.e.* 63.

[677] Cf. xx. 4, xxxix. 6.

praise. 12. And she said: "Blessed be the Lord God, and may His holy name be blessed for ever and ever, who hath given me Jacob as a pure son and a holy seed; for He is Thine, and Thine shall his seed be continually and throughout all the generations for evermore. 13. Bless him, O Lord, and place in my mouth the blessing of righteousness, that I may bless him." 14. And at that hour, when the spirit of righteousness [678]descended into her mouth, she placed both her hands on the head of Jacob, and said: 15. "Blessed art thou, Lord of righteousness and God of the ages; And may He bless thee beyond all the generations of men. May He give thee, my son, the path of righteousness, And reveal righteousness to thy seed. 16. And may He make thy sons many during thy life,

And may they arise according to the number of the months of the year. And may their sons become many and great beyond the stars of heaven, And their numbers be more than the sand of the sea.

17.And may He give them this goodly land--as He said He would give it to Abraham and to his seed after him alway [679]--

And may they hold it as a possession for ever.

18.And may I see (born) unto thee, my son, blessed children during my life, And a blessed and holy seed may all thy seed be.

19. And as thou hast refreshed thy mother's spirit during †my†[680] life, The womb of her that bare thee blesseth thee,

[My affection] and my breasts bless thee

And my mouth and my tongue praise thee greatly.

20.Increase and spread over the earth,

And may thy seed be perfect in the joy of heaven and earth for ever;

And may thy seed rejoice,

And on the great day of peace may it have peace.

21.And may thy name and thy seed endure to all the ages,

And may the Most High God be their God,

And may the God of righteousness dwell with them,

And by them may His sanctuary be built unto all the ages. [681]

22.Blessed be he that blesseth thee,

And all flesh that curseth thee falsely may it be cursed."[682]

23.And she kissed him, and said to him

"May the Lord of the world love thee

As the heart of thy mother and her affection rejoice in thee and bless thee." And she ceased from blessing.

Jacob obtains the Blessing of the Firstborn (xxvi. 1-35; cf. Gen. xxvii.).

XXVI. And in the seventh year of this week (2114 A.M.) Isaac called Esau, his elder son, and said unto him: "I am old, my son, and behold my eyes are dim in seeing, and I know not the day of my death. 2. And now take thy hunting weapons, thy quiver and thy bow, and go out to the field, and hunt and catch me (venison), my son, and make me savoury meat, such as my soul loveth, and bring it to me that I may eat, and that my soul may bless thee before I die." 3. But Rebecca heard Isaac speaking to Esau. 4. And Esau went forth early to the field to hunt and catch and bring home to his father. 5. And Rebecca called Jacob, her son, and said unto him: "Behold, I heard Isaac, thy father, speak unto Esau, thy brother, saying: 'Hunt for me, and make me savoury

---

[678] Cf. John xiv. 17, XV. 26, xvi. 13 (τ πλε μα τ ς ληθείας) variant reading here is "Holy Spirit."

[679] Cf. Luke i. 55.

[680] Read "thy" (Charles).

[681] Cf. i. 29.

[682] Cf. Gen. xxvii. 29.

meat, and bring (it) to me that I may eat and bless thee before the Lord before I die.' 6. And now, my son, obey my voice in that which I command thee: Go to thy flock and fetch me two good kids of the goats, and I will make them savoury meat for thy father, such as he loveth, and thou shalt bring (it) to thy father that he may eat and bless thee before the Lord before he die, and that thou mayst be blessed." 7. And Jacob said to Rebecca his mother: "Mother, I shall not withhold anything which my father would eat, and which would please him: only I fear, my mother, that he will recognise my voice and wish to touch me. 8. And thou knowest that I am smooth, and Esau, my brother, is hairy, and I shall appear before his eyes as an evildoer, and shall do a deed which he had not commanded me, and he will be wroth with me, and I shall bring upon myself a curse, and not a blessing." 9. And Rebecca, his mother, said unto him: "Upon me be thy curse, my son, only obey my voice." 10. And Jacob obeyed the voice of Rebecca, his mother, and went and fetched two good and fat kids of the goats, and brought them to his mother, and his mother made them (savoury meat) such as he loved. 11. And Rebecca took the goodly raiment of Esau, her elder son, which was with her in the house, and she clothed Jacob, her younger son, (with them), and she put the skins of the kids upon his hands and on the exposed parts of his neck. 12. And she gave the meat and the bread which she had prepared into the hand of her son Jacob. 13. And Jacob went in to his father and said: "I am thy son: I have done according as thou badest me: arise and sit and eat of that which I have caught, father, that thy soul may bless me." 14. And Isaac said to his son: "How hast thou found so quickly, my son?" 15. And Jacob said: "Because (the Lord) thy God caused me to find." 16. And Isaac said unto him: "Come near, that I may feel thee, my son, if thou art my son Esau or not." 17. And Jacob went near to Isaac, his father, and he felt him and said: 18. "The voice is Jacob's voice, but the hands are the hands of Esau," and he discerned him not, because it was a dispensation from heaven [683]to remove his power of perception and Isaac discerned not, for his hands were hairy as (his brother) Esau's, so that he blessed him. 19. And he said: "Art thou my son Esau?" and he said: "I am thy son and he said, "Bring near to me that I may eat of that which thou hast caught, my son, that my soul may bless thee." 20. And he brought near to him, and he did eat, and he brought him wine and he drank. 21. And Isaac, his father, said unto him: "Come near and kiss me, my son." And he came near and kissed him. 22. And he smelled the smell of his raiment, and he blessed him and said: "Behold, the smell of my son is as the smell of a (full) [684] field which the Lord hath blessed.

23.And may the Lord give thee of the dew of heaven

And of the dew[685] of the earth, and plenty of corn and oil: [686]

Let nations serve thee,

And peoples bow down to thee.

24.Be lord over thy brethren,

And let thy mother's sons bow down to thee;

And may all the blessings wherewith the Lord hath blessed me and blessed Abraham, my father, [687]Be imparted to thee and to thy seed for ever Cursed be he that curseth thee, And blessed be he that blesseth thee." 25. And it came to pass as soon as Isaac had made an end of blessing his son Jacob, and Jacob had gone forth from Isaac his father †the hid himself and† [688]Esau, his brother, came in from his hunting. 26. And he also made savoury meat, and brought (it) to his father, and said unto his father: "Let my father arise, and eat of my venison that thy soul may bless me." 27. And Isaac, his father, said unto him: "Who art thou?" And he said unto him: "I am thy first born, thy son Esau: I have done as thou hast commanded me." 28. And Isaac was very greatly astonished, and said: "Who is he that hath hunted and caught and brought (it) to me, and I have eaten of all before thou camest, and have blessed him: (and) he shall be blessed, and all his seed for ever." 29. And it came to pass when Esau heard the words of his father Isaac that he cried with an exceeding great and bitter cry, and said unto his father: "Bless me, (even) me also, father." 30. And he said unto him: "Thy brother came with

---

[683] Cf. 1 Kings xii. 15.

[684] So Latin here, and Sam. LXX and Vulg. in Gen. xxvii. 27: MT omits.

[685] Text of Gen. xxvii. 28 has "fatness."

[686] Text of Genesis has "wine."

[687] Cf. Gen; xxviii. 4.

[688] Charles suspects this to be an addition to the text: read "that."

guile, and hath taken away thy blessing." And he said: "Now I know why his name is named Jacob: behold, he hath supplanted me these two times: he took away my birth-right, and now he hath taken away my blessing." 31. And he said: "Hast thou not reserved a blessing for me, father?" and Isaac answered and said unto Esau:

"Behold, I have made him thy lord,

And all his brethren have I given to him for servants,

And with plenty of com and wine and oil have I strengthened him: And what now shall I do for thee, my son?"

32. And Esau said to Isaac, his father:

"Hast thou but one blessing, O father? Bless me, (even) me also, father":

And Esau lifted up his voice and wept.

33. And Isaac answered and said unto him:

"Behold, far from the dew of the earth shall be thy dwelling, And far from the dew of heaven from above.

34. And by thy sword wilt thou live,

And thou wilt serve thy brother.

And it shall come to pass when thou becomest great,[689]

And dost shake his yoke from off thy neck,

Thou wilt sin a complete sin unto death, [690]

And thy seed will be rooted out from under heaven."

35. And Esau kept threatening Jacob because of the blessing wherewith his father blessed him, and he said in his heart:

"May the days of mourning for my father now come, so that I may slay my brother Jacob."

Rebecca induces Isaac to send Jacob to Mesopotamia. Jacob's Dream and View at Bethel (xxvii. 1-27; cf. Gen. xxviii.).

XXVII. And the words of Esau, her elder son, were told to Rebecca in a dream, and Rebecca sent and called Jacob her younger son, and said unto him: 2. "Behold Esau thy brother will take vengeance on thee so as to kill thee. 3. Now, therefore, my son, obey my voice, and arise and flee thou to Laban, my brother, to Haran, and tarry with him a few days until thy brother's anger turneth away, and he remove his anger from thee, and forget all that thou hast done; then I will send and fetch thee from thence." 4. And Jacob said: "I am not afraid; if he wisheth to kill me, I will kill him." 5. But she said unto him: "Let me not be bereft of both my sons on one day." 6. And Jacob said to Rebecca his mother: "Behold, thou knowest that my father hath become old, and doth not see because his eyes are dull, and if I leave him it will be evil in his eyes, because I leave him and go away from you, and my father will be angry, and will curse me. I will not go; [691]when he sendeth me, then only will I go." 7. And Rebecca said to Jacob: "I will go in and speak to him, and he will send thee away." 8. And Rebecca went in and said to Isaac: "I loathe my life because of the two daughters of Heth, whom Esau hath taken him as wives; and if Jacob take a wife from among the daughters of the land such as these, for what purpose do I further live; for the daughters of Canaan are evil." [692]9. And Isaac called Jacob and blessed him, and admonished him and said unto him: 10. "Do not take thee a wife of any of the daughters of Canaan; arise and go to Mesopotamia, to the house of Bethuel, thy mother's father, and take thee a wife from thence of the daughters of Laban, thy mother's brother. 11. And God Almighty bless thee and increase and multiply thee that thou mayest become a company of nations, and give thee the blessings of my father Abraham, to thee and to thy seed after thee, that thou mayest inherit the land of thy sojournings and all the land which God gave to Abraham: go, my son, in peace." 12. And Isaac sent Jacob away, and he went to Mesopotamia, to Laban the son of Bethuel the Syrian, the brother of Rebecca, Jacob's mother. 13. And it came to pass after Jacob had arisen

---

[689] So Sam. of Gen. xxvii. 40: MT "when Thou shalt break loose."

[690] This line is a complete departure from the original text, which has: "thou shalt shake his yoke from off thy neck." The interpretation here given in the text has no support elsewhere.

[691] The author desires to relieve Jacob of the reproach of leaving his father in his old age.

[692] Cf. Gen. xxvii. 46.

to go to Mesopotamia that the spirit of Rebecca was grieved after her son, and she wept. 14. And Isaac said to Rebecca: "My sister, [693]weep not on account of Jacob, my son; for he goeth in peace, and in peace will he return. 15. The Most High God will preserve him from all evil, and will be with him; for He will not forsake him all his days; 16. For I know that his ways will be prospered in all things wherever he goeth, until he return in peace to us, and we see him in peace. 17. Fear not on his account my sister, for he is on the upright path and he is a perfect man: and he is faithful and will not perish. Weep not." 18. And Isaac comforted Rebecca on account of her son Jacob, and blessed him. 19. And Jacob went from the Well of the Oath to go to Haran on the first year of the second week in the forty-fourth Jubilee, and he came to Luz on the mountains, that is, Bethel, on the new moon of the first month of this week (2115 A.M.), and he came to the place at even and turned from the way to the west of the road that night: and he slept there; for the sun had set. 20. And he took one of the stones of that place and laid it (at his head) under the tree, [694]and he was journeying alone, and he slept. 21. And he dreamt that night, and behold a ladder set up on the earth, and the top of it reached to heaven, and behold, the angels of the Lord ascended and descended on it: and behold, the Lord stood upon it. 22. And He spake to Jacob and said: "I am the Lord God of Abraham, thy father, and the God of Isaac; the land whereon thou art sleeping, to thee shall I give it, and to thy-seed after thee. 23. And thy seed will be as the dust of the earth, and thou wilt increase to the west and to the east, to the north and the south, and in thee and in thy seed will all the families of the nations be blessed. 24. And behold, I shall be with thee, and shall keep thee whithersoever thou goest, and I shall bring thee again into this land in peace; for I shall not leave thee until I do everything that I told thee of." 25. And Jacob awoke from his sleep, and said, "Truly this place is the house of the Lord, and I knew it not." And he was afraid and said:" Dreadful is this place which is none other than the house of God, and this is the gate of heaven." 26. And Jacob arose early in the morning, and took the stone which he had put under his head and set it up as a pillar for a sign, and he poured oil upon the top of it. And he called the name of that place Bethel; but the name of the place was Luz at the first. 27. And Jacob vowed a vow unto the Lord, saying: "If the Lord will be with me, and will keep me in this way that I go, and give me bread to eat and raiment to put on, so that I come again to my father's house in peace, then shall the Lord be my God, and this stone which I have set up as a pillar for a sign in this place, shall be the Lord's house, and of all that thou givest me, I shall give the tenth to thee, my God."

Jacob's Marriage to Leah and Rachel; his Children and Riches (xxviii. i-30; cf. Gen. xxix., xxx., xxxi. 1-2).

XXVIII. And he went on his journey, and came to the land of the east, to Laban, the brother of Rebecca, and he was with him, and served him for Rachel his daughter one week. [695]2.[696]And in the first year of the third week (2122 A.M) he said unto him: "Give me my wife, for whom I have served thee seven years;" and Laban said unto Jacob. "I will give thee thy wife." 3. And Laban made a feast, and took Leah his elder daughter, and gave (her) to Jacob as a wife, and gave her Zilpah his handmaid for an handmaid; and Jacob did not know, for he thought that she was Rachel. 4. And he went in unto her, and behold, she was Leah; and Jacob was angry with Laban, and said unto him: "Why hast thou dealt thus with me? Did not I serve thee for Rachel and not for Leah? Why hast thou wronged me? Take thy daughter, and I will go; for thou hast done evil to me." 5. For Jacob loved Rachel more than Leah; for Leah's eyes were weak, but her form was very handsome; but Rachel had beautiful eyes and a beautiful and very handsome form. [697]6. And Laban said to Jacob: "It is not so done in our country, to give the younger before the elder." [698]And it is not right to do this; for thus it is ordained and

---

[693] The use of "sister" as a term of endearment (to a wife) may be illustrated from Tobit V. 20, vii. 16; Canticles iv. 9, etc., but appears to be unknown to Rabbinic literature. Its use here may be designed to justify Isaac's having called Rebecca his sister at Abimelech's court.

[694] ? which marked a shrine.

[695] *i. e.* seven years. For 1 cf. Gen. xxix. 1, 20

[696] For 2-4 cf. Gen. xxix. 21-25.

[697] Cf. Gen. xxix. 17-18*a*.

[698] Cf. Gen. xxix. 26.

written in the heavenly tables,[699] that no one should give his younger daughter before the elder--but the elder one giveth first and after her the younger--and the man who doeth so, they set down guilt against him in heaven, and none is righteous that doeth this thing, for this deed is evil before the Lord. 7. And command thou the children of Israel that they do not this thing; let them neither take nor give the younger before they have given the elder, for it is very wicked. 8. [700]And Laban said to Jacob: "Let the seven days of the feast of this one pass by, and I shall give thee Rachel, [701]that thou mayest serve me another seven years, that thou mayest pasture my sheep as thou didst in the former week." 9. And on the day when the seven days of the feast of Leah had passed, Laban gave Rachel to Jacob, that he might serve him another seven years, and he gave to Rachel Bilhah, the sister of Zilpah [702]as a handmaid. 10. And he served yet other seven years for Rachel, for Leah had been given to him for nothing. 11. And the Lord opened the womb of Leah, and she conceived and bare Jacob a son, and he [703]called his name Reuben, [704]on the fourteenth day of the ninth month, in the first year of the third week. (2122 A.M.) 12. But the womb of Rachel was closed, for the Lord saw that Leah was hated and Rachel loved. 13. And again Jacob went in unto Leah, and she conceived, and bare Jacob a second son, and he called his name Simeon, on the twenty-first of the tenth month, and in the third year of this week. (2124 A.M.) 14. And again Jacob went in unto Leah, and she conceived, and bare him a third son, and he called his name Levi, in the new moon of the first month in the sixth year of this week. (2127 A.M.) 15. And again Jacob went in unto her, and she conceived, and bare him a fourth son, and he called his name Judah, on the fifteenth of the third month, (2129 A.M.) in the †first† year of the †fourth† week. 16. And on account of all this Rachel envied Leah, for she did not bear, and she said to Jacob: "Give me children "; and Jacob said: "Have I withheld from thee the fruits of thy womb? Have I forsaken thee?" 17. And when Rachel saw that Leah had borne four sons to Jacob, Reuben and Simeon and Levi and Judah, she said unto him: "Go in unto Bilhah my handmaid, and she will conceive, and bear a son unto me." 18. (And she gave (him) Bilhah her handmaid to wife.) And he went in unto her, and she conceived, and bare him a son, and he called his name Dan, on the ninth of the sixth month, in the †sixth† year of the †third† week. (2127 A.M.)19. And Jacob went in again unto Bilhah a second time, and she conceived, and bare Jacob another son, and Rachel called his name Naphtali, on the fifth of the seventh month, in the second year of the fourth week. 20. And when Leah saw that she had become sterile and did not bear, A.M. she envied (Rachel) and she also gave her handmaid Zilpah to Jacob to wife, and she conceived, and bare a son, and Leah called his name Gad, on the twelfth of the eighth month, in the third year of the fourth week. 21. And h e went in again unto her, and she conceived, and bare him a second son, and Leah called his name Asher, on the second of the eleventh month, in the †fifth† year of the fourth week. 22. And Jacob went in unto Leah, and she conceived, and bare a son, and she called his name Issachar, on the fourth of the fifth month, in the †fourth† year of the fourth week, and she gave him to a nurse. 23. And Jacob went in again unto her, and she conceived, and bare two (children), a son and a daughter, and she called the name of the son Zebulon, and the name of the daughter Dinah, in the seventh of the seventh month, in the sixth year of the fourth week. 24. And the Lord was gracious to Rachel, and opened her womb, and she conceived, and bare a son, and she called his name Joseph, on the new moon of the fourth month, in the †sixth† year in this fourth week. (2134 A.M.) 25. And in the days when Joseph was born, Jacob said to Laban: "Give me my wives and sons, and let me go to my father Isaac, and let me make me an house; for I have completed the years in which I have served thee for thy two daughters, and I will go to the house of my father." 26. And Laban said to Jacob:

---

[699] The comment of the angels. This rule seems to be unknown to tradition.

[700] For 8-10 cf. Gen. xxix. 27-29.

[701] The marriage of two living sisters to the same man is expressly forbidden in the Mosaic Law; cf. Lev. xviii. 18.

[702] According to *Test. Naphtali* i. also, Bilhah and Zilpah were sisters. in later Jewish tradition they are represented as daughters of Laban; cf. *e. g. Pirke de R. Eliezer*, xxxvi.

[703] Gen. xxix. 32 has "she called.".

[704] The twelve sons of Jacob appear in our text in the same order as in Gen. xxix. 32-34, xxx. 1-24, xxxv. 17-18, viz. (1) Reuben; (2) Simeon; (3) Levi; (4) Judah; (5) Dan; (6) Naphtali; (7) Gad; (8) Asher; (9) Issachar; (110) Zebulon; (11) Joseph; (12) Benjamin. A different order is given in Gen. xlix. and in the *Test. XII Patriarchs*. The order of birth, as given in *Jubilees*, is complicated by textual difficulties; see Charles *ad loc.*

"†Tarry with me for thy wages†[705], and pasture my flock for me again, and take thy wages." 27. And they agreed with one another that he should give him as his wages those of the lambs and kids which were born black and spotted and white,[706] (these) were to be his wages. 28. And all the sheep brought forth spotted and speckled and black, variously marked, [707]and they brought forth again lambs like themselves, and all that were spotted were Jacob's and those which were not were Laban's. 29. And Jacob's possessions multiplied exceedingly, and he possessed oxen and sheep [708]and asses and camels, and menservants and maidservants. 30. And Laban and his sons envied Jacob, and Laban took back his sheep from him, and he observed him with evil intent.

Jacob's Flight with his Family: his Covenant with Laban (xxix. 1-12; cf. Gen, xxxi.).

XXIX. And it came to pass when Rachel had borne Joseph, that Laban went to shear his sheep; for they were distant from him a three days' journey. 2. And Jacob saw that Laban was going to shear his sheep, and Jacob called Leah and Rachel, and spake kindly unto them that they should come with him to the land of Canaan. 3. For he told them how he had seen everything in a dream, even all that He had spoken unto him that he should return to his father's house; and they said: "To every place whither thou goest we will go with thee." 4. And Jacob blessed the God of Isaac his father, and the God of Abraham his father's father, and he arose and mounted his wives and his children, and took all his possessions and crossed the river, and came to the land of Gilead, and Jacob hid [709]his intention from Laban and told him not. 5. And in the seventh year of the fourth week (2135 A.M..) Jacob turned (his face) toward Gilead in the first month, on the twenty-first thereof. And Laban pursued after him and overtook Jacob in the mountain of Gilead in the third month, on the thirteenth thereof. 6. And the Lord did not suffer him to injure Jacob; for He appeared to him in a dream by night. And Laban spake to Jacob, 7. And on the fifteenth of those days Jacob made a feast for Laban, and for all who came with him, and Jacob sware to Laban that day, and Laban also to Jacob, that neither should cross the mountain of Gilead to the other with evil purpose. 8. And he made there a heap for a witness; wherefore the name of that place is called: "The Heap of Witness," after this heap. [710]9. But before they used to call the land of Gilead the land of the Rephaim; [711]for it was the land of the Rephaim, and the Rephaim were born (there), giants whose height was ten, nine, eight down to seven cubits. 10. [712]And their habitation was from the land of the children of Ammon to Mount Hermon, and the seats of their kingdom were Karnaim and Ashtaroth, [713]and Edrei, and Mîsûr, [714]and Beon. [715]11. And the Lord destroyed them because of the evil of their deeds; for they were very malignant, and the Amorites dwelt in their stead, wicked and sinful, and there is no people to-day which hath

---

[705] Gen. XXX. 28 has "appoint me thy wages."

[706] A wrong rendering of the Hebrew (Gen. xxx. 32), which means "speckled" (nā ōd).

[707] Speckled and black, variously marked LXX ποικίλα κα σποδοιεδ αντά does not represent σποδοειδ.

[708] And sheep so LXX (Gen. xxx. 43); but MT and other versions omit.

[709] So LXX (Gen. xxxi. 20) and Targ. Onkelos; but MT Sam., Vulg., "stole" (the heart of Laban).

[710] Cf. Gen. xxxi. 47 ("Galeed" = "Heap of Witness").

[711] Cf. Gen. xiv. 5.

[712] The places here mentioned were, perhaps, associated with Maccabean victories in the mind of our author (Charles).

[713] In MT of Gen. xiv. 5, Asheroth-karnaim is one place; but Syr. and some MSS. of LXX support our text. Karnaim was captured by. Judas Maccabæus (1 Macc. 43 f.).

[714] In Deut. iii. 10 "plain" = mîshôr.

[715] = probably the Bæan of 1 Macc. v. 4 f., which was destroyed by Judas.

wrought to the full all their sins, and they have no longer length of life on the earth. [716]12. And Jacob sent away Laban, and he departed into Mesopotamia, the land of the East, and Jacob returned to the land of Gilead.

Jacob, reconciled with Esau, dwells in Canaan and supports his Parents (xxix. 1320; Cf. Gen. xxxii., xxxiii.).

13. And he passed over the Jabbok [717]in the ninth month, on the eleventh thereof. And on that day Esau, his brother, came to him, and he was reconciled to him, and departed from him unto the land of Seir, but Jacob dwelt in tents. 14. And in the first year of the fifth week in this jubilee (2136 A.M.) he crossed the Jordan, and dwelt beyond the Jordan, and he pastured his sheep from the sea †of the heap† [718]unto Bethshan, [719]and unto Dothan and unto the †forest† [720]of Akrabbim. 15. And he sent to his father Isaac of all his substance, clothing, and food, and meat, and drink, and milk, and butter, and cheese, and some dates of the valley, 16. And to his mother Rebecca also four times a year, between the times of the months, between ploughing and reaping, and between autumn and the rain (season) and between winter and spring, to the tower of Abraham. 17. For Isaac had returned from the Well of the Oath and gone up to the tower of his father Abraham, and he dwelt there apart from his son Esau. 18. For in the days when Jacob went to Mesopotamia, Esau took to himself a wife Mahalath, the daughter of Ishmael, and he gathered together all the flocks of his father and his wives, and went up and dwelt on Mount Seir, and left Isaac his father at the Well of the Oath alone. [721]19. And Isaac went up from the Well of the Oath and dwelt in the tower of Abraham his father on the mountains of Hebron, 20. And thither Jacob sent all that he did send to his father and his mother from time to time, all they needed, and they blessed Jacob with all their heart and with all their soul.

Dinah ravished. Slaughter of the Shechemites. Laws against Intermarriage between Israel and the Heathen. The Choice of Levi (xxx. 1-26; cf. Gen. xxxiv.).

XXX. And in the first year of the sixth week (2143 A.M.) he went up to Salem, to the east of Shechem, in peace,[722] in the fourth month. 2. And there they carried off Dinah, the daughter of Jacob, into the house of Shechem, the son of Hamor, the Hivite, the prince of the land, and he lay with her and defiled her, and she was a little girl, a child of twelve years. 3. And he besought his father and her brothers that she might be given to him to wife. And Jacob and his sons were wroth because of the men of Shechem; [723]for they had defiled Dinah, their sister, and they spake to them with evil intent and dealt deceitfully with them and beguiled them. 4. And Simeon and Levi came unexpectedly to Shechem and executed judgment on all the men of Shechem, and slew all the men whom they found in it, and left not a single one remaining in it: they slew all in torments because they had dishonoured their sister Dinah. 5. And thus let it not again be done from henceforth that a daughter of Israel be defiled; for judgment is ordained in heaven against them that they should destroy with the sword all the men of the Shechemites because they had wrought shame in Israel. 6. And the Lord delivered them into the hands of the sons of Jacob that they might exterminate them with the sword and execute judgment upon them, and that it might not thus again be done in Israel that a virgin of Israel should be defiled. 7. And if there is any man who wisheth in Israel to give his daughter or his sister to any man who is of the seed of the Gentiles

---

[716] Judas "must have nearly annihilated" the Amorites (Charles).

[717] Cf. Gen. xxxi. 22.

[718] Text corrupt. Latin has "from the Salt Sea."

[719] Cf. 1 Macc. v. 52, xii. 10.

[720] ? read "ascent" (cf. Num. xxxiv. 4; Josh. xv. 3). Judas fought in this district (of Idumea); cf. 1 Macc. v. 3.

[721] Cf. Gen. xxviii. 9, xxxvi. 6, 8. In contrast with Jacob's conduct to his parents, Esau's is unfilial.

[722] Based upon xxxiii. 18 (cf. R.V. marg.). Our text combines two readings ("Shalem," the name of a city, and shālōm, "peace").

[723] Our author omits all reference to the circumcision of the Shechemites, because he approves of the conduct of Simeon and Levi, and extols it. On the other hand, their conduct in the matter is severely reprobated in Gen. xlix. 5-7. Our author's view seems to reflect a bitter feeling against the people of Shechem. which prevailed in his time.

he shall surely die, and they shall stone him with stones; for he hath wrought shame in Israel; and they shall burn the woman with fire, because she hath dishonoured the name of the house of her father, and she shall be rooted out of Israel. 724 8. And let not an adulteress and no uncleanness be found in Israel throughout all the days of the generations of the earth; for Israel is holy unto the Lord, and every man who hath defiled (it) shall surely die: they shall stone him with stones. 9. For thus hath it been ordained and written in the heavenly tables regarding all the seed of Israel: he who defileth (it) shall surely die, and he shall be stoned with stones. 10. And to this law there is no limit of days, and no remission, nor any atonement: but the man who hath defiled his daughter shall be rooted out in the midst of all Israel, because he hath p. 155 given of his seed to Moloch, 725and wrought impiously so as to defile it. 11. And do thou, Moses, command the children of Israel and exhort them not to give their daughters to the Gentiles, and not to take for their sons any of the daughters of the Gentiles, for this is abominable before the Lord. 12. For this reason I have written for thee in the words of the Law all the deeds of the Shechemites, which they wrought against Dinah, and how the sons of Jacob spake, saying: "We shall not give our daughter to a man who is uncircumcised; for that were a reproach unto us." 13. And it is a reproach to Israel, to those who give, and to those who take the daughters of the Gentiles; for this is unclean and abominable to Israel. 14. 726And Israel will not be free from this uncleanness if it hath a wife of the daughters of the Gentiles, or hath given any of its daughters to a man who is of any of the Gentiles. 15. For there will be plague upon plague, and curse upon curse, and every judgment and plague and curse will come (upon him): if he do this thing, or hide his eyes from 727those who commit uncleanness, or those who defile the sanctuary of the Lord, or those who profane His holy name, 728(then) will the whole nation 729together be judged for all the uncleanness and profanation of this (man). 16. And there will be no respect of persons [and no consideration of persons], 730and no receiving at his hands of fruits and offerings and burnt-offerings and fat, nor the fragrance of sweet savour, so as to accept it: and so fare every man or woman in Israel who defileth the sanctuary. 17. For this reason I have commanded thee, saying: "Testify this testimony to Israel: see how the Shechemites fared and their sons: how they were delivered into the hands of two sons of Jacob, and they slew them under tortures, and it was (reckoned) unto them for righteousness, and it is written down to them for righteousness. 18. And the seed of Levi was chosen for the priesthood, and to be Levites, that they might minister before the Lord, as we, continually, and that Levi and his sons may be blessed for ever; for he was zealous to execute righteousness and judgment and vengeance on all those who arose against Israel. 73119. And so they inscribe as a testimony in his favour on the heavenly tables blessing and righteousness before the God of all: 20. And we remember the righteousness which the man fulfilled during his life, at all periods of the year; until a thousand generations they will record it, and it will come to him and to his descendants after him, and he hath been recorded on the heavenly tables as a friend 732and a righteous man. 21. All this account I have written for thee, and have commanded thee to say to the children of Israel, that they should not commit sin nor transgress the ordinances nor break the covenant which hath been ordained for them, (but) that they should fulfil it and be recorded as friends. 73322. But if they transgress and work uncleanness in every way, they

---

724 Notice the passionate denunciation of mixed marriages. The burning of the woman with fire, according to the Mosaic Law (Lev. xxi. 9), was reserved for the priest's daughter who played the harlot.

725 Cf. Lev. xviii. 21: here the prohibition in Lev. against making "any of thy seed pass through the fire to Molech" is interpreted as = to give one's child in marriage to a Gentile; so, also, Targ. Ps.-Jonathan on this verse. In later times the rule has not always been strictly enjoined.

726 14-15 are based upon Lev. xx. 2-4.

727 *i. e.* "ignore"; cf. Lev. xx. 4.

728 Cf. Lev. xx. 3.

729 In Lev. xx. 5, only the guilty man's family is involved.

730 Bracketed as a dittograph

731 A different reason for Levi's choice for the priesthood is given in xxxii. 3; cf. also *Test. Levi* iv. 2.

732 *sc.* of God.
733 *sc.* of God.

will be recorded on the heavenly tables as adversaries, and they will be destroyed out of the book of life, [734]and they will be recorded in the book of those who will be destroyed and with those who will be rooted out of the earth. 23. And on the day when the sons of Jacob slew Shechem a writing was recorded in their favour in heaven that they had executed righteousness and uprightness and vengeance on the sinners, and it was written for a blessing. 24. And they brought Dinah, their sister, out of the house of Shechem, and they took captive everything that was in Shechem, their sheep and their oxen and their asses, and all their wealth, and all their flocks, and brought them all to Jacob their father. 25. And he reproached them because they had put the city to the sword; [735]for he feared those who dwelt in the land, the Canaanites and the Perizzites. 26. And the dread of the Lord was upon all the cities which are around about Shechem, and they did not rise to pursue after the sons of Jacob; for terror had fallen upon them. [736]

Jacob's Journey to Bethel and Hebron. Isaac blesses Levi and Judah (xxxi. 1-25; cf. Gen. xxxv.).

XXXI. And on the new moon of the month Jacob spake to all the people of his house, saying: "Purify yourselves and change your garments, and let us arise and go up to Bethel, where I vowed a vow to Him on the day when I fled from the face of Esau my brother, because He hath been with me and brought me into this land in peace, and put ye away the strange gods that are among you." 2. And they gave up the strange gods and that which was in their ears and which was †on their necks,† *(corrupt)* and the idols which Rachel stole from Laban her brother she gave wholly to Jacob. And he burnt and brake them to pieces and destroyed them, and hid them under an oak which is in the land of Shechem. 3. And he went up on the new moon of the seventh month to Bethel. And he built an altar at the place where he had slept, and he set up a pillar there, and he sent word to his father Isaac to come to him to his sacrifice, and to his mother Rebecca.

4. And Isaac said: "Let my son Jacob come, and let me see him before I die." [737]5. And Jacob went to his father Isaac and to his mother Rebecca, to the house of his father Abraham, [738]and he took two of his sons with him, Levi and Judah, and he came to his father Isaac and to his mother Rebecca. [739] 6. And Rebecca came forth from the tower to the front of it to kiss Jacob and embrace him; for her spirit had revived when she heard: "Behold Jacob thy son hath come"; and she kissed him. 7. And she saw his two sons, and she recognised them, and said unto him: "Are these thy sons, my son?" and she embraced them and kissed them, and blessed them, saying: "In you shall the seed of Abraham become illustrious, and ye will prove a blessing on the earth." 8. And Jacob went in to Isaac his father, to the chamber where he lay, and his two sons were with him, and he took the hand of his father, and stooping down he kissed him, and Isaac clung to the neck of Jacob his son, and wept upon his neck. 9. And the darkness left the eyes of Isaac, and he saw the two sons of Jacob, Levi and Judah, and he said: "Are these thy sons, my son? for they are like thee." 10. And he said unto him that they were truly his sons: "And thou hast truly seen that they are truly my sons." 11. And they came near to him, and he turned and kissed them and embraced them both together. 12. And the spirit of prophecy came down into his mouth, and he took Levi by his right hand and Judah by his left. 13. And he turned to Levi first, [740]and began to bless him first, and said unto him:, 'May the God of all, the very Lord of all the ages, bless thee and thy children throughout all the ages. 14. And may the Lord give to thee and to thy seed †greatness and great glory†, and cause thee and thy seed, from among all flesh, to approach Him to serve in His sanctuary as the angels of the

---

[734] This expression, derived from the O.T. (cf. Ps. lxix. 28; Exod. xxxii. 32) had reference originally to the temporal blessings of the theocracy, and this may be its meaning here; but later the meaning was extended to eternal life. It occurs frequently in the N.T. (cf. Rev. iii. 5, xiii. 8, etc.); cf. also 1 Enoch xlvii. 3.

[735] Cf. *Test. Levi* vi.

[736] Cf. Gen. xxxv. 5.

[737] 1 Isaac refused to go to Bethel; cf. Test. Levi ix. 2.

[738] i. e. to Hebron

[739] This last meeting of Jacob with Isaac is not referred to in the Rabbinical Haggada.

[740] Cf. *Test. Levi* ix. 1 f. The primacy of Levi is here marked.

presence and as the holy ones. [741](Even) as they, will the seed of thy sons be for glory and greatness and holiness, and may He make them great unto all the ages. 15. And they will be princes and judges, and chiefs [742]of all the seed of the sons of Jacob;

They will speak the word of the Lord in righteousness,

 And they will judge all His judgments in righteousness.

And they will declare My ways to Jacob And My paths to Israel.

The blessing of the Lord will be given in their mouths [743]
To bless all the seed of the beloved. [744]

16.Thy mother hath called thy name Levi,
And justly hath she called thy name;
Thou wilt be joined [745]to the Lord
And be the companion of all the sons of Jacob;
Let His table be thine, [746]
And do thou and thy sons eat thereof;

And may thy table be full unto all generations,

And thy food fail not unto all the ages.

17. And let all who hate thee fall down before thee,

And let all thy adversaries be rooted out and perish;

And blessed be he that blesseth thee,

And cursed be every nation that curseth thee.

18. And to Judah he said:

May the Lord give thee strength and power

To tread down all that hate thee;

A prince shalt thou be, thou and one of thy sons, [747]over the sons of Jacob;

May thy name and the name of thy sons [748]go forth and traverse every land and region.
Then will the Gentiles fear before thy face,
And all the nations will quake
[And all the peoples will quake].[749]
19.In thee shall be the help of Jacob,
And in thee be found the salvation of Israel.
20.And when thou sittest on the throne of the honour of thy righteousness,

---

[741] Levi is to serve in the sanctuary as the two highest orders of angels serve in the highest heaven.

[742] Levi's descendants are not only to be priests but also rulers of the nation. This double function was exercised by the Maccabean priest-princes: cf. *Test. Levi* viii. ii ff.

[743] *i. e.* the priestly blessing; cf. Ecclus. l. 20.

[744] *i. e.* of Abraham.

[745] A play on the name "Levi" (= *attaché*); cf. Gen. xxix. 34 (R.V. marg.); also Num. xviii. 2, 4.

[746] Cf. *Test. Levi* viii. 16 ("and the table of the Lord shall thy seed apportion").

[747] *i. e.?* the Messiah who is to spring from Judah: but if so the expression of the hope is somewhat vague. More probably the reference is to the historical David.

[748] *i. e.* the name of the Jewish people.

[749] Bracketed as a dittograph.

There will be great peace for all the seed of the sons of the beloved, [750]
And blessed will he be that blesseth thee;
And all that hate thee and afflict thee and curse thee
Shall be rooted out and destroyed from the earth and accursed."

21. And turning he kissed him again and embraced him, and rejoiced greatly; for he had seen the sons of Jacob his son in very truth. 22. And he went forth from between his feet and fell down and worshipped him. And he blessed them. And (Jacob) rested there with Isaac his father that night, and they ate and drank with joy. 23. And he made the two sons of Jacob sleep, the one on his right hand and the other on his left and it was counted to him for righteousness. 24. And Jacob told his father everything during the night, how the Lord had shown him great mercy, and how He had prospered (him in) all his ways, and protected him from all evil. 25. And Isaac blessed the God of his father Abraham, who had not withdrawn His mercy and His righteousness from the sons of His servant Isaac.

Rebecca journeys with Jacob to Bethel (xxxi. 26-32).

26. And in the morning Jacob told his father Isaac the vow which he had vowed to the Lord, and the vision which he had seen, and that he had built an altar, [751] and that everything was ready for the sacrifice to be made before the Lord as he had vowed, and that he had come to set him on an ass.

27. And Isaac said unto Jacob his son: "I am not able to go with thee; for I am old, and not able to bear the way: go, my son, in peace; for I am one hundred and sixty-five years this day; I am no longer able to journey, set thy mother (on an ass) and let her go with thee. 28. And I know, my son, that thou hast come on my account, and may this day be blessed on which thou hast seen me alive, and I also have seen thee, my son. 29. Mayest thou prosper and fulfil the vow which thou hast vowed, and put not off thy vow; for thou wilt be called to account as touching the vow;[752] now therefore make haste to perform it, and may He be pleased who hath made all things, to whom thou hast vowed the vow." 30. And he said to Rebecca: "Go with Jacob thy son"; and Rebecca went with Jacob her son, and Deborah with her, and they came to Bethel. 31. And Jacob remembered the prayer with which his father had blessed him and his two sons, Levi and Judah, and he rejoiced and blessed the God of his fathers, Abraham and Isaac. 32. And he said: "Now I know that I have an eternal hope, and my sons also, before the God of all;" and thus is it ordained concerning the two; and they record it as an eternal testimony unto them on the heavenly tables how Isaac blessed them.

Levi's Dream at Bethel; he is appointed to the Priesthood. Jacob celebrates the Feast of Tabernacles and offers Tithes. The Institution of Tithes (xxxii. 1-15; cf. Gen. xxxv.),

XXXII. And he abode that night at Bethel, and Levi dreamed [753] that they had ordained and made him the priest of the Most High God, [754] him and his sons for ever; and he awoke from his sleep and blessed the Lord. 2. And Jacob rose early in the morning, on the fourteenth of this month, and he gave a tithe of all that came with him, both of men and cattle, both of gold and every vessel and garment, yea, he gave tithes of all. 3. And in those days Rachel became pregnant with her son

---

[750] *i. e.* of Abraham.

[751] At Bethel; cf. Gen. xxviii. 18-22.

[752] Note the emphasis on the obligation to keep a vow.

[753] Cf. *Test. Levi* viii. (which describes Levi's dream-vision of seven men in white as having taken place at Bethel); also v. of the same work (in ix. 3 Jacob has this dream also).

[754] Cf. Gen. xiv. 18-20 (Melchizedek). The title, "Priest of the Most High God," was appropriated by the Maccabean priest-kings. Apparently it was expected in certain quarters that the Messiah would spring from this priestly ruling house; cf. Ps. cx., especially ver. 4.

Benjamin. And Jacob counted his sons from him [755]upwards and Levi fell to the portion of the Lord,[756] and his father clothed him in the garments of the priesthood and filled his hands. [757]4. And on the fifteenth of this month, he brought to the altar fourteen oxen from amongst the cattle, and twenty-eight rams, and forty-nine sheep, and seven lambs, and twenty-one kids of the goats as a burnt-offering on the altar of sacrifice, well pleasing for a sweet savour before God. [758]5. This was his offering, in consequence of the vow which he had vowed that he would give a tenth, [759]with their fruit offerings and their drink-offerings. 6. And when the fire had consumed it, he burnt incense on the fire over the fire, and for a thank-offering two oxen and four rams and four sheep, four he-goats, and two sheep of a year old, and two kids of the goats; and thus he did daily for seven days. 7. And he and all his sons and his men were eating (this) with joy there during seven days and blessing and thanking the Lord, who had delivered him out of all his tribulation and had given him his vow. 8. And he tithed all the clean animals, and made a burnt sacrifice, but the unclean animals he gave (not) to Levi his son, and he gave him all the souls of the men. [760]9. And Levi discharged the priestly office at Bethel before Jacob his father in preference to his ten brothers, and he was a priest there, and Jacob gave his vow: thus he tithed again the tithe [761]to the Lord and sanctified it, and it became holy unto Him. 10. And for this reason it is ordained on the heavenly tables as a law for the tithing again the tithe to eat before the Lord from year to year, [762]in the place where it is chosen that His name should dwell, and to this law there is no limit of days for ever. 11. This ordinance is written that it may be fulfilled from year to year in eating the second tithe before the Lord in the place where it hath been chosen, and nothing shall remain over from it from this year to the year following. 12. For in its year shall the seed be eaten till the days of the gathering of the seed of the year, and the wine till the days of the wine, and the oil till the days of its season. 13. And all that is left thereof and becometh old, let it be regarded as polluted: let it be burnt with fire, for it is unclean. 14. And thus let them eat it together in the sanctuary, and let them not suffer it to become old. 15. And all the tithes of the oxen and sheep shall be holy unto the Lord, [763]and shall belong to His priests, which they will eat before Him from year to year; for thus is it ordained and engraven regarding the tithe on the heavenly tables.

Jacob's Visions. He celebrates the eighth day of Tabernacles. The Birth of Benjamin and Death of Rachel (xxxii. 16-34; cf. Gen. xxxv.).

And on the following night, on the twenty-second day of this month, Jacob resolved to build that place, and to surround the court with a wall, and to sanctify it and make it holy for ever, for himself and his children after him. 17. And the Lord appeared to him by night and blessed him and said unto him: "Thy name shall not be called Jacob, but Israel shall they name thy name." 18. And He said unto him again: "I am the Lord who created the heaven and the earth, and I shall increase thee and multiply thee exceedingly, and kings will come forth from thee, and they will judge everywhere wherever the foot of the sons of men hath trodden. 19. Ana I shall

---

[755] *i.e.* from Benjamin.

[756] Levi, as the tenth son (counting backwards from Benjamin), fell, under the law of tithe, to the Lord, and was consecrated to the priesthood; cf. also *Pire de R. Eliezer* xxxvii., where Levi is counted (by a different method) as tenth "and was reckoned as the tithe, holy to God" (cf. Lev. xxvii. 32).

[757] A technical expression meaning appointment to the priesthood; cf. Exod. xxviii. 41 (R.V. marg.); xxix. 9.

[758] The number of victims does not agree with the prescriptions of the Mosaic Law regarding the Feast of Tabernacles; cf. Num. xxix. 12-40; Lev. xxiii. 34-36, 39-44.

[759] Cf. Gen. xxviii. 22.

[760] Cf. *Test. Levi* ix. 3 ("And he [Jacob] paid tithes of all to the Lord through me").

[761] *i. e.* the second tithe; cf. Num. xviii. 26.

[762] Cf. Deut. xiv. 23 (Tobit i. 7).

[763] Cf. Lev. xxvii. 32; 2 Chron. xxxi. 6. These tithes are not otherwise attested in the O.T.

give to thy seed all the earth [764]which is under heaven, and they will judge all the nations according to their desires, and after that they will get possession of the whole earth and inherit it for ever." 20. And He finished speaking with him, and He went up from him, and Jacob looked till He had ascended into heaven.[765] 21. And he saw in a vision of the night, and behold an angel descended from heaven with seven tablets[766] in his hands, and he gave them to Jacob, and he read them and knew all that was written therein which would befall him and his sons throughout all the ages. [767] 22. And he showed him all that was written on the tablets, and said unto him: "Do not build this place, and do not make it an eternal sanctuary,[768] and do not dwell here; for this is not the place. Go to the house of Abraham thy father and dwell with Isaac thy father until the day of the death of thy father. 23. For in Egypt thou wilt die in peace, and in this land thou wilt be buried with honour in the sepulchre of thy fathers, with Abraham and Isaac. 24. Fear not, for as thou hast seen and read it, thus will it all be; and do thou write down everything as thou hast seen and read." 25. And Jacob said: "Lord, how can I remember all that I have read and seen?" And he said unto him: "I will bring all things to thy remembrance." [769] 26. And he went up from him, and he awoke from his sleep, and he remembered everything which he had read and seen, and he wrote down all the words which he had read and seen. 27. And he celebrated there yet another day, [770]and he sacrificed thereon according to all that he sacrificed on the former days, and called its name †"Addition,"†[771] for †this day was added,† and the former days he called "The Feast." [772] 28. And thus it was manifested that it should be, and it is written on the heavenly tables: wherefore it was revealed to him that he should celebrate it, and add it to the seven days of the feast. 29. [773]And its name was called †"Addition," † †because that† it was recorded amongst the days of the feast days, †according to† the number of the days of the year. 30. And in the night, on the twenty-third of this month, Deborah Rebecca's nurse died, and they buried her beneath the city under the oak of the river, and he called the name of this place, "The river of Deborah," and the oak, "The oak of the mourning of Deborah." [774] 31. And Rebecca went and returned to her house to his father Isaac, and Jacob sent by her hand rams and sheep and he-goats that she should prepare a meal for his father such as he desired. 32. And he went after his mother till he came to the land of Kabrâtân, [775]and he dwelt there. 33. And Rachel bare a son in the night, and called his name "Son of my sorrow"; for she suffered in giving him birth: but his father called his name Benjamin, on the eleventh of the eighth month in the first of the sixth

---

[764] For 17-18 cf. Gen. xxxv. 10-12. Notice that the whole inhabited earth (not merely Palestine, as in Gen. xxxv. 12) is here promised to Israel.

[765] Cf. Gen. xxxv. 13.

[766] Cf. 4 Ezra xiv. 24.

[767] Cf. xlv. 4.

[768] The sanctuary at Bethel was not to be the one central shrine, where alone acceptable worship was to be offered.

[769] In 4 Ezra xiv. 40, Ezra's memory is said to have been miraculously strengthened after he had received the cup of inspiration; cf. also John xiv. 26.

[770] *i. e.* the eighth day of the Feast of Tabernacles.

[771] The Hebrew name is *'aṣereth* (*'aṣarta*), from a root meaning "detain" (*'āar*). Hence, perhaps, we may emend here "keeping back," for on that day he was kept back (Charles).

[772] So in Rabbinic the Feast of Tabernacles was called, *par excellence*, "the Feast."

[773] 29 is very corrupt. Charles suggests that it should be read: "And its name was called 'a keeping back' (*i.e. 'a   ereth*) when it was recorded amongst the days of the feast days in the number of the days of the year."

[774] Cf. Gen. xxxv. 8 (R.V. marg.).

[775] Due to a misunderstanding of the words rendered "some distance" (*kibrath hā'areṣ*) in Gen. xxxv. 16. The LXX also took kibrath to be a proper name (Χιβραθο).

week of this jubilee. (2143 A.M.) 34. And Rachel died there and she was buried in the land [776]of Ephrath, the same is

Bethlehem, and Jacob built a pillar on the grave of Rachel, on the road above her grave.

Reuben's Sin with Bilhah. Laws regarding Incest. Jacob's Children (xxxiii. 1-23; Cf. Gen. xxxv. 21-27).

XXXIII. And Jacob went and dwelt to the south of Magdalâdrâ'êf. [777]And he went to his father Isaac, he and Leah his wife, on the new moon of the tenth month. 2. And Reuben saw Bilhah, Rachel's maid, the concubine of his father, bathing in water in a secret place, and he loved her. 3. And he hid himself at night, and he entered the house of Bilhah [at night], and he found her sleeping alone on a bed in her house. 4. And he lay with her, and she awoke and saw, and behold Reuben was lying with her in the bed, and she uncovered the border of her covering and seized him, and cried out, and discovered that it was Reuben. 5. And she was ashamed because of him, and released her hand from him, and he fled. 6. And she lamented because of this thing exceedingly, and did not tell it to any one. 7. And when Jacob returned and sought her, she said unto him: "I am not clean for thee, for I have been defiled as regards thee; for Reuben hath defiled me, and hath lain with me in the night, and I was asleep, and did not discover until he uncovered my skirt and slept with me." 8. And Jacob was exceedingly wroth with Reuben because he had lain with Bilhah, because he had uncovered his father's skirt. [778]9. And Jacob did not approach her again because Reuben had defiled her. And as for any man who uncovereth his father's skirt his deed is wicked exceedingly, for he is abominable before the Lord. 10. For this reason it is written and ordained on the heavenly tables that a man should not lie with his father's wife, and should not uncover his father's skirt, for this is unclean: they shall surely die together, [779]the man who lieth with his father's wife and the woman also, for they have wrought uncleanness on the earth. 11. And there shall be nothing unclean before our God in the nation which He hath chosen for Himself as a possession. 12. And again, it is written a second time: "Cursed he be who lieth with the wife of his father, for he hath uncovered his father's shame"; and all the holy ones of the Lord said "So be it; so be it." [780]13. And do thou, Moses, command the children of Israel that they observe this word; for it (entaileth) a punishment of death; and it is unclean, and there is no atonement for ever to atone for the man who hath committed this, but he is to be put to death and slain, and stoned with stones, and rooted out from the midst of the people of our God. 14. For to no man who doeth so in Israel is it permitted to remain alive a single day on the earth, for he is abominable and unclean. 15. And let them not say: to Reuben was granted life and forgiveness after he had lain with his father's concubine, and to her also though she had a husband, and her husband Jacob, his father, was still alive. 16. For until that time there had not been revealed the ordinance and judgment and law in its completeness for all, but in thy days (it hath been revealed) as a law of seasons and of days, and an everlasting law for the everlasting generations. [781]17. And for this law there is no consummation of days, and no atonement for it, but they must both be rooted out in the midst of the nation: on the day whereon they committed it they shall slay them. 18. And do thou, Moses, write (it) down for Israel that they may observe it, and do according to these words, and not commit a sin unto death; [782]for the Lord our God is judge, who respecteth not persons and accepteth not gifts. [783]19. And tell them these words of the covenant, that they may hear and observe, and be on their guard

---

[776] "On the way to" in the text of Gen. xxxv. 19.

[777] A compound of migdal 'eder 'ephrāth ("the tower of Eder of Ephrath"); cf. Gen. xxxv. 21, also *Test. Reuben* iii. 9--15, where the same incident is narrated. In later Jewish tradition an explanation is given which exculpates Reuben (cf. Targ. Ps.-Jon. on Gen. xxxv. 22).

[778] Cf. Deut. xxii. 30.

[779] Cf. Lev. xx. 11.

[780] Cf. Deut. xxvii. 20.

[781] "Where there is no law there is no transgression" (Rom. iv. 15).

[782] Cf. xxi. 22.

[783] Cf. v. 16, xl. 8.

with respect to them, and not be destroyed and rooted out of the land; for an uncleanness, and an abomination, and a contamination, and a pollution are all they who commit it on the earth before our God. 20. And there is no greater sin than the fornication which they commit on earth; for Israel is a holy nation unto the Lord its God, and a nation of inheritance, and a priestly and royal nation and for (His own) possession; [784]and there shall no such uncleanness appear in the midst of the holy nation.

21. And in the third year of this sixth week (2145 A.M.) Jacob and all his sons went and dwelt in the house of Abraham, near Isaac his father and Rebecca his mother. 22. [785]And these were the names of the sons of Jacob: the first-born Reuben, Simeon, Levi, Judah, Issachar, Zebulon, the sons of Leah; and the sons of Rachel, Joseph and Benjamin; and the sons of Bilhah, Dan and Naphtali, and the sons of Zilpah, Gad and Asher; and Dinah, the daughter of Leah, the only daughter of Jacob. 23. And they came and bowed themselves to Isaac and Rebecca, and when they saw them they blessed Jacob and all his sons, and Isaac rejoiced exceedingly, for he saw the sons of Jacob, his younger son, and he blessed them.

War of the Amorite Kings against Jacob and his Sons. Joseph sold into Egypt (cf. Gen. xxxvii.). The Death of Bilhah and Dinah (xxxiv. 1-19).

XXXIV. And in the sixth year of this week of this forty-fourth jubilee (2148 A.M.)Jacob sent his sons to pasture their sheep, and his servants with them, to the pastures of Shechem. 2. [786]And the seven kings of the Amorites assembled themselves together against them, to slay them, hiding themselves under the trees, and to take their cattle as a prey. 3. And Jacob and Levi and Judah and Joseph were in the house with Isaac their father; for his spirit was sorrowful, and they could not leave him: and Benjamin was the youngest, and for this reason remained with his father. 4. And there came the king[s] [787]of Tâphû, [788] and the king[s][789] of †'Arêsa,† [790]and the king[s] of Sêragân, [791]and the king[s] of Sêlô, [792]and the king[s] of Gâ'as, [793]and the king of Bêthôrôn, [794]and the king of †Ma'anîsâkîr,† [795]and all those who dwell in these mountains (and) who dwell in the woods in the land of Canaan. 5. And they announced this to Jacob saying: "Behold, the kings of the Amorites have surrounded thy sons, and plundered their herds." 6. And he arose from his housel he and his three sons and all the servants of his father, and his own servants, and he went against them with six thousand [796]men, who carried swords. 7. And he slew them in the pastures of Shechem, and pursued those who fled, and he slew them

---

[784] Cf. xvi. 18 (note).

[785] For 22 cf. Gen. xxxv. 23-27.

[786] The account given in 2-8 of the conquest of Shechem is given in a fuller form in the *Test. Judah* iii-vii., and in the Midrash Wajjissau (cf. Gaster, *Chronicles of Jerahmeel*, pp. 80-87). The legend evidently has an old basis, for it harmonizes with the statement given in Gen. xlviii. 22, which refers to Jacob's conquest of Shechem (cf. RX. margin). This form of the story is obviously independent of, and possibly older than, that given in Gen. xxxiv.

[787] Read "king."

[788] = Tappuah (Josh. xv. 53, xvi. 8). It is the Tephon mentioned in 1 Macc. ix. 50. This and the following places mentioned may have been specially interesting to our author because of events connected with them in Maccabean times.

[789] Read "king."

[790] Read "Asor," *i. e.* Hazer, the scene of a great victory by Jonathan, 1 Macc. xi. 67 ff.

[791] Unknown.

[792] *i. e.* Shiloh

[793] =? Gaash (Josh. xxiv. 30).

[794] The scene of more than one Maccabean victory; cf. 1 Macc. iii. 13 ff vii. 39 ff.

[795] Corrupt for Shakir-Maani."

[796] Another reading is "800."

with the edge of the sword, and he slew [797]†'Arêsa † and Tâphû and Sarêgân and Sêlô and †'Amânîsakîr† and Gâ[gâ]'as, and he recovered his herds. 8. And he prevailed over them, and imposed tribute on them that they should pay him tribute, five fruit products of their land, and he built Rôbêl[798] and Tamnâtârês [799]9. And he returned in peace, and made peace with them, and they became his servants, until the day that he and his sons went down into Egypt. 10. [800]And in the seventh year of this week (2149 A.M.) he sent Joseph to learn about the welfare of his brothers from his house to the land of Shechem, and he found them in the land of Dothan. 11. And they dealt treacherously with him, and formed a plot against him to slay him, but changing their minds, they sold him to Ishmaelite merchants, and they brought him down into Egypt, and they sold him to Potiphar, the eunuch[801] of Pharaoh, the chief of the cooks, [802]priest of the city of 'Êlêw. [803]12. And the sons of Jacob slaughtered a kid, and dipped the coat of Joseph in the blood, and sent (it) to Jacob their father on the tenth of the seventh month. 13. And he mourned all that night, for they had brought it to him in the evening, and he became feverish with mourning for his death, and he said: "An evil beast hath devoured Joseph"; and all the members of his house [mourned with him that day, and they] [804]were grieving and mourning with him all that day. 14. And his sons and his daughter rose up to comfort him, but he refused to be comforted for his son. 15. And on that day Bilhah heard that Joseph had perished, and she died mourning him, and she was living in †Qafrâtêf† [805]and Dinah also, his daughter, died after Joseph had perished. And there came these three mournings upon Israel in one month. 16. And they buried Bilhah over against the tomb of Rachel, and Dinah also, his daughter, they buried there. 17. And he mourned for Joseph one year, and did not cease, for he said "Let me go down to the grave mourning for my son." [806]18. For this reason [807]it is ordained for the children of Israel that they should afflict themselves[808] on the tenth of the seventh month--on the day that the news which made him weep for Joseph came to Jacob his father--that they should make atonement for themselves thereon with a young goat on the tenth of the seventh month, once a year, for their sins; for they had grieved the affection of their father regarding Joseph his son. 19. And this day hath been ordained that they should grieve thereon for their sins, and for all their transgressions and for all their errors, so that they might cleanse themselves on that day once a year.

The Wives of Jacob's Sons (xxxiv. 20-21).

20. And after Joseph perished, the sons of Jacob took unto themselves wives. The name of Reuben's wife is 'Adâ and the name of Simeon's wife is 'Adîbâ'a, a Canaanite; [809]and the name of Levi's wife is Mêlkâ, [810]of

---

[797] Six out of the seven kings are slain; so *Test. Judah* iv. [For the names see notes on 4 above.]

[798] Perhaps corrupt for "Arbael" = Arbela (1 Macc. ix. 2).

[799] = *Timnath-heres* (Jud. ii. 9); cf. 1 Macc. ix. 50.

[800] For 10-11 cf. Gen. xxxvii. 12 ff.

[801] Or "court official."

[802] So LXX of Gen. xxxvii. 36 (ρχιμάγειρος), misunderstanding the Hebrew (= "captain of the guard").

[803] *i. e.* Heliopolis (LXX λίου πόλεωσ, Gen. xli. 45, 50), *i. e.* "On."

[804] Bracketed as a dittograph.

[805] ? = "Kabrâtân," xxxii. 32

[806] Cf. Gen. xxxvii. 35.

[807] The reason here given for the institution of the Day of Atonement (cf. Lev. xvi.) seems to be peculiar to our Book.

[808] = "fast," cf. Lev. xvi. 31, etc.

[809] Cf. Gen. xlvi. 10. According to xxx. 7 ff. such a marriage (with a Canaanitish woman) was punishable with death.

[810] Cf. *Test. Levi* xi. i.

the daughters of Aram, of the seed of the sons of Terah; and the name of Judah's wife, Bêtasû'êl, [811]a Canaanite; and the name of Issachar's wife, Hêzaqâ; and the name of Zebulon's wife, †Nî'îmân†; [812]and the name of Dan's wife, 'Êglâ; and the name of Naphtali's wife, Rasû'û, of Mesopotamia; and the name of Gad's wife, Mâka; and the name of Asher's wife, 'Îjônâ; and the name of Joseph's wife, Asenath, [813]the Egyptian; and the name of Benjamin's wife, 'Îjasaka. 21. And Simeon repented, and took a second wife from Mesopotamia as his brothers.

Rebecca's Last Admonitions and Death (xxxv. 1-27).

XXXV. And in the first year of the first week of the forty-fifth jubilee (2157 A.M.) Rebecca called Jacob, her son, and commanded him regarding his father and regarding his brother, that he should honour them all the days of his life. 2. And Jacob said: "I will do everything as thou hast commanded me; for this thing will be honour and greatness to me, and righteousness before the Lord, that I should honour them. 3. And thou too, mother, knowest from the time I was born until this day, all my deeds and all that is in my heart, that I always think good concerning all. 4. And how should I not do this thing which thou hast commanded me, that I should honour my father and my brother! 5. Tell me, mother, what perversity hast thou seen in me and I shall turn away from it, and mercy will be upon me." 6. And she said unto him: "My son, I have not seen in thee all my days any perverse but (only) upright deeds. And yet I shall tell thee the truth, my son: I shall die this, year, and I shall not survive this year in my life; for I have seen in a dream the day of my death, that I should not live beyond a hundred and fifty-five years: and behold I have completed all the days of my life which I am to live." 7. And Jacob laughed at the words of his mother, because his mother had said unto him that she should die; and she was sitting opposite to him in possession of her strength, and she was not infirm in her strength; for she went in and out and saw, and her teeth were strong, and no ailment had touched her all the days of her life. 8. And Jacob said unto her: "Blessed am I, mother, if my days approach the days of thy life, and my strength remain with me thus as thy strength: and thou wilt not die, for thou art jesting idly with me regarding thy death." 9. And she went in to Isaac and said unto him: "One petition I make unto thee: make Esau swear that he will not injure Jacob, nor pursue him with enmity; for thou knowest Esau's thoughts that they are perverse from his youth, and there is no goodness in him; for he desireth after thy death to kill him. 10. And thou knowest all that he hath done since the day Jacob his brother went to Haran until this day; how he hath forsaken us with his whole heart, and hath done evil to us; thy flocks he hath taken to himself, and carried off all thy possessions from before thy face. 11. And when we implored and besought him for what was our own, he did as a man who was taking pity on us. 12. And he is bitter against thee because thou didst bless Jacob thy perfect and upright son; for there is no evil but only goodness in him, and since he came from Haran unto this day he hath not robbed us of aught, for he bringeth us everything in its season always, and rejoiceth with all his heart when we take at his hands, and he blesseth us, and hath not parted from us since he came from Haran until this day, and he remaineth with us continually at home honouring us." 13. And Isaac said unto her: "I, too, know and see the deeds of Jacob who is with us, how that with all his heart he honoureth us; but I loved Esau formerly more than Jacob, because he was the first-born; but now I love Jacob more than Esau, for he hath done manifold evil deeds, and there is no righteousness in him, for all his ways are unrighteousness and violence, [and there is no righteousness around him]. [814]14. And now my heart is troubled because of all his deeds, and neither he nor his seed is to be saved, for they are those who will be destroyed from the earth, and who will be rooted out from under heaven, for he hath forsaken the God of Abraham and gone after his wives and after their uncleanness and after their error, he and his children. 15. And thou dost bid me make him swear that he will not slay Jacob, his brother; even if he swear he will not abide by his oath, and he will not do good but evil only. 16. But if he desireth to slay Jacob, his brother, into Jacob's hands will he be given, and he will not escape from his hands, [for he will descend into his hands.] [815]17. And fear thou not on account of Jacob;

---

[811] Cf. xli. 7. The name goes back to "Bath-shua" (*i. e.* "daughter of Shua"); cf. *Test. Judah* viii. 2, etc.; cf. Gen. xxxviii. 2.

[812] The name is doubtful. Some Ethiopic MSS. omit it.

[813] Cf. Gen. xli. 45.

[814] ? a dittograph.

[815] ? bracketed words a gloss; cf. xxxvi. 9.

for the guardian [816]of Jacob is great and powerful and honoured, and praised more than the guardian of Esau." 18. And Rebecca sent and called Esau, and he came to her, and she said unto him: "I have a petition, my son, to make unto thee, and do thou promise to do it, my son." 19. And he said: "I will do everything that thou sayest unto me, and I will not refuse thy petition." 20. And she said unto him: "I ask you that the day I die, thou wilt take me in and bury me near Sarah, thy father's mother, and that thou and Jacob will love each other, and that neither will desire evil against the other, but mutual love only, and (so) ye will prosper, my sons, and be honoured in the midst of the land, and no enemy will rejoice over you, and ye will be a blessing and a mercy in the eyes of all those that love you." 21. And he said: "I will do all that thou hast told me, and I shall bury thee on the day thou diest near Sarah, my father's mother, as thou hast desired that her bones may be near thy bones. 22. And Jacob, my brother, also, I shall love above all flesh; for I have not a brother in all the earth but him only: and this is no great merit for me if I love him; for he is my brother, and we were sown together in thy body, and together came we forth from thy womb, and if I do not love my brother, whom shall I love? 23. And I, myself, beg thee to exhort Jacob concerning me and concerning my sons, for I know that he will assuredly be king over me and my sons, for on the day my father blessed him he made him the higher and me the lower. 24. And I swear unto thee that I shall love him, and not desire evil against him all the days of my life but good only." And he sware unto her regarding all this matter. 25. And she called Jacob before the eyes of Esau, and gave him commandment according to the words which she had spoken to Esau. 26. And he said: "I shall do thy pleasure; believe me that no evil will proceed from me or from my sons against Esau, and I shall be first in naught save in love only." 27. And they ate and drank, she and her sons that night, and she died, three jubilees and one week and one year old, on that night, and her two sons, Esau and Jacob, buried her in the double cave [817]near Sarah, their father's mother.

Isaac's Last Words and Admonitions: his Death. The Death of Leah (xxxvi. 1-24).

XXXVI. And in the sixth year of this week (2162 A.M.) Isaac called his two sons, Esau and Jacob, and they came to him, and he said unto them: "My sons, I am going the way of my fathers, to the eternal house [818]where my fathers are. 2. Wherefore bury me near Abraham my father, in the double cave in the field of Ephron the Hittite, where Abraham purchased a sepulchre to bury in; in the sepulchre which I digged for myself, there bury me. 3. And this I command you, my sons, that ye practise righteousness and uprightness on the earth, so that the Lord may bring upon you all that the Lord said that he would do to Abraham and to his seed. 4. And love one another, my sons, your brothers [819]as a man who loveth his own soul, and let each seek in what he may benefit his brother, and act together on the earth; and let them love each other as their own souls. 5. And concerning the question of idols, I command and admonish you to reject them and hate them, and love them not; for they are full of deception for those that worship them and for those that bow down to them. 6. Remember ye, my sons, the Lord God of Abraham your father, and how I too worshipped Him and served Him in righteousness and in joy, that He might multiply you and increase your seed as the stars of heaven in multitude, and establish you on the earth as the plant of righteousness [820]which will not be rooted out unto all the generations for ever. 7. And now I shall make you swear a great oath--for there is no oath which is greater than it by the name glorious and honoured and great and splendid and wonderful and mighty, which created the heavens and the earth and all things together--that ye will fear Him and worship Him. 8. And that each will love his brother with affection and righteousness, and that neither will desire evil against his brother from henceforth for ever all the days of your life, so that ye may prosper in all your deeds and not be destroyed. 9. And if either of you deviseth evil against his brother, know that from henceforth every one that deviseth evil against his brother will fall into his hand, and will be rooted out of the land of the living, and his seed will be destroyed from under heaven. 10. But on the day of turbulence and execration and indignation and anger, with flaming devouring fire as He burnt Sodom, so likewise will He burn his land and his city and all that is his, and

---

[816] ? the guardian-angel; cf. Matt. xviii. 10; Acts xii. 15; Heb. i. 14.

[817] *i. e.* Machpelah.

[818] Cf. Eccles. xii. 5 ("man goeth to his long home," lit. "to his eternal house").

[819] "Your brothers" probably a gloss.

[820] Cf. i. 16, xvi. 26, xxi. 24.

he will be blotted out of the book of the discipline of the children of men, and not be recorded in the book of life, [821]but in that which is appointed to destruction, and he will depart into eternal execration; so that their condemnation may be always renewed in hate and in execration and in wrath and in torment and in indignation and in plagues and in disease for ever. 11. I say and testify to you, my sons, according to the judgment which will come upon the man who wisheth to injure his brother." 12. And he divided all his possessions between the two on that day, and he gave the larger portion to him that was the first-born, and the tower and all that was about it, and all that Abraham possessed at the Well of the Oath. 13. And he said, "This larger portion I shall give to the first-born." 14. And Esau said, "I have sold to Jacob and given my birthright to Jacob; to him let it be given, and I have not a single word to say regarding it, for it is his." 15. And Isaac said, "May a blessing rest upon you, my sons, and upon your seed this day, for ye have given me rest, and my heart is not pained concerning the birthright, lest thou shouldest work wickedness on account of it. 16. May the Most High God [822]bless the man that worketh righteousness, him and his seed for ever." 17. And he ended commanding them and blessing them, and they ate and drank together before him, and he rejoiced because there was one mind between them, and they went forth from him and rested that day and slept. 18. And Isaac slept on his bed that day rejoicing; and he slept the eternal sleep, and died one hundred and eighty years old. He completed twenty-five weeks and five years; and his two sons Esau and Jacob buried him. [823]19. And Esau went to the land of Edom, to the mountains of Seir, and dwelt there. 20. And Jacob dwelt in the mountains of Hebron, in the tower of the land of the sojournings of his father Abraham, and he worshipped the Lord with all his heart and according to the visible commands according as He had divided the days of his generations. [824]21. And Leah his wife died in the fourth year of the second week of the forty-fifth jubilee (2167 A.M.), and he buried her in the double cave near Rebecca his mother, to the left of the grave of Sarah, his father's mother. 22. And all her sons and his sons came to mourn over Leah his wife with him, and to comfort him regarding her, for he was lamenting her. 23. For he loved her exceedingly after Rachel her sister died; for she was perfect and upright in all her ways and honoured Jacob, and all the days that she lived with him he did not hear from her mouth a harsh word, for she was gentle and peaceable and upright and honourable. 24. And he remembered all her deeds which she had done during her life, and he lamented her exceedingly; for he loved her with all his heart and with all his soul.

Esau and his Sons wage War with Jacob (xxxvii. 1-25).

XXXVII. [825]And on the day that Isaac the father of Jacob and Esau died, (2162 A.M.) the sons of Esau heard that Isaac had given the portion of the elder to his younger son Jacob and they were very angry. 2. And they strove with their father, saying: "Why hath thy father given Jacob the portion of the elder and passed over thee, although thou art the elder and Jacob the younger?" 3. And he said unto them "Because I sold my birthright to Jacob for a small mess of lentils; and on the day my father sent me to hunt and catch and bring him something that he should eat and bless me, he came with guile and brought my father food and drink, and my father blessed him and put me under his hand. 4. And now our father hath caused us to swear, me and him, that we shall not mutually devise evil, either against his brother, and that we shall continue in love and in peace each with his brother and not make our ways corrupt." [826]5. And they said unto him, "We shall not hearken unto thee to make peace with him; for our strength is greater than his strength, and we are more powerful than he; we shall go against him and slay him, and destroy him and his sons. And if thou wilt not go with us, we shall

---

[821] Cf. XXX. 22.

[822] This divine title occurs frequently in our Book, and in Ecclus. (48 times), and Daniel (13 times). In the Pentateuch, outside Gen. xiv. (where it occurs four times), it is only found twice. Its use was revived in *Ap. Bar.* (23 times), and in 4 Ezra.

[823] Cf. Gen. xxxv. 29.

[824] These commands had been made visible to Jacob on the seven tables which the angel had shown him in a vision; Cf. xxxii. 21.

[825] The legend of the wars between the sons of Jacob and Esau contained in chaps. xxxviixxxviii. here seems to be ancient. It is also found in *Test. Judah* ix. and in the Jewish Midrashic literature. Our text contains the oldest form.

[826] This representation gives a favourable view of Esau's own attitude. In the later form of the legend (in the *Yal   ut*) this is altered to Esau's disadvantage.

do hurt to thee also. 6. And now hearken unto us: Let us send to Aram [827]and Philistia [828]and Moab and Ammon, [829]and let us choose for ourselves chosen men who are ardent for battle, and let us go against him and do battle with him, and let us exterminate him from the earth before he groweth strong." 7. And their father said unto them, "Do not go and do not make war with him lest ye fall before him." 8. And they said unto him, "This too, is exactly thy mode of action from thy youth until this day, and thou art putting thy neck under his yoke. We shall not hearken to these words." 9. And they sent to Aram, and to 'Adurâm[830] to the friend of their father, and they hired along with them one thousand fighting men, chosen men of war. 10. And there came to them from Moab and from the children of Ammon, those who were hired, one thousand chosen men, and from Philistia, one thousand chosen men of war, and from Edom [831]and from the Horites one thousand chosen fighting men, and from the Kittim [832]mighty men of war. 11. And they said unto their father: "Go forth with them and lead them, else we shall slay thee." 12. And he was filled with wrath and indignation on seeing that his sons were forcing him to go before (them) to lead them against Jacob his brother. 13. But afterward he remembered all the evil which lay hidden in his heart against Jacob his brother; and he remembered not the oath which he had sworn to his father and to his mother that he would devise no evil all his days against Jacob his brother. 14. And notwithstanding all this, Jacob knew not that they were coming against him to battle, and he was mourning for Leah, his wife, until they approached very near to the tower with four thousand warriors and chosen men of war. 15. And the men of Hebron sent to him saying, "Behold thy brother hath come against thee, to fight thee, with four thousand girt with the sword, and they carry shields and weapons"; for they loved Jacob more than Esau. So they told him; for Jacob was a more liberal and merciful man than Esau. 16. But Jacob would not believe until they came very near to the tower. 17. And he closed the gates of the tower; and he stood on the battlements and spake to his brother Esau and said, "Noble is the comfort wherewith thou hast come to comfort me for my wife who hath died. Is this the oath that thou didst swear to thy father and again to thy mother before they died? Thou hast broken the oath, and on the moment that thou didst swear to thy father wast thou condemned." 18. And then Esau answered and said unto him, "Neither the children of men nor the beasts of the earth have any oath of righteousness which in swearing they have sworn (an oath valid) for ever; but every day they devise evil one against another, and how each may slay his adversary and foe. 19. And thou dost hate me and my children for ever. And there is no observing the tie of brotherhood with thee. 20. Hear these words which I declare unto thee, If the boar can change its skin and make its bristles as soft as wool, Or if it can cause horns to sprout forth on its head like the horns of a stag or of a sheep, Then shall I observe the tie of brotherhood with thee. [833] [And if the breasts separated themselves from their mother; for thou hast not been a brother to me.] [834]

21.And if the wolves make peace with the lambs so as not to devour or do them violence, And if their hearts are towards them for good, Then there will be peace in my heart towards thee.

22.And if the lion becometh the friend of the ox and maketh peace with him,

And if he is bound under one yoke with him and plougheth with him,

Then shall I make peace with thee.

---

[827] The peoples mentioned here and in the context nearly all played a prominent part in the campaigns of the Maccabees. "Aram," *i. e.* Syria, was, of course, the suzerain power in their day, who sought to oppress the Jews, and whose yoke was ultimately entirely thrown off.

[828] Cf. xxiv. 28 (note).

[829] Cf. 1 Macc. v. 6-8.

[830] An Aramaean; cf. xxxviii. 3.

[831] Cf. 1 Macc. v. 3, 65 (also iv. 29, 61).

[832] Cf. xxiv. 28.

[833] For the construction of such sayings cf. the rebuke administered to A   iba (when the latter recognized Bar-Kokba as the Messiah) by Jochanan ben Torta: "Sooner shall grass grow from thy beard, A   iba, than that Messiah should appear." The "boar" may symbolize Esau.

[834] Charles thinks the bracketed words may be out of place or corrupt.

23.And when the raven becometh white as the râzâ, [835]

Then know that -I have loved thee

And shall make peace with thee.

Thou shalt be rooted out,

And thy sons shall be rooted out,

And there shall be no peace for thee."

24. And when Jacob saw that he was (so) evilly disposed towards him with his heart, and with all his soul as to slay him, and that he had come springing like the wild boar which cometh upon the spear that pierceth and killeth it, and recoileth not from it; 25. Then he spake to his own and to his servants that they should attack him and all his companions.

The War between Jacob and Esau at the Tower of Hebron. The Death of Esau and Overthrow of his Forces (xxxviii. 1-4).

XXXVIII. And after that Judah spake to Jacob, his father, and said unto him: "Bend thy bow, father, and send forth thy arrows and cast down the adversary and slay the enemy; and mayest thou have the power, for we shall not slay thy brother, for he is such as thou, and he is like thee: let us give him (this) honour." 2. Then Jacob bent his bow and sent forth the arrow and struck Esau, his brother, (on his right breast) and slew him. [836]3. And again he sent forth an arrow and struck 'Adôrân the Aramaean, [837]on the left breast, and drove him backward and slew him. 4. And then went forth the sons of Jacob, they and their servants, dividing themselves into companies on the four sides of the tower. 5. And Judah went forth in front, and Naphtali and Gad with him and fifty servants with him on the south side of the tower, and they slew all they found before them, and not one individual of them escaped. 6. And Levi and Dan and Asher went forth on the east side of the tower, and fifty (men) with them, and they slew the fighting men of Moab and Ammon. 7. And Reuben and Issachar and Zebulon went forth on the north side of the tower, and fifty men with them, and they slew the fighting men of the Philistines. 8. And Simeon and Benjamin and Enoch, Reuben's son, went forth on the west side of the tower, and fifty (men) with them, and they slew of Edom and of the Horites four hundred men, stout warriors; and six hundred fled, and four of the sons of Esau fled with them, and left their father lying slain, as he had fallen on the hill which is in 'Adûrâm. [838]9. And the sons of Jacob pursued after them to the mountains of Seir. And Jacob buried his brother on the hill which is in 'Adûrâm, and he returned to his house. 10. And the sons of Jacob pressed hard upon the sons of Esau in the mountains of Seir, and bowed their necks so that they became servants of the sons of Jacob. 11. And they sent to their father (to inquire) whether they should make peace with them or slay them. 12. And Jacob sent word to his sons that they should make peace, and they made peace with them, and placed the yoke of servitude upon them, so that they paid tribute to Jacob and to his sons always. 13. And they continued to pay tribute to Jacob until the day that he went down into Egypt. [839]14. And the sons of Edom have not got quit of the yoke of servitude which the twelve sons of Jacob had imposed on them until this day.[840]

The Kings of Edom (xxxviii. 15-24; cf. Gen. xxxvi. 31-39)

---

[835] "A large white bird which eats grasshoppers" (Isenberg, quoted by Charles).

[836] According to later Jewish tradition Esau was killed by Chushim, son of Dan, at the cave of Machpelah when Jacob's corpse had arrived there for burial; cf. *Pirke de R. Eliezer* xxxix. (towards end).

[837] Cf. xxxvii. 9.

[838] A city in Idumaea (Edom) identical with the "Adora" mentioned in 1 Macc. xiii. 20. It was captured by John Hyrcanus and forced to accept circumcision. in *Test. Judah* ix. 3 the name appears as *Anoniram*.

[839] For 11-13 cf. *Test. Judah* ix. 7-8.

[840] *i. e.* the author's day. Edom was finally made tributary to Israel by John Hyrcanus.

15. And these are the kings that reigned in Edom before there reigned any king over the children of Israel [until this day] in the land of Edom. 16. And Bâlâq, [841]the son of Beor, reigned in Edom, and the name of his city was Danâbâ. [842]17. And Bâlâq died, and Jobab, the son of Zârâ of Bôsêr,[843] reigned in his stead. 18. And Jobab died, and 'Asâm, [844]of the land of Têmân, reigned in his stead. 19. And 'Asâm died, and 'Adâth, [845]the son of Barad, [846]who slew Midian in the field of Moab, reigned in his stead, and the name of his city was Avith. 20. And 'Adâth died, and Salman, [847]from 'Amâsêqâ, [848]reigned in his stead. 21. And Salman died, and Saul of Râ'abôth [849](by the) river, reigned in his stead. 22. And Saul died, and Ba'êlûnân, [850]the son of Achbor, reigned in his stead.

23. And Ba'êlûnân, the son of Achbor, died, and 'Adâth [851]reigned in his stead, and the name of his wife was Maiabîth, [852]the daughter of Mâarat, [853]the daughter of Mêtabêdzâ'ab. [854]24. These are the kings who reigned in the land of Edom.

Joseph's Service with Potiphar; his Purity and Imprisonment (xxxix. 1-13; cf. Gen. xxxix.).

XXXIX. And Jacob dwelt in the land of his father's sojournings in the land of Canaan. 2. These are the generations of Jacob. And Joseph was seventeen years old [855]when they took him down into the land of Egypt, and Potiphar, an eunuch of Pharaoh, the chief cook [856]bought him. 3. And he set Joseph over all his house, and the blessing of the Lord came upon the house of the Egyptian on account of Joseph, and the Lord prospered him in all that he did. 4. And the Egyptian committed everything into the hands of Joseph; for he saw that the Lord was with him, and that the Lord prospered him in all that he did. 5. And Joseph's appearance was comely and very beautiful was his appearance, and his master's wife lifted up her eyes and saw Joseph, and she loved him, and besought him to lie with her. 6. But he did not surrender his soul, and he remembered the Lord and

---

[841] LXX (Gen. xxxvi. 22) Βάλακ= Heb. *Belă*.

[842] MT *Dinhabah*.

[843] MT *Bozrah*.

[844] LXX σόμ, MT *Husham*.

[845] MT *Hadad*.

[846] LXX Βαράθ, MT *Bedad*.

[847] LXX Σαλαμά, MT *Samlah*.

[848] MT *Masrekah*.

[849] LXX οωβώθ, MT *Rehoboth*.

[850] LXX Βαλαεννάν, MT *Baal-hanan*.

[851] MT *Hadar*.

[852] MT *Mehetabel*.

[853] MT *Matred* (LXX Ματαρείθ).

[854] MT *Me-zahab*.

[855] Cf. Gen. xxxvii. 2.

[856] Cf. xxxiv. ii (note).

the words which Jacob, his father, used to read from amongst the words of Abraham, [857]that no man should commit fornication with a woman who hath a husband; that for him the punishment of death hath been ordained in the heavens before the Most High God, and the sin will be recorded against him in the eternal books continually before the Lord. 7. And Joseph remembered these words and refused to lie with her. 8. And she besought him for a year, but he refused and would not listen. 9. But she embraced him and held him fast in the house in order to force him to lie with her, and closed the doors of the house and held him fast; but he left his garment in her hands and broke through the door and fled without from her presence. 10. And the woman saw that he would not lie with her, and she calumniated him in the presence of his lord, saying: "Thy Hebrew servant, whom thou lovest, sought to force me so that he might lie with me; and it came to pass when I lifted up my voice that he fled and left his garment in my hands when I held him, and he brake through the door." 11. And the Egyptian saw the garment of Joseph and the broken door, and heard the words of his wife, and cast Joseph into prison into the place where the prisoners were kept whom the king imprisoned. 12. And he was there in the prison; and the Lord gave Joseph favour in the sight of the chief of the prison guards and compassion before him, for he saw that the Lord was with him, and that the Lord made all that he did to prosper. 13. And he committed all things into his hands, and the chief of -the prison guards knew of nothing that was with him, [858]for Joseph did everything, and the Lord perfected it.

Joseph interprets the Dreams of the Chief Butler and the Chief Baker (xxxix. 1418; cf. Gen. xl.).,

14. And he remained there two years. [859]And in those days Pharaoh, king of Egypt, was wroth against his two eunuchs, against the chief butler and against the chief baker, and he put them in ward in the house of the chief cook,[860] in the prison where Joseph was kept. 15. And the chief of the prison guards appointed Joseph to serve them; and he served before them. 16. And they both dreamed a dream, the chief butler and the chief baker, and they told it to Joseph. 17. And as he interpreted to them so it befell them, and Pharaoh restored the chief butler to his office, and the (chief) baker he slew, as Joseph had interpreted to them. 18. But the chief butler forgot Joseph in the prison, although he had informed him what would befall him, and did not remember to inform Pharaoh how Joseph had told him for he forgot.

Pharaoh's Dreams and their Interpretation. Joseph's Elevation and Marriage (xl. 1-13; cf. Gen. xli.).

XL. And in those days Pharaoh dreamed two dreams in one night concerning a famine which was to be in all the land, and he awoke from his sleep and called all the interpreters of dreams that were in Egypt, and magicians, and told them his two dreams, and they were not able to declare (them). 2. And then the chief butler remembered Joseph and spake of him to the king, and he brought him forth from the prison, and he told his two dreams before him. 3. And he said before Pharaoh that his two dreams were one, and he said unto him: "Seven years will come (in which there will be) plenty over all the land of Egypt, and after that seven years of famine, such a famine as hath not been in all the land. 4. And now let Pharaoh appoint overseers[861] in all the land of Egypt, and let them store up food in every city throughout the days of the years of plenty, and there will be food for the seven years of famine, and the land will not perish through the famine, for it will be very severe." 5. And the Lord gave Joseph favour and mercy in the eyes of Pharaoh, and Pharaoh said unto his servants: "We shall not find such a wise and discreet man as this man, for the spirit of the Lord is with him." 6. And he appointed him the second in all his kingdom and gave him authority over all Egypt, and caused him to ride in the second chariot of Pharaoh. 7. And he clothed him with byssus garments, and he put a gold chain upon his

---

[857] Cf. xx. 4, xxv. 7.

[858] Cf. Gen. xxxix. 8.

[859] Cf. Gen. xli. 1.

[860] Cf. xxxiv. 11 (note).

[861] Cf. Gen. xli. 34.

neck, and (a herald) proclaimed before him "'Êl 'Êl wa' Abîrĕr," [862]and he placed a ring on his hand and made him ruler over all his house, and magnified him, and said unto him: "Only on the throne shall I be greater than thou." 8. And Joseph ruled over all the land of Egypt, and all the princes of Pharaoh, and all his servants, and all who did the king's business loved him, for he walked in uprightness, for he was without pride and arrogance, and he had no respect of persons, and did not accept gifts, but he judged in uprightness all the people of the land. 9. And the land of Egypt was at peace before Pharaoh because of Joseph, for the Lord was with him, and gave him favour and mercy for all his generations before all those who knew him and those who heard concerning him, and Pharaoh's kingdom was well ordered, and there was no Satan [863]and no evil person (therein). 10. And the king called Joseph's name Sĕphân îphâns, [864]and gave Joseph to wife the daughter of Potiphar, the daughter of the priest of Heliopolis, the chief cook. [865]11. And on the day that Joseph stood before Pharaoh he was thirty years old [when he stood before Pharaoh]. 12. And in that year Isaac died. And it came to pass as Joseph had said in the interpretation of his two dreams, according as he had said it, there were seven years of plenty over all the land of Egypt, and the land of Egypt produced abundantly, one measure (producing) eighteen hundred measures. 13. And Joseph gathered food into every city until they were full of corn until they could no longer count and measure it for its multitude.

Judah's Incest with Tamar; his Repentance and Forgiveness (xli. 1-28; Cf. Gen. xxxviii.).

2 XLI. And in the forty-fifth jubilee, in the second week, (and) in the second year, (2165 A.M.) Judah took for his first-born Er, a wife from the daughters of Aram, [866]named Tamar. 2. But he hated, and did not lie with her, because his mother was of the daughters of Canaan, and he wished to take him a wife of the kinsfolk of his mother, but Judah, his father, would not permit him. 3. And this Er, the first-born of Judah, was wicked, and the Lord slew him. 4. And Judah said unto Onan, his brother: "Go in unto thy brother's wife and perform the duty of a husband's brother unto her, [867]and raise up seed unto thy brother." 5. And Onan knew that the seed would not be his, (but) his brother's only, and he went into the house of his brother's wife, and spilt the seed on the ground, and he was wicked in the eyes of the Lord, and He slew him. 6. And Judah said unto Tamar, his daughter-inlaw: "Remain in thy father's house as a widow till Shelah my son be grown up, and I shall give thee to him to wife." 7. And he grew up; but Bêdsû'êl, [868]the wife of Judah, did not permit her son Shelah to marry. And Bêdsû'êl, the wife of Judah, died in the fifth year of this week. 8. And in the sixth year Judah went up to shear his sheep at Timnah. And they told Tamar: "Behold thy father-in-law goeth up to Timnah to shear his A.M. sheep." 9. And she put off her widow's clothes, and put on a veil, and adorned herself, and sat in the gate adjoining the way to Timnah. 10. And as Judah was going along he found her, and thought her to be an harlot, and he said unto her: "Let me come in unto thee"; and she said unto him: "Come in," and he went in. 11. And she said unto him: "Give me my hire"; and he said unto her: "I have nothing in my hand save my ring that is on my finger, and my necklace, and my staff which is in my hand." 12. And she said unto him: "Give them to me until thou dost send me my hire"; and he said unto her: "I will send unto thee a kid of the goats"; and he gave them to her, (and he went in unto her,) and she conceived by him. 13. And Judah went unto his sheep, and she went to her father's house. 14. And Judah sent a kid of the goats by the hand of his shepherd, an Adullamite, and he found her not; and he asked the people of the place, saying: "Where is the harlot who was here?" And they said unto him: "There is no harlot here with us." 15. And he returned and informed him, and

---

[862] 'Êl 'Êl wa' Abîrĕr = Heb. 'el 'el wa'ăbîr 'el, "God, God, the mighty one of God." This is a peculiar amplification of the Hebrew 'abrēk (R.V. "bow the knee ") of Gen. xli. 43. "Mighty one of God" may be a technical term for a great magician; cf. Acts viii. 10.

[863] A sign of great felicity; cf. xxiii. 29.

[864] *i. e.* Zaphenath-paneah (Gen. xli. 45).

[865] The author identifies Potiphar of Gen. xxxvii. 36 with Potiphera of Gen. xli. 45. In later Jewish legend Asenath (Joseph's wife) is represented as a Jewess, a daughter of Dinah, who was brought up in the family of Potiphera (cf. *Pirke de R. Eliezer* xxxviii.). The difficulty of Joseph's heathen marriage is thus removed.

[866] Cf. *Test. Judah* x. ("from Mesopotamia").

[867] Cf. Gen. xxxviii. 8; Deut. xxv. 5.

[868] *i. e.* Bathshua; Cf. xxxiv. 20.

said unto him that he had not found her; "I asked the people of the place, and they said unto me: 'There is no harlot here.'" And he said: "Let her keep (them) lest we become a cause of derision." 16. And when she had completed three months, it was manifest that she was with child, and they told Judah, saying: "Behold Tamar, thy daughter-in-law, is with child by whoredom." 17. And Judah went to the house of her father, and said unto her father and her brothers: "Bring her forth, and let them burn her, [869]for she hath wrought uncleanness in Israel." 18. And it came to pass when they brought her forth to bum her that she sent to her father-in-law the ring and the necklace, and the staff, saying: "Discern whose are these, for by him am I with child." 19. And Judah acknowledged, and said: "Tamar is more righteous than I am. And therefore let them burn her not." 20. And for that reason she was not given to Shelah, and he did not again approach her. 21. And after that she bare two sons, Perez and Zerah, in the seventh year of this second week. (2170 A.M.) 22. And thereupon the seven years of fruitfulness were accomplished, of which Joseph spake to Pharaoh. [870]23. And Judah acknowledged that the deed which he had done was evil, for he had lain with his daughter-in-law, and he esteemed it hateful in his eyes, and he acknowledged that he had transgressed and gone astray; for he had uncovered the skirt of his son, and he began to lament and to supplicate before the Lord because of his transgression. 24. And we told him in a dream that it was forgiven him because he supplicated earnestly, and lamented, and did not again commit it. 25. And he received forgiveness because he turned from his sin and from his ignorance, for he transgressed greatly before our God; and every one that acteth thus, every one who lieth with his mother-in-law, let them burn him with fire that he may bum therein, [871]for there is uncleanness and pollution upon them; with fire let them bum them. 26. And do thou command the children of Israel that there be no uncleanness amongst them, for every one who lieth with his daughter-in-law [872]or with his mother-in-law hath wrought uncleanness; with fire let them bum the man who hath lain with her, and likewise the woman, and He will turn away wrath and punishment from Israel. 27. And unto Judah we said that his two sons had not lain with her, and for this reason his seed was established for a second generation, and would not be rooted out. 28. For in singleness of eye he had gone and sought for punishment, namely, according to the judgment of Abraham,[873] which he had commanded his sons, Judah had sought to burn her with fire.

The Two Journeys of the Sons of Jacob to Egypt (xlii. 1-25; cf. Gen. xlii., xliii.).

XLII. And in the first year of the third week of the forty-fifth jubilee (2171 A.M.) the famine began to come into the land, and the rain refused to be given to the earth, for none whatever fell. 2. And the earth grew barren, but in the land of Egypt there was food, for Joseph had gathered the seed of the land in the seven years of plenty and had preserved it. [874]3. And the Egyptians came to Joseph that he might give them food, and he opened the storehouses where was the grain of the first year, and he sold it to the people of the land for gold. [875]4. (Now the famine was very sore in the land of Canaan), and Jacob heard that there was food in Egypt, and he sent his ten sons that they should procure food for him in Egypt; but Benjamin he did not send, and (the ten sons of Jacob) arrived (in Egypt) among those that went (there.) 5. And Joseph recognized them, but they did not recognize him, and he spake unto them and questioned them, and he said unto them: "Are ye not spies, and have ye not come to explore the approaches of the land?" And he put them in ward. 6. And after that he set them free again, and detained Simeon alone and sent off his nine brothers. 7. And he filled their sacks with corn, and he put their gold in their sacks, and they did not know. 8. And he commanded them to bring their younger brother, for they had told him their father was living and their younger brother. 9. And they went up from the land of Egypt and they came to the land of Canaan; and they told their father all that had befallen

---

[869] The punishment appointed for such an offence on the part of a priest's daughter (Lev. xxi. 9); cf. xxx. 7 above. According to the Targum (Ps.-Jon.), on Gen. xxxviii. 6, 24, Tamar was the daughter of a priest.

[870] Cf. Gen. xli. 53.

[871] Cf. Lev. xx. 14.

[872] Cf. Lev. xviii. 15, XX. 12 (mode of death not specified; but Gen. xxxviii. 24 presupposes burning by fire).

[873] Cf. xx. 4 (note).

[874] Cf. Gen. xli. 54.

[875] Cf. Gen. xli. 56.

them, and how the lord of the country had spoken roughly to them, and had seized Simeon till they should bring Benjamin. 10. And Jacob said: "Me have ye bereaved of my children! Joseph is not and Simeon also is not, and ye will take Benjamin away. On me hath your wickedness come." [876] 11. And he said: "My son will not go down with you lest perchance he fall sick; for their mother gave birth to two sons, and one hath perished, and this one also ye will take from me. If perchance he took a fever on the road, [877] ye would bring down my old age with sorrow unto death." 12. For he saw that their money had been returned to every man in his sack, and for this reason he feared to send him. 13. And the famine increased and became sore in the land of Canaan, and in all lands save in the land of Egypt, for many of the children of the Egyptians had stored up their seed for food from the time when they saw Joseph gathering seed together and putting it in storehouses and preserving it for the years of famine. 14. And the people of Egypt fed themselves thereon during the first year of their famine. 15. But when Israel saw that the famine was very sore in the land, and there was no deliverance, he said unto his sons: "Go again, and procure food for us that we die not." 16. And they said: "We shall not go; unless our youngest brother go with us, we shall not go." 17. And Israel saw that if he did not send him with them, they should all perish by reason of the famine. 18. And Reuben said: "Give him into my hand, and if I do not bring him back to thee, slay my two sons instead of his soul." And he said unto him He will not go with thee." 19. And Judah came near and said: "Send him with me, and if I do not bring him back to thee, let me bear the blame before thee all the days of my life." 20. And he sent him with them in the second year of this week on the first day of the month, and they came to the land of Egypt with all those who 2172 went, and (they had) presents in their hands, stacte and almonds and terebinth nuts and A.M. pure honey. 21. And they went and stood before Joseph, and he saw Benjamin his brother, and he knew him, and said unto them: "Is this your youngest brother?" And they said unto him: "It is he." And he said: "The Lord be gracious to thee, my son!" 22. And he sent him into his house and he brought forth Simeon unto them and he made a feast for them, and they presented to him the gift which they had brought in their hands. 23. And they ate before him and he gave them all a portion, but the portion of Benjamin was seven times larger than that of any of theirs. 24. And they ate and drank and arose and remained with their asses. 25. And Joseph devised a plan whereby he might learn their thoughts as to whether thoughts of peace prevailed amongst them, and he said to the steward who was over his house: "Fill all their sacks with food, and return their money unto them into their vessels, and my cup, the silver cup out of which I drink, put it in the sack of the youngest, and send them away." [878]

Joseph finally tests his Brethren, and then makes himself known to them (xliii. 124; cf. Gen. xliv., xlv.).

XLIII. And he did as Joseph had told him, and filled all their sacks for them with food and put their money in their sacks, and put the cup in Benjamin's sack. 2. And early in the morning they departed, and it came to pass that, when they had gone from thence, Joseph said unto the steward of his house: "Pursue them, run and seize them, saying, 'For good ye have requited me with evil; you have stolen from me the silver cup out of which my lord drinks.' And bring back to me their youngest brother, and fetch (him) quickly before I go forth to my seat of judgment." 3. And he ran after them and said unto them according to these words. 4. And they said unto him: "God forbid that thy servants should do this thing, and steal from the house of thy lord any utensil, and the money also which we found in our sacks the first time, we thy servants brought back from the land of Canaan. 5. How then should we steal any utensil? Behold here are we and our sacks; search, and wherever thou findest the cup in the sack of any man amongst us, let him be slain, and we and our asses will serve thy lord." 6. And he said unto them: "Not so, the man with whom I find, him only shall I take as a servant, and ye will return in peace unto your house." 7. And as he was searching in their vessels, beginning with the eldest and ending with the youngest, it was found in Benjamin's sack. 8. And they rent their garments, and laded their asses, and returned to the city and came to the house of Joseph, and they all bowed themselves on their faces to the ground before him. 9. And Joseph said unto them: "Ye have done evil." And they said: "What shall we say and how shall we defend ourselves? Our lord hath discovered the transgression of his servants; behold we are the servants of our lord, and our asses also." 10. And Joseph said unto them: "I too fear the Lord; as for you, go ye to your homes and let your brother be my servant, for ye have done evil.. Know ye not that a man

---

[876] ? An interpretation of Gen. xlii. 36 (" All these things are against me ").

[877] "If mischief befall him by the way in the which ye go" (Gen. xlii. 38).

[878] Cf. Gen. xliv. 1, 2.

delighteth in his cup as I with this cup? [879]And yet ye have stolen it from me." 11. And Judah said: "O my lord, let thy servant, I pray thee, speak a word in my lord's ear; two brothers did thy servant's mother bear to our father; one went away and was lost, and hath not been found, and he alone is left of his mother, and thy servant our father loveth him, and his life also is bound up with the life of this (lad). 12. And it will come to pass, when we go to thy servant our father, and the lad is not with us, that he will die, and we shall bring down our father with sorrow unto death. 13. Now rather let me, thy servant, abide instead of the boy as a bondsman unto my lord, and let the lad go with his brethren, for I became surety for him at the hand of thy servant our father, and if I do not bring him back, thy servant will bear the blame to our father for ever." 14. And Joseph saw that they were all accordant in goodness one with another, and he could not refrain himself, and he told them that he was Joseph. 15. And he conversed with them in the Hebrew tongue[880] and fell on their neck and wept. But they knew him not and they began to weep. 16. And he said unto them: "Weep not over me, but hasten and bring my father to me; and ye see that it is my mouth that speaketh and the eyes of my brother Benjamin see. 17. For behold this is the second year of the famine, and there are still five years without harvest or fruit of trees or ploughing. 18. Come down quickly ye and your households, so that ye perish not through the famine, and do not be grieved for your possessions, for the Lord sent me before you to set things in order that many people might live. 19. And tell my father that I am still alive, and ye, behold, ye see that the Lord hath made me as a father to Pharaoh, and ruler over his house and over all the land of Egypt. 20. And tell my father of all my glory, and all the riches and glory that the Lord hath given Me." 21. And by the command of the mouth of Pharaoh he gave them chariots and provisions for the way, and he gave them all many-coloured raiment and silver. 22. And to their father he sent raiment and silver and ten asses which carried com, and he sent them away. 23. And they went up and told their father that Joseph was alive, and was measuring out corn to all the nations of the earth, and that he was ruler over all the land of Egypt. 24. And their father did not believe it, for he was beside himself in his mind; but when he saw the wagons which Joseph had sent, the life of his spirit revived, and he said: "It is enough for me if Joseph liveth; I will go down and see him before I die."

Jacob celebrates the Feast of First-fruits and journeys to Egypt. List of his Descendants. (xliv. 1-34; cf. Gen. xlvi. 1-28).

XLIV. And Israel took his journey from †Haran† [881]from his house on the new moon of the third month, and he went on the way of the Well of the Oath, [882]and he offered a sacrifice to the God of his father Isaac on the seventh of this month. 2. And Jacob remembered the dream that he had seen at Bethel, [883]and he feared to go down into Egypt. 3. And while he was thinking of sending word to Joseph to come to him, and that he would not go down, he remained there seven days, if perchance he should see a vision as to whether he should remain or go down. 4. And he celebrated the harvest festival of the first-fruits [884]with old grain, for in all the land of Canaan there was not a handful of seed (in the land), for the famine was over all the beasts and cattle and birds, and also over man. 5. And on the sixteenth the Lord appeared unto him, and said unto him, "Jacob, Jacob"; and he said, "Here am I." And He said unto him: "I am the God of thy fathers, the God of Abraham and Isaac; fear not to go down into Egypt, for I will there make of thee a great nation. 6. I shall go down with thee, and I shall bring thee up[885] (again), and in this land wilt thou be buried, and Joseph will put his hands upon thy eyes. Fear not; go down into Egypt." 7. And his sons rose up, and his sons' sons, and they placed their father and their possessions upon wagons. 8. And Israel rose up from the Well of the Oath on the sixteenth of this third

---

[879] Gen. xliv. 15 ("Know ye not that such a man as I can indeed divine?"). The change in our text may be deliberate.

[880] A Midrashic touch; so *Bereshith rabba* xciii.

[881] Probably corrupt for "Hebron"; cf. Gen. xxxvii. 14.

[882] Beersheba.

[883] Cf. xxvii. 22.

[884] Cf. Gen. xlvi. i (the feast was celebrated on the 15th of the third month).

[885] Cf. xxvii. 24, xxxii. 23.

month, and he went to the land of Egypt. 9. And Israel sent Judah before him to his son Joseph to examine[886] the Land of Goshen, for Joseph had told his brothers that they should come and dwell there that they might be near him.

10. And this was the goodliest (land) in the land of Egypt, and near to him, for all (of them) and also for the cattle. 11. And these are the names of the sons of Jacob who went into Egypt with Jacob their father. 12. [887]Reuben, the first-born of Israel; and these are the names of his sons: Enoch, and Pallu, and Hezron and Carmi--five. [888]13. Simeon and his sons; and these are the names of his sons: Jemuel, and Jamin, and Ohad, and Jachin, and Zohar, and Shaul, the son of the Zephathite [889]woman--seven. 14. Levi and his sons; and these are the names of his sons: Gershon, and Kohath, and Merari--four. 15. Judah and his sons; and these are the names of his sons: Shela, and Perez, and Zerah--four. 16. Issachar and his sons; and these are the names of his sons: Tola, and Phûa, [890]and Jâsûb, [891]and Shimron--five. 17. Zebulon and his sons; and these are the names of his sons: Sered, and Elon, and Jahleel--four. 18. And these are the sons of Jacob, and their sons, whom Leah bore to Jacob in Mesopotamia, six, and their one sister, Dinah: and all the souls of the sons of Leah, and their sons, who went with Jacob their father into Egypt, were twenty-nine, and Jacob their father being with them, they were thirty. 19. And the sons of Zilpah, Leah's handmaid, the wife of Jacob, whom she bore unto Jacob, Gad and Asher. 20. And these are the names of their sons who went with him into Egypt: the sons of Gad: Ziphion, and Haggi, and Shuni, and Ezbon, (and Eri) and Areli, and Arodi--eight. 21. And the sons of Asher: Imnah, and Ishvah, (and Ishvi), and Beriah, and Serah, their one sister--six. 22. All the souls were fourteen, and all those of Leah were forty-four. 23. And the sons of Rachel, the wife of Jacob: Joseph and Benjamin. 24. And there were born to Joseph in Egypt before his father came into Egypt, those whom Asenath, daughter of Potiphar priest of Heliopolis bare unto him, Manasseh, and Ephraim--three. 25. And the sons of Benjamin: Bela and Becher, and Ashbel, Gera, and Naaman, and Ehi, and Rosh, and Muppim, and Huppim, and Ard--eleven. 26. And all the souls of Rachel were fourteen. 27. And the sons of Bilhah, the handmaid of Rachel, the wife of Jacob, whom she bare to Jacob, were Dan and Naphtali. 28. And these are the names of their sons who went with them into Egypt. And the sons of Dan were Hushim, and Sâmôn, and Asûdî, and 'Îjâka, and Salômôn--six. 29. And they died the year in which they entered into Egypt, and there was left to Dan Hushim alone. [892]30. And these are the names of the sons of Naphtali: Jahziel, and Guni, and Jezer, and Shallum, and 'Îv. [893]31. And 'Îv, who was born after the years of famine, died in Egypt. 32. And all the souls of Rachel were twenty-six. 33. And all the souls of Jacob which went into Egypt were seventy souls. These are his children and his children's children, in all seventy; but five died in Egypt before Joseph, and had no children. 34. And in the land of Canaan two sons of Judah died, Er and Onan, and they had no children, and the children of Israel buried those who perished, and they were reckoned among the seventy Gentile nations.

Joseph receives Jacob. The Land of Egypt is acquired for Pharaoh. Jacob's Death and Burial (xlv. 1-16; cf. Gen. xlvi. 28 ff., xlvii. 11 ff.).

XLV. And Israel went into the country of Egypt, 2 into the land of Goshen, on the new moon of the fourth month, in the second year of the third week of the forty-fifth jubilee. (2172 A.M)2. And Joseph went to meet his father Jacob, to the land of Goshen, and he fell on his father's neck and wept. 3. And Israel said unto Joseph:

---

886 "To show the way" (Gen. xlvi. 28).

887 The number 70, according to our text, includes Jacob with his descendants. Another reckoning makes up the number by excluding Jacob himself: cf. Exod. i. 5 and Gen. xlvi. 15, 18, 21, 25, 27. The number 75, in Acts vii. 14. is due to the LXX of Exod. i. 5 and Deut. X. 22. There are certain differences in detail between the list in our text and the details given in Genesis; see Charles *ad loc.*

888 The father is included in each case.

889 *i. e.* a native of the Canaanite city Zephath; cf. Judg. i. 17.

890 So LXX, Sam. and other versions. MT *Puvah* (Gen. xlvi. 13).

891 So Sam. (Gen. xlvi. 13) and LXX = MT *Iob.*

892 in Gen. xlvi. 23 "Hushim" (MT) is mentioned alone.

893 Cf. Gen. xlvi. 24 and 1 Chron. vii. 13: *'Iv* is omitted in both texts.

"Now let me die since I have seen thee, and now may the Lord God of Israel be blessed, the God of Abraham and the God of Isaac who hath not withheld His mercy and His grace from His servant Jacob. 4. It is enough for me that I have seen thy face whilst †I am† [894]yet alive; yea, true is the vision which I saw at Bethel. Blessed be the Lord my God for ever and ever, and blessed be His name." 5. And Joseph and his brothers ate bread before their father and drank wine, and Jacob rejoiced with exceeding great joy because he saw Joseph eating with his brothers and drinking before him, and he blessed the Creator of all things who had preserved him, and had preserved for him his twelve sons. 6. [895]And Joseph had given to his father and to his brothers as a gift the right of dwelling in the land of Goshen and in Rameses and all the region round about, which he ruled over before Pharaoh. And Israel and his sons dwelt in the land of Goshen, the best part of the land of Egypt; and Israel was one hundred and thirty years old when he came into Egypt, 7. And Joseph nourished his father and his brethren and also their possessions with bread as much as sufficed them[896] for the seven years of the famine. 8. And the land of Egypt suffered by reason of the famine, and Joseph acquired all the land of Egypt for Pharaoh in return for food, and he got possession of the people and their cattle and everything for Pharaoh. 9. And the years of the famine were accomplished, and Joseph gave to the people in the land seed and food that they might sow (the land) in the eighth year, for the river had overflowed all the land of Egypt. 10. For in the seven years of the famine it had not overflowed and had irrigated only a few places on the banks of the river, but now it overflowed and the Egyptians sowed the land, and it bore much corn that year. 11. And this was the first year of the fourth week of the forty-fifth jubilee. (2178 A.M.) 12. And Joseph took of the corn of the harvest the fifth part for the king and left four parts for them for food and for seed, and Joseph made it an ordinance for the land of Egypt until this day. 13. And Israel lived in the land of Egypt seventeen years, and all the days which he lived were three jubilees, one hundred and forty-seven years, and he died in the fourth year of the fifth week of the forty-fifth jubilee. (2188 A.M.) 14. And Israel blessed his sons before he died and told them everything [897]that would befall them in the land of Egypt; and he made known to them what would come upon them in the last days, and blessed them and gave to Joseph two portions [898]in the land. 15. And he slept with his fathers, and he was buried in the double cave in the land of Canaan, near Abraham his father in the grave which he dug for himself in the double cave in the land of Hebron. [899]16. And he gave all his books and the books of his fathers to Levi his son that he might preserve them and renew them for his children until this day. [900]

The Death of Joseph. The Bones of Jacob's Sons (except Joseph) interred at Hebron. The Oppression of Israel by Egypt (xlvi. 1-16; cf. Gen. l.; Exod. i.).

XLVI. And it came to pass that after Jacob died the children of Israel multiplied in the land of Egypt, and they became a great nation, and they were of one accord in heart, so that brother loved brother and every man helped his brother, and they increased abundantly and multiplied exceedingly, ten weeks of years (2242 A.M.), all the days of the life of Joseph. [901]2. And there was no Satan [902]nor any evil all the days of the life of Joseph which he lived after his father Jacob, for all the Egyptians honoured the children of Israel all the days of the life of Joseph. 3. And Joseph died being a hundred and ten years old; [903]seventeen years he lived in the land of

---

[894] MT (Gen. xlvi. 30) "that thou art."

[895] Cf. Gen. xlvii. 11.

[896] MT (Gen. xlvii. 12) "`according to their families."

[897] Cf. Gen. xlix. i ff.

[898] Cf. Gen. xlvii. 22.

[899] Cf. Gen. l. 13

[900] Note that the tribal traditions are represented by our author as in the keeping of the priests (Levi and his descendants).

[901] Cf. Exod. i.

[902] Cf. xxiii. 29.

[903] Cf. Gen. l. 22, 26; Exod. i. 6.

Canaan, and ten years he was a servant, and three years in prison, and eighty years he was under the king, ruling all the land of Egypt. 4. And he died and all his brethren and all that generation. 5. And he commanded the children of Israel before he died that they should carry his bones with them when they went forth from the land of Egypt. [904]6. And he made them swear regarding his bones, for he knew that the Egyptians would not again bring forth and bury him in the land of Canaan,[905] for Mâkamârôn,[906] king of Canaan, while dwelling in the land of Assyria, fought in the valley with the king of Egypt and slew him there, and pursued after the Egyptians to the gates of 'Êrmôn. [907]7. But he was not able to enter, for another, a new king, had become king of Egypt, [908]and he was stronger than he, and he returned to the land of Canaan, and the gates of Egypt were closed, and none went out and none came into Egypt. 8. And Joseph died in the forty-sixth jubilee, in the sixth week, in the second year, (2242 A.M.) and they buried him in the land of Egypt, and his brethren died after him. 9. And the king of Egypt went forth to war with the king of Canaan in the forty-seventh jubilee, in the second week in the second year (2263 A.M.), and the children of Israel brought forth all the bones of the children of Jacob save the bones of Joseph, and they buried them in the field in the double cave in the mountain. 10. And the most (of them) returned to Egypt, but a few of them remained in the mountains of Hebron, and Amram thy father remained with them [909]

11. And the king of Canaan was victorious over the king of Egypt, and he closed the gates of Egypt. 12. And he devised an evil device against the children of Israel of afflicting them; and he said unto the people of Egypt: 13. "Behold the people of the children of Israel have increased and multiplied more than we. Come and let us deal wisely with them before they become too many, and let us afflict them with slavery before war come upon us and before they too fight against us; else they will join themselves unto our enemies and get them up out of our land, for their hearts and faces are towards the land of Canaan." 14. And he set over them taskmasters to afflict them with slavery; and they built strong [910]cities for Pharaoh, Pithom and Raamses, and they built all the walls and all the fortifications which had fallen in the cities of Egypt. 15. And they made them serve with rigour, and the more they dealt evilly with them, the more they increased and multiplied. 16. And the people of Egypt abominated the children of Israel.

The Birth and Early Years of Moses (xlvii. 1-12; cf. Exod. ii.).

XLVII. And in the seventh week, in the seventh year, in the forty-seventh jubilee, (2303 A.M.) thy father [911]went forth from the land of Canaan, and thou wast born in the fourth week, in the sixth year thereof, in the forty-eighth jubilee (2330 A.M.); this was the time of tribulation on the children of Israel. 2. And Pharaoh, king of Egypt, issued a command regarding them that they should cast all their male children which were born into the river. 3. And they cast them in for seven months until the day that thou wast born. And thy mother hid thee for three months, and they told regarding her. 4. And she made an ark for thee, and covered it with pitch and asphalt, and placed it in the flags on the bank of the river, and she placed thee in it seven days, and thy mother came by night and suckled thee, and by day Miriam, thy sister, guarded thee from the birds. 5. And in those

---

[904] Cf. Gen. l. 25.

[905] Cf. *Test. Simeon* viii. 3 f. ("For the bones of Joseph the Egyptians guarded in the tombs of the kings. For the sorcerers told them that on the departure of the bones of Joseph there should be throughout all the land darkness and gloom," etc.).

[906] Identification unknown.

[907] *i. e.* Heroônpolis (close to the desert).

[908] ? Rameses III (1202-1171), founder of the 20th dynasty, who repulsed an invasion of peoples from the north and twice marched through Canaan, and in North Canaan defeated the invaders. The war between Egypt and Canaan, mentioned in our text, is referred to in *Test. Simeon* viii. 2. A war between Cush and Egypt, in which Moses led the Egyptians, is referred to by Josephus (*Ant.* ii. 10). In *Chron. Jerahmeel* xlv. it is between Cush and Syria.

[909] This interesting statement apparently implies that some of the Hebrew tribes were already in Canaan before the Exodus. Or is it a reminiscence of the fact that the tribe of Judah absorbed some South Canaanitish tribes which were never in Egypt? Cf. Burney in *Journal of Theological Studies*, 1908, pp. 321-352.

[910] So LXX (Exod. i. ii); MT =? "store cities."

[911] *i. e.* Moses' father, Amram.

days Tharmuth, [912]the daughter of Pharaoh, came to bathe in the river, and she heard thy voice crying, and she told her maidens to bring thee forth, and they brought thee unto her. 6. And she took thee out of the ark, and she had compassion on thee. 7. And thy sister said unto her: "Shall I go and call unto thee one of the Hebrew women to nurse and suckle this babe for thee?" And she said (unto her): "Go." 8. And she went and called thy mother Jochebed, [913]and she gave her wages, and she nursed thee. 9. And afterwards, when thou wast grown up, they brought thee unto the daughter of Pharaoh, and thou didst become her son, and Amram thy father taught thee writing, [914]and after thou hadst completed three weeks they brought thee into the royal court. 10. And thou wast three weeks of years (2351-2372 A.M.) at court until the time when thou didst go forth from the royal court and didst see an Egyptian smiting thy friend who was of the children of Israel, and thou didst slay him and hide him in the sand. 11. And on the second day thou didst find two of the children of Israel striving together, and thou didst say to him who was doing the wrong: "Why dost thou smite thy brother? 12. And he was angry and indignant, and said "Who made thee a prince and a judge over us? Thinkest thou to kill me as thou killedst the Egyptian yesterday?" And thou didst fear and flee on account of these words.

From the Flight of Moses to the Exodus (xlviii. 1-19; cf. Exod. ii. 15 ff., iv. 19-24, vii-xiv.).

XLVIII. And in the sixth year of the third week (2372 A.M.) of the forty-ninth jubilee thou didst depart and dwell in the land of Midian [915]five weeks and one year. And thou didst return into Egypt [916]in the second week in the second year in the fiftieth jubilee. (2410 A.M.) 2. And thou thyself knowest what He spake unto thee on Mount Sinai, and what prince Mastêmâ [917]desired to do with thee when thou wast returning into Egypt on the way when thou didst meet him at the lodging-place. 3. Did he not with all his power seek to slay thee and deliver the Egyptians out of thy hand when he saw that thou wast sent to execute judgment and vengeance on the Egyptians? [918]4. And I delivered thee out of his hand, and thou didst perform the signs and wonders which thou wast sent to perform in Egypt against Pharaoh, and against all his house, and against his servants and his people. 5. And the Lord executed a great vengeance on them for Israel's sake, and smote them through (the plagues of) blood and frogs, lice and dog-flies, and malignant boils breaking forth in blains; and their cattle by death; and by hail-stones, thereby He destroyed everything that grew for them; and by locusts which devoured the residue which had been left by the hail, and by darkness; and (by the death) of the first-born of men and animals, and on all their idols the Lord took vengeance and burned them with fire. [919]6. And everything was sent through thy hand, that thou shouldst declare (these things) before they were done, and thou didst speak with the king of Egypt before all his servants and before his people. 7. And everything took place according to thy words; ten great and terrible judgments came on the land of Egypt that thou mightest execute vengeance on it for Israel. 8. And the Lord did everything for Israel's sake, and according to His covenant, which He had ordained with Abraham that He would take vengeance on them as they had brought them by force into bondage. [920]9. And the prince of the Mastêmâ stood up against thee, and sought to cast thee into the hands of Pharaoh, and he helped the Egyptian sorcerers, and they stood up and wrought before thee. 10. The evils indeed

---

[912] Thermuthis (Josephus, *Ant.* ii. 9, 5, 7).

[913] Cf. Exod. vi. 20; Num. xxvi. 59.

[914] Contrast Acts vii. 22.

[915] Cf. Exod. ii. 15.

[916] Cf. Exod. iv. 19.

[917] Notice here the substitution of Satanic agency where the original text of Scripture ascribes the action directly to Jahveh (cf. Exod. iv. 24); another instance in our Book is xvii. 16. The same tendency can be illustrated from 1 Chron. xxi. 1 compared with 2 Sam. xxiv. 1.

[918] This explanation of the incident described in Exod. iv. 24 ff. seems to be peculiar to our author, the real explanation being that Moses had failed to circumcise his son (so Targ. Ps.-Jon. *in loc.*).

[919] An enumeration of the ten plagues.

[920] Cf. Gen. xv. 13, 14.

we permitted them to work, but the remedies we did not allow to be wrought by their hands. 11. And the Lord smote them with malignant ulcers, and they were not able to stand [921] for we destroyed them so that they could not perform a single sign. 12. And notwithstanding all (these) signs and wonders the prince of the Mastêmâ was not put to shame because he took courage and cried to the Egyptians to pursue after thee with all the powers of the Egyptians, with their chariots, and with their horses, and with all the hosts of the peoples of Egypt. [922] 13. And I stood between the Egyptians and Israel, and we delivered Israel out of his hand, and out of the hand of his people, and the Lord brought them through the midst of the sea as if it were dry land. 14. And all the peoples whom he brought to pursue after Israel, the Lord our God cast them into the midst of the sea, into the depths of the abyss beneath the children of Israel, even as the people of Egypt had cast their children into the river. [923] He took vengeance on 1,000,000 of them, and one thousand strong and energetic men were destroyed on account of one suckling of the children of thy people which they had thrown into the river. [924]15. And on the fourteenth day and on the fifteenth and on the sixteenth and on the seventeenth and on the eighteenth the prince of the Mastêmâ was bound and imprisoned behind the children of Israel that he might not accuse them. 16. And on the nineteenth we let them loose that they might help the Egyptians and pursue the children of Israel. 17. And he [925]hardened their hearts and made them stubborn, and the device was devised by the Lord our God that He might smite the Egyptians and cast them into the sea. 18. And on the fourteenth we bound him that he might not accuse the children of Israel on the day when they asked the Egyptians for vessels and garments, vessels of silver, and vessels of gold, and vessels of bronze, in order to despoil the Egyptians [926]in return for the bondage in which they had forced them to serve. 19. And we did not lead forth the children of Israel from Egypt empty handed.

Regulations regarding the Passover (xlix. 1-23; cf. Exod. xii)

XLIX. Remember the commandment which the Lord commanded thee concerning the passover, that thou shouldst celebrate it in its season on the fourteenth of the first month, that thou shouldst kill it before it is evening, and that they should eat it by night on the evening [927]of the fifteenth from the time of the setting of the sun. 2. For on this night--the beginning of the festival and the beginning of the joy--ye were eating the passover in Egypt, when all the powers of Mastêmâ [928]had been let loose to slay all the first-born in the land of Egypt, from the firstborn of Pharaoh to the first-born of the captive maidservant in the mill, and to the cattle. 3. And this is the sign which the Lord gave them: Into every house on the lintels of which they saw the blood of a lamb of the first year, into (that) house they should not enter to slay, but should pass by (it), that all those should be saved that were in the house because the sign of the blood was on its lintels. 4. And the powers of the Lord did everything according as the Lord commanded them, and they passed by all the children of Israel, and the plague came not upon them to destroy from amongst them any soul either of cattle, or man, or dog.

5. And the plague was very grievous in Egypt, and there was no house in Egypt where there was not one dead, and weeping and lamentation. 6. And all Israel was eating the flesh of the paschal lamb, and drinking the wine, [929]and was lauding and blessing, and giving thanks to the Lord God of their fathers, and was ready to go

---

[921] Cf. Ex. ix. 11.

[922] Cf. Ex. xiv. 8, 9.

[923] Another example of the *lex talionis* (cf. iv 31), though a distinction may be drawn between 'eye for eye' (a principle of human justice) and 'measure for measure' (a theory of divine retribution); cf. Abrahams, *Studies in Pharisaism and the Gospels*, p. 154 (series i).

[924] Cf. Wisdom xviii. 5.

[925] *i. e.* the prince of the Mastêmâ (substituted for Jahveh in Exod. xiv. 8).

[926] Cf. Exod. xii. 35 f.

[927] Cf. Exod. xii. 6.

[928] In Exod. xii. 29 it is Jahveh Himself who smites all the first-born.

[929] The use of wine at the Passover feast is attested here for the first time. For the later prescriptions about the four cups of wine drunk at the feast see Mishna, *Pesaḥim* x.

forth from under the yoke of Egypt; and from the evil bondage. 7. And remember thou this day all the days of thy life, and observe it from year to year all the days of thy life, once a year, on its day, according to all the law thereof, and do not adjourn (it) from day to day, or from month to month. 8. For it is an eternal ordinance, and engraven on the heavenly tables regarding all the children of Israel that they should observe it every year on its day once a year, throughout all their generations; [930]and there is no limit of days, for this is ordained for ever. 9. And the man who is free from uncleanness, and doth not come to observe it on occasion of its day, so as to bring an acceptable offering before the Lord, and to eat and to drink before the Lord on the day of its festival, that man who is clean and close at hand will be cut off; because he offered not the oblation of the Lord in its appointed season, he will take the guilt upon himself. [931]10. Let the children of Israel come and observe the passover on the day of its fixed time, on the fourteenth day of the first month, between the evenings, from the third part of the day to the third part of the night, for two portions of the day are given to the light, and a third part to the evening. [932]11. That is that which the Lord commanded thee that thou shouldst observe it between the evenings. 12. And it is not permissible to slay it during any period of the light, but during the period bordering on the evening, [933]and let them eat it at the time of the evening until the third part of the night, [934]and whatever is leftover of all its flesh from the third part of the night and onwards, let them burn it with fire. 13. And they shall not cook it with water, nor shall they eat it raw, but roast on the fire: [935]they shall eat it with diligence, [936]its head with the inwards thereof [937]and its feet they shall roast with fire, and not break any bone thereof;[938] for †of the children of Israel no bone shall be crushed†. [939]14. For this reason the Lord commanded the children of Israel to observe the passover on the day of its fixed time, and they shall not break a bone thereof; for it is a festival day, and a day commanded, and p. 210 there may be no passing over from day to day, and month to month, but on the day of its festival let it be observed. 15. And do thou command the children of Israel to observe the passover throughout their days, every year, once a year on the day of its fixed time, and it will come for a memorial well pleasing before the Lord, and no plague will come upon them to slay or to smite [940]in that year in which they celebrate the passover in its season in every respect according to His command. 16. And they shall not eat it outside the sanctuary [941] of the Lord, but before the sanctuary of the Lord, and all the people of the congregation of Israel shall celebrate it in its appointed season. 17. And every man who hath come upon its day shall eat it in the sanctuary of your God before the Lord from twenty years old [942] and upward; for thus is it written and ordained that they should eat it in the sanctuary of the Lord. 18. And when

---

[930] For 7-8 cf. vi. 20, 22.

[931] Cf. Num. ix. 13.

[932] The Jews divided the night into three parts, or watches (6-10 p.m., 10 P.M.-2 a.m., 2-6 a.m.). The corresponding parts of the day would be 6-10 a.m., 10 a.m.-2 p.m., and 2 p.m.-6 p.m. Our text says the last of these was "given" to the evening.

[933] This is an interpretation of the Biblical phrase "between the two evenings" (Exod. xii. 6; cf. R.V. marg.). This was interpreted by the Sadducees and Samaritans to mean between sunset and complete darkness (and may possibly have that meaning here), but by the Pharisees it was understood to refer to the earlier afternoon (3-6).

[934] *i. e.* any time between 6 p.m. and 6 a.m. The Rabbis limited the eating to midnight.

[935] Cf. Exod. xii. 9.

[936] Cf. LXX (σπουδαίωσ): Heb. (Exod. xii. ii), "in haste."

[937] Cf. Exod. xii. 9.

[938] Cf. Exod. xii. 46.

[939] The Latin, which is to be preferred, reads: "There shall be no tribulation among the sons of Israel on this day."

[940] Cf. Exod. xii. 13.

[941] Cf. 20 below

[942] *i. e.* the age when maturity is first attained; cf. Exod. xxx. 14; Num. i. 32.

the children of Israel come into the land which they are to possess, into the land of Canaan, and set up the tabernacle of the Lord in the midst of the land in one of their tribes until the sanctuary of the Lord hath been built in the land, let them come and celebrate the passover in the midst of the tabernacle of the Lord, and let them slay it before the Lord from year to year. 19. And in the days when the house hath been built in the name of the Lord in the land of their inheritance, they shall go there and slay the passover in the evening, at sunset, at the third part of the day. 20. And they will offer its blood on the threshold of the altar, and shall place its fat on the fire which is upon the altar, and they shall eat its flesh roasted with fire in the court of the house [943] which hath been sanctified in the name of the Lord. 21. And they may not celebrate the passover in their cities, nor in any place save before the tabernacle of the Lord, or before His house where His name hath dwelt; and they will not go astray from the Lord. 22. And do thou, Moses, command the children of Israel to observe the ordinances of the passover, as it was commanded unto thee; declare thou unto them every year †and the day of its days, and† 2 the festival of unleavened bread, that they should eat unleavened bread seven days, (and) that they should observe its festival, and that they bring an oblation every day during those seven days of joy before the Lord on the altar of your God. 23. For ye celebrated this festival with haste 3 when ye went forth from Egypt till ye entered into the wilderness of Shur; 4 for on the shore of the sea ye completed it.

Laws regarding the Jubilees and the Sabbath (l. 1-13).

L. And after this law I made known to thee the days of the Sabbaths in the desert of Sin[ai], which is between Elim and Sinai. 2. And I told thee of the Sabbaths of the land on Mount Sinai, and I told thee of the jubilee years in the sabbaths of years: but the year thereof have I not told thee till ye enter the land which ye are to possess. 3. And the land also will keep its sabbaths while they dwell upon it, and they will know the jubilee year. 4. Wherefore I have ordained for thee the yearweeks and the years and the jubilees: there are forty-nine jubilees from the days of Adam until this day, and one week and two years (2410 A.M.) and there are yet forty years to come (lit. "distant for learning the commandments of the Lord, until they pass over into the land of Canaan, crossing the Jordan to the west. (2450 A.M.) 5. And the jubilees will pass by, until Israel is cleansed from all guilt of fornication, and uncleanness, and pollution, and sin, and error, and dwelleth with confidence in all the land, and there will be no more a Satan or any evil one, and the land will be clean from that time for evermore.

6. And behold the commandment regarding the Sabbaths--I have written (them) down for thee and all the judgments of its laws. 7. Six days wilt thou labour, but on the seventh day is the Sabbath of the Lord your God. In it ye shall do no manner of work, ye and your sons, and your men-servants and your maid-servants, and all your cattle and the sojourner also who is with you. 8. And the man that doeth any work on it shall die: whoever desecrateth that day, whoever lieth with (his) wife or whoever saith he will do something on it, that he will set out on a journey thereon in regard to any buying or selling: and whoever draweth water thereon which he had not prepared for himself on the sixth day, and whoever taketh up any burden to carry it out of his tent or out of his house shall die. 9. Ye shall do no work whatever on the Sabbath day save that ye have prepared for yourselves on the sixth day, so as to eat, and drink, and rest, and keep Sabbath from all work on that day, and to bless the Lord your God, who has given you a day of festival, and a holy day: and a day of the holy kingdom for all Israel is this day among their days for ever. 10. For great is the honour which the Lord hath given to Israel that they should eat and drink and be satisfied on this festival day, and rest thereon from all labour which belongeth to the labour of the children of men, save burning frankincense and bringing oblations and sacrifices before the Lord for days and for Sabbaths. 11. This work alone shall be done on the Sabbath-days in the sanctuary of the Lord your God; that they may atone for Israel with sacrifice continually from day to day for a memorial wellpleasing before the Lord, and that He may receive them always from day to day according as thou hast been commanded. 12. And every man who doeth any work thereon, or goeth a journey, or tilleth (his) farm, whether in his house or any other place, and whoever lighteth a fire, or rideth on any beast, or travelleth by ship on the sea, and whoever striketh or killeth anything, or slaughtereth a beast or a bird, or whoever catcheth an animal or a bird or a fish, or whoever fasteth or maketh war on the Sabbaths: 13. The man who doeth any of these things on the Sabbath shall die, so that the children of Israel shall observe the Sabbaths according to the commandments regarding the Sabbaths of the land, as it is written in the tables, which He gave into my hands that I should write out for thee the laws of the seasons, and the seasons according to the division of their days.

Herewith is completed the account of the division of the days.

---

[943] Cf. Deut. xvi. 7. In later times the Passover lamb was slaughtered in the Temple, but eaten at home, *i. e.* in a house in Jerusalem. The vast numbers of pilgrims present necessitated this extension (cf. Josephus, *War*, vi. 9,3. ii. 14, 3).

Made in the USA
Middletown, DE
16 September 2024

61000090R00222